INSIDERS' GUIDE® TO
THE TWIN CITIES

Help Us Keep This Guide Up to Date

Every effort has been made by the authors and editors to make this guide as accurate and useful as possible. However, many things can change after a guide is published—establishments close, phone numbers change, hiking trails are rerouted, facilities come under new management, etc.

We would love to hear from you concerning your experiences with this guide and how you feel it could be improved and be kept up to date. While we may not be able to respond to all comments and suggestions, we'll take them to heart and we'll also make certain to share them with the authors. Please send your comments and suggestions to the following address:

The Globe Pequot Press
Reader Response/Editorial Department
P.O. Box 480
Guilford, CT 06437

Or you may e-mail us at:

editorial@GlobePequot.com

Thanks for your input, and happy travels!

INSIDERS' GUIDE® SERIES

Insiders' Guide®
to the Twin Cities

FOURTH EDITION

Todd R. Berger, Holly Day, and Sherman Wick

Guilford, Connecticut

An imprint of The Globe Pequot Press

The prices and rates in this guidebook were confirmed at press time. We recommend, however, that you call establishments before traveling to obtain current information.

Front cover photo by Don Romero, Index Stock
Back cover and spine photos © 2003 www.clipart.com
Maps created by XNR Productions Inc. © The Globe Pequot Press

ISSN 1525-7460
ISBN 0-7627-2808-6

Manufactured in the United States of America
Fourth Edition/First Printing

Contents

Directory of Maps

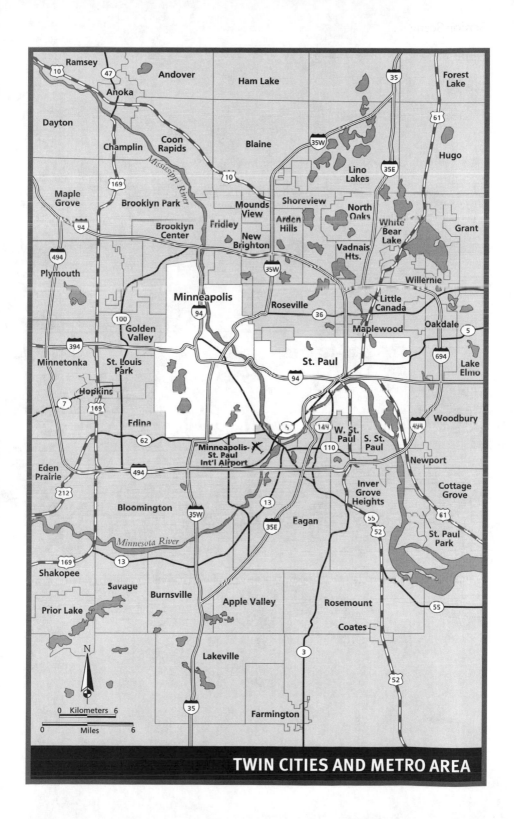

TWIN CITIES AND METRO AREA

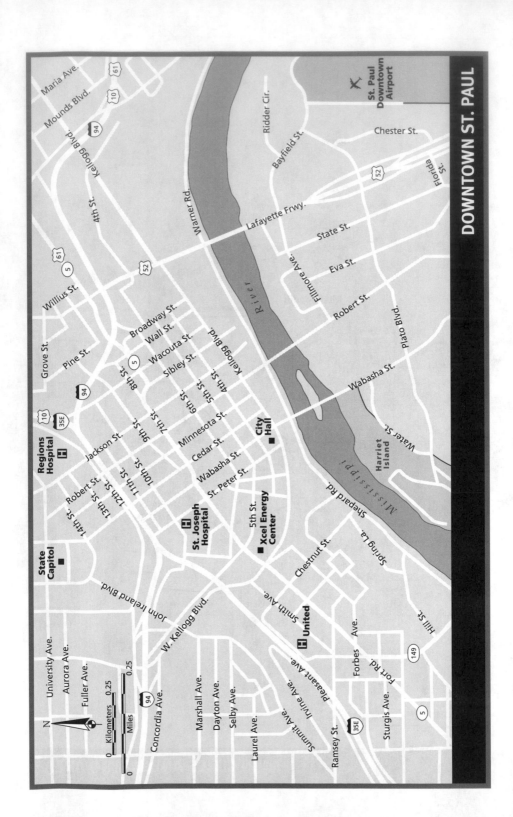

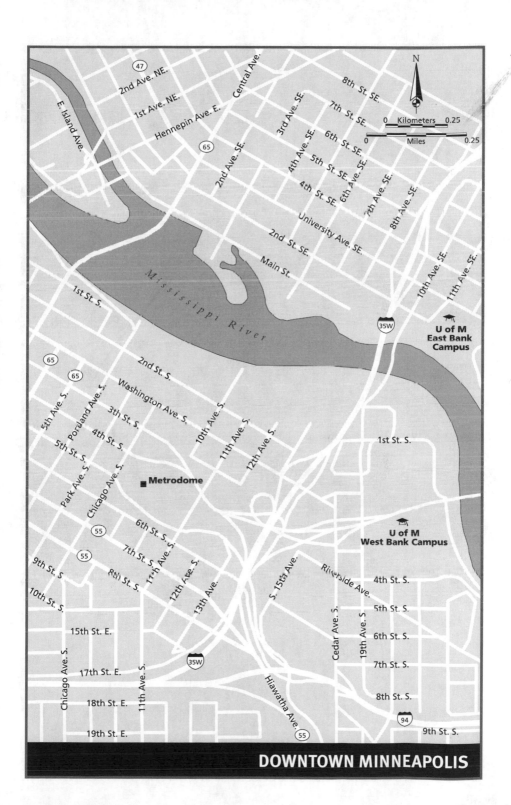

DOWNTOWN MINNEAPOLIS

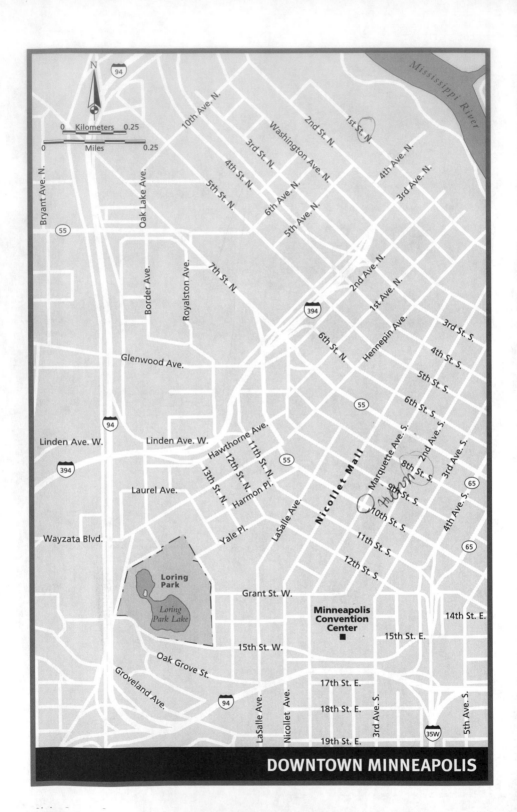

DOWNTOWN MINNEAPOLIS

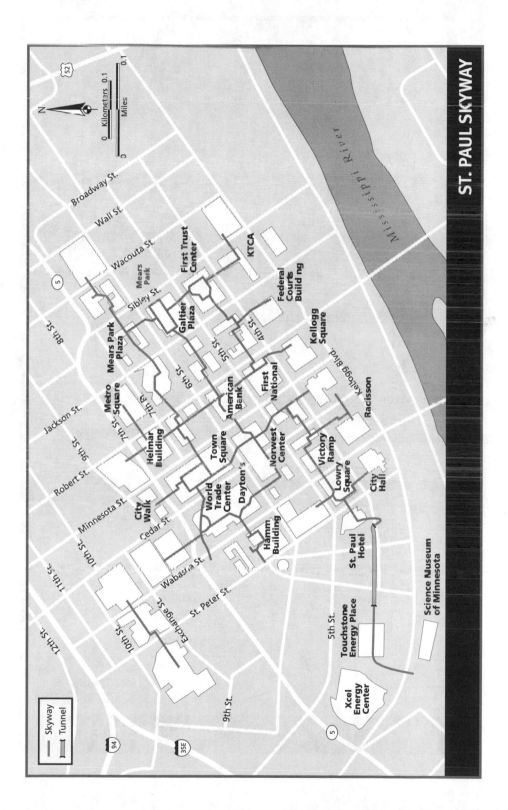

ST. PAUL SKYWAY

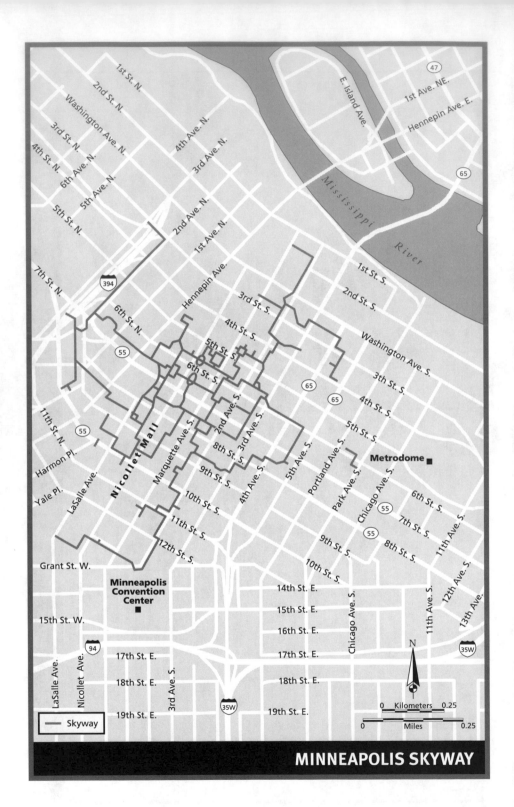

MINNEAPOLIS SKYWAY

Preface

I love the Twin Cities. During my decade living here, I've gotten frostbite, crashed two cars on the freeway sliding on ice, dumped and been dumped by many female Minnesotans, and had my car stolen by joyriders. But during my time in the Metro, I've also pursued and become unimaginably successful as a writer and editor, shopped like someone in a far higher income bracket in downtown Minneapolis, rekindled my passion for the outdoors through Twin Cities parks and annual trips up north, attended the first performances of musicals such as the *Lion King* that went on to spectacular Broadway runs, eaten meals so orgasmic that my girlfriend and I practically sprinted back to my place for a "nightcap," witnessed firsthand the return of the Minnesota Twins to greatness, and nurtured friendships that will last a lifetime. I may well give middle names to my future children of "St. Paul" and "Minneapolis," much to their later dismay.

Updating the *Insiders' Guide to the Twin Cities* was not easy, nor did I take my role lightly. What follows is the result of hundreds, perhaps thousands, of hours of research, phone calls, late-night writing frenzies, confusing drives to parts of the Cities I had never seen, a camera cracking while shooting in far too cold temperatures (fixable with Super Glue, however), and a willingness to venture into places normally outside my realm of expertise and comfort—with the sometimes surprising outcome that I had discovered a side of myself I did not know existed.

I did all of this to save you from the same kind of trouble—and hopefully to guide you to spots you will find delightful, intriguing, delicious, mind-expanding, and memorable. Well, I did it for money, too. Enjoy.

Todd R. Berger

Acknowledgments

Updating a guidebook of this nature involved not only Herculean efforts on the part of myself but also the wonderful assistance, support, generosity, and enthusiasm of numerous individuals. First and foremost, I would like to thank my girlfriend, Bonnie Platt, who helped with research, shot a quite lovely author photo, put up with my canceling plans with her so that I could write, tolerated subzero temperatures keeping me company as I photographed sites across the Twin Cities, and provided perspective and a calming influence when I was about ready to throw the whole manuscript (and my computer) out the iced-over window. I would also like to thank the following persons at The Globe Pequot Press: Jeff Serena, editorial director, for his willingness to take a chance on me to do freelance work for his company that ultimately led to the updating of this book; Paula Brisco, former managing editor, for her faith in my abilities shown throughout our working relationship, culminating in the contract to do this book; Liz Taylor, former assistant managing editor and now managing editor, for her straightforward advice, sense of humor, and guidance; and Joan Wheal, project editor, who took on the unenviable task to incorporate (and polish) my updates to the book.

I am not the first author of this book. Holly Day and Sherman Wick did a fine job updating the third edition, and much of their writing remains in this edition. Having just gone through the process that they went through two years ago, I am awestruck and thankful for their first-rate efforts and sidewalk-pounding work that remains a part of this book and that I was able to build upon.

I would also like to thank Pat Laurel at the Saint Paul Convention and Visitors Bureau for providing high-quality scans of images he took of the city and allowing us to use them in this book and Susan Scofield at the Greater Minneapolis Convention & Visitors Association for allowing us to use images from her organization. Hundreds of restaurateurs, hoteliers, shopkeepers, park employees, attraction managers, public relations employees, and others patiently and, in many cases, enthusiastically answered my questions when I'm certain they had much more pressing things to do; I thank each of them with equivalent enthusiasm. In particular, I would like to thank the generous and kind Gerard Viardin, general manager of the Marquette Hotel; the informative staff at TeaSource in St. Paul; Kathy Jarvis, general manager of the Afton House Inn; Stephanie Schultz, general manager of the Nicollet Island Inn; John T. Sloss, general manager of the Holiday Inn Express–Bandana Square; Joe Witterschein, director of marketing at Mystic Lake Casino Hotel; Michael Goodman of Pazzaluna; Benjamin of Al's Breakfast; Ed Runyon at Fabulous Fern's; the staff at the St. Clair Broiler for never letting me down during hundreds of breakfasts eaten at their establishment (when I should have been working on the book); Christophe Marchand, assistant front-of-the-house manager at Vincent; Susanne Novak of The Saint Paul Hotel; the entire staff at the Bryant-Lake Bowl; Kari Bohlen, administrative assistant at the Radisson Plaza Hotel; Jay Henahan at La Belle Vie; Nathan Kasselder, sales assistant at The Grand Hotel; the staff of the University of Minnesota Athletics Media Relations; and the speedy and high-quality development and printing of many rolls of black and white film at Shutterbug on Grand. Without the help of these persons and many others, the pages in this book would not be the font of Twin Cities information they are.

How to Use This Book

For the most part, those of us who live in the Twin Cities don't consider ourselves Twin Cities residents—in the Metro we're either from Minneapolis or St. Paul. While both cities have much in common, there are also differences in architecture, city layout, history, and industry to set St. Paul and Minneapolis apart. Each has enough points of interest to fill a separate book by itself.

The *Insiders' Guide to the Twin Cities* is organized so that information can be accessed as quickly as possible. Besides the comprehensive Table of Contents and Index, each separate chapter includes multiple subheadings. Chapters are divided by city where appropriate for easier navigation through the Cities.

New to this edition is a chapter on relocation, with pertinent information for those thinking of moving to the Twin Cities or those already here from points elsewhere. You will also find greatly expanded and more detailed information on Minneapolis–St. Paul International Airport, the forthcoming light-rail system, many new restaurant suggestions, streamlined listings to get to the heart of a site, and recommendations for some more intimate, eclectic places to stay while visiting the Cities.

The book is structured with the reader in mind: I constantly strove to write from the point of view of someone moving to or visiting the Twin Cities for the first time or visiting a given establishment for the first time. Accurate, useful information was the standard, and although perfection is never attainable, excellence is. You can feel confident that this book will steer you in the right direction 99 percent of the time as you use it to make choices based on your own preferences. Negative comments are few; if a certain restaurant, attraction, park, or hotel would rate such negative words, it is not listed here. Why recommend rudeness, poor service, lousy food, bad atmosphere, or uninteresting "attractions"? That said, there are numerous worthy establishments in the Cities that do not appear in these pages because of time constraints, space constraints, or the ignorance of the author. Although I encourage you to use this guidebook and am confident that you will choose to visit places to your liking, I also encourage you to stop by that intriguing Ethiopian restaurant, visit that interesting shop selling bobblehead dolls or what-have-you, or buy a house in a neighborhood that "feels right," whether or not it is included in this book. This book is a diving board to get you into the pool; once there, you can swim wherever you like.

The modern skyscrapers of downtown Minneapolis. PHOTO: GREATER MINNEAPOLIS CONVENTION & VISITORS ASSOCIATION

Area Overview

Legend has it that the many lakes that cover the face of Minnesota are actually the filled-in footprints of Paul Bunyan and his mighty blue ox, Babe, created as they stomped around the countryside when Paul was just a boy. If this is true, then he must have been doing jumping jacks in the Twin Cities: St. Paul and Minneapolis alone have 22 lakes within their borders, with many more just outside their borders. There are, of course, much more logical explanations of why there are so many lakes in the area, but the Paul Bunyan theory is by far the most fun.

Even with all its beautiful historic buildings, bridges, and recent whimsical experiments in architecture, the most remarkable physical feature about the Twin Cities has always been their natural beauty. Where else can you find wildlife preservations, rich fossil beds, and fishing lakes, all a short walk from the two downtowns? We who live in either city are fully aware of how lucky we are, and any possibly detrimental change to the landscape, whether it be a proposed road-widening in an area near a park or leveling of a historic building, is met with much more opposition than your average city planner is prepared for.

This, of course, was not always so. Minneapolis was partially built on the lumber industry, and thousands and thousands of old-growth trees were leveled and shipped out-of-state, almost completely destroying the "Big Woods," a maple, oak, and basswood forest that once covered most of southern Minnesota. The Mississippi River Valley Native American populations were decimated along with the forests that had been their home for thousands of years, and many of their spiritual centers, including the ill-fated Spirit Island that once rose out of the Mississippi River below St. Anthony Falls, were either gutted or dynamited in the name of progress.

With the founding of the two cities in the mid-1800s, however, a new level of civility and sophistication came to the residents. Multiple parks boards were established to protect wildlife areas, and even more groomed areas were set aside for outdoor activities. Today, Twin Citians have the luxury of being able to walk past wetlands full of migratory waterfowl and turtles on their way to downtown Minneapolis, or through thickly forested areas housing species of rare native animals and birds just minutes outside downtown St. Paul. Kids who grow up in the Twin Cities get to share in pleasures usually reserved for children who grow up in the country, whether it be fishing in one of the many regularly stocked urban lakes, berry picking, or just enjoying being surrounded by trees, songbirds, and wildflowers in parks practically in their own backyards.

1680: Father Louis Hennepin, after being held captive in a village of the Mille Lacs Dakota, is the first European to see the Falls of St. Anthony.

1819: The United States establishes Fort St. Anthony (renamed Fort Snelling in 1825) to protect the confluence of the Minnesota and Mississippi Rivers.

1837: Governor Henry Dodge of Wisconsin signs a treaty at Fort Snelling with the Ojibwe, who agree to cede all their pine lands on the St. Croix and its tributaries. A treaty is also signed at Washington, D.C., with representatives of the Dakota for their lands east of the Mississippi. These treaties lead the way for extensive white settlements within the area of Minnesota.

1838: Franklin Steele establishes a claim at the Falls of St. Anthony in what is today Minneapolis; Pierre "Pig's Eye" Parrant builds a shanty and settles on the present site of the city of St. Paul, then called Pig's Eye.

1841: The Chapel of St. Paul is built and consecrated, giving the name to the future capital of the state.

1848: On August 26, after the admission of Wisconsin to the Union, the Stillwater Convention adopts measures calling for a separate territory to be named Minnesota. On October 30, Henry Hastings Sibley is elected delegate to Congress for the Minnesota Territory.

1855: On January 23, the first bridge to span the main channel of the Mississippi River anywhere along its length is opened between Minneapolis and St. Anthony.

1858: Minnesota becomes the 32nd state on May 11. At the time of its entry, Minnesota is the third-largest state in land area—only Texas and California are larger.

1861: On April 14, Governor Alexander Ramsey offers President Lincoln 1,000 men for the Civil War effort, making Minnesota the first state to offer troops to the Union. The first Minnesota regiment leaves Fort Snelling on June 22.

1862: The first railroad in Minnesota is opened between Minneapolis and St. Paul.

1881: Technological advances in flour milling made during the 1870s help turn Minneapolis into the flour milling capital of the world.

1883: The Northern Pacific Railroad completes its transcontinental route from Minnesota to the Pacific.

1884: The first iron ore is shipped from Minnesota, a product of the Soudan Mine on the Vermillion Range. Six years later iron is discovered on the Mesabi Range and shipped from there beginning in 1892.

1930: Minnesotan Frank B. Kellogg, serving as U.S. Secretary of State, is awarded the Nobel Peace Prize for his work on the Kellogg-Briand Peace Pact, signed in Paris in 1928.

1944: The Democratic and Farmer-Labor Parties merge to form the Minnesota Democratic-Farmer-Labor Party (DFL).

1947: Engineering Research Associates, Inc., designs the ATLAS—the beginning of Minnesota's computer industry.

1948: The value of manufactured products exceeds cash farm receipts in the state for the first time.

1965: Hubert H. Humphrey becomes the first Minnesotan to win election to national executive office when he is sworn in as vice president on January 20.

1969: Warren Burger of St. Paul becomes Chief Justice of the United States Supreme Court.

1977: Walter Mondale becomes the second Minnesotan to win election to national executive office when he is sworn in as vice president on January 20.

1977: Rosalie Wahl becomes the first woman to serve on the state supreme court.

1987: The Minnesota Twins win the World Series.

1990: The Minnesota Supreme Court becomes the first state supreme court in the nation to have a majority of women seated as justices, following the appointment of Appeals Court Judge Sandra Gardebring.

1991: Casino gambling becomes legal in and around Minnesota's reservations.

1991: The Minnesota Twins win their second world championship in five years.

1992: The Mall of America, the nation's largest shopping and entertainment complex, opens in Bloomington.

1993: Minnesota loses professional hockey when the Minnesota North Stars move to Dallas.

1993: Sharon Sayles Belton is elected mayor of Minneapolis, the first African-American woman to preside over a major American city.

1999: On January 3, Reform Party candidate Jesse Ventura, whose only previous political experience was as the mayor of the Minneapolis suburb of Brooklyn Park, is sworn in as Minnesota's governor.

2000: NHL hockey returns to Minnesota on September 29 when the Minnesota Wild play their first game before a sold-out crowd at the brand-new Xcel Energy Center in downtown St. Paul.

2002: On October 25, 11 days before the election, U.S. Senator Paul Wellstone of Minnesota, his wife, daughter, three campaign workers, and two pilots die in a plane crash in northern Minnesota.

The Personality of the Cities

Minnesota has long suffered a reputation of being an American Siberia peopled with blond-haired, blue-eyed Scandinavian-types that drive around in pickup trucks. And while it's true that some parts of the state do have six-month cold seasons, often complete with snow for the entire six months, the Twin Cities have been particularly blessed with relatively mild temperatures, partly due to our proximity to the swift-moving Mississippi River. Summers can top the scale at 100 degrees occasionally, and, conversely, winters can drop below zero. A good rule of thumb is to just be prepared for it to get cold in the winter and warm in the summer, and dress accordingly.

While most residents of the Twin Cities will go on and on about how much we love the changing of the seasons, to the point of ridiculing visitors who complain about "a little snow," fact is, as soon as any of us have enough money to take a vacation somewhere warm during the winter, we're gone. Our "snow bird" migrations—RV-driving senior citizens who winter in the South and summer in Minnesota—are legendary. A brief jaunt to a tropical clime in the dead of winter is not an act of infidelity on any level—rather, we just want to protect the treasured memories we have of glorious old-growth trees covered with palm-sized green or flame-colored leaves, of hordes of Canada geese sunning them-

Founded: Minneapolis: 1848; St. Paul: 1819

Incorporated: Minneapolis: 1867; St. Paul: 1854

Size: Minneapolis: 54.9 square miles; St. Paul: 52.8 square miles

Elevation: 824 feet above sea level

Population: Minneapolis: 382,618; St. Paul: 287,151

Mayor: Minneapolis: R. T. Rybak; St. Paul: Randy Kelly

Governor: Tim Pawlenty

Airport: Minneapolis–St. Paul International Airport

Average temperatures: July: 73 degrees F
January: 13 degrees F

Average yearly precipitation: 28 inches

Colleges and universities:
Minneapolis: Augsburg College, Capella University, Dunwoody Institute, Minneapolis College of Art and Design, Minneapolis Community and Technical College, Music Tech, Northwestern Health Science University, The University of Minnesota–Twin Cities, Walden University
St. Paul: Bethel College and Seminary, The College of St. Catherine, Concordia University-St. Paul, Hamline University, Luther Seminary, Macalester College, Metropolitan State University, William Mitchell College of Law, Northwestern College, St. Paul Technical College, University of St. Thomas

Daily newspapers: *Star Tribune, St. Paul Pioneer Press*

Radio stations: 38

Television stations: 8

Driving laws: Driver's license at age 16; maximum speed limit 65 mph (except in a few semirural stretches in the outer-ring suburbs where the speed limit is 70); seat belts mandatory for driver and all passengers; child seats mandatory for children under five or under 45 pounds; helmets mandatory for motorcycle riders.

selves along the shores of the Mississippi, or of the way the brilliant white riverboats look heading down the St. Croix River in the middle of summer, mirror-reflected in the clear, tannin-tinted waters.

As soon as the weather is nice, however, anyone who can go outside, is outside. City parks get used here in the Twin Cities, from huge group picnics to locally organized volleyball and baseball games.

Almost every neighborhood park has a splash pool for kids, and at any given time during the summer, families can be seen splashing around in the ridiculously shallow waters. At night, the streets of downtown Minneapolis and St. Paul are full of people either out for a late-night walk in the balmy evening air or heading out on foot for a night on the town.

Hollywood and the Twin Cities

Minnesota has long been a favorite filming spot for moviemakers, especially those who need to shoot in snowy, cold areas with lots of open spaces. The Twin Cities are also a logical spot to find actors and actresses to fill these scenes, as both Minneapolis and St. Paul have more than enough talent trained on the many professional and amateur theater stages in the area. Some of the films that have been shot in the Twin Cities metro area include *Airport, Beautiful Girls, Drop Dead Fred, Equinox, Fargo, Feeling Minnesota, Foolin' Around, Grumpy Old Men, Grumpier Old Men, Jingle All the Way, Mall Rats, The Mighty Ducks (I, II, and III), The Personals, Twenty Bucks,* and *Untamed Heart.* Brothers Joel and Ethan Coen, formerly from St. Louis Park, film directors and producers of such films as *Raising Arizona, Blood Simple, Barton Fink, Fargo,* and *O Brother Where Art Thou,* are from here, as is *Twin Peaks* producer Mark Frost and director of *The Sting,* George Roy Hill.

Television and big picture actors and actresses that hail from the Twin Cities include Eddie Albert (*Roman Holiday, Green Acres*), Loni Anderson (*WKRP in Cincinnati*), Richard Dean Anderson (*General Hospital, MacGyver, Stargate SG–1*), James Arness (*Gunsmoke*), Julia Duffy (*Newhart, Designing Women*), Mike Farrell (*M*A*S*H, Providence*), Al Franken (*Saturday Night Live*), Peter Graves (*Mission: Impossible*), Tippi Hedren (*The Birds*), Charlie Korsmo (*Hook, Dick Tracy*), Dorothy Lyman (*All My Children, Mama's Family*), Kelly Lynch (*Drugstore Cowboy*), Mike Nelson (*Mystery Science Theater*), Kevin Sorbo (*Hercules, Andromeda*), Lea Thompson (*Back To the Future I, II, III; Howard the Duck, Caroline in the City*), and Robert Vaughn (*The Man From U.N.C.L.E.*).

St. Paul honors its native son Charles Schultz with Peanuts characters sprinkled throughout the city during the summer. The statues are later auctioned off, and some St. Paul businesses keep them on permanent display. PHOTO: TODD R. BERGER

good book—or sit down and write one. Some literary luminaries from the Twin Cities area have included *Prairie Home Companion*'s Garrison Keillor, Sinclair Lewis, F. Scott Fitzgerald, Meridel Le Sueur, Harvey Mackay, Robert Bly, Gordon Parks, cartoonist Charles Schultz, and journalist Eric Severeid. Folksinger Bob Dylan, blues legends Koerner, Ray and Glover, former Replacements' lead singer Paul Westerberg, Soul Asylum singer Dave Pirner, and Prince Rogers Nelson (a.k.a. Prince) also all made Minneapolis or St. Paul their home at one time or another.

Literature and Music

There's nothing like a long, Minnesota winter to make you want to curl up with a

Geology

The state of Minnesota is known throughout the world for its once-productive iron

Many downtown St. Paul intersections are bricked over, and many of the newer buildings, like this parking ramp, have elegant facades. PHOTO: TODD R. BERGER

beneath shallow continental seas. During the Ordovician period (505 to 438 million years ago), Minnesota was located 10 to 40 degrees south of the equator, making the area about as tropical as Hawaii is today. The waters were rich with primitive animal life, much of which can be seen today as layers in the fossil record at paleontology digs throughout the state. Large amounts of corals, trilobites, snails, mussel and clam shells, and the ancestors of modern-day octopus and squid have been unearthed at sites such as Harriet Island/Lilydale Park and Shadow Falls in St. Paul, and near Cannon Falls in Goodhue County.

Most of Minnesota is part of the Canadian Shield—a core of Precambrian rocks that contains the record of the history of the North American continent from about 3,600 million to 600 million years ago and is some of the oldest exposed rock in the world. Much of this ancient shield had been protected by the covering of the Ordovician seas, and later by layers of sediment and earth, but was again exposed by the eroding progress of glaciers over a mile thick that covered the area more than 12,000 years ago—the same glaciers that eventually carved out the 15,000-plus lakes and rivers that cross the face of the state today.

The Original Settlers

Before European settlement, Dakota (Sioux) and Ojibwe (Chippewa) tribes populated the Twin Cities area, and before that, an amalgam of people known as the Woodland Indians (or Hopewell Indians), who left behind thousands of burial mounds throughout the Midwest, six of which can still be seen at Mounds Park in St. Paul. The Mississippian cultures of the Dakota and Ojibwe replaced these American Indians circa A.D. 800 to 1000.

While the Ojibwe's origins were to the east and north, the Dakota were western Plains Indians, who at the time of European exploration occupied the Twin Cities, western and southern Minnesota, and much of present-day North and South

mines as well as its quarries of beautiful St. Peter sandstone and marble deposits. Of more scientific interest, some of the oldest exposed rock known in the world is also located in the Minnesota River Valley, the Morton gneiss, which was formed approximately 3,600 million years ago. The Morton gneiss and "younger" (1,700 to 1,800 million-year-old) quarries of Minnesota granite and basalt have been prized as building materials throughout the world for years, as has St. Peter sandstone, marble, and fossil-rich kaolinite clay.

Millions of years ago, the area now known as Minnesota lay submerged

Dakota. The French referred to the Dakota as Sioux, a meaningless abridgement of the Ojibwe term, *Nadouissouix,* which meant "little viper" or "lesser enemy." The derogatory name stuck for centuries until recently, when the tribe began referring to themselves by their original name. Both the Dakota and Ojibwe were hunting societies, and their hunting techniques evolved by incorporating European tools, wares, and implements, such as guns, hatchets, blankets, knives, and kettles. On a cultural level, the European introduction of glass beads and colored cloth and yarn to the native peoples resulted in a revolution in Native American artwork, producing the spectacular woven blankets and intricate beadwork that we associate with Native American craftwork today.

The Twin Cities is home to the largest urban population of Native Americans in the United States and is the birthplace of the American Indian Movement (AIM). AIM produces a large volume of locally and nationally distributed literature that addresses Native American concerns on everything from legal issues to finding hospitals that practice Native American medicine.

St. Paul

Home to thousands of Native Americans for centuries, the earliest known name for St. Paul is that which it was called by the Indians: *Im-in-i-ja ska,* which translated into English means "White Rock," taken from the high limestone bluffs in the area. Fort Snelling (originally named Fort St. Anthony), the first European settlement in the area, was built in 1819, and soon after, seeking the nearby protection of the fort, the thriving community of Mendota was established.

Soon, the more privileged military officers and the residents of Mendota became disturbed at the lifestyle of the residents of the squatters camp, most of whom were refugees from the ill-fated Selkirk Colony in Manitoba. They were especially disturbed about the activities of a notorious and highly popular retired fur trapper whose talents had been turned to moon-

shining, Pierre "Pig's Eye" Parrant. The whiskey trade quickly infuriated the strait-laced Major Talliaferro, Fort Snelling's Indian Agent, who issued a proclamation banishing the squatters from lands controlled by the fort. This forced them to move down the river to the northeast, just outside the fort's jurisdiction.

This site, then known as Fountain Cave, was located near what is now the southern part of St. Paul. A small monument today marks a spot on the riverbank near where the small group settled. Soon after they set up their new squatter camp, Major Talliaferro decided they were not quite far enough out of his sight and extended the jurisdiction of the fort to include the Fountain Cave site, sending his soldiers to burn the Fountain Cave encampment. The settlers were again forced to move farther down the river, this time settling on the north bank in what is now part of downtown St. Paul.

Institutions such as government and the Roman Catholic Church have been central to St. Paul's history since its earliest days. Since the beginnings of Minnesota Territory in 1849, St. Paul has served as the capital. At about the same time, it also became a Catholic diocese established by Father Lucian Galtier, who had come to save the souls in the crassly named settlement of "Pig's Eye."

Industry and technology were paramount in the historical development of St. Paul. Minnesota Mining and Manufacturing Company (3M) is one of the cities' most important companies. 3M's history began in 1902 in Two Harbors, a small town north of Duluth, as a manufacturer

Insiders' Tip

AIM—the American Indian Movement—was founded and is headquartered in Minneapolis.

on the Mississippi, in Minneapolis and St. Anthony, because of the falls. To businessmen in the area, the falls represented an unbridled source of energy for milling the vast wheat crops in the area, which rapidly expanded as Minnesota and the upper Midwest were settled. The milling industry became increasingly decentralized as the largest and most successful Twin Cities milling companies gradually diversified into related industries.

of sandpaper. The company relocated to St. Paul in 1909, where sandpaper is one of numerous important 3M products today. However, 3M has always placed a premium on producing and developing diverse new and innovative products. Products such as Scotch brand tape and Post-It notes are also important product lines. As time has passed 3M has grown into an international corporation and remains essentially a St. Paul company, even after relocating its headquarters to the adjoining suburb of Maplewood.

Minneapolis

The emergence of the other Twin City, Minneapolis, was far less colorful. In 1680 Father Louis Hennepin happened upon St. Anthony Falls, and 140 years later, soldiers from nearby Fort Snelling constructed a sawmill and flour mill at the falls. Minneapolis and the across-the-river town of St. Anthony both began in the 1840s as milling and lumbering centers, when Franklin Steele settled in St. Anthony in 1838 and began his successful flour and sawmills. By the 1840s the village of St. Anthony had been established on the east bank of the Mississippi and the village of Minneapolis on the west bank. The two towns were soon linked by a suspension bridge, and in 1872 Minneapolis and St. Anthony were united to form one city.

Historically, Minneapolis was founded to process Minnesota grain with the tremendous power-generating capabilities of St. Anthony Falls, and by the late 19th century, Minneapolis became nationally known as the "Mill City." Milling began

The Cities Together

Since the beginning of the 20th century, the Twin Cities economy has become increasingly diverse, depending less on a single industry, such as lumber, milling, or mining. The end result was an area economy consistently among the strongest in the United States. While the rest of the nation's economy began to decline in the '60s, '70s, and '80s, the Twin Cities economy was prepared. Its footholds in the technological, medical, retail, and agricultural fields kept the state from plunging into a serious recession.

Since World War II, high tech has played an increasingly important role in the Twin Cities economy. Some companies' roots often reach back to industry and manufacturing that began in the late 19th and early 20th century, as is the case with the 3M Corporation, while others quickly became important businesses in the area because of technological innovation. Medtronic founder, Earl Bakken, began his company in a northeast Minneapolis garage in 1949, and it became the first of many medical supply companies that have made their home in the Twin Cities.

The Twin Cities is also home to one of the nation's largest retailers, the Target Corporation. For most of its long history in the Twin Cities, Target was known as Dayton Corporation, and later the Dayton Hudson Corporation. George Dayton opened the first Dayton's in downtown Minneapolis in 1902, and in 1962, Dayton Corporation's most nationally known retail store, Target, opened its door for the first time in nearby Roseville. Dayton

Hudson officially changed its name to the Target Corporation in 2000, in an effort to improve market visibility for investors interested in purchasing stock.

Recent immigration is transforming the composition of the Twin Cities, much as it did in the late 19th and early 20th centuries. These new immigrant populations include Vietnamese, Laotians, Khmers (Cambodia), Hmong (Laos), east Africans, Russians, and Bosnians. With the exception of the Russians and Bosnians, following the wake of the conflict in the former Yugoslavia, Europeans are a relatively small component of the new immigration. The Twin Cities, in particular St. Paul, have the largest Hmong population in the nation. The Hmong and other Southeast Asians have started more than 400 area businesses and have transformed St. Paul's Frogtown and Midway neighborhoods.

The new wave of immigration is just one parallel linking the Twin Cities past and present. Both Minneapolis and St. Paul are reviving important elements of their past on the Mississippi riverfront. Since the late '80s Minneapolis has focused on regaining its greatest historical assets—the Mississippi River and the Mill District. Down the river in St. Paul, the renovated Harriet Island Regional Park celebrates its city's rich history.

The Seven County Metro Area

Anoka County

Anoka County's history starts as far back as 1849, when the Minnesota territorial legislature organized the counties of Washington, Ramsey, and Benton. What is now Anoka County was originally parts of both Ramsey and Benton Counties, with the Rum River dividing the two counties. As more settlers came into the area, the plot of land bordering the Rum River's shores was given the name Anoka. The name originated from an American Indian word meaning "on both sides."

Anoka County was formed from Ramsey County on May 23, 1857. The original eight townships included Anoka, Watertown (Ramsey), Round Lake (Andover), Bethel, Columbus, St. Francis, Oak Grove, and Centerville. The original boundaries of Anoka County were the same as today except for a small portion of the southeastern tip of the county along the Mississippi River. This strip was a tiny county created from Ramsey County, possibly by a surveying miscalculation, the same day Anoka County was created. This tiny county was given the name of Manomin and occupied only about one-third of a congressional township; it functioned as an organized county until abolished and attached to Anoka County by constitutional amendment November 2, 1869. As an organized township of Anoka County, Manomin kept this name until it was changed to Fridley in 1879.

Anoka County has grown from a largely rural area in 1857 to the present-day urban center. It is one of the largest and fastest growing counties in the state. Anoka County, with its county seat in the city of Anoka, encompasses a 430-square-mile area, has a population of approximately 298,948 and is the fourth-largest county in Minnesota. Anoka County is also the third most densely populated county in the state, following Ramsey and Hennepin Counties, and includes the cities of Andover, Anoka, Bethel, Blaine, Burns, Centerville, Circle Pines, Columbia Heights, Columbus, Coon Rapids, East Bethel, Fridley, Ham Lake, Hilltop, Lexington, Lino Lakes, Linwood, Oak Grove, Ramsey, St. Francis, and Spring Lake Park within its borders.

Carver County

With the signing of the treaty of Traverse de Sioux in March 1855, the formerly Native American lands that soon became Carver County were opened for settlement by white pioneers. The county was named in honor of explorer Jonathan Carver. The original county seat was in San Francisco Township, but in 1856 voters moved it to Chaska, where it remains today.

Riverboats ply the waters of the Mississippi and St. Croix Rivers in the Twin Cities Metro during the summer. PHOTO: GREATER MINNEAPOLIS CONVENTION & VISITORS ASSOCIATION

Many of Carver County's initial settlers were from the East Coast, but by the 1860s, many of the area's new settlers were immigrants from Germany or Sweden. The Germans founded towns like Hamburg, New Germany, and Cologne, while the Swedes settled in East Union and Watertown.

Farming was the chief occupation of Carver County for 100 years. While many grew crops, others were dairy farmers, and creameries were so numerous that the county started calling itself "The Golden Buckle of the Dairy Belt." Oak Grove Dairy in Norwood-Young America and Bongards Creameries are still important forces in the dairy industry.

Carver County's most historically important farmer was Wendelin Grimm, a German immigrant who settled in Chanhassen. Grimm's claim to fame was in creating his own strain of hardy alfalfa, named Grimm alfalfa, which was at the time considered to be the most winter-hardy strain available. Grimm alfalfa was used throughout North America between 1910 and 1940 and is one of Minnesota's leading contributions to the history of agriculture.

Today, Carver County has a population of approximately 68,000 people, divided among the cities of Carver, Chanhassen, Chaska, Cologne, Hamburg, Mayer, New Germany, Norwood, Norwood-Young America, Victoria, Waconia, and Watertown.

Dakota County

Located minutes south of the Twin Cities, Dakota County offers the amenities of the metropolitan area with the charm and serenity of a small town. Approximately 350,000 people live within the county's limits, making it the third most populous county in the state of Minnesota, while still having an amazing one-half of its land left undeveloped or rural.

The quality of life in Dakota County is high due to its excellent schools, its proximity to renowned healthcare facilities, and pleasant neighborhoods. Parks, fishing lakes, trail systems, and recreation areas are in abundance, as well as the spacious grounds of the Minnesota Zoo, the second-largest zoo in the country. Businesses with roots and holdings in Dakota County include Con Agra, Hudson Manufacturing, Alexis Baily, Vineyard, Mead Papper, and Gumby Fancy, providing long-term employment for residents of the area.

Dakota County cities include Apple Valley, Burnsville, Eagan, Farmington, Hastings, Inver Grove Heights, Lakeville, Lilydale, Mendota, Mendota Heights, Miesville, New Trier, Randolph, Rosemount, Sunfish Lake, South St. Paul, and West St. Paul.

Hennepin County

Hennepin County, incorporated in 1852, forms part of one of the nation's major metropolitan areas, with Minneapolis as its largest city and county seat. The county has a broad-based economy with strong trade, service, and manufacturing sectors, and many major corporations are headquartered in the county. The employment base is diverse, and employment remains relatively stable. The county's unemployment rate has consistently remained below the state and national averages.

More than 1,100,000 people live in the 611 square miles that make up Hennepin County, with the greatest percentage living in Minneapolis and the rest distributed among the cities of Bloomington, Brooklyn Center, Brooklyn Park, Champlin, Chanhassen, Corcoran, Crystal, Dayton, Deephaven, Eden Prairie, Edina, Excelsior, Golden Valley, Greenfield, Hamel, Hanover, Hopkins, Howard Lake, Independence, Long Lake, Loretto, Maple Grove, Maple Plain, Medicine Lake, Medina, Minnetonka, Minnetonka Beach, Minnetonka Mills, Minnetrista, Mound, Navarre, New Hope, Orono, Osseo, Plymouth, Richfield, Robbinsdale, Rockford, Rogers, Saint Anthony, Saint Bonifacius, Saint Louis Park, Spring Park, Tonka Bay, Wayzata, Woodland, and Young America.

The largest employers with holdings in Hennepin County include the state government, the University of Minnesota, General Mills, Cargill, Target Corporation, and the U.S. Postal Service.

Ramsey County

Ramsey County, established in 1849, is home to Minnesota's state capital, the city of St. Paul. More than 487,000 people live in the 156 square miles that make up the county, which includes the cities of Arden Hills, Blaine, Falcon Heights, Gem Lake, Lauderdale, Little Canada, Maplewood, Mounds View, New Brighton, North Oaks, North St. Paul, Roseville, St. Anthony, St. Paul, Shoreview, Spring Lake Park, Vadnais Heights, and White Bear Lake.

Ramsey County is the site of many popular attractions, both man-made and natural, including Como Park Zoo and Conservatory, Indian Mounds Park, Harriet Island and Lilydale Parks, and the Alexander Ramsey House. St. Paul's suburbs are particularly blessed with beautiful, historic neighborhoods built around lakes and parks for summer and winter recreation alike.

Scott County

Scott County, established in 1853 and named after General Winfield Scott, is an area of 375 square miles located in the southwest corner of the Twin Cities metro area. The Minnesota River forms the northern border of the county, while the broad river valley cuts though glacial sediment into some of the oldest exposed rock beds in the state. The savanna that makes up most of Scott County once bordered the "Big Woods," a hardwood forest that covered a majority of the state before it was logged in the mid-19th century.

Shakopee, the county seat, began in 1851 as a trading post nearby to the Dakota village of Chief Shakopee (or Shakpay). Townsites were established along transportation routes provided by the Minnesota River and the numerous oxcart trails that crisscrossed the region. Years later, the railroad was the choice of transport in Minnesota, and highways developed along the oxcart trails and between communities.

Today, urban sprawl and suburbanization are threatening this primarily rural county. Industry has taken hold, and transportation issues today play a primary role in development decisions, just as they did in the past.

The county currently has a population of approximately 81,990 and is expected to increase to approximately 109,000 persons by the year 2010, according to Metropolitan Council estimates. Located within the county lines are the cities of Elko, Jordan, New Prague, Prior Lake, and Savage.

Washington County

Washington County is located on the eastern edge of the Metro. Incorporated in 1849, its 423 square miles now house more than 205,000 people divided among the cities of Afton, Bayport, Birchwood, Cottage Grove, Dellwood, Forest Lake, Hastings, Hugo, Lake Elmo, Lake St. Croix Beach, Lakeland, Lakeland Shores, Landfall, Marine on St. Croix, Newport, Oak Park Heights, Oakdale, Pine Springs, Saint Mary's Point, Saint Paul Park, Scandia, Stillwater, Willernie, and Woodbury. The county seat is located in Stillwater, along the St. Croix River. Originally full of lumber towns, with an economy fueled by the lumber industry and made possible by the St. Croix River, industry in Washington County has grown to include major employers such as Anderson Windows, State Farm Insurance, 3M, and the Minnesota Correctional Facilities in Bayport and Oak Park Heights.

Washington County is full of historic sites that played key parts in the formation of the state. In 1849 the Minnesota territorial legislature met in Stillwater (at 102 South Main Street) and created nine counties in the new Minnesota Territory, including Washington County. Other historic places in the county include Gammelgården, Scandia, the site of the first Swedish settlement in Minnesota, and Cottage Grove, the birthplace of commercial agriculture in Minnesota.

Washington County has more than its share of beautiful natural areas as well. Located within county lines are Afton State Park, Lake Elmo Park Reserve, St. Croix Bluffs Regional Park, and Square Lake Park, as well as dozens of smaller protected wilderness areas. The county is bordered by the Lower St. Croix National Scenic Riverway.

Getting Here, Getting Around

Air Travel

Train Travel

Bus Travel

Car Travel

Snow Emergency
Information

Parking

Public Transportation

Transportation has long played a crucial role in shaping the Twin Cities. In the beginning, the Mississippi, Minnesota, and St. Croix Rivers all made the lumber industry possible in Minnesota, turning communities like Stillwater, St. Anthony, and Minneapolis into important centers of commerce and trade. The rivers were also important in transporting iron, granite, sandstone, and marble from Minnesota to the rest of the world, and for bringing military supplies and luxury items from the rest of the world to Minnesota. Trains later replaced the great ships as the preferred means of transporting raw materials, and commuter trains became Twin Cities residents' favorite means of personal transportation. The Great Northern Depot in St. Paul, built in 1914, connected passengers to nearby resort destinations like Minnehaha Park and White Bear Lake, as well as the East and West Coast.

Electric streetcars made their debut in the Twin Cities in 1889, and by the 1920s Minneapolis and St. Paul were home to one of the largest streetcar systems in the world. More than 1,000 cars on 500 miles of track took commuters to work and back home again each day, and the system was so extensive that it was possible to take a streetcar from downtown Minneapolis all the way to Stillwater or Excelsior. Unfortunately, the streetcar system was abandoned in the 1950s, partly due to rising pressure from auto manufacturers. In 1954 street buses replaced the electric streetcars, and the electric tracks that crisscrossed the metro area were paved over to facilitate automobile use.

Today the Twin Cities are home to one large international airport and six smaller ones and a bus line that runs 24 hours a day in the busy downtown areas. Even if you're new to the area, fleets of friendly, reliable taxicabs and helpful bus drivers and information operators will make sure you get to your destination safely.

Air Travel

Minneapolis-St. Paul International Airport
Charles A. Lindbergh Terminal
4300 Glumack Drive, St. Paul
(612) 726–5555

Hubert H. Humphrey Terminal
7150 Humphrey Drive, Minneapolis
(612) 726–5800
www.mspairport.com
Minneapolis-St. Paul International Airport (MSP) is a sprawling complex of two terminals serving 25 passenger airlines, 19 cargo airlines, and 34 million people annually. The airport is located between Minneapolis and St. Paul on the southern side of the Metro, with relatively quick access to both downtowns and the rest of the Twin Cities region. MSP is a hub for Northwest Airlines (the company is based in Eagan, a St. Paul suburb) and, with a steady stream of takeoffs and landings, ranks as the eighth busiest airport in the nation.

The Lindbergh Terminal at Minneapolis-St. Paul International Airport hums with activity nearly around the clock. PHOTO: TODD R. BERGER

Getting to the Airport

MSP encompasses two terminals—the Lindbergh Terminal and the Humphrey Terminal. The Lindbergh Terminal is accessible from Minnesota Highway 5 via the Lindbergh Terminal exit. The Humphrey Terminal is accessible from Interstate 494 via the 34th Avenue South exit. Most commercial passenger airlines fly into Lindbergh, while Humphrey is the landing site for many charter airlines. Check your ticket carefully to determine your terminal before driving to the airport or instructing someone where to pick you up, although if you end up at the wrong terminal, you can hop

on a shuttle bus (or a light rail car by late 2004) to quickly get back on track.

Design

If you havn't been through MSP for a few years, you probably won't recognize either of the terminals today. MSP and the six reliever airports operated by the Metropolitan Airports Commission (MAC) are undergoing a $3.1 billion reconstruction project known as MSP 2010, and things have come a long way since work began in 1996.

Despite the changes, it is not difficult to find your way around either the Lindbergh or Humphrey Terminal. The top level of the Lindbergh Terminal is for ticketing and departures. You can be dropped off at this level via the elevated roadway just outside the doors. The gate concourses at Lindbergh are lettered sequentially, A through G. Generally, if your concourse letter is A through E, you will veer right after passing through the security checkpoints in between the check-in counters; if your concourse letter is F or G, you will veer left. You can easily find your gate by observing the concourse number and gate (for example, E8 would be Gate 8 on Concourse E). The lower the number of the gate, the shorter your walk down the concourse. Note that Concourses A and B, designated for smaller commuter airlines, are at the *end* of Concourse C.

People-mover walkways carry passengers down Concourses C and G, the two longest at MSP, and across the Skyway Connector between Concourses C and G. An aboveground shuttle tram also carries passengers the length of Concourse C, with several stops along the way, and an underground Hub Tram runs from Level T, two floors below the ticketing and departures concourse, to escalators leading to the Skyway Connector. This tram also carries passengers to the outer Blue and Red parking ramps and to the Transit Center, where you will find the rental car counters, city bus stop, a stop for the shuttle to the Humphrey Terminal, and (in late 2004) the light rail station.

At Lindbergh, the baggage claim area is one floor below the ticketing and departures concourse. Electronic displays on this level indicate which of the 14 baggage carousels will deliver the luggage from your flight.

The much-smaller Humphrey Terminal, which reopened in a brand new terminal building in May 2001, will not make your feet as sore. Ticketing and departure counters, as well as the baggage claim area, are all located on the first floor of the terminal. The gates are one floor up and accessible via a short escalator ride. The shuttle bus to the Lindbergh Terminal leaves from the east side of the terminal; taxis and shuttles to rental car centers leave from the front of the building at Door 4.

Airlines

As noted, MSP is a hub for Northwest Airlines, and the carrier dominates air traffic in and out of the airport, controlling 78 percent of the gates. Some studies have concluded that Minneapolis-St. Paul's hub status leads to higher ticket fares. Then, again, it also means that Twin Citians and visitors have a large selection of nonstop flights to multiple destinations worldwide. If you are flexible about your departure time, plan far enough in advance, and look for sale fares through travel agents and online, you'll be less likely to experience sticker shock after flying in or out of MSP.

Given the dominance of Northwest in Minneapolis-St. Paul, it is worth checking the airline's Web site (www.nwa.com) for deals if you are planning a trip to or from the Twin Cities. The airline offers weekly specials, released every Wednesday, for departures the following Saturday with returns on Monday or Tuesday. If you can plan on the fly and the special happens to be to or from your city, you can get a steep discount on your seat. On the Web site you can sign up for e-mail notices of these special fares.

Of course, Northwest isn't the only game in town. With the exception of Southwest Airlines, all major American carriers serve MSP, as do three international airlines and six charter airlines.

Charter flights also often can get you a deal on your airline seat, although in Minneapolis-St. Paul most charter flights are from the Cities to warm-weather destinations, particularly in winter. You may have trouble finding a charter flight into MSP, but shop around if you want to save your money for fun while in the Twin Cities.

Domestic Airlines

AirTran Airways, (800) 247-8726; www.airtran.com
America West, (800) 235-9292; www.americawest.com
American Airlines/TWA, (800) 433-7300; www.aa.com
American Trans Air, (800) 435-9282; www.ata.com
Comair Airlines (operated by Delta), (800) 221-1212; www.comair.com
Continental Airlines, (800) 525-0280; www.continental.com
Delta Airlines, (800) 221-1212; www.delta.com
Frontier Airlines, (800) 432-1359; www.frontierairlines.com
Great Lakes Aviation (United Express), (800) 241-6522; www.greatlakesav.com
Mesaba (Northwest Airlines Airlink), (800) 225-2525; www.mesaba.com
Northwest Airlines, (800) 225-2525; www.nwa.com
Skyway Airlines (Midwest Express), (800) 452-2022; www2.midwestexpress.com/home.asp
SkyWest Airlines, (800) 221-1212 or (800) 241-6522; www.skywest.com
Sun Country Airlines, (800) 359-6786; www.suncountry.com
United Airlines, (800) 241-6522; www.ual.com
US Airways, (800) 428-4322; www.usairways.com

International Airlines

Air Canada, (800) 247-2262; www.aircanada.com
Icelandair, (800) 223-5500; www.icelandair.com

KLM Royal Dutch Airlines,
(800) 225–2525; www.nwa.com

Charter Airlines

Casino Express, (800) 258–8800;
www.redlioncasino.com
Champion Air, (800) 922–2606;
www.championair.com
Miami Air International, (305) 876–3600;
www.miamiair.com
Omni Air International, (877) 718–8901;
www.omniairintl.com
Ryan International, (888) 464–7926;
www.flyryan.com
Transmeridian Airlines, (888) 733–6373;
www.transmeridian-airlines.com

Ground Transportation

You can get to or from the airport via a variety of means. For the Lindbergh Terminal: For car rentals, city buses, the shuttle to the Humphrey Terminal, hotel shuttles, or (in late 2004) the light rail station, take the Hub Tram on Level T to the Transit Center. For taxis follow the signs on Level T to the escalators to the taxi station.

Car rental agencies that have rental locations at the airport include **National Car Rental** (800–227–7368; www.national car.com); **Budget Car & Truck Rental** (612–527–7000; www.budget.com); **AVIS Rent A Car** (800–831–2847; www.avis.com); **Alamo** (800–327–9633; www.alamo.com); and **Hertz** (800–654–3131; www.hertz.com).

At the airport it is easiest to catch a taxi at the taxi station, where you simply wait in line for the next available taxi. Let the attendant know if you have special needs, such as a cab that takes credit cards. For a list of taxi companies and their contact information, see the Taxis section later in this chapter.

City buses are far and away the cheapest way to get to and from the airport. If you're traveling light and in no big hurry, you can catch a city bus at the Transit Center. Contact **Metro Transit** at (612) 373–3333 or visit www.metrotransit.org for route and schedule information.

Scheduled to open for service to both airport terminals in late 2004, Minneapolis-St. Paul's first light rail line, the Hiawatha LRT, will connect downtown Minneapolis with the Mall of America, with 17 stops along the route. The light rail station at Lindbergh will be underground and accessible via the Transit Center. The light rail station at Humphrey will be aboveground inside the new parking ramp across from the terminal. For more information about service and the Hiawatha LRT route, see the Light Rail section later in this chapter or contact Metro Transit.

Parking

There are convenient parking facilities adjacent to both the Lindbergh and Humphrey Terminals at MSP. These lots include general, short-term, wheelchair-accessible, and valet parking (Lindbergh Terminal only). There are also several privately owned off-airport parking facilities to meet your needs.

Lindbergh Terminal offers short-term, long-term, and valet parking in the four ramps surrounded by the terminal concourses. Follow the signs as you enter the terminal area. Short-term parking is designed for stays of less than two hours; long-term parking is designed for stays longer than two hours. You can access the terminal from any of the ramps via enclosed skyways, the Hub Tram (accessible from the Transit Center), or Level T.

Humphrey Terminal offers short- and long-term parking in the ramp across the street from the terminal. Travelers can get to the terminal by walking across the street or using the enclosed skyway on the second level.

For off-airport parking, the following lots offer shuttle transportation to and from MSP every 5 to 10 minutes, 24 hours a day:

EZ Air Park (651–777–7275); at 2804 Lexington Avenue in Eagan

Park 'N Go (952–854–3386; www. park ngo.net); Interstate 494 and 34th Avenue in Bloomington

Park 'N Fly (952–854–0606; www.pnf. com); 3700 East 80th Street in Bloomington

Park 'N Jet, (651–690–1200); 1400 Davern Street and Shepard Road in St. Paul

For parking availability and information, call the **MSP Parking Information Line** at (952) 826-7000.

Amenities

With the last big series of expansions made to MSP in the '90s, the Lindbergh Terminal's waiting area went from being a midsize airport to a minimall of shopping opportunities with several restaurant courts. The centerpiece of the terminal's lobby is Northstar Crossing, a collection of more than 65 retail shops and restaurants in the Lindbergh Terminal. The area features Minnesota-themed shops and nationally known retailers, including the first airport-based Lands' End and Liz Claiborne stores. Throughout the terminal can be found McDonald's, Burger King, Cinnabon, Pizza Hut, Miami Subs & Grill, and Pretzel Mania; for libations (Lindbergh Terminal only) there are several City Martinis, a PS Air Pub, and the MSP Brewhouse. The Humphrey Terminal offers more limited services, with one full-service restaurant and two shops selling magazines, newspapers, snacks, and gifts.

For disabled passengers, all airlines operating out of MSP provide wheelchairs for the flight. For carts, wheelchairs, or medical transportation, airline passengers should contact their travel agent, ticketing agents, flight attendants, or gate agents. Travelers Assistance (TA) can also help with wheelchair requests. TA volunteers may be reached by calling (612) 726-5500. Wheelchairs are also available for check out at the information booth on Level T and at security checkpoints.

If you lose something at either of the terminals, call **Airport Lost and Found** at (612) 726-5141.

The Metropolitan Airports Commission invites members of public and private groups alike to MSP. One-hour tours are offered Monday through Friday between 9:00 A.M. and 3:00 P.M. Children's groups must be at a first-grade level or older and include a minimum of one chaperone per six children; the minimum group size is 10 and the maximum group size is 30. Contact the tour coordinator at (612) 726-5574 for more information or to reserve your tour time.

Train Travel

Amtrak
Twin Cities Passenger Station
730 Transfer Road, St. Paul
(651) 644-1127 or (800) 872-7245
www.amtrak.com

The Twin Cities share a train station in the industrial Midway District of St. Paul. To get to the station, take the Cretin Avenue/Vandalia Street exit from Interstate 94 and turn north at the stoplights. Turn west (right) at University Avenue, and then turn north (left) at the next stoplight (Transfer Road). The station is about a block up on the right. You can also get to the station from downtown Minneapolis or St. Paul on Metro Transit bus route 16 along University Avenue. The station and ticket counter are open 6:30 A.M. to 11:30 P.M. daily.

A single passenger train, the Empire Builder between Chicago and Seattle, stops at the station twice a day (once in each direction). If you're headed for points far afield, you can make connections in Chicago or Seattle to stations throughout the country.

Within Minnesota, Amtrak is less useful than other transportation options. Although the Empire Builder stops at Winona, Red Wing, St. Cloud, Staples,

---

Insiders' Tip

Some of the buses in downtown Minneapolis run 24 hours a day, year-round. Call Metro Transit at (612) 373-3333 for specific bus information.

Detroit Lakes, and Fargo-Moorhead, you will arrive at those stations in the middle of the night, regardless of whether you are on the east- or westbound train.

Bus Travel

Greyhound Bus Lines
166 West University Avenue, St. Paul
(651) 222–0507
950 Hawthorne Avenue, Minneapolis
(612) 371–3325
www.greyhound.com

Greyhound is a Minnesota company, founded in Hibbing on northern Minnesota's Iron Range in 1914. St. Paul and Minneapolis each have a Greyhound station. St. Paul's station is just west of the State Capitol building on University Avenue and is open 6:15 A.M. to 9:00 P.M. daily. The sparkling new downtown Minneapolis station is inside the Hawthorne Transportation Center, a few blocks west of Target Center (First Avenue becomes Hawthorne Avenue as it heads west), and is open 5:30 A.M. to 1:00 A.M. daily.

Jefferson Bus Lines serves both Greyhound terminals as well as the Lindbergh Terminal at Minneapolis-St. Paul International Airport. Call (612) 332–3224 for more information.

Car Travel

Highways

Minneapolis-St. Paul has well-thought-out arterial and surrounding highways. However, politics and not-so-well-thought-out plans limit the number of lanes on many area highways, causing traffic jams and bottlenecks with predictable frequency. If you are driving to your destination in the Twin Cities, be aware that the major highways become parking lots during the morning and evening rush hours.

The Twin Cities are ringed by the Interstate 494/Interstate 694 loop. I-494 starts at the interchange with I-94 in the eastern suburb of Woodbury; arcs south around South St. Paul; heads due west through Eagan, Bloomington, and Eden Prairie; and then swings north through the western suburbs to reunite with I-94 in the suburb of Maple Grove northwest of Minneapolis. I-694 also starts at the

I–94 in downtown St. Paul winds its way through the city and on to Minneapolis. PHOTO: TODD R. BERGER

ing times of heavy congestion), and its ramps take you right into the heart of Minneapolis's Warehouse District.

Several other federal and state highways crosshatch the I–494/I–694 loop. U.S. Highway 169 arrives in the Metro from southwestern Minnesota in the suburb of Eden Prairie, on the southwestern edge of the Cities, and then shoots due north through the western suburbs, crossing I–694 in Maple Grove just east of the intersection of I–694 and I–494. US 169 and the roughly parallel Minnesota Highway 100 are the principal north-south routes in the western suburbs.

Minnesota Highway 62 is the major east-west route through the southern Metro north of I–494. MN 62, referred to locally as the Crosstown, runs from its intersection with US 169 in Minnetonka in the southwestern Metro to its intersection with Minnesota Highway 55, just north of Minneapolis-St. Paul International Airport. The Crosstown looks convenient on a map, but the highway briefly merges with I–35W in Richfield, and the resulting bottleneck is considered one of the worst in the nation.

Other useful highways in the south central Metro include Minnesota Highway 77, which runs from the southern suburb of Apple Valley to its intersection with the Crosstown in the Lake Nokomis area of south Minneapolis. This highway passes, among other things, the Minnesota Zoo, the Mall of America, and MSP airport. Minnesota Highway 55 stretches all the way from the town of Hastings, 20 miles southeast of St. Paul, to downtown Minneapolis, passing over the Minnesota River via the 4,119-foot concrete-arch Fort Snelling-Mendota Bridge and skirting Fort Snelling State Park, MSP airport, and Minnehaha Park before gliding through the commercial districts of south Minneapolis. Known as Hiawatha Avenue along its path inside Minneapolis, this road will be the route of the Hiawatha LRT leg from downtown Minneapolis to the airport. There are stoplights along parts of this route, but it can be a quick alternative to get downtown from the southeastern Metro.

intersection with I–94 in Woodbury but heads north through Oakdale, swings west to the intersection with Interstate 35E in Little Canada, and then meanders roughly northwest through the suburbs of New Brighton, Fridley, Brooklyn Center, Brooklyn Park, and Maple Grove, where it meets I–94 again.

The rough rectangle made by the I–494/I–694 loop is sliced by two branches of I–35 heading north-south through the Metro. I–35 splits into I–35W and I–35E in the southern suburb of Burnsville. I–35W heads due north through the western part of the Metro into downtown Minneapolis and then wiggles northeast of downtown through the northern suburbs to merge with I–35E in Lino Lakes and become I–35 again. I–35E heads northeast from Burnsville into downtown St. Paul and then shoots north to briefly merge with I–694 before stretching north again for its eventual reunion with I–35W.

I–94 and I–394 split the I–494/I–694 rectangle east-west. I–94 rolls into the eastern Metro from Wisconsin, bouncing along through downtown St. Paul and downtown Minneapolis before abruptly swinging north, where it merges for a few miles with I–694 in Brooklyn Center before going it alone again in its long march westward. Interstate 394 runs from the western suburbs to downtown Minneapolis. The newest of the Twin Cities freeways, I–394 includes separate carpool lanes (open dur-

The view of downtown St. Paul from Cathedral Hill in winter. PHOTO: TODD R. BERGER

The principal highways in the eastern Metro include Minnesota Highway 110, which starts at its intersection with I-494 just west of the intersection with U.S. Highway 52, then takes a short tour of the St. Paul suburbs of Inver Grove Heights, Sunfish Lake, West St. Paul, and Mendota Heights before intersecting with MN 55 just before the Fort Snelling–Mendota Bridge over the Minnesota River.

US 52 is perhaps more useful, arriving from southern Minnesota and intersecting I-494 in the southern St. Paul suburb of Inver Grove Heights. From there the highway conveniently heads through the suburbs of South St. Paul and West St. Paul right to downtown St. Paul, passing St. Paul Downtown Holman Field airport and crossing the Mississippi River in the process. The route into the city along US 52, particularly at night, provides some of the most spectacular views of the St. Paul skyline.

U.S. Highways 10 and 61 unite in Hastings and follow the Mississippi River to I-94 just east of downtown St. Paul, passing through the suburbs of Cottage Grove, St. Paul Park, and Newport in the process. From there, US 61 veers north at Arcade Street, following city streets until hitting the suburb of Maplewood and then spiking north through the suburbs of Mahtomedi, Gem Lake, White Bear Lake, and Hugo before ending just north of Forest Lake about 25 miles north of downtown St. Paul. US 61 roughly parallels I-35E in the northern suburbs, and the interstate is almost always a better choice except during heavy rush hour-traffic.

US 10 takes the easy route after intersecting I-94 by merging with the interstate in the westbound direction, then turning north and merging with I-35E for a few miles, and then merging with I-694 and heading northwest to the northern suburb of Arden Hills. From there US 10 briefly follows its own route northwest, then merges with I-35W in Mounds View for a few miles, finally going it alone through the suburbs of Blaine, Coon Rapids, Anoka, Ramsey, and Elk River before skipping out of the Metro.

Minnesota Highway 36 is another useful eastern Metro highway, running from its intersection with I 35W in the northern suburb of Roseville through Little Canada, Maplewood, North St. Paul, and Oakdale all the way to Stillwater on the St. Croix River. This highway has some stoplights, particularly in the stretch between I-35E and I-694 and on the approach into Stillwater, and is prone to gridlocked traffic during rush hours; but it is the quickest outlet to the St. Croix Valley and a convenient artery leading to many shopping areas in the first-tier northern suburbs.

Minnesota Highway 280 provides an appreciated shortcut for motorists on I-94 on the western edges of St. Paul intent on reaching the northern suburbs. The highway runs from its intersection with I-94 just east of the Minneapolis city boundary due north through Lauderdale to intersect I-35W in Roseville after just a few miles. The highway provides access not only to the retail outlets of Roseville but also to the University of Minnesota–St. Paul Campus and Luther Seminary.

Twin Cities Streets

Minneapolis and St. Paul are two distinctly governed municipalities, separated along much of one boundary by the Mississippi River. For this reason, Minneapolis and St. Paul share a few important streets, which include University and Como Avenues. However, several streets change their names when crossing the Mississippi. Most notably, Larpenteur Avenue in St. Paul becomes East Hennepin Avenue in Minneapolis, and Marshall Avenue in St. Paul changes its name to Lake Street after crossing the Mississippi into Minneapolis. So don't be alarmed if you just crossed the beautiful Mississippi on Marshall Avenue and now find yourself on Lake Street. More confusingly, both cities have streets that share names, but are not connected to their counterparts across the river. Just a few examples include Minnehaha and Grand

Avenues. Always keep in mind the city you are in, and realize these streets are quite frequently not connected when navigating Twin Cities streets.

St. Paul Streets

In downtown St. Paul, Kellogg Boulevard is the major thoroughfare. It connects the "Lowertown" section of downtown to the myriad attractions located on the southwest part of the boulevard; e.g., the Ordway Music Center, the Science Museum of Minnesota, the Xcel Energy Center, and the Minnesota Historical Center. Wabasha Street is the major street moving northwest and southwest through the city. It travels over the bridge of the same name and passes Harriet Island, one of the city's loveliest parks. Both streets are prone to congestion, especially when an event is taking place downtown, but they are not as busy as many other Minneapolis streets during rush hour. Seventh Street is another important downtown street because it moves traffic northeast and southwest. Passing through the heart of downtown St. Paul, the street is often congested. It also serves as a link to several

Insiders' Tip

Numerous Twin Cities events offer park and ride opportunities. For example, the Minnesota State Fair has park and ride lots at the University of Minnesota, Har Mar Mall (in Roseville), and at other locations. Park and ride is an excellent way to avoid traffic and the hassle of commuting to popular Twin Cities events.

additional significant streets. Grand Avenue is one of them. Beginning on the edge of downtown, Grand Avenue travels up one of the city's largest bluffs and is St. Paul's favorite street for shopping. It stretches east-west through much of the city and is one of the most well-known streets. University Avenue begins near the Minnesota State Capitol just north of downtown, where it passes across St. Paul, Minneapolis, and the northern suburbs of the Twin Cities. Through St. Paul, it serves as a major east-west street. Much slower than I–94, which runs parallel to the avenue, it presents a more intimate overview of the area. In addition, Larpenteur, Maryland, East Minnehaha, and Como Avenues also serve as important east-west routes through St. Paul.

If you're headed north-south on surface streets in the western part of St. Paul, you will probably find yourself on Snelling Avenue. The major thoroughfare, which is also Minnesota Highway 51, runs through the city from West Seventh Street east of MSP airport and past the St. Paul neighborhood of Highland Park, as well as Macalester College, Hamline University, and the Minnesota State Fairgrounds, intersecting such major routes as Grand Avenue, I–94, University Avenue, and Larpenteur Avenue along the way. The major north-south surface streets in the eastern part of the city include Arcade Street (US 61) and White Bear Avenue, which stretches from Battle Creek Regional Park across I–94, following a straight-north route to the northern suburbs.

Minneapolis Streets

Minneapolis streets, as in its sister Twin City, take some experience to understand. The more populous Minneapolis has many more one-way streets, so always pay attention to signs. For example, when driving through the University of Minnesota, University Avenue splits into two one-way streets (one continues as University Avenue, the other is Southeast Fourth Street). Again, do not worry, the streets come together before entering northeast Minneapolis.

Hennepin Avenue is downtown's most renowned street. Historically the theater district of the city, it is reemerging with the same role and is also a popular place to eat, drink, and be merry. For automobile travel, Hennepin Avenue downtown is closed to traffic headed southwest, where drivers must instead follow First Avenue, a one-way street. Hennepin Avenue also leads to the Walker Art Center and into the shopping and dining of the Uptown neighborhood in south Minneapolis. Lake Street moves east-west from Lake Calhoun, then splits into one-way streets through densely populated Uptown and south Minneapolis. Downtown Minneapolis has numerous one-way streets, almost all on the grid arranged to move northwest-southeast and northeast-southwest. Each of these streets in downtown is extremely congested during the rush hours but otherwise presents an astounding view of the city's skyline. Through the northern part of the city east of I-94, Central Avenue and University Avenue Northeast are the major thoroughfares. In the northwestern part of the city, Lyndale Avenue North and Penn Avenue North are the principal surface routes.

Snow Emergency Information

Although the words "snow emergency" may sound ominous to the uninitiated,

such events are declared primarily so that the city of Minneapolis or St. Paul can get people to park their cars in the proper places to allow the plows to get through. Declaration of such an "emergency" does not (necessarily) mean that you will need to stock up on batteries or canned chipped beef. Both Minneapolis and St. Paul have extensive and different snow emergency ordinances. In some situations, not complying with snow removal rules will result in the towing of a vehicle or a hefty fine, so beware. Snow emergencies are announced through the local media. You can also check to see if restrictions are in effect in Minneapolis by calling (612) 348-SNOW or visiting www.ci.minneapolis.mn.us/snow. For St. Paul call (651) 266-PLOW, or check the Web at www.ci.saint-paul.mn.us/depts/publicworks/snowplow. It is your responsibility to check whether a snow emergency has been declared; pleading ignorance will not get you out of paying a fine or towing fees. The following is a list of guidelines and helpful hints for snow emergencies.

Minneapolis

Minneapolis does not set a minimum amount of snowfall to declare a snow emergency other than to describe it as "significant." Once a snow emergency is declared, the entire city enters a three-day cycle that dictates where you can park your car. On the first day of a snow emergency, from 9:00 P.M. to 8:00 A.M., the city allows no parking on either side of Snow Emergency Routes, which are marked with red signs along the side of the street or blue street-name signs (non-snow emergency routes have green or brown street-name signs). You can park on either side of any non-snow emergency route and on parkways. On the second day of the snow emergency, from 8:00 A.M. to 8:00 P.M., there is no parking on either side of parkways or on the even-numbered side of non-snow emergency routes; however, you can now park on plowed Snow Emergency Routes. From 8:00 P.M. to 8:00 A.M. on the second night of the snow emergency, you cannot park on the odd-numbered side of non-snow emergency

Insiders' Tip

Are you concerned about road conditions? Check out the Minnesota Department of Transportation Web site (www.dot.state.mn.us) or give them a call at (651) 296-3000 or (800) 657-3774.

There is no overnight parking on this street during Snow Emergencies in St. Paul. Residents also need to find another place to park their cars overnight on Sundays, when the city sometimes cleans the streets. Parking here during these times will likely lead to a costly ticket or a more costly towing of your vehicle.

PHOTO: TODD R. BERGER

routes. On the third day of the snow emergency, the parking ban continues on the odd-numbered side of non–snow emergency routes until the street is plowed to the curb.

Minneapolis offers free or reduced-fee parking on the first night of a snow emergency at several parking ramps downtown and around the University of Minnesota. Call the Minneapolis snow emergency line or check out the Web site for more information.

St. Paul

St. Paul declares snow emergencies after 3 or more inches of snow accumulation over a couple of days. St. Paul divides its streets into "night plow" and "day plow" routes. The night plow routes are plowed between 9:00 P.M. and 6:00 A.M. on the night the snow emergency is declared. These routes are marked with permanent night plow zone signs. Note that some north-south residential streets have signs reading

NIGHT PLOW ROUTE THIS SIDE OF STREET. You *can* park on the nonsigned sides of these streets during the first night of a snow emergency. The snow is removed on day plow routes from 8:00 A.M. to 5:00 P.M. These routes, which are not marked with signs, include east-west residential streets and north-south residential streets without plowing signs.

Parking

The rates at downtown Minneapolis and St. Paul parking ramps and lots range widely based on location, time of day, the owner of the facility, and whether a sporting event or other major happening is occurring in the area. Generally you can expect to pay $1.50 minimum for the first half-hour at downtown lots in either city and considerably more than that for lots and ramps owned by private companies and located in choice spots. To get the best price, look for municipal ramps and lots on the fringes of either city's downtown.

Both cities have extensive street-level parking, most with parking meters. Rates and enforcement times vary, so check the signs carefully, carry plenty of quarters, and consult your timepiece before strolling away from your car. In downtown Minneapolis parking charges can be avoided by patronizing stores and restaurants that participate in the "Do the Town" parking program, where a $20 purchase after 4:00 P.M. and all day on weekends will get you a parking validation. If you're going to be spending the money anyway, why not spend it on something nice for yourself, instead of putting the money down just to keep your car from being towed?

Keep in mind when parking downtown that you do not necessarily have to park right next to your destination when the winter winds blow and the temperatures plummet. In both downtown Minneapolis and downtown St. Paul, many buildings and parking ramps are connected through the Cities' respective Skyway systems.

The Skyway systems provide an added bonus in the summer, too—walking over the main pedestrian thoroughfares means you don't have to stop for traffic lights or crosswalks—or watch out for puddles or rogue automobiles.

Park and Ride Lots

Over 8,000 free parking spaces are available for city bus passengers at more than 120 Park & Ride lots throughout the Twin Cities metro area. For locations, call Metro Commuter Services at (651) 602-1602, or visit their Web site at www.metro transit.org.

Public Transportation

City Bus

Metro Transit
(612) 373-3333
www.metrotransit.org

Metro Transit, the principal transportation provider in the Minneapolis and St. Paul area, is one of the country's largest transit systems, providing roughly 95 percent of the 65 million bus trips taken annually in the Twin Cities. Each weekday, customers board Metro Transit buses an average of 200,000 times. Buses run between the Cities and the suburbs every day and evening—some downtown Minneapolis lines even run 24 hours a day. The system is made up of 109 routes served by a fleet of 888 buses, and Metro Transit has its own police department.

Adult rates for Metro Transit buses are $1.25 during non–rush-hour times and $2.00 for rush-hour times for local bus routes and $2.00 outside rush hour and $2.75 during rush hour for express routes. Rush hour is defined as 6:00 to 9:00 A.M. and 3:00 to 6:30 P.M., Monday through Friday (except holidays). Seniors over 65 and youth under 12 can ride at reduced fares during non–rush-hour times. Persons with disabilities can ride for 50 cents anytime.

Metro Transit buses are reliable and travel widely dispersed routes within the cities of Minneapolis and St. Paul, and it is very possible to live in either St. Paul or Minneapolis and not own a car. Service to the outer suburbs is spotty, with only a few lines running out of town each day—usually one an hour at most. Downtown Minneapolis, downtown St. Paul, Uptown Minneapolis, and the Mall of America are Metro Transit's four main hubs, where most routes converge and transfers are easy to make. A quick phone call to Metro Transit will put you in touch with an operator who will mail you all the schedules you need to get around the area (please specify which ones you need, because there are hundreds of routes to choose from). Transit System maps are also available from Metro Transit for a small fee.

On Metro Transit's Web site, you can determine routes, view route maps, print schedules, and plan itineraries by entering origination and destination addresses or nearest street intersections.

Light Rail

The Twin Cities first light rail line, the Hiawatha LRT, is scheduled to begin operations in spring 2004. When complete, the line will stretch 11.6 miles from downtown Minneapolis, past the Metrodome and through the University of Minnesota West Bank Campus, and then follow Hiawatha Avenue through south Minneapolis past Lake Street, tunnel under Minnehaha Park, resurface to pause at the Veterans' Administration Medical Center, and then move on to Fort Snelling State Park. The line will dive underground again via tunnels to the Lindbergh Terminal and emerge to stop at the Humphrey Terminal at MSP airport, then travel on to the Mall of America in Bloomington. Riders will be able to board trains on the first section of the Hiawatha LRT line, from downtown Minneapolis to Fort Snelling, in April 2004; the remainder of the line, from Fort Snelling to the Mall of America, will open for service in December 2004.

The line will feature 17 stations, all individually designed to fit in with the surrounding neighborhoods. Though fares were not available at the time of this writing, Metro Transit expects them to parallel the bus fare structure noted earlier.

The Hiawatha LRT line has been a source of great public debate for many years in the Twin Cities and in Minnesota state government—not surprising given the project's $675.4 million price tag (in 2002 dollars). However, when the first south Minneapolis residents ride to the Mall of America, the first conventioneers board a train at the airport and skim to their downtown Minneapolis hotels, and the first Metro commuters take advantage of the several park and ride lots for quick trips to their downtown jobs, the arguments will slowly move to the side and the long-overdue system will become as much a part of the Twin Cities landscape as the IDS Center, the Mall of America, and the desperately overcrowded freeways.

Suburban Bus Systems

Several suburban areas have smaller bus systems serving outlying communities, with connections to the larger Metro Transit system in the Twin Cities. For more information on bus service in specific areas, contact the following organizations.

Northwestern Suburbs

Anoka County Transit Services
(763) 422–7075
www.co.anoka.mn.us/departments/trans portation/index

Anoka County Transit Services maintains bus routes serving the northwestern communities of Anoka, Blaine, and Coon Rapids.

Far Southern Suburbs

Minnesota Valley Transit Authority
(952) 882–7500
www.mvta.com

The Minnesota Valley Transit Authority serves five southern suburbs just south of the Minnesota River: Apple Valley, Burnsville, Eagan, Rosemount, and Savage.

Southwestern Suburbs

Southwest Metro Transit
(952) 974–3107
www.swtransit.org

Southwest Metro Transit serves the communities of Eden Prairie, Chanhassen, and Chaska, with express service also available to downtown Minneapolis, Southdale Center in Edina, and the University of Minnesota West Bank and East Bank campuses in Minneapolis.

Taxis

While taxicabs have become a common sight in both downtown Minneapolis and St. Paul, flagging one down on the street is nearly impossible. Your best bet is to call a cab company and have them send a ride over to you instead of trying to randomly flag one down.

The one exception to this rule is, like in most other cities, at the airport. Parked cabs waiting for fares line up at the taxi station at Lindbergh Terminal and at the curb in front of Humphrey Terminal.

The following taxi companies provide

service throughout the Twin Cities. Many localized cab companies in the Cities serve either the eastern or western Metro—but not both—so consult the Minneapolis or St. Paul Yellow Pages for further options.

Airport Taxi/Town Taxi
Airport Service: (952) 928–0000
Minneapolis and St. Paul Service:
(612) 331–8294

Yellow Cab Company
Airport Service: (651) 644–3212
Minneapolis Service: (612) 824–4444
St. Paul Service: (651) 222–4433

Green & White/Suburban Taxi
Airport Service: (952) 884–8888
Minneapolis Service: (612) 522–2222
St. Paul Service: (651) 222–2222

History

When arriving in Minnesota, many visitors are struck by a peculiarity among Twin Cities residents: their concern with the weather. As time has passed, the weather's impact on Twin Citians' lives has decreased considerably, and industry, and later technology, have replaced the area's reliance on natural resources and agriculture. Still, in a state where temperatures have ranged from –60 degrees F to 114 degrees F, and an Indian summer afternoon can transmogrify into a chilling winter blizzard in less than an hour, the interest remains. After all, the Twin Cities were built on their abundant natural resources and fecund lands. Milling, mining, and lumbering were the cornerstones of the early Minnesota economy. These industries created links to numerous allied businesses that developed into the component parts of the area's diverse and dynamic 21st-century economy. So when you visit the Twin Cities, remember the area's concern with weather has an important historical antecedent. The number of farmers, millers, and lumberjacks may have dramatically decreased, but it is the basis of the area's early history. And at least indirectly, it continues to affect the personal and economic livelihood of Twin Citians.

The Origins of the Twin Cities

The history of the Twin Cities begins with two cities, Minneapolis and St. Paul, each with distinct yet similar developments. Minneapolis is nicknamed the "City of Lakes" and the "Mill City." In stark contrast, St. Paul is the "Saintly City" and the "Capital City." These differences have exacerbated competition between the cities. Residents of both cities become angered when one of the cities is mentioned and the other is left out, as was the case during Super Bowl XXVI at the Metrodome in Minneapolis on January 26, 1992. St. Paul residents felt the national media focused too much attention on Minneapolis, where the event took place. Incidents like these have been common throughout the Twin Cities history, where frequently good-natured competition has occurred. However, there are more similarities than differences between the cities. One commonality in the two cities' history is the first inhabitants of the area, the American Indians.

Before European settlement, the Dakota and Ojibwe populated the Twin Cities area. However, Native American presence predates the Dakota and Ojibwe. Archeologists and historians actually know more about the Woodland Indians because of the rich fossil record they left behind. Woodland Indian burial mounds were scattered throughout Minnesota when the state was settled. Mounds Park, overlooking downtown St. Paul, has one of the area's finest examples of Hopewell Indian mounds. The Mississippian cultures of the Dakota and Ojibwe replaced these early peoples. Archeologists posit that this occurred between A.D. 800 and 1000. Unlike in the past, the mounds and their human remains, tools, and other artifacts are now protected as the historical record of the first Twin Citians.

The Ojibwe, or Ojibwa, were in the past more often referred to as the Chippewa and had origins in the area near Sault Ste. Marie, Michigan. The skilled hunters' territories expanded to include parts of the northern metropolitan Twin Cities. While the Ojibwe's origins were to the east and north, the Dakota were western Plains Indians, who at the time of European exploration occupied the Twin Cities, western and southern Minnesota, and much of present-day North Dakota and South Dakota. The French referred to the Dakota as Sioux, a meaningless abridgement of the Ojibwe term, *Nadouissoutx*. The word translates as "little viper" or "lesser enemy." The derogatory name stuck for centuries, until recently when the tribe was called the more respectful name Dakota. Both Indian tribes were hunting societies, and evolved tremendously by incorporating European tools, wares, and implements such as guns, hatchets, blankets, knives, and kettles. The contact and cultural exchange transformed the local American Indians and the Europeans. The Europeans rapidly pushed the less densely populated American Indians from their lands through treaties and warfare. Frequently internecine warfare occurred between the Dakota, usually supported and supplied by the British, and the Ojibwe, supported by the French. However, the French voyageurs were the first Europeans to leave a mark on the area, even if they did not establish a permanent settlement.

The names of French explorers and traders are common among the streets, avenues, counties, and institutions in the Twin Cities. Father Louis Hennepin, a Belgian, explored French territories that included the area that became the Twin Cities in 1680 and three years later wrote the then best-selling book *Description of Louisiana*, in which he exaggerated the splendor of the area's natural wonders. During his visit he named the Falls of St. Anthony after his patron saint. St. Anthony is located across the Mississippi River from the later birthplace of Minneapolis. In 1872 St. Anthony and Minneapolis merged. Hennepin's name is commemorated in Minneapolis's most famous thoroughfare, Hennepin Avenue, and the county of the same name. Fur trapping remained important in the area for well over a century, but a permanent settlement in the area did not occur until the United States won independence from England.

Fort Snelling was the first site permanently settled in Minnesota. The federal government established the fort to protect the most northwestern edge of the United States. Henry Leavenworth came to the present site of Fort Snelling in 1819, at the confluence of the Mississippi and Minnesota Rivers. The current location adjoins Minneapolis-St. Paul International Airport. Leavenworth failed miserably and was quickly replaced by Josiah Snelling. He performed his duties so well the federal government named it in his honor in 1825. The fort sits on a cliff overlooking the rivers, allowing for easy protection of the area. It remains one of the Twin Cities' most scenic overlooks. When Fort Snelling was constructed, civilians began squatting in the area in order to serve the needs of soldiers and take advantage of the protection of the U.S. military.

The birth of St. Paul was an extremely colorful page of Twin Cities history. Pierre "Pig's Eye" Parrant, a 60-year-old former voyageur, was the liquor bootlegger for the soldiers and citizens around Fort Snelling. Parrant's nickname, "Pig's Eye," was the result of his disfigured and blind eye, and was the original name given to St. Paul. Not surprisingly, the thorny name for the city did not last. In 1840 a young Catholic priest, Lucian Galtier, arrived in Pig's Eye, where he christened the Chapel of St. Paul. Afterward the city was generally referred to as St. Paul's Landing. Following the arrival of the post office in 1846, the city's name was simply shortened to St. Paul.

Just up the Mississippi, the emergence of the other twin city, Minneapolis, was less colorful. Minneapolis and St. Anthony began in the 1840s as milling and lumbering centers; at first the two industries developed gradually. Franklin Steele settled St. Anthony in 1838, where he began successful flour and sawmills.

On the other side of the Mississippi, Minneapolis was not founded until 1852, when Congress rescinded 26,000 acres from Fort Snelling's control. This allowed squatters such as Colonel John H. Stevens to claim and develop the land that would become downtown Minneapolis.

Minneapolis's name has interesting origins. It is an amalgam of words from two languages, the Dakota word "minne," meaning "sky-tinted water," and "polis," the Greek word for "city." Minneapolis was founded on the west bank of the Mississippi River and St. Anthony on the east bank. In the 21st century it is difficult to believe that St. Anthony's importance early in its history eclipsed Minneapolis's, which had a relatively late start and was not chartered until 1867. But as time marched on, Minneapolis's growth significantly outpaced St. Anthony's. In 1855 a suspension bridge was constructed to link the two communities. It was the first permanent bridge anywhere across the Mississippi, and it created extensive commercial and civic ties between the rapidly expanding urban centers. The two cities merged in 1872, which established a much larger Minneapolis. The Twin Cities' growth had a significant impact on Minnesota, which became a territory in 1849 and the thirty-second state in 1858.

The Mill City

In the late 19th and early 20th centuries Minneapolis became nationally prominent as the "Mill City." The emergence of milling came as the lumbering industry began to decline because of competition from the west. The ascendancy of milling also created numerous allied industries and was important to the development of the diverse Minneapolis economy in the 20th century.

Milling began on the Mississippi, in Minneapolis and St. Anthony, because of the falls. Since the 19th century, industry and government programs have tamed much of the turbulence of St. Anthony Falls. To businessmen in the area, the falls represented an unbridled source of energy for milling the vast wheat crops in the area, which rapidly expanded as Minnesota and the upper Midwest were settled. As time progressed, each succeeding generation of mills became larger. Of course, this led to further consolidation, and industry leaders, internationally recognizable even today, emerged to dominate Minneapolis's market.

Innovations were instrumental in the development and dominance of General Mills. The corporation emerged gradually after a succession of mergers in Minneapolis's milling industry. Washburn-Crosby and Company is the major component of General Mills. The star of the company skyrocketed following an important innovation, "new process flour," which was brought to Washburn-Crosby and Company in 1871. The revolutionary new process flour involved milling spring wheat into white flour. No longer was "winter wheat" preferred. Quickly, many Minneapolis mills acquired the revolutionary technology for producing new process flour. Many competitors acquired the information dubiously. Washburn-Crosby and Company found tremendous success again in 1880, when they won the gold medal at the Millers' Exhibition in Cincinnati; thereafter the company marketed the Gold Medal brand of flour. The new technology catapulted General Mills and other Minneapolis mills to prominence as the nation's leading milling companies. By 1890 Minneapolis was the largest wheat market in the nation.

Minneapolis spawned many of the world's largest and most important mills, and they have had a profound impact on the Cities' development. Pillsbury is another Minnesota-based company, and it began milling on the Mississippi in Minneapolis. The world's largest agribusiness company—Cargill—also has origins in Minneapolis, where it remains to this day, headquartered in Minnetonka, a Minneapolis suburb. Milling's influence still deeply pervades Minneapolis culture. Even the minor league baseball team was named the Millers. Moreover, the call letters of one of Minneapolis's radio and television stations is WCCO. The station takes its name

St. Paul has always been a river city, having grown up on the banks of the Mississippi. PHOTO: SAINT PAUL CONVENTION AND VISITORS BUREAU

from Washburn-Crosby and Company, an early owner of the station. Diversification like this has spurred the increasingly dynamic Minnesota economy.

The Capital City

The nicknames of St. Paul are fundamental to its history. As the "Capital City" and the "Saintly City," institutions play a pivotal role in the city's development. Unlike Minneapolis, St. Paul's economic history is not dominated by a single industry, but corporations such as 3M have been instrumental throughout the city's history.

Institutions such as government and the Roman Catholic Church are central to St. Paul's history. Since the beginnings of the Minnesota Territory in 1849, St. Paul has served as the capital city. Although early in its territorial history, it almost lost the capital to St. Peter in 1857. Joe Rolette, a territorial councilman, pocketed a bill passed by both houses of the legislature calling for

relocating the territorial capital to St. Peter (south on the Minnesota River). Rolette hid with the bill for a week, but a copy of the bill was passed on to the governor, who signed it. Fortunately for St. Paul, the territorial governor was not reappointed. Later, a federal district judge ruled that Minnesota Territory could not name another capital site. The capital remained in St. Paul. Since then, as the capital of Minnesota, political events have continued to play an important role in St. Paul's history.

The Roman Catholic Church is another important institution in the city's history. Catholicism has always found more adherents in St. Paul. The city includes larger populations of Irish, German Catholics, and a small but significant number of Italian immigrants, while Minneapolis's immigration in the 19th century was dominated by Scandinavian and German Lutherans. Catholicism profoundly affected St. Paul's history. It began with the arrival of Father Lucian Galtier, who came to save the souls in "Pig's Eye." St. Paul was established as a diocese by 1850, and in 1888 it was expanded to become the archdiocese of St. Paul. The first archbishop of St. Paul, John Ireland, was instrumental in the development of Catholicism in the archdiocese. Born in Ireland, he attended the antecedent of Cretin-Derham Hall and was groomed for his position as archbishop. Ireland was also involved in Irish immigration societies with St. Paul railroad magnate James J. Hill. The society populated the city and greater Minnesota with Catholics. In 1918 Ireland died, after initiating the erection of the spectacular Cathedral of St. Paul, which continues today as one the city's most important landmarks. The archdiocese of St. Paul and Minneapolis remains headquartered in St. Paul, and it is an institution of essential importance in the city's history.

Industry and technology were paramount in the historical development of St. Paul. Minnesota Mining and Manufacturing Company is one of the Cities' most important companies. 3M's history began in Two Harbors, a small town north of Duluth, in 1902 as a manufacturer of sandpaper. The company relocated to St. Paul in 1909 and has always placed a premium on producing and developing diverse, new, and innovative products. Sandpaper, Scotch brand tape and Post-It self-sticking notes are important product lines. Over time 3M has grown into an international corporation and remains essentially a St. Paul company, even after relocating its headquarters to the adjoining suburb of Maplewood.

Europeans Settle the Twin Cities

Minnesota immigration in the 19th and early 20th centuries for the most part mirrored patterns throughout the United States. However, there were exceptions specific to the state of Minnesota and the Twin Cities. The national perception of Minnesota is of a state dominated by Scandinavians. This generalization is fairly accurate, if slightly exaggerated. In fact, German heritage is the most common ethnic background, followed closely by Norwegian, Swedish, and Irish ancestry.

Germans were certainly not the first Europeans to immigrate to Minnesota. As an ethnic group, Germans came to the state in greatest numbers from 1875 to 1900. Germans' contributions have been significant, especially in communities like New Ulm. In the south and west metropolitan area, there are numerous communities with German names and origins, such as New Germany, Hamburg, and Heidelberg. However, for the most part German heritage has been assimilated into the overall culture of the Twin Cities and Minnesota.

Minnesota's second most numerous group of immigrants, not surprisingly, were the Norwegians. Only slightly larger in numbers than the Swedish, the Norwegian immigrants' legacy is profoundly felt to this day. From 1875 until 1910 Norwegian immigrants came to Minnesota in the greatest numbers. O. E. Rolvaag was among this paramount immigrant group. He wrote *Giants in the Earth* (1927), a classic novel about Norwegian immigrant farmers. His son, Karl Rolvaag, served as governor of Minnesota.

The Swedish are the third-largest ancestral group in Minnesota. The Swedes fol-

Insiders' Tip
Reflecting the transitory course of the United States' nation building, before becoming Minnesota Territory in 1849, the future state of Minnesota was part of Illinois, Indiana, Michigan, Missouri, Wisconsin, and Iowa Territories at some time during its history.

lowed similar immigration patterns as the Norwegians, and the two quickly became largely indistinguishable, at least to outsiders. The legacy of Scandinavians is manifest in the names of several towns and villages around the Twin Cities. The extreme northeast metropolitan area has several cities founded and settled by Scandinavians, e.g., Scandia and Lindstrom. Moreover, public facilities bear the name of important past citizens of Scandinavian heritage. Olson Memorial Highway is named after Governor Floyd B. Olson, who died suddenly in 1936 while running for the U.S. Senate.

Scandinavians have dominated Minnesota politics during much of the state's history. Since Knute Nelson was elected governor in 1893, there have been 25 additional heads of state, and of this number only 6 were not of Scandinavian heritage. Even today, Scandinavian heritage is an important asset for Minnesota politicians. Congressman Martin Olav Sabo of Minneapolis makes his ancestry apparent by emphasizing his Scandinavian middle name.

The Irish are also an essential component of Minnesota's ethnic heritage. The Irish were particularly influential in the development of St. Paul, especially in the formation of the Catholic Church under the leadership of Archbishop John Ireland. Heavy Irish immigration began in the 1860s and ended about 1890. The ethnic group quickly integrated into the community and ascended to government positions.

Of course, numerous additional immigrant groups came to Minnesota and the Twin Cities. From 1820 to 1890 small groups of Swiss, Belgians, and Dutch also settled the area. Later, echoing national trends, southern, central, and eastern Europeans came to the Twin Cities. Compared with many other areas of the nation, they were smaller in number. However, they were a significant immigrant group from 1890 until 1920. Primarily Russians and various groups from the Austro-Hungarian Empire were included in this wave of immigrants. Unlike many other areas of the country, Italians and Greeks were a rela-

tively insignificant immigrant group during this time in Minnesota. Minnesota and the Twin Cities population was preponderantly of European heritage, but since the 1960s the background of immigrants arriving in the area has become strikingly diverse.

The Diverse Twin Cities 20th-Century Economy

As the Twin Cities proceeded through the 20th century, the Twin Cities economy became increasingly diverse. The end result was an area economy consistently among the strongest in the United States. When the nation's economy began to adjust to global pressures in the '60s, '70s, and '80s, the Twin Cities economy was prepared. It was not concentrated in a single industry, as were Pittsburgh (steel), Detroit (automobiles), and many of the nation's other industrial centers. Certainly, there were definite periods of ebb and flow in the Twin Cities economy, but the evolving diversity of the area's economy provided recessions instead of a localized depression, and transitions as opposed to decline. For example, when Pittsburgh's steel industry largely relocated overseas, there were years of moribund local economy before medicine and high-technology industry took its place and the local economy recovered. The same transition occurred incrementally, and less messily, in Minneapolis's largest industry, milling.

The milling industry became increasingly decentralized, as the largest and most successful Twin Cities milling companies gradually diversified into related industries. The decline of Minneapolis milling occurred fairly rapidly, and in the 1920s flour production was halved from the production levels of the glory years before and immediately after the turn of the 20th century. Despite the local decline of the industry, milling increasingly became dispersed throughout the nation. Today Minneapolis is once again the largest producer of flour in the United States but holds considerably less domination over the industry, where it accounts for only 10 percent of the national total.

Washburn-Crosby and Company changed its name to General Mills in 1928. The name change represented the growing national focus of the company. Reflecting this change, General Mills expanded further into several additional businesses. Before the creation of General Mills, the corporation had developed Wheaties breakfast cereal in 1924 and Betty Crocker, a globally recognized cake mix, in 1921. Later, General Mills moved into other food-related businesses, including numerous breakfast foods, dough mixes, and frozen foods.

Pillsbury followed a similar path, diversifying its food lines and businesses throughout the 20th century. The home of the Pillsbury Doughboy moved into prepared doughs, as well as frozen and canned foods. The company entered the restaurant business in 1967, acquiring Burger King, and later became involved in several additional restaurant ventures. However, Pillsbury underwent a significant change in 1989, foreshadowing the experience of many other Twin Cities businesses in the late 20th century. As the traditional industries of the Twin Cities diversified, new high-tech businesses asserted themselves as an important component of the local economy.

Since World War II, high tech has played an increasingly important role in the Twin Cities economy. Some companies' roots often reach back to industry and manufacturing that began in the late 19th and early 20th centuries, as is the case with the 3M Corporation, while others quickly became important businesses in the area because of technological innovation.

One such Twin Cities company is Medtronic Inc. Earl Bakken, a University of Minnesota graduate student, began his company in a northeast Minneapolis garage in 1949. Medtronic's first big success came with the development of an implantable pacemaker in 1960. After this invention, Medtronic diversified into numerous medical technology fields and today is an internationally recognized corporation.

Honeywell is another important Twin Cities high-technology company. The origins of Honeywell date back to a failed spring-powered thermostat company developed by A.M. Butz in 1885. Over time, and numerous name changes, the fledgling company honed its technological devices. After success with its thermostat line, the company moved into heating, air-conditioning, and varied technological devices for industry and Cold War defense programs. Honeywell's military products became an important component of the company's revenues. As the Cold War came to an end following the fall of the Soviet Union, Honeywell ran into economic hard times.

The Twin Cities are also home to one of the nation's largest retailers, the Target Corporation. For most of its long history in the Twin Cities, Target was known as the Dayton Company, and later the Dayton Hudson Corporation. The Dayton Company opened for business in downtown Minneapolis in 1902. George Dayton started the business at a site in downtown Minneapolis that, to this day, remains Dayton's. The Dayton Company started its most nationally recognized retail store, Target, in suburban Roseville, in 1962. Dayton Hudson officially changed its name to the Target Corporation in 2000, in an effort to improve market visibility for investors interested in purchasing stock.

As the 20th century came to a close, the Twin Cities underwent significant corporate reorganization. Larger domestic and multinational corporations acquired several local firms. Several Twin Cities economists questioned the vitality of the area's economy, while many others felt the event was simply emblematic of global restructuring of the economy.

The Twin Cities Enter the New Millennium

The Twin Cities underwent a substantial transformation during the late '90s. The economy is still a hot issue and a topic of incessant conversation because of acquisitions and mergers of several "blue chip" Twin Cities firms. Reflecting the strength of the local economy, there was a sharp increase in immigration over the past decade. The most recent Twin Cities immigrants are largely from Asia, Africa, and areas of the world that before the late '70s were absent from area demographics. Despite their brief history, the dynamic new immigrant population has significantly contributed to the complex "salad bowl" of Twin Cities ethnicity.

Corporations outside the Twin Cities recently acquired several area firms. Minneapolis-based ReliaStar, a financial products firm, was purchased by ING Group of Amsterdam, the Netherlands, in September 2000. Norwest, a bank headquartered in the Twin Cities, was purchased by Wells Fargo of San Francisco. Even prior to these acquisitions, Honeywell merged with a Morristown, New Jersey, company and more recently was bought by General Electric.

The aforementioned events stirred apprehension in local economists. The most notable response came from Dean David Kidwell of the University of Minnesota's Carlson School of Business Management. On March 7, 2000, Kidwell gave a controversial speech at the institution titled "Has the Twin Cities Economy Lost Its Blue Chip Status?" Kidwell discussed the recent acquisitions, and emphasized that the Twin Cities economy must remain competitive. In addition, he said that efforts must be made to develop and nurture new high-technology firms or the economy may falter.

Rapid growth and new construction in downtown St. Paul in recent years, particularly around the Xcel Energy Center, have fueled many new businesses in the downtown region. PHOTO: TODD R. BERGER

Larry Millett, Author

"I always tell people the most interesting place in the world is the place where you grew up," says Larry Millett, author of the award-winning books *Lost Twin Cities* and *Twin Cities Then and Now,* as well as several Sherlock Holmes mysteries that take place in Minnesota. "I've sort of been a fan of local history for a long time because I find it intriguing. I grew up in the Cities and went to school in downtown Minneapolis and saw first-hand the demolition of the Gateway District. My father's family goes way back in Minneapolis—my grandfather owned a bar on Washington Avenue, and his wife was the granddaughter of one of the early founders of the city. So I kind of have deep roots in this area."

Millett, who has worked as a reporter and editor at the *St. Paul Pioneer Press* for more than 30 years, has taken his love for architecture and history to write some of the most amazing and heartbreaking literary tours of the Twin Cities. Using photos kept on record at the Minnesota History Center for more than 150 years, Millett's books show in great detail how much the cities have both changed and stayed the same over the past century. *Lost Twin Cities* is composed completely of photographs and the histories of the many architectural wonders that were destroyed over the years—including the beautiful Gateway Park, which became a hangout for homeless people during the Depression—while *Twin Cities Then and Now* provides side-by-side pictures of various Twin Cities neighborhoods and business districts at various points in time.

"The cities are not hugely distinctive from each other architecturally, I think," says Millett about the Twin Cities today. "What happened historically is that there was a different set of architects for St. Paul and Minneapolis, so there were initial differences from the individual hands involved. But what's happened in St. Paul since is that it's probably got a better stock of historic buildings than Minneapolis, while Minneapolis probably has a better stock of newer buildings. St. Paul has been more fortunate in preserving its historic housing stock than Minneapolis, and there are reasons for that that have more to do with relative lack of development and change than any great historic sentiment, I think. Minneapolis, since the turn of the century, has been a more dynamic city, and the more dynamic a city is, the more quickly its architecture tends to change."

Millett's favorite buildings today? "I love St. Paul's city hall," he says. "I think it's one of our country's great Art Deco buildings, as is the county courthouse. The public library in St. Paul, and the Hill Reference Library, which is next door and is part of the same building but a different institution. Of course Landmark Center, the State Capitol, St. Paul Cathedral, the basics. In Minneapolis, I'm very fond of the IDS building, I think that's a nationally, and internationally significant skyscraper, and the Norwest Tower's (renamed the Wells Fargo Center) very nice for its kind, too.

"It's amazing as a researcher to find out how many places aren't documented," finishes Millett. "There are places in both cities where basically there's no clue to how it looked 100 years ago because there are no pictures in the public collection. That's especially true of some of the residential neighborhoods. The downtowns of both cities are well documented, but once you get out to the residential districts, the documentation is much spottier. It all depends on how good a job the city's photographer did at the time. The Minnesota Historical Society has more than 140,000 images on their Web site (www.mnhs.org), so you can cruise through all those on their Web site now. It's really phenomenal what they have, all the images of the Twin Cities in particular."

Recent immigration is transforming the composition of the Twin Cities, much as it did in late-19th- and early-20th-century Minnesota. The new wave of immigrants began to arrive in the late '70s. The new immigrant populations are largely émigrés who came to the United States to escape political tumult, repression, and warfare. The recent Twin Citians are remarkably diverse and follow national trends in immigration, where Europeans no longer predominate. With the exception of Bosnians, in the wake of the conflict in the former Yugoslavia, Europeans are a relatively small component of the new immigration. The Twin Cities' dynamic immigration began after the Vietnam conflict. The first group to arrive were displaced Vietnamese, who were followed by numerous other Southeast Asian groups, which included Laotians, Khmers (Cambodia), and the Hmong (Laos).

The Hmong are a significant immigrant group in the Twin Cities. Since the late '70s they have come from Laos, or relocated to the area from other American cities, to take advantage of the area's low unemployment and booming economy. The Hmong are mountain people from Laos, who were the United States' allies in the Vietnam conflict. As a result, when their enemies, the Pathet Lao, came to power in Laos, many were considered pariahs and without a home. Today there are more than 200,000 Hmong living in the United States. The Twin Cities, in particular St. Paul, have the largest Hmong population in the nation. The Hmong and other Southeast Asians have started more than 400 area businesses and have transformed St. Paul's Frogtown and Midway neighborhoods.

An even more recent trend has seen large groups of East Africans settling in the Twin Cities. The first significant wave of African immigrants came from Ethiopia in the late '80s, and arrived in increasingly greater numbers during Eritrea's successful war for independence from Ethiopia in the early '90s. The Twin Cities Ethiopian and Eritrean population has since firmly established themselves in the community. Ethiopians and Eritrean restaurant businesses are scattered throughout the Twin

Cities, and many now hold government positions, such as working for the U.S. Post Office.

The Somalis are another East African immigrant group. An estimated 40,000 Somalis currently live in the United States, and approximately 20,000 reside in Minnesota. However, members of the Somali community feel the government numbers are extremely low and believe there may be as many as 90,000 in Minnesota. After Somalia fell into anarchy and the United States sponsored "Operation Restore Hope," many have come to the Twin Cities, particularly south Minneapolis. The Somalis' presence is felt in the many small businesses owned and operated by the community.

The new wave of immigration is just one parallel linking the Twin Cities' past and present. Both Minneapolis and St. Paul are reviving important elements of their past on the Mississippi riverfront.

Since the late '80s, Minneapolis has focused on regaining its greatest historical assets—the Mississippi River and the Mill District. After years of decay, the Mill City is restoring its most important historical area. It began with the restoration of the James J. Hill Stone Arch Bridge—one of Minneapolis's most scenic vistas—and is nearing its climax with the recently founded Mill City Museum. Opened in 2003, the museum is located in the historic Washburn-Crosby A Mill ruins. The museum celebrates the city's former status as the world's largest producer of flour. In addition, the Minneapolis Park and Recreation Board has completed the Mill Ruins Park. It is an exciting time in Minneapolis as the past and the present are brought together on the historic Mississippi River.

Down river in St. Paul, the renovated Harriet Island Regional Park celebrates its city's rich history. During late summer 2000 more than 50,000 citizens attended the reopening of the park. The park represents the Cities' commitment to the riverfront. The importance of the riverfront in the Twin Cities and other American cities was forgotten. Fortunately, Minneapolis and St. Paul have revived their historic riverfronts.

Architecture

Twin Cities Architectural History: An Eclectic Mix

Like other major metropolitan areas across the country, the architectural styles in the Twin Cities have been influenced by the times. In addition, the Twin Cities are composed of two cities with distinctly different histories and perspectives on architecture. In the aggregate, both cities draw architectural inspiration from different sources, and it is reflected in their respective architecture.

St. Paul has always looked to the east, and in particular Boston, as a source for civic inspiration. The design of the city reflects this perspective and was in large part developed by transplanted old-stock New Englanders. The streets, like Boston's, were platted much narrower than in Minneapolis. St. Paul views itself as a city of tradition and as the "Capital City." With a few exceptions, most notably the Minnesota World Trade Center, St. Paul's architecture has concerned itself with human scale structures of elegance. St. Paul's rival across the river has taken a considerably different approach to architecture.

In contrast, Minneapolis has always embraced progress and modernity. This distinction between the cities has only been exacerbated as Minneapolis architecture has increasingly grown vertically. Also, the streets are wider and for the most part straighter than in St. Paul. Street addresses are much easier to follow because each block contains 100 potential addresses, thus addresses are clearly demarcated by intersections. These distinctions have guided Minneapolis and St. Paul's architecture, to some extent, throughout the Cities' histories.

Function First: The Birth of the Twin Cities

Early Twin Cities architecture reflects national trends. When America was settled, functionality was of primary importance. Homes and civic structures were erected with safety and survival as primary concerns. During this time settlers faced several significant problems; most notably, they required protection from American Indians and the severe Minnesota winters. Hence, the most numerous early examples of architecture in the Twin Cities were log cabins, sod houses, and simple wooden structures.

Fort Snelling was the first permanent white settlement in the Twin Cities. Completed in 1820, it protected the northwestern-most edge of the United States. Thereafter, small wooden pieces of architecture were constructed in the two fledgling cities. Father Lucian Galtier dedicated a small log chapel in honor of St. Paul in November of 1841. Down the Mississippi almost a decade later, John Stevens created the first humble structure in the area that would soon be named Minneapolis. The little white house was soon surrounded by many similar structures.

The massive Cathedral of St. Paul towers over downtown St. Paul from its perch on Cathedral Hill. PHOTO: TODD R. BERGER

Minneapolis and St. Paul rapidly developed into nationally prominent cities. During this epoch, buildings were constructed as quickly as possible in order to meet the needs of the expanding cities. As the cities developed, municipal institutions became necessary. Public buildings were the first opulent pieces of architecture in both cities, and they were important as public declarations of the emergence of the cities on the national scene.

The Emergence of the Twin Cities

The Minneapolis City Hall (1906) represented the cities' emergence as a nationally prominent municipality. In 1856 Minneapolis's population was 4,607, but by 1895 it had swelled to 192,823 and was then the eighteenth largest city in the nation.

St. Paul also created several structures to celebrate the Cities' ascendancy at the turn of the 20th century. The most significant architectural work was the Min-

nesota State Capitol, completed in 1904. Cass Gilbert designed the neoclassical structure, which is a matter of civic pride for St. Paul and the entire state of Minnesota. It is one of several outstanding pieces of government architecture in St. Paul. Government and institutional structures marked St. Paul's entrance into the modern age. In contrast, Minneapolis was poised to begin its ascent skyward, which began with the Foshay Tower.

The Foshay Tower was the first skyscraper constructed in the Twin Cities. When it was completed in 1929, it was considered a feat of modern architecture. The 31-story obelisk was the largest building in the Twin Cities for more than 40 years. During the late 19th and early 20th centuries both cities expanded upward with large concrete and metal structures, but none were as grand in scale as the Foshay.

Since the IDS Center was completed in 1973, immense skyscrapers have become an increasingly more prominent part of downtown Minneapolis. After exceeding the Foshay by 26 stories, the IDS was briefly lonesome atop the skyline. However, the situation changed significantly in the '80s and '90s and continues today. Skyscrapers constructed of glass, concrete, and steel now dominate downtown, and most of these immense structures are named after large corporations. The architecture is an eclectic modern mix of styles ranging from the interesting Art Deco–influenced Wells Fargo Center to less distinctive massive glass structures like the Piper Jaffray Tower. Unfortunately, the most recent additions to downtown, particularly on the south side of the Nicollet Mall, are less architecturally ambitious.

St. Paul also expanded upward in the late 20th century, but skyscrapers are not as prominent downtown. The sixth-tallest building in Minneapolis, the Pillsbury Center, is taller than any building in St. Paul. However, the best architecture in downtown St. Paul is the city's government buildings. The St. Paul City Hall is a stunning structure, particularly its lobby, a fine example of Art Deco/Moderne design. The Cathedral of St. Paul is another architectural masterpiece; the baroque interior of the building suggests Europe rather than St. Paul, Minnesota. St. Paul architecture is not as vertically oriented as Minneapolis; however, the Minnesota State Capitol and the Cathedral of St. Paul make up for it in sheer size.

Into the 21st Century

As the Twin Cities enter the 21st century, both cities have recommitted themselves to the historic riverfront. Architecture and landscape design in the last decade has placed an emphasis on the Mississippi River. The Twin Cities, like many other cities around the nation, now make a significant effort to emphasize the river and not turn their back on it. Several projects have recently been completed or are currently in progress in both cities.

In St. Paul, there have been a number of architectural projects on the Mississippi. A few years ago the new Science Museum of Minnesota opened on the bluff above the river. Besides creating a state-of-the-art museum, the facility makes fine use of its location with several scenic overviews of the river. In addition, the city reopened one of its most scenic parks, Harriet Island. The park is across the river from downtown and underwent extensive landscape architecture to restore its links to the river. One important feature is the large concrete steps leading down to the river, where visitors can dangle their feet in the water. There are a number of other proposals. Plans to redevelop the beautiful riverfront property to make better use of the river are in various stages of implementation. There is also a plan for residential development in the historic Irvine Park neighborhood on the Mississippi. St. Paul has made the redevelopment of the riverfront a top priority for the city's future.

Minneapolis has also shown a commitment to redeveloping the Mississippi riverfront with several projects of its own. The first major project was the James J. Hill Stone Arch Bridge, which was renovated in 1994 by the Minnesota Department of Transportation. Since then, the city has embarked on creating its most ambitious project, the Mill City Museum (see Close-Up on page 56 for further details). The Minneapolis firm of Meyer, Scherer, and Rockcastle Ltd. created the design for the museum, which opened in September 2003.

As the Twin Cities begin the 21st century, both cities are reclaiming the location of their origins on the historic Mississippi River. Architecture has played an important role in this process, and it has linked the architecture of the past to the present.

Twin Cities Architecture in Detail

The Downtown Minneapolis Skyline

The Minneapolis skyline has been expanding skyward since the arrival of the IDS Center in 1973. However, the first skyscraper located in downtown Minneapolis was the Foshay Tower, which today is a midget among the giants of the city's impressive skyline. The following are but a few of the buildings erected in successive waves during the '80s and '90s and continuing today, when there seems to be no limit to the immense glass corporate structures that dominate today's Minneapolis skyline.

Campbell Mithun Tower
222 South Ninth Street, Minneapolis
(612) 342–6000

Immense glass skyscrapers have transformed the look of downtown Minneapolis. This is manifest throughout the city. Looking down Ninth Street, the chasm between the past and present is highly visible. On the corner of Marquette Avenue and Ninth is the reigning king of the skies for more than 40 years, the 31-story Foshay Tower. Continuing down Ninth Street to Third Avenue South is the Campbell Mithun Tower. By no means is it one of the most well-known pieces of architecture in Minneapolis, yet the structure easily eclipses the once giant Foshay Tower in sheer size. Rising 42 stories, the Campbell Mithun Tower is the fifth-tallest building in the city. Constructed in 1985, it was an early addition to the skyward growth of downtown.

Dain Rauscher Plaza
60 South Sixth Street, Minneapolis

This is one of the many large glass skyscrapers erected in downtown Minneapolis in the '90s. Like all of the recent additions to the Minneapolis skyline, it has a system of skyways connecting it to the neighboring monuments to large corporations. However, the Dain Rauscher skyway offers connections on the second and fourth levels to the Wells Fargo Center. At 539 feet and 40 stories, it is the seventh-tallest building in Minneapolis and, like many of the new structures, is constructed of glass.

The Foshay Tower
821 Marquette Avenue South, Minneapolis
(612) 359–3030

When visiting downtown Minneapolis it is difficult to imagine this obelisk once stood as the tallest skyscraper west of Chicago. It dominated the Minneapolis skyline and was the tallest building in the Twin Cities until the completion of the IDS Center in 1973. Today the Foshay Tower is surrounded by the modern glass-and-steel giants, which dwarf what is now the sixteenth-tallest building.

The Foshay Tower offers an interesting piece of local history. It draws its name from the financier behind its construction, Wilbur H. Foshay. Foshay, a utilities magnate, became wealthy enough during the boom of the "Roaring Twenties" economy to begin constructing his dream in 1926—a building modeled on one that he adored since his visit to the nation's capital when he was 15 years old—the Washington Monument. The 32-story obelisk was topped with 10-foot-high letters that spelled out FOSHAY. The Foshay's dedication in 1929 was one of the most lavish in the city's history. The festivities included fireworks and a 75-piece brass band conducted by John Philip Sousa, which included his latest composition "Foshay Tower—Washington Memorial March." Unfortunately for Foshay, the good times were not to last for long. Shortly afterward the stock market crashed and ushered in the Great Depression. Foshay's finances were decimated; in addition, he was convicted of fraud and sentenced to 15 years at Fort Leavenworth. President Franklin Delano Roosevelt pardoned Foshay after he had served three years. This less-than-auspicious start for the 447-foot Goliath, fortunately, led to a far less noteworthy and more stable recent history.

To be sure, the Foshay is one of the Twin Cities' memorable sights with its lights illuminating the Minneapolis sky. And it does this despite its relatively diminutive stature alongside the many larger skyscrapers built in the wake of the '80s and '90s. Features such as the open-air observatory are timeless and offer one of the most panoramic views of Minneapolis. Access is limited to late spring, summer, and early fall days because of the area's frequently inclement weather. For further information about the observation deck and prices, call (612) 359–3030. The Foshay Tower is a view not to be missed, especially during the splendor of a beautiful Minneapolis summer evening.

Hennepin County Government Center
300 South Sixth Street, Minneapolis
(612) 348-3000

The twin tower exterior of the Hennepin County Government Center is unassuming enough. However, the 24-story atrium provides a truly impressive view. The center of the building is open and provides for a spectacular view, which grows as you ascend the 25 stories of the building. In addition, there is another interesting feature to the building—Sixth Street passes directly under the structure.

The building was completed in 1977, and it serves Hennepin County (Minneapolis and suburbs) well. In addition to the wonderful atrium, the building also includes an immense water fountain. The Hennepin Government Center has hosted a number of public political rallies over the years. Prior to the 1992 election, former President Bill Clinton spoke at a huge rally on a lovely late summer evening.

IDS Center
80 South Eighth Street, Minneapolis
(612) 376-8000

The IDS Center supplanted the Foshay Tower as the tallest building in the Twin Cities when it opened in 1973—a position it has not relinquished to this day. The IDS Center is also, arguably, the most well-known building in the Twin Cities, and is recognized as the centerpiece of the Min-

neapolis skyline. When visiting downtown Minneapolis, and even the suburbs, the IDS Center looms large in the distance.

Besides its immense size, the IDS Center distinguishes itself in several other ways. The 57-story, 775-foot structure has more than 42,000 panes of glass, as well as a 105-foot waterfall in Crystal Court, which was added during the 1998 renovation. Designed by world-renowned architects Philip Johnson and John Burgee, the skyscraper has frequently attracted national attention. Johnson is nationally known for Glass House (1949), an example of his architecture that is closely imitative of Mies Van Der Rohe (New Canaan, Connecticut), and later works, which more fully demonstrate the development of his style, such as the Amon Carter Museum in Fort Worth, Texas (1961), and the New York State Theatre for the Lincoln Art Center in New York (1962-64).

The grandeur of Crystal Court was featured in the *Mary Tyler Moore Show* and two motion pictures. In addition, the IDS observatory was a major Twin Cities attraction for years. Unfortunately, the observatory has since closed; however, Crystal Court is still one of the most beautiful shopping areas in the Twin Cities, and the IDS Center remains the centerpiece of the Minneapolis skyline.

Pillsbury Center
200 South Sixth Street, Minneapolis

Minneapolis was known throughout the nation as the "Mill City" during the 19th and early 20th centuries. As time has passed, the importance of milling has been de-emphasized, and the "City of Lakes" nickname has moved to the forefront. However, milling and its many allied services and industries remain a vital part of the area's dynamic economy.

After all, the Minneapolis area remains home to three nationally recognized companies that began milling in the city. General Mills, Cargill, and Pillsbury have, since their inceptions, vastly expanded beyond milling. Unfortunately, of the three, only Pillsbury remains headquartered in downtown Minneapolis.

Pillsbury Center is in the heart of downtown Minneapolis, where the 41-story building overlooks the city with its immense neighbors. The Pillsbury Center has two towers, and the beautiful atrium distinguishes it from other structures, with its eight stories of enclosed open space. Recently Pillsbury was spun off by its parent company, multinational Diageo Plc, and now is a part of General Mills. The structure, completed in 1981, is not historically significant, but the corporation is an important part of the Twin Cities community for the past, present, and future.

225 South Sixth
225 South Sixth Street, Minneapolis

225 South Sixth is recognizable throughout Minneapolis by the crown that sits atop the large glass skyscraper. The building is the second-tallest in Minneapolis. It was completed in 1992 as First Bank Place. The name was changed to U.S. Bank Place a few years ago in order to reflect the company's new identity and then to 225 South Sixth in 2002 when U.S. Bancorp moved its headquarters to Nicollet Mall. The nationally respected firm of Pei, Cobb, Freed and Partners designed the 56-story 225 South Sixth, which, despite its size, receives far less attention than the Wells Fargo Center and the IDS Center.

Wells Fargo Center
90 South Seventh Street, Minneapolis
(612) 344-1200

The Wells Fargo Center sits at the heart of downtown and perhaps is Minneapolis's most recognizable building at night with its yellow-hued glow. The third-tallest building in the Twin Cities, like its neighbor the IDS Center it is 57 stories high. The building was completed in 1988 as the Norwest Center. The name changed when the Norwest and Wells Fargo banks merged.

The Norwest Center was constructed in the ashes of tragedy. A Thanksgiving '82 fire destroyed the Northwestern National Bank Building, then the name of the company. The structure itself was not as important a piece of architecture to the community as the "weatherball," which provided weather news 24/7 to Minneapolis. Norwest set out to construct a replacement.

The Norwest Center was completed in 1989. The heavily Art Deco–derived building was the work of Cesar Pelli and features a 100-foot-high domed ceiling rotunda, as well as a more traditional lobby. The Wells Fargo Center is among the Minneapolis skyline's most recognizable buildings.

Minneapolis Architectural Landmarks

American Swedish Institute
2600 Park Avenue, Minneapolis
(612) 871-4907
www.americanswedishinst.org

Less than 100 years ago, Minneapolis's wealthy resided on Park Avenue beside the American Swedish Institute. In St. Paul, Summit Avenue retains its old-money status, but on Park Avenue the affluent relocated many years ago and have left the elegant American Swedish Institute behind.

Constructed in 1904, the palatial 33-room mansion was once a single-family residence. The Chateauesque-style mansion was constructed for Swan and Christina Turnblad and their daughter, Lillian. The Turnblad family amassed their fortune through the *Svenska Amerikanska Posten*, a Swedish-language newspaper with a circulation of 40,000 at its zenith. The Turn-

The American Swedish Institute in south Minneapolis during SwedishFest. PHOTO: GREATER MINNEAPOLIS CONVENTION & VISITORS ASSOCIATION

blads donated the mansion to the American Institute for Swedish Arts, Literature and Science. The rooms inside the mansion display interesting architectural details. For example, there is a Rococo Revival salon, a two-story fireplace in the Grand Hall made of carved mahogany, and 11 Swedish "kaklugnar" (porcelain stoves) in various rooms of the mansion. Besides the spectacular architecture, the institute is the oldest museum of Swedish-American history and culture in the United States. Appropriately, it is located on Park Avenue, where many rags-to-riches millionaires like the Turnblads once resided. Sadly, many of the avenue's breathtaking mansions have been razed. However, the American Swedish Institute

Butler Square
Sixth Street and First Avenue,
Minneapolis
(612) 339-4343

Butler Square is perhaps the finest example of a renovated warehouse in Minneapolis. The building, formerly known as Butler Brothers Warehouse, is situated on the southwestern edge of the historic Warehouse District. The Warehouse District is filled with classic buildings that once housed Minneapolis's bustling industrial and shipping sector.

As time passed, many businesses closed or left the warehouses for the suburbs. The Warehouse District, like much of the city, was neglected in the era following World War II as people flocked to the suburbs. As this process unfolded, much of the Warehouse District sat dormant, which was a fate much better than the neighboring Gateway District of downtown. The Warehouse District was spared the wrecking ball of urban renewal because the property was too far from downtown and not considered financially lucrative enough. In the '70s urban revitalization gradually began in the Warehouse District, and buildings such as Butler Square were some of the first converted for modern use. Today the once-moribund section of Minneapolis is a sparkling beauty, filled with converted warehouses that today serve as office space, restaurants, bars, art galleries, and retail shops.

Butler Square's architecture is based on its past strengths combined with a superb renovation in 1973. The exterior is dark brick, and it distinguishes itself with a Moorish-style turret atop the building. However, the interior is where the building sets itself apart. The renovation maximized the building's open space. The building's original wood beams were cleaned and left exposed and windows were installed to gaze out at the atrium. There are two large atriums from floor to ceiling, and sculptures such as George Segal's *Acrobats* accent the interior's striking beauty. After the success of Butler

Square, many other renovations followed in the Warehouse District, but none have matched its architectural grandeur.

Hennepin Center for the Arts
528 Hennepin Avenue, Minneapolis
(612) 332–4478

An example of 19th-century Richardsonian Romanesque architecture, the Hennepin Center for the Arts was completed in 1889 as the Masonic Temple. Like its neighbor the Lumber Exchange, it is an excellent example of the architecture that coexisted with the Hennepin Avenue Theater District until after World War II. Thereafter, it was neglected and the architecture modified. The onion dome on the top corner facing Fifth Street and Hennepin Avenue was lopped off. However, after years of neglect, parts of downtown were reborn. In the last score of years, many of the avenue's lovely theaters have been renovated. Today the Hennepin Center for the Arts thrives as a performance arts building.

Lumber Exchange Building
425 Hennepin Avenue, Minneapolis
(612) 334–3011

In the late 19th century, downtown Minneapolis was lined with large stone structures like the Lumber Exchange Building. Constructed in 1886, it is an example of Minneapolis's first skyscrapers. Modifications were made since the building's construction. Most significantly, two floors were added to the top of the building, and oddly enough, they do not match. Today downtown is dominated by immense glass, steel, and concrete buildings occupied by large corporations. Opinions on the Lumber Exchange vary markedly; some feel it is a quirky link to the past, while others malign it as a monstrosity. The Lumber Exchange retains the character of the city when it first rose to prominence, and it exudes the ambience that once pervaded the city.

Minneapolis City Hall
350 South Fifth Street, Minneapolis
(612) 673–3000

The Minneapolis City Hall was an extraordinarily expensive and time-consuming project that marked the city's arrival on the national scene. Constructed between 1889 and 1905, the city hall came at great financial costs but symbolically represented much more for the fledgling upstart city. The city hall covers an entire city block, and is distinguished by its 341-foot-high clock tower, which rings daily throughout downtown.

Minneapolis Post Office
100 South First Street, Minneapolis
(612) 321–5957

The Minneapolis Post Office is a colossal 2-block Moderne structure located in the heart of the birthplace of the city. The building was completed in 1933, and the architecture reflects its WPA origins. With millions of Americans out of work, projects like the post office were paramount in bolstering the nation's confidence.

The site of the post office is among the most architecturally historic in Minneapolis. Near the present location of the post office (on the riverfront), Minneapolis and Hennepin County were organized. Colonel John H. Stevens's home was where these two important events took place. He was also the first permanent settler of European heritage on the site. Early pictures show Stevens's home and American Indian tepees peacefully coexisting. Stevens received permission to build in 1852 when Congress severed control of the land from Fort Snelling. On the site, Stevens constructed the first building in the future city of Minneapolis—a small white frame house. This important piece of architecture was relocated to Minnehaha Park in south Minneapolis, where it can be visited today.

When the post office was completed, the Gateway District, the confluence of Nicollet and Hennepin Avenues, was entering its decline. The Gateway was just outside the post office's door and was the heart of downtown during much of its early history. However, the Gateway was a casualty to urban renewal in the '50s and '60s. Since then the vicinity of the post office is no longer one of the more important areas in Minneapolis. The post office, like many other buildings in Minneapolis, turned its back on the Cities' roots on the Mississippi River.

The post office is an excellent example of the fine government structures built by the WPA. The interior is particularly stunning, and it is one of the best examples of Art Deco in downtown Minneapolis. The lobby includes plenty of fine stone, brass, and glass, which is immaculately maintained. The exterior is more subdued and is constructed of stone with large metal grilles over the two entrances. The post office exudes the confidence that was necessary during the darkest days of the Great Depression.

Shubert Theater
Fifth Street and Hennepin Avenue, Minneapolis

The Shubert Theater is one of the Twin Cities' most contentious pieces of architecture. The grand old theater sat vacant for years on the corner of Seventh Street and First Avenue, where it was once a part of Minneapolis's extensive Hennepin Avenue and Seventh Street theater district. But much had changed since the Shubert's construction. The Shubert had fallen from its glory, but unlike most of the downtown theaters, the old hulk avoided a date with the wrecking ball.

Local leaders and business interests called for the theater's demolition, especially in light of its location on the lucrative, vacant, and, until recently, undeveloped Block E. The theater stood in the way of development on the highly sought piece of property. A plan made for the theater's destruction was met by resistance from local arts organizations. Fortunately, the theater was spared; however, it was moved 2 blocks away beside the Hennepin Center for the Arts. The Shubert weighs an astounding 5,816,000 pounds or 2,908 tons, and its move set a world record for the largest structure relocated. Since the move the Shubert has not received a facelift. Instead, it patiently awaits its return to glory as one of the renovated downtown theaters.

University of Minnesota– Twin Cities: Minneapolis Campus

Throughout the University of Minnesota's history, the institution has played a pivotal role in many aspects of the community. Architecture is yet another area where the school shines. The university celebrated its sesquicentennial in 2001, and the school has taken important steps to preserve the wealth of architecture, particularly on the immense Minneapolis campus. The following buildings are only a few of the fine pieces of architecture on the flagship campus of the University of Minnesota, the state's largest public institution of higher learning.

Civil Engineering
500 Pillsbury Drive SE, Minneapolis

Civil Engineering stands in stark contrast to the variations of classic architecture that dominate the campus. More than 95 percent of the building was constructed underground, and it extends 110 feet below the surface. Civil Engineering was built during the OPEC oil embargo of 1974. The Minnesota Legislature became seriously concerned about sustainable energy sources and allocated funds for numerous experimental features in the structure. Both active and passive solar heating is included for research purposes. The future did not arrive as fast as many critics were predicting. During the nadir of the OPEC oil embargo, however, the building was simultaneously an architectural curiosity and a source for research into more efficient energy and land use.

McNamara Alumni Center
200 Oak Street SE, Minneapolis

The McNamara Alumni Center is the most recent addition to the Minneapolis campus of the University of Minnesota. The structure is an apt bridge between the alumni and present students and contains something for the admirers of both the school's august history and daring architecture.

Both downtown Minneapolis and St. Paul have extensive skyway systems between buildings, allowing visitors and workers to get around most of the downtowns without ever setting foot outside. PHOTO: GREATER MINNEAPOLIS CONVENTION & VISITORS ASSOCIATION

Until the '80s the McNamara Alumni Center was the site of Memorial Stadium. The stadium served as the home for the Minnesota Golden Gophers football team. Today the restored Memorial Stadium arch serves as the entrance to the Curtis L. and Arleen Carlson Heritage Gallery, where the University of Minnesota's alumni and faculty are honored with artifacts, images, and stories.

In addition, the McNamara is the home of the University of Minnesota Alumni Association (UMAA). The two office blocks are copper faced, which represents the maroon and gold team colors of the Gophers. The structure is a domed 90-foot geode, which encloses the office space and heritage gallery. The outside of the building is also covered in copper and sits on the eastern edge of the campus. The McNamara Alumni Center is a $35 million monument to the rich history created in the area by the school's alumni.

Northrop Memorial Auditorium
84 Church Street SE, Minneapolis
(651) 624–2345

The Northrop Memorial Auditorium stands out elegantly on the north end of the mall. The mall is lined with stunning architecture, and it was the dream of Cass Gilbert that the mall would stretch to the banks of the Mississippi River. Gilbert created the Minnesota State Capitol and the Woolworth's Building in downtown New York City. Unfortunately his dreams were thwarted, and the Coffman Memorial Union was constructed at the base of the bluff above the Mississippi. Since then the union has stared across the mall at the Northrop Auditorium, and Gilbert's plan has not been revived.

The neoclassical building is among the most beautiful and storied on campus. The large brick structure features a ten-column facade and was named after University of Minnesota president Cyrus Northrop (1884–1911). Completed in 1929, Northrop Memorial Auditorium serves as an auditorium concert hall. And with more than 4,800 seats, the auditorium is one of the area's most beautiful venues. Over the years, Northrop Memorial Auditorium has featured a wide range of concerts, graduations, theater events, and much more. Another important feature is the Westminster chimes and carillon bells, which have chimed on the hour since their installation in 1948. The beauty of Northrop Memorial Auditorium is difficult to deny—and even more difficult to miss when visiting the University of Minnesota's Minneapolis campus.

Walter Library
Pleasant Avenue SE, Minneapolis

Under the leadership of former President Mark Yudof, the University of Minnesota demonstrated a commitment to restoring and preserving its architectural heritage. Walter Library, currently undergoing a massive $53.6 million renovation, is a building with important history to the campus and the Twin Cities.

Constructed in 1924, it was the third principal library and soon will serve as the Digital Technology Center and the Science and Engineering Library. The impressive architecture of Walter Library has benefited from recent extensive renovation, which included restoring the staircase, lobby, and reading rooms to their original glory. The structure is built in the Roman Renaissance style, the dominant style of the campus's architectural epicenter, the Northrop Mall. It has the most decorative facade on the mall, making use of red brick and limestone trim. Walter Library has been an important piece of architecture since its construction and continues to be since its renovation and reopening in fall 2001.

Weisman Art Museum
333 East River Road, Minneapolis
(612) 625-9494

The Frederick R. Weisman Art Museum is one of the Twin Cities' most distinctive pieces of architecture. Opinions on the museum vary widely. Detractors have called the structure an ugly, discombobulated homage to the tin man in *The Wizard of Oz*, while enthusiasts glow incessantly about Frank Gehry's internationally acclaimed style. However, one fact is for certain: Gehry created a museum that is not, in the words of a former University of Minnesota president, Nils Hasselmo,

The Weisman Art Museum along the banks of the Mississippi River on the East Bank Campus of the University of Minnesota is one of the most striking buildings in the Twin Cities. PHOTO: GREATER MINNEAPOLIS CONVENTION & VISITORS ASSOCIATION

"…another brick lump."

Critics from as far away as New York have lauded the Weisman. The museum features brushed stainless steel arranged in bold undulating angles. Gehry links the museum to the more architecturally conservative buildings with terra-cotta bricks on the south and east sides. The interior of the museum includes extensive use of natural lighting sources, whether it is the skylights or large picture windows tastefully framing the view of downtown Minneapolis. The Weisman houses five galleries. Gehry has agreed to design an expansion, which is due to the art museum's success, despite Gehry's extremely busy schedule (the great architect has just completed his plans for the 40-story Guggenheim Museum in Manhattan).

The Weisman has been home to the University of Minnesota's art collection since it opened in 1993. The museum emphasizes art of the recent vintage, just as the building is among the Twin Cities' most ambitious pieces of modern architecture. The Weisman is definitely worth a visit both for its fine galleries as well as its astounding architecture.

St. Paul's Architectural Treasures

Like Minneapolis, St. Paul has plenty of interesting and historic architecture. In contrast to the enormous modern skyscrapers that dominate Minneapolis, the architecture of the St. Paul skyline is not as large in scale. However, as the "capital city," it contains numerous striking government buildings. St. Paul has always, of the two cities, been the city of tradition, and it shows in the number of beautiful works of architecture.

Bandana Square
1021 East Bandana Boulevard, St. Paul
(651) 642-1509

During the past century, the site of present-day Bandana Square has served several different roles. The structure was constructed to serve as a train repair shop. Then, as the importance of the railroad industry declined, the repair shop closed. After sitting vacant the huge building was spared the fate of meeting the wrecking ball. The structure was renovated in the '80s and reopened as a shopping mall. Unfortunately, like many other urban shopping complexes, the beautiful shopping center did not fare well. A few businesses have remained, but, for the most part, offices are the most common tenants at Bandana Square. Bandana Square hosts a link to its past—the Twin Cities Model Railroad Club—where fans of architecture can revisit the old train garage in miniature surrounded by facades of the historic Twin Cities.

Fort Snelling
Minnesota Highways 5 and 55 , St. Paul
(651) 725-2413

Fort Snelling was the first permanent settlement in Minnesota and was once the most northwestern military post of the United States. The restored fort features numerous examples of 19th-century architecture, which emphasizes practical, defense-oriented architecture over opulence. On the site are a hospital, forge, and of course, a garrison for defending the confluence of the Mississippi and the Minnesota Rivers. Minnesota, like much of the Midwest, has a relatively brief history, and at Fort Snelling visitors can examine a restored version of the architecture of the first Minnesotans of European heritage.

Governor's Residence
1006 Summit Avenue, St. Paul
(651) 297-8177

The location of the governor's residence is ideal. Summit Avenue is the historical home of St. Paul's old wealth. The beautiful wide parkway is lined with trees and elegant Victorian homes and was the childhood home of F. Scott Fitzgerald and railroad baron James J. Hill.

The governor's residence is a fairly recent tradition in Minnesota. Since the 1960s Minnesota's governor has called 240 Summit Avenue home. Prior to that date, the governors lived in their own homes and rented facilities for political events. William Channing Whitney, a prominent Twin Cities architect, designed the governor's residence. The residence is in the English Tudor Revival style, while the interior has been renovated several times. Tours are available occasionally and by appointment.

James J. Hill House
240 Summit Avenue, St. Paul
(651) 296-6126

The James J. Hill House was once one of the largest mansions in the Midwest, appropriately built for one of St. Paul's wealthiest and most powerful men. In the age of barons of industry, Hill was one of the area's most prominent citizens. Mansions like Hill's helped create the reputation Summit Avenue retains even

The Governor's Residence on Summit Avenue in St. Paul. PHOTO: TODD R. BERGER

today—as the street where St. Paul's old money resides.

James J. Hill, ironically, arrived via riverboat at age 17 from Ontario, Canada, in 1838. Hill was to play a central role in the development of another conveyance, the railroad, in the rapidly developing United States. Hill built a railroad empire, the Great Northern Railroad, from his adopted home of St. Paul.

Perhaps the most impressive aspect of the Hill House is its sheer size. The beautiful home was constructed with red sandstone and many examples of skilled craftsmanship. The carved woodwork and stained glass are of the finest quality. There are 32 rooms, 13 bathrooms, and 22 fireplaces, which were a necessity for Minnesota's harsh winters when the house was constructed in 1891. Boasting 36,000 square feet of living space, it was a fitting residence for one of Minnesota's, and the nation's, greatest railroad tycoons.

Landmark Center
75 West Fifth Street, St. Paul
(651) 292–3228

The Landmark Center is one of many architectural gems in downtown St. Paul's cultural quarter, which includes the Ordway Music Theatre, the Children's Museum, and the Science Museum. The Landmark Center was erected in 1906 as the Federal Courthouse, where St. Paul's famous gangsters were once prosecuted. Today, the Landmark Center serves as the gallery for the Minnesota Museum of American Art, but the architecture continues to convey the structure's history. The building's tower overlooks Rice Park, which is surrounded by several of St. Paul's most attractive pieces of architecture.

Marjorie McNeely Conservatory at Como Park
Estabrook Drive and Aida Place, St. Paul
(651) 632–5111

The Marjorie McNeely Conservatory at Como Park is the architectural centerpiece of this lovely St. Paul public park. The park itself was originally designed by one of St. Paul's most important landscape architects, Horace W. S. Cleveland, and a German immigrant, Frederick

St. Paul's historic Landmark Center on Rice Park. PHOTO: SAINT PAUL CONVENTION AND VISITORS BUREAU

Nussbaumer. Later, Nussbaumer drew up the plans for the conservatory, which was inspired by London's Crystal Palace in Kew Garden.

The conservatory features a palm dome in the center of this glass structure, and the building is split into several different wings displaying a vast array of seasonally blooming flora. The conservatory is expertly integrated into the landscape of the rolling hills, ravine, and gardens that surround the structure. However, over time the conservatory grew and unfortunately deteriorated. In 1993 a major face-lift was completed, and it restored the conservatory to a splendor far eclipsing when it opened in 1915. The combination of architecture and flowers make the conservatory a treat for Twin Citians throughout the year.

Minnesota State Capitol
75 Constitution Avenue, St. Paul
(651) 297–3521
The Minnesota State Capitol is one of the

area's architectural landmarks for several reasons. The 223-foot unsupported marble dome is the largest in the world. The architectural splendor does not stop with the breathtaking dome, but also includes statues, columns, arches, and murals.

Cass Gilbert won a capitol design competition in 1898. Gilbert designed several Twin Cities buildings and the plan for the University of Minnesota's Northrop Mall (which was significantly modified) before moving on to national prominence with designs such as the Woolworth Building in New York City. The capitol was completed in 1904, and the cost of the new structure was the subject of great controversy. The third state capitol, most Minnesotans would agree today, was worth the hefty price tag.

St. Paul City Hall and Ramsey County
Courthouse
15 West Kellogg Boulevard, St. Paul
(651) 266–8023

The St. Paul City Hall and Ramsey County Courthouse is an exemplary combination of neoclassical and Art Deco. The building's facade is an example of neoclassical style, while the Art Deco interior is where the building shines. It shares with New York's Rockefeller Center the then-modern Art Deco style that is paired with unmatched attention to materials and detail.

Constructed during the middle of the Great Depression, the St. Paul City Hall overflows with the finest craftsmanship. When the nation's economy hit rock bottom, many of the nation's most talented artists and artisans were unemployed. In addition, not only did the cost of labor plummet, but also the price paid for materials. The results are breathtaking, particularly in the lobby, which glitters with black marble walls. Moreover, the lobby features a 36-foot-high rotating statue named *Visions of Peace*. The original 1931 structure was renovated in 1993, restoring any luster that may have diminished over the years.

St. Paul Public Library
80 West Fourth Street, St. Paul
(651) 227–9531

Twin Cities libraries are often distinguished by fine architecture. The St. Paul Public Library is an exceptional example, especially the James J. Hill Reference Library Reading Room. The reading room is an exemplar of Beaux Arts classicism, and the two-story reading room is surrounded by the book stacks and Ionic columns, with abundant fine crafted woodwork and granite floors. Large comfy tables and chairs entice visitors to enjoy the resources available or quietly absorb the architecture. Recently renovated, the library is one of downtown St. Paul's many beautiful public buildings.

Union Depot
214 East Fourth Street, St. Paul

The Union Depot was constructed between 1917 and 1923. At the time, the railroad was a prominent means of transportation, and a serpentine labyrinth of tracks circled the depot. Since then the importance of the railroad has signifi-

cantly dwindled. However, the depot remains—although it serves a different purpose. Today the Union Depot is an awe-inspiring architectural work that takes advantage of a high ceiling, balconies, and plenty of stone. Restaurants now occupy the immense lobby, where passengers once arrived and departed, and visitors may dine in one of St. Paul's most historic and architecturally attractive settings.

Minnesota World Trade Center
30 East Seventh Street, St. Paul
(651) 297–1580

The Minnesota World Trade Center, completed in 1987, sits high atop the St. Paul skyline. It is the tallest building in St. Paul, and at 40 stories high, the building would fit in the much loftier Minneapolis

St. Paul's tallest building, the Minnesota World Trade Center, towers over the surrounding structures of the Capital City. PHOTO: TODD R. BERGER

skyline. The building is leased by a variety of different firms. The architectural design of the trade center is similar to many of the colossal Minneapolis structures. The exterior has plenty of dark glass, which reflects light on sunny summer days. Even in St. Paul, a city where tradition has always been emphasized, the Minnesota World Trade Center (a modern skyscraper) dominates the skyline.

Houses of Worship

St. Paul

Assumption Church
51 West Seventh Street, St. Paul
(651) 224–7536

The Assumption Church was constructed between 1869 and 1874. Located in an area of downtown St. Paul where architectural change has occurred at a rapid pace, the church remains a distinct and important piece of architecture.

As St. Paul developed, religious communities constructed churches to fulfill their spiritual needs. Of course, the ethnic heritage and denomination of the church often profoundly influenced the architecture of individual churches. This was certainly the case with the Assumption Church, which was formed to meet the needs of German Catholics. The Ludwigskirche in Munich heavily influenced the German Romanesque revival design of the church. For materials, the church makes use of Minnesota limestone. However, the twin towers are the most distinguishable features of the church. The Assumption Church's twin towers rise 210 feet high and are a perennial landmark in the ephemeral architecture of downtown St. Paul.

Cathedral of Saint Paul
239 Selby Avenue, St. Paul
(651) 228–1766

The Cathedral of Saint Paul is one of the Twin Cities' most recognizable landmarks. The sheer size of the structure is daunting, and it stands like a sentinel atop Cathedral Hill, where it overlooks

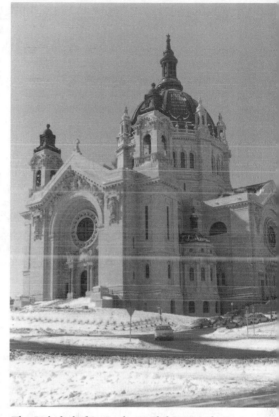

The Cathedral of St. Paul overwhelms everything that surrounds it with its sheer size. PHOTO: TODD R. BERGER

downtown St. Paul, directly across the interstate from the massive Minnesota State Capitol.

The grand scale of the Cathedral of Saint Paul reflects its source of inspiration. The cathedral was modeled after Saint Peter's Cathedral in Rome, and designed by Emmanuel L. Masqueray. Also instrumental in the erection of the cathedral was Archbishop John Ireland, who envisioned and raised the money for the cathedral as a tribute to the faith of the archdiocese.

The features of the cathedral, completed in 1915, are breathtaking. The interior is baroque in design, and makes use of Minnesota granite and travertine, and is decorated with stained glass and religion-inspired paintings which include several

Mill City Museum

Minneapolis is most commonly known to visitors as the "City of Lakes." The city's first nickname, and the name that elevated the city to national prominence, the "Mill City," is rarely used today. Instead, the city has focused on its "chain of lakes," most notably Lake Calhoun, Lake Harriet, Lake Nokomis, and Lake of the Isles. Annually the city commemorates the lakes' importance during the Aquatennial, the only city-wide annual event. However, the riverfront has undergone a renaissance in recent years as, piece by piece, elements of Minneapolis's past have been revived. The Mill City Museum, which opened in September 2003, reclaimed the once buried and nearly forgotten history of the city, and restored it to the prominent position it deserves as the birthplace of a world-class city.

The Mill City Museum is located in the heart of Minneapolis's historic milling district. Shortly after the city was founded in 1852, small mills congregated on both the east bank (until 1872, St. Anthony) and the west bank of the Mississippi near St. Anthony Falls. At this only waterfall on the Mississippi, the river provided an exceptional source of power for milling the increasingly limitless wheat of the upper Midwest, and the number and size of the mills swelled. By 1890 Minneapolis had established itself as the nation's largest wheat market, and Washburn-Crosby and Company (the antecedent of General Mills) was among the Cities' leaders in the industry with their nationally recognized trademark, "Gold Medal Flour."

To serve these needs, the company constructed the Washburn A Mill. Like its predecessor, the A Mill was plagued by fire, but not nearly as deadly as the May 2, 1878, explosion, which killed 18. For many years the A Mill was left dormant, during which time the structure was seriously damaged. Parts of the old mill were totally destroyed and enormous gaping holes were left, exposing the structure to Minneapolis's harsh weather. This was the challenge for the Minneapolis architectural firm of Meyer, Scherer & Rockcastle Ltd., which designed the Mill City Museum. Surprisingly, the design uses the former dilapidation of the A Mill to the museum's advantage.

Architect Tom Meyer has adapted this unique structure for the numerous attractions at the Mill City Museum. The museum emphasizes hands-on experiences, like the Minnesota Historical Society, and includes a water power laboratory and a test kitchen. In addition, the eight-story "Flour Tower" ride features regional history. Another attraction is the open-air courtyard within the walls of the mill ruins.

Beyond milling, the museum features several historical exhibits. The influence of water power both in milling and in allied industries on the Mississippi River are examined. The museum demonstrates the role of milling in the development of Minneapolis's dynamic economy and its impact on paramount issues, such as immigration patterns, railroad development, and agriculture. The museum's architecture is an essential component in conveying the history of early Minneapolis.

The Mill City Museum design maximizes preservation of the historic ruins. Retained are many elements of the old mill e.g., milling machinery, flour bins, rail corridor, engine house, and wheat house. While much of the mill has been restored to its former glory, in some cases the architect has exploited scenic views created by fire damage. For example, the fire destroyed a portion of the mill, but created a breathtaking view of St. Anthony Falls. The structure presented a challenge for the architects; however, the design met the challenge by successfully integrating the mill ruins with new construction.

In addition to the museum, the structure includes a bookstore to provide further information about the mill, the Twin Cities, and Minnesota. Also, the mill incorporates classrooms for educational purposes and a restaurant. And finally, the mill provides one of the most innovative and scenic living opportunities in the Twin Cities. The Brighton Development is located in the top five floors of the mill, with lofts available. The Brighton Development promises to become a part of an emerging neighborhood in downtown.

The Mill City Museum has a $24 million budget. Of these funds $20 million are from the state and federal government. In addition, the project has been the recipient of many endowments and private sector donations. The largest donations were received from the McKnight Foundation (3M) and Cargill Incorporated. Ironically, Cargill, like General Mills, got its start in milling in Minneapolis.

104 S. 2nd St

beautiful frescoes. The dome extends 175 feet above the cathedral, and can be seen from great distances. Guided tours are held Monday, Wednesday, and Friday at 1:00 P.M., where visitors may enjoy the Cathedral of Saint Paul's astounding beauty.

St. Clement's Episcopal Church
901 Portland Avenue, St. Paul
(651) 228–1164

Many are surprised to hear that this attractive and quaint church was designed by Cass Gilbert, who later served as architect for the colossal Minnesota State Capitol. The structure makes fine use of material but on a much smaller scale. Intimacy is stressed. The church is constructed of slate, stone, and wood; conveys a sense of solace; and is scaled to parishioner's size. St. Clement's Episcopal Church was completed in 1894, after which Gilbert went on to bigger, but not necessarily better, architectural projects.

Mount Zion Temple
1300 Summit Avenue, St. Paul
(651) 698–3881
www.mzion.org

The first Jewish house of worship in the Twin Cities was located at the first Mount Zion Temple. The present building is located, oddly enough, on Summit Avenue, where the old money in St. Paul resides. Eric Mendelsohn, an internation-

ally renowned architect, designed the stylish, modern building.

Minneapolis

The Basilica of Saint Mary
88 North 17th Street, Minneapolis
(612) 333–1381

The Basilica of Saint Mary celebrated its first Mass on May 31, 1914, as a then unique Catholic place for worship. It was the first basilica in America, an institution created to serve the needs of Minneapolis. While St. Paul completed its own breathtakingly beautiful cathedral in 1915 to serve its parishioners, the other Twin City was allowed by the Vatican to construct the basilica. As with the Cathedral of Saint Paul, Emmanuel L. Masqueray (1861–1917) was the architect for the Basilica of Saint Mary.

Masqueray unveiled his design in 1906. The colossal basilica features a 200-foot dome and an impressive nave. At the time of its construction, the 140-foot by 82-foot nave was considered the widest in the world. The stained-glass windows, designed by Thomas Gaytee, are another extraordinary feature of the basilica.

The life of the namesake of the basilica, Mary, mother of Jesus, is artfully displayed on the stained-glass windows. The basilica excels architecturally in its use of details like these and others. For example, the rose windows on both sides of the sanctuary portray the Immaculate Conception and the Crowning of Mary Queen of Heaven. In addition, there are the archangels in the windows of the entrance, which guard everyone who enters the basilica. Furthermore, sculptures play a significant role in the architecture of the basilica and its grounds. The 12 apostles are depicted in the sanctuary, and there are half-scale replicas of the sculptures at Saint John Lateran in Rome. These are just a few of the sculptures, which include Father Louis Hennepin, who brought Catholicism to the area and looks out on the street that today bears his name (Hennepin Avenue).

Location is yet another superlative feature of the building's architecture. Located on the edge of downtown Minneapolis, it sits across the street from Loring Park, and is within walking distance of the internationally acclaimed Walker Art Center and the numerous beautiful churches lining Hennepin Avenue (Hennepin Avenue United Methodist and Cathedral Church of St. Mark). All of these churches are definitely examples of excellent Beaux Arts architecture, but the Basilica of Saint Mary is certainly the largest in scale.

Cathedral Church of St. Mark
519 Oak Grove Street, Minneapolis
(612) 870–7800

The Cathedral Church of St. Mark was designed by one of the Twin Cities' most renowned architectural firms in the early 20th century, Brown and Hewitt. Between 1904 and 1930, the firm created several outstanding pieces of architecture, including this church, created in 1911. Edwin H. Hewitt was the primary designer of most of the firm's work, which was heavily influenced by the eclectic Beaux Arts style. Emphasizing revivalism in architectural designs, Beaux Arts works are symmetrical and balanced. The style was a popular foil of modernism.

As a member of the church, Hewitt set out to create a design appropriate to his faith. Denominationally, the church is Episcopalian; the design reflects this heritage. English Gothic Revival dominates the church's architectural style. The tower is inspired by the example found at Magdalen College at Oxford, albeit significantly scaled down. Adding to the church's splendor is its location on the edge of Loring Park, which is one of Minneapolis's most beautiful parks.

Christ Church Lutheran
3244 34th Avenue South, Minneapolis
(612) 721–6611

Built in a humble working class neighborhood in south Minneapolis, the Christ Lutheran Church is the last design of Eliel Saarinen. Appropriately, the world-famous architect created a design for the state of Minnesota, where Scandinavian Lutherans abound.

Saarinen constructed the church from 1949 to 1950, with the assistance of his architect son, Eero. Saarinen, the 76-year-old master, was nearing the end of his long illustrious life. The church followed a number of his great architectural pieces, which began with the railway station in Helsinki (1905–1914). Then he went on to design a series of central European railway stations. Later, Saarinen emigrated to the United States, where his work culminated with the Cranbrook School (c. 1925). For his last architectural triumph, he was selected for the Christ Church Lutheran's design.

Saarinen's forte was creating excellent institutional architecture, but he faced a formidable challenge with the church. Unlike many of his earlier pieces of architecture, the church's coffers did not overflow with money for a distinctive design. Hence, Saarinen created a work of great beauty out of a relatively limited budget. The church is small and intimate, and the exterior design is composed of minimalistic blocks. As parishioners or visitors approach the church, they walk under a large stone canopy. Inside the building are two wings, with a sanctuary on one end, and a fellowship hall, offices, and classrooms on the other. The interior is finely detailed, and makes abundant use of yellow brick and complementary shaded wood. The exterior of the sanctuary has four sculptures representing faith, love, church, and hope. Saarinen died in 1950, the year Christ Church Lutheran was completed. However, the architect's legacy continues with one of the Twin Cities' most attractive small churches.

Hennepin Avenue United Methodist Church
511 Groveland Avenue, Minneapolis
(612) 871-5303
www.themethodistchurch.org

The Hennepin Avenue United Methodist Church is yet another impressive piece of architecture on Hennepin Avenue. Like the Cathedral Church of St. Mark, it was designed by Hewitt and Brown and is once again an example of English Gothic Revival work. The octagonal base of the steeple and tall, slender spire set the church apart and position it among the Twin Cities' most spectacular architectural churches.

Our Lady of Lourdes Church
One Lourdes Place, Minneapolis
(612) 379-2259
www.ourladyoflourdes.com

Not only is Our Lady of Lourdes the oldest standing church in Minneapolis, but it also has a simultaneously tumultuous and intriguing history. The church's architecture plays a pivotal role in its history. During each successive turn in the history of the church, at least minimal architectural alterations were made. Surprisingly, despite the cobbled nature of the church's construction, it is an awe-inspiring work and a landmark in historic St. Anthony.

The church dates back to 1854, when the First Universalist Church constructed the original structure. The front nave was built from native limestone. The original Greek temple–style church was significantly smaller than it is today. In 1877 the church was purchased by a group of Catholic French Canadian settlers in the area and rechristened Our Lady of Lourdes. Substantial alterations were made to

reflect this change. The Canadians added the mansard roof, which remains on the eastern side of the church. In toto, the structure was transformed into the French Provincial style, which was one of the seven styles of church architecture then constructed in Quebec. Shortly thereafter, the church added a bell tower, sacristy, and a vestibule. Stained-glass windows were installed from the 1890s through the 1910s. However, the church was increasingly neglected over time.

In 1968 church leaders decided to demolish the church, but just as it was to meet the wrecking ball the Minneapolis city council intervened. They argued the church was too valuable a piece of the area's architectural history, and the church was spared. The Minneapolis city council also recognized the vital role the church played in historic St. Anthony, where Father Louis Hennepin sighted the falls in 1680 and the area's history began. Since 1968 the church has undergone several renovations in order to restore it to its previous glory. In 1991 carillon bells were mounted in the church tower. Today their sonorous chiming can be heard throughout historic St. Anthony.

West

Colonial Church of Edina
6200 Colonial Way, Edina
(952) 925-2711

The Colonial Church of Edina is a visible curiosity that stands in stark contrast to the architecture most common on Minnesota Highway 62. The church's design was modeled on a New England colonial village.

Architect Richard Hammel actually visited a church in Barnstable, Massachusetts, that was built by the Pilgrims in the 17th century. The design, in keeping with the original architecture, is simple and subdued. The church makes use of gray with white trim and features a bell tower at the center. The colonial village design includes space for a sanctuary, lounges, and additional rooms for church activities. It comes as no surprise to Twin Citians that the Colonial Church is located in Edina, which was one of the first wealthy suburbs in Minneapolis, and continues as one of the area's most exclusive cities.

East

St. Michael's Catholic Church
611 South Third Street, Stillwater
(651) 439–4400
www.stmichael.stillwater.mn.us

The Catholic missionaries arrived in Stillwater in 1849. The city, founded in 1843, is home to numerous historic sites. The city rapidly developed as one of Minnesota's most important cities, which was due largely to the lumbering industry.

In 1873 the construction of St. Michael's Catholic Church began. The site of the church sits atop a bluff overlooking the city of Stillwater and the St. Croix River Valley. The structure was built of native, blond Kasota stone. The church has impressive dimensions of 140 by 180 feet, with the gorgeous spire extending 190 feet above. In 1883 the church added the first chimes in the area, which to this day ring mellifluously above the valley, although today they chime via automation. Over the years St. Michael's has been renovated several times to maintain its striking beauty. In a city filled with architectural treasures, St. Michael's Church stands out as one of the city's most stunning pieces of architecture.

Insiders' Tip
The Stone Arch Bridge is the best place in Minneapolis to view both Minneapolis's historic milling district architecture and the city's skyline.

Insiders' Tip
The first Hennepin Avenue Bridge, completed in 1855, was the first permanent span across the Mississippi in the entire nation.

Twin Cities Bridges

Hennepin Avenue Suspension Bridge
Main Street SE and Hennepin Avenue, Minneapolis

The Hennepin Avenue Suspension Bridge is an essential piece of Minneapolis's architectural history. The first Hennepin Avenue Bridge was completed in 1855; it was the first permanent span across the Mississippi. Furthermore, the bridge was necessary for the creation of Minneapolis in 1872. The cities of St. Anthony (east bank) and Minneapolis (west bank) could not have merged without the bridge.

The current bridge is the fourth structure on the site in Minneapolis's history. It is a larger, architecturally scaled down version of the bridge that occupied the site in the late 19th century. Three minimal, relatively short towers sit on both sides of the Mississippi. Despite its subdued architecture for a grand suspension bridge, it serves an important function and provides a panoramic view of the city's architecture.

High Bridge
Smith Avenue, St. Paul

The High Bridge is a landmark that provides one of the best scenic views of St. Paul. The original High Bridge was constructed in the late 19th century to link St. Paul's West Seventh Street and the upper West Side. The span of the bridge was an astounding 2,770 feet in length and constructed of over one million

The Hennepin Avenue Suspension Bridge stands on the spot of the first bridge across the Mississippi River.

PHOTO: GREATER MINNEAPOLIS CONVENTION & VISITORS ASSOCIATION

pieces of iron. It was no small accomplishment for its epoch; however, the bridge deteriorated over the course of almost a century. The bridge was razed in 1985 after being closed for a year.

St. Paul began the construction of a replica High Bridge. Once again, the bridge had a steep 4 percent grade. In addition, the bridge consisted of 11 spans. The largest span is an astounding 520 feet. Just as it did in the past, the bridge provides one of the best views of St. Paul and its numerous fine pieces of architecture.

Stillwater Lift Bridge
Wisconsin Minnesota Highway 64 and Water Street, Stillwater

The Stillwater Bridge is one of the many pieces of architecture in the historic city, but its future is uncertain. The span linking Stillwater, Minnesota to Wisconsin was constructed in 1931. It is a vertical-lift bridge, which must be raised for large vessels on the St. Croix River. Today, there are only three extant examples of vertical-lift bridges in Minnesota, and Wisconsin. Despite the bridge's architectural significance, it has a questionable future because of the population growth in the St. Croix River Valley.

Stone Arch Bridge
Main Street SE and Fifth Avenue, Minneapolis

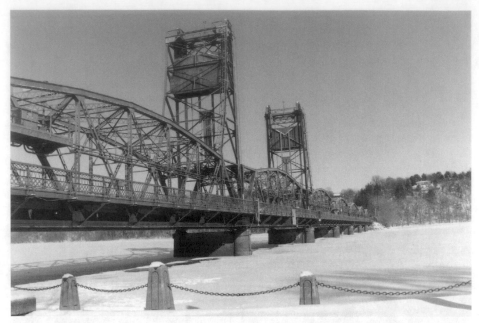

Stillwater's famous Lift Bridge spans the St. Croix River, connecting Minnesota and Wisconsin. PHOTO: TODD R. BERGER

The Stone Arch Bridge is an important piece of Minneapolis's history. It was constructed in 1883 for James J. Hill's Great Northern Railway. The bridge spanning the Mississippi took two years to complete. In 1982 the bridge was closed because of decreased train traffic. The bridge remained dormant until the state of Minnesota purchased it in 1992, and it was renovated to appear as it did during its glory days. The only significant alteration is that the bridge now serves as a pedestrian walkway linking the old milling district and historic St. Anthony. Besides serving as an important piece of Minneapolis's architectural history, it also provides one of the best panoramic views of downtown.

Accommodations

Minneapolis
St. Paul
Neighboring
   Communities
Bed and Breakfasts

There are a few good rules to remember when trying to find hotel accommodations in the Twin Cities. First of all, winter rates for rooms are almost half that of spring and summer rates. Second, staying in St. Paul is quite a bit cheaper than staying in Minneapolis, although this may change with the recent building of the new Xcel Energy Center in downtown St. Paul. So we're at a bit of a loss quoting actual rates for hotel rooms, since the rates can change so drastically from month to month depending on what conventions are in town, sports events, high-profile local festivals, and rumors of a final break in winter or the first sign of fall. Most hotels in the Cities, however, have package plans that can knock up to a couple hundred dollars off the price of a room if you reserve the room a few months in advance and you plan to stay for two or more days. All major credit cards are accepted at the following establishments except where noted. Also, all the following hotels have both smoking and nonsmoking rooms unless otherwise noted; however, none of the bed-and-breakfasts listed here allow smoking inside the rooms. All hotels in the metro area are required to have wheelchair-accessible ramps outside and inside the hotels, although winter conditions may make some of these ramps harder to navigate if they're not properly maintained.

If you do end up visiting the Twin Cities during the chilly winter months, try to find a hotel connected to either the Minneapolis or the St. Paul Skyway system. These wonderful second-floor walkways are climate-controlled and link most of the downtown businesses, so you don't actually have to step outside unless you want to. You can enter the skyway system through the parking garages in both cities, and posted maps let you know where you are in the city at every junction.

Price Code

The following rate information is based on the present cost of a standard, double-occupancy room in springtime (May–June), which is generally considered to be the peak tourist season in the Twin Cities.

$ . . . . Less than $100
$$ . . . . $101–$150
$$$ . . . . $151–$200
$$$$ . . . . $201–$250
$$$$$ . . . . $251 and higher

Minneapolis

Best Western Normandy Downtown $
405 South Eighth Street, Minneapolis
(612) 370–1400 or (800) 372–3131

Conveniently located in the heart of downtown Minneapolis, this hotel is just steps away from the downtown Skyway system and all the shopping, businesses, and entertainment of the area. The hotel offers guests a complimentary continental breakfast, an indoor pool and Jacuzzi, fitness room, laundromat, and free local and long-distance phone access.

Crowne Plaza Northstar Hotel $$$
618 Second Avenue South, Minneapolis
(612) 338–2288 or (800) 586–7827
www.msp-northstar.crowneplaza.com

This recently renovated hotel offers a comfortable stay for tourists and business travelers alike, with an eighth-floor Skygarden patio for relaxing outdoor seating May through October and a fitness center for the rest of the year. Each room includes an oversized desk with an ergonomic chair, individually controlled heating and air-conditioning, and high-speed Internet access to make your business trip even more productive. For those here on pleasure, the hotel is right in the middle of downtown Minneapolis, and minutes away from all the entertainment venues and shopping the area has to offer.

Days Inn University of Minneapolis $
2407 University Avenue SE, Minneapolis
(612) 623-3999

This friendly six-story hotel is located on the eastern edge of the University of Minneapolis campus and is walking distance from Dinkytown and all its shopping and restaurants. The hotel offers guests a complimentary continental breakfast as well as free lot parking and complimentary shuttle service to and from the U of M campus and the U of M Hospital and Clinics.

Embassy Suites $$$$
425 South Seventh Street, Minneapolis
(612) 333-3111

This all-suite hotel features an open atrium and immediate access to the downtown Skyway system. Suite amenities include a separate bedroom, living area, and a fully equipped kitchen; hotel facilities include a gym, an indoor swimming pool, and two on-site restaurants that are also available for room service.

Insiders' Tip
The downtown Minneapolis trolley stops at most downtown hotels to pick up passengers in summer. Ask your hotel concierge for more information.

Four Points Sheraton Minneapolis $$$$
1330 Industrial Boulevard, Minneapolis
(612) 331-1900

Just minutes away from the Metrodome, the Target Center, and the State Fairgrounds, this AAA 3 Diamond property is close to all the sights and sounds you come to the Twin Cities for. For your dining pleasure, there's The Anchorage and the attached Anchorage Lounge, one of the best seafood restaurants in the area and an exclusive to the hotel. Amenities include a heated indoor pool, sauna, and a private gym.

The Grand Hotel Minneapolis $$$$$
615 Second Avenue South, Minneapolis
(612) 288-8888 or (866) THE-GRAND
www.grandhotelminneapolis.com

Originally the home of the historic Minneapolis Athletic Club, the Grand Hotel Minneapolis remodeled and reopened as a hotel in 2000. Based on the AAA rating system, the hotel is the top luxury hotel in downtown Minneapolis. Although you will pay for the experience, you will be pampered from the moment you step in the door. The 140 rooms of the hotel all feature such indulgences as Egyptian cotton sheets, silk bathrobes, Aveda bath products, leather-topped desks, and Tuscan furniture. Guests also enjoy their choice of complimentary newspapers delivered to their door, complimentary shoe shines, the Martini Blu Restaurant and Night Club, the Martini Blu Sushi Bar, the Grande Finale Lobby Bar, and an Aveda Concept Salon and Spa. Guests are allowed free use of the on-site 58,000-square-foot Minneapolis Lifetime Athletic Club, with such features as an indoor lap pool, racquetball and squash courts, fitness center, boxing studio, sauna, and a eucalyptus steam room. The hotel is connected to the Skyway system, and is within easy walking distance of the luxurious Gaviidae Common shopping center (anchored by such stores as Neiman Marcus and Saks Fifth Avenue), the Minneapolis Convention Center, Nicollet Mall, and the Hennepin Theater District.

Hilton Minneapolis $$$$
1001 Marquette Avenue,
Minneapolis
(612) 376–1000
www.minneapolis.hilton.com

The Hilton Minneapolis is located next door to Orchestra Hall in the center of downtown and is connected to the Skyway system. The 25-story Victorian-style brick hotel has 821 rooms, all featuring large windows and hand-carved oak trim. The hotel has an on site health club, including a full gym, whirlpool, sauna, and swimming pool, as well as security-controlled parking, 24-hour concierge service, same-day laundry service, and complimentary transportation to Mystic Lake Casino. Harmony's coffee shop, located in the hotel, serves breakfast, lunch, and dinner.

Holiday Inn Express Hotel & Suites $$
225 South 11th Street, Minneapolis
(612) 341–3300 or (800) 870–0114
www.hiexpress.com/msp-downtown

Like many other hotels in the area, this Holiday Inn reclaimed a beautiful old brick building and refurbished it, making it even more pleasurable to stay at if you're even slightly interested in architecture or the history of the Twin Cities mill industry. The location is great, too, with an entrance to the downtown Skyway right across the street and 2 blocks away from the Minneapolis Convention Center and Nicollet Mall. Amenities include an indoor pool, complimentary breakfast, free local phone calls, and an on-site fitness center.

The Holiday Inn Metrodome $$$$
1500 Washington Avenue South,
Minneapolis
(612) 333–4646

Located on the eastern edge of the downtown Minneapolis business district with the University of Minnesota on one side and the Metrodome on the other, the Holiday Inn Metrodome has one of the best hotel locations for sports fans in Minneapolis. The 265-room hotel has an indoor pool, whirlpool and sauna, a gym, and a restaurant (The Grill Room Restau-

Insiders' Tip
Making hotel reservations at least two months in advance can save you a lot of money. Also, most hotels have discount plans for stays of two days or more.

rant and 7th Corner Lounge) on site and offers guests shuttle transportation within a 3-mile radius.

Hyatt Regency Hotel $$$$$
1300 Nicollet Mall, Minneapolis
(612) 370–1234

This 24-story hotel is located right on the Nicollet Avenue pedestrian "mall," with access to the Skyway from the second floor of the four-story atrium. With 533 guest rooms and suites, four restaurants, an indoor pool, a full service athletic club, and a retail area that includes clothing stores, hair, nail, and tanning salons, gourmet coffee shops, and delis, this is one of the more comfortable places to stay as you ease yourself into the bustle of Minneapolis. The hotel also features the city's finest "flown-in daily" seafood restaurant, the Oceannaire, whose menu changes depending on which seafood specialties are available for the day.

Marquette Hotel $$$
710 Marquette Avenue, Minneapolis
(612) 333–4545 or (800) 328–4782

Located in the heart of downtown Minneapolis, the Marquette has the distinct advantage of being connected to the IDS Center complex, which is connected to the downtown Skyway system, linking the hotel to more than 65 blocks of shops, restaurants, and the Minneapolis Convention Center. The rooms are large with great views of the downtown area from all sides, and the hotel's restaurant, Basil's, has a pianist serenading patrons on weekends. The entire hotel was renovated during spring and summer 2003. The Marquette also operates Windows on Minnesota, a banquet and meeting space on the 50th floor of the IDS Center, a location very popular with wedding couples looking to celebrate their nuptials with an unrivaled panoramic view of the Twin Cities.

Le Méridien Minneapolis $$$$
601 First Avenue, Minneapolis
(612) 677–1100 or (800) 543–4300
www.lemeridien.minneapolis.com

Downtown Minneapolis's newest hotel, opened in March 2003, is across the street from the Target Center in the Block E entertainment and shopping complex and is connected to the Skyway system. The hotel is the first "Art & Tech" hotel opened in the United States by the Le Méridien chain, with features such as glass-etched, handcrafted headboards, backlit photographs inspired by Twin Cities culture, 42-inch plasma televisions, high-speed Internet access, and artisti-

cally designed bathrooms. In addition to an on-site health club, the hotel has a restaurant (Cosmos) and a street-level bar (Infinity Room).

Minneapolis Marriott City Center $$$$
30 South Seventh Street, Minneapolis
(612) 349–4000 or (800) 228–9290
www.marriotthotels.com/mspcc

Connected to the City Center Mall and the Minneapolis Convention Center via the Skyway, this 4-Diamond, Pinnacle Award–winning hotel is conveniently located near all the main shopping areas and restaurants in downtown Minneapolis. The hotel also provides guests with a private, Nautilus-equipped health club and an on-site restaurant—Northern Shores Grille, a cheery, casual dining establishment.

Nicollet Island Inn $$$
95 Merriam Street, Minneapolis
(612) 331–1800
www.nicolletislandinn.com

The Nicollet Island Inn sits in the middle of the Mississippi River on Nicollet Island

Minneapolis's Nicollet Island Inn is a cozy spot on the Mississippi River, just across from downtown Minneapolis. PHOTO: TODD R. BERGER

across from downtown Minneapolis and easily accessible from the Warehouse District via the Hennepin Avenue Bridge. The building that houses the inn was built in 1893 as the factory for the Island Door and Sash Company, a maker of window shades and blinds. Today the National Historic Building includes 24 individually decorated guest rooms, many with nice views of the downtown skyline and the river. The Nicollet Island Inn also has a romantic restaurant well known throughout the Cities for its wonderful brunch.

Quality Inn & Suites $$
41 North 10th Street, Minneapolis
(612) 339–9311 or (800) 423–4100
www.qualityminneapolis.com

This inexpensive hotel chain is one of the few places in downtown Minneapolis that offers free parking to its guests. Since it's located near several major bus lines, it's a good place to just leave your car while exploring the downtown area so that you won't have to pay for parking in one of the lots or metered spaces. The hotel offers a complimentary continental breakfast and has an indoor pool, gym, whirlpool, and outdoor patio for guests to use.

Radisson Metrodome $$
615 Southeast Washington Avenue, Minneapolis
(612) 379–8888 or (800) 379 MPLS
www.radisson.com/minneapolismn_metrodome

The Radisson Metrodome is set on the University of Minnesota–Minneapolis campus. A short walk from U of M sporting venues and Dinkytown—the main college kid hangout—this is a great place to catch most of the sports action in town, college or otherwise. The hotel offers a wide selection of amenities, including two on-site restaurants, a full-service bank, a travel agency, and a beauty salon. Guests are also allowed to use the university's Rec Sports Center next to the hotel free of charge, and complimentary shuttle service to any destination within 5 miles of the hotel is offered on an appointment basis.

> ## Insiders' Tip
> Finding a parking place in downtown Minneapolis is just about impossible during business hours. Your best bet is to leave the car at the hotel and catch one of the buses heading up and down Nicollet Mall. And don't worry about getting a bus home—many of the buses on Nicollet run 24 hours a day.

Radisson Plaza Hotel Minneapolis $$$$
35 South Seventh Street, Minneapolis
(612) 339–4900 or (800) 333–3333
www.radisson.com/minneapolismn_plaza

Located in the heart of downtown Minneapolis, this luxury hotel has the added bonus of being connected to the Minneapolis Skyway system. The Radisson Plaza features two restaurants, two lounges, and the Radisson Health Club. Through the Skyway, you can easily reach most of downtown Minneapolis's attractions and shopping, including the Target Center, the Minneapolis Convention Center, and Nicollet Mall.

The Whitney Hotel $$$
150 Portland Avenue, Minneapolis
(612) 339–9300
www.thewhitneyhotel.com

The Whitney Hotel, part of the Hyatt Regency chain, opened in 1987 inside a historic 1879 flour mill in the heart of the Minneapolis West Side Milling District. Listed on the National Register of Historic Places as part of the St. Anthony Falls Historic District, the Whitney sits on the banks of the Mississippi River at the falls. The beautiful hotel has 97 guest rooms, many with spectacular views of

The Whitney Hotel was built inside an old flour mill on the banks of the Mississippi in downtown Minneapolis. PHOTO: TODD R. BERGER

the river, the Stone Arch Bridge, the Metrodome, and downtown Minneapolis's skyscrapers. The hotel has a restaurant, the Whitney Grille (see the Restaurants chapter), and a bar, the Whitney Lounge, as well as a fitness center. Guests receive complimentary copies of *USA Today,* minifridges in their rooms, and many other nice touches at this reasonably priced luxury hotel.

St. Paul

Best Western Kelly Inn $
161 St. Anthony Avenue, St. Paul
(651) 227-8711

A short walk from the State Capitol in St. Paul, with a great view of St. Paul's Cathedral, this hotel offers guests comfortable, inexpensive rooms in one of the more scenic historic neighborhoods in the metro area. Amenities include an indoor swimming pool and sauna as well as cable and satellite TV and room service for all guests.

Embassy Suites St. Paul $$
175 East 10th Street, St. Paul
(651) 224-5400 or (800) EMBASSY
www.embassystpaul.com

Located in downtown St. Paul, the Embassy Suites St. Paul has 210 rooms, all two-room suites. Hotel amenities include a swimming pool, fitness club, whirlpool, sauna, downtown shuttle service, full-service restaurant (Woolley's), and an Irish sports bar (Cork's Pub), which features a nightly happy hour. The price of the room includes breakfast, and the tropical atrium belies the Northern Plains climate beyond the glass. The hotel is within walking distance of many St. Paul sites, including the Minnesota State Capitol building and the F. Scott Fitzgerald Theatre (where Garrison Keillor's *A Prairie Home Companion* radio show is performed).

Four Points Sheraton St. Paul/Midway $
400 Hamline Avenue, St. Paul
(651) 642-1234 or (800) 535-2339

Located right between Minneapolis and St. Paul, this hotel has the advantage of offering easy and equal access to the features and attractions of both cities. Amenities include an indoor pool, whirlpool and exercise room, an on-site airline ticket counter, a nearby golf course and jogging track, and complimentary transportation to the Mall of America and the airport by appointment.

Holiday Inn RiverCentre $$
175 West Seventh Street, St. Paul
(651) 225-1515

Located right across the street from the Xcel Energy Center, home of the Minnesota Wild NHL team, and the RiverCentre convention center, this hotel is also within 4 blocks of the Science Museum of Minnesota, the Children's Museum, and the Ordway Theater. It's also a short walk from the Minnesota State Capitol, the Minnesota History Center, and the Fitzgerald Theatre. The hotel has been completely renovated, with all new carpeting, furniture, and fixtures. Guest amenities include an indoor pool and gym.

Holiday Inn Express—Bandana Square $
1010 Bandana Boulevard West, St. Paul
(651) 647-1637

Built inside the original shell of a Northern Pacific Railroad foundry repair shop, this beautiful yellow-brick hotel is also connected to the stores of historic Bandana Square. The facilities include an indoor pool and hot tub. The hotel is about 3 miles away from all the attractions and museums of downtown St. Paul.

Radisson Riverfront Hotel St. Paul $$
11 East Kellogg Boulevard, St. Paul
(651) 292-1900 or (800) 333-3333
www.radisson.com

Right across the boulevard from the Mississippi River and in the heart of downtown St. Paul, this hotel sports the Twin Cities' only revolving restaurant, the Carousal Restaurant, located on the 22nd floor and offering a panoramic view of the Mississippi River. Hotel amenities include a heated indoor pool, a fitness center, and a T1 high-speed Internet connection.

The Radisson Riverfront Hotel in St. Paul offers traditional elegance and the Twin Cities' only revolving restaurant. PHOTO: SAINT PAUL CONVENTION AND VISITORS BUREAU

Saint Paul Hotel $$$
350 Market Street, St. Paul
(651) 292-9292 or (800) 292-9292
www.stpaulhotel.com

Built in 1910 and located in the center of St. Paul on historic Market Street, this premier luxury hotel is a member of the Historic Hotels of America. Fully restored to its original splendor, the hotel offers guests a unique combination of turn-of-the-century charm and modern convenience. The hotel is within walking distance of St. Paul's RiverCentre, the Ordway Center for the Performing Arts, the new Minnesota Science Museum, and Xcel Energy Center, as well as the Missis-

The historic Saint Paul Hotel overlooks Rice Park in the heart of the city. PHOTO: SAINT PAUL CONVENTION AND VISITORS BUREAU

sippi River walk, and business and shopping districts via the climate-controlled St. Paul downtown skyway. Amenities include daily turndown service with mineral water delivered to each room, a complimentary newspaper and coffee each morning, 24-hour security, full-time concierge services, indoor parking and valet service, and a rooftop fitness center. The hotel has two restaurants, the elegant Saint Paul Grill and The Cafe. (For more information on eating at the Saint Paul Grill, see the Restaurants chapter.)

Neighboring Communities

Afton House Inn $$
3291 St. Croix Trail South, Afton
(651) 436–8883 or (877) 436–8883
www.aftonhouseinn.com

The Afton House Inn is located about 20 miles east of downtown St. Paul in the quaint town of Afton on the St. Croix River. Built in 1867 as a hotel/restaurant, the 25-room hotel is on the National Register of Historic Places. The nicely furnished rooms include such amenities as gas fireplaces and Jacuzzis. The hotel also operates Afton Cruise Lines, with several boats that cruise the St. Croix.

Amerisuites $$
7800 International Drive, Bloomington
(952) 854–0700

This all-suite hotel is within a mile of the Mall of America and MSP airport. The 128 rooms all have either king or queen beds, coffeemakers, minifridges, and other amenities. The hotel has a swimming pool and exercise room for its guests' use and operates a shuttle service to the airport. This is a good choice for business travelers wishing to be near the airport and visitors coming to the Cities primarily to shop at the megamall.

Comfort Inn $
2715 Long Lake Road, Roseville
(651) 636–5800 or (800) 451–7258

Just outside of the metro area, the recently renovated Comfort Inn provides easy access to the freeways that will take you back into the Twin Cities. Roseville is a pleasant, quiet suburb with several full-size shopping centers as well as some great local swimming holes in summer and ice skating and hockey rinks in winter.

Courtyard by Marriott $$
2905 Centre Pointe Drive, Roseville
(651) 746–8000 or (800) 321–2211
www.courtyard.com

The Courtyard by Marriott in Roseville is close to area shopping centers, and the nearby freeways allow for quick access to downtown Minneapolis and St. Paul, as well as the northern suburbs. The hotel has a restaurant, lounge, swimming pool, whirlpool, and fitness center on site and features an outdoor courtyard with fish ponds and a gazebo. Rooms include

The Afton House Inn is a short drive from the Twin Cities in the little town of Afton on the St. Croix River. PHOTO: SAINT PAUL CONVENTION AND VISITORS BUREAU

either one king or two queen beds, coffeemaker, and complimentary copies of *USA Today*. Some rooms also have DSL Internet connections.

Hampton Inn Airport/Mall of America $$
7745 Lyndale Avenue, Richfield
(612) 861-1000 or (800) 551-ROOM
www.hamptoninnrichfield.com

This comfortable hotel with few frills is set up especially with the business traveler in mind, with desks and modem hookups in many rooms. The hotel provides free shuttle transportation to the Mall of America and Minneapolis-St. Paul International Airport, and there is an indoor swimming pool and whirlpool on the premises. There is no additional charge for making local phone calls.

The Lowell Inn $$$
102 North Second Street, Stillwater
(651) 439-1100 or (888) 569-3554
www.lowellinn.com

The elegant Lowell Inn in Stillwater (20 miles east of downtown St. Paul) harbors

21 individually decorated rooms featuring period antiques. Elmore Lowell established the Sawyer House on the land where the Lowell Inn now stands in 1848, the year Stillwater was incorporated as the Minnesota Territory's first city. The colonial inn standing today dates from 1930, and the interior brings to mind the regal atmosphere of Southern plantation homes. The Lowell has three distinct dining rooms (see the Restaurants chapter for more information); guests can also relax during a Minnesota winter in front of the colonial fireplace in the Front Parlor. Room rates range widely depending on the room and its amenities, the day of the week (prices are higher on weekends), and whether guests prefer a package price including room, dinner for two, and breakfast.

Mystic Lake Casino Hotel $
2400 Mystic Lake Boulevard, Prior Lake
(952) 445-9000 or (800) 813-7349
www.mysticlake.com

About 25 miles southwest of downtown Minneapolis, the 416-room Mystic Lake

Casino Hotel rises next to the casino of the same name. The hotel features such amenities as an Olympic-sized pool with waterslide, 18-hole golf course, fitness center, and the largest casino in the Upper Midwest, with some 3,300 slot machines and 88 blackjack tables. Major celebrities regularly headline at the Celebrity Palace, and guests can partake in the massive buffet, routinely honored as the Best Buffet in the Twin Cities according to readers of *Mpls/St. Paul Magazine*. The hotel is also near Canterbury Park, which features betting on live horse racing during summer months and a card room year-round.

Radisson Hotel & Conference Center $$
3131 Campus Drive, Plymouth
(763) 559–6600 or (800) 333–3333
www.radisson.com/
minneapolismn_plymouth

The Radisson Plymouth is located in a parklike setting overlooking a 25-acre marshland preserve. All guest rooms include a minibar, two telephones, and a lighted work desk. Hotel facilities include a full-service fitness center and an indoor pool.

Sofitel Minneapolis $$$
5601 West 78th Street, Bloomington
(952) 835–1900 or (800) 876–6303
www.sofitelminneapolis.com

The French-style Sofitel is located at the intersection of Interstate 494 and Minnesota Highway 100 on the Bloomington

Strip. The hotel is about 10 minutes from the Mall of America, MSP airport, and downtown Minneapolis and offers shuttle service to the airport and the megamall. The 282-room hotel pampers guests with such tantalizing extras as an on-call masseuse, Parisian bath and shower products, and nightly turndown service with a complimentary rose and bottle of Evian.

Bed and Breakfasts

Chatsworth Bed and Breakfast $$$$
984 Ashland Avenue, St. Paul
(651) 227–4288 or (877) 978–4837
www.chatsworth-bb.com

Opened in 1986, the Chatsworth was the first B&B established in St. Paul. The 1904 Victorian house has five guest rooms with differing features, including canopied beds, whirlpools, period antiques, and private baths. The house has elegant woodwork throughout, and you can warm yourself in front of the fireplace in the main sitting room on chilly winter nights. Everything served for breakfast at the Chatsworth is homemade in the kitchen of the B&B's full-time chef, and recent meals have included Memphis vanilla gem muffins, baked cream cheese–stuffed French toast over sautéed apples, and cheese soufflés. The Chatsworth is within easy walking distance of the shops and restaurants along Grand Avenue and a short drive west of downtown St. Paul.

Covington Inn Bed and Breakfast $$$
100 Yacht Club, Pier One, Harriet Island,
St. Paul
(651) 292–1411
www.covingtoninn.com

The only floating bed and breakfast in the Twin Cities, the Covington Inn is a renovated tugboat first launched in 1946 and now moored in the Mississippi River across from downtown St. Paul. Open year-round, the B&B has four comfortable rooms, some with fireplaces, French doors, minifridges, and portholes. All rooms have private baths. The inn's common areas are trimmed in bronze, brass,

reasonable rates. Hundreds of visitors from more than 68 countries have stayed in this antique-furnished turn-of-the-20th-century home, with stays ranging from one night to one year (room rates decrease significantly according to length of stay). The living rooms, which are open to guests, include a four-season porch, large front parlor, fireplace room, lounge, dining room, and kitchen. Outside, guests can use the front patio. Amenities include free continental breakfast, private telephones in each room with free local calls, a furnished guest kitchen, on-site laundry, and a cleaning service.

and mahogany, and many salvaged fixtures suggest what it must have been like when the tug *Covington* pushed barges up and down the river. You can sit out on the deck and watch the mighty river flow by. The Covington's Harriet Island dock is a short walk from the Wabasha Street Bridge, which spans the Mississippi and leads to the museums, theaters, restaurants, and shops of downtown St. Paul.

Wales House $
1115 Southeast Fifth Street, Minneapolis
(612) 331-3931

Since opening to the public in 1994, this 10-bedroom bed-and-breakfast has been providing the charm of an Old World inn for faculty, staff, and other visitors to the University of Minnesota for extremely

William Sauntry Mansion $$$
626 North Fourth Street, Stillwater
(651) 430-2653 or (800) 828-2653
www.sauntrymansion.com

Lumber baron William Sauntry had his 25-room Victorian mansion built in the booming sawmill town of Stillwater on the St. Croix River in 1881. Today this B&B, listed on the National Register of Historic Places, has six guest rooms, all with fireplaces, private baths, and double whirlpool tubs. The ornate house features wood floors, the original chandeliers, stained-glass windows, and Victorian furnishings. The William Sauntry Mansion is close to downtown Stillwater, with its quaint antiques stores, lovely cafes, and antiquarian bookshops.

Restaurants

With approximately 3,500 restaurants in the metropolitan area, the Twin Cities boast one of the best dining scenes in the country. Once considered the land of the smorgasbord or simple meat-and-potato fare, the Twin Cities today offer a vast array of culinary choices. Whether it's fine dining or exotic ethnic cuisine, it can be found in the Twin Cities, not to mention the many unique coffeehouses and ice cream parlors in the area. The area also features several dining institutions that have been perennial favorites.

Traditional American and European fine-dining options are plentiful in the Twin Cities. The area features numerous upscale steak houses, both national chains and local institutions, as well as posh seafood, French, and Italian restaurants and much more. Nicollet Mall, located in the heart of downtown Minneapolis, offers the highest concentration of fine-dining opportunities in the Twin Cities, including Aquavit Restaurant, Brasserie Zinc, Oceanaire, and Manny's Steakhouse. St. Paul also boasts numerous fine-dining opportunities in downtown and the thriving Cathedral Hill neighborhood. Whether diners are looking for a posh restaurant for a special occasion, business, or rest and relaxation, there is something for everyone in the Twin Cities. But the options for diners only begin with fine dining; the area is also home to a seemingly endless array of ethnic dining choices.

The Twin Cities restaurant scene is extremely diverse. Besides the more standard ethnic fare such as Chinese, Mexican, Thai, Middle Eastern, and Indian foods, the area also boasts Kurdish, Cambodian, Afghani, Eastern European, and Ethiopian cuisine. Ethnic dining in the area starts on Nicollet Avenue, or Eat Street, which begins on the Nicollet Mall in downtown Minneapolis and leads into south Minneapolis. On Eat Street, diners will find some of the best Southeast Asian and Mexican restaurants in the Twin Cities as well as longtime favorites such as the Black Forest Inn. The Twin Cities have witnessed a renaissance in Mexican dining over the past decade, where authentic Mexican food is showcased. The Twin Cities now include Mexican eateries such as the cafeteria-style El Burrito Mercado in St. Paul and the wonderful flavors and immense portions served at El Mariachi on Eat Street in Minneapolis. These are only a few of the ethnic food possibilities in the Twin Cities.

Another trend in the past decade has been the emergence of much more diverse dining options in the suburban Twin Cities. Today there are numerous options in the suburbs, especially the St. Croix River Valley east of the Twin

Cities. Among the choices available is the avant-garde cuisine of the Bayport Cookery, the tropical flavors of the San Pedro Cafe, and the fine dining of La Belle Vie in Stillwater. The suburbs are also home to numerous ethnic restaurants. In fact, there are many more Indian restaurants in the suburbs than in Minneapolis and St. Paul. One of the best Indian restaurants is the India Palace in Roseville. There are also plenty of Chinese and Vietnamese restaurants in the suburbs, a few of which regularly top critics' polls, such as Singapore! Cuisine of China and Malaysia (Maplewood) and My Le Hoa (Chinese cuisine in Little Canada).

The chapter has been divided so that readers can easily find the type of food and location of individual restaurants. Cuisines are listed alphabetically. In addition, the listings are divided into Minneapolis, St. Paul, North, South, East, and West. Also listed for most restaurants are business hours, reservation policies, and credit card policies. If the listing does not say otherwise, you can assume that the restaurant accepts all major credit cards. These policies frequently change, so call the restaurant if you have any questions.

Price Code

Twin Cities restaurants feature a wide range of meal prices. We have developed a price code to guide readers in selecting restaurants. Whether diners are looking for an elegant traditional American dinner or an inexpensive ethnic lunch, there is a restaurant in the Twin Cities for everyone and every occasion. We cannot make any assumptions about the size of your group, so the price code is based on one adult entrée, without beverage, gratuity, and tax

$	under $10
$$	$11–$20
$$$	$21–$30
$$$$	$31–$40

Afghani

St. Paul

Khyber Pass Café $–$$
1571 Grand Avenue, St. Paul
(651) 690–0505

Khyber Pass Café has served delicious Afghani cuisine for more than 16 years. When entering the restaurant, the diner is immediately struck by its personality, charm, and aesthetic sense. The Khyber Pass Café stands in stark contrast to the generic and sterile decor dominant in

many restaurants today. The restaurant has a comfortable, clean, and cobbled-together feel, which integrates potted plants and Afghani crafts with numerous tasteful paintings.

The menu is composed of several well-executed entrees. The possibilities include chicken, lamb, beef, and vegetarian dishes. The korma-e-murgh, boneless chicken in curry sauce with potatoes and peas, is one savory option. Another interesting choice is kofta chalau, which is made of meat balls, onions, and spices. There are also several vegetarian entrees. The restaurant is open Tuesday through Saturday for dinner only.

South

Da Afghan Restaurant $$
929 West 80th Street, Bloomington
(952) 888–5829
www.daafghan.com

Da Afghan serves Southwest Asian and Middle Eastern specialties, including spring lamb chops, kabeli palow with chicken or lamb, mantou, and many kinds of kabob. The beautiful restaurant is decorated with Afghani artifacts and Afghani rugs on the tabletops. Beer and wine are served. Da Afghan is open for dinner Tuesday through Saturday and lunch on Thursday and Friday.

American

Minneapolis

Al's Breakfast $
413 14th Avenue SE, Minneapolis
(612) 331–9991

This tiny hole-in-the-wall near the U of M has been serving customers since the 1940s. College students and folks from the neighborhood have been known to line up around the block waiting for the place to open or to get a seat. Eggs, hash browns, and pancakes are served, as well as exotic omelettes, many of which are named after Al's patrons or employees. Al's is open for breakfast and lunch (serving dishes off the breakfast menu) daily. Al's is a Twin Cities institution, and if you don't mind the wait or the grease, get your day started the wrong way at Al's. Al's accepts no credit cards.

Annie's Parlour $
313 14th Avenue SE, Minneapolis
(612) 379–0744

Located just a couple of blocks from the University of Minnesota and the Bell Museum, Annie's Parlour is a great place to stop and get a bite to eat. This Dinkytown malt shop is as much a part of the University of Minnesota as Goldy Gopher himself, serving juicy burgers, chicken sandwiches, french fries, creamy malts, hot fudge sundaes, and banana splits. Since the restaurant is so appealing to college kids, this is the spot where many Twin Cities young ones are introduced to the U—they come to campus for a play or concert and Mom and Dad feed them here.

Aster Café $
125 Southeast Main Street, Minneapolis
(612) 379–3138

Located across the Mississippi River from downtown Minneapolis, this little cafe is the perfect place to stop by for lunch or grab a cup of coffee or a beer in the evening. The menu includes a variety of premade sandwiches and homemade soups, cookies, focaccia bread pizzas, and dessert bars. The dining area inside is large and opens up into the art gallery next door, and there's also a beautiful fenced-in outside patio that's nice for summer lounging. They infrequently book acoustic music during the summer, but most of the entertainment is provided by people wandering in to play the piano set up in the corner of the shop. The cafe also keeps about a dozen board and card games on hand for patrons who want to hang out past lunch—they also have a bowl full of dog biscuits under the counter for hounds accompanying patrons.

Birchwood Café $
3311 East 25th Street, Minneapolis
(612) 722–4474
www.birchwoodcafe.com

Birchwood, formerly a dairy and grocery store, has an old-fashioned stay-a-spell sense of welcome that makes it Seward's informal community center. The fifties-era dining room has both indoor seating and an outdoor patio in summer and serves sandwiches on fresh country bread, rustic pizzas, daily changing entrees such as enchiladas and curries, soups, and half a dozen salads. Known for its fresh organic ingredients and extensive vegetarian and vegan dishes, the Birchwood menu also includes nonvegetarian items. Service is semi-cafeteria style; you get your salads, desserts, and beverages (no alcohol) at the counter, and hot or custom-made items are brought to your birchwood-topped table.

The Brothers Deli $
50 South Sixth Street, Minneapolis
(612) 341–8007

The Brothers Deli offers authentic New York–style deli fare in downtown Minneapolis. This small deli, located on a busy second-floor skyway route in downtown, serves mouthwatering delicacies composed of only the best breads, meats, toppings, and condiments. The Broadway Danny Rose is a combination of corned beef and pastrami on fresh rye bread. Another top-notch sandwich is the Brother Sam, which melds the tastes of beef brisket and cheddar cheese on rye. The menu also features grilled sandwiches such as the tuna melt and Reuben, as well as matzo ball, chicken noodle, and tomato basil soups. Meals include potato salad, fresh pickles, and the best condiments available at a local deli. Brothers Deli accepts American Express.

Bryant-Lake Bowl $–$$
810 West Lake Street, Minneapolis
(612) 825–3737
www.bryantlakebowl.com

A bowling alley? Well, yes, but the Bryant-Lake Bowl in Uptown belies every stereotype of bowling alley eats, atmosphere, and culture that might come to mind. The atmosphere inside the restaurant is vintage 1940s, with beautiful woodwork and closely placed tables for intimate eating (with patrons at your neighboring table, as well as your tablemates). Famous for its cheap-but-delicious breakfasts, including corned beef hash, several BLB Scrambles (eggs scrambled with a choice of ingredients), and the ridiculously yummy Amy's Breakfast Burrito, the BLB serves lunch and dinner as well. Diners favor such specialties as the turkey, avocado, and bacon sandwich; grilled ahi tuna; and basmati rice and vegetables (with tofu or chicken optional). The BLB has a full bar, with many microbrews on tap. In addition to the 1950's-era bowling lanes, where you get to relearn the lost art of scoring your game by hand, the BLB is attached to a cabaret theater, where you can also order from the full menu. (See The Arts chapter for more information on the Bryant-Lake Bowl Theatre.)

Café Brenda $$$
300 1st Avenue North, Minneapolis
(612) 342–9230
www.cafebrenda.com

Café Brenda is a chic little bistro where the emphasis is on natural foods—ingredients obtained, as often as possible, from local farmers and prepared in ways that emphasize the current season. This spot is many vegetarians' favorite restaurant, thanks to Brenda Langston's takes on such fares as miso-herb pâté or her mock duck tacos. The cafe also serves omnivorous fare including fresh fish, such as Icelandic charr

Insiders Tip
Monday night from 6:30 P.M. to 12:30 A.M. is "Cheap Date Night" at the Bryant-Lake Bowl. For a paltry 25 bucks, you and your sweetie get two special entrees, a bottle of red or white wine, and a round of bowling.

and Wisconsin rainbow trout; shrimp quesadillas; and free-range chicken dishes. Vegetarians and vegans will find something to like in the menu of macrobiotic and whole-grain dishes created by chef-owner Langston, who is among an elite group setting new standards for vegetarian cuisine. Her touch manifests itself especially in the Asian hummus and tart pomegranate dips with pita. The macrobiotic sozai of brown rice comes with ginger and maple-seasoned red beans, sautéed tofu, and pickled cabbage; and the creamy mushroom stroganoff is served with crunchy broccoli.

Chino Latino $$–$$$
2916 Hennepin Avenue South, Minneapolis
(612) 824-7878

A popular spot for the hip dinner crowd, the foods of Thailand, Mexico, Jamaica, Polynesia, and Korea are represented on Chino Latino's true melting pot of a menu. Chino Latino's menu changes daily, and the foods here run the gamut of these countries' spiciest cuisines, including five-spice duck, taco plates, and peppery steamed mussels. They also serve a variety of sakes and tequilas to accompany your meal—and just about the biggest banana split in the state to finish it off. The global menu is perfectly matched with the wild, complicated decor, with its cushioned orange-vinyl wall, a satay bar, giant round booths, semi-unisex bathrooms (shared sinks), and an open kitchen.

The 510 Restaurant $$–$$$
510 Groveland Avenue, Minneapolis
(612) 874–6440
www.510restaurant.com

The 510 Restaurant offers traditional American and French fine dining at reasonable prices. Dinner selections include the sweet citrus-glazed salmon with a lemon-cilantro butter sauce and grilled filet mignon with green peppercorn–cognac cream sauce. The wines are also excellent at the 510, with American, South American, and European reds and whites to suit all taste buds and wallet sizes.

French Meadow Bakery & Café $
2610 Lyndale Avenue South, Minneapolis
(612) 870–7855
www.frenchmeadow.com

There's no disputing the quality of the food at this trendy eatery in the Wedge neighborhood, which sells organic sourdough breads, coffees, elaborate cakes, and several kinds of quiches. French Meadow uses no fat, no preservatives, and no yeast in producing chewy and flavorful organic loaves in flavors ranging from seven-grain to oatmeal raisin to Anaheim pepper. Step to the counter to order up a French Meadow sandwich and you can request any of those breads with a tasty topping of hummus, roasted eggplant, rosemary chicken salad, whitefish, or smoked turkey. With a comfortable country decor that includes simple tables and chairs, dried grapevines winding up the walls, and enough antiques to keep you intrigued but not overwhelmed, French Meadow is the perfect place to get a cup of coffee and a sandwich for lunch.

Goodfellow's $$$$
40 South Seventh Street, Minneapolis
(612) 332–4800
www.goodfellowsrestaurant.com

Set in an incredible sage-and-silver Art Deco decor, this restaurant has one of the most extensive wine lists in the Cities. Polite servers deliver treats such as grilled pork tenderloin with pork mu shu and foie gras, pheasant breast with acorn squash chili, and Maine lobster and Nantucket

Bay scallop enchiladas with house-smoked bacon. Kids are treated to fruit and cheese plates, made with cheeses kids actually like.

Hamlin's Coffee Shop $
512 Nicollet Avenue, Minneapolis
(612) 333–3876

Hamlin's serves golden, skin-on fries, hash browns made of real potatoes, giant onion rings, and pancakes, burgers, turkey melts, and grilled cheeses. They also make homemade pies, which usually disappear with the morning crowd and won't be made again until the next day. One step into this little coffee shop in Xcel Energy's Renaissance Square Building on Nicollet Mall and you can pretend you're in the middle of small-town America and not in the bustling metropolis of Minneapolis.

Hell's Kitchen $–$$$
89 South 10th Street, Minneapolis
(612) 332–4700

Hell's Kitchen took over the space formerly occupied by downtown Minneapolis's Du Jour Casual Café, and this new breakfast, brunch (on weekends), and lunch spot holds up quite well against the delicious menu of its predecessor. Hell's Kitchen features wonderfully inventive dishes such as eggs Benedict with bison flank steak and tangerine-jalapeño hollandaise sauce, wild-rice porridge, and walleye hash. Despite higher prices than most other breakfast places in the Twin Cities, Hell's Kitchen serves food that is a cut above the rest.

Jax Café $$$$
1928 University Avenue NE, Minneapolis
(612) 789–7297

Jax has been a strange combination of kitsch and elegance since it opened its doors in 1933 (right after Prohibition ended), with a long wooden bar accented by a stained-glass window depicting the seven dwarfs, and a trout stream in back. The menu includes shrimp cocktail, crab cakes, gigantic aged steaks, and salmon. In winter you'll want to be near the fireplace in the dark Roundtable Room. During spring and summer request a place on the outside patio, where you can catch your own rainbow trout in the stream (and have the cook pan-fry it for you) or drink a cocktail and watch elegantly dressed patrons attempting to catch the wily fish themselves.

Joe's Garage $-$$
1610 Harmon Place, Minneapolis
(612) 904-1163
www.joes-garage.com

Loring Park is one of the most urbane areas in the Twin Cities. So it comes as no surprise that a restaurant like Joe's Garage exists at its location. Joe's integrates the culinary flavors of the world with traditional American fare. Burgers are among the menu items available. An offering typical of the menu is the sun-dried tomato falafel burger, a Middle Eastern take on a traditional burger, made of falafel topped with feta, cucumber, tomato, and spinach on a pita. Other offerings include the spicy Asian pork burger, and the classic beef burger. Pasta and risotto are also prominently featured on the menu.

The Malt Shop $
809 West 50th Street, Minneapolis
(612) 824-1352
Snelling Avenue at Interstate 94, St. Paul
(651) 645-4643

The Malt Shop serves gourmet burgers and sandwiches as well as shakes and malts. Besides the standard cheeseburgers and reubens, there are items like the Malibu chicken, a sautéed chicken breast with Swiss cheese, bacon, and avocado. Most important are the malts and shakes, available in almost 40 flavors. They range from strawberry and chocolate to black cherry and cookies 'n' cream.

Manny's Steakhouse $$$$
1300 Nicollet Mall (Hyatt Regency Hotel), Minneapolis
(612) 339-9900

With the bad rap cholesterol gets these days, it's hard not to feel a little bit naughty eating here. This bustling, Manhattan-style steakhouse serves obscenely huge and gloriously tender steaks, lobster, salmon,

and chops—and that's about it besides the great wine list and a couple of desserts. Be prepared to either share dinner with a companion or get a doggy bag to go, because there's almost no way for one person to eat a whole dinner entree here.

Market Bar-B-Que $$
1414 Nicollet Avenue, Minneapolis
(612) 872-1111
www.marketbbq.com

Established in 1946 (although not always at this location), Market Bar-B-Que's been a Twin Cities family tradition for years. Their menu includes fabulous, lean spareribs and beef tips, barbecue meat sandwiches, and an amazing "dessert trough" including Key lime pie and chocolate mud sundaes. They also have an extensive wine list, printed on the side of giant empty wine bottles set on the tables. The decor is simple and comfortable, with large carved wooden booths and tables and black-and-white photographs of celebrities that have dined at Market, including Bobby McFerrin and Willie Mays, and each table is equipped with a small jukebox that carries popular music selections from the '50s to the present.

Matt's Bar $
3500 Cedar Avenue South, Minneapolis
(612) 722-7072

Matt's Bar is famous for one dish—the Jucy Lucy. And, yes, that is the correct spelling of the south Minneapolis supercheeseburger. Matt's makes the best Jucy Lucy, although a couple of south Minneapolis bars disagree on where it was first created in the Twin Cities. The burger is composed of two beef patties surrounding a pool of American cheese. Jucy Lucy novices beware; the burger, when removed from the grill, is filled with steaming hot cheese. Diners are rewarded for their patience when the burger cools by the sumptuous taste of this south Minneapolis specialty. The menu also includes additional burger selections and sandwiches.

Modern Café $-$$
337 13th Avenue NE, Minneapolis
(612) 378-9882

The Modern is a magnet for university students and arty types who miss their mom's home cooking but don't want to eat at an actual diner. The restaurant serves pot roast with carrots, pork sandwiches on apple bread, omelettes, and giant malts and milk shakes. To mix it up a bit, they also make walleye egg rolls, penne with goat cheese and crimini mushrooms, tomato risotto with capers and lemon zest, and heavenly chocolate crème brûlée.

Murray's $$–$$$$
26 South Sixth Street, Minneapolis
(612) 339–0909
www.murraysrestaurant.com

The double New York sirloin is a tradition for Twin Cities upscale dining. For three generations Murray's has satisfied its legion of dedicated customers with the Silver Butter Knife Steak, which is available for two or three diners. Other menu items are offered, but the many regulars come in droves for the steaks and the charming and elegant dining room. Reservations are a necessity. Even then, diners must compete with the regulars for a good table.

Rosen's Bar & Grill $–$$
430 First Avenue North, Minneapolis
(612) 338–1926

Rosen's is the popular restaurant and bar of longtime WCCO television sportscaster Mark Rosen. The location in downtown Minneapolis's Warehouse District is an especially busy spot on weekends, not only for the libations but also for the food. To accompany the suds there are appetizers such as fries, chicken fingers, and Rosen's Jumbo Buffalo Wings. For lighter appetites salads and stir-fries are included, and for hardier diners there is a certified Angus burger as well as entrees such as steaks, pork chops, and a Minnesota favorite, pan-fried walleye. Plus, several pasta choices are available. Rosen's is open daily for lunch and dinner.

St. Martin's Table $
2001 Riverside Avenue, Minneapolis
(612) 339–3920

This small vegetarian restaurant run by the community of St. Martin will convert even the most agnostic palates with its menu (which changes daily) of fresh-baked breads, ingenious sandwiches, and savory soups. The restaurant uses organic produce, non–bovine growth hormone milk, and purified water in its dishes and is committed to serving simple, nutritious food that sustains our natural resources and supports growers. St. Martin's wait-staff is all volunteer, and they donate their tips to local, national, and international charities. St. Martin's Table is open for lunch only Monday through Saturday. The restaurant does not serve alcohol. You dine well, and all for a higher purpose.

Sapor Café and Bar $$–$$$
428 Washington Avenue North, Minneapolis
(612) 375–1971
www.saporcafe.com

Diners in search of a sophisticated and difficult to classify fusion cuisine will love the Sapor Café. Entrees meld together high-quality, seemingly disparate ingredients to create piquant culinary delights. Dinners include a miso-baked salmon and a pork chop in jerk spices. A relatively new Twin Cities restaurant, the Sapor is quickly becoming a Twin Cities favorite for fine dining. The restaurant features a comfortable bar, which is frequented by a hip crowd.

Tavern on Grand $–$$
656 Grand Avenue, St. Paul
(651) 228–9030

Tavern on Grand is a Minnesota classic, serving up plates of walleye fillets to the masses. Sure, you can also come here for Black Angus top sirloin, baked chicken, and slow-roasted ribs, but you're unlikely to order walleye in Memphis, so get with the program and order up a plate of the exalted fish with all the trimmings. The restaurant has a north-woodsy feel like a lakefront lodge, complete with built-in fish tank, and the walleye is simply spectacular. Options abound, including a choice of a grilled or deep-fried (with "secret batter") one- or two-fillet dinner, the walleye basket, the walleye sandwich, and the Lakeshore Special, which includes a fillet and an eight-ounce steak. You can also add a flaky fillet to any meal as a side order, if spaghetti, meatballs, and walleye is your thing. The waitstaff won't bat an eye.

Ted Cook's 19th Hole Bar-B-Que $-$$
2814 East 38th Street, Minneapolis
(612) 721-2023

Ted Cook's is a small take-out-only restaurant in south Minneapolis that serves some of the best barbecue in the Twin Cities. The restaurant is decorated minimally and functionally, and Ted Cook's elevates barbecue to an art. All aspects of the meats, sides, and desserts are carefully executed, and the end result is outstanding. The meats include pork ribs, beef ribs, and barbecue chicken and beef. The tender meat is accompanied by the rich and tasty barbecue sauce, which can be ordered mild or spicy. With each dinner, jo jo potatoes, coleslaw, and bread are served. In addition, items from Mom's kitchen—greens with corn muffins, black-eyed peas, and red beans and rice—are available as well as peach cobbler and sweet potato pie for dessert. Prices are very reasonable at Ted Cook's and even cheaper with lunch sandwich combinations. Ted Cook's is slightly off the beaten path but is well worth the trip south on Hiawatha Avenue (Minnesota Highway 55). In winter a picnic just down the avenue at Minnehaha Park sounds great. Unfortunately, the conditions outdoors won't allow it, but there is always Ted Cook's scrumptious take-out for an indoor picnic.

The Times Bar & Café $$-$$$
201 East Hennepin Avenue, Minneapolis
(612) 617-8098
www.timesbarandcafe.com

The Times's big draw is its fondue—pots of cheese, oil, or chocolate are brought bubbling with a host of goodies for dipping. Beyond that, the menu features burgers, sandwiches, pizza, and pasta. On weekdays the menu offers Blue Plate Special lunch items that are exceptional deals, ranging from zingy tortilla wraps stuffed with chicken and cilantro to minipizzas and open-face roast turkey sandwiches. Most

evenings the Times hosts live jazz or Latin bands (see the Web site for the restaurant's entertainment calendar).

Tuggs Tavern $
219 Southeast Main Street, Minneapolis
(612) 379-4404

The main thing this upscale burger joint and bar has going for it is the wonderful view from the dining porch. The food is good—they have several specialty stuffed burgers as well as a good fish-and-chips basket, and they make excellent fresh-squeezed lemonade—but they are literally the only restaurant on the St. Anthony's Wharf strip that has an unobstructed view of the Mississippi River and the downtown Minneapolis skyline. On hot summer nights, this is a beautiful spot to take a date to enjoy the cool breezes coming off the river and watch the full moon and the lights of downtown reflected on the water. The bar makes great mixed drinks and uses their wonderful fresh-squeezed lemonade in their house specialties.

Vera's Café $
2901 Lyndale Avenue South, Minneapolis
(612) 822-3871
www.verascafe.com

Open until 1:00 A.M. seven nights a week, Vera's is the premier late-night dining establishment in Uptown, serving homemade soups, huge sandwiches, six kinds of scrambled eggs, and European coffees. During the summer months, the gated patio is a beautiful place to take in lunch or to hang out after a movie. Inside, Vera's is outfitted with antique-looking tables, ice cream parlor chairs, and velvet and mohair couches.

Whitney Grille $$$
150 Portland Avenue, Minneapolis
(612) 372-6405

Built out of the shell of a former flour mill, the elegant Whitney Grille looks out over the Mississippi River from the middle of what was once the biggest milling district in the country. The often-changing menu is not extensive but is innovative, including appetizers like house-smoked tiger prawn cocktail with spicy Caribbean sauce, stuffed portobello mushrooms, and entrees that include walleye, herb-crusted salmon, rack of lamb, and phyllo-wrapped chicken accompanied by wild rice and cranberries. On Sunday the draw is a spectacular brunch, from mimosas and smoked salmon to omelettes and ribs.

St. Paul

Andy's Garage $
1825 University Avenue West, St. Paul
(651) 917–2332
www.andysgaragecafe.com

Andy's Garage specializes in '50s-style American diner food. Several burgers, sandwiches, soups, and salads are on the menu, as well as daily specials and roasted turkey or beef sandwiches. The fries are especially good. The restaurant is particularly popular for its excellent desserts, root beer floats, malts, and shakes. The thick, rich, silky malts are reminiscent of the glory days of the '50s that the restaurant's decor celebrates. The restaurant was originally a garage but was converted to the charming diner it is today. Andy's is located in the heart of University Avenue's

summertime classic car cruising strip, where the retro '50s diner is greatly appreciated. Children love Andy's, not only for its treats but also because of the six "Little Mechanics" items offered. They include peanut butter and jelly sandwiches, corn dogs, and hamburgers. The restaurant also goes out of its way to entertain children. One example is the Etch-A-Sketches provided to occupy kids. Andy's offers something for all members of the family in a casual environment.

Café Minnesota $
345 West Kellogg Boulevard West (Minnesota History Center), St. Paul
(651) 297–4097

In most cases museums and attractions are not known for their food. However, Café Minnesota is a pleasant exception to the rule. Where most museums serve bland variations of American favorites, this cafe offers much more. So if you are tired of hamburgers, chicken nuggets, and fries at the museum, this is the place to visit. The cafe is cafeteria style and serves breakfast and dinner daily. Each week the restaurant offers a menu that

Andy's Garage in St. Paul's Midway neighborhood offers fifties-diner–style food in a converted service station. PHOTO: SAINT PAUL CONVENTION AND VISITORS BUREAU

includes an item from each of the following: the soup tureen, the Minnesota grill, the chef's carvery, the main course, and the feature sauté. Examples of dishes available on a given day include spicy sausage and shrimp soup, rosemary roasted pork loin, and linguini and white clam sauce. The Café Minnesota is a great casual place for a bite to eat when enjoying the numerous attractions at the Minnesota History Center.

Cecil's Restaurant, Delicatessen & Bakery
$
651 South Cleveland Avenue, St. Paul
(651) 698-0334
www.cecilsdeli.com

Cecil's is St. Paul's best deli. The front of the building is a huge deli with fresh meats, cheeses, breads, and baked goods; in the back is a modest restaurant. But don't be confused by the decor, which looks much as it did decades ago. The food is also as outstanding as it always has been and has not yielded to the prepared and health food trends that now dominate the restaurant business. The menu contains almost every hot and cold sandwich imaginable. There are also several kosher selections. Cecil's house specialty sandwiches include the Nosher, which comprises roast beef, lettuce, and spicy dressing on a fresh kaiser roll, and five different Reubens, including a vegetarian version.

Day by Day Café **$**
477 West Seventh Street, St. Paul
(651) 227-0654
www.daybyday.com

Day by Day is a lovely spot just southwest of downtown St. Paul. The restaurant meanders through several rooms of multiple storefronts on busy West Seventh Street, and the plants, bookshelves, and tables at odd angles will make visitors feel right at home. Breakfast highlights include homemade buckwheat cakes, the Earth Breakfast (two eggs scrambled with hash browns and onions and covered with melted cheese), and the breakfast burrito. For lunch and dinner the restaurant features a guacamole burger, triple-decker

Insiders' Tip

Show up at the Day by Day Café between 6:00 and 7:00 A.M., and you can stuff yourself with two eggs, hash browns or American fries, bacon or sausage, and toast, or two pancakes, two eggs, and bacon or sausage at a big discount.

clubhouse sandwich, and stir-fried sesame chicken or tofu. Each menu has a hand-drawn cover, courtesy of children who have eaten at the café (ask at the register to have your munchkin create a masterpiece for future guests).

Fabulous Fern's Bar & Grill **$$**
400 Selby Avenue, St. Paul
(651) 225-9414
www.fabulousferns.com

Located in St. Paul's historic Cathedral Hill neighborhood of brownstone town homes, Fabulous Fern's is a casual spot with plenty of comfort food and an active bar. Restaurant specialties include wild rice and chicken salad with cranberry-vinaigrette dressing, meat loaf sandwich, blackened ribeye steak with Louisiana cream sauce, and pecan-crusted walleye. Popular with sports fans, who flock to Fabulous Fern's to watch the bar's four plasma TVs and ten regular TVs, the place really gets hopping during Vikings games.

Forepaugh's **$$-$$$**
276 South Exchange Street, St. Paul
(651) 224-5606

Named for Joe Forepaugh, the dry-goods merchant who built the house in 1870, this Victorian beauty is neighbor to the equally impressive home of Alexander Ramsey, Minnesota's first territorial governor. Soft light in nine cozy dining rooms offers the warmth of Grandma's parlor, lace curtains and all. Forepaugh's main courses include duck, lamb, veal, steak, and the best beef Wellington in town. Forepaugh's offers a shuttle ride to and from the Ordway in downtown St. Paul, very helpful if your evening includes a concert or show, or if you plan to attend a Wild game at the Xcel Energy Center next to the Ordway. Ask about the shuttle when you make your reservations, which are recommended. The restaurant is open for lunch and dinner Monday through Saturday and for brunch and dinner on Sunday.

Hickory Hut $
647 University Avenue West, St. Paul
(651) 224–9464

The Hickory Hut serves up great barbecue in a fast-food and take-out environment. Wings, barbecue sandwiches, and ribs are the most popular items. In addition, catfish, shrimp, and at least a dozen side dishes are available. All items come in large portions and are inexpensive. The barbecue sauce is superb and comes in both mild and spicy. If you are on the go and looking

for barbecue or take-out, the Hickory Hut will certainly satiate your craving.

Keys Restaurant $–$$
767 Raymond Avenue, St. Paul
(651) 646–5756
Six additional Twin Cities locations

Since 1973 Keys has been a favorite place for breakfast and traditional diner fare in the Twin Cities. Barbara Hunn established the first Keys on Raymond Avenue in St. Paul. Keys specializes in breakfast and lunch (Keys is not open for dinner), which it serves in immense, heaping portions. The menu includes a vast array of omelettes, pancakes, eggs, and combination breakfasts. The lunch menu is huge, and it features such American favorites as burgers, salads, and soups. Fresh fruit pies and cakes are featured for dessert. Hours vary significantly at Keys locations.

Mickey's Diner $
36 West Seventh Street, St. Paul
(651) 222–5633

Mickey's, one of only two diners in the country on the National Register of His-

St. Paul's historic Mickey's Diner is wildly popular among the downtown lunch crowd and curious tourists. PHOTO: TODD R. BERGER

toric Places, serves up real ice cream malts, eggs any way you like 'em, burgers and fries, Mulligan stew, and pancakes 24 hours a day. Set in a '30s-era dining car with a chrome and Formica interior, the diner has been family owned and operated since 1939. Almost inevitably, movies shot in Minnesota, including *Jingle All the Way, The Mighty Ducks,* and the two *Mighty Ducks* sequels, feature downtown St. Paul's most camera-friendly diner.

Mildred Pierce Café $–$$
786 Randolph Avenue, St. Paul
(651) 222–7430

Mildred Pierce's cuisine is strikingly similar to the Joan Crawford film it is named after. The film is a combination domestic drama and film noir. The restaurant also balances traditional American cuisine with a touch of the edginess found in the gourmet touches given to the '40s-style food items. Like old-fashioned American diners, Mildred Pierce emphasizes breakfast. The breakfast options include omelettes, waffles, and eggs Benedict. However, Mildred Pierce has updated these traditional items. An example is an omelette with mushrooms, spinach, and cream cheese. The omelettes are huge and come accompanied by four pieces of toast and plenty of potato wedges. In contrast to the hearty omelettes, items such as a delicious delicate blueberry waffle with a sweet berry sauce are also offered. Lunch and dinner options include daily specials as well as sandwiches, soups, and risotto. Mildred Pierce is open for breakfast, lunch, and dinner on weekdays. On Saturday and Sunday the restaurant serves only brunch.

Muffuletta Café $$
2260 Como Avenue, St. Paul
(651) 644–9116

Located in the beautiful St. Anthony Park neighborhood near the University of Minnesota's St. Paul campus, Muffuletta serves an eclectic menu in a colorful, casual-yet-classy atmosphere. Specialties include tortellini with cream, peas, mushrooms, and prosciutto; pork tenderloin crusted with rosemary and pancetta; and the grilled chicken sandwich with grilled onions, avocado, and chipotle mayo. Muffuletta serves beer and wine, including a fabulous wine list courtesy of the sommelier on staff. The restaurant is open for lunch and dinner Monday through Friday, dinner only on Saturday, and brunch only on Sunday.

128 Café $$–$$$
128 Cleveland Avenue North, St. Paul
(651) 645–4128
www.128cafe.net

The 128 Café serves posh American cuisine from the basement of an apartment building in St. Paul. The restaurant features a seasonal menu developed by Brock and Natalie Obee, who serve as both chefs and owners. The 60-seat restaurant serves dishes such as penne, pork tenderloin, ribs, and much more. The penne is a combination of smoked chicken, sweet corn, bacon, leeks, cilantro, sun-dried tomatoes, and chipotle goat cheese. The baby back ribs are covered with barbecue sauce and accompanied by sautéed vegetables and garlic mashed potatoes. The restaurant also offers prix fixe dinners (a reasonably priced three-course meal). The 128 is open for dinner. In addition, the restaurant serves an excellent Sunday brunch (10:00 A.M. to 2:00 P.M.). Reservations are recommended.

Porky's $
1890 University Avenue West, St. Paul
(651) 644–1790

In the early 21st century, there are few drive-in restaurants. Porky's is one of them. And the pickup window is open regardless of Twin Cities weather. That's right, drive-in food is available 12 months a year at Porky's. The restaurant is a modified drive-in where you have the option of ordering at the drive-through pickup window or at a counter inside the restaurant. Diners may enjoy their food in their car under the large awning or, when weather permits, on the half dozen picnic tables provided by the restaurant. Porky's menu is filled with drive-in favorites such as hamburgers, cheeseburgers, fried chicken, chicken wings, pork sandwiches, catfish, shakes, fries, and much more. Porky's opened in 1953, then closed briefly before reopening about a decade ago. Today Porky's serves as a meeting place for classic cars when the MSRA (Minnesota Streetrod Association) holds local events in the summertime. Porky's offers classic American drive-in food in a '50s environment.

St. Clair Broiler $–$$
1580 St. Clair Avenue West, St. Paul
(651) 698–7055

The St. Clair Broiler cooks up some of the best traditional American diner food in the Twin Cities. The highlights here are plentiful. First, the daily specials include roast turkey, Greek chicken, meat loaf sandwiches, and one of the best Friday all-you-can-eat fish fries in this area. The milk shakes and malts are as delicious as they were in the less health conscious '50s and enormous enough to easily feed two. Kids' menus and seniors' specials are available. The Broiler is also a popular breakfast spot, with extra-large omelettes, golden French toast, and choice steak and eggs.

St. Paul Grill $$–$$$
350 Market Street, St. Paul
(651) 224–7455
www.stpaulhotel.com

If you enjoy traditional American dining in an elegant hotel, the St. Paul Grill is ideal. Located in the four-star St. Paul Hotel, the restaurant overlooks Rice Park. Moreover, the restaurant is within walking distance of several cultural attractions including the Ordway Theater, the Xcel Energy Center, and the Science Museum, as well as numerous downtown retail shops.

Insiders' Tip

The walleye is Minnesota's favorite fish and is readily available in restaurants throughout the Twin Cities.

Besides the superb location, the St. Paul Grill serves upscale food and spirits. The menu includes beef and poultry as well as pasta, salads, and soups. The restaurant features an excellent wine list, which, like the cuisine, has received countless local and national awards. Reservations are highly recommended. The St. Paul Grill is open for lunch and dinner Monday through Sunday.

W. A. Frost and Company $$$
374 Selby Avenue, St. Paul
(651) 224–5715
www.wafrost.com

W. A. Frost is located in the Cathedral Hill neighborhood of St. Paul in the elegant 19th-century Dacotah Building. The menu is brief but well executed and includes chicken breast, walleye, New York strip, and more. Since 1975 the beautiful old brownstone restaurant has been an integral part of the lovely neighborhood and has enticed diners to visit for food and spirits in one of the Twin Cities' most charming spots. During summer the restaurant serves meals on its expansive patio, one of the most beautiful and romantic locations for outdoor dining in the Twin Cities. W. A. Frost is open daily for lunch and dinner. Reservations are highly recommended.

South

Joe Senser's Sports Grill & Bar $–$$
4217 West 80th Street, Bloomington
(952) 835–1191
2350 Cleveland Avenue, Roseville
(651) 631–1781
3010 Eagandale Place, Eagan
(651) 687–9333

The three Joe Senser's Sports Grills are favorite places to watch sports and enjoy burgers, sandwiches, soups, or entrees. Unlike many sports bars, there are plenty of choices. Featured are several burgers and sandwiches, such as the Flying Buffalo Chicken sandwich and the turkey bacon parmesan sandwich. Also included are entrees such as barbecue ribs, pork chops, walleye, and pastas. Besides the food, of course, there are the beers and the big screen televisions.

East

The Bayport Cookery $$$$
328 Fifth Avenue North, Bayport
(651) 430–1066
www.bayportcookery.com

The Bayport Cookery is recognized locally and nationally for adventurous fine dining. The core of the restaurant's menu, which has monthly themes and varies weekly, is avant-garde cuisine. However, unlike any other fine restaurant of its kind, the foods of Minnesota are emphasized. The Cookery is a favorite among local foodies and tourists, who make the half-hour trek from downtown Minneapolis to the scenic St. Croix. The menu is based on availability of fresh items. For example, the month of January showcases five courses of truffles. Due to supply, the savory menu often changes on a daily basis. The prix fixe menu varies greatly from month to month. Reservations are required.

Chickadee Cottage Restaurant $–$$
9900 Valley Creek Road, Woodbury
(651) 578–8118

The Chickadee Cottage Restaurant offers an extensive menu of American and European-influenced favorites. The cottage theme pervades the restaurant, with each room having a particular cottage motif (e.g., rustic lodge or rural getaway). Chickadee's breakfast menu is enormous and includes many fresh-baked goods as well as pancakes, waffles, eggs, omelettes, and much more. The lunch and dinner menus also provide plenty to choose from, e.g., meat loaf sandwiches, grilled Caesar salad, scallops and shrimp, vegetable lasagna, and smoky apple pork chops. In addition, the restaurant is very family friendly. Children are provided crayons and a menu that includes pancakes and scrambled eggs for breakfast and grilled cheese or peanut butter and jelly sandwiches for dinner. Chickadee Cottage Restaurant is open Tuesday through Sunday for breakfast, lunch, and dinner.

The Lowell Inn $$$–$$$$
102 North Second Street, Stillwater
(651) 439–1100 or (888) 569–3554
www.lowellinn.com

The Lowell Inn is widely known for its Swiss fondue, served in the Stillwater Inn's Matterhorn Room. But at the Lowell, the Swiss cheese fondue is just the starter of a four-course meal (with optional wine accompaniment) featuring beef tenderloin, duck breast, or jumbo prawns with Minnesota wild rice pilaf. Desserts include grapes Devonshire and Swiss chocolate fondue. The whole shebang is delivered tableside for a set price. On Friday and Saturday nights, diners can also choose the set-price game platter, with such entrees as paprika rabbit, ribeye bison steak, or braised pheasant, followed by bread pudding with a praline pecan sauce. For those looking to choose individual dishes rather than a multicourse extravaganza, the Lowell's George Washington Room offers such entrees as duck breast, filet mignon, and lobster tail. (For more information on the Lowell Inn's guest rooms, see the Accommodations chapter.)

West

Park Tavern $
3401 Louisiana Avenue, St. Louis Park
(952) 929–6810

Bar and bowling alley food is generally not highly regarded for its taste, but rather frequently purchased out of necessity. The Park Tavern is an exception to the rule. The appetizers are tasty and edible, with or without suds for lubrication, and include nachos, quesadillas, and chicken strips. Also featured are top-notch burgers and sandwiches such as the French dip au jus and the prime melt sandwich, which features prime rib topped with sautéed onions and cheese. Salads are another option for less ravenous diners.

Zaroff's Delicatessen Restaurant $–$$
11300 Wayzata Boulevard, Minnetonka
(952) 543–8687

When patrons open Zaroff's menu they first notice the glossary of terms. Despite the restaurant's Minneapolis suburban location—Minnetonka—the menu proudly proclaims its Jewish deli roots. There are almost 20 Yiddish terms to aid patrons not yet experienced with Jewish-American culinary traditions. The extensive menu includes appetizers, numerous sandwich selections, entrees, burgers and franks, and eggs. Just a few highlights are the hot brisket of beef, the hot pastrami sandwich, and the Hebrew National frank on a bun. Besides these classics, there are several specialty items, such as sautéed chicken livers, Hungarian goulash, and borscht. Zaroff's offers a wide selection of dessert items, including chocolate cake, apple pie, and ice cream. The cakes and cheesecake are flown in from the Carnegie Deli in New York. The full-service deli also has a wine and beer list. In Minnesota, authentic New York-style delis are few and far between, and Zaroff's annually receives kudos for its fine foods.

Cajun/Southern

St. Paul

Dixies on Grand $–$$$
695 Grand Avenue, St. Paul
(651) 222-7345

There are only a few Cajun and Southern restaurants in the North Star State of Minnesota. Since Dixies opened in 1985, many other restaurants have incorporated Cajun items in their menu, but few have had the success of Dixies because they lack their dedication and specialization. Cajun and Southern cooking purists may balk at the menu since it includes such foods as calamari and Cuban black bean soup and fusion foods like the Cajun burger. However, the vast majority of items are from the Cajun and Southern food traditions. A few specialty dishes are jambalaya, blackened catfish, shrimp and crawfish étouffée, and Carolina crab cakes. The ribs are another specialty at Dixies and are available in baby back and country-style pork ribs. Barbecue chicken is another popular menu item. Although dinner can be expensive, lunch offers much cheaper menu selections. Dixies has an extensive wine list as well as a large selection of domestic and imported beers. On Sunday the restaurant hosts a brunch, which includes red beans and rice, corn bread, country ham, barbecue chicken, and much more. In addition, the entire menu is available for take-out. Reservations for dinner are recommended, especially on weekend evenings. A second Dixies is located near Lake Calhoun in south Minneapolis at 2730 West Lake Street; (612) 920-5000.

Cambodian

St. Paul

Cheng Heng $
448 University Avenue West, St. Paul
(651) 222-5577

Definitely a diamond in the rough, Cheng Heng is one of the most amazing deals (and best-kept secrets) in town. Located in one of the more dilapidated parts of St. Paul, Cheng Heng looks, to the casual observer, like just one more uninviting sign in a line of strip malls. However, this is the only place in town where you can get a

Insiders' Tip

If you are an ethnic food novice but would like to sample the cuisine of another culture, many Twin Cities ethnic restaurants feature lunch buffets. The buffets provide an excellent overview of a culture's food at reasonable prices and allow the diner to select dishes.

pile of beautifully steamed mussels in black bean sauce for under $10, and that's about the most expensive selection on the menu. The family-owned restaurant has won numerous critics' choice awards—just about annually—for everything from their egg roll salad to their shrimp-stuffed spring rolls. The couple that run the place take hospitality to new levels, positioning fans to cool down your table when it's hot out, and fussing over you as though you were their house guest and not just another restaurant customer. They offer suggestions and menus with pictures to make even the pickiest of eaters comfortable with ordering Cambodian food for the first time and are more than willing to share their cooking secrets with curious customers. This has long been a favorite place to take relatives for special occasions or wow out-of-town friends when they come to visit. Cheng Heng is open daily for breakfast, lunch, and dinner.

Caribbean

St. Paul

West Indies Soul Café $
625 University Avenue, Suite 102, St. Paul
(651) 665–0115

West Indies Soul began serving the Twin Cities at annual neighborhood festivals. The savory tastes of the Caribbean created a demand for catering and later a restaurant to serve jerk chicken, curry chicken and goat, fried plantains, and roti (Caribbean breads filled with meats). Though not a fast-food restaurant, the order-in and take-out counter-style dining facilitates quick service. Diners may select large or regular-size portions, and a sample platter is available for those interested in a culinary overview of the restaurant. Wraps and sandwiches, salads, and baskets are another option. They include a few non-Caribbean baskets such as rib tips and catfish strips. The restaurant serves homemade drinks of carrot punch, ginger beer, and lemonade but does not serve alcohol. West Indies Soul is open for lunch and dinner Tuesday through Saturday.

East

San Pedro Café $–$$
426 Second Street, Hudson, Wisconsin
(715) 386–4003

San Pedro Café offers Mediterranean and tropical cuisine and atmosphere in scenic Hudson, Wisconsin. Still considered a day trip to some Twin Citians, this community on the beautiful St. Croix River has become home to many people in the area. As a result, there has been a restaurant boom in Hudson in the last five years.

The menu overflows with flavor. There are sandwiches, wraps, pastas, salads, seafood, and Neapolitan pizzas. One fine example is an excellent Caribbean jerk chicken. Besides the delicious food, the decor is pleasant and relies heavily on tropical blues and reds and exposed brick. The restaurant is located in a wonderful restored building in downtown Hudson and is packed with customers at all times of the day. Ten years ago Twin Citians would have laughed if someone said Hudson and Stillwater would have some of the best restaurants in the area; today it is a well-established fact. The San Pedro Café is one of the best examples of the wealth of fine dining in the greater Twin Cities.

Chinese

Minneapolis

China Express $–$$
409 14th Avenue SE, Minneapolis
(612) 379–6378, (612) 379–6374

China Express's lunch express is an excellent fast-food alternative, where diners may select two items with white rice or pork fried rice for a very low price. In addition, there are lunch specials such as kung pao shrimp, pepper steak, and moo goo gai pan. Numerous Chinese dinner specialties include dragon and phoenix (jumbo shrimp and chicken), and General Tso's chicken. China Express is open daily for lunch and dinner, and offers delivery for orders over $15.

1st Wok $–$$
3236 West Lake Street,
Minneapolis
(612) 922–8883

1st Wok features an extensive menu of Hunan and Szechwan-style Chinese food. Fine renditions of sesame chicken, kung pao chicken, lo mein, and pepper steak are served, as well as numerous seafood items. The restaurant also features several specialties such as sesame shrimp, double wonder, and princess chicken and shrimp. Daily lunch specials are a steal and include an entree plus soup and fried rice. Vegetarian items are also featured and include bean curd selections (kung pao bean curd and spicy bean curd Szechwan-style). 1st Wok is open daily for lunch and dinner.

Hong Kong Noodles Restaurant $–$$
901 Washington Avenue SE, Minneapolis
(612) 379–9472

Several excellent Chinese restaurants are in the vicinity of the University of Minnesota—this is arguably one of the best. The restaurant is rather small and seats no more than 50 people in an often packed room. However, it is the food that garners the restaurant accolades from its regular patrons and critics alike. With almost 300 menu items, Hong Kong Noodles offers plenty to choose from, but noodles are the restaurant's specialty. The menu is divided into extensive soup, chicken, beef, fried rice, hot pot, seafood, pork, and vegetable choices. In addition, the restaurant offers chef specialties and daily specials based on the availability of fresh produce and seafood. Finally, there is the restaurant's wide selection of noodles, which include rice noodles, pan-fried noodles, and lo mein. A few standouts are the Singapore-style rice noodles, seafood lo mein, and beef brisket fun. Hong Kong Noodles is open late on a daily basis, which is relatively uncommon in the Twin Cities. Hence, the restaurant does a booming business until midnight on Sunday through Thursday. On Friday and Saturday evenings, the restaurant stays open until 2:00 A.M.

Peking Garden Chinese Restaurant $–$$
2324 University Avenue SE, Minneapolis
(612) 623–3989 or (612) 623–3992

The Peking Garden is one of the Twin Cities' favorite traditional Chinese restaurants. Located near the University of Minnesota, it draws large crowds of students, professors, and lovers of fine Chinese food. There are literally hundreds of choices on the extensive menu. Besides the typical beef, chicken, and pork entrees, there are numerous seafood, duck, and soup choices.

Rainbow Chinese Restaurant & Bar $–$$
2739 Nicollet Avenue, Minneapolis
(612) 870–7084
www.rainbowrestaurant.com

Rainbow Chinese is one of the Twin Cities' favorite Chinese restaurants. The menu features exciting examples of Chinese cuisine prepared with fresh ingredients. Rainbow's signature dishes include Szechuan wontons, honey-walnut shrimp and Singapore chow mai fun, and fried walleye pike with black bean sauce. There are many other options, including multiple vegetarian choices. Alcohol is available with meals and at the lovely bar, where diners can feel free to bask in the comely decor of the restaurant, which is superbly decorated in greens and yellows. Reservations are only accepted for groups of four or more. The restaurant serves lunch and dinner Monday through Friday but closes between 2:00 and 4:30 P.M. The restaurant is open all day on Saturday and Sunday.

Shuang Cheng Restaurant $–$$$
1320 Fourth Street SE, Minneapolis
(612) 378–0208

Food critics and diners consistently recognize Shuang Cheng as one of the Twin Cities' best seafood restaurants. Shuang Cheng is modestly decorated with small, slightly uncomfortable chairs and a few booths along the wall. However, the food stands in stark contrast to the decor. It is located in Dinkytown, just outside the University of Minnesota campus. On weekends it draws huge crowds, mainly for the delicious seafood prepared with a tantalizing Chinese flair. The menu includes shrimp, crab, scallops, oysters, clams, lobster, squid, and four walleye dishes. Beyond seafood, chicken, beef, pork, and vegetarian options are available. Various daily specials are posted on a whiteboard and erased when the item sells out. Here are just a few of the ever-changing daily specials: live lobster, stir-fried bok choy, seafood and asparagus, and Black Sea bass. Shuang Cheng serves inexpensive lunch combinations aimed at thrifty University of Minnesota students.

Village Wok Restaurant $–$$
610 Washington Avenue SE, Minneapolis
(612) 331–9041
www.villagewok.com

The Village Wok does some of the briskest business in the Twin Cities. Located on the edge of the University of Minnesota, it attracts a regular lunch, dinner, and late-night crowd of students, professors, and doctors. In addition, the restaurant draws throngs of Chinese diners with its traditional Chinese cuisine, especially the large seafood menu. They may have the largest menu in the Twin Cities, with sections dedicated to fried rice, chow mein, Cantonese specialties, Szechwan specialties, duck, hot pot, shrimp, scallops, squid, four types of noodle selections, plus the lengthy list of chef's selections and the late-night special menu. The menu features daily lunch combination specials, such as shrimp Szechwan, cheese wonton and fried rice or sweet and sour chicken, egg roll, and fried rice. All lunch combinations are served for less than $5.00. The Cantonese style dinners are another delicious bargain; they include beef with black bean sauce, roast duck, and shrimp with broccoli. Each of these enormous dinners is served with a choice of soup and a large bowl of rice and, at slightly more than $5.00, has fed countless financially strapped University of Minnesota students.

Besides the Village Wok's Chinese dinner specials, the seafood menu is one of the largest in the area. Diners may choose from several different preparations of trout, sole, salmon, and walleye. Each fish is prepared in a sauce such as black bean sauce, lemon sauce, or ginger sauce. A popular fish selection is the crispy whole walleye Hunan-style. Other seafood items include baked and fried lobster and oysters. The Village Wok is open for lunch and dinner daily. Unlike most area restaurants, it has late-night hours and does not close until 2:00 A.M. daily.

St. Paul

Cleveland Wok Chinese Restaurant $
767 Cleveland Avenue South, St. Paul
(651) 699–3141

The Cleveland Wok offers an extensive menu of Chinese specialties. The restaurant follows the trend of many new Chinese restaurants in the Twin Cities—they provide an expanded menu of seafood and Chinese noodle items. Among the noodle selections are choices between pan-fried noodles (either egg noodles or rice noodles), lo mein, or chow fun. An excellent noodle item is the Singapore curry rice noodles, which marries roasted pork, shrimp, fried egg, carrots, green peppers, and lemongrass in a spicy complex combination that creates a savory sauce. There are also several chef's combo specials, where an entree such as curry chicken, kung pao chicken, or sesame chicken comes accompanied by fried rice and an egg roll or egg foo young. In addition, there are numerous chicken, pork, and beef items available. Cleveland Wok serves beer and wine. The restaurant is open Monday through Saturday for lunch and dinner.

My Le Hoa $–$$
2900 Rice Street (Market Place Shopping Center), Little Canada
(651) 484–5353

Located in a suburban shopping center in St. Paul, My Le Hoa is routinely named one of the Twin Cities' favorite Chinese restaurants. Besides chow mein, fried rice, and egg foo young, the restaurant serves Cantonese noodle dishes, chicken, pork, beef, and numerous seafood items. Prawns, scallops, squid, and fish are all prepared in sauces ranging from curry and satay sauce to black bean and oyster sauce. The fish selection is impressive and includes salmon, sole, walleye, and cod prepared with various sauces. In addition, the restaurant offers four duck dishes. Duck is available half or whole. My Le Hoa is open for lunch and dinner Tuesday through Sunday.

North

Willow Gate $
1885 West Perimeter Drive, Roseville
(651) 628–0990

Willow Gate's menu is extensive and features several hundred Chinese and Vietnamese items. At lunch there are numerous combination meals for under $5.00, which include several seafood items. The curry shrimp and chicken fried rice are two favorites. Each is accompanied by a choice of two chicken wings or cheese wontons. Dinner offers larger combination plates as well as traditional Chinese fare, such as lo mein, egg foo young, fried rice, and seafood. Willow Gate serves beer and wine, and lunch and dinner are served daily.

South

Hunan Restaurant $
8066 Morgan Circle, Bloomington
(952) 881–2280

Hunan Restaurant is one of the many excellent Twin Cities Chinese restaurants located in a suburban strip mall. The menu is extensive and includes chicken, beef, pork, and seafood items. Hunan specialties include kung pao chicken, Hunan lamb (sliced leg of lamb with onions), sesame chicken, and Lake Tung Ting scallops. The scallops are served in a spicy wine garlic sauce with bamboo shoots and water chestnuts. In addition, the restaurant features Peking and Szechwan-style Chinese cuisine. And for lunch there are bargains galore that include lunch specials and a buffet (Monday through Friday).

East

Singapore! Cuisine of China & Malaysia
$–$$
1715 Beam Avenue Suite A, Maplewood
(651) 777–7999

Singapore quickly became one of the Twin Cities' favorite Asian restaurants. Despite its unlikely location, suburban Maplewood, the restaurant features some of the area's most outstanding dishes. The suburban location has not deterred its many fans from frequently visiting this gem. What sets the restaurant apart from the multitude of area Asian restaurants? It's not the restaurant's superb versions of Chinese dishes, which are among the best in the area. Instead, the complex and savory Malaysian items distinguish Singapore from the crowd.

Singapore is the only Twin Cities restaurant to feature an extensive Malaysian menu, created by Chef Kin Lee. Included are sambals, a Malaysian specialty made of shrimp paste, ground chili peppers, and shallots. There are several sambal options, ranging from mixed vegetables to prawns, scallops, shrimp, and other seafood choices. Complexly spiced curries and rendangs (a dry curry) are also prominent menu items. The savory Captain's Curry boasts an astounding 27 spices. It is hard to go wrong at Singapore because all menu items are deft combinations of fresh vegetables, meats, and spices. And for vegetarians, there are several excellent choices. If diners have any questions, the friendly servers are more than happy to make suggestions or ask the chef to alter dishes to meet desired spice levels.

There are many excellent Chinese menu items for less adventurous diners. Despite the serious cuisine, Singapore is a relatively casual restaurant. But it is in the food where the restaurant truly shines. It comes as no surprise to local Asian food connoisseurs that the restaurant routinely wins awards from local weeklies and periodicals. Singapore is open Tuesday through Sunday for lunch and dinner.

West

Yangtze Chinese Restaurant $-$$
5625 Wayzata Boulevard, St. Louis Park
(952) 541-9469

The Yangtze Restaurant serves Szechwan, Cantonese, and Mandarin Chinese dishes. Menu favorites include sesame chicken, Mandarin shrimp, pan-fried noodles, pot stickers, and sizzling duck. Yangtze Restaurant is open daily for lunch and dinner, and on weekends features one of the best dim sum in the Twin Cities.

Cuban

Minneapolis

Café Havana $-$$
119 Washington Avenue North, Minneapolis
(612) 338-8484

In the 1950s cosmopolitan Havana spawned sizzling nightclubs, Latin rhythms, and a reckless, live-for-today attitude. Café Havana re-creates this paradise of privilege through telling details: the red carpet leading to the door, huge sprays of flowers, sumptuous velveteen chairs and curtains, the whiff of good cigars, and the black dial telephone. Fans of true Cuban food—rice and pork dishes, plantains, and creamy three-milk cakes—will love Café Havana, which is also home to one of the posher bar scenes in the Cities. There's even a cigar room for postdinner stogies. Owners Gladys and Peter Mendoza (mother and son) say that their family recipes are faithful to the Cuban dishes they left behind in 1969. Black beans and rice, the national dish, accompany many entrees, along with fried plantains (starchier, less-sweet cousins of bananas). Items from cornmeal-crusted conch fritters to grilled chorizo with peppers and onions serve as appetizers. There's no goat on the menu, but the lamb shank and the traditional ropa vieja (shredded beef slow-cooked in sherry-tomato sauce) are satisfying and delicious, and the seafood tastes as though it's just off the boat.

Victor's 1959 Café $
3756 Grand Avenue South, Minneapolis
(612) 827-8948

Serving Cuban and American breakfast and lunch cuisine, this tiny restaurant is packed with photographs and memorabilia of both Cuba and Castro. The yellow walls give a Caribbean feel to the restaurant, as does the Cuban music in the background. The menu includes eggs Havana, mango waffles, ranchero Cubano, the Bay of Pigs pork sandwich, fried yucca, both sweet plantains and fried green plantains, and Cuban coffee. The restaurant is a very popular neighborhood stop, and with fewer than ten tables inside, the wait to get seated can be an hour or so. Victor's accepts Visa and MasterCard only.

Eastern European

Kramarczuk Sausage Company $
215 Hennepin Avenue East, Minneapolis
(612) 379-3018

Specializing in the cuisine of Poland, Ukraine, and Russia, the casual Kramarczuk Sausage Company serves delicious, cheap eats in their cafeteria-style restaurant across the river from downtown Minneapolis. Specialties include varenyky (dumplings stuffed with meat, cheese and potato, or sauerkraut), holubets (cabbage rolls stuffed with rice and meat and topped with tomato sauce), szegedin goulash (meat, sauerkraut, and onions in a paprika sauce), and several selections of sausages. Soups include borscht and sausage vegetable, and Kramarczuk serves beer and wine. The restaurant also has an on-site deli and market. Live accordion music livens things up on Saturday night. Kramarczuk is open for lunch and dinner Monday through Saturday; the market and deli are also open in the morning for sausages (and many other items) to take home and grill.

Eat Street

Restaurants are an important component of any urban center's vitality. The great cities of the world, in part, draw their identity from these sections. Whether it's Chinatown in New York, Rush Street or Devon Avenue in Chicago, or Market Street in San Francisco, dining districts are essential in defining the character of cities. The Twin Cities, like most other great metropolitan areas, boast several sections renowned for their dining opportunities.

Since the Twin Cities are composed of two distinct cities, each with its own lively restaurant scenes, the options for dining are almost endless. Diners are given ample gastronomical possibilities in several locations in the metropolitan area, where excellent eateries congregate en masse. St. Paul features the numerous Southeast Asian restaurants lining University Avenue in the Midway and Frogtown neighborhoods, the Mexican restaurant district situated on the West Side, and the emerging restaurant scene on West Seventh Street near the new Xcel Energy Center. Minneapolis also boasts several important dining districts. The heaviest concentration of fine dining in the Twin Cities is on the Nicollet Mall, where diners may choose between Manny's Steakhouse, Oceanaire, and Aquavit, to name just a few possibilities. Another area of Minneapolis with tremendous choices available is Hennepin Avenue in Uptown. There are restaurants of all price ranges and culinary backgrounds offered. And don't forget desserts and ice cream, served at Sebastian Joe's Ice Cream Café and Häagen-Dazs Ice Cream Shop, to name just a few. However, the most renowned dining district in the Twin Cities is probably the dense distribution of ethnic restaurants on Nicollet Avenue just south of downtown.

This stretch of Nicollet Avenue is known as "Eat Street." It received its name from the heavy concentration of diverse restaurants along the avenue. The strip along Nicollet Avenue showcases more than 50 restaurants and food markets and is still growing. Eat Street features several American restaurants, but the number of high-quality, diverse ethnic restaurants is where the street truly shines. With some of the best Middle Eastern, Greek, Chinese, Vietnamese, and Mexican restaurants in the Twin Cities, Eat Street has something to offer everyone who loves ethnic food.

Eat Street's location is an important asset. It begins just south of the fine shopping on Nicollet Mall, which is closed to automobile traffic (except buses and taxis). The 17-block culinary journey terminates just north of Lake Street. Eat Street begins just walking distance from the Minneapolis Convention Center. In addition, Eat Street is conveniently located near several attractions, most notably the Minneapolis Institute of Arts. However, the restaurants truly define Eat Street.

Less than a decade ago, the section of Nicollet Avenue now known as Eat Street was viewed as a neighborhood in a state of decline. However, it was just the beginning of the conversion of the avenue into the most ethnically diverse and concentrated confluence of restaurants in the Twin Cities. The renaissance of Nicollet Avenue was due in large part to the influx of nascent Asian and Chicano restaurants in the area. Today Eat Street features a diverse cross section of the Twin Cities' best ethnic foods and more.

Asian restaurants offer the largest and most diverse cuisine available on Eat Street. Diners are afforded a variety of superb choices from Asian seafood and authentic Chinese cuisine to outstanding Vietnamese foods. The Seafood Palace specializes in a wide array of fresh seafood items such as crab, mussels, and shrimp prepared in several piquant sauces. Another excellent Asian choice is the Quang

Restaurant. During its short existence the Quang Restaurant has topped numerous local polls as the best Vietnamese restaurant. As diners travel a few buildings south on the 2700 block of Eat Street, they will reach one of the Twin Cities' favorite Chinese restaurants. Rainbow Chinese Restaurant serves some of the best authentic Chinese cuisine in the Twin Cities. A few favorites at Rainbow are the orange peel chicken, beef with mustard green, and Singapore chow mai fun (noodles). These are only a few of the Asian restaurants on Eat Street, which is constantly adding exciting new Asian food dining choices.

Mexican dining has undergone a renaissance of sorts over the past decade in Minneapolis, and nowhere is this more manifest than on Eat Street. These restaurants present a variety of authentic Mexican flavors as opposed to bland, compromised versions of meaty tacos and burritos covered with American cheese. Tacos and burritos can be found on Eat Street, but certainly not the dull, overly Americanized rendition. El Mariachi is the best example of authentic Mexican food on Eat Street. Meals begin with fresh chips accompanied by savory salsa. Unlike local Mexican restaurants in the recent past, seafood is a prominent menu item, and the menu includes both soups and entrees. Besides El Mariachi, Eat Street features an abundance of Mexican eateries and grocery stores. The Mexican dining possibilities are

Eat Street, also known as Nicollet Avenue and Nicollet Mall, hosts dozens of restaurants along its route through downtown and south Minneapolis. PHOTO: TODD R. BERGER

burgeoning on Eat Street, where new restaurants often sprout up on a monthly basis.

Greek food connoisseurs may select from traditional Greek fare at Christos Greek Restaurant and the less familiar regional specialties at Kypros Greek Restaurant. Plus, there are several excellent Middle Eastern restaurants, the foremost being Jerusalem's Restaurant, a perennial poll topper and diner favorite. Eat Street also features the Black Forest Inn, a favorite place for decades to enjoy German food and outdoor dining.

There are numerous additional dining choices available on Eat Street, which is easily accessible to visiting diners. Among the options available are the Arts and Eats Express, a shuttle provided by Metro Transit, and the River City Trolley, (612) 378–7833, which visits Eat Street on its city tour. Diners are provided myriad options in close proximity on Eat Street.

Ethiopian

Minneapolis

Blue Nile $–$$
2027 Franklin Avenue East, Minneapolis
(612) 338–3000

For more than a decade a thriving population of Ethiopians and Eritreans have
lived in the Twin Cities. The immigrants
have enriched the area with the wealth of
their culture. One highly visible result of
the group's impact is the many Ethiopian
restaurants scattered throughout Minneapolis and St. Paul. Blue Nile was one
of the first Ethiopian restaurants in the
area. Its first location was in south Minneapolis, but they later relocated to their
present location in Minneapolis's Seward
neighborhood. The Blue Nile moved into
an expansive former supper club, where
there is a huge dining room, bar, and
space for dancing and live music.

The Blue Nile features a menu filled
with Ethiopian specialty dishes as well as
Middle Eastern specialties. Menu items
include the maraka hoolaa, which is lamb
flavored with ginger root and other exotic
spices. The restaurant also features a shish
kebab combo. In addition, vegetarian
menu selections are available. And for an
excellent overview of the culinary treats
offered at the Blue Nile, try the gosa-gosa
C, which is a sampler of two of the menu's
vegetarian entrees and maraka (Ethiopian
stewed meat dishes). The Blue Nile is open
for dinner Monday through Sunday.

St. Paul

Queen of Sheba Café & Restaurant $–$$
2447 West Seventh Street, St. Paul
(651) 690–0068

Queen of Sheba serves primarily Ethiopian
food—stewed beef, chicken, and vegetables
spiced and served with injera (delicious,
spongy pieces of flat bread made with
ultrafine grain)—but the menu also has
hot dogs, french fries, and hamburgers. It's
a strange mixture of elegant and casual, as
the restaurant is beautifully decorated
with hand-embroidered tablecloths and

framed needlepoints, but all the food is
prepared to be eaten with your hands
alone, although if you ask, they'll gladly
bring you silverware. A counter at one side
of the restaurant serves Ethiopian coffee.

French

Minneapolis

Café Un Deux Trois $$$–$$$$
114 South Ninth Street, Minneapolis
(612) 673–0686

Located in the historic Foshay Tower, this
hot spot for business power lunches serves
French food such as frites, moules, cheesy
French onion soup, escargots steeped in
garlic and herbs, steak tartare, heaping
bowls of mussels, braised lamb shank,
grilled salmon with lobster-infused
risotto, liver and onions, and salade
Niçoise. Drawing paper and crayons are
set on each table to entertain patrons
while they wait for their food, while owner
Michael Morse is always there, snapping
his fingers, greeting customers, and mak-
ing sure everything works. Café Un Deux
Trois is open for lunch and dinner Mon-
day through Friday and dinner only on
Saturday. Valet parking is available, and
reservations are recommended.

Restaurant Alma $$–$$$
528 University Avenue SE, Minneapolis
(612) 379–4909

Chef Alex Roberts, a veteran hailing from
such restaurant kitchens as New York
City's Bouley and Union Square Café,
serves up incredible dishes following clas-
sic French techniques. Typical menu
items include a Portuguese-style stew
crowned with tender, in-the-shell clams,
buttery squares of chicken, and spicy
chorizo in a tomato broth; vegetarian
corn crespelle; and prime, dry-aged ribeye
steak. Reservations are highly recom-
mended, especially on weekends.

Table of Contents $$$–$$$$
1310 Hennepin Avenue South, Minneapolis
(612) 339–1133

Chef Philip Corwart loves to show off his

cooking skills on such luxuries as sea urchin, wild boar, bison, soft-shell crabs, dandelion greens, steamed cattails, frog leg pizza, or duck breast, but Table of Contents' menu is also loaded with more conservative options like pork loin, pasta, chicken, and fish. The vegetarian specials can be quite extraordinary, and the restaurant also sports a full bar specializing in martinis and carrying a wine list with more than 100 selections to choose from.

Vincent $$$
1100 Nicollet Mall, Minneapolis
(612) 630-1183

Vincent, named for head chef and owner Vincent Francoual, is a lovely spot for casual fine dining. Beautiful oak woodwork, high ceilings, and large windows overlooking Nicollet Mall and Orchestra Hall provide the upscale atmosphere for the restaurant's French-American specialties. The menu changes every two months, but some recent dishes include pan-seared scallops with an orange sauce, seafood "cappuccino" with crab custard and a lobster froth, and fennel seed-crusted Atlantic salmon. Vincent is open for lunch Monday through Friday and dinner daily; reservations are recommended, particularly on weekends.

St. Paul

Tulips Restaurant $-$$$
452 Selby Avenue, St. Paul
(651) 221-1061

Tulips Restaurant serves fine French country cuisine in the charming Cathedral Hill neighborhood of St. Paul. The restaurant features dinners such as salmon with honey mustard, baked halibut and shrimp, and filet mignon. For lunch and brunch the menu items are smaller and less expensive. The Saturday and Sunday brunch includes eggs Benedict, waffle with berries, and a smoked salmon plate. Tulips Restaurant is open Monday through Friday for lunch and dinner. On Saturday and Sunday the restaurant features brunch. Dinner is also offered on Saturday.

East

La Belle Vie $$$$
312 Main Street, Stillwater
(651) 430-3545

La Belle Vie serves exquisite French and Mediterranean cuisine in Stillwater's charming downtown. The restaurant provides the perfect setting for a romantic dinner. The chef behind this favorite place for fine dining is Tim McKee, who has received numerous awards locally and nationally for his skill in the kitchen. In 1997 *Food & Wine* magazine recognized him as one of the nation's best young chefs. In the wake of the honor, McKee was showered with many more awards; most notably he was honored by *City Pages* as the best chef in the Twin Cities. The restaurant's creative menu incorporates foods and culinary traditions that extend beyond French cuisine to include entrees such as grilled lamb with cannellini and charmoula, grilled ahi tuna with saffron and tomato confit, and bouillabaisse. Also offered is a large wine list to complete a fine meal. The restaurant is open for dinner daily, and reservations are highly recommended.

South

La Fougasse $$$
Sofitel Minneapolis Hotel, 5601 West 78th Street, Bloomington
(952) 835-0126

This hotel restaurant, formerly the site of two smaller French restaurants, serves a wide variety of elegant French dishes, including excellent onion soup, fougasse, and a huge collection of scrumptious desserts. Warm saffron, deep red, and azure blue monopolize every inch of this restaurant, giving it the ultimate Mediterranean look. Reservations are almost always required, as the place fills up quickly with hotel guests.

German

Minneapolis

Black Forest Inn $$
1 East 26th Street, Minneapolis
(612) 872–0812

The Black Forest Inn has been a favorite German restaurant for more than 30 years. It is located on the increasingly popular ethnic restaurant area of Eat Street (Nicollet Avenue). The restaurant has stood the test of time and remains a popular hangout for German food and, in summertime, outdoor dining. In the Twin Cities, beautiful summer days take on exceptional significance, and the restaurant is perennially where locals dine alfresco. A canopy of trees with lots of green flora and a fountain shade the outdoor dining area. Another asset at the restaurant is the large bar stocked with imported German and domestic beers, which go great with the hearty German food, including such specialties as wiener schnitzel, sauerbraten, and hasenpfeffer, as well as sauerkraut and spaetzle (German dumplings somewhat similar to thick, doughy noodles). Dessert is outstanding, too, especially the decadent Black Forest cake.

St. Paul

Glockenspiel $–$$
605 West Seventh Street, St. Paul
(651) 292–9421

When Glockenspiel opened the Twin Cities was prepared for something special. After all, two of the restaurant's co-owners are the Wildmos, David and Mary, who own one of St. Paul's favorite restaurants, the Tavern on Grand. The location, a Czech and Slovak fraternal hall, is one of the restaurant's greatest assets. On entering the restaurant, there is a huge bar stocked with German beers. The dining area is a classy continuation of the bar, and is decked out in plenty of blue against a large mural in the long, narrow, spacious dining area.

German specialties, especially pork, fill the large menu. The restaurant has daily specials, which include venison medallions on Saturday evenings. Other specials during the week are salmon fillets and beef rouladen (beef rolled around a pickle). A few other entrees are schweinhaxe (pork hocks), Eisbach pfeffersteak (a German version of sirloin steak), and schweinrippchen (pork spare ribs). And for those with a smaller appetite, there are kleine speise (lighter fare) such as bratwurst, weisswurst, and a Reuben sandwich. Finally, for dessert the restaurant features tortes, cakes, and other German delights. Glockenspiel is open for lunch and dinner daily.

East

Gasthaus Bavarian Hunter $–$$
8390 Lofton Avenue North, Stillwater
(651) 439–7128
www.gasthausbavarianhunter.com

Gasthaus has specialized in the cuisine of south Germany since 1966, and the extensive menu offers something for everyone. The restaurant has the largest variety of schnitzels (cutlets) in the Twin Cities. Also featured are sausages, sauerbraten (a tangy beef), and, for large appetites, a couple of Bavarian combination platters. Surprisingly, the meaty restaurant has two *kein fleisch* (no meat) meals—vegetable rouladen and vegetable casserole. And don't forget to wash the meal down with a German beer, especially since the restaurant does not stock domestic beers. For diners' entertainment, polka music is performed on Friday and Sunday as well as for the many German events. The Gasthaus Bavarian Hunter is open daily for lunch and dinner.

The Gasthaus packs them in for its three annual festivals: Sommerfest in June, Waldfest on Labor Day, and Oktoberfest later in September. Sommerfest and Oktoberfest feature food, German beer in traditional one-liter Mass mugs (and in smaller sizes), and polka music under the big tent in front of the restaurant. If you plan to partake in the festivities, make sure someone in your party is the designated driver, because the beer goes down fast and the location of the rural Stillwater-area restaurant makes for an expensive taxi ride back to the Cities.

Winzer Stube $$
516 Second Street, Hudson, Wisconsin
(715) 381-5092

One of the Twin Cities' best German restaurants is located in Hudson, Wisconsin, 25 miles east of downtown St. Paul. The restaurant, which opened in November 1999, has become a popular destination for Twin Citians who desire authentic German cuisine at reasonable prices. Located in the basement of the old opera house in downtown Hudson, the restaurant is decorated with lots of wood and German motifs.

The menu features several excellent dishes. One savory item is the roulade mit speck und gurke. The flavorful beef roll-ups are wrapped around a tasty pickle. Also outstanding is the jägerschnitzel. The fine pork cutlet is the restaurant's biggest seller and comes accompanied by spaetzle (homemade noodles) and rotkraut (red cabbage). The schweinhaxe (pork hocks) is a popular daily special that occasionally sells out during lunch. For smaller appetites there are soups and sausage platters (bratwurst, weisswurst, bauern mettwurst, and knackwurst) on the menu. The restaurant has a children's menu, and to end the meal there are outstanding dessert options such as Black Forest cake, apple strudel, and chocolate torte.

Greek

Minneapolis

Gardens of Salonica New Greek Café and Deli $-$$
19 Northeast Fifth Street, Minneapolis
(612) 378-0611

Anna and Lazaros Christoforide's sunny restaurant serves fresh bread with delightful dips, like their zingy skordalia (potatoes, lemon juice, and garlic), and tyro

(feta cheese blended with roasted peppers, garlic, and herbs); chicken souvlaki and lamb-and-beef gyro sandwiches; and fancier dishes like rice-stuffed squid baked in red wine sauce and the fresh artichoke-and-braised-lamb dish that's a spring special. The house specialty, popular for lunch or dessert, is boughatsa: phyllo pastries that come in sweet and savory varieties. Located in a turn-of-the-20th-century storefront on an obscure side street, this family-owned Greek cafe and deli draws patrons from all over the Metro.

It's Greek to Me $$
626 West Lake Street, Minneapolis
(612) 825-9922

This restaurant is casual and welcoming, with high pressed-tin ceilings, freshly painted wall murals, and new terra-cotta-like tiled floors. It's also inexpensive, considering that a dinner-size portion of anything costs around $10 and will usually leave you enough for tomorrow's lunch. The menu offers nearly two dozen appetizer options to precede classic Greek specialties such as souvlaki and spanakopita, fried smelt, octopus, chicken gyros, and flaming cheese. It's Greek to Me maintains its status as one of the Lyn-Lake neighborhood's most popular eateries. Every night, the place bustles with couples, small families, and intimate clusters of friends devouring spicy-hot feta cheese spread, roast leg of lamb, or vegetarian dolmades.

St. Paul

Acropol Inn Restaurant $
748 Grand Avenue, St. Paul
(651) 298-0151

The Acropol Inn is one of the Twin Cities' oldest Greek restaurants. The Apostolou family opened the restaurant in 1975 to serve gyros and other Greek specialties. The restaurant serves all the traditional Greek standards—moussaka (meat and eggplant), dolmades (grape leaves stuffed with rice and meat), and pasticcio (a Greek version of lasagna). Wash the Greek cuisine down with a cold beer or glass of wine. The Acropol Inn Restaurant is open Monday through Saturday for lunch and dinner.

Christos Greek Restaurant $–$$
214 East Fourth Street, St. Paul
(651) 224–6000
2632 Nicollet Avenue, Minneapolis
(612) 871–2111

Christos serves all your Greek favorites from two Twin Cities locations. The St. Paul restaurant is one the most beautiful and historical dining spots in the area, the Union Depot Place. Christos is situated in the middle of the immense former Union Depot, atop a riser, and is surrounded by columns and plenty of big windows and marble. It's hard for a restaurant to fail with such grandeur and beauty.

Both locations feature tasty versions of Greek cuisine. The menu includes gyros, dolmades, spanakopita, moussaka, and many other traditional Greek dishes. The prices are reasonable, especially for lunch, when the St. Paul location serves a buffet Monday through Friday. The buffet offers a relatively inexpensive introduction for Greek food novices as well as connoisseurs. The food selections are always delicious, and the unmatched ambience is free.

Spiro's Mediterranean Market $
2264 University Avenue West, St. Paul
(651) 645–4607

Besides a well-stocked Mediterranean market, Spiro's features a deli counter. There are two sandwiches offered—an Italian beef sandwich and, of course, a gyro. The gyro is big and tasty. The succulent gyro meat is surrounded by a fresh pita and topped with onions, tomatoes, and creamy Greek sauce. Also available are Greek salads and the deli's delicious homemade hummus. The hummus is among the best in the Twin Cities, with a tangy citrus taste in combination with the pureed chickpeas. Don't forget dessert. A couple of dessert treats are provided, and the baklava is a particularly good mix of phyllo dough, nuts, and honey. Spiro's is open for lunch Monday through Friday and early dinner (until 7:00 P.M. on weekdays and 5:00 P.M. on Saturday).

The Minneapolis branch of Christos on Nicollet Avenue in south Minneapolis. PHOTO: TODD R. BERGER

West

Santorini $–$$$
9920 Wayzata Boulevard, St. Louis Park
(952) 546–6722

Greek cuisine and American specialties dominate the menu at Santorini. For lunch and dinner there are numerous choices. Sandwiches ranging from a traditional burger to the Moroccan chicken, which features a unique pepper spread, onions, and cucumbers, are served along with pastas and more elaborate entrees. Shrimp, steaks, lamb chops, and much more are available as well as Greek combination platters.

Indian

Minneapolis

Passage to India $–$$
1401 West Lake Street, Minneapolis
(612) 827–7518
Passage to India is one of the many fine Indian restaurants in the Twin Cities. A few years ago this restaurant opened in the Uptown area of Minneapolis. With its opening came great expectations, since another branch is regarded as one of the best Indian restaurants in New York City. The Passage to India met most critics' expectations by providing a number of savory options. The numerous breads and tandoori choices are outstanding as are the special dinners. Each offers soup, appetizer, main course, and dessert for under $20. Passage to India is open until midnight most nights—a blessing in the Twin Cities, where so few restaurants have late-night hours.

North

India Palace $–$$
2570 Cleveland Avenue North, Roseville
(651) 631–1222
India Palace creates some of the area's best cuisine. Besides the facade of the building, the restaurant shows no signs of its previous tenants, a fast-food chain. Decorated with subtle Indian art, the restaurant is a favorite. Featured menu items include tandoori specialties, curries, and vindaloos. Also available is the lunch buffet, where seven days a week, diners may enjoy the flavors of India. In addition, the restaurant offers take-out as well as an extensive beer and wine list. India Palace is open daily for lunch and dinner.

South

Tandoor Restaurant $–$$
8062 Morgan Circle South, Bloomington
(952) 885–9060
True to its name, the specialty of Tandoor Restaurant is the meats, seafood, and other foods cooked in their tandoor, a clay oven heated to high heat using charcoal. Favorites included tandoori chicken, tandoori naan bread, lamb rogan nosh, and chicken makhani, as well as various curry dishes. The restaurant also features a lunch buffet. Tandoor Restaurant is open daily for lunch and dinner.

East

Taste of India $–$$
1745 Cope Avenue East, Maplewood
(651) 773–5477
www.tasteofindiamn.com
This Taste of India has different ownership than the St. Louis Park location and a slightly different menu. The restaurant features an extensive list of mainly north Indian dishes. Curries and tandoori specialties dominate the menu. In addition, the restaurant provides a daily lunch buffet, where diners can sample the flavors of India. Then wash it down with an exotic Indian drink, a beer, or wine. Taste of India serves lunch and dinner daily.

West

Taste of India $–$$
5617 Wayzata Boulevard, St. Louis Park
(952) 541–4865
The Taste of India offers an extensive menu of excellently prepared curries and tandoori (clay oven) specialties. The Taste of India was one of the first restaurants of its kind in the area. Located in a comfortable strip mall in the suburbs, the restaurant specializes in north Indian cuisine, with treats from throughout the subcontinent thrown in to enthrall the taste buds. The tandoori items are especially tasty. The tandoori shrimp is an incredibly savory item. Large shrimp are covered in the tasty yogurt glaze and spices and then cooked to perfection; the shrimp is moist and packed with flavor. Indian specialty drinks (mango milk shakes, mango lassis, etc.) as well as wines and beers, both imported and domestic, are offered. The restaurant features a daily lunch buffet

with one of the largest spreads in the Twin Cities. Taste of India is open daily for lunch and dinner.

Irish

Minneapolis

Kieran's Irish Pub $–$$
330 Second Avenue South (Towle Building), Minneapolis
(612) 339–4499
www.kierans.com

Kieran's Irish Pub is a popular place to imbibe in the gaiety of the Emerald Isle. Owner Kieran Folliard satisfies the Twin Cities' love of Irish culture by providing beer, liquor, music, and food. The menu includes such Irish classics as lamb stew and corned beef and cabbage, as well as American favorites like the grilled New York strip. All menu items are influenced by Ireland; even the New York strip has an Irish flair (Irish whiskey sauce). And don't forget to order a Guinness to accompany the Irish fare. Kieran's is especially busy during lunch and happy hour because of the immense downtown Minneapolis worker population. The restaurant is open daily for lunch and dinner.

The Local $–$$
931 Nicollet Mall, Minneapolis
(612) 904–1000
www.the-local.com

The Local is another successful restaurant created by Kieran Folliard. In 1997 Folliard developed an elegant Irish eatery where diners may select either inexpensive or haute cuisine food items. However, all food is served in a lovely dining room draped with velvet curtains and a charming bar, which is amply stocked with Irish, local, and domestic beers. The menu includes reasonably priced sandwiches and entrees. Among the sandwiches offered are the pot roast beef, chicken breast, and an Irish specialty, corned beef (topped with Swiss cheese). For lighter appetites, diners may choose from a half dozen salads. Entrees include salmon, sirloin steak, fish-and-chips, and lamb steak.

Reservations are recommended. The Local is open Monday through Friday for lunch and dinner. On the weekends, in addition to dinner the Local serves brunch until 2:00 P.M.

Italian

Minneapolis

Auriga $$$
1930 Hennepin Avenue South, Minneapolis
(612) 871–0777

Exotic cheeses, just-made breads, and European comfort food like sautéed polenta with organic scrambled eggs and baked Parmesan rind are the standbys here. Elegant foods include chestnut-and-duck-egg ravioli with watercress and truffle butter, special treats for special nights. The brief menu, which changes every two or three weeks, offers fish, chicken, beef or pork, game, and vegetarian dishes, including parsley root and porcini mushrooms generously dressing homemade pasta, brown rice-and-walnut croquettes, portobello mushrooms, and thin parsnip crisps. Deep jewel tones, metallic paints, and Prairie School light fixtures shine up the place, while stripped-to-concrete floors, industrial hardware, and candles lend a monastic simplicity.

Bobino Café and Wine Bar $$–$$$
222 East Hennepin Avenue, Minneapolis
(612) 623–3301
www.bobino.com

Named for the Monte Carlo theater where Josephine Baker last sang, Bobino's is a romantic little spot with citrus-colored walls, warm lighting, alcoves, arches, and artful windows that set the stage for romance. The five or six entrees offered each night might include grilled hanger steak, mussels, and a selection of fresh fish. (The menu changes monthly.) More than 50 wines and 20 tap beers are also served here, as well as a half dozen tapas plates and some really extraordinary desserts, such as champagne-infused vanilla custard poured over fresh fruit and rich chocolate tortes. The Bobino Starlite Lounge (212 East Hennepin Avenue; 612-623-3301), a martini bar, is nearby.

Broders' Cucina Italiana $
2308 West 50th Street, Minneapolis
(612) 925-3113

Back in the early 1950s, Tom and Molly Broder founded this amazing neighborhood deli that served handmade pastas, imported olive oils, olives, cheese, meats, and other high-quality imported and homemade ingredients. Since then, they've added spicy pizzas sold by the slice, sandwiches, take-out homemade pasta sauces, and deli treats from grilled asparagus to homemade cannolis to the menu. And they don't skimp on anything. Standbys include sandwiches such as the Tramezzino (roasted vegetables and feta on homemade focaccia), Genovese (tuna salad with red peppers, Dijon mayonnaise, tomatoes, and greens on French bread), and Prosciutto Cotto (roasted ham, baby Swiss cheese, and greens on focaccia). The deli serves a full range of desserts, including triple-chocolate cheesecake and tiramisu.

Broders' Southside Pasta Bar $$
5000 Penn Avenue South, Minneapolis
(612) 925-9202

Made by hand by the excellent chefs at Broders', the different styles of pasta served here are all amazingly tender and rich, complemented by sauces and toppings that range from fresh Prince Edward Island mussels paired with beautiful, wine-soaked wild mushrooms to broiled fish and fresh herbs. It's about as far away from ordinary spaghetti as you can get, and for a price that's more than reasonable, especially for the quality of food Broders' serves. The one drawback is their no-reservation policy, and mere minutes after the doors open for dinner (generally 5:00 P.M.), the place is packed. In summer, guests can sip drinks on the modest outdoor patio while waiting for a seat, but in winter, latecomers will more than likely be left out in the cold.

Buca di Beppo $$
1204 Harmon Place, Minneapolis
(612) 288-0138
7711 Mitchell Road, Eden Prairie
(952) 724-7266
2728 Gannon Road, St. Paul
(651) 772-4388
14300 Burnhaven Drive, Burnsville
(952) 892-7272
www.bucadibeppo.com

Now a national chain, the first Buca di Beppo opened in a charming basement in Minneapolis—hence, the restaurant's name, which means Joe's basement in Italian. The south Italian family-style restaurant has become a popular place for Twin Citians to celebrate. Diners order immense portions of Italian favorites from a chalkboard. The family-style meals are best enjoyed with large groups so that more items can be ordered and shared. Menu items are ordered a la carte and include numerous appetizers, salads, pizzas, pastas, and side dishes. All menu items are enormous. A few standouts include chicken marsala, chicken cacciatore, pizzas, and much more. The pasta choices are extensive and include standards ranging from spaghetti marinara to linguini frutti di mare, a combination of mussels, clams, and calamari. In addition, the restaurant serves a large selection of wines. Reservations are accepted at all area Buca di Beppos. The Minneapolis Buca is open for dinner Monday through Saturday. On Sunday, the restaurant opens for lunch and dinner.

Campiello $$$
1320 West Lake Street, Minneapolis
(612) 825-2222
6411 City West Parkway, Eden Prairie
(952) 941-6868

Campiello is a great place to impress a date. The smart lighting makes everyone look fabulous, and the stunning presentations make everyone look like a big spender without breaking the bank. Campiello is high-class without being snobby, as is the waitstaff. Bond in his tuxedo might feel a little overdressed, but everyone else, from the blue-jeaned to the all-in-black, fits right in. On the menu, the crackly thin-crusted pizzas make for stunning appetizers, the salads are solid, and the entrees (especially the pastas and the rotisserie meats) are absolutely top-drawer.

D'Amico & Sons $
2210 Hennepin Avenue, Minneapolis
(612) 374–1858
www.damico.com
Nine additional Twin Cities locations

D'Amico & Sons specializes in high-quality deli fare for casual eating in or take-out. Where the D'Amico Cucina serves upscale cuisine, this restaurant creates delicious, reasonably priced items. The restaurant features salads, pastas, pizza, and sandwiches prepared with fresh ingredients. In addition, beers and wines are available. D'Amico has the classiest and highest quality casual dining in the Twin Cities. D'Amico & Sons (Hennepin Avenue) is open Monday through Sunday for lunch and dinner.

D'Amico Cucina $$$
100 North Sixth Street, Minneapolis
(612) 338–2401
www.damico.com

The D'Amicos own restaurants throughout the Twin Cities. The D'Amico Cucina is their fine Italian dining restaurant. The restaurant prepares some of the best northern Italian cuisine in the area. For wine lovers, the restaurant has a spectacular wine list of vintages found nowhere else in Minneapolis. D'Amico Cucina is open daily for dinner only. Reservations are highly recommended.

Davanni's Pizza & Hot Hoagies $
2500 Riverside Avenue, Minneapolis
(612) 332–5551
Seventeen additional Twin Cities locations
www.davannis.com

Since 1975 Davanni's has been one of the Twin Cities' favorite places for pizza and hot hoagies. The casual restaurant is a great place for students and families to enjoy one of the many delicious menu items. Diners have an option of three crust types: traditional, thin, and Chicago deep dish. The deep dish is especially tasty. The thick light crust is topped with a tangy tomato sauce, and the toppings and cheese

are always fresh. Another popular menu item is the almost 20 hoagies, including salami, turkey, roast beef, meatball, pizza, and tuna. Delivery is also an important part of Davanni's business. They are almost annually named the best take-out and pizza delivery in the Twin Cities.

Fat Lorenzo's $
5600 Cedar Avenue South, Minneapolis
(612) 822–2040

A southside neighborhood institution, Fat Lorenzo's tables are covered with white butcher paper for customers to doodle on with supplied crayons while they wait for their pizzas to show up. The menu features New York–style pizza and a variety of Italian specialties such as lasagna, baked rigatoni, spaghetti, and chicken cacciatore. A variety of hot and cold hoagies (including meatball, turkey, and roast beef) round the menu off nicely.

Figlio Restaurant and Bar $$
3001 Hennepin Avenue, Minneapolis
(612) 822–1688
www.figlio.com

Located inside the Calhoun Square mall, this is where the wealthy, hip young crowd comes to drink and hold their power lunches. Figlio's servings are generous, and their specialty dishes are absolutely decadent. Their seafood and pasta dishes are excellent, and their desserts have won numerous awards throughout the Twin Cities. The Death By Chocolate concoction is especially wonderful: layers of soft chocolate molded around a chocolate torte filled with chocolate mousse and drenched in warm chocolate sauce. You may want to call ahead for a reservation on weekend nights or holidays—this place fills up fast. Serving a full menu until 1:00 A.M. during the week and until 2:00 A.M. on Friday and Saturday nights, Figlio is a popular stop for patrons fresh from the bars and clubs of Uptown.

Golooney's East Coast Pizza $
2329 Hennepin Avenue, Minneapolis
(612) 377–8555

New York–style pizza shops are frequently

imitated in the Twin Cities, but Golooney's East Coast Pizza is one of the best. The pizza is thick and cheesy with a fresh, piquant tomato sauce and a variety of delicious toppings. An important part of the restaurant's business is pizza by the slice, which serves the hungry, young, and hip Uptown neighborhood. For thrifty diners, lunch specials are offered as well as takeout service. The menu also includes salads, sub sandwiches, and pitas. Golooney's is open daily for lunch and dinner.

Green Mill $–$$
2626 Hennepin Avenue, Minneapolis
(612) 374–2131
Nine additional Twin Cities locations

Since 1976 the Green Mill has been one of the Twin Cities' favorite places for pizza. Since then the Green Mill has opened 20 franchises in five states and expanded the scope of its menu to include pasta, calzones, sandwiches, fish, fowl, and much more. The pizza remains the standout and the restaurant's best value. Green Mill offers flat, deep-dish, pescara, and numerous specialty pizzas.

La Toscana Ristorante $$$
3220 West Lake Street (Calhoun Village), Minneapolis
(612) 926–6668

Located in Calhoun Village, this mall restaurant is much more than a place to stop for a quick bite to eat while shopping. The decor includes oversized, gilt-framed Picasso reproductions on the walls and dark-wood tables illuminated by tiny overhead lights. The best dishes here are the grilled quail, the lobster fettuccini in yellow tomato sauce, and steamed chocolate pudding drenched in chocolate and pistachio sauces. Other standouts from the menu include the insalata timballo (layered salad), fried calamari, melanzane arrostite (grilled eggplant and roasted-pepper Napoleon), mushroom risotto, grilled salmon, and balsamic roasted chicken. There's also a wide selection of specialty salads and quick meals for the lunch crowd.

Green Mill has expanded throughout the Twin Cities and to some other cities in the Midwest. The pizza parlor and brewpub serves up some of the tastiest pizza pie in the Metro. PHOTO: TODD R. BERGER

Pane Vino Dolce $$
819 West 50th Street, Minneapolis
(612) 825–3201

Pane Vino Dolce offers fine Italian cuisine in a small, busy dining room. The menu includes small pizzas, risotto, and ravioli, as well as seafood. All are prepared with fresh ingredients, and great attention is paid to presentation. Daily specials are also offered at the eatery. The restaurant is open daily for lunch and Monday through Friday for dinner. Pane Vino Dolce does not accept credit cards.

Pizza Lucé $–$$
119 North Fourth Street, Minneapolis
(612) 333-7359
3200 Lyndale Avenue South, Minneapolis
(612) 827-5978
www.pizzaluce.com

Pizza Lucé specializes in, well, pizza, and many Twin Citians consider the restaurant's pies the best in town. Including the classic taste of The Lucé, which is made of Italian sausage, onions, garlic, and extra cheese, there are many gourmet pizza choices, such as the barbecue chicken and the luau (Canadian bacon, pineapple, green onions, and mozzarella). And if the large selection of gourmet pizzas doesn't meet your needs, then build your own pizza. The menu of more than 50 fresh ingredients includes meats, seafood, vegetables, and eight cheeses. In addition to pizza, the restaurant serves hoagies, spaghetti, lasagna, mostaccioli, and several vegetarian and vegan dishes. The Lyndale location serves beer and wine; the downtown location has a full bar.

Both restaurants are open late. The Lyndale location closes at 1:00 A.M.; the North Fourth Street location in the downtown Warehouse District stays open until 2:00 A.M. Sunday through Thursday and until 3:00 A.M. on Friday and Saturday, making Pizza Lucé a popular post-bartime nosh spot for the downtown club crowd.

Zelo $$–$$$
831 Nicollet Mall, Minneapolis
(612) 333-7000

This splashy restaurant is doing everything right to please couples in search of a memorable date, combining impeccable services with an accessible menu and a nicely focused wine list. Daily fish specials are the highlight, such as flaky walleye Milanese with a golden crown of Italian bread crumbs or a lusciously rare grilled ahi tuna moistened with Chinese mustard vinaigrette and served with green wasabi mashed potatoes. The next best thing to the fish is the filettini—delicate, pounded pork tenderloin slices in green peppercorn-cream-brandy sauce. Steaks, veal chops, and lemon-herb chicken round out the entrees, while commendable pizzas and pastas present more economical options. Their most popular dessert is their incredible tiramisu layered with mascarpone.

St. Paul

Carmelo's $$
238 South Snelling Avenue, St. Paul
(651) 699-2448

Carmelo's is a small, intimate Italian restaurant near the intersection of Snelling and St. Clair Avenues in St. Paul's Mac-Groveland neighborhood. The busy, family-run restaurant is a nice choice for a romantic evening, with a hand-picked selection of wines and beers to complement such made-from-scratch dishes as chicken carmelo, seafood canneloni, and spinach and cheese ravioli. The restaurant is open for lunch Tuesday through Friday and dinner Monday through Saturday. If you can't find a parking place out front, park in the lot next to Sweeney Cleaners at the intersection of Snelling and St. Clair. Reservations are highly recommended for dinner, especially on the weekend.

Chet's Taverna $$–$$$
791 Raymond Avenue, St. Paul
(651) 646-2655

On the brief retail district on Raymond Avenue just off bustling University Avenue in St. Paul is Chet's Taverna. The restaurant's prices reflect the middle-class neighborhood by offering moderately priced lunches and wines. The neighborhood bistro offers pasta, pizza, and entrees for lunch and dinner. Chet's chefs use regional, seasonal, organic ingredients in most of the restaurant's dishes and work closely with regional farmers to support sustainable and organic agriculture. The menu changes seasonally but has included such menu items as eggplant caporata bruschetta, duck leg confit, and various lamb entrees. Lunch offers smaller, but equally complex flavors e.g., a sandwich composed of Serrano ham with shaved manchego cheese on a toasted roll. Chet's Taverna is open for lunch Tuesday through Friday and for dinner Tuesday through Sunday. Reservations are recommended.

Cossetta Italian Market & Pizzeria $
211 West Seventh Street, St. Paul
(651) 222–3476

Cossetta's is one of the busiest lunch spots in St. Paul. It draws throngs of patrons because of the fine pizzas and pastas prepared for eating in or take-out. The Chicago-style pizza is some of the best in the Twin Cities. The delicious chewy thick crust is topped with a piquant marinara sauce and tasty mozzarella and fresh ingredients. Huge pieces of pizza are ready to eat at the counter. Another counter offers lasagna, sausage and peppers, chicken marsala, sausage calabrase, chicken cacciatore, and more a la carte items. Ample seating is provided on two floors, where Italian-American singers such as Tony Bennett and Frank Sinatra are played over the sound system. A wine list is also available for those who enjoy imbibing with their meals. Michael and Irene Cossetta opened the adjoining market in 1911 where the now sprawling market and restaurant began. Today Cossetta's does booming business for lunch and dinner daily, and looks to expand in the wake of the construction of the Xcel Energy Center just down the street.

Dari-ette Drive Inn $
1440 Minnehaha Avenue, St. Paul
(651) 776–3470

Not much to look at from the outside, this small drive-in Italian restaurant carries a huge selection of dishes you can eat right in your car. The menu includes wonderful, thick meatball, sausage, and pizza sandwiches (for a little extra, you can order peppers, onions, or mushrooms to go on the sandwich), hamburgers, Coney dogs, and fried shrimp baskets. The sandwiches come with either french fries or spaghetti on the side—we recommend getting the spaghetti because it is good, although a little messy to eat in the car. For dessert, there are ice cream shakes, malts, sundaes, and excellent, cheap banana splits.

Luci Ancora $$–$$$
2060 Randolph Avenue, St. Paul
(651) 698–6889

Luci Ancora is another restaurant from the husband-and-wife team of Al and Lucille Smith and their large family. Unlike the southern Italian–themed Ristorante Luci, Luci Ancora specializes in northern Italian fare. The menu is brief, but all dishes are well executed. Each evening a four-course prezzo fisso meal is offered, which includes antipasto, soup or salad, pasta, and fish. In addition, wine and delicious desserts are offered. Call ahead for reservations. Luci Ancora is open for lunch and dinner Monday through Friday and for dinner only on Saturday and Sunday.

Paisano's Pizza & Hot Hoagies $
619 Selby Avenue, St. Paul
(651) 224–3350

Paisano's deep-dish pizza is sold by the slice as well as in large, medium, and "solo" sizes. There are several specialty pizzas, which include the Classic, pepperoni, sausage, mushrooms, green peppers, and onions; the Tuscan, white sauce, Canadian bacon, red onion, fresh basil, and sun-dried tomatoes; and the Mediterranean, sun-dried tomatoes, artichoke hearts, feta cheese, Kalamata olives, and fresh spinach. There are a couple more specialty pies as well as 24 toppings to build a pizza to your liking. In addition, there are eight varieties of cold and hot hoagies. For the health conscious, house, classic Caesar, and Mediterranean salads are available. Paisano's is open seven days a week for lunch and dinner.

Pazzaluna Urban Trattoria and Bar $$$
360 St. Peter Street, St. Paul
(651) 223–7000
www.pazzaluna.com

Pazzaluna serves upscale regional Italian cuisine in downtown St. Paul. Specialties of the house include risotto alla Milanese, gnocchi alla Bolognese, medalione di manzo, and carpaccio di manzo alla Piemontese. A full bar features many Italian wines and several varieties of grappa, as well as single-malt scotches and numerous cordials. The elegant bar has a happy hour from 4:00 to 6:00 P.M. Tuesday through Friday, with live music after 9:00 P.M. on Thursday and Friday. Open for dinner only, Pazzaluna is closed Monday. Reservations are recommended, and valet parking is available for bar and restaurant patrons.

Punch Neapolitan Pizza $–$$
704 Cleveland Avenue South, St. Paul
(651) 696–1066

Punch takes its plate-sized Neapolitan pizzas very seriously. In fact, since the restaurant opened in 1996, it has been a member of the Associazione Vera Pizza Napoletana, an Italian organization that regulates pizza purity. Since Punch's inception, owner John Soranno has adhered to the organization's guidelines requiring only the highest quality ingredients and methods. The result is an outstanding pizza. All pizzas are thin crusted and vary only in their high-quality toppings, such as the Puttanesca, which includes anchovies, capers, olives, onions, and oregano. With more than 20 pizzas, the choices are almost endless. Calzones and salads are other options on the menu. A wine list is also provided. Punch is open Tuesday through Saturday for dinner.

Red's Savoy Pizza $
421 East Seventh Street, St. Paul
(651) 227–1437
Two additional Twin Cities locations

Red's offers an excellent rendition of flat-crust pizza. The pizza has a zippy sauce and fresh cheese and ingredients. Diners may select from numerous popular pizzas, such as pepperoni and sausage, or atypical pies, such as the tomato, bacon, and pickle. The pizzas are very inexpensive, and they are available in regular or large. In addition, the restaurant serves burgers and several pastas. Another bonus at Red's is the dark and interesting ambience of the restaurant/bar, which feels like a movie gangster hangout.

Ristorante Luci $$–$$$
470 Cleveland Avenue South, St. Paul
(651) 699–8258

Ristorante Luci serves spectacular southern Italian cuisine in a modestly decorated location. The restaurant is owned by the Smith family, Al and Lucille, who own another restaurant, Luci Ancora, across the street. The restaurant specializes in pastas and seafood, which are prepared to perfection. This is one of the reasons the neighborhood restaurant is a perennial favorite. Another is the wine list and the excellent desserts. Reservations are recommended. Ristorante Luci is open for dinner Tuesday through Sunday.

West

Daniel's Italian Restaurant $$
3220 West 70th Street (Galleria Mall), Edina
(952) 920–3338

Daniel's Italian Restaurant serves fine foods in the luxurious Galleria Mall in Edina. Of course, pasta is a featured menu choice as well as several seafood and veal dishes. Menu items include tortellini, chicken parmigiana, and salmon lasagna. Plenty of free parking is available in the Galleria's parking lot. Daniel's is open for lunch and dinner.

Vescio's Italian Restaurant $–$$
4001 Minnesota Highway 7, St. Louis Park
(952) 920–0733
406 14th Avenue SE, Minneapolis
(612) 378–1747

Vescio's is a traditional place for Twin Citians to enjoy Italian food and more.

The restaurant serves ravioli, rigatoni, tortellini, fettuccine, and spaghetti as well as sandwiches. The sandwiches are Italian-inspired creations that include the Big Boy Italiano (various meats and cheeses on French loaf) and Sweet Fried Pepper Sandwich. And don't forget Vescio's pizza. The pizzas are available in small and large and include one notable specialty: Sid's Special Pizza is topped with sausage, mushrooms, pepperoni, sweet fried peppers, extra cheese, and special seasoning, and is named after longtime Minneapolis *Star-Tribune* sports columnist Sid Hartman, who often frequents the restaurant. The restaurant also goes out of its way to accommodate special diets. There are sections dedicated to diet dining, vegetarian selections, and a children's menu.

Japanese

Minneapolis

Fuji Ya Japanese Restaurant $$
600 West Lake Street, Minneapolis
(612) 871-4055

Fuji Ya is located in the Lyn-Lake neighborhood of south Minneapolis. It is the fourth location in the long history of the restaurant, which first opened its doors in downtown Minneapolis in 1959. Fuji Ya offers a wide array of Japanese food items in all price ranges. For lunch, the restaurant's noodle soups as well as more expensive items are available, and there is also a sushi bar to satisfy lovers of the Japanese delicacy. Dinner specialties include shrimp tempura, sukiyaki and chicken teriyaki. Fuji Ya has an extensive list of beers and wines. Lunch is served Tuesday through Friday; dinner is provided Tuesday through Sunday. Reservations are recommended.

Kikugawa $$-$$$
43 Main Street SE, Minneapolis
(612) 378-3006
www.kikugawa-sushi.com

The best seats in the house are in the Kikugawa atrium, from which restaurant patrons can look out over the Mississippi and beyond to the Minneapolis downtown skyline. Inside, the lighting is romantically dim, reflecting off the large gold-leaf fans decorating the walls. Their sukiyaki (a simmered beef dish) is the best in town, and they also have a large selection of sushi to choose from and pickled vegetable appetizers. To drink, there's a large selection of Japanese beers and flavored sakes to choose from. At night (if you're lucky) drinking businessmen and big-spending hipsters take turns at the karaoke machine, belting out hits from the '60s on up.

Koyi Sushi $-$$
122 North Fourth Street, Minneapolis
(612) 375-9811

Koyi Sushi serves fresh sushi at some of the best prices in town, with some very tasty renditions. Some of the more popular choices include the Dynamite Roll (spicy salmon and yellowtail), the Dragon Roll (cooked tuna, masago, and spicy mayo topped with unagi and avocado), and the Marilyn Monroll (grilled chicken, asparagus, and avocado). Koyi offers sushi a la carte (two pieces per serving), as well as small and large rolls. Non-sushi offerings include kalbee (marinated and grilled beef ribs served with Korean vegetables) and seafood tempura. The restaurant is open daily for dinner.

St. Paul

Sakura Restaurant and Sushi Bar $-$$$$
350 St. Peter Street, St. Paul
(651) 224-0185

The price ranges speak loudly about the possibilities at this fine downtown St. Paul restaurant. For novices to Japanese cuisine or those who are financially strapped for funds, lunch provides several options for under $10. The menu is divided into tempura, teriyaki, donburi, noodles, salads, and of course, sushi. Sushi is the most important menu item—although there are many other standouts from the rest of the large menu.

The sushi bar is prominently placed at the center of a large open room. With more than 30 types of the freshest sushi in town connoisseurs have plenty of choices.

The sushi bar offers California rolls, salmon egg, shrimp, crab, albacore tuna, scallop, and sea eel; all are beautifully presented. The restaurant has a relaxed atmosphere, and lacks the snobbishness of some other Japanese restaurants. Servers are happy to help patrons navigate the menu. The excellent service resonates from owner Miyoko Omori, who frequently greets and seats customers. Reservations are recommended for dinner, which is offered late on Friday and Saturday. Sakura is open daily for both lunch and dinner.

Tanpopo Noodle Shop $
367 Selby Avenue, St. Paul
(651) 228-9967

There are numerous Vietnamese noodle shops in the area but few Japanese restaurants specializing in the fine delicacy. The act of making noodles is elevated to an art at Tanpopo. The menu changes seasonally at the noodle shop, and the restaurant concentrates on a concise, inexpensive, well-executed menu for lunch and dinner composed of various udon (wheat flour noodles), soba (buckwheat flour noodles), and teishoku soups as well as a few side dishes. The Nabayaki Udon is one superb selection, which includes shrimp tempura, chicken, mushrooms, vegetables, and fish cake. There is also a vegetarian item, the tanpopo tofu teishoku. For dessert, fresh truffles (from Just Truffles) as well as green tea ice cream are included. The noodle shop is a beautiful 32-seat restaurant in the charming Cathedral Hill neighborhood of St. Paul. They are currently not accepting credit cards and are open for lunch and dinner Tuesday through Sunday.

Korean

St. Paul

Mirror of Korea $-$$
761 Snelling Avenue North, St. Paul
(651) 647-9004

Snelling Avenue has several Korean restaurants. The Mirror of Korea was one of the first of its kind on the block. The restaurant moved into a building previously occupied by a pizza and sandwich shop. Its large menu belies the humbly decorated restaurant. Soups, stir-fries, and stews fill out the menu. One excellent dish is the chop chae, a traditional Korean dish of beef, vegetables, and rice noodles. There are also several more exotic dishes, like the yook hwae (raw beef). The restaurant also offers several Korean lunch specials. Mirror of Korea is open for lunch and dinner daily, except on Tuesday when the restaurant is closed.

Shilla Korean Restaurant $-$$
694 Snelling Avenue North, St. Paul
(651) 645-0006

Shilla Korean Restaurant is much larger than its neighbor, Mirror of Korea, just down the avenue, but both share many of the same menu items. The restaurant is a combination of '70s decor accented with Korean motifs and serves as the meeting place for many activities in the local Korean community. The menu is extensive and includes all of your Korean favorites. A few standout dishes are bi bim bop (vegetable salad with a boiled egg) and man do (pork and vegetable dumplings). Bargain hunters will be happy to hear that the restaurant offers several lunch specials. Take-out is also available. Shilla is open Tuesday through Sunday for lunch and dinner and does not accept reservations.

Sole Café $-$$
684 Snelling Avenue North, St. Paul
(651) 644-2068

In an area with two additional Korean restaurants within walking distance, this restaurant is certainly the most authentic and arguably the best. The Sole Café is a friendly mom-and-pop operation, with usually one server for several tables. Despite this potential problem, the servers manage to be extremely friendly and attentive to the needs of diners. The decor is a comfortable dining room with Korean motifs and a large bar at the front of the restaurant. Unlike its neighboring Korean restaurants, the menu is not extensive. It is, however, remarkably well executed. The menu includes traditional Korean favorites, such as bulgogi (the spicy Korean version of barbecue), kim chi soup, and chop chae, as well as less familiar items for American diners. The chop chae is an outstanding dish of tender beef and cellophane noodles, mushrooms, thinly sliced carrots, lemongrass, scallions, onions, and mild peppers. Soups and seafood are also prominent menu items, such as the tae chee gae, a swordfish soup with vegetables, and grilled salt adka fish. Sole Café is closed on Wednesday but open Thursday through Tuesday for lunch and dinner.

South

Hoban $
1989 Silver Bell Road, Eagan
(651) 688–3447

Hoban serves Korean dishes from their southeast suburban location in an Eagan strip mall. The casual, small restaurant specializes in favorites such as dolsot bibimbop (steamed vegetables over rice) and kalbee (thinly sliced marinated beef ribs that are grilled). The restaurant serves beer and wine and is open for lunch and dinner Tuesday through Sunday. The restaurant accepts Visa and MasterCard only.

Kurdish

St. Paul

Babani's Kurdish Restaurant $–$$
544 St. Peter Street, St. Paul
(651) 602–9964

Babani's Kurdish is the first restaurant of its kind in the United States. The beautiful building on the outskirts of downtown St. Paul is decorated with Kurdish designs on rugs, pictures, and green curtains. The Kurds are a people without a national homeland, who live today in Iran, Iraq, Syria, and Turkey. A small population of Kurds now resides in the Twin Cities. The restaurant provides an excellent opportunity to learn about Kurdish

culture and cuisine. The servers are extremely attentive and eager to answer questions regarding Kurdish food, which includes heavy influences of Middle Eastern, Indian, and Mediterranean cuisine. Chicken tawa, a sautéed chicken in lemon with vegetables over rice, is an excellent choice. The biryani (rice with almonds, raisins, vegetables, and spices) is also excellent and quite similar to the Indian dish of the same name. In total, there are almost a dozen entrees for dinner on the menu, and each is served with a choice of soup or salad. Lunches are smaller and less expensive versions of dinner. Babani's serves lunch Monday through Friday and is open for dinner seven days a week.

Latin American

Minneapolis

Conga Latin Bistro $$–$$$
501 East Hennepin Avenue, Minneapolis
(612) 331–3360
www.congalatinbistro.com

Latin American cuisine has experienced a tremendous boom over the past year in the Twin Cities. Several trendy Latin restaurants have opened, but few have the pedigree of Conga. The owners of Conga, the Thunstrom family, are also responsible for the perennially popular south Minneapolis Latin restaurant, El Meson. The nuevo Latino menu features a couple of paellas, the popular Spanish rice and seafood dish, as well as a wide selection of chicken, pork, beef, and seafood items. Other choices include the seafood casserole and Jamaican chicken. The beer and wine list is extensive, and there is also ample opportunity for dancing.

Machu Picchu $$–$$$
2940 Lyndale Avenue South, Minneapolis
(612) 822–2125

Machu Picchu is a Peruvian restaurant that specializes in Latin seafood. Located in the heart of the Lyn-Lake neighborhood, an area overflowing with shopping, theaters, and coffee shops, the restaurant attracts a hip crowd looking for an exotic dining experience. Arroz con mariscos is a featured entree, and the Peruvian paella, which is composed of saffron rice studded with shrimp, clams, squid, mussels, and crab legs, is among the best seafood dishes in the Twin Cities. There are several additional seafood items, including specialty seafood soups. The parihuela is an ocean-full of fresh seafood that includes shrimp, halibut, squid, clams, mussels, and crab legs in a spicy broth. Machu Picchu is open for dinner Tuesday through Saturday.

Machu Picchu in the Lyn-Lake neighborhood of south Minneapolis. PHOTO: TODD R. BERGER

Mexican

Minneapolis

Chiapas Restaurant $
2416 Central Avenue NE, Minneapolis
(612) 789–2971

Chiapas Restaurant serves authentic Mexican food in northeast Minneapolis. Silverio Perez, who also owns the Pancho Villa restaurant in south Minneapolis, operates this 50-seat eatery. The restaurant specialties include chile relleño, enchiladas, and fajitas. Also featured are several vegetarian items. Chiapas is open daily for late breakfast, lunch, and dinner.

El Mariachi Restaurant $
2750 Nicollet Avenue South, Minneapolis
(612) 871–5200

El Mariachi serves up a terrific carne asada, marinated with lots of lime and

grilled to a chewy, charred perfection. They also make a wonderful puerco en salsa verde with citrus-rich tomatillo sauce and delicious tacos filled with pork, chicken, or beef cooked in a variety of ways with homemade tortillas. Friday, Saturday, and Sunday nights you can listen to live Mariachi music while you eat. On Friday night between 9:00 and 10:00 P.M., uninhibited customers can get up and sing with the musicians.

Me Gusta Mexican Cuisine $–$$
1507 East Lake Street, Minneapolis
(612) 724–6007

Me Gusta Mexican Cuisine is a Minneapolis favorite. For decades it has satisfied Twin Citians' needs for authentic

Mexican cuisine. Today, there are numerous authentic Mexican restaurants in the area, but not that long ago Me Gusta was an oasis in a sea of bland, tasteless pseudo-Mexican eateries. The restaurant has introduced many Twin Citians to the savory tastes of Mexico.

Diners receive a complimentary bowl of homemade chips and salsa. Like the rest of the menu, the chips are fresh and the salsa is spicy. Then satisfy your thirst with Mexican beer, wine, or Jarritos, a sweet Mexican soda. The comidas (dinners) are large and are accompanied by refried beans, rice, and lettuce and tomatoes. The menu includes several burrito, fajita, and enchilada dinners and, for more adventurous diners, nopales asados (grilled cactus), the chile relleño, or the enchildas en mole. Several seafood items have recently been added to the menu. Me Gusta is open daily for lunch and dinner.

Pepito's Mexi-Go Deli $
4624 Nicollet Avenue South, Minneapolis
(612) 825–6311
www.pepitosrestaurant.com

At a completely different, sister restaurant, Pepito's owner, Joe Senkyr, played actor Christian Slater's boss in the movie *Untamed Heart*. In reality, Senkyr's small local chain of Mexican restaurants and delis carries an amazing selection of Mexican foods at reasonable prices, including vegetarian enchiladas and tacos, Azteca sandwiches served on teleta-style Mexican bread, huge nacho plates, and quesadillas made with homemade tortillas, all of which are excellent when topped with one of the six fresh made salsas offered at the salad table. You can also take home buckets of pre-prepared ground beef, grilled chicken, bags of homemade corn chips and tortillas, and lots of side dishes and sauces to use at your next get-together.

Taco Morelos $
1515 East Lake Street, Minneapolis
(612) 728–5437
Two additional Twin Cities locations

Taco Morelos serves authentic Mexican cuisine just around the corner from Eat Street. In an area of Minneapolis with numerous authentic Mexican restaurants, Taco Morelos was among the first. The restaurant features tacos, tamales, fajitas, enchiladas, burritos and all the Mexican standards. Wine and beer are also offered at this comfortable and casual restaurant. The restaurant is open daily for lunch and dinner.

Tacqueria Don Blass $–$$
3764 Nicollet Avenue, Minneapolis
(612) 825–5410

Tacqueria Don Blass serves authentic Mexican food in a homey atmosphere. The service is often slow, and the ambience is nothing to write home about, but the food is inexpensive and wholesome. The menu features tortas (Mexican sandwiches), soups, combination platters, and a few seafood items. A lunch buffet is also served and provides an overview of some of the house specialties. Several types of meat are served with rice and beans. Delicious fresh tortillas are also included. The chicken mole is especially tasty. Quesadillas, tamales, and soup are available for a cheap and less filling lunch.

St. Paul

El Burrito Mercado $
175 Concord Street, St. Paul
(651) 227–2192
www.elburritomercado.com

St. Paul's West Side is a historically diverse neighborhood and one of the first Chicano settlements in the Twin Cities. In this enclave, there is a large Mexican grocery, bakery, and the cafeteria-style restaurant, El Burrito Mercado. Tucked in the back of the complex, it does astounding business by serving excellent Mexican food at reasonable prices. Get in line and make a selection from the menu, which features tortas, quesadillas, tamales, tacos, and burritos. After a shorter wait than at many fast-food restaurants, take a seat and enjoy a fine Mexican meal. El Burrito Mercado also serves breakfast, and don't forget to visit their bakery and grocery.

Middle Eastern

Minneapolis

Caspian Bistro & Marketplace $
2418 University Avenue SE, Minneapolis
(612) 623–1113

The Caspian Bistro serves the best kabobs in the Twin Cities. The kabob options include beef, chicken, and lamb accompanied by basmati rice and salad. The menu also includes Middle Eastern treats such as gyro and lamb shank. Since 1986 the restaurant has served the nearby University of Minnesota with scrumptious Persian foods. The adjoining marketplace allows diners to purchase ethnic groceries for home. The 60-seat restaurant is open for lunch and dinner Tuesday through Saturday.

Falafel King $
701 West Lake Street, Minneapolis
(612) 824–7887
Two additional Twin Cities locations

The Falafel King provides Middle Eastern foods in a casual atmosphere. From the counter, diners may select from numerous appetizers, salads, sandwiches, combinations, and dinner entrees. Middle Eastern favorites such as kabobs, hummus, and falafel are served. Fettuccine Alfredo, chicken shish tawk (grilled chicken and vegetables), and foule muddammas (Egyptian fava bean dip) are also featured. The restaurant also serves omelettes, and Greek and Middle Eastern–style breakfasts. The Falafel King is open daily and offers lunch and dinner buffets.

Holy Land Bakery, Grocery & Deli $
2513 Central Avenue NE, Minneapolis
(612) 781–2627

Holy Land is not only one of the best ethnic markets in the area but also serves enormous portions of outstanding Middle Eastern cuisine on a disposable plate. The choices include kabobs, falafel, hummus, spinach pie, shawarma (gyro), and much more. The menu offers large pita sandwiches and much larger dinners, which generally include a salad and rice or hummus paired with one of several meats (shawarma, kabobs, combinations, etc.) and a basket of fresh pita. Select a self-service drink, and there will be plenty of leftovers for less than $10. The shawarma platter is colossal. Plus, there are sampler plates of Middle Eastern cuisine as well as vegetarian meals. The deli offers halal meals to meet the dietary needs of Muslims upon request. Holy Land does not serve alcohol. The busy restaurant provides seating beside the deli and grocery and has additional seating on the second floor. The Holy Land is open daily for lunch and dinner.

Jerusalem's $-$$
1518 Nicollet Avenue South, Minneapolis
(612) 871–8883

Jerusalem's, a perennial Best of the Twin Cities winner among readers of *City Pages,* dishes up the flavors and ambience of the Middle East in a surprisingly intimate atmosphere. The restaurant is topped by a mosquelike onion dome, and stepping inside the otherwise unassuming building on Nicollet Avenue just before the bridge over I-94 will transport you to another world filled with exotic spices, sights, and sounds.

Jerusalem's serves a pan–Middle Eastern menu. Lovers of hummus, kibby (bulgur, beef, onion, and pine nuts), and stuffed grape leaves will find plenty of choices to satisfy their taste buds. Entrees include shawarma (thin slices of spiced beef and lamb), spinach pie, chicken shish kebab, and the lamb curry dinner. Many of the dinner dishes are available in smaller plate or sandwich form for lunchtime diners and take-out.

Desserts are simple but tasty, including baklava and krima. Do not leave the table without a demitasse of Turkish coffee; the restaurant serves a just-sweet-enough version with a floating cardamom seed that is perhaps the best this side of Ankara.

If your schedule allows, come to Jerusalem's on a Friday or Saturday night, when belly dancing wiggles on stage and through the dining room, although be sure to call ahead for reservations; the small restaurant is often packed on those nights. The sword dance is a crowd pleaser, and don't be shy about sticking a few bucks in the myriad elastic bands on the dancer's costume when she shimmies by your table. You'll get a big smile and a few extra wiggles in return.

The Signature Café $-$$
130 Warwick Street SE, Minneapolis
(612) 378-0237

If you are looking for Egyptian cuisine, you'll find it in an unexpected area in Minneapolis. The Signature Café is located in the ritzy Prospect Park neighborhood, where it sits in the middle of a residential block. The cafe's exterior suggests the successions of diners that once occupied this lovely spot. Egyptian music and decorations greet patrons upon entering, and the aromas of the kitchen fill the air. The menu is divided into several sections ranging from lighter fare—salads, soups, and sandwiches—to Egyptian main courses. Also featured are a couple of pasta selections. The options include kofta, falafel, and shawarma. Vegetarians are in luck at the cafe, where almost half the menu satisfies their dietary needs. Koshary, an Egyptian comfort food, is included and is made of garbanzo beans, fried onions, lentils, and tomato sauce served over rice. In addition, there are a few children's menu items. And don't forget the selection of desserts and Egyptian drinks. The Signature Café is open Monday through Saturday for lunch and dinner.

Sindbad Café & Market $-$$
2528 Nicollet Avenue, Minneapolis
(612) 871-6505

Sindbad Café & Market is a Middle Eastern grocery store and restaurant. Food may be ordered for take-out or in the comfortable sit-down restaurant. The menu includes falafel, spinach pie, gyro, and most Middle Eastern favorites, as well as Moroccan couscous. The restaurant also features Turkish coffee, mango drink, hibiscus drink, baklava, and several more dessert and beverage options.

Trieste Café $
10 South Fifth Street, Minneapolis
(612) 333-4658

Trieste Café is an international eatery with flair. The beverage list is extensive, with several types of coffee, lemonade, mineral waters, malts, and shakes. The menu also has hot hoagies, subs, international favorites, and salads. The international favorites are where the Trieste Café shines. The gyro is of particular note and recognized by many as one of the best in the Twin Cities. Other international items include hummus, falafel, spanakopita, and tabbouleh salad. The Trieste Café occupies a small, cramped space on the ground floor of the historic Lumber Exchange building and is open from breakfast until 6:00 P.M. on weekdays. Hurry over before the end of rush hour, when the Trieste's doors close, and enjoy one of the best gyros in town.

North

El Bustan $-$$
4757 Central Avenue NE, Columbia Heights
(763) 502-8888

As the Twin Cities Middle Eastern population has grown, restaurants like El Bustan have appeared to meet the needs of this burgeoning community. The Columbia Heights restaurant features halal foods (in accordance with Islamic dietary laws), no alcohol, and a shisha, a traditional water pipe. The menu is an extensive survey of Middle Eastern standards and includes delicious hummus, kabobs, and shrimp sayyadiya. The dish is a spicy combination of shrimp in tomato sauce served over a bed of rice. El Bustan is open daily and accepts Visa and MasterCard.

The Olive Tree Restaurant and Market $
3700 Central Avenue NE, Columbia Heights
(763) 782-9900

The Olive Tree offers Middle Eastern fare at rock-bottom prices. Two people can easily eat a filling lunch for less than $10. The menu is composed of salads, appetizers, sandwiches, and entrees. It ranges from Middle Eastern favorites like shawarma, kabobs, and falafel, to lamb chops and chicken musahab, a Cornish hen marinated and charbroiled in a special sauce. The deli is cramped next to the market, but the lunch bargains more than make up for this slight inconvenience.

Nepali and Tibetan

St. Paul

Everest on Grand
1278 Grand Avenue, St. Paul
(651) 696–1666
www.hotmomo.com

Everest on Grand fills a much-needed spot in Twin Cities cuisine, serving Nepali and Tibetan dishes to tuna casserole-leaning Midwesterners. The restaurant specializes in Tibetan momos, tasty steamed dumplings mixed with vegetables, pork and turkey, or yak. Nepali specialties include a variety of vegetarian and meat or fish (chicken, goat, lamb, cod, or shrimp) curries and daal-bhatt, traditional Nepali combination meals. During the week the restaurant features a lunch buffet, allowing patrons to sample many of the kitchen's Himalayan dishes at a set price.

North African

Minneapolis

Asase-Yaa Organic Juices and Foods
2922 Bryant Avenue South, Minneapolis
(612) 821–6484

This cozy little restaurant/cafe is a great place to stop for lunch when in northeast Minneapolis. The food is North African inspired, with myriad changing chicken and vegetable-based dishes and soups, doled out in extremely generous portions with a large side of rice and mixed fresh vegetables to round your meal out. The menu also includes coffee, espresso, and more than 20 different kinds of fresh-made fruit smoothies (including mango-banana) and a wide selection of fresh-made veggie juices ranging from carrot to wheat

grass juice. For customers who feel like hanging around after their meal to properly digest, there's a chess set and a backgammon set on hand to entertain while you do so.

Puerto Rican

Puerta Azul $–$$
1811 Selby Avenue, St. Paul
(651) 646–7003

This friendly, beautifully lit and decorated restaurant is considered by many a St. Paul treasure, serving a small but enticing menu of Puerto Rican food that leaves customers waffling between exactly what to get and coming back to try whatever it was they didn't get the last time. Chef Sonia Gonzales Sadr grew up in Puerto Rico, and the wonderful dishes served at Puerta Azul are either from traditional recipes or her own variations. The base of many is sofrito, a blend of garlic, onions, green pepper, cilantro and tomato, which stands out in the arroz con pollo and the beans and rice. Sofrito-flavored beans or fried plantain are served with most entrees, such as their excellent pork kebabs or roast marinated in garlic and ginger, marinated sliced beef fried with onions, and fish in Spanish sauce. Using a sweeter base is the mango chicken and the guava chicken dishes, which are also as close to perfect as you can get. For dessert, the coconut mango ice cream is sweet and refreshing, while the cream cheese flan with homemade caramel sauce is indescribably delicious. The restaurant serves beer and wine. Puerta Azul is open daily for lunch and dinner and accepts Visa and MasterCard only.

Scandinavian

Minneapolis

Aquavit
80 South Eighth Street (IDS Center Crystal Court), Minneapolis
(612) 343–3333
www.aquavit.org

Ranked by *Gourmet* magazine as one of the top 50 restaurants in the country, Aquavit is, arguably, the finest restaurant in the Twin Cities. Named after the Scandinavian fruit- or herb-flavored aperitif (numerous choices of the specialty are on the drink menu), Aquavit serves Scandinavian cuisine in a space with a crisp, modern ambience. Sample specialties include rare seared tuna and scallops with braised bok choy and shiitake mushrooms, smoked duck breast, and foie gras ganache, as well as a six-course tasting menu. The waitstaff is extremely attentive; among other touches, it is standard for the waiter or waitress to fold the patron's napkin and place it over the chair arm if the customer steps away from the table to use the rest room. An extensive, extremely well-chosen wine list complements the menu, and the desserts are truly something to behold. Aquavit is open for lunch and dinner Monday through Saturday, and reservations are recommended.

Seafood

Minneapolis

McCormick & Schmick's Seafood Restaurant $$$
800 Nicollet Mall, Minneapolis
(612) 338-3300

The best downtown happy-hour food is to be found in the bar here from 4:00 to 6:00 P.M. and again from 10:00 to 11:00 P.M., as that's when a couple of bucks will get you a luscious pan of mussels, a cheeseburger with fries, or a fish taco plate. The restaurant's dark rich wood, shiny brass, and sparkling beveled glass decor sets off the Tiffany-style stained-glass ceiling beautifully, making this the place to take people you want to impress. Fresh seafood is flown in twice daily: scallops from Florida, swordfish from Hawaii, and oysters from British Columbia, and the menu includes big and beautiful Dungeness crab and bay shrimp cakes with red pepper aioli, fresh oysters, and excellent clam chowder.

Oceanaire Seafood Room $$$$
1300 Nicollet Mall (in the Hyatt Regency Hotel), Minneapolis
(612) 333-2277

A sidecar, clams casino, and lobster thermidor are just a few factors that make up the Oceanaire's decor. The fish here is all fresh, flown in daily from both coasts, and, depending on the catch(es) of the day, the restaurant serves meals like black bass in black butter; a zesty cioppino boasting an immense catch of mussels, clams, shrimp, and fish; yellowfin tuna with wild mushrooms and rich red-wine sauce; Chilean sea bass; and a fantastic oyster bar. The menu changes daily, according to what's available, and the fish fresh on any given day are identified at the top of the menu with a check mark.

Seafood Palace Chinese Restaurant $-$$
2523 Nicollet Avenue, Minneapolis
(612) 874-7721

As Chinese restaurants have diversified over the past decade, several specialty restaurants have opened. The Seafood Palace Chinese Restaurant has met the need for fresh seafood. The restaurant's menu begins with extremely reasonable lunch specials, then moves on to the dinner specialties, which include shrimp, scallops, mussels, lobster, and crab as well as traditional Chinese favorites like fried crispy duck, sweet and sour pork, and vegetarian dishes such as bean curd with brown sauce and mushrooms with Chinese cabbage. Dinner prices are inexpensive for seafood, especially for lobster and Vancouver Dungeness crab, and both are served in black bean sauce. Shrimp choices are numerous and include chow fun, honey-walnut, fried rice, lo mein, black bean sauce, and many more.

St. Paul

Mac's Fish & Chips $
1330 Larpenteur Avenue West, St. Paul
(651) 489-5299

Mac's is tiny, none-too-fancy, and takeout oriented, but for fish-and-chips that would make a Londoner proud, it is a must-visit restaurant in the Twin Cities. Mac's specializes in halibut fillets, and the lightly breaded deep-fried fish pieces seem as light as clouds and taste otherworldly. You can get the best deal if you buy a basket, which includes halibut fillets, shrimp, chicken strips, or a combination thereof, along with fries, coleslaw, bread, and a beverage. You can also buy the halibut fillets and shrimp by the piece, chicken strips in six-strip servings, half and full orders of fries, and plenty of slaw, allowing you to customize the size of your meal. Mac's harbors a few tables in its dining room, but it is best to call ahead and pick up your order, heading back to your hotel or home with a basket or two of fish-and-chips for a low-key, inexpensive, filling feast.

Southwestern

Minneapolis

Bar Abilene $–$$
1300 Lagoon Avenue, Minneapolis
(612) 825–2525

The flavors of the Southwest are available in the Twin Cities at Bar Abilene. Located in the Uptown neighborhood of Minneapolis, the restaurant does brisk business and draws a hip clientele. For starters the menu features Texas tapas that include potato chipotle gouda flautas, Maryland blue crab-corn quesadillas, and tortilla soup. Dinner is divided into burgers and Southwestern specialties. The burgers include several restaurant specialties such as the Hill Country Burger, which combines mild green chili and Monterey jack cheese on an onion bun. The restaurant's other specialties range from the savory jalapeño skewered shrimp to the wild mushroom quesadillas.

West

Tejas $$
3910 West 50th Street, Edina
(952) 926–0800
www.tejasrestaurant.com

Tejas is a casual, rustic, eclectic restaurant serving Southwestern-influenced dishes. House specialties include the chicken burrito with mango/habañero sauce, braised lamb shank with horseradish whipped potatoes, and wood-roasted beef tenderloin with barbecue béarnaise sauce and cayenne onion rings. Closed Sunday, Tejas is open for lunch and dinner every other day of the week.

Spanish

Minneapolis

El Meson $–$$
3450 Lyndale Avenue South, Minneapolis
(612) 822–8062

El Meson features Spanish and Caribbean cuisine in a relaxed, comfortable atmosphere. A few popular dishes include the arroz con mariscos (rice with seafood) and the paellas (a Spanish rice and seafood dish). In addition, the restaurant serves various chicken and pork dishes with savory rice and beans. For lunch the restaurant offers an ever-popular buffet of home-style Latin favorites. The restaurant has repeatedly received kudos for its delicious, nutritious cuisine. El Meson also serves beer and wine.

La Bodega Tapas Bar $$–$$$
3005 Lyndale Avenue South, Minneapolis
(612) 823–2661

Tapas, a small Spanish food dish, have become a trendy cuisine nationally. The Twin Cities' first tapas bar, La Bodega is a popular restaurant in the Lyn-Lake neighborhood of south Minneapolis. The tapas are small portions, and the majority of diners purchase at least two or three. Seafood is featured prominently among the tapas choices, which include fried calamari and garlic shrimp. The restaurant offers extensive wine selections to accompany the tapas as well as Spanish flamenco music and dancing on weekends. La Bodega is open daily for lunch and dinner.

Sri Lankan

Sri Lanka Restaurant $$–$$$
3226 West Lake Street, Minneapolis
(612) 926–0110

This lovely restaurant specializes in the bounty of tastes from Sri Lanka, where fresh fruits, vegetables, meats, and spices are combined to make some of the most exciting dishes in the area. A warning to those who are inexperienced with Sri Lankan cuisine: Spice is very important. However, the cooks will spice the dishes to meet diners' tastes. Seafood and vegetarian items are prominent among the menu choices. The malu curry is a complex combination of halibut or salmon with Asian mustard and vegetables. The Harak Mas Mallum is one of several dishes served exclusively at the restaurant. The dish is composed of sliced beef and vegetables, which are flavored by an imported fish from the Maldive Islands. Several roti (breads) and noodle entrees are also offered. The restaurant also serves a brunch on Friday, Saturday, and Sunday. The brunch is one of the best in the area and features salads, meats, vegetables, and desserts. The range of flavors and combinations of tastes are astounding. Besides brunch, Sri Lanka Restaurant is open daily for dinner; reservations are recommended.

Thai

St. Paul

Pad Thai Grand Café $–$$
1659 Grand Avenue, St. Paul
(651) 690–1393
www.padthaigrandcafe.com

Pad Thai Grand Café specializes in authentic Thai food in a beautifully decorated restaurant. The decor is loaded with Thai elephant motifs, murals, and lots of plants. Red is abundant and complements the exposed brick. Besides the lovely indoor dining space, outdoor seating is also available.

The food at the Pad Thai Grand Café also includes some excellent items. The spring rolls are delicious and unique and come with a tangy spicy fish sauce. The pad Thai, their specialty, is also superb. A wonderful mixture of contrasting flavors are melded together including rice noodles, bean sprouts, onions, ground peanuts, and lemon. The menu also includes many seafood and vegetarian options as well as a wine list. The service is friendly, and the chef will spice dishes according to patrons' desired heat level. Pad Thai is open Monday through Saturday for lunch and dinner and Sunday for dinner only.

Ruam Mit Thai Café $–$$
475 St. Peter Street, St. Paul
(651) 290–0067

Ruam Mit Thai Café is tucked into a quiet stretch of St. Peter Street in downtown St. Paul, near the Fitzgerald Theatre and the Minnesota Children's Museum. The restaurant, which opened in 1989, is considered by many the finest Thai restaurant in the Twin Cities. The menu includes many Thai favorites, such as spring rolls, pad Thai, roast duck curry, and bamboo shoot salad. The restaurant serves beer and wine and is open for lunch and dinner Monday through Saturday. During weekdays the restaurant serves a very popular lunch buffet.

Taste of Thailand $
1671 Selby Avenue, St. Paul
(651) 644–3997
1753 Old Hudson Road, St. Paul
(651) 774–6905
7890 University Avenue NE, Fridley
(763) 571–1188

The main location of Taste of Thailand, in a residential area on Selby Avenue west of Snelling Avenue in St. Paul, won't wow you with its intimate atmosphere. But for what the restaurant lacks in ambience, it more than makes up for with its extensive menu of wonderful Thai dishes. The restaurant has all the classics, including oh-so-light spring rolls, fiery miang kham, the house specialty tom yum soup, and the ever-popular pad Thai. Other notable dishes include pad goong, pad med mamnang himaphane, and gaeng ped pla. If it's summertime, wash it all down with a glass of Thai lemonade.

North

Royal Orchid $–$$
2401 Fairview Avenue, Roseville, MN
(651) 639–9999
www.thebestthaifood.com
Royal Orchid serves authentic Thai cuisine in a restaurant decorated in subdued pastel purple and lilac with a few murals featuring elephants and other Thai motifs. Beyond the pleasant ambience, Royal Orchid creates unique Thai cuisine. Instead of cooking with cliché tastes and using shortcuts, the Royal Orchid marries complex spices, vegetables, and meats. The masmon curry is like no other because of just this. Besides the pad Thai and curries, the menu includes several interesting salads, such as the Moslem salad, which includes lettuce, cucumber, scallion, tofu, peanut dressing, and sweet potato chips. The entree selection is also extensive. Pineapple rice and Thai-flavor fish are two standouts. Also available are beef, chicken, pork, tofu, scallops, and shrimp, which all can be prepared with eight different sauce choices, from garlic to saffron curry, satay, and mock ginger chili with green beans. Royal Orchid accepts Visa and Master-Card only and is open for lunch and dinner Monday through Saturday.

Vietnamese

Minneapolis

Camdi Chinese-Vietnamese Restaurant $
1325 Fourth Street SE, Minneapolis
(612) 331–4194
Camdi Chinese-Vietnamese Restaurant's daily lunch special is one of the best bargains in the Twin Cities. For under $4.00 diners may select one of the specials, which include curry chicken, Vietnamese chow mein, hot and spicy chicken, sweet and sour chicken, Buddha's delight (a vegetarian dish), and several more choices.

The lunch specials are big and tasty. The menu includes a number of larger dinners and wonderful egg rolls with fish sauce. The small, humble restaurant has served the Dinkytown neighborhood (next to the University of Minnesota) for years with its inexpensive Vietnamese cuisine.

The Lotus Restaurant $
313 Southeast Oak Street, Minneapolis
(612) 331–1781
Three additional Twin Cities locations
Each Lotus location has its own unique character, and this location reflects its proximity to the University of Minnesota. For starters the Lotus has many fine options, especially the egg rolls and spring rolls. The menu includes favorites such as Vietnamese beef salad and curried chicken Vietnamese-style. Lunch specials are also offered; the Mustard Chicken is particularly good and includes chicken and onions in a spicy mustard sauce. The Lotus Restaurant is closed Monday but provides a casual environment for lunch and dinner the rest of the week.

Lucky Dragon Riverside Restaurant $–$$
1827 Riverside Avenue, Minneapolis
(612) 375–1690
Lucky Dragon specializes in reasonably priced Vietnamese and Chinese fare. Lucky Dragon's menu includes soups, combination meals, noodles, stir-fried entrees, and numerous Vietnamese specialties. There are many vegetarian items available, and the entire menu contains no MSG. There is also a large lunch and dinner buffet Monday through Friday. Lucky Dragon features one of the best Vietnamese buffets in the Twin Cities. The egg rolls, hot and spicy chicken, and beef in black bean sauce are exceptional and usually available with the buffet.

Quang Restaurant $–$$
2719 Nicollet Avenue South, Minneapolis
(612) 870–4739
The Quang Restaurant has received local and national attention for innovative versions of traditional Vietnamese cuisine. The *New York Times* praised the restaurant

as one of the best restaurants for business travelers, which came as no surprise to many Twin Citians. The hip restaurant serves fine renditions of Vietnamese favorites. Popular menu items include caramelized lemongrass chicken, grilled pork chops, and the seafood noodle soups. In addition to fine versions of egg rolls and spring rolls, the menu features such dishes as grilled sugarcane shrimp (banh hoi choi). The restaurant does not serve alcohol. The Quang Restaurant is closed Tuesday and open for lunch and dinner the rest of the week.

St. Paul

Saigon Restaurant & Bakery $
601 University Avenue West, St. Paul
(651) 225-8751

The Saigon Restaurant is the best and most affordable authentic Vietnamese restaurant in the Twin Cities. The specialties are pho and banh mi. Pho, the national dish of Vietnam, is a huge bowl of soup. It includes vegetables, noodles, and a choice of meats from roast pork to several delicious seafood combinations. Another signature dish at the Saigon Restaurant is the banh mi, a savory Vietnamese sandwich composed of pâté, cilantro, cucumber, Vietnamese mayo, and any of a number of meats combined on a fresh baguette. There is a deli counter where banh mi and baked goods are available for take-out, all at incredibly low prices.

Vina Highland Vietnamese Restaurant $
756 Cleveland Avenue South, St. Paul
(651) 698-8408
Two additional Twin Cities locations

The casual Vina serves delicious, inexpensive dishes. The menu is filled with Vietnamese favorites such as curry shrimp, egg roll salad, and hot and spicy chicken. The hot and spicy chicken is an excellent rendition of the Vietnamese favorite and it is composed of chicken with onions, lemongrass, and red peppers. All items are spiced to order and contain no MSG. For lunch, Vina features more inexpensive combination meals, where the Chinese menu items are an important part. Vina is

open seven days a week for lunch and dinner. There are two additional locations in the Twin Cities with slightly different hours and menu items. They are Vina Vietnamese Restaurant (6401 Nicollet Avenue, Richfield; 612-866-5034) and Vina Plus (1821 University Avenue, St. Paul; 651-644-1384).

South

Kimson Vietnamese Cuisine $
8654 Lyndale Avenue South, Bloomington
(952) 885-0230

Kimson is another one of the excellent Vietnamese restaurants in the Twin Cities. With more than 200 items, there are plenty of pork, chicken, beef, tofu, seafood, and vegetarian selections available. Vietnamese favorites including hot and spicy chicken, sautéed beef over fried potatoes, curry chicken, and egg rolls are offered. Plus, the menu serves extensive vegetarian items and six types of eggplant, e.g., curry eggplant and eggplant with bean curd, broccoli, and celery. There are nearly a dozen tofu entrees, which range from chow mein and sweet and sour to ginger bean curd. Kimson is open daily for lunch and dinner.

Kinhdo Restaurant $
6345 Penn Avenue South, Richfield
(612) 861-2491
2755 Hennepin Avenue, Minneapolis
(612) 870-1295
2709 Winnetka Avenue North, New Hope
(763) 544-8490

If you enjoy excellent Vietnamese cuisine, there are numerous opportunities in the Twin Cities. Kinhdo Restaurant has three unique Twin Cities locations, but all serve excellent renditions of Vietnamese cuisine as well as a few favorite Chinese food items. The Richfield restaurant reflects its decidedly working-class neighborhood by featuring a popular daily lunch and dinner buffet. The menu features numerous exceptional values on Vietnamese favorites like hot and spicy chicken, beef and potatoes, and egg rolls with fish sauce. The menu also features such Chinese items as chow mein, egg foo young, and a great version of sweet and sour chicken. Kinhdo Restaurant (Richfield) is open daily for lunch and dinner.

Sweets and Treats

Minneapolis

Award Baking International $
1101 Northeast Stinson Boulevard, Suite 3, Minneapolis
(612) 331–3523 or (800) 333–3523
www.oblaten.com

Award Baking International is the place to go to get oblaten—those thin, crisp, delicately flavored cookies that upscale ice cream parlors serve with sundaes—as well as biscotti, both of which are made by Award Baking. The little store—hidden behind a nondescript door in the side of a warehouse building—also carries a good selection of teas and imported English fruit candies and licorice.

Caruso's Gelato Cafe $
3001 Hennepin Avenue South, Calhoun Square, Minneapolis
(612) 822–2629

The gelato fad has finally reached the Midwest, and Caruso's promises to be only the first of many such cafes to spring up throughout the Twin Cities. Caruso's carries more than 30 flavors of the creamy, sticky Italian dessert, including chocolate chip, cappuccino, mango, coconut, strawberry cheesecake, lemon, banana, and tiramisu, which can be carried out either in a waffle cone or in a cup.

Dairy Sales Room Store $
Andrew Boss Meat Science Building
University of Minnesota
1354 Eckles Avenue, St. Paul

If your timing is right, you can find some of the best ice cream and cheeses in the Twin Cities in this little-known and rarely open outlet on the University of Minnesota's St. Paul Campus. Open only 3:00 to 5:00 P.M. Wednesdays, customers line up early to get their hands on excess dairy products produced by university students and researchers. Don't worry, no failed experiments make it to the sales floor, and if you're willing to make the effort to find the store, you will be treated to rich (12 percent fat!) and creamy ice cream in a variety of flavors and a range of cheeses, the weekly selection depending on what is available from the university's work and the time of year. The store may (or may not) have on hand such favorites as Gopher Gold (French vanilla and raspberry), aged cheddar, and Nuworld, a spreadable variety of blue cheese that is all white. Quantities available for sale are always limited: Arrive early for the best selection.

Livingston's Organic Ice Cream and Coffee $
2037 Riverside Avenue, Minneapolis
(612) 333–5692

This parlor is committed to supporting sustainable agriculture and family farming, and makes its ice cream from a single herd of family-owned dairy cows. The ice cream is made in the shop and in only two flavors: absolutely amazing vanilla and Ghirardelli chocolate. The creamy delicacy is sold by the weight, not the number of scoops. Livingston's also sells a good variety of homemade danishes, cookies, brownies, and gourmet coffee.

Sebastian Joe's $
1007 Franklin Avenue West, Minneapolis
(612) 870–0065

When Italian immigrant Sebastiano Pellizer arrived in the Twin Cities in the 1930s, he was almost immediately rechristened Joe by his employer, a construction-crew chief. The moniker stuck, and in 1984 when his grandchildren Mike and Todd founded this ice cream shop, Sebastiano gave them permission to use his name. Sebastian Joe's has become nearly synonymous with handmade ice cream in the Twin Cities. The ice cream list tops 80 flavors (15 daily) and includes both new spins and old favorites, such as basil-strawberry, chocolate, fresh strawberry, vanilla made from ground vanilla beans, ginger-cream, and cayenne pepper–laced Chocolate Coyote.

Wuollet Bakery $
2447 Hennepin Avenue, Minneapolis
(612) 381–9400
1080 Grand Avenue, St. Paul
(651) 292–9035
Two additional Twin Cities locations
What began more than 70 years ago as a neighborhood bread-baking concern grew to include cakes, pastries, and a following. Yet Wuollet is still a family-run bakery, watched over by two brothers, their uncle, and a cousin. In the hands of Wuollet's cake artists, traditional white-on-white wedding cakes can ascend to seven tiers covered in white chocolate ropes, orchids, and other amazements, while soufflé cakes featuring genoise (egg-rich sponge cake) disappear under drifts of Bavarian cream. A sweets table covered in profiteroles, fancy French pastries, cheesecake, and trifle is a reception addition that uses Wuollet's skills to their tastiest advantage. Wuollet also offers chocolate long johns smothered in rich chocolate frosting, brownies, and blondies so buttery they melt on the tongue like the richest fudge or caramel. They also sell delicious doughnuts and princess tortes layered in Bavarian cream and raspberry preserves.

St. Paul

Café Latte $
850 Grand Avenue, St. Paul
(651) 224–5687
Look no further than Café Latte to find the ultimate in cheesecakes in a myriad of flavors, including their Tin Roof Cheesecake with layers of nuts and chocolate. Latte is renowned for its decadent turtle cake—dark chocolate cake layers separated by and topped with buttery caramel and pecans, as well as their tart key lime pies, raspberry marzipan, thick scones served with crème fraiche, jams, and fresh fruit and fudge tarts.

Grand Ole Creamery $
750 Grand Avenue, St. Paul
(651) 293–1655
The Grand Ole Creamery has been creating some of the most imaginative and delicious ice cream flavors in its parlor since 1984. And the flavors, including Irish coffee eggnog and chocolate malt banana, aren't just interesting experiments in flavor, they're also very, very good.

The store serves up to 32 flavors from a master list of more than 100, and customers can satisfy their chocolate, strawberry, or vanilla cravings or get reckless with unusual flavors such as black walnut, cinnamon, and sweet cream. At the bottom of each ice cream cone is a malted milk ball lovingly placed so that the ice cream doesn't leak out onto your shirt. The prices (around $4.00 for a single-scoop waffle cone) are a little high but well worth the extra expense to true ice cream connoisseurs. The store also makes thick, rich malts and shakes, banana splits, and sundaes. During the dog days of summer, folks line up out the door to indulge in this stuff.

Grand Ole Creamery on Grand Avenue in St. Paul. PHOTO: TODD R. BERGER

Izzy's Ice Cream Cafe $
2034 Marshall Avenue, St. Paul
(651) 603–1458
www.izzysicecream.com

This 16-seat ice creamery, open since 2000, is sparse and clean, with outdoor seating and tables for kids. The store serves an amazing variety of homemade ice cream, including lemon raisin bar, blueberry cheesecake yogurt, granola, chocolate cherry, ginger, hazelnut, pistachio, crème de menthe, pineapple, Oreo cookie, and coffee ice cream that's flecked with coffee grounds. The beauty of it all is that if there's another flavor that you weren't really sure on but would like to try, you can ask the server to make that flavor your izzy—a small scoop added to the top of your first choice. If you're not in the mood for a homemade waffle cone, you can order a malt, shake, float, sundae, or an egg cream. Izzy's is closed from Thanksgiving to March 1.

Just Truffles $
1326 Grand Avenue, St. Paul
(651) 690–0075

Like its name, this store carries just truffles: thick, rich, gigantic homemade chocolate truffles kept in a refrigerated glass case until purchase. Originally located in the famous St. Paul Hotel, this store sells its chocolates to locals and celebrities passing through (their autographed pictures line the walls of the confectionery) in dozens of flavors, including champagne, peanut butter, Kahlua, and raspberry. Their edible chocolate boxes are a special and delicious way to send the truffles as a gift.

Regina's Candy Kitchen & Store $
2073 St. Clair Avenue, St. Paul
(651) 698–8603
1905 South Robert Street,
Southview Square,
West St. Paul
(651) 455–8864

Founded in 1926 by a young Greek craftsman and his bride, Regina, and passed on to their children and grandchildren, Regina's uses Old World craftsmanship in making its amazing (and amazingly inexpensive) caramels, chocolates, toffees, and more than 20 flavors of dark chocolate truffles. You can't tell from the nondescript painted-brick building that Regina's Candies is much more than a hole-in-the-wall with a block-letter sign on the bright blue awning, but inside you'll find a timeless candy-filled shop with enough kinds of chocolates to make your head spin.

Taste of Scandinavia Catering and Bakery
$
2232 Carter Avenue, St. Paul
(651) 645–9181
9900 Valley Creek Road, Woodbury
(651) 501–0807
845 Village Center Drive, North Oaks
(651) 482–8876

This charming European bakery is tucked under the other businesses in the Tudor-style Carter Square. Luscious desserts spin inside a glass case—the strawberry torte layers yellow sponge cake separated by chocolate mousse, fresh banana slices, and raspberry preserves and is covered in strawberries and peaks of cream. Sweets from elegantly decorated layer cakes to muffins and cookies to Finnish cinnamon pulla can also be found. On late afternoons, the bakery offers many half-price deals, so stop in late and indulge yourself.

Coffeehouses and Teashops

Minneapolis

Acadia Café $
1931 Nicollet Avenue, Minneapolis
(612) 874–8702

If you weren't hungry when you first walked in, a few seconds of standing by the counter and inhaling all the wonderful scents of fresh chocolate croissants and cookies baking is sure to start your stomach rumbling. Aside from all the coffee and espresso drinks you could ever want, Acadia makes fresh soups, sandwiches, store-made bread, yogurt parfaits, and homemade Belgian waffles with fruit and whipped cream that are worth waking up early for. There's lots of comfortable seating and large tables for eating, too, making this more than just a place to drop by to grab a cup of coffee and a quick bite to eat.

Recorded light jazz and blues fill the open, airy coffeehouse, where owner and commercial photographer Tom Berthiaume displays his black-and-white portraits against exposed-brick walls. If you'd like to see more artwork, a full-fledged gallery with changing shows is connected.

Blue Moon Coffee Café $
3822 East Lake Street, Minneapolis
(612) 721 9230

Everything about the Blue Moon breathes comfort and relaxation. The soothing purple and blue color scheme and sparkling strings of white and colored Christmas lights make the cafe the perfect place for a calming evening of quiet revitalization. There are many coffee drinks on the menu and a choice of eight different kinds of coffee, 20 types of tea, homemade biscotti, pastries, sandwiches, and a big ice cream cooler that carries Häagen-Dazs bars and other treats. Outside seating is available, but the large selection of comfy couches is hard to resist even on the nicest summer evenings.

Bob's Java Hut $
2651 Lyndale Avenue South, Minneapolis
(612) 871-4485

This funky little coffeeshop stays open past midnight in the summer months and closes earlier depending on how many customers are hanging around in the winter. Don't be intimidated by the rough-looking crowd that hangs out here—they're mostly just art students with time on their hands and a budget that includes copious amounts of hair dye. The menu is mostly coffee drinks and juice, with a few baked goods for the morning and lunch crowds. The house specialty is Kool-Aid. No one else in town bothers putting it on their menu, and lots of people who come here order it. On warm days and nights, the large storefront window rolls back to let fresh air and conversation from the outside patio in.

Dunn Bros. Coffee $
201 Third Avenue South, Minneapolis
(612) 692-8530

This old brick warehouse building is the home of one of the nicer Dunn Bros. coffeehouses in town (there are about two dozen throughout the Twin Cities), with live music most summer weekend nights and a beautiful, comfortable interior, furnished with large potted plants that make it feel like it's springtime year-round. The best thing about the coffee shop, however, is the location—attached to the Milwaukee Road building, an indoor ice-skating rink/farmers' market (depending on season) that was once a train depot and was only recently renovated and opened to the public. The shop serves all the coffee and espresso drinks you could want as well as cookies, muffins, and a changing menu of other treats, depending on the mood of the staff.

Europe@n Grind $
815 Washington Avenue SE, Minneapolis
(612) 331-7700

This is the coolest of the University of Minnesota–neighborhood coffeehouses. The decor is strangely futuristic-looking, with mock Louis VIII–style furniture—elegant high-backed loveseats and armchairs and heavy, ancient-looking coffeetables—paired with fully loaded PCs and framed prints of European churches and German train schedules hanging on the walls. You can also buy guidebooks on traveling through Europe here, Eurail and youth hostel passes, plane tickets, and general transatlantic info. The Grind offers Internet access for about $5.00 an hour as well as Internet accounts for customers. The rest rooms are large, with hand-painted designs on the walls, and the toilet lids are shaped and painted like acoustic guitar bodies. The shop is also divided into smoking and nonsmoking sections, with the smoking section well enough away from the front counter so that you don't actually have to pass through it to order your food and drinks. Lots of different coffee and espresso drinks are included in the menu, as well as more than a dozen flavors of syrup shots for those with an extreme sweet tooth. There's also home-made soup, cookies, and fruit smoothies made in the kitchen.

La Société du Thé $
2708 Lyndale Avenue South, Minneapolis
(612) 871–5148

This well-stocked, comfortable teahouse offers 130 varieties of specialty and whole-leaf teas, ranging from $20 to $200 per pound. The helpful staff gives careful instructions about heating water, steeping time, and the story behind each particular type of tea, all of which are preserved in air-tight canisters. Come in for a soothing cup of boiled leaves—come away understanding at least part of the spiritual art of making and drinking tea.

May Day Café $
3440 Bloomington Avenue South,
Minneapolis
(612) 729–5627

Situated in the old Powderhorn Co-Op grocery spot just off the edge of Powderhorn Park, this small, cozy place is remarkable for its quality coffee and wonderful sweet breads (sweet potato pound cake, cranberry, and zucchini bread in season).

Muddy Waters $
2401 Lyndale Avenue South, Minneapolis
(612) 872–2232

This long-established coffeehouse, furnished like a college student's first apartment, caters specifically to the quirky hipster crowd, with menu items like Pop Tarts and Spaghetti-Os. There's lots of indoor seating, and in the summertime the crowds of caffeine addicts spill out to fill the tables spread out in front of the building. Saturday morning cartoons are often featured on the TV screens.

Pandora's Cup $
2516 Hennepin Avenue South, Minneapolis
(612) 381–0700

This old two-story house-turned-cafe in Uptown offers two roomy front porches (one downstairs, one upstairs) that look out onto the bustle of Hennepin Avenue. The cozy rooms inside are crowded with mismatched kitchen and living-room furniture, video games, bookshelves, local artwork, and chain-smoking teens and twenty-somethings. Pandora's Cup has a full coffee/espresso menu, lots of loose teas, a wide selection of lesser-known soda pops, including Rat Bastard Root Beer, sandwiches (tomato, basil pesto, and cheese; peanut butter and jelly), vegetarian soups, and a pile of cookies and muffins. With tons of great music on their 100-CD changer, Pandora's has become a home away from home for urban and suburban teenagers, who crowd the modest space at night.

Purple Onion $
326 14th Avenue SE, Minneapolis
(612) 378–7763

This low-frills coffeehouse revels somewhat in its hipness, with loud alternative music playing at all times on the stereo and purposefully blank walls offsetting the large, comfortable, and insular wooden booths and tables (perfect for reading or studying) that may or may not have been left over from the diner that was once here. The shop is divided into two large smoking and nonsmoking sections, separated by a short flight of stairs. This is almost strictly a coffee/espresso-serving establishment, with just a few other items on the menu.

Sister's Sludge Coffee Café $
4557 Bloomington Avenue South, Minneapolis
(612) 722–3933
330 2nd Avenue South, Minneapolis
(612) 371–4395

This funky little neighborhood coffeehouse serves a wide variety of coffee, espresso, and chai drinks to patrons either crowded into the small shop or spread out comfortably among the tables set outside. The menu is small and consists mostly of Rice Krispie bars, muffins, and cookies, but it's a comfortable place to spend an afternoon or catch a cup of coffee before officially starting your day.

Windom Park Café $
1903 Northeast Johnson Street, Minneapolis
(612) 781–7817
www.wpcafe.com

Like most of the Windom Park neighborhood, the Windom Park Café is small and unassuming on the outside. Once inside, however, you'll see this is more than just a place to stop by for a quick cup of overheated coffee. The main room of the shop is large enough for six or seven well-spaced small tables, while off in the far corner, two computer terminals are set up for customers to check their e-mail or just to sit and work. The menu of the café is pretty extensive, too, offering a wide selection of homemade sandwiches, soups, smoothies, quesadillas, and salads all day—and, if you call in a $25 order, they'll deliver food and drinks right to your door. Of course, they have all the espresso drinks and coffee specialties that are standard to today's coffeehouses. The main difference here is that this place is really trying to be a community hangout—and doing a good job of making their customers feel right at home.

St. Paul

Bean Counter Coffee Company $
769 Cleveland Avenue South, St. Paul
(651) 699-5448

Since 1993, Bean Counter Coffee Co. has been a local coffee distributor as well as a great neighborhood coffeehouse. The Highland Park establishment has worked hard to integrate itself into the culture of its classy St. Paul neighborhood, providing both a wonderful selection of baked goods, including homemade caramel rolls and filled croissants, sandwiches, coffee and espresso drinks, and an increasing roster of reasons to just hang out and enjoy the atmosphere. The shop holds drawings weekly to see which lucky patron gets a prize of either free food or coffee, and there are lots of daily lunch specials to lure people in from work. They're extremely kid-friendly, too, and have two or three tiny kid-size tables and chairs as well as a huge stack of coloring books and drawing pads on hand for any children that come in. For adults, there are regular tables and chairs as well as some extremely comfortable couches and armchairs to lounge around on.

Brewberry's—The Coffee Place $
475 Fairview Avenue South, St. Paul
(651) 699-1117

Located across the street from the College of St. Catherine, this coffeehouse has a huge and loyal clientele of professors, students, and people from the neighborhood who come here in the morning to loudly discuss everything from modern politics to classical literature. While it is a nice neighborhood coffeehouse, the feel is somewhat cafeteria-like, probably because it is so busy, with three to four counter-persons running around at all times trying to keep up with customer orders. There are two rooms to sit in, though, and the smaller front room is much quieter and more relaxed than the back room, so if you don't want to get dragged into the heady conversations of the day, you can hide out here to read your newspaper—this is also the room with the free newspaper and magazine rack. The menu includes made-to-order sandwiches and soups, fruit smoothies, many flavors of biscotti, and a wide variety of baked desserts, as well as all the coffee and espresso drinks you could ever need.

Ginkgo Coffeehouse $
721 Snelling Avenue North, St. Paul
(651) 645-2647
Ginkgo in the Park
2300 Como Avenue, St. Paul
(651) 644-7699

By day, Ginkgo is a friendly java joint with mismatched furniture, potted plants, and a few outdoor tables in summer. A couple of nights a week, however, the atmosphere changes, and this coffeehouse on the edge of St. Paul's Hamline University campus becomes a dimly lit, cozy, acoustic-music venue. In addition to local singer-songwriters trying out their material on an invariably friendly audience, acoustic acts from throughout North America stop by to perform and sell CDs and demo tapes here. If the artist is particularly popular, arrive early.

The smaller of the two Ginkgos, Ginkgo in the Park, has a more neighborhood feel to it, with tables set out on the patio and a cozy sitting area inside for customers, including little-kid-size chairs for smaller customers. The menu includes homemade soups and breakfast sandwiches, ice cream floats, shakes, cones, fruit smoothies, a wide selection of bakery treats, and two chalkboards full of coffee and espresso drinks. The waitstaff is consistently pleasant here, too, which makes visiting this coffeehouse all the more worthwhile.

Lori's Coffee House $
1441 Cleveland Avenue North, St. Paul
(651) 647–9007

Lori's is a nice little corner coffeehouse that makes wonderful, homemade soups on site and throws a couple of huge slices of also-homemade bread in for free. There's also coffee and espresso, as well as cookies, muffins, a good selection of bottled juices to pick from, and fresh-squeezed orange juice. Lots of college kids hang out here, and there's definitely room for them—while the inside is spacious and airy, most people opt to sit around one of the many tables spread out on the lawn.

Prairie Star Coffee House $
2399 University Avenue West, St. Paul
(651) 646–7827

This is a comfortable little nook that is definitely trying to bring in the neighborhood. The decor is sweet, with large, mismatched, and primary color–painted wooden furniture that reminds one of doll's furniture, stained glass, Christmas lights, and a beautiful piano set up in one corner. There's a large selection of eatables served here, including ice cream, cookies, and pastries, all your standard coffee and espresso drinks, and fresh-squeezed lemonade.

Sarah Jo's Coffee Café $
327 West Seventh Street, St. Paul
(651) 224–3890

This nonsmoking establishment caters specifically to the breakfast and lunch crowd, opening earlier than most places in the neighborhood and closing around

5:00 p.m. The menu is wonderfully diverse, with a large selection of hot and cold fresh sandwiches to choose from—including beef French dip and barbecue meatball—as well as homemade soup, smoothies, muffins, and all the usual selections of coffee and espresso drinks. There's lots of seating space in here, and the tables are actually big enough for two or three to set down their food and drinks. The coffee shop is also walking distance from the Xcel arena and downtown St. Paul, making it a great place to park and stop before seeing the sights of the area.

Tea Source $
752 Cleveland Avenue South, St. Paul
(651) 690–9822
www.teasource.com

Owner Bill Waddington personally selects the fine teas he sells to customers of all tastes. Although Tea Source is a retail store selling loose teas, you can also stop in the Highland Park store just north of Ford Parkway and enjoy a cup or pot of your favorite tea in the store—a perfect spot for an afternoon read, a break from shopping, or conversation. With dozens of options among black, green, oolong, tisanes (herbal teas), and blends, you can also pick out a few ounces of your favorite or an adventurous alternative to take home. A detailed guide available in the store helps make sense of the inventory (which can be overwhelming to those used to gas station coffee), and Tea Source offers similar information in their catalog and on-line.

North

The Corner Coffee House $
87 West County Road C, Little Canada
(651) 482–1114

One of the few true coffeehouses in the suburbs, the Corner Coffee House is a big, friendly-looking, yellow two-story house with a large back patio and several cozy rooms inside for neighborhood get-togethers, and lots of lot parking. The menu includes a couple dozen coffee and espresso drinks, huge fresh fruit smoothies topped with whipped cream, breakfast pastries, and Italian desserts. There is also art and knickknacks for sale, most of which are made by local artists, and live musicians stop by to play weekend afternoons and evenings. If you don't feel like stopping in but still want the coffee, there's even a drive-through window in back for a quick pickup.

Nightlife

A casual drive throughout the Twin Cities might lead you to think that Minnesotans must have a serious drinking problem. There are literally hundreds of little drinking holes throughout the region, sometimes spaced less than a city block apart from another. However, the truth is that Minnesotans just like to be together, especially in the winter. Around December, the local bar takes the place of most people's front rooms by providing a place for people to gather to play Trivial Pursuit, watch TV, and buy tickets to win the traditional bar "meat raffle," which usually consists of some lucky customer winning 10 pounds of bologna or olive loaf. There's no better fun in January than getting bundled up tight as the sun goes down and heading out to the neighborhood bar to meet with friends and neighbors—you'll find that the colder the evening gets, the less likely the bartenders are to announce "last call" on time.

If your idea of a night on the town is catching a good live band, you're in luck—nearly all the bars and coffee shops in the Twin Cities metro area offer at least one night of local or acoustic live music a week. There are clubs that cater to just about every musical taste you can imagine. Downtown Minneapolis, particularly the Warehouse District, has the largest concentration of dance clubs. The Uptown area of Minneapolis has many hip bars, some with live music, and the area around the University of Minnesota has numerous, somewhat grittier bars filled with younger, drunker patrons. Downtown St. Paul is much tamer in terms of live music, though new brewpubs and bars that have sprung up near Rice Park and around the Xcel Energy Center are certainly livening things up. Several elegant drinking establishments inhabit the Selby-Dale area just west of the cathedral, and St. Paul has two first-class jazz clubs, the Dakota in the Midway and the Artists' Quarter downtown, as well as two excellent spots for live Irish music, Half Time Rec near Como Park and the Dubliner Pub in the Midway. The numerous pubs in neighborhoods across the Saintly City offer plenty of local color.

Alternative Music and Rock Clubs

Minneapolis

400 Bar
400 Cedar Avenue South, Minneapolis
(612) 332-2903
www.400bar.com

The bartender's surly, the beer's expensive, and the doorman thinks everybody who comes in is up to no good; but the sound man knows what he's doing, and a lot of touring acts stop here specifically because they sound so incredibly good in this club. The owners' former association with Soul Asylum helped bring people into the club when the band was big, but it's the club's reputation as a good venue to play that brings the bands in now. Everything from alternative rock to folk to blues acts (and everything in between) from all over the world make this club a regular stop on their tours. If you don't get here when the doors open, you probably won't be able to get in because of the huge crowds.

The Cabooze
917 Cedar Avenue, Minneapolis
(612) 338–6425
www.cabooze.com

Since 1974, the Cabooze has opened its doors to both nationally recognized touring rock, folk, and instrumental acts as well as many local bands that never get outside the Twin Cities. The club often pairs lesser-known local acts with major touring bands, too, giving good smaller bands the greater exposure they need to hit the tour circuit themselves. The Cabooze features musical acts almost every night of the week and has a large dance floor for those who don't feel like just standing around, as well as the largest bar in the Twin Cities.

Fine Line Music Café
318 First Avenue North, Minneapolis
(612) 338–8100
www.finelinemusic.com

Offering a decent blend of folk music, light rock, jazz, and sometimes strangely experimental acts, the Fine Line is a fairly small, intimate, and comfortable club on good nights and extremely packed and uncomfortable on bad nights. The stage is poorly placed way in the back of the club, and when an act has a good draw, it's nearly impossible to see the stage from anywhere but directly in front of the stage. The bar serves decent Italian fare, and their Sunday gospel brunch is excellent, both in the quality of the soul food and the soulful gospel singers brought in to serenade and inspire the early-afternoon crowds.

First Avenue/Seventh Street Entry
701 First Avenue North, Minneapolis
(612) 332–1775
www.first-avenue.com

Despite rumors to the contrary, Prince never actually owned First Avenue, nor did much more than hang out there—he only pretended to be the club's owner in the movie *Purple Rain*. The world-famous First Avenue site has been a popular hangout for bands and musicians and clubgoers for more than 30 years, since Joe Cocker first took the stage on opening night in 1970. Since then, the club has indiscriminately featured Top 40, alternative, and classic rock acts at least one night a week, usually more, and opened its floors on weekends to crowds dancing to techno, house music, salsa, swing, and pretty much everything in between. The 21-plus section upstairs is a great place to retreat from the downstairs crowd, with a fully stocked bar and a wall-length window that provides views of the dance floor below. However, the real beauty about First Avenue is the layout; no matter where you stand in the club, whether it be on the floor or upstairs at the bar, you can always get a decent view of the stage.

Set in a side room of First Avenue, the Entry is the much more intimate venue of the two. Again, the stage setting is great here, and though the room gets packed quickly (and smoke-filled even quicker), on good nights this is about as close to having a major label act play in your living room as you can get. The dress code also is about as informal as you can get, and this is the cheapest place in town to get tap beer. For the most part, expect to pay less than 10 bucks for a cover charge, and feel free to

> ### Insiders' Tip
> First Avenue/Seventh Street Entry gives out free passes to upcoming shows and events with each ticket purchased. Usually, if you buy one ticket, you get enough free tickets to get you into three or four other shows or dance club nights.

cross back and forth between the Entry and the much-roomier First Avenue after receiving a hand stamp. There are usually shows at least three nights a week in the main room, and in summer the club's booked almost every night. Ticket prices for both clubs vary widely depending on the acts playing, so it's a good idea to either pick up a club schedule (found at any record store in the Twin Cities, both venues are listed on the same schedule), check out their Web site, or just give them a call.

Ground Zero/The Front
15 Northeast Fourth Street, Minneapolis
(612) 378–5115

Ground Zero offers diverse theme nights four times a week. One of the club's most popular dance nights is "Bondage a go-go," where every Thursday dancers perform relatively tame S&M; the crowd dresses in corresponding attire. On a lighter note, Saturday features "'80s Excessive," showcasing dance hits of the '80s with a sprinkling of '90s favorites.

Besides the large dance floor, Ground Zero has a smaller, cozier lounge room, the Front. Prince fans will enjoy every Wednesday, when the club pays homage to the Minneapolis native with a selection of his hits and numerous deeper tracks. Other theme nights at the Front include "Astro Lounge," "Trans-Euro Express," and "Funky Friday." Beer prices are inexpensive in both clubs, and specials can be found almost daily.

Lee's Liquor Lounge
101 Glenwood Avenue, Minneapolis
(612) 338–9491
www.leesliquorlounge.com

Located in a former industrial area just south of downtown's Warehouse District, Lee's seems a little off the beaten path, and the one-way streets in the area sometimes make it tricky to find. But Lee's has the feel of a slightly rough-around-the-edges rockin' roadhouse, and the place gets hopping when local acts grab the stage. Most tables in the bar have a good view of the stage, and the small dance floor attracts an energetic, sweaty crowd. Lee's hosts live music almost every night, and covers generally run $5.00 or less. If you want to toss back a few beers and bob your head to the steady beat or do your thing on the dance floor, you will find Lee's quite stimulating.

Mayslacks Polka Lounge
1428 Northeast Fourth Street, Minneapolis
(612) 789–9862
www.mayslacks.com

This place can be the best bang for your buck so far as seeing live music. The cover is rarely more than $3.00, and bands usually play for a good two or three hours—and for the low cover, you can see anything from a brand-new band made up of neighborhood kids to a major label act. The downside of this is that there are rarely opening bands for acts, so by the time the headliners are finished playing, they're sometimes panting, out of breath, and usually very drunk. The sound system is better than you might expect from a local neighborhood bar, though, and a lot of groups play here just because they like the way they sound on the stage. The beer's moderately priced, too, and on football/soccer/hockey/bartender's-in-a-good-mood nights, they have some really great specials.

New Union
3141 Central Avenue NE, Minneapolis
(612) 781–8488

Kind of a rarity in the Twin Cities, especially with the recent demise of everyone's favorite all-ages club, the Foxfire, the New Union is an alcohol-free, smoke-free nightclub for audiences age 15 and up. The club mostly books politically correct punk bands and Christian rock, but the occasional acoustic act makes its way in now and again.

The Quest Club
110 North Fifth Street, Minneapolis
(612) 338–3383

The Quest is a really beautiful nightclub that brings in some major national acts, with several conveniently located bars on both floors so that you don't have to fight too much to get a bartender's attention. The brightly lit stage is set so that you can see the performers pretty much anywhere you stand in the club, and the second floor has very comfortable booths and tables you can wrestle other patrons to secure. The club is tucked away in an unassuming stately old office building, and the main floor's ceiling stretches up all the way to the top of the building, giving it an open, airy feeling even when the floor is packed. The VIP room, too, is amazing, with fake palm trees, fiberoptic twinkling stars, and an active fountain that completes the illusion of actually being outside perfectly. One drawback of the club is that they do push their house dress code occasionally, but they're pretty lenient about it depending on the band you're coming to see.

Terminal Bar
409 Hennepin Avenue East, Minneapolis
(612) 623–4545

The rumor is that this is the best place in Minneapolis to meet members of the opposite sex. Most of the patrons of this bar are people from the neighborhood that like to stop by after work for a beer and kids coming to see local bands perform on the small stage in the back. The draft beer is a little high priced, but there's a popcorn machine always full of popcorn, and if you ask nicely, the owner's son will cook for you, which may or may not be a good thing (his repertoire includes serving a hard-boiled egg on a Ritz cracker with a little mustard). The cover charge, if there is one, is usually around $3.00, a relative bargain in Minneapolis. During winter, the bar has weekly Trivial Pursuit contests (the prize is a free beer) to try to lure people out of their nice, warm houses into the bar for a drink.

The Uptown Bar and Café
3018 Hennepin Avenue South, Minneapolis
(612) 823–4719

Once known for attracting the loudest national and local acts, the Uptown Bar and Café briefly stopped booking bands in the mid-1990s; despite good attendance, the bar was losing money and decided to concentrate only on food and drink. When the bar returned to booking bands, it featured a scaled-back all-local

schedule, mostly composed of roots rock and acoustic music. Once again, the bar drew well in Minneapolis's hip Uptown neighborhood and has expanded to music on Wednesday through Saturday.

Whiskey Junction
901 Cedar Avenue, Minneapolis
(612) 338–9550
www.whiskeyjunction.com

With local music on the weekends and beer and food specials every other day, Whiskey Junction, just down the street from the Cabooze, attracts a slightly grungy crowd, including plenty of students from the nearby U of M and Augsburg College. Two bars keep thirsty patrons busy, and the bar has several pool tables and 10 TVs, often flickering with various sporting events (the bar is the base for the unofficial Cleveland Browns Fan Club, making a brave statement in Vikings country). Whiskey Junction has an excellent selection of tap beers, including the local favorite, Summit, as well as rarer finds on tap, such as Beamish Stout, Boddington Cream Ale, Fullers India Pale Ale, and Paulaner Hefe Weizen.

The Whole Music Café
Coffman Memorial Union
300 Washington Avenue SE, Minneapolis
(612) 624–8638
www.coffman.umn.edu/whole

The Whole, originally called the Gopher Hole, occupies the basement of Coffman Union on the University of Minnesota–Minneapolis campus. The 40-year-old venue has a venerable history, including early days as a coffeehouse featuring folky songsters and poets and later as a haven for new wave, punk, and indie rock bands and their devoted student (mostly) fans. Coffman Union recently underwent a $71 million renovation, and the improvements to the Whole included such coveted features as bathrooms and a rocking sound system. But the architects wisely left the gritty, down-in-the-cellar atmosphere much as it always has been, a nod to the tradition of this little underground club in the heart of the university.

St. Paul

Christiansen's Big V's Saloon
1567 University Avenue West, St. Paul
(651) 645–8472

Another relic of the old days of St. Paul, Christiansen's Big V's Saloon features live music from mostly local bands every weekend and most weekdays. The decor of the bar is fabulous—the walls are covered with old menus from the '40s and '50s (don't try ordering the 15-cent pancake breakfast, because it doesn't actually exist), while the bar itself is a classy antique curved wooden affair with a mirrored backdrop. The placing of the stage is a little inconvenient, tucked way in the back where only patrons in the back room can actually see the stage, but considering that they don't usually charge more than $5.00 for a full night, not many people complain.

Fourth Street Station and the Lab
201 East Fourth Street, St. Paul
(651) 298–0173

The Fourth Street Station and the Lab is the newest incarnation of Ryan's, St. Paul's favorite metal club. The venue has altered its schedule to reflect this change. The music is aimed at a younger demographic. Local hard rock and rap/metal are the most common bookings with a smidgen of ska. The club is divided into two parts, one with a long bar and plenty of pool tables, the other for the music. There is a large stage and lots of seating for the young bar crowd, who on weekends fill Fourth Street Station and the Lab.

Turf Club/Clown Lounge
1601 University Avenue, St. Paul
(651) 647–0486
www.turfclub.net

Billing itself as the "Best Relic of the '40s," St. Paul's Turf Club combines upscale sophistication with the feel of an old-fashioned cowboy bar. There are many local, domestic, and imported beers on tap, and the club features an elegant, curved wooden bar for customers to perch at, as well as booths and tables throughout the establishment. Long having a reputation for giving local bands a much-needed performance outlet, the Turf Club is one of the hippest hangouts in the Twin Cities, with music almost every night for ridiculously low cover charges. The Turf Club clientele is refreshingly free of the "beautiful people" crowd found at many downtown Minneapolis dance clubs, and the music here ranges from foot-stomping country to ska. Downstairs from the Turf Bar is the Clown Lounge, which features a more eclectic selection of performances, from art shows in the ladies' rest room to book signings by local writers and poets to puppet shows, DJs, karaoke, and a wide range of musical acts.

The Suburbs

Medina Entertainment Center
500 Highway 55, Medina
(763) 478–6661
www.medinaentertainment.com

About 5 miles west of I–494 in the western suburb of Medina, the Medina Entertainment Center hosts everything from local bands like the disco kings Boogie Wonderland to "Yoga with Ruth" on Monday night. On Wednesday and Thursday in Rascals Bar within the complex, you can consult with psychic Ruth Lordan for insight into your present and future. In addition to live music, you can ham it up at the Medina during Friday and Saturday karaoke nights.

Sharky's Grill'n'Bar
4880 Central Avenue NE,
Columbia Heights
(763) 571–8643

Featuring live music seven nights a week, Sharky's brings in a wide variety of performers from local bands to nationally-known touring bands. It's mostly local entertainment, but the range goes from punk rock bands to jam bands and country. The cover charge is usually under $5.00, and the bar prices are extremely reasonable. The bar itself is a little on the divey side, though, so if rough-looking crowds make you nervous, this isn't the place for you.

Coffeehouses

Minneapolis

Asase-Yaa Organic Juices and Foods
2922 Bryant Avenue South, Minneapolis
(612) 821–6484

This combination juice bar and restaurant opens its doors late each Tuesday night to present live music and poetry from whoever shows and signs up to perform. If you want to perform, get in early to sign the performance sheet, because this little neighborhood mainstay gets a lot of business, and the performance roster fills up fast.

Europe@n Grind
815 Washington Avenue SE, Minneapolis
(612) 331–7700

This is yet another college campus–area coffeehouse that opens its doors most nights to live, usually local bands. The ambience here is great for just hanging out, with big, beautiful furniture to relax on, lots of art on display, a decent DJ/counterperson selecting the background music when the bands are offstage, and three PCs with DSL connections to play on for as long as you want (although politeness and common courtesy will dictate exactly how long that is). You can also buy books on traveling through Europe here, including information on hostels and backpacking vacations.

St. Paul

Bean Counter Coffee Company
769 Cleveland Avenue South, St. Paul
(651) 699–5448

This great neighborhood coffeehouse has live local music performances at least five nights a week year-round. It doesn't stay open that late (usually closes before midnight), but it's a nice place to swing by for a relaxing early evening on the town.

Lori's Coffeehouse
1441 Cleveland Avenue North, St. Paul
(651) 647–9007

Located near the University of St. Thomas campus, Lori's holds almost nightly poetry readings and live (mostly acoustic) music for the entertainment of the clientele. They're not so great about posting a schedule, though, so you'll have to just swing by and take your chances on who's actually performing. The upside of this, though, is that there's never a cover charge, and this is really a pretty pleasant place to hang out to get the feel of the neighborhood.

Prairie Star Coffeehouse
2399 University Avenue West, St. Paul
(651) 646–7827

This cozy little neighborhood coffeehouse opens its doors every Thursday and Friday night to live acoustic acts that either perform on the beautiful piano already set up in the corner or on their own instruments. So far, there's been no cover charge to attend the intimate little in-store shows, and the coffee and food's good and cheap enough that you don't feel like you've been tricked into paying for the music.

Comedy Clubs

Minneapolis

Acme Comedy Company
708 North First Street, Minneapolis
(612) 338–6393
www.acmecomedycompany.com

Acme hosts local and national comedians in its Warehouse District space inside the Itasca Building. The club has shows nightly except Monday, with two shows nightly on Friday and Saturday. The on-site restaurant serves pasta, steaks, and ribs, and you have the choice of buying a ticket for the comedy show alone or a dinner and show special, which includes an entree off the menu (up to $14) and a show ticket, for $22.

ComedySportz
Calhoun Square, 3001 Hennepin Avenue South, Minneapolis
(612) 870–1230
www.comedysportztc.com

Part of the national ComedySportz chain,

this club sets up refereed comedy teams that compete for the biggest laughs and the most points for their unscripted, improvisational performances. Audience members are encouraged to heckle the teams as well as throw out suggestions for comedy themes. But make sure your suggestions are clean, or the referee could call the "Brown Bag Foul" on you and you'll end up wearing a paper bag over your head. Shows are every Friday and Saturday at 8:00 P.M. and 10:30 P.M.

Dance Clubs

Minneapolis

Banana Joe's
15 South Fifth Street, Minneapolis
(612) 333–6500

The Minneapolis branch of this national chain of dance clubs features, like many of the other dance clubs in the area, a charmingly tacky, tropical setting that seems more like a hangover vision of *Beach Blanket Bingo* than the Miami scene it's trying to imitate. The menu is secondary to the parade of tropical drinks and tap beers that fuel each evening's dancing and socializing, and the DJ's selections run the gamut of Top 40 hits from the '70s, '80s, and '90s, with house music playing in one of the back rooms and the occasional tribute to Jimmy Buffett. The cover charge is a bit steep, but this is a great place to meet and mingle with the 20-something crowd.

South Beach
323 First Avenue North, Minneapolis
(612) 204–0790

Kind of an anomaly on the Twin Cities nightlife scene, this South Florida–themed dance club has actual dress codes that the burly doormen are only too willing to enforce. However, once you get in, you can almost imagine you're in a similar dance club in Miami, with swirling lights; perpetual fog; loud, thumping dance music; and every kind of mixed drink under the sun— if there's a drink the bartender hasn't heard of, he'll certainly try to make it. Grooving here is seen as sort of a status

symbol among suburbanite hipsters, partly because actually being able to get in is a status symbol in itself.

Tropix Beach Club
400 Third Avenue North, Minneapolis
(612) 333–1006

You can tell Tropix is nearby half a block before you even turn the corner, because the music is loud, loud, loud. Another Miami-themed nightclub, Tropix is a bit more relaxed on the dress code and is therefore a popular hangout for post-collegiate Twin Cities girls and boys who want to relax, dance, and meet members of the opposite sex.

Folk, Irish, and Acoustic Music

Minneapolis

Cedar Cultural Centre
416 Cedar Avenue South, Minneapolis
(612) 338–2674
www.thecedar.org

The Cedar Cultural Centre is an absolutely amazing place to see musicians perform. The auditorium is designed specifically for listening to music, with beautiful hardwood floors, a large raised stage in the front, excellent acoustics, and a soundman who actually pays attention to musicians' cues. A host of exciting acts perform at this venue, from traditional Irish bands to folk duos to world-famous acoustic soloists such as Pierre Bensusan and Didier Malherbe. The Cedar Cultural Centre is also the home of the annual Nordic Roots festival, a four-day-long event that features elemental, contemporary, and experimental groups from the Nordic countries. The refreshment bar is worth noting here, too— this nonsmoking establishment includes cheap, good beer on tap, wine, homemade cookies, and Indian samosas on their menu.

Jitters at the Times
205 Hennepin Avenue East, Minneapolis
(612) 617–1111

Originally a downtown Minneapolis coffee shop, restaurant, and bar famous for introducing new bands and local spoken word performers to the Cities, Jitters recently moved to northeast Minneapolis to become almost exclusively a bar with a limited menu and an even more limited repertoire of live shows. The decor is interesting, almost as though someone went piano bar–hopping in Vegas and picked out a selection of disparate elements from those clubs to make one big one. The walls are made of metal siding and silver paint, the couches are covered in red velvet fabric; the tables are small, Art Deco affairs set with roses in mismatched vases; and the lighting is provided by metal lamps that look as though they were stolen from the Renaissance Faire. However, there's no admission charge, the beer is cheap, and the music is free.

Kieran's Irish Pub & Restaurant
330 Second Avenue South, Minneapolis
(612) 339–4499
www.klerans.com

One of the few truly Irish bars in Minneapolis, Kieran's has a full bar and an excellent menu that includes traditional U.K. foods like fish-and-chips and bangers-and-mash. The bar usually has live Irish and folk music playing on two different stages Friday and Saturday nights and infrequently during the week, with the occasional open mic night and scheduled poetry readings on the smaller stage. During the summer, Kieran's sets up an outside bar and lots of tables for clients, with the occasional live band set up outside as well to serenade both patrons and random passersby.

St. Paul

The Dubliner Pub
2162 University Avenue West, St. Paul
(651) 646–5551

The Dubliner Pub is an old-style Irish theme bar for its working class industrial location. The cozy, box-shaped pub is painted green and has a beautiful long bar, where numerous Irish, English, and domestic beers are available on tap. There

is also a small stage for Irish music on the weekends as well as darts and free popcorn.

Half Time Rec
1013 Front Avenue, St. Paul
(651) 488–8245

The Half Time Rec is the most authentic neighborhood Irish bar in the Twin Cities. It began as a bar catering to the new Irish immigrants who began arriving in St. Paul during the '70s but has gone on to serve a much larger cross section of the Twin Cities population. Weekend business is extremely busy, and attracts young and old as well as people from the Como Park neighborhood where it is located.

The Half Time Rec features a long, comfortable, U-shaped bar and an adjoining room with a stage for music Tuesday through Saturday. The rooms are comfortably furnished, and the stage is draped with both the Irish and the American flags. At the Half Time Rec, patrons vociferously have fun. They frequently sing along with the music or get up and dance to the authentic Irish music, which sometimes includes a few American via Ireland–inspired covers. The beers are reasonably priced and the Guinness is prepared with the correct amount of head. In addition, for patrons' enjoyment, there is a boccie court in the basement. The Half Time Rec is a few miles from the major thoroughfares, but it is well worth the effort if you enjoy authentic Irish music and fun.

Gay Bars

Minneapolis

Gay Nineties Theatre Cafe & Bar
408 Hennepin Avenue, Minneapolis
(612) 333–7755

The state's largest gay club, the Gay Nineties pretty much offers something for everyone, from live music to a weekly (and very popular) drag show at the La Femme Show Lounge on the second floor. The club has a dedicated straight following as well, who come for the very strong mixed drinks and the excellent dance music, with no cover charged—Friday and Saturday nights are extremely packed, and there's nearly always a line to get inside. The club has nine different bars on the premises, two discos, a supper club, male strippers, and a game room.

The Saloon
830 Hennepin Avenue, Minneapolis
(612) 332–0835

The Saloon is one of the most popular bars and dance floors for Twin Cities gay men, featuring a large, dark dance floor with plenty of loud music and a large bar in the back for socializing and imbibing. The Saloon is conveniently located on busy Hennepin Avenue in downtown Minneapolis.

Jazz, Blues, and R&B

Minneapolis

Bunker's Music Bar & Grill
716 Washington Avenue North, Minneapolis
(612) 338–8188

A popular lunch spot serving soups and sandwiches during the day, this neighborhood bar turns into a blues and rock club at night. The acts booked range from pop and alternative rock bands to blues, R&B, and jazz acts. The cover charge is pretty low—usually under $5.00—and there are also pool tables and video games for entertainment.

Famous Dave's Bar-B-Que Uptown
3001 Hennepin Avenue South, Calhoun Square, Minneapolis
(612) 822–9900

Not only does Famous Dave's have some of the best barbecue ribs and fried catfish in the Twin Cities (especially for a chain restaurant), the Uptown branch also books some of the rawest blues in the area. Bands perform after 9:00 P.M. most nights of the week, giving parents time to feed their kids and drop them off at the sitters' before coming back to sit in on blues sessions. The music is free, and the drinks are reasonably priced.

JazzMine's
123 North Third Street, Minneapolis
(612) 630–JAZZ
www.jazzmines.com

JazzMine's motto is "eat, drink, and keep the beat!" This nightclub is one of the most beautifully furnished and decorated in the Twin Cities; because of this, cover prices tend to be expensive for the area. JazzMine's provides R&B, Latin, soul, and, of course, jazz. JazzMine's also features a Sunday jazz brunch.

Sophia
65 Southeast Main Street, Minneapolis
(612) 379–1111

Located right next to the Mississippi River in St. Anthony Main, Sophia serves a wide selection of fairly expensive dishes and has a full bar. Starting around 8:00 P.M. almost every night, local soft jazz acts take the small stage set near the bar and play until closing. There's no cover charge for the music, although there is a two-drink minimum after 9:00 P.M. Nominated by local papers time and again for the best romantic restaurant and best jazz club in Minneapolis for its classy music and dancing, this is an excellent place to take a date you want to impress.

The Viking Bar
1829 Riverside Avenue South, Minneapolis
(612) 332–4259

The Viking Bar does not live up to the image its name projects. It is not a Minnesota Vikings sports bar, nor is it involved in the preservation of Scandinavian culture. Instead, the Viking is one of the Twin Cities' grittiest venues for American roots music. Local R&B, jazz, and blues musicians play the small stage and even smaller stage. The Viking Bar is as close as the Twin Cities get to the seedy clubs in New Orleans and Chicago, with all their inherent charm and oddness.

St. Paul

Artists' Quarter
408 St. Peter Street, St. Paul
(651) 292–1359
www.mnjazz.com

This basement jazz club has great potential that has yet to be realized. The acoustics are great in the small basement space, the stage is big enough to hold a full piano and an accompanying band, and the bar serves clean, cheap tap beer as well as liquor, but so few nationally recognized jazz acts pass through the Twin Cities that most nights are booked by local artists that have a lot more heart than talent. Still, the club is a great place to stop by late at night to unwind—the bartenders are friendly, the cover charge is usually under $5.00 (rare for jazz clubs here), and if you're not a jazz purist, the bands that do play here are usually a lot of fun.

The Dakota Bar & Grill
Bandana Square, 1021 East Bandana
Boulevard, St. Paul
(651) 642–1442
www.dakotacooks.com

At least once a week, a national headlining jazz act comes through town to play at this club, and while the ticket prices are high (usually around $20) for the area, jazz fans will definitely get their money's worth. The cuisine served is elegant and as improvisational as the music: trout in maple sauce, walleye cheeks with pepper-garlic sauce, and the signature brie-and-apple soup. There's also an extensive wine list, a full bar, and a happy hour Monday through Friday from 4:30 to 6:30 P.M.

Lounges, Pubs, and Brewpubs

Minneapolis

Brit's Pub & Eating Establishment
1110 Nicollet Mall, Minneapolis
(612) 332–3908

This upscale downtown bar is almost always packed on weekends, usually with drinking-age kids from college or graduate school. The main room is lavishly furnished with mock-Georgian lounges and armchairs, as well as beautiful wooden bar stools set next to tables and wall outcroppings to set your beer on throughout the room. The far walls are also hung with large mirrors, giving the illusion that the main room is a lot larger than it actually is. There's a large back room to Brit's as well, but it's usually reserved for private parties at night. During summer, Britt's opens its rooftop patio for outdoor libations surrounded by Minneapolis's skyscrapers. You can also watch lawn bowlers practicing their avocation on the neighboring rooftop grassy field, the only elevated lawn bowling field in the country. For a fee, you can also attempt to roll your "bowl" as close as possible to the "jack."

Chatterbox Pub
2229 East 35th Street, Minneapolis
(612) 728–9871

This bar's big claim to fame is their huge collection of Atari video games available for customers to use. In short, this bar's perfect for those who like tipping back a few while bathing in the warm green and blue glow of Frogger and Space Invaders. It's an interesting idea, and no one else in the area is doing it.

Club Ashe
322 First Avenue North, Minneapolis
(612) 673–9694

Located next door to the Fine Line Music Café (they share the same front entrance), Club Ashe is a sophisticated little hideaway featuring a full bar that includes a few exotic and extremely strong drinks that the bartenders have concocted themselves. The seating consists of large, comfortable booths for those who want to spend time by themselves or with their guests, as well as plenty of seating and standing room on the main floor. Although they do occasionally book local acid jazz bands to play in the background, the music and atmosphere is mostly provided by a DJ and a fog machine.

Gluek's Restaurant & Bar
16 North Sixth Street, Minneapolis
(612) 338–6621
www.glueks.com

Gluek's is Minneapolis's original brewpub. Since 1902 Gluek's has served Minneapolis with the "big Gluek's," 34 ounces of their delicious and uniquely tasty beer. Located in the historic Warehouse District, Gluek's draws huge crowds with their brew, other domestic and foreign beers, and liquors. Gluek's is across the street from the Target Center, home of the Minnesota Timberwolves, and within walking distance of downtown Minneapolis. With all these advantages, it is no surprise Gluek's remains one of Minneapolis's great brewpubs.

The Herkimer Pub & Brewery
2922 Lyndale Avenue South, Minneapolis
(612) 821–0101

The Herkimer Pub & Brewery offers a large selection of fresh beers at reasonable prices. Despite its location in the Lyn-Lake neighborhood, the beers made in-house cost less than a bottle of domestic. Lyn-Lake is a neighborhood at the intersection of Lyndale Avenue and Lake Street and abuts the Uptown neighborhood of Minneapolis. In recent years there has been significant renewal at the intersection of two of the city's major thoroughfares. Many shops and restaurants, including the Herkimer, call Lyn-Lake home.

The Herkimer specializes in its in-house-brewed beer. Each day there are different "Today's Brews" written on a chalkboard, including light lagers and heavier dunkels (German for dark). The restaurant and bar is clean and comfortable, with plenty of booths as well as tables. The Herkimer serves food and appetizers until midnight, all reasonably priced, as is the beer.

Lyle's Bar and Restaurant
2021 Hennepin Avenue South, Minneapolis
(612) 870–8183

On the edge of Uptown, one would think that Liquor Lyle's, as most area residents call this establishment, would tend toward a hipster crowd. But this neighborhood watering hole attracts everyone from construction workers to artists to its somewhat smudgy, dated-yet-colorful ambience. The booths have vinyl seats, the men's rest rooms have trough urinals, and the bouncer is big and hairy; but if you want to share a pitcher of beer and a basket of deep-fried cheese curds with a friend on a day when you haven't taken a shower, Lyle's is hard to beat.

MacKenzie
918 Hennepin Avenue, Minneapolis
(612) 333–7268

MacKenzie specializes in Scottish beers and liquors but also has a large selection of American libations, all at reasonable prices. The inside of the bar is decorated with Scottish decor and theater posters on lots of beautiful exposed brick. Located next to the historic Orpheum Theatre, and within walking distance of several others, MacKenzie is a great stop before or after Hennepin Avenue theater events.

Insiders' Tip

"Bar time" in Minnesota is 2:00 A.M. although many bars close earlier. Some bars and restaurants, such as First Avenue and Figlio, stay open later but do not continue to serve alcohol. Liquor stores in the Twin Cities can be open from 8:00 A.M. to 8:00 P.M. Monday through Thursday and until 10:00 P.M. Friday and Saturday, as well as on July 3 and New Year's Eve. Liquor stores are closed on Sunday, though some convenience stores sell 3.2 beer on Sunday.

The Herkimer Pub & Brewery on Lyndale Avenue in south Minneapolis. PHOTO. TODD R. BERGER

Mario's Keller Bar
2300 University Avenue NE, Minneapolis
(612) 781-3860

Mario's Keller Bar occupies the large and comfortable basement of the Gasthof zur Gemuetlichkeit Restaurant. Not surprisingly, the Keller Bar features polka on Friday and Saturday nights and rock music Tuesday through Thursday. In addition, the bar hosts "Swing Dance Sunday," where dance lessons are available for only $4.00. A festive atmosphere overtakes the club, especially on weekends, when many fraternity members pack the dance floor and consume massive quantities of beer, which comes as no surprise considering the excellent selection of imported German beers on tap and available by the glass, pint, or enormous glass boot. Connoisseurs of German beers will enjoy the bar's selection, which runs a bit pricey, while many others will revel in the joyous German beer hall atmosphere.

O'Donovan's Irish Pub
700 First Avenue North, Minneapolis
(612) 317-8896

O'Donovan's is a recent addition to the small Twin Cities Irish pub scene. Unlike the Dubliner Pub or Kieran's Irish Pub, O'Donovan's authenticity to all that is Irish is mostly left to the beautiful decor. The walls are covered with Irish murals and the rooms are furnished with comfortable booths. O'Donovan's draws a young, collegiate-type crowd, who enjoy the pub's live music selection, which is not Irish reels but often includes Top 40 hits performed on a keyboard. Location is a prime asset for O'Donovan's—the Target Center, and First Avenue and the Seventh Street Entry, are directly across the street.

Triple Rock Social Club
629 Cedar Avenue South, Minneapolis
(612) 333-7399

The Triple Rock Social Club is the punk rock bar and restaurant of the Twin Cities. Owned by Erik Funk, a member of local punk legend Dillinger 4, it provides beer and food in a comfortable and relaxed atmosphere. The jukebox is particularly interesting—filled with a surprisingly eclectic range of music, from punk to R&B

to metal—patrons' selections never cease to amaze and create an interesting atmosphere. Also of note is the wide selection of beers on tap, a dozen at last count, served at reasonable prices. The Triple Rock's menu contains sandwiches, salads, burgers, and one of the Twin Cities' largest and best selections of vegetarian items.

Urban Wildlife Bar & Grill
128 North Fourth Street, Minneapolis
(612) 339–4665
www.urbanwildlifebar.com
Urban Wildlife is one of the most popular Twin Cities hangouts for hip 20-somethings. During the summer, the bar and outside seating are packed, particularly during the weekends. This is not surprising considering its location in the heart of the cool and busy Warehouse District of Minneapolis. Urban Wildlife takes advantage of the view by having windows along the perimeter of the two exposed walls. A small menu of bar food is also available.

Whitey's World Famous Saloon
400 Hennepin Avenue East, Minneapolis
(612) 623–9478
Geared somewhat to the college crowd, Whitey's is your standard, comfortable neighborhood bar that has weekend specials on Jägermeister shots and about half a dozen domestic and locally brewed beers on tap. The interior is beautiful—the bar is an elegant, curved length of carved wood surrounded by high-backed stools, and in summertime, customers can choose whether they want to sit inside the bar or at the tables set outside on the fenced-in patio.

St. Paul

Great Waters Brewing Company
426 St. Peter Street, St. Paul
(651) 224–2739
www.greatwatersbc.com
A relative newcomer to downtown St. Paul, the Great Waters Brewing Company serves flavorful microbrews from their location inside the Hamm Building. The brewpub's beers include cask-conditioned ales, served at cellar temperature of 52 degrees F and "hand pulled" from casks in the basement, and pushed beers, which are served at 38 degrees F, similar to other tap beers in the United States. Beers include the award-winning Old Bastard English Ale, as well as Martin's Bitter, Brown Trout Brown Ale, and Pot Hole Porter. Great Waters also brews their own root beer and has an outdoor patio and full menu, featuring several pastas, grilled duck breast, and a top-notch London broil.

O'Gara's Bar & Grill
164 Snelling Avenue North, St. Paul
(651) 644–3333
www.ogaras.com
O'Gara's is a popular St. Paul bar for several reasons. First, the beer prices are reasonable, with some taps as cheap as a couple bucks. Second, they have plenty of comfortable space, nicely decorated with beautiful exposed brick, for enjoying the libations. Third, they have an entire wall dedicated to the late *Peanuts* cartoon cre-

ator, Charles Schulz. Schulz grew up in one of the apartments above O'Gara's, and his father also worked at a barbershop that today is part of O'Gara's Bar. A barber pole, Snoopy cartoons, and prints commemorate the bar's place in history.

O'Gara's also features a brewpub. They have several of their own beers, some of which are seasonal; a few specialty brews include Sligo Red, Oktoberfest, Light Amber Ale, and, for more adventurous beer connoisseurs, selections such as Dublin Apricot Wheat, which includes a subtle hint of apricot.

Sweeney's Saloon
96 North Dale Street, St. Paul
(651) 221-9157

Sweeney's is a local pub with beautiful woodwork and a secluded (though usually packed) patio bar open during the summer. With many excellent beers on tap, lots of booths, and a pub-food menu, Sweeney's is a neighborhood institution attracting young, cute singles and attached (or not) 30-somethings looking for a pint or a pitcher in a busy, friendly setting.

Vine Park Brewing Company
242 West Seventh Street, St. Paul
(651) 228-1355
www.vinepark.com

The Vine Park Brewing Company is one of the many excellent bars in the shadow of the new Xcel Energy Center in downtown St. Paul. The Xcel opened for the expansion Minnesota Wild hockey team and has transformed the nightlife in St. Paul. Only a few blocks from the Xcel, Vine Park does great business by brewing some of the best beer in the Twin Cities, such as the bittersweet Eelpout Stout and the sweet and nutty Walnut Brown Ale. Their menu includes three other handcrafted beers plus seasonal specialties or a sampler of all five; all the brews taste great and are reasonably priced. Vine Park also offers a full food menu, with such specialties as smoked duck chili, mahi-mahi po'boy, garlic roasted pot roast, and avocado-stuffed salmon.

Movie Theaters

Movie theaters are an important part of Twin Cities nightlife. And with a wide variety of diverse venues for viewing movies, there is a theater available for everyone. Besides several classic theaters in Minneapolis and St. Paul, there has been a recent explosion of stadium seat megaplexes in the suburbs. So whether you enjoy box office hits, Hong Kong cinema, or film revivals, there is a place for every moviegoer in the Twin Cities.

Minneapolis

Asian Media Access
3028 Oregon Avenue South, Minneapolis
(612) 376-7715
www.amamedia.org

Asian Media Access specializes in the best of Hong Kong and Asian cinema from the present and the past. Lacking a theater of their own, they rent two local theaters on a regular basis for screenings. Currently they have a morning and a midnight program at the Oak Street Cinema. Additionally, they continue to have Friday and Saturday midnight showings at the Riverview Theater. Asian Media Access consistently provides action-packed Hong Kong cinema, with beautiful costumes, martial arts, and all you expect from the genre. Be sure to call or check their Web site before planning to attend an event, since theaters and showing times occasionally change.

Block E 15
Block E, 600 Hennepin Avenue, Minneapolis
(612) 338-5900

Minneapolis's newest theater complex and the only cinema downtown, the Block E 15 inside the new Block E shopping and entertainment complex shows first-run movies in full digital sound with stadium seating. Students with an ID get a discount, and parking in the complex's underground ramp is free for up to three hours.

Landmark's Lagoon Cinema
1320 Lagoon Avenue, Minneapolis
(612) 825–6006

Lagoon Cinema is part of the Landmark's national art theater chain. Arty, indie, and a few foreign hits are often held over at the Lagoon after playing its sister theater, the Uptown. The Lagoon screens smaller-budget films for a longer duration and others that would not otherwise have been shown. The five theaters in this multiplex are roomy and comfortable, with excellent sound and large movie screens, but they lack the charm of the Uptown Theatre.

Oak Street Cinema
309 Southeast Oak Street, Minneapolis
(612) 331–3134
www.oakstreetcinema.org

Oak Street Cinema is the only Twin Cities theater dedicated to classic film revivals. Occasionally new films from famous directors or student films are shown, but beyond that Oak Street Cinema sticks to reviving cinema's illustrious as well as forgotten past.

The nonprofit organization is the place where Twin Cities cineastes catch their fix of film's rich history. Recent schedules have included great films of the '70s, the French New Wave, and the films of directors such as Tarkovsky, Bergman, Mel Brooks, Bunuel, and a host of others. Thematic scheduling such as the best of vampire films or silent films is common. Oak Street Cinema recently celebrated its fifth anniversary and hopefully will continue for years to come, as it is one of the Twin Cities great artistic treasures.

Parkway Theater
4814 Chicago Avenue South, Minneapolis
(612) 822–3030
www.parkwaytheater.com

This south Minneapolis theater has a knack for consistently showing the best of second-run indie and mainstream films. Despite the Parkway's less than spectacular ambience, this old mom-and-pop theater more than makes up for it in value. Ticket prices are low, and concession

prices are a steal. Finally, if you are curious about what is playing at the Parkway, give them a call; the answering machine is always homey and interesting.

Riverview Theatre
3800 42nd Avenue South, Minneapolis
(612) 729–7369
www.riverviewtheatre.com

The Riverview Theatre presents second-run movies in one of the Cities' most beautiful facilities. The theater is a fine example of Art Deco architecture and furnishings. The lobby is of particular distinction—appearing today as it probably did 50 years ago—decorated with Art Deco lamps and sofas.

Films screened at the Riverview are usually popular second-run films. However, there are occasional deviations from the normal booking policy. *The Wizard of Oz* and other cinema classics have been shown at this Minneapolis gem. Prices for tickets are a bargain ($2.00 for all shows), and concessions are much cheaper than at the suburban multiplexes, especially if you purchase a combo. The seats are comfortable, with stadium seating available in the back of the theater. The Riverview is a treasure, providing its south Minneapolis neighborhood with inexpensive entertainment in a wonderful theater.

St. Anthony Main Theatre
115 Southeast Main Street, Minneapolis
(612) 331–4723

This theater is in Minneapolis's beautiful St. Anthony area. It is also within walking distance of Nicollet Island and the Stone Arch Bridge and close to downtown.

St. Anthony Main Theatre has much more charm than your average suburban multiplex. The individual theaters and seating are comfortable and the concessions comparable to other theaters in town, but once again, the theater's real selling point is its location, right next to the picturesque St. Anthony area. Go for a walk and enjoy the grandeur and the sites of downtown and St. Anthony, then stop by the theater for a movie.

Suburban World Theater
3022 Hennepin Avenue South, Minneapolis
(612) 825-0717

The historic Suburban World Theater was recently renovated into a one-screen cinema and restaurant. When the restoration was completed in June, the theater appropriately opened with *Some Like It Hot*. The theater reflects the Uptown neighborhood, so the food and beverages are different from the usual grub and movies. The menu includes the usual burgers and pizza as well as wraps, salads, tapas, and sandwiches, plus wine and beer—all served during shows. Also included is the exceptional beauty of the theater.

The Suburban World first opened in 1928 as the Granada Theatre. It was and is an example of Spanish-Moorish architecture, adorned with stucco facades of balconies, plants, and statues. The combination of the food and the architecture make this an interesting place to see a revival or second-run film. Also, the theater now hosts special television sports events, concerts, and live performances.

U Film Society
U of M Campus, Bell Auditorium,
17th Avenue SE at University Avenue SE,
Minneapolis
(612) 627-4430
www.ufilm.org

U Film offers eclectic and piquant films from around the world. No issue or subject matter is off limits here: A recent series was on marijuana. For over 25 years Al Milgrom has been the director of the U Film Society, where he has screened a vast array of domestic and foreign films. Additionally, two of the most important Twin Cities film events are held here annually: the Minneapolis/St. Paul International Film Festival and the Twin Cities Gay, Lesbian, and Transgender Film Festival. The Rivertown Film Festival screens films from Russia, China, Brazil, and Australia. All the corners of the world are brought together at this wonderful and inexpensive event for cineastes.

Uptown Theatre
2906 Hennepin Avenue South, Minneapolis
(612) 825-6006

The Uptown Theatre is where most art and indie cinema debuts in the Twin Cities. Films frequently are screened at the Uptown exclusively before moving to Landmark's Lagoon Cinema and suburban Twin Cities theaters.

In the heart of Minneapolis's hip Uptown neighborhood, the Uptown Theatre is a stunning piece of architecture. Since the 1930s it has been the best single-screen theater in the area, in part because of its size—as large as most of the suburban multiplexes. The balcony is huge and the seating is comfortable. Unfortunately, despite its breathtaking architecture, details such as the rest rooms and paint on the walls have not been as well maintained. Nevertheless, the Uptown Theatre remains one of the most enjoyable movie venues in the Twin Cities.

St. Paul

Grandview Theater
1830 Grand Avenue, St. Paul
(651) 698-3344

Two neighborhood theaters showing first-run movies survive in St. Paul, and the Grandview, opened in 1933, lives on at its Grand Avenue location near Macalester College and the University of St. Thomas. The theater has two screens, a large theater downstairs and a smaller room upstairs (originally the theater's balcony). Designed in the Art Moderne style, the classic theater is a neighborhood treasure.

Highland Theater
760 Cleveland Avenue South, St. Paul
(651) 698-3085

The future of the 1938 Art Deco Highland Theater in St. Paul's Highland Park neighborhood is in doubt at the time of this writing, although the classic cinema currently continues to show first-run movies. Competition from suburban megacomplexes has hit many one- and two-screen cinemas in the Cities hard over the years, and the Highland, along with its sister theater, the Grandview, is a holdover from another era. Stepping Stone Theater, a children's theater currently in Galtier Plaza in downtown St. Paul, signed a purchase agreement to buy the theater and convert it into their new playhouse, but the sale has not yet gone through. Neighborhood councils and area residents are battling the sale by attempting to have the theater designated a Historic Preservation Site and maintained as a first-run movie house. So get down to the Highland Theater while you still can, and enjoy the latest Hollywood has to offer in a classic neighborhood theater.

The Suburbs

Har Mar 11
2100 North Snelling Avenue, Roseville
(651) 636–2664
www.generalcinema.com

If you want to see the most recent Hollywood blockbuster hits with a few indie and art house film leftovers, this is the spot. Har Mar and the retail complexes in Roseville are some of the largest in the Twin Cities, with the exception of the Mall of America, so go ahead and catch a film and do some shopping all in one visit. There are three large theaters where the most recent box office smashes are shown daily on big screens and eight smaller theaters with a much smaller multiplex feel.

Heights Theatre
3951 Central Avenue NE,
Columbia Heights
(763) 788–9079

Once a dilapidated second-run theater, the Heights has been transformed into one of the most beautiful theaters in the Twin Cities. A few years ago the restoration began: The inside and outside were painted, comfortable new seats were installed, and a vintage theater organ was installed. The organ allows silent film classics to be scored for the audience's pleasure.

Besides occasional silent film revivals, the Heights also books second-run and classic films, as well as special events such

St. Paul's historic Grandview Theater plays first-run movies in its cozy spot on Grand Avenue in St. Paul. PHOTO: TODD R. BERGER

as Tromafest, a festival dedicated to the kitschy horror of Troma Studios. For this event, Lloyd Kaufman came to the Heights for a special screening of his newest film and a book signing. For adventurous film lovers the Heights is one of the most interesting movie theaters in the Twin Cities.

Pavilion at Crossroads
County Road B-2 and Snelling Avenue,
Roseville
(651) 777–FILM

These theaters are part of the United Artists theater chain and show the Hollywood hits with a few art and indie films. Pavilion at Crossroads has excellent sound and seating and has the advantage of proximity to Minneapolis and St. Paul and easy accessibility via Minnesota Highway 36.

Regal Cinemas Brooklyn Center 20
Minnesota Highway 252 at I–94 and I–694
(763) 566–3456
www.regalcinemas.com

Regal Cinemas Brooklyn Center 20 has the most screens and the most modern theaters in the Twin Cities. Carmike Oakdale Stadium 20 is the only other theater in the area with 20 screens. The new Regal Cinemas, like the other megaplexes, has stadium seating, high-back adjustable chairs, and digital sound in all of its theaters. Besides these amenities, Regal Cinemas feels more comfortable due to its design, which includes larger individual theaters decorated with minimalistic murals. This immense yet comfortable megaplex also includes a cafe stocked with many coffees and ice creams and a video game room for kids of all ages.

Roseville 4 Theatres
1211 Larpenteur Avenue West, Roseville
(651) 488–4242

Roseville 4 shows all the Hollywood blockbuster hits—and does it for cheap. Tuesday night tickets are only $1.00 and concessions are reasonably priced. These bargains make Roseville 4 a perennially favorite hangout for teens in the Twin Cities. The theater is located conveniently near the busy Roseville shopping area.

Showplace 16 Theatres
Minnesota Highway 52 at Upper 55th Street, Inver Grove Heights
(651) 453 1016
www.kerasotes.com

One of the first mammoth megaplexes in the Twin Cities, Showplace 16 Theatres is also one of the best. With some of the largest movie screens, comfortable stadium seating, and a great view of the screen anywhere, Showplace 16 is one of the many new colossal multiplexes in the Twin Cities suburban area. Summer hits are usually booked on several screens, assuring an expeditious showing of current hits.

Mall of America

General Cinema Mall of America 14
401 South Avenue, Mall of America,
60 East Broadway, Bloomington
(952) 851–0074

This is one of the better theaters for watching movies in the Twin Cities. The theaters are large and comfortable, with huge screens and clear sound. General Cinema Mall of America occasionally is the site for local and even national premieres as well as quirky bookings. The "Terror at the Mall" Halloween series is one great example. For the past three years, recent and classic horror films have been shown at midnight during the month of October. But there are disadvantages at the Mall of America. The theaters are almost always busy; however, the complex is well designed for handling large crowds. In addition, the concessions are as extensive as any theater in the Twin Cities. Pizza and coffee are available as well as the more traditional theater fare, popcorn and soda.

Sports Bars

Minneapolis

Big Ten Restaurant & Bar
606 Washington Avenue SE, Minneapolis
(612) 378–0467

The Big Ten Restaurant & Bar is a University of Minnesota institution, known both for good subs and for covering Minnesota Golden Gopher athletics. The restaurant and bar is filled with memorabilia from Gophers sports; included are numerous autographed photos of triumphs in football, basketball, and hockey. For atmosphere alone, this is the place to catch a Gopher game, not to mention the beer and the excellent bar food. The televisions may not be as large and fancy as at the suburban bars, but they make up for it in spirit and tradition—and isn't that what college athletics are about after all?

The Heights

Once considered an eyesore in an already-run-down part of town, the Heights The-atre has been reborn as the centerpiece of a cultural revolution in the Columbia Heights suburb of Minneapolis. Under the guidance of proprietors Tom Letness and Dave Holmgren, who bought the theater in 1998 and funded the renovation with profits from the Dairy Queen franchise they own right next door, the tacky turquoise aluminum siding facade was stripped to reveal the beautiful brickwork underneath. Inside, the garish green walls were replaced with red velvet drapes and a deep purple coat of paint. The sound system and projectors were replaced with up-to-date equip-ment as well as an antiquated 70mm projector. With this new hardware, it's now pos-sible for the Heights to screen silent Frank Capra classics, the original 70mm prints of Lawrence of Arabia, and an amazing selection of "Bollywood" Hindi-language action films that have packed the 410-seat theater to capacity on a regular basis. They've also recently put in a restored Wurlitzer theater organ, and classic silent films now have the live organ accompaniment they did when they were first screened.

Aside from the wide selection of art house, classic, and foreign films they show, the Heights also holds special, irregularly scheduled events where independent film-makers passing through town come into the theater to speak about their work and sign autographs. In 2000, Lloyd Kaufman of Troma Films stopped in on his way to the Sundance Film Festival to lecture, sign copies of his book about the history of his com-pany, and give out free T-shirts and video copies of his movies to audience members. The event was accompanied by a weeklong film retrospective of Troma classics. The Heights also hosts the Minnesota Film Festival in conjunction with the area's annual spring Art-A-Whirl gallery tours as well as the annual late summer Minneapolis/St. Paul International Film Festival. All during the holiday season (starting with Hal-loween), holiday-specific classics and new films are shown.

The neighborhood the Heights is nestled in has undergone a similar reawaken-ing. With the influx of immigrants coming into the Twin Cities metro areas, every-thing from Balkan coffee shops serving Bosnian foods to Middle Eastern restaurants and grocery stores have taken root and blossomed in northeast Minneapolis. Gone are the days of tiny diners and bowling alleys being the main source of entertainment found in the shadows of the giant cereal factories and industrial warehouses— northeast Minneapolis today is a true, working melting pot of customs and cultures.

Despite being an art house theater on par with those in uptown Minneapolis, the Heights still retains its everyman's appeal. With its more-than-reasonable door prices (usually $5.00 per adult), cheap concessions, and free street parking, the Heights has managed to keep itself accessible to the working-class Columbia Heights neighbor-hood, which only recently started having coffee shops that were more than greasy spoons. They don't pretend to be a highbrow establishment either, mixing black-and-white horror and science fiction "classics" with popular second-run films and true "art" films. The theater has a loyal core crowd of locals that show up to see every-thing the theater runs, and, depending on what's on for the night, the rest of the audience comes from every imaginable walk of life to the suburban theater.

City Billiards Bar & Café
25 North Fourth Street, Minneapolis
(612) 338–BALL

City Billiards is the pool hall for downtown Minneapolis. Though smaller than its suburban counterparts, it has the advantage of being situated in the shadows of Minneapolis's skyline. Also available at City Billiards are beer, sandwiches, and pizza. The prices are reasonable for the pricey Warehouse District, and numerous specials are available for pool, food, and drinks.

Dub's Pub & Grill
412 14th Avenue SE, Minneapolis
(612) 331–4111

Over the years, this has been the site of numerous restaurants, bars, and grills. All have served a similar purpose as the local watering hole for the student population of the University of Minnesota. Dub's is a popular place to go for Minnesota Golden Gopher basketball, football, and hockey. The big-screen television and the reasonably priced burgers and subs are also big draws. So if you visit the state and are curious about Minnesotan's obsession with hockey—or would like a tall glass of tap beer—stop by Dub's.

William's Uptown Pub & Peanut Bar
2911 Hennepin Avenue South, Minneapolis
(612) 823–6271

If you are looking for variety in domestic and imported beers, William's is the place. This Uptown establishment boasts 217 different bottled beers from around the world, including Russia, Thailand, Africa, Finland, and Greece. In addition, William's offers plenty of daily specials on domestic beers and appetizers. The appetizers are enormous and go great with their wide selection of tap beers. William's is divided into a pub on the first floor and a more casual peanut bar in the basement where, not surprisingly, peanuts and popcorn are complimentary. Despite the sophisticated beer selection, the clientele at William's is mostly the young Uptown set, who enjoy the billiards and darts available on both floors.

St. Paul

Billy's on Grand
857 Grand Avenue, St. Paul
(651) 292–9140

Billy's on Grand offers something for all who are looking for a drink and a good time. The rooms at Billy's provide unlimited possibilities, from sports bar to lodge to patio seating in the summer. The beer prices are reasonable, too. Also available is a full menu, which includes burgers and prime rib. The variety of options available at Billy's is one of the reasons it is extremely busy on weekends and is such a popular nightlife spot among young St. Paulites.

Tom Reid's Hockey City Pub
258 West Seventh Street, St. Paul
(651) 292–9916

The name of this pub says it all. Hockey returned to Minnesota in fall 2000 at the Xcel Energy Center in St. Paul; in its wake, many new bars and restaurants have sprung up. And who better to open a pub than Tom Reid, a sports announcer and former National Hockey League player with the Minnesota North Stars (now the Dallas Stars). Not only does the pub broadcast the game on numerous television screens, but it also hosts a radio pre-game on KFAN, the local sports radio station.

The Suburbs

Biff's Sports Bar & Grill
7777 NE Minnesota Highway 65,
Spring Lake Park
(763) 784–9446

Biff's provides inexpensive pool, darts, food, and sports viewing for the northern suburbs of the Twin Cities. Televisions range in size from big to bigger screens at Biff's, where you can watch all your Vikings game day action. Besides the sports bar there are more than 25 pool tables, where the local working-class clientele play in organized pool leagues and enjoy Biff's many beer specials.

Billiard Street Café
7178 University Avenue NE, Fridley
(763) 574–1399
www.billiardstreet.com

Since 1988 Billiard Street Café has served as a pool hall for local teens. Unlike Biff's Sports Bar and Grill, Billiard Street Café is a no-alcohol pool hall with a cafe and a proshop. It is inconspicuously located in a strip mall; despite this, it is one of the area's largest billiard clubs, with more than 50 pool tables. In-house eight ball leagues make the Billiard Street Café busy, and it is sometimes difficult to reserve a table on weekday evenings, although they are usually available after a wait. Their late night/morning hours also provide ample opportunity for billiards. If you are looking to play pool in the Twin Cities, Billiard Street Café might be the place for you.

Joe Senser's Sports Grill & Bar
2350 Cleveland Avenue, Roseville
(651) 631–1781
4217 West 80th Street, Bloomington
(952) 835–1191
3010 Eagandale Place, St. Paul
(651) 687–9333

Joe Senser's Sports Grill & Bar is a popular spot for Minnesota Vikings fans. With three locations, it easily serves much of the area and provides excellent coverage on several big-screen televisions, as well as numerous smaller monitors. Joe Senser, a former Minnesota Viking, is the local legend/owner and also participates in a Vikings post-game show, "Vikings Unsensored" (on Twin Cities sports radio station, KFAN), after each game. In addition, Senser's features college football and basketball, as well as professional basketball, baseball, and hockey. Besides a wide selection of beers, Senser's has plenty of food to accompany the suds, such as a Friday and Saturday prime rib special from 5:00 to 11:00 P.M.

Park Tavern
3401 Louisiana Avenue, St. Louis Park
(952) 929–6810
5221 Viking Drive, Bloomington
(952) 844–0335

The Park Tavern is one of the Twin Cities' premier sports bars. Twin Citians come in hordes to watch sports on the big-screen televisions and enjoy the kitchen's excellent food. This is where they have the competition beat. Many other sports bars treat the food as secondary, but the Park Tavern excels, with delicious burgers and sandwiches, not the everyday bar fare. Plus, they have some of the best beer specials in town for Vikings games, and the St. Louis Park location boasts the best bowling alley in the Twin Cities.

Unique to the Twin Cities

Grumpy's Downtown
1111 Washington Avenue South, Minneapolis
(612) 340–9738
www.grumpysbar.com/downtown.html

Although we're told this looks kind of divey from the outside, especially since the interior lights are kept low at all times, this is actually a really interesting bar to check out. Intermittently, tables are moved around to make way for performance artists, poets, and acoustic and electric bands to set up in one corner, or a movie screen and projector are brought in and art house films, black-and-white classics, and new films from local filmmakers are showcased, including those from the ex-Minnesotan Coen brothers. There are also several pool tables and an ATM on the premises. There are about a dozen beers on tap, too, as well as a decent selection of food on the menu—especially for a bar—and the waitstaff is extremely attentive and friendly.

Nye's Polonaise Room
112 Hennepin Avenue East, Minneapolis
(612) 379–2021
www.nyespolonaise.com

Now this is a fun place to drink. Nye's, a northeast Minneapolis tradition since 1949, features live polka music in the basement and a piano bar upstairs most nights of the week, and everyone comes here to dance. The crowd is about as mixed as you can get, with senior citizens manning the accordions in Ruth Adams' Polka Band and barely 21-year-old hipsters hanging out on the dance floor. The bar looks much the same as it did when it first opened, with scarlet walls and carpets and dark, polished wood accents everywhere. The upstairs bar also serves Polish and American food that's good enough to come in for even if you don't want to polka.

Shopping

"Shopping trip" means so many different things when in the Twin Cities. It could mean you're planning a sunny, summer walk down picturesque Grand Avenue in St. Paul, where beautiful two-story Victorian houses have been converted into antiques shops, custom clothiers, or flower shops with multi-hued wares spilling out onto the sidewalk. It could mean window-shopping in the busy downtown districts of either city, where importers, clothiers, and jewelers have set up shop in the ornate storefronts of 100-plus-year-old buildings. It could mean braving the immense Mall of America, the largest indoor mall in the country.

But whatever "shopping trip" means to you, you're sure to find satisfaction shopping in the Twin Cities. There are tiny neighborhood shops, heady metropolitan areas, and suburban malls that carry everything from sports to celebrity memorabilia; specialty grocery complexes that sell novelty items and foods from around the world; and stores that carry everything you'd ever need to have a successful and beautiful wedding, professional social event, or child's theme birthday party.

Antiques Shops

Minneapolis

City Salvage and Antiques
505 First Avenue NE, Minneapolis
(612) 627–9107

Part art studio, part antiques shop, part salvage service, and part lamp gallery, this store's odd collection of stuff makes for highly entertaining shopping. Mantels, archways, buffets, stained glass, and other high-end items salvaged from old buildings or from people's basements fill the store, as well as a changing inventory that has at times included Charlie the Tuna lamps, a full bar complete with booths, and church pews. Owners John and Barbara Eckley have more than two decades' experience in architectural salvage.

Mildred's
1517 West Lake Street, Minneapolis
(612) 824–3347

This prettily restored three-story Eastlake Victorian home has many small rooms filled with pottery, dolls, art, linens, and glassware, specializing in Art Deco and 1950s kitsch. The side room is hung with long formal dresses, fur wraps, and ornate hats, while the jewelry case is full of brilliant rhinestone necklaces, earrings, and rings, as well as antique silver and gold

Insiders' Tip
There is no sales tax on clothing or groceries in Minnesota.

jewelry. There's also a large box full of bags of loose glass beads and buttons by the cash register for sale at extremely reasonable prices.

St. Paul

Wescott Station Antiques
226 West Seventh Street, St. Paul
(651) 227-2469
Wescott Station Antiques is a family-run antiques business offering seven rooms full of antique furniture, glassware, lamps, and more. Literally thousands of antiques and collectibles line the walls of this tightly packed store, making a visit here as much a treasure hunt as it is a shopping spree.

West Suburbs

Battlefield Military Antiques
3915 Minnesota Highway 7, St. Louis Park
(952) 920-3820
Battlefield Military Antiques is absolutely packed with war memorabilia, including rows and rows of books, magazines, and unopened boxes of model soldiers, frontiersmen, warplanes, and boats. The books, new and used, cover every era of combat from Hadrian's Wall to Vietnam, in incredible levels of both technical and strategic detail. What catches the eye first, though, are the neatly racked and displayed antiques: a clothing store's worth of old uniforms, helmets worn by both good guys and bad guys, blue and green caps topping the shelves in perfect rows, ribbons, and medals. Collectors will also appreciate the boxes of limited-edition G.I. Joes, for those whose ideal soldier stands under a foot tall.

Blake Antiques
8450 Excelsior Boulevard, Hopkins
(952) 930-0477
Blake Antiques carries a wide selection of refinished antique furniture ready to bring home and display without even needing to be dusted. Besides furniture, the store carries fine sterling jewelry and

flatware, original oil paintings, Oriental rugs, fine porcelain (including unusual Arts and Crafts designs), pottery, and an eclectic collection of costume and fine jewelry.

Bookstores

Minneapolis

Amazon Books Co-Operative
4432 Chicago Avenue South, Minneapolis
(612) 821-9630
www.amazonfembks.com
Amazon Books Co-Op opened in the late 1960s, the first bookstore in the country dedicated to women/lesbian books. It remains today one of only a handful of bookstores in the United States specializing in books "by, for, and about women." The bookstore in south Minneapolis stocks some 10,000 fiction and nonfiction titles, as well as gifts, music, and art. The bookstore, which specializes in titles from small feminist presses, is a worker cooperative, and the friendly staff will steer you to titles of interest.

Big Brain Comics
81 South 10th Street, Minneapolis
(612) 338-4390
This small, well-stocked comic book store focuses more on unusual and underground comic books and magazines than the superhero type that Marvel and DC put out. There are lots of imported comics in the stacks here, as well as American independent and collectible comic books.

The Bokhandel
2600 Park Avenue, Minneapolis
(612) 871-4907
www.americanswedishinst.org
Located inside the beautiful American Swedish Institute building, the Bokhandel sells books, prints, cards, gift items, compact discs, and cassette tapes relating to Sweden and Scandinavia. Titles are available in both English and Swedish.

Book House in Dinkytown
429 14th Avenue SE, Minneapolis
(612) 331–1430

The Book House has been a mainstay of the University's Dinkytown area for more than 20 years, carrying hardcover and softcover books. With more than 150,000 volumes in stock, this store has bookshelves that run from floor to ceiling and has excellent fiction, drama, and poetry sections, not to mention rows and rows of foreign language material and an entire basement level dedicated to scholarly works. Book House buys tons of used books, so it's worth checking back regularly to see what's new in stock.

B H Biermaier's Books
809 Fourth Street SE, Minneapolis
(612) 378–0129

Bill Biermaier has been selling books from his Minneapolis location for a quarter century and is proud of his success in locating hard-to-find copies of out-of-print or obscure books. Arts, literature, and children's books dominate the store's collection in sheer number, but Biermaier's is a good source for just about any genre of book you're looking for, including rare and collectors' editions. With ceiling-high stacks and books spilling out into the aisles, this place practically begs you to browse for hours. Finding a specific book can become a daylong challenge, but if you need to get out in a hurry, Bill can find it for you awfully quick.

BookSmart
2919 Hennepin Avenue South, Minneapolis
(612) 823–5612

BookSmart is the place to go to buy cheap used books, with a huge selection of mysteries and a great biography section. Turnover is quick (especially since they throw 99-cent inventory clearance sales on a regular basis), so if you see something you want in stock, you'd better buy it quick or someone else will.

Cummings Books
318 14th Avenue SE, Minneapolis
(612) 331–1424

Jim Cummings, son of Book House owner Kristen Cummings, struck out on his own a few years ago to found this bright new used-and-rare shop. In his shop, fiction is an especially strong presence, as are literary criticism, special interest books, and, for some reason, Canadian history. If you can't find what you're looking for, Cummings Books's friendly staff is more than willing to help you look.

DreamHaven Books & Comics
1309 Fourth Street SE, Minneapolis
(612) 379–8924
912 West Lake Street, Minneapolis
(612) 823–6161
www.dreamhavenbooks.com

In addition to Jupiter-size selections of new and used books, DreamHaven is a dream destination for fans of comic books, Japanese anime, kung fu movies, and everything pop-cultural, from Dr. Who to Asterix. A free monthly catalog and a mail-order service mean that even out-of-state patrons can enjoy DreamHaven. DreamHaven is also responsible for putting on some of the larger science fiction and fantasy fan conventions in the Twin Cities and holds many in-store book signings when science fiction and fantasy authors pass through town.

Lien's Bookstore
507 Hennepin Avenue East, Minneapolis
(612) 362–0763

Not your ordinary used bookstore, Lien's is a treasury of the printed word. First editions and rare, out-of-print, and gorgeous art and history volumes live in this picturesque corner-store collection. The store holds 4,000 square feet of books and specializes in European and American history, with a particular emphasis on military books as well as classic literature. The knowledgeable staff will help track down those hard-to-find old books the store may not have on hand.

Magus Books & Herbs
1316 Fourth Street SE, Minneapolis
(612) 379–7669
www.magusbooks.com

Magus Books sells new books on t'ai chi, Wicca, magic, tarot, astrology, and the like, as well as herbs, candles, incense, scented oils, jewelry, and meditation and New Age tapes and CDs. Their staff is very informative and can direct you to exactly whatever it is you're looking for, as well as provide helpful historical background information on products you purchase.

Paperback Exchange
2227 West 50th Street, Minneapolis
(612) 929–8801

Paperback Exchange carries thousands of used paperback books covering pretty much all subjects, from pulp mystery to criticism, depending on what's in their current, quick-turnover stock. The store also rents hardcover books for nominal charges, many of which are brand-new and not yet available at local libraries.

Present Moment Books & Herbs
3546 Grand Avenue South, Minneapolis
(612) 824–3157
www.presentmoment.com

In addition to being one of the nation's largest purveyors of herbs and homeopathic remedies, Present Moment offers more than 36,000 new and used book titles. Whether your New Age and wellness needs run to *Cooking with Herbs* or *Infinite Mind: The Science of Human Vibrations, Compassion in Action,* or *The Spirit of Place: A Workbook for Sacred Alignment,* it's present at Present Moment. Their specialties include books on alternative health, world religions, New Age, Wiccan, and yoga, as well as women's studies and environmental publications.

St. Martin's Table/St. Martin's Bookstore
2001 Riverside Avenue, Minneapolis
(612) 339–3920

St. Martin's Bookstore is located at the back of St. Martin's Table (see the Restaurants chapter for more information about St. Martin's Table), with racks of books devoted to peace, religion, and social-justice issues. The bookstore also holds special Friday-night readings and performances September through May.

Shinders
733 Hennepin Avenue, Minneapolis
(612) 333–3628

With 13 locations throughout the Twin Cities metro area, locally owned Shinders is a great place to pick up major newspapers from around the country, comic books, games, sports collectibles and trading cards, hard-to-find independent magazines, and books from both major and independent publishing houses.

Uncle Edgar's Mystery Bookstore/Uncle Hugo's Science Fiction Bookstore
2864 Chicago Avenue South, Minneapolis
(612) 824–9984 or (612) 824–6347
www.unclehugo.com or www.uncleedgar.com

Specialization is the name of the game for many independent booksellers in these days of giant chain bookstores, but Uncle Edgar's/Uncle Hugo's was at it long before the trend began in the late '80s. Uncle Hugo's opened in 1974, and Uncle Edgar's opened in 1980. The two shops merged into one location in south Minneapolis in 1984. With a huge selection of their respective genres, both new and used, they sponsor many author readings every month. Check their respective Web sites for more information about upcoming events.

St. Paul

Bound to Be Read
870 Grand Avenue, St. Paul
(651) 646–BOOK or (866) 230–BOOK
www.boundtoberead.com

Independently owned, with stores in Albuquerque, New Mexico; Key Largo, Florida; and St. Paul, Bound to Be Read is the Twin Cities' newest purveyor of new general-interest books. The spacious bookstore in the heart of the Grand Avenue shopping district stocks thousands of titles in virtually all genres and sponsors many monthly author readings and signings.

Midway Used & Rare Books
1579 University Avenue West, St. Paul
(651) 644–7605

With three stories of used and rare books that include huge pulp fiction and small press poetry sections, this store seems as though it's almost too good to be true. The prices are incredibly reasonable, and if whatever it was you originally came here to find isn't available, you're sure to find one or two things that are easily good enough to take home instead.

The Red Balloon Bookshop
891 Grand Avenue, St. Paul
(651) 224–8320
www.redballoonbookshop.com

This spacious bookstore, specializing in educational and fun books for kids, is located in a beautiful converted Victorian house on St. Paul's Grand Avenue. The store carries more than 50,000 books, audio- and videotapes, and selected toys for young people from birth to junior high age. The bookstore offers free gift wrapping, a book-of-the-month club, and non-profit discounts; takes mail and phone orders; and sends out a regular newsletter with a calendar of in-store events. Several times a year, visiting authors and educators speak at the Red Balloon, and the store holds teacher/parent events during the school year.

Ruminator Books
1648 Grand Avenue, St. Paul
(651) 699–0587
www.ruminator.com

This nationally known, locally owned bookstore (formerly known as the Hungry Mind) is a regular stop for visiting authors to perform and hold book signings throughout the year. The store has an excellent magazine rack of both national and independent publications as well as a huge collection of literary and nonfiction works in stock. The bookstore's nationally distributed publica-

St. Paul's Ruminator Books, formerly known as Hungry Mind, serves the general book-buying public as well as students at neighboring Macalester College. PHOTO: TODD R. BERGER

tion, the *Ruminator Review*, features new titles and related articles.

Sixth Chamber Used Books
1332 Grand Avenue, St. Paul
(651) 690–9463
www.sixthchamber.com

Sixth Chamber Used Books is a clean, well-organized, and spacious used bookstore featuring hardcover and paperback editions in most major categories. Especially notable is their used science fiction and fantasy section, which takes up several ceiling-to-floor shelves in the back of the store. Their prices are extremely reasonable, and their staff is both quick and efficient. Sixth Chamber also holds irregular in-store book signings and author readings.

Clothing Stores

Minneapolis

Hubert White
South Seventh Street and Nicollet Mall,
IDS Crystal Court, Minneapolis
(612) 339–9200

Hubert White has been the quality standard for men's apparel since they opened their first store in Minneapolis in 1916. Today the thriving chain of men's clothiers carries a wide selection of brand-name men's contemporary, casual, and formal wear, including Hugo Boss, Gran Sasso, Bobby Jones, Scott Barber, Canali, Oxxford, Tallia, and Gitman. Their very professional staff is helpful in both assisting with selecting purchases and arranging alterations at the last minute.

Lava Lounge
3037 Lyndale Avenue South, Minneapolis
(612) 824–5631

Lava Lounge's inventory makes it a one-stop shop for club clothes. Beyond the staples—shiny, leathered, feathered, synthetic clothes—it also carries an impressive array of skateboards, handbags, hair dye, glitter, and headdresses, with brand names like Playboy, Billabong, and Kangal stocked

for all seasons. Lava Lounge's annual patio sale occurs during the Lyn-Lake Festival in August, when prices on cool clothes are significantly dropped.

Nate's Clothing Company
37 North Fourth Street, Minneapolis
(612) 333–1401

A fixture in the Minneapolis Warehouse District since 1916, Nate's carries a staggering collection of worsted wool, nubby tweed, and linen suits and shirts. The store carries suits and sportcoats from designers like Bill Blass and Ralph Lauren, and Nate's expert staff can find something sharp and classy for even hard-to-size guys. The store's sales are legendary, so sign up for Nate's mailings for the inside scoop on sale dates.

Saint Sabrina's Parlor in Purgatory
2751 Hennepin Avenue, Minneapolis
(612) 874–7360

Decorated in deep black and red tones, Saint Sabrina's is a decadent shopping experience. The store has a wide selection of club clothes, sunglasses, shoes, bondage clothes, leather jackets, and even an in-store piercing booth. The clearance rack is a good place to pick up marked-down stuff that was cool yesterday and will probably be cool and expensive again tomorrow.

Top Shelf Clothiers & Consultants
3040 Lyndale Avenue South, Minneapolis
(612) 824–2800

Located inside a turn-of-the 20th-century former home, Top Shelf is divided into many small, friendly rooms that are perfect for the personalized business of creating custom clothing. A formal dining room now acts as the library for a collection of the finest offerings of suit, sportcoat, pant, and topcoat materials from the woolen mills of England, Italy, Spain, and the United States. Well-known fabric lines such as Zegna, Loro Piana, Roger La Viale, Scabal, Reda, Barberis, Cerruti, Holland, Sherry, and many others are available for custom designs, including shirts. From the selection of fabric to measurement

Minneapolis's Nicollet Mall offers upscale chain shopping as well as several local stores, attracting shoppers of all persuasions to downtown Minneapolis. PHOTO: GREATER MINNEAPOLIS CONVENTION & VISITORS ASSOCIATION

and styling, the customer is encouraged to follow the process and participate in laying the groundwork for satisfying future orders.

St. Paul

Annette's: A Unique Boutique
867 Grand Avenue, St. Paul
(651) 222–9798

Located in the Victoria Crossing shopping center, Annette's carries some of the most unusual, beautiful, high-quality clothes and jewelry in the Twin Cities. Strings of black pearls are suspended on silver wire like iridescent sprigs of wheat, while beautiful, brightly colored silk jackets and woolen capes fringed with soft fur or tufts of pheasant feathers hang from the racks. Although the price tags may seem a bit high, considering the quality of the fabrics and material used in these pieces, they're actually reasonable.

Artgarbs Gallery
794 Grand Avenue, St. Paul
(651) 229–0204

Each piece of clothing in Artgarbs Gallery is an original concept and design, and all are hand painted by resident artist Lisa J. Omodt. The clothing is 100 percent cotton or linen, and is machine washable. The designs, inspired by everyday activities and summer outdoor play, are limited editions and signed by the artist.

C'est Fou Showroom
1128 Grand Avenue, St. Paul
(651) 602–9133

This French boutique–style retail store carries one-of-a-kind and custom-made clothes, as well as elegant shoes and eclectic and glamorous jewelry and accessories. The store offers free alterations on all clothes purchased here, with an emphasis on creating a flattering fit for all customers. The store also displays and sells a rotating stock of artwork and jewelry created by local artists.

Coat of Many Colors
1666 Grand Avenue, St. Paul
(651) 690–5255

This Grand Avenue store specializes in natural fabric women's clothing in sizes small to 3X, as well as jewelry and gifts from around the world. Most of the jewelry here is handmade, focusing on sterling silver set with semiprecious stones, bone, seeds, and metals. Coat of Many Colors is a socially and environmentally conscious store that returns 20 percent of their profits to Third World development projects.

Grand Jeté
975 Grand Avenue, St. Paul
(651) 227–0331

Grand Jeté is a retail store carrying a full line of dancewear for children and adults, including dance tights, leotards, and skirts and ballet, pointe, tap, and jazz shoes in a full range of sizes. The store staff is especially helpful in assisting customers in the selection and proper fit of pointe shoes.

West Suburbs

Oh Baby!
3515 Galleria, Edina
(952) 928–9119
743 East Lake Street, Wayzata
(952) 404–0170

Oh Baby! offers some of the Twin Cities' most precious selection of clothing for infants, toddlers, and growing boys and girls, along with bedding, furnishings, accessories, and gifts. Much of the inventory is imported from Europe, while in-house designers can be hired to fully customize children's rooms with hand-painted walls, furniture, and custom bedding.

Whymsy
3360 Galleria, Edina
(952) 924–4176

Whymsy is a retailer of unique, creative attire and accessories for women, including

distinctive one-of-a-kind and limited-edition items. The store is full of brand-name lines of upscale, coordinated women's clothing and accessories, with a focus on elegant casual and special occasion attire for the nontraditional woman.

Farmers' Markets

Minnesota has long been a major exporter of fruits, grains, legumes, and even flowers, and the variety of plants that actually grow here is never more apparent than at the farmers' markets and roadside produce stands that spring up just about everywhere during summer and early fall. Everything from gigantic pumpkins and unhusked ears of corn to baskets of plump, red strawberries and juicy blueberries can be picked and purchased during the season. Here are just a few of the many sites where you can buy these homegrown delicacies (check for official summer opening dates and business hours, as they're subject to change and are dependent on growing seasons).

Adelmann's Farm Market
24149 Chippendale Avenue West,
Farmington
(651) 463–3543
www.herb man.com

9:00 A.M. to 6:00 P.M. Monday through Saturday, noon to 5:00 P.M. Sunday.

Aldrich Arena Farmers' Market
1850 White Bear Avenue, St. Paul
(651) 227–6856
www.stpaulfarmersmarket.com

8:00 A.M. to 12:30 P.M. Wednesday.

At the Farm
8880 Minnesota Highway 5, Waconia
(952) 442–4816

10:00 A.M. to 7:00 P.M. daily.

Axdahl's Garden Farm
7452 Manning Avenue, Stillwater
(651) 439–2460

9:30 A.M. to 6:30 P.M. daily.

Boorsma's Organically Grown Vegetables
MN 5 and Minnewashta Place, Victoria
(952) 443–2068
8:00 A.M. to noon Monday through Saturday.

Burnsville Farmers' Market
Diamondhead Senior Campus, 200 West
Burnsville Parkway, Burnsville
(952) 227–6856
www.stpaulfarmersmarket.com
7:00 A.M. to 1:00 P.M. Saturday.

Cal's Market and Greenhouse
6403 Eagan Drive, Savage
(952) 447–5215
8:00 A.M. to 9:00 P.M. Monday through Saturday, 10:00 A.M. to 6:00 P.M. Sunday.

Cottage Grove Farmers' Market
Cottage Grove Square Mall, 8200 80th
Avenue, Cottage Grove
(651) 227–6856
www.stpaulfarmersmarket.com
2:00 to 6:00 P.M. Sunday.

Dinkytown Farmers' Market
15th Avenue and Fourth Street SE,
Minneapolis
(612) 379–3913
8:00 A.M. to 4:00 P.M. Friday.

Excelsior Farmers' Market
Lyman Park on Water Street, Excelsior
(952) 474–3145
2:00 to 6:00 P.M. Thursday.

Gerten's Farm Market
2900 East 65th Street, Inver Grove Heights
(651) 450–0001
9:00 A.M. to 6:00 P.M. daily.

Greenfingers Farm, Inc.
7140 Casey Parkway, Prior Lake
(952) 447–8945
9:00 A.M. to 7:00 P.M. Monday through Saturday, noon to 5:00 P.M. Sunday.

Healthy Powderhorn Farmers' Market
Mount Olive Lutheran Church, East 31st
Street and Chicago Avenue South,
Minneapolis
(612) 721–5745
9:00 A.M. to 1:00 P.M. Saturday.

Hopkins Farmers' Market
16 Ninth Avenue South, Hopkins
(952) 922–7703
7:30 A.M. to noon Saturday.

Johnson's Whistling Well Farm
County Roads 21 and 76, Hastings
(651) 436–7314
Noon to dusk Saturday and Sunday.

Jordan Ranch
6400 Upper Afton Road, Woodbury
(651) 738–3422
9:00 A.M. to 6:00 P.M. Tuesday through
Sunday.

Marketfest
3rd Street and Washington, White Bear Lake
(651) 426–2271
6:00 to 9:00 P.M. Thursday.

Minneapolis Farmers' Market
312 Lyndale Avenue North, Minneapolis
(612) 333–1737
www.mplsfarmersmarket.com
6:00 A.M. to 1:00 P.M. weekdays, 6:00 A.M. to
2:00 P.M. weekends.

Minneapolis Farmers' Market on Nicollet
Mall
Nicollet Mall between 4th and 10th Street,
Minneapolis
(612) 333–1737
www.mplsfarmersmarket.com
6:00 A.M. to 6:00 P.M. Thursday, 9:00 A.M. to
3:00 P.M. Saturday. The Saturday market
may be closed during Nicollet Mall events.

Father and son inspect the produce at the Minneapolis Farmers' Market on Nicollet Mall. PHOTO: GREATER MINNEAPOLIS CONVENTION & VISITORS ASSOCIATION

Morrie's Market
7170 Minnesota Highway 7, Excelsior
(952) 472-1135
Open daily from July to October; hours vary.

Northfield Farmers' Market
Riverside Park on Seventh Street, Northfield
(651) 463-3577
Call for hours and dates.

Pahl's Market
6885 160th Street, Apple Valley
(952) 431-4345
9:00 A.M. to 8:00 P.M. Saturday, 10:00 A.M. to 5:00 P.M. Sunday.

Peterson Produce
8910 Minnesota Highway 12, Delano
(763) 972-2052
10:00 A.M. to 6:00 P.M. daily.

Richfield Farmers' Market
6335 Portland Avenue, Richfield
(612) 861-9385
www.ci.richfield.mn.us
7:00 A.M. to noon Saturday.

Riverside Farm Market
Minnesota Highway 10, Elk River
(763) 427-6023
8:00 A.M. to 7:00 P.M. daily.

Roseville Farmers' Market
HarMar Mall, 2100 Snelling Avenue, Roseville
8:00 A.M. to noon Tuesday.

Seventh Place Mall Farmers' Market
7th Street and Wabasha Street, St. Paul
(651) 227-6856
www.stpaulfarmersmarket.com
10:00 A.M. to 2:00 P.M. Tuesday and Thursday.

St. Luke's Church Farmers' Market
1079 Summit Avenue, St. Paul
(651) 227–6856
www.stpaulfarmersmarket.com
1:15 to 5:00 P.M. Friday.

St. Paul Downtown Farmers' Market
5th Street and Wall Street, St. Paul
(651) 227–6856
www.stpaulfarmersmarket.com
6:00 A.M. to 1:00 P.M. Saturday, 8:00 A.M. to
1:00 P.M. Sunday.

St. Paul Farmers' Market
Signal Hills Shopping Center, Butler and
Robert Street, West St. Paul
(651) 227–6856
8:00 A.M. to noon Friday.

Westonka Farmers' Market
County Roads 15 and 110, Mound
(763) 491–8045
8:00 A.M. to noon Saturday, noon to 5:00
P.M. Monday and Wednesday.

White Bear Lake Farmers' Market
Corner of Third Street and Washington
Square, White Bear Lake
(651) 429–8566
8:00 A.M. to 1:00 P.M. Friday.

Woodbury Farmers' Market
Woodbury City Hall, 8301 Valley Creek Road,
Woodbury
(651) 227–6856
8:00 A.M. to 1:00 P.M. Sunday.

Flower and Garden Shops

Minneapolis

Brown & Greene
4400 Beard Avenue South,
Minneapolis
(612) 928–3778

Brown & Greene floral designer Lyn Williams has been creating beautiful, non-traditional arrangements from her historic neighborhood store since 1989. Her designs are centered around customers'

color choices and feature unusual flower choices like gerberas and black calla lilies to go with roses and more conventional flowers. Bouquet prices range from $30 to more than $200, depending on the arrangements, and reservations for weddings must be made at least six months in advance.

Indulge & Bloom
1320 Hennepin Avenue South,
Minneapolis
(612) 343–0000

Indulge & Bloom carries beautiful, strange, and unusual flowers and plants from all over the world, including Ecuadorian roses, orchids, and topiaries. Staff members dress in head-to-toe black and pride themselves on their professionalism; wedding arrangements are their specialty. Wedding flowers can range from $1,000 to $30,000 and up, and reservations should be made 9 to 12 months in advance of the wedding. The store also features home-decor items, Waterford crystal, bath-and-body products, garden-related items, ornaments, books, cards, truffles, and children's gifts.

St. Paul

Laurel Street Flowers
1129 Grand Avenue, St. Paul
(651) 221–9700
www.laurelstreetflowers.com

Located in a cottage house on historic and picturesque Grand Avenue, this store's arrangements fit perfectly into its surroundings. The shop's guiding style leans to English and French Provincial, and typical arrangements include fresh blooms such as tulips and lilies of the valley in spring and summer to boutonnieres shaped as miniature Christmas wreaths for winter weddings. Owner and designer Paula Flom uses a European hand-tie method in her bouquets instead of plastic holders, and her creations often include such unusual choices as mixed fruits in dark colors dripping from centerpieces and viney garlands hanging from chandeliers. Prices run the gamut of boutonnieres starting at $9.50 to wedding bouquets costing around $125.00. Flom starts wedding couples with a free consultation and estimate and suggests that couples make arrangements a year before the wedding date.

Stems & Vines
949 Grand Avenue, St. Paul
(651) 228-1450
Four additional Twin Cities locations

Housed in a renovated Victorian home on Grand Avenue, the store's location in historic St. Paul adds to its ambience and charm. Tia Stern, one of the top designers at Stems & Vines, designs flower bouquets and events around personalities instead of colors and styles; and specializes in arranging flowers for weddings at an average cost of $3,000 for the entire event. Although Stern says that no bride is turned away, Stems & Vines designers are booked well in advance; it's recommended that reservations be made no later than nine months prior to your wedding date. Stems & Vines is a sponsor of the Twin Cities Bridal Association and holds exhibitions at every bridal and floral event in town.

Music Stores

Minneapolis

Cheapo Discs
1300 West Lake Street, Minneapolis
(612) 827-8238
1417 Southeast Fourth Street, Minneapolis
(612) 362-0136
5151 Central Avenue NE, Fridley
(763) 574-2308
80 North Snelling Avenue, St. Paul
(651) 644-8981

Cheapo is the Twin Cities' largest independent seller of new and used CDs. The store opened decades ago as Cheapo Records but since the arrival of CDs has moved into the more popular format for recorded music. Today Cheapo has four Twin Cities locations, where new and used rock, country, R&B, and much more are bought and sold 365 days a year until midnight. The largest location, in the Uptown neighborhood of Minneapolis, also houses

Applause, Cheapo's new and used classical and jazz CD store. A second Applause store is located across the street from the St. Paul store, at 71 North Snelling Avenue (651-644-5115). The Uptown and St. Paul locations also feature new and used records and tapes.

Electric Fetus
2000 Fourth Avenue South, Minneapolis
(612) 870-9300
www.efetus.com

The Electric Fetus is one of the Twin Cities' favorite stores to purchase CDs because of its wide selection of releases in all genres. In addition, the store features plenty of sales and reduced-price items. Besides stocking a superb selection of rock and pop, the store has a wide selection of jazz, blues, country, reggae, and ska. Also available are used CDs as well as clothing, gifts, and tobacco-related accessories.

Extreme Noise Records
407 West Lake Street, Minneapolis
(612) 824-0100

Extreme Noise Records specializes in punk rock records and CDs. The store sells its merchandise at lower prices because of the largely volunteer staff. Whether you are looking for classic Buzzcocks, the Ramones, the Germs, or G. G Allin, or more recent punk stars such as Dillinger 4, Extreme Noise usually will have it. Punk records and CDs are available from throughout the world. The store also features a wide selection of "zines," books, and videos regarding the punk rock lifestyle. In addition to selling records unavailable at other Twin Cities music sellers, the store also serves as an important part of the local community by supporting punk rock in the area.

Let It Be Records
1001 Nicollet Mall, Minneapolis
(612) 339-7439
www.letitbe.com

Let It Be is loaded with unique LPs and CDs. Many uncommon items can be found at the store, including a wide selection of indie and import records. Besides rock, the store stocks numerous avant-garde, jazz, soundtracks, blues, and under-recognized groups and musicians. Let It Be also features a wide selection of dance records. Plus, the store has plenty of classic and rare vinyl as well as videos, books, and magazines.

Roadrunner Records
4304 Nicollet Avenue, Minneapolis
(612) 822–0613
www.landspeedrecords.com
Roadrunner Records specializes in CDs and vinyl in all genres of music. The largest selection can be found in the rock area; however, the store also features a wide selection of jazz, punk, and world music. Roadrunner's world music selection is one of the best in the Twin Cities.

St. Paul

Root Cellar Records
636 North Snelling Avenue, St. Paul
(651) 644–2070 or 1 (888) 663–2070
www.vinylust.com
Root Cellar Records is an interesting St. Paul record store. It's owned by Earl Root, who for years has hosted *Root of All Evil* on Saturday night/Sunday morning on community radio station KFAI. The program showcases metal, but the contents of Root's store include numerous rock, jazz, soundtracks, and difficult-to-categorize music. The store stocks plenty of oddities, including '70s German psychedelic music and cartoon and monster movie soundtracks. The store also features a bargain basement and LPs as well as CDs and has the largest selection of metal LPs and CDs in the Twin Cities.

Odds 'n' Ends

Minneapolis

Beezwax Candles, Etc.
3001 Hennepin Avenue South, Calhoun Square, Minneapolis
(612) 822–6169

Beezwax Candles, Etc., carries one of the Cities' largest arrays of both scented and unscented candles in all shapes and sizes. Made from a natural, renewable resource, these pure beeswax candles are clean burning and long lasting. Also in stock are beautifully scented natural aromatherapy candles, more than 30 brands of incense, perfume oils, aromatherapy oils, bath products, and scent diffusers. You can also display your candle purchases in their unique selection of home decor, including chandeliers, wall sconces, and candle holders of all sizes.

Colección y Elegancia
1515 East Lake Street, #118,
Mercado Central, Minneapolis
(612) 728–5416
Colección y Elegancia, a small store tucked into Mercado Central, carries beautiful music boxes, snowglobes, porcelain figurines, and other things that have to be put on high shelves where they won't be destroyed. The prices are very reasonable for the quality of work that is displayed here, and their inventory moves quickly because of it.

Golden Leaf, Ltd.
3001 Hennepin Avenue South, Calhoun Square, Minneapolis
(612) 824–1867
Golden Leaf has a large selection of premium cigars from the leading companies in the industry. The walk-in humidor contains more than 250 brands of the freshest and best-priced cigars in Minnesota. Other products for sale include accessories, humidors, pipes, tobacco, candy, newspapers, lottery tickets, lighters, and other gifts.

Ingebretsen Scandinavian Gifts & Foods
1601 East Lake Street, Minneapolis
(612) 729–9333
www.ingebretsens.com
Ingebretsen carries Norwegian pewter, Scandinavian crystal (Hadeland, iittala, Nybro), dinnerware from Porsgrund, candles and holders, housewares, linens, wood carvings, rosemaling and other folk art,

Norwegian sweaters, jackets and skirts, T-shirts, and sweatshirts. In their jewelry case are beautiful pieces wrought in silver, pewter, bronze, leather, porcelain, enamel, and wood, while at the needlework shop next door, you can find fabrics, kits, books, and supplies for Danish counted cross-stitch, Hardanger embroidery, Norwegian "Klostersøm" needlepoint, lace making, and Norwegian knitting. Their select food section includes such Scandinavian delights as lutefisk and lefse, Swedish meatballs and sausage, herring, cheeses, lingonberries, chocolate, and flat bread. They also carry cookware for making specialty items like lefse, krumkake, aebleskiver, kransekake, rosettes, and other treats in your own kitchen. The library in back contains folk tales, children's books, language materials, cookbooks, fiction, culture and tradition, travel, emigration, history, art, music, and picture books for sale as well as CDs and cassettes of Scandinavian folk music, classical, jazz, and popular music and Nordic humor.

Kitchen Window
3001 Hennepin Avenue South, Calhoun Square, Minneapolis
(612) 824-4417
www.kitchenwindow.com

Kitchen Window is ranked by houseware vendors as one of the top kitchen stores in the country and is considered a key destination for quality kitchen products in the Twin Cities metro area.

The store is filled with such brands as All Clad, Berndes, Chantal, Calphalon, Cuprinox, and Le Creuset cookware; Wusthof Trident, Chef's Choice, and Lamson cutlery; Rosle kitchen tools; Kaiser and Chicago Metallic bakeware; and Cuisinart, Kitchen Aid, Krups, and Panasonic small appliances. Kitchen Window also features a large selection of espresso machines and coffeemakers, teamakers, mugs, carafes, and press pots. Parts for Cuisinart food processors and replacement carafes for Krups, Bodum, and Braun are also available. They also carry items for ethnic cooking that range from lefse griddles and krumkake irons to pasta makers, tortilla presses, sushi mats, and gadgets of all

kinds. Kitchen Window also holds cooking classes irregularly. Check the Web site or call for more information.

Paper Source
2404 Hennepin Avenue, Minneapolis
(612) 377-0700

This aptly named shop carries a staggering range of paper-related products—from stationery sets to bookbinding glue, greeting cards, rubber stamps, blank books, and lots and lots of paper. The paper stock runs from affordable typing and computer paper to beautiful imported sheets of handmade paper worthy of being framed and displayed. Every inch of the store is decorated with vintage graphics and paper creations made by the store's own staff, making Paper Source equal parts art supply store, gift shop, and gallery.

Party City
1630 New Brighton Boulevard, Minneapolis
(612) 781-9025
Three additional Twin Cities locations

Whether you're looking to buy small rubber dinosaurs, warming trays, balloons, or paper plates in bulk, Party City is the greatest place to stop for kids' and adults' party supplies. Their extensive wedding section includes paper samples for invitations, a huge selection of cake toppers, and cake decorating kits. Their all-season aisles hold every color of plastic flatware (with matching plates and napkins) you can imagine. They also sell warming trays, racks, and canned heat at extremely reasonable prices (around $1.00 per piece), as well as plastic punch bowls and ladles.

Patina
1009 Franklin Avenue West, Minneapolis
(612) 872-0880
5001 Bryant Avenue South, Minneapolis
(612) 821-9315
2305 18th Avenue NE, Minneapolis
(612) 788-8933

Patina is a great little gift store for stylish and relatively inexpensive gift options—many under $25. The variety is great, and they even carry gifts for pets, just in case you feel guilty for buying yourself that

Hello Kitty lunchbox without picking up a new designer collar for your cat as well. For the Hello Kitty and Badtz-Maru collector, there are lunchboxes, beaded purses, scrapbooks, and candies. For everyone else, there are impressive candles, nightlamps, and knickknacks that often look much more expensive than their actual marked prices.

SaraCura Silver
3001 Hennepin Avenue South, Calhoun Square, Minneapolis
(612) 821–8885

SaraCura sells some of the most exquisite stone-set silver jewelry in Uptown and sells it at such reasonable prices that it's nearly impossible to leave the mall without purchasing something from the store—that is, if you like pretty stuff. The store carries everything from gorgeous semiprecious-stone necklaces, rings, and bracelets set in silver, as well as Egyptian and African art and loose charms from all over the world. On weekends, artists at the store offer traditional henna painting to customers.

Sister Fun
1604 West Lake Street, Minneapolis
(612) 672–0263

The name says it all—this store is just amazingly fun to poke around in. File cabinet drawers reveal everything from tiny plastic airplanes to tin trains with wind-up cranks, baby doll parts, and cheap novelty keychains. On the shelves can be found 3D renditions of *The Last Supper*, coin purses with pictures of the Pope on them, Elvis paraphernalia, snowglobes with tiny nuns in them, Brady Bunch lunchboxes, reissues of Godzilla movies, mood rings, miniature tin carousels, etc., etc., etc. You can get lost in this place, but

---

Insiders' Tip

Ax Man Surplus offers senior citizens a whopping 20 percent discount on purchases every Tuesday.

---

don't worry—everything in here is priced much, much lower than you'd expect, despite being such a chic, campy, and popular shopping stop for college kids, artists, and adults going through their second childhood.

St. Paul

Ax Man Surplus
1639 University Avenue West, St. Paul
(651) 646–8653

Ax Man has everything you want that you never thought you wanted at more than reasonable prices, including iron lungs, ancient airplane models, antiquated TI-80 computer keyboards, beads, buttons, Pogs, snail shells, seashells, remote control wiring, police tape, public address horns, maps, huge bags of shredded money, rock videos, tapes of old television shows, copper cable, bar magnets, refrigerator magnets, transformers, all sizes of electrical motors, music box innards, marbles, bicycle tires, and doll heads. The stock is constantly changing, and some truly strange things wind up here for sale, including school bus fenders and fake cheese.

The Bead Monkey
867 Grand Avenue, St. Paul
(651) 222–7729

With several other locations spread throughout the Twin Cities, The Bead Monkey is the place to go to buy pipes of inexpensive glass beads, charms, jewelry-making supplies, beading needles and wire, and semiprecious stones. If you like beading but aren't sure how to go about a project, the extremely knowledgeable staff can either help you on the spot or refer you to one of their many beading classes for persons of all ages.

The Crossroads Shoppe of Crocus Hill
619 Grand Avenue, St. Paul
(651) 225–4467

The Crossroads Shoppe presents the largest selection of heirloom-quality Amish handcrafted quilts and furniture in the Twin Cities. Some of the Amish-crafted items sold here include gorgeously embroidered wall hangings, tablerunners, thick quilts, braided and woven rugs, straw baskets, and cloth dolls.

Garden of Eden
867 Grand Avenue, St. Paul
(651) 293–1300
1418 West Lake Street, Minneapolis
(612) 824–3715
Two additional Twin Cities locations

This luxury bath shop carries a huge selection of scented soaps, oils, perfumes, bath candles, and aromatherapy items. Soaps include handmade bars of glycerin with ribbons of flowers and herbs in them to novelty bars with "Satan Be Gone" emblazoned across the package. While most of the items here are aimed at women, they also carry aftershave and some men's soap.

Grand Remnants
1136 Grand Avenue, St. Paul
(651) 222–0221

This unique store specializes in vintage textiles, including swaths of colored and print fabrics, chenilles, hand-tatted lace, and linens; loose metal, bone, and wooden buttons; and vintage clothes for men and women. They also carry antiques, pottery, furniture, and more.

Irish on Grand
1124 Grand Avenue, St. Paul
(651) 222–5151

Irish on Grand, the premier Irish shop in the upper Midwest, offers a huge selection of Irish products, including music, books, food, teas, crystal, china, artwork, and much more. Aside from the usual T-shirts with shamrock themes, Irish on Grand carries beautiful woolen capes and throws, sweaters, mittens, scarves, and hats, as well as fine silver and gold jewelry.

Legacy Art & Gifts
1209 Grand Avenue, St. Paul
(651) 221–9094

Legacy Art & Gifts carries a wide selection of items created by local and nationally known artists showcased in a fabulous converted Victorian house. The shop features pottery, etchings, handblown glass, watercolors, textiles, wood boxes, one-of-a-kind jewelry, and more.

Irish on Grand occupies a former home on the busy retail and residential street, selling all things Irish.
PHOTO: TODD R. BERGER

St. Patrick's Guild
1554 Randolph Avenue, St. Paul
(651) 690–1506

St. Patrick's Guild, established in 1949, is a huge Catholic-themed store that carries religious books, drawers full of rosaries, medallions dedicated to about 30 different saints, holy water bottles, religious figurines, children's bibles, and concrete garden statues.

Stogies on Grand
961 Grand Avenue, St. Paul
(651) 222–8700

Stogies on Grand is a premier tobacconist that also offers a comfortable smoking lounge, complete with big-screen TV, newspapers, and board games, for those who want to immediately try out the cigars and tobacco they just purchased. Stogies carries more than 300 premium cigars in their large walk-in humidor and a wide selection of pipes, tobacco, humidors, lighters, cutters, and other tobacco-related accessories.

Ten Thousand Villages
867 Grand Avenue, St. Paul
(651) 225–1043

Ten Thousand Villages, located in Victoria Crossing West shopping mall, is a nonprofit shop featuring handcrafted jewelry, gifts, clothing, and home furnishings from around the world, with many pieces contributed by native artists in developing nations. The profits from purchases made at Ten Thousand Villages go directly back to the artists of these nations in an effort to provide them with a fair living income for their work.

Twin Cities Magic & Costume
241 West Seventh Street, St. Paul
(651) 227–7888

It's hard to miss Twin Cities Magic & Costume—the innocuous little white storefront manages to stand out from the rest of the neighborhood by having a giant silver flying saucer perched on the roof. Inside, the store has just about everything you need to embark on your career as a magician or a bank robber disguised as a gorilla, Little Bo Peep, or Dracula. They have a huge selection of costumes, theatrical supplies, and special effects equipment for sale and rent, including fog machines, strobe lights, explosive paper and powders, and dry ice. The store also provides magicians for hire and offers magic lessons for beginners and professionals alike.

West Suburbs

Ampersand
5034 France Avenue South, Edina
(952) 920–2118

Ampersand carries an incredible stock of everything you might possibly need for a party, whether it be a very formal affair or a casual lawn party. Ampersand has boxed invitations for every event under the sun, including birthdays, weddings, showers, anniversaries, barbecues, and cocktail parties, as well as silver olive forks, Italian pottery, designer cork tops, hand-painted dishware, flatware, elegant crystal punchbowls, and a huge selection of candles. As well as party supplies, Ampersand sells kids' books, blank journal books, baby toys, parenting books, stationery, giftboxes and wrapping paper, diaries, high-end bath supplies, and even stained-glass nightlights.

Bockstruck Jewelers
3624 Galleria, Edina
(952) 929–3143
400 St. Peter Street, St. Paul
(651) 222–1858

Family owned and operated since 1883, Bockstruck Jewelers has an incredibly eclectic collection of custom jewelry, brand-name watches and jewelry, crystal and glass sculptures, and artwork. Brand names such as Rolex, Ebel, Tag Heuer, Mikimoto, Penny Preville, and Philippe Charriol fill their cases, while exquisite blown-glass vases and lead crystal abstractions line the shelves. A member of the American Gem Society, Bockstruck Jewelers has a GIA-certified appraiser and a nationally acclaimed custom designer on staff.

Gabberts Furniture & Design Studio
3501 Galleria, Edina
(952) 927-1500

Voted the number-one home furnishings retailer in America by *House Beautiful* magazine, Gabberts has earned acclaim for its vast selection of fine home furnishings that suit every lifestyle and span the spectrum of design from traditional to casual to contemporary. The stock changes with the seasons and times and is always amazing—hand-painted desks, tables, and chairs with farm motifs or ocean scenes, or primary color furniture that looks like adult versions of a kid's playset. They also carry lush, soft leather couches, beautiful lamps, chandeliers, and pretty much anything else you need to make your home truly yours.

Que Sera
3580 Galleria, Edina
(952) 924-6390

This eclectic store, identified in front by a detailed chipped-tile mosaic, carries vintage-inspired home furnishings, lighting, beautiful costume jewelry, and knick-knacks of all sorts. Que Sera offers custom upholstery and slipcovered sofas and chairs incorporating vintage fabrics, hand-painted furniture, custom iron and wood beds, custom bedding, hand-blown glass chandeliers, table lamps, candles, mirrors, frames, and more.

South Suburbs

BareBones
100 North Garden, Mall of America, 60 East Broadway, Bloomington
(952) 858-8652

BareBones is a wonderful "toy" store for kids and adults alike, a place where the doctor's office meets the novelty store. BareBones carries a wide assortment of toys and books dealing with human anatomy, including 3D puzzles, sex-ed books, human anatomy posters, and coffee-table books.

Specialty Grocers

Minneapolis

Holy Land Bakery, Grocery and Deli
2513 Central Avenue NE, Minneapolis
(612) 781-2627

This Mediterranean deli and grocery store sells everything you need to make your own lamb kebobs, hummus, spinach pie, and falafel, although chances are you probably won't be able to make them quite as good as the Holy Land deli counter does. The store stocks items such as pita bread (made fresh in the bakery every day), meats, gigantic bags of basmati rice, roasted and dried chickpeas, at least six types of feta cheese, black and green olives, specialty coffees, and a wide selection of Middle Eastern cookies, candies, and specialty chocolates.

Shuang Hur Oriental Market
2710 Nicollet Avenue, Minneapolis
(612) 872-8606

Shuang Hur is the largest Asian supermarket on Eat Street, carrying thousands of products from China, Taiwan, and Thailand. The full-service grocery store has a large fresh produce section with melons, bean sprouts, and crates of aged duck eggs; freezers full of egg roll and spring roll wraps and desserts; and a Chinese BBQ deli that carries whole roasted pigs and BBQ duck and chicken meat. In the dry goods sections are rows and rows of dried mushrooms, noodles, soups, spices, rice, and shrimp crackers. A couple of rows over are about a hundred different types of festively colored packaged candy and cookies.

Surdyk's
303 East Hennepin Avenue, Minneapolis
(612) 379-3232

This Minneapolis shop is a wine connoisseur's dream come true. Surdyk's carries a great selection of wines and other spirits,

Thrifty Outfitters, located upstairs inside the Midwest Mountaineering store in Minneapolis, sells new and used outdoors equipment, clothing, and boots at steep discounts.

plus a gourmet cheese shop that makes this the place to consider when planning cocktail or dinner parties. Cigar smokers will appreciate the large humidor, which was a part of the store long before puffing cigars became trendy.

St. Paul

El Burrito Mercado
175 Concord Street, St. Paul
(651) 227–2192

El Burrito Mercado is an all-purpose Mexican and Latin grocery store located in St. Paul's West Side. The immense store features a bakery where you can purchase fresh pastries, fruit turnovers, breads, and cookies; a meat counter that carries fresh seafood, shredded pork, chicken, and beef, as well as gigantic fried pork rinds; a restaurant that whips up tacos, quesadillas, and burritos as quick as most fast-food restaurants, except the ingredients here are fresh, spicy, and good for you; and a full-service grocery carrying everything from Mexican coffees and candies to fresh, homemade corn chips and statues of tiny, sombrero-wearing skeletons playing guitars.

Spiros Mediterranean Market
2264 University Avenue West, St. Paul
(651) 645–4607

This wonderful Greek deli and grocery carries a huge selection of items for making Greek foods, like frozen beef and lamb for gyros, cucumber sauce, and a good selection of cheeses. The grocery section has a wide variety of Mediterranean candies, coffees, beans, pastas, fruit preserves, nuts, flour, jars of olives, pickled squid, and anchovy paste. The deli counter has some of the best baklava in town, as well as hummus and Greek salad, and makes gyros and other sandwiches fresh to order. In the freezer section are trays of moussaka and frozen spinach pies made fresh in the store.

Sports and Recreation Outfitters

Minneapolis

Alternative Bike & Board Shop
2408 Hennepin Avenue, Minneapolis
(612) 374–3635

Alternative Bike & Board Shop has been an Uptown institution since 1974, carrying all the respected bicycle and snowboard brands like Burton, Clicker, Nitro, and K2. They also carry clothing, accessories, and gear and have a knowledgeable staff that can help set you up with anything you need to get out on the road or on the slopes. A trustworthy repair department offers a quick turnaround time on repairs for a reasonable price.

Erik's Bike Shop
1312 Fourth Street SE, Minneapolis
(612) 617–8002
www.eriksbikeshop.com
Seven additional Twin Cities locations

This chain of local shops offers an excellent selection of equipment and is operated by a knowledgeable staff who can help you out with everything from information about bike and ski trails to what kind of equipment would suit you best. Cyclists will find an extensive assortment of mountain, road, touring, and BMX bikes from GT, Cannondale, Specialized, Yakima, and Haro, as well as cycling accessories, including car racks, helmets, parts, and apparel. Winter enthusiasts will be pleased by Erik's selection of snowboards, clothing, boots, and even snowshoes from

Palmer, Rossignol, Nitro, and Tubbs. Erik's also has a full-service bike shop for quickie to major repairs and offers regular in-store clinics that'll teach you how to make the repairs yourself.

Freewheel Bike
1812 South Sixth Street, Minneapolis
(612) 339-2219
www.freewheelbike.com

Freewheel Bike carries a good selection of mountain, road, and tandem bikes from Trek, Fisher, LeMond, Schwinn, Univega, Bontrager, Klein, and Santana, but its best feature is arguably the Public Shop, where, for under $10 an hour you can use the store's racks and tools to fix your bike—if you get in over your head, the staff is on hand to offer assistance. Freewheel also hosts maintenance classes jointly with Open U, rents bikes, and sponsors riding groups and teams.

Midwest Mountaineering
309 Cedar Avenue South, Minneapolis
(612) 339-3433
www.midwestmountaineering.com

Midwest Mountaineering takes up nearly an entire block of Cedar Avenue on the University of Minnesota's West Bank and is one of the most complete retail stores for brand-name outdoor adventure gear (including a giant outdoors-related book section) and one of the few outfitters to rent kayaks and other gear for whitewater paddling. The store's "cave" offers bouldering opportunities for climbers looking to try out equipment or just wanting a quick overhang workout, while an outside vertical ice wall is available for climbers during the winter. Once you sign a waiver, you're free to hit the walls. The store's staff is extremely helpful and can direct you to some of the better climbing, rafting, or hiking opportunities in the region.

St. Paul

Finn-Sisu
1841 University Avenue West, St. Paul
(651) 645-2443

This tiny Midway shop stocks a fabulous selection of cross-country and racing skis as well as equipment and supplies by all the top makers. The prices are a little high, but it's all top-quality merchandise, and the staff is very good at matching people with just the right gear. The store is also conveniently located near Como Park, giving you a chance to try out your new toys mere minutes after leaving the store.

Joe's Sporting Goods
935 North Dale Street, St. Paul
(651) 488-5511
www.joesportinggoods.com

Joe's carries a solid selection of top-of-the-line fishing equipment, from rods, reels, and flies to clothes, boots, and hats, as well as a complete array of hunting and skiing gear. No classes or clinics are offered here, but the knowledgeable sales staff is quick to answer any questions you might have or direct you to someone who can help.

Summit Fly Fishing Company
940 Grand Avenue, St. Paul
(651) 225-1200
www.summitflyfishing.com

Summit Fly Fishing Company is St. Paul's only full-service fly shop and carries the largest selection of flies in Minnesota. The store sells top-of-the-line angling equipment from Filson, Simms, Mastery, and Sage for serious-minded sportsfolk. For those just beginning, owner Paul Mueller conducts fly-tying, fishing, and casting clinics throughout the year.

East Suburbs

P. J. Asch Otterfitters
413 East Nelson Street, Stillwater
(651) 430-2286
www.pjaschotterfitters.com

The owners of P. J. Asch Otterfitters converted four old grain bins in downtown Stillwater into four cozy climbing rooms, then added an outdoor store to augment the climbing facilities. With 6,000 square feet of climbing surface—and walls that reach 42 feet—the place attracts climbers of all skill levels. Nearly half the business

Stillwater's P. J. Asch Otterfitters, about a block from the Lower St. Croix National Scenic Riverway, has a climbing wall inside its converted-grain-bin retail space. PHOTO: TODD R. BERGER

comes from first-time climbers, so plenty of beginner routes and lessons are provided, with instructors on hand to teach you the ropes. For experienced climbers, P. J. Asch also has four advanced climbing routes (with corner smears and a lieback crack). You also can rent sea kayaks here, mostly for use on the nearby St. Croix River.

West Suburbs

White Wolf
1601 MN 7, Hopkins
(952) 933–1047
Every store in the White Wolf chain is jammed to the rafters with downhill equipment from top makers (Rossignol,

Salomon, Nordica, K2) and ski clothing from top designers (North Face, Obermeyer, Helly-Hansen). The store carries snowboards, clothing, and gear by Burton, Liquid, Beacon, and Ride, and the in-store service center caters to both skiers and boarders.

Vintage Clothes and Thrift Stores

Minneapolis

Corner Store
900 West Lake Street, Minneapolis
(612) 823–1270
The Corner Store specializes in brand-name jeans and Western apparel such as cowboy boots, brass belt buckles, and fringed suede jackets, as well as motorcycle jackets, costume jewelry, and sequined clothing. For more elegant occasions, they also carry a wide selection of vintage tuxedos for rent.

Everyday People Clothing Exchange
323 14th Avenue SE, Minneapolis
(612) 623–9095
This vintage and resale store carries an eclectic (and sometimes hilarious) collection of disco clothes, out-of-date band T-shirts, go-go boots, comfortably broken-in Levis, and studded leather and plastic belts. The owners of this locally owned business are meticulous about everything they sell, and it shows. Anything in here with holes in it has them for a good and fashionable reason.

Repeat Performance Vintage Clothing
3404 Lyndale Avenue South, Minneapolis
(612) 824–3035
The proprietors of Repeat Performance are true fashion historians, and after some gentle prying, they're more than happy to tell you everything about why and when pant legs and skirt hems have changed over the years and other tidbits about American and European fashion. Repeat Performance is like a minimuseum filled

with history-lesson surprises: petticoats for the ladies and spats for the dapper gentlemen of the 1910s, and '40s loungewear for the night crowds, as well as beautiful handbags and coin purses, Bakelite jewelry, accessories, and much, much more.

Tatters
2928 Lyndale Avenue South, Minneapolis
(612) 823–5285

Originally called Tatters and Platters, a retailer selling apparel and vinyl, Tatters has been a Twin Cities retro-alternative clothing establishment for many years. Tatters has a huge selection of freshly laundered used and vintage clothing that spans decades, carrying seasoned motorcycle and letter jackets, Hawaiian and bowling shirts, party dresses from the 1940s onward, and lots and lots of Levis. They also stock new apparel ranging from partywear to T-shirts and underwear.

St. Paul

J.T.'s Feathered Denim
1583 North Hamline Avenue, St. Paul
(651) 649–1452

J.T.'s is the vintage clothing store of your dreams, carrying just about anything you could possibly want in a resale store, including Adidas track suits, bowling shirts, bow ties, ballgowns, flashy high heels, and amazing hats. And while it isn't the cheapest thrift store in town, its selection is so phenomenal that even the pickiest of shoppers should be able to come away with something.

Lula
1587 Selby Avenue, St. Paul
(651) 644–4110

Lula is stocked with crazy cocktail dresses, marvelous minis, and fabulous flapper suits for all your theme-party needs. Lula even stocks stylish vintage clothes for guys and super-cool shoes—if you're lucky enough to find your size. The owner has a knack for fitting customers and loading their dressing rooms with nifty possibilities that might have been overlooked.

For the stylish in a vintage sort of way, Lula is likely to stock duds that will attract attention (the good kind). PHOTO: TODD R. BERGER

Unique Thrift Store
1657 Rice Street, St. Paul
(651) 489–5083
2201 37th Avenue NE, Columbia Heights
(763) 788–5250
4471 Winnetka Avenue West, New Hope
(763) 535–0200

Once a year, *City Pages* puts out its "Best of the Twin Cities" list of stores in the metro area, and when they do, the Unique Thrift Store almost always gets the best thrift store award. Unfortunately, for about two weeks after receiving the award, prices in the store go up, the selection of great shoes and clothes gets cleaned out by a mad new-customer rush, and it's suddenly just another thrift store stocked with dusty junk at outrageous prices. Before and after this annual tradition, however, all three Unique Thrift Store locations are the place to go to get beautiful, barely worn summer dresses, business suits, boots and shoes, ice skates, in-line skates, leather jackets, winter coats, and kids' stuff at unbelievable prices. You can pretty much buy a fashionable, brand-name wardrobe for your son or daughter for a whole growing season, including shoes and a coat, for under $50; prices on adult clothes and shoes are just as reasonable.

Insiders' Tip

In October, you can pick up a working bicycle at the Unique Thrift Store for about $2.00. In April this is the place to look for ice skates.

Attractions

There is never a reason to be truly bored in the Twin Cities. On top of all the educational opportunities and artistic venues the area is famous for, the metro area is host to two wicked amusement parks—one indoor, one outdoor—a bevy of hands-on historical exhibits, one of the largest zoos and one of the best free zoos in the country, and lots of interesting spots to just hang out for the day. In winter, flocks of teenagers and adults head to the Mall of America to spend the day walking among the still-green trees and surreal landscape that make up the always-summery Camp Snoopy, or to the tropical canopies of wild orchid displays that fill Como Park's spectacular Marjorie McNeely Conservatory. In summer there's no excuse for staying inside running the air conditioner (unless you have to work)—Valleyfair! Amusement Park is nothing but cool, watery roller coasters, wave machines, and swimming pools.

Price Code

The following price code is based on the cost for general admission for one adult. Most sites offer considerably discounted tickets for children and seniors, and some allow discounts or even free entry for employees, members of the military, and certain organizations. Some sites, such as the Metrodome, Mall of America, and casinos, have no price code because the prices range widely depending on the event, how much you want to spend shopping, or how much you are willing to wager.

Free
$ .... $5 and under
$$ .... $6–$15
$$$ .... $16–$30
$$$$ .... $31 and up

Amusement Parks

Knott's Camp Snoopy $$
Mall of America, 60 East Broadway,
Bloomington
(952) 883–8600
www.campsnoopy.com

Located at the center of Mall of America, this seven-acre indoor theme park offers more than 25 rides and attractions. The largest indoor theme park in the nation, Knott's Camp Snoopy sits right on top of the old Met Stadium site—in place of a baseball diamond are 400 live trees, artificial cliffs meant to evoke the St. Croix River, all of those rides, and, of course, Snoopy and the rest of the *Peanuts* gang. Unlike outdoor amusement parks such as Valleyfair!, a stroll through Camp Snoopy costs you nothing (in fact, cutting through the park is often the fastest route between stores at the MOA). Rides require tickets, which you can buy at booths or at automated machines. Tickets for rides and attractions are based on a point system. A point is worth 75 cents, with rides and attractions costing three to six points each. You can also purchase Ticket Point Packages and all-day wristbands, two money-saving options if the little ones (or you) plan to get on a lot of Camp Snoopy rides.

For small children, there's the Americana Carousel, a hand-painted contemporary version of the classic carousel, and Li'l Shaver, a smaller, slower version of the roller coaster that circles the park (the Ripsaw Roller Coaster). For everyone else, there's the Skyscraper Ferris Wheel that takes visitors 74 feet high, Paul Bunyan's Log Chute—a watery ride that includes a drop over a 40-foot waterfall—and more than enough other rides and features to take your mind off shopping, including the Mighty Axe, the Screaming Eagle, and the Kite-Eating Tree. There's also a full-service child care facility at Camp Snoopy, Kids Quest, which charges by the hour and entertains kids with toys, video games, and heavily supervised walks around the park.

Valleyfair! Amusement Park $$$$
1 Valleyfair Drive, Shakopee
(952) 445–7600 or (800) 386–7433
www.valleyfair.com

With more than 75 rides, the Midwest's largest theme park has something to offer the littlest kid and the bravest adult alike. You can take an inner tube down a gently sloping canal for a relaxing, meditative ride; bumper cars and electric car tracks; exciting water rides like the Flume, which sends passenger boats off a 50-foot drop at the end of the ride; and the Excalibur, a high-speed wooden roller coaster with a 105-foot drop and lots of quick twists and turns. The new Steel Venom impulse coaster plummets at speeds up to 68 mph, corkscrewing you straight toward the ground before veering to a horizontal ride just before impact. For those with no fear of heights, the 275-foot Power Tower will take you high in the air and then, well, drop you. There are lots of rides for the really little guys, too, from bumble bee–shaped electric cars to Berenstain Bear Spooky Tree Children's Slide to an antique carousel. An IMAX theater is an added attraction to the park and a great

Insiders' Tip

For a reasonable charge, kids can buy Dixie cups of fish to throw to the seals at Como Zoo.

place to hide out during sudden late-summer showers. The park is open mid-May through September, with special Halloween and Christmas events during the off-season.

Animals and Plants

Como Zoo/Marjorie McNeely
Conservatory at Como Park   Free
1250 Kaufman Drive, St. Paul
(651) 487–8229
www.comopark.com

Minnesota's only free zoo offers intimate exhibits housing great apes, giraffes, zebras, wolves, and more. One of only four free metropolitan-area zoos in the country, Como Zoo has been an institution in St. Paul for more than 100 years. The first Siberian tigers successfully bred in captivity were born here in 1958, and the big cat display is still one of the best features of the zoo, including a single breeding pair of lions that has had several healthy pairs of cubs over the past decade. There is also a great primate exhibit here, with about a dozen ring-tailed and brown lemurs, spider monkeys, a couple of breeding pairs of tamarins that have successfully given birth every spring, and orangutans and gorillas that have been with the zoo for more than 10 years.

Located right next door to the zoo is the Marjorie McNeely Conservatory at Como Park, the region's largest botanical garden. The Victorian-style, glass-domed conservatory features hundreds of plants from throughout the world valued at several million dollars and is divided into six sections featuring palms, ferns, tropical food plants, bonsai trees, and seasonal flowers, as well as a Gallery Garden dedicated to showcasing youth artwork set among a changing selection of flowers and plants. In summer a side door opens into the Como Ordway Japanese Garden, a Sansui (mountain and water) design created by St. Paul's sister city, Nagasaki, Japan, for the park.

The newest feature of the zoo is the antique wooden Cafesjian's Carousel, formerly located in downtown St. Paul.

A delighted small fry on Cafesjian's Carousel at Como Zoo in St. Paul. PHOTO: SAINT PAUL CONVENTION AND VISITORS BUREAU

Beautifully restored, the brightly painted and mirrored wooden animals are available to ride throughout the summer for a nominal charge.

Both the Como Zoo and the Marjorie McNeely Conservatory at Como Park are open year-round.

Minnesota Landscape Arboretum $
3675 Arboretum Drive, Chanhassen
(952) 443-1400
www.arboretum.umn.edu

The Minnesota Landscape Arboretum, Minnesota's largest public garden, is part of the Department of Horticultural Science at the University of Minnesota. Its mission is to provide a community and national resource for horticultural and environmental information, research, and public education; to develop and evaluate plants and horticultural practices for cold climates; and to inspire all visitors with beautiful, healthy plants in well-designed and maintained displays, collections, model landscapes, and conservation areas.

The arboretum features 1,000 acres of public gardens, including spectacular annual and perennial display gardens, collections of plants developed for northern climates, natural and native areas, and demonstration gardens. The arboretum grounds include miles of summer hiking trails and winter cross-country ski trails that take you through northern woodlands, native prairie, and natural marshes. In spring, summer, and fall, trams can be boarded for a guided tour around the beautiful 3-mile drive, and volunteer-guided walking tours can be taken through the many display gardens for free.

The arboretum is open daily from 8:00 A.M. until 5:30 P.M., November through April, and until sunset May through September. Volunteer-guided walking tours that focus on the plant collections near the building (dwarf conifers, roses, perennials, herbs, annuals, host glade, Japanese gardens, and home demonstration gardens) generally last 60 to 90 minutes. Visitors can take their own personal 30-minute audio walking tour of the demonstration gardens (equipment is available in the lobby of the Snyder Building for no extra charge).

Minnesota Zoo $$–$$$
13000 Zoo Boulevard, Apple Valley
(952) 431–9500 or (800) 366–7811
www.mnzoo.com

Located in the southern suburb of Apple Valley and housing more than 3,000 species of animals from five different continents, the Minnesota Zoo and its IMAX theater see more than a million visitors per year; the zoo is considered by wildlife experts to be one of the 10 best zoos in the country. The second-largest zoo in the United States, the zoo's 500 acres include an indoor tropical rain forest populated by an amazing variety of birds and animals, a family of gibbons, and a large and smelly South American tapir. At Discovery Bay, there are dolphins that officially perform for audiences every afternoon and unofficially any time enough people gather around their huge, glass-walled tank; a walk-through aquarium with sharks, fish, and deep-sea plants; an education center where kids can pet everything from snakes to chinchillas, depending on what the zoo personnel bring in that day; and a Minnesota animal exhibit with beavers, foxes, fruit bats, and porcupines. Outside the main exhibit building, you can find ducks and swans, a prairie dog town, wild horses, camels, tigers, and many, many other animals, some of which are on the endangered species lists and are almost an exclusive at the zoo, such as the red panda. Domesticated animals like pigs and chickens get their day in the sun at the Wells Fargo Family Farm exhibit. It's also home to three cloned cows.

Also at the zoo is the 600-seat 3D IMAX theater. In the Weesner Family Amphitheater, the zoo often features big-name human stars, like Los Lobos and the Brian Setzer Orchestra.

UnderWater Adventures $$
Mall of America, 60 East Broadway, Bloomington
(952) 883–0202 or (888) DIVE–TIME
www.underwateradventures.net

UnderWater Adventures is a huge (1.2 million gallons) walk-through aquarium located in the basement of the Mall of America. The facility features more than 3,000 different sea creatures from around the world in seven different displays. For a one-time admission charge, visitors can walk through a 300-foot see-through acrylic tunnel that leads them underneath and through the middle of the three freshwater exhibits: Northwoods (featuring fish from Minnesota, including muskies and walleye), Fisherman's Hollow, and the Mighty Mississippi, and four ocean exhibits: Shark Cove, Rainbow Reef, Seven Seas Gallery, and Starfish Beach, where children can touch a variety of harmless sharks and stingrays.

Casinos and Racetracks

Canterbury Park Racetrack and Card Club
1100 Canterbury Road, Shakopee
(952) 445–7223 or (800) 340–6361
www.canterburypark.com

Canterbury Park, located about 25 miles southwest of downtown Minneapolis, hosts live horse racing with on-site parimutuel betting mid-May through the beginning of September and on-site teleracing betting on simulcast horse races around the country throughout the year. Canterbury also has a card room, including the Poker Room, featuring such games as Texas hold'em, seven-card stud, and Omaha, and the Casino Games Room, with games like blackjack, Caribbean stud, and Super 9. Canterbury is about 3 miles from both Mystic Lake and Little Six Casinos.

Little Six Casino
2354 Sioux Trail NW, Prior Lake
(952) 445–6000 or (800) 262–7799

Located 25 miles southwest of the Twin Cities, the Little Six Casino, like the much-larger and nearby Mystic Lake Casino, is run by the Shakopee Mdewakanton Sioux (Dakota) Community. The casino has 576 slot machines and eight blackjack tables.

Mystic Lake Casino
2400 Mystic Lake Boulevard, Prior Lake
(800) 262–7799
www.mysticlake.com

Besides its trademark high-stakes bingo,

Mystic Lake Casino has 3,300 slots and 88 blackjack tables as well as restaurants, including a huge buffet. The gaming facility also offers concerts, celebrity shows (comedian Louie Anderson and entertainer Charo were recent performers here), a shopping mall, a hotel, and an RV park. It is operated by the Shakopee Mdewakanton Sioux (Dakota) Community.

Treasure Island Casino
off Minnesota Highways 61 and 316,
Red Wing
(800) 222-7077
www.treasureislandcasino.com

Located 45 minutes southeast of St. Paul near the Mississippi river town of Red Wing, Treasure Island Casino features 2,500 slots, 44 blackjack tables, high-stakes bingo, and a nonsmoking casino. Aside from the gambling facilities, guests can take a cruise down the scenic Mississippi River aboard the *Spirit of the Water*, the casino's 150-passenger yacht. There's also a venue for live, nationally known celebrity entertainment as well as several smaller entertainment stages inside the casino for not-so-nationally-known performers.

Should you get hungry, there are plenty of great places to eat at Treasure Island, including the Tradewinds all-you-can-eat buffet and Java's seafood restaurant for meals ranging from steak to seafood.

Guided Excursions

Capital City Trolley $$
Downtown St. Paul
(651) 223-5600

History tours of downtown St. Paul and nearby neighborhoods are the specialty of the Capital City Trolley cars. Trolley guides impart the history of the city—including the railroad barons, gangsters, historic buildings, the State Capitol, and river life—as the trolley cars wind through downtown St. Paul, the government district around the Capitol, and the mansions of Summit Avenue.

The tours operate on Thursday only, May through October.

Minneapolis RiverCity Trolley $$
(612) 204-0000
www.minneapolis.org/gmcva/trolley

Sit back and enjoy the ride on the RiverCity

The Minneapolis RiverCity Trolley carries the curious all over the place from May through October.
PHOTO: GREATER MINNEAPOLIS CONVENTION & VISITORS ASSOCIATION

Trolley as friendly conductors tell the history of the "City of Lakes" during this 60-minute tour of turn-of-the-20th-century city buildings, skyscrapers, and other points of interest. The trolley travels along the Mississippi River past St. Anthony Falls to Main Street in the heart of the historic milling district—extended rides take you past the Walker Art Center, the State and Orpheum Theatres, and the Minneapolis Sculpture Garden.

Kids will love riding on the brightly painted, Mr. Rogers–style trolley cars. The trolleys are climate controlled and comfortable, and the seats are high enough that it's easy for smaller children to look out the windows. Your best bet is to get an all-day pass so that you can hop on and off the trolley throughout the day while you take in the sights of either the milling district and St. Anthony Falls (Downtown Minneapolis Tour) or the shores of the many beautiful lakes (Chain of Lakes Tour). Look for trolley signs around downtown, where you can hop on or off at your leisure. The season runs from May to October, seven days a week.

Padelford Packet Boat Company, Inc.
$$–$$$$
Harriet Island Park, St. Paul
Boom Island Park, Minneapolis
(651) 227–1100 or (800) 543–3908
www.riverrides.com
Hop on one of four riverboats leaving daily from Boom Island in Minneapolis and Harriet Island in St. Paul for a Mississippi River excursion. These paddleboat river tours offer an excellent way to experience the river up close.

One of the riverboats, the *Harriet Bishop,* named for St. Paul's first schoolteacher, is the newest and largest Mississippi riverboat. The riverboat offers two enclosed decks that seat 300 for dinner plus the open third deck. Bars and rest rooms can be found on all three decks, and the top deck features a dance/band area as well as a 48-tone Tangley calliope.

Another of the riverboats, one of the few truly authentic sternwheelers on the Mississippi river, the all-steel *Jonathan Padelford* is named for the tenth great maternal grandfather of Captain William D. Bowell Sr., owner of the Padelford Packet Boat Company, Inc. The engines are identical to the old steam engines but run hydraulically.

Padelford Packet Boat Company, Inc., offers two narrated daily public excursions from both cities seven days a week in June, July, and August, as well as elegant evening dinner cruises on weekends and a Sunday brunch cruise. In October the boats take passengers on a special Fall Colors sightseeing cruise down the Mississippi on Sunday afternoons.

Historical Attractions

Alexander Ramsey House $$
265 South Exchange Street, St. Paul
(651) 296–8760
www.mnhs.org/places/sites/arh
Completed in 1872, this is one of the country's best-preserved Victorian homes. The Ramsey House is one of the most detailed and intimate historical sites in the Twin Cities. The only owners were the Ramsey family, and so the history stayed in the house. More than 90 percent of the furnishings are original, which is rare for historical sites.

Costumed guides lead visitors on a tour of the impressive home of Alexander and Anna Ramsey. Ramsey was the first territorial governor and the second state governor, and he held many other prominent positions in public life.

The Ramsey House features original furniture, crystal chandeliers, carved walnut woodwork, and marble fireplaces. Tours change monthly, highlighting different facets of Victorian lifestyle in Minnesota. The costumed interpreters offer more than just a dry recitation of facts, playing out vignettes showing the life of the times. Free fresh-baked cookies are handed out by the "servants." Tours run year-round on Friday and Saturday between 10:00 A.M. and 3:00 P.M. with expanded hours during the holiday season.

American Swedish Institute $
2600 Park Avenue, Minneapolis
(612) 871–4907
www.americanswedishinst.com

Set in a spectacular, 33-room turn-of-the-20th-century mansion that looks more like a castle than a former residence, the American Swedish Institute is the largest and oldest museum of Swedish culture, arts, and history in the country. Completed in 1908, the French chateauesque structure is all ornately carved Indiana limestone on the outside. The inside is a marvel of hand-carved wood, with intricate designs lining the walls, and each sculpted plaster ceiling is a work of art. There's also a kakelugner in each room, which, to those of us who don't speak Swedish, is basically a colorful, porcelain-wrapped Swedish fireplace. Once the home of Swan J. Turnblad, publisher of America's foremost Swedish-language newspaper, the house was donated to the American Swedish Institute (which Turnblad founded) in 1929.

While taking in the decor, expect also to be taken with tales of immigrants who left Scandinavia to settle in Minnesota, which bears similar scenery, albeit sans mountains and fjords. The museum is a rich resource for local history, as well as a showcase for artwork by Swedish and Swedish-American artists and artisans. There are also concerts and theater performances in the upper rooms and lectures and other events in the modernized basement. (It's a special treat to visit when the mansion is decked out at Christmas time.)

Also exhibited at the museum are Scandinavian artifacts from the Turnblad family, including their clothes, family photographs, books, and toys. There are also fiddling and dancing groups that come through to entertain visitors, special festivals with music and food, and guage classes for kids and ad

The Ard Godfrey House $$
45 Ortman Street SE, Minneap
(612) 379–9707

Built in 1849, the Ard Godfrey House was the family residence for the Maine millwright who helped build the first dam and sawmills to put the waterpower of the Falls of St. Anthony to use. The oldest frame house in the Twin Cities and built with the first lumber sawn at the mill, this Greek revival structure was restored and refurbished by the Woman's Club of Minneapolis with assistance from the Building and Construction Trade Council, the Minneapolis Park and Recreation Board, and the Historical Societies.

The Godfrey House was reopened to the public in 1979. Today the house is available for tours, led by guides who are pioneer descendants themselves. Their stories are so personal, so embedded in their lives, you feel almost as though you're invading someone's privacy. The house is open to the public weekends June through September and for private tours by appointment year-round.

Fort Snelling $$
Highways 5 and 55, St. Paul
(612) 726–1171
www.mnhs.org/places/sites/hfs

Built on a high bluff overlooking the Mississippi and Minnesota Rivers in 1827, Fort Snelling was once the westernmost United States outpost in the mostly unexplored wilds of the north and was the center of frontier commerce and government on the upper Mississippi. At the time, an outpost on the confluence of the Minnesota and Mississippi Rivers meant control of river traffic throughout the Minnesota Territory; British fur traders, American outlaws, and warring American Indian nations could be held in check. Today a variety of themed tours provide insight into what life was like at the fort, with costumed guides reenacting scenes from military, civilian, and Native American life of the 1800s. Not only are these some of the oldest surviving buildings in the state, but both Twin Cities

their pedigrees to the fort. Soldiers ɔm the fort built the first sawmill at St. Anthony Falls, and the first residents of St. Paul were moved there after being sheltered as immigrants.

This reconstruction of the first permanent settlement in Minnesota is open May through October and is staffed by costumed guides portraying fort life in 1827. Exhibitions at the fort include hands-on crafts and theatrical presentations, veterans and expert discussions on World War II, watching or joining in with residents of the 1820s military post as they prepare the harvest for storage and winter use, and book readings and lectures from Minnesota authors and historians. Around Halloween, the fort holds candlelight tours led by the "ghost" of Indian Agent Lawrence Taliaferro. In July the fort breaks out its finery, roasts a whole pig (free samples if your timing's right), and stages entertaining plays throughout the day.

Gibbs Farm Museum $$
2097 Larpenteur Avenue, Falcon Heights
(651) 646–8629
www.rchs.com/gbbsfm2.htm

Amid the farm fields that make up the northern border of the University of Minnesota's agriculturally focused St. Paul campus, you'll find this quaint little barn and farmhouse, which date to the 19th century. They're preserved in their original state as an educational opportunity for those who would like to step back in time. On summer weekends, expect to see people in period dress driving horse-drawn plows and churning butter on the porch. Interpreters share the process and results of their extensive archeology of this site, displaying excavated artifacts and explaining their historic significance to the public. The Gibbs Farm's medicine and vegetable gardens are especially interesting, with many native plants that no longer exist "naturally" in the area but were especially important to Native Americans and pioneer settlers.

A point of interest to note to both politically correct parents and otherwise is that the history most spoken about at this archeological site is that of Jane Gibbs, a young girl raised by missionaries and used as an interpreter between the Dakota Indians and settlers for many years, and not that of her husband, Heman Gibbs, who helped build the two houses on the property as well as the barn in back. The Gibbses, who first moved to the Minnesota property in the 1840s from Illinois, lived for five years in a tiny sod house—replicated in astounding detail and now a part of the tour—before building the main house. Guided tours cover everything that's left of the original Gibbs property. Gibbs Farm is open May through mid-November.

Henry Sibley House Historic Site $
1357 Sibley Memorial Highway, Mendota
(651) 452–1596
www.mnhs.org/places/sites/hts

Henry Sibley, a fur trader and Minnesota's first governor, lived in a rambling trading-post-turned-house in the riverside hamlet of Mendota. Today visitors can walk through two 1830s limestone houses in Minnesota's oldest European-American settlement, home to Sibley and his neighbor, Jean Baptiste Faribault. Sibley's restored house is full of fur trade stuff and the trappings of frontier gentility—pelts, muskets, and loads of blue china. The guides' stories of Sibley and company are vivid snapshots of the difficulties faced by these tough frontiersmen living in a wild world.

The Sibley House offers many theme tours and events, including Children's Day, where kids can learn about Dakota techniques used since the 1680s for turning natural materials into tepees, bowstrings, and fishing lines, and the 1850 Holiday Theme Tours, where visitors of all ages can tour the Sibley and Faribault Houses decorated as they were for winter holidays in 1849–50. During the Holiday Tours, guides discuss the different celebrations by Yankees and French-Canadians, upper and lower classes, Presbyterians and Catholics, and the Dakota peoples. The site is open May through October and is closed Tuesday and Wednesday.

John H. Stevens House $
East Minnehaha Parkway and Hiawatha
Avenue, Minneapolis
(612) 722–2220

The John H. Stevens House, built in 1850 and originally located in the present-day riverfront spot of the Minneapolis Post Office, is the first permanent settler's home in Minneapolis. The home of Colonel Stevens and his family served as the social and civic hub of the new city. People met here to discuss a name for the city and to organize local schools and government. In addition, it was here that John Stevens named Hennepin County and drew up the original territorial boundaries for the county. The first elections were held here, and the first Board of County Commissioners met here in 1852.

The house was reopened to the public in 1985 after being closed since the turn of the last century. It was brought to Minnehaha Park in 1896 by more than 70,000 schoolchildren in the first act of historic preservation in the state of Minnesota, but lack of funding prevented it from being anything but a curious landmark in the park for decades. Now an interpretive museum, exhibits, and tour guides inside the house tell the story of the city, founding father Stevens, and the importance of this little white house. The Stevens House is open year-round in the afternoon and on weekends.

Minnesota State Capitol   Free
75 Constitution Avenue, St. Paul
(651) 296–2881
www.mnhs.org/places/sites/msc

Soaring domes, monumental arches, columns, statues, and symbolic murals dominate the scene for visitors today as they did when the State Capitol was completed in 1905. The first two capitols, each outgrown, were in downtown St. Paul. When it came time to build the third in 1904, land was too expensive, so legislators acquired an old livery stable instead and built on that property. The result is the stark, white capitol topped by the world's largest freestanding dome and the four golden horses—the Quadriga—that

The Minnesota State Capitol building in St. Paul. PHOTO: TODD R. BERGER

are usually what people remember after their visit to this masterpiece of Italian Renaissance architecture.

Today the State Senate, House of Representatives, and Supreme Court have been restored to their original appearances, as has the Rathskellar Cafe, now open to the public. Guided tours of the capitol leave every hour; self-guided tour brochures are available at the front entrance. The State House, Senate, and Supreme Court are open for visitors, and if your timing's right, you can hear important issues being decided. The tours follow the chronological sequence of amply captioned oil portraits of Minnesota governors around the atrium and give insight to the history of the building through stories of art, history, power, politics, and public service, as well as architect Cass Gilbert's role in selecting decorations, art, and furnishings for his magnum opus. The capitol is open daily year-round.

Murphy's Landing $$
2187 East Highway 101, Shakopee
(952) 445–6901
www.murphyslanding.org

Murphy's Landing is a living-history site that preserves and interprets 19th-century life in the Minnesota River Valley. More than 40 period buildings were moved here from 1969 to 1972 with the intent of re-creating a 19th-century village; today the village includes a fur trading post, a homestead, and a storefront, all of which are arranged in chronological order according to when they were built. Costumed interpreters demonstrate the rigors of the daily life of Minnesota's settlers, from metalsmiths to weavers and merchants. Special seasonal events are planned around the holidays for history buffs of all ages. This Minnesota River site is listed on the National Register of Historic Places. Murphy's Landing is open daily year-round.

St. Anthony Falls Historic District
Minneapolis
(612) 627–5433

Located on the Mississippi riverfront, St. Anthony Falls defined Minneapolis as the world leader in flour milling for more than 50 years. With the completion of the restored Stone Arch Bridge and various revitalization projects, the area is a rediscovered historical treasure. The Minnesota Historical Society offers a variety of walking and biking tours to help you "step back into the past" and uncover the history of this landmark district.

Originally called "curling waters" by the Dakota Indians, St. Anthony Falls were renamed by Father Louis Hennepin after his patron saint, Saint Anthony of Padua. Known as the birthplace of Minneapolis, this landmark is the only waterfall on the Mississippi River. Great viewing of the falls is available from the Stone Arch Bridge. The falls originally traversed a limestone ledge and, in their natural state, fell 16 feet to rapids below. In the 1950s, when the Upper Lock and Dam was constructed, the degrading ledge was covered with a concrete apron to protect it from further erosion. Today the falls stand between 12 and 15 feet above water level, dependent on the level of the Mississippi River.

A year-round walking trail provides a self-guided tour of the St. Anthony Falls Historic District with its nationally significant homes, buildings, and archeological ruins of former flour mills. Visitors can follow the Heritage Trail around St. Anthony Falls and learn about historic structures and archeological sites from exhibits or join a Minnesota Historical Society tour to get extra insight into the area from a trained guide. Either way, the trail offers a spectacular view of the river from the historic Stone Arch Bridge and is a great way to get away from the bustle of the city without actually leaving Minneapolis.

Head across the bridge and back in time on Nicollet Island. Nicollet Island was the stepping-stone to the settlement of Minneapolis, and many of the 19th-century homes and row houses are still on the island. The Historical Society offers guided tours of this area as well—for an extra treat, a horse and carriage ride around the island can be picked up at Nicollet Island Inn.

Wabasha Street Caves $$–$$$
215 South Wabasha Street, St. Paul
(651) 292–1220
www.wabashastreetcaves.com

Burrowed into the sandstone bluffs that line the Mississippi River on St. Paul's West Side, this is the site of the late Castle Royal nightclub, which was a speakeasy during the days of Prohibition and, before that, a mushroom farm. There's a lot of St. Paul history here, especially for those interested in the city's incarnation as a gangster mecca. Considering that the city of St. Paul was built around a cave (Pig's Eye Parrant's cavern and tavern), a cave is an appropriate dwelling for a night out. An annual Halloween collection of ghostly musings has been among the attractions here, as well as jovial evenings of storytelling about the gangster massacres that took place here and in the neighborhood during Prohibition days. The Historic Cave Tour covers the history of the Wabasha Street Caves, while the St. Paul Gangster Tour stops at several sites outside the caves where infamous crimes took place. The caves are open year-round (call for tour times and reservations).

Indoor Recreation

Hubert H. Humphrey Metrodome
900 South Fifth Street, Minneapolis
(612) 332–0386
www.msfc.com

This multipurpose facility, home of the Minnesota Vikings, Twins, and the U of M Gopher football team, features a variety of events year-round. First-time visitors to the Metrodome are awed by its interior volume; regular fans sometimes feel they're watching "theater," not sports. It's the city's only indoor facility big enough to host motocross events and monster-truck rallies as well as football games, occasional rock concerts, and inline skaters.

During evenings when there's not a previously scheduled event, the Metrodome turns into the Rollerdome—hordes of skaters take over its half-mile concourses, taking advantage of the tremendous work-

The Hubert H. Humphrey Metrodome forms the most horizontal part of the downtown Minneapolis skyline. PHOTO: GREATER MINNEAPOLIS CONVENTION & VISITORS ASSOCIATION

out the field provides. Skaters addicted to speed zoom around the upper concourse, which has a pacer clock, while less-rabid skaters enjoy the Dome's smooth skating surface on the lower concourse. It's a great cure for cabin fever and an excellent way to keep up your chops for snaking around the lakes in summer.

No one gets turned away wearing traditional skates, but Rollerdome is Inline Central. Rollerblade sponsors these skating sessions, where free protective gear is dispensed on a first-come, first-served basis and safety teams patrol to keep in-liners in line.

Parking for Rollerdome and the Metrodome is free in the Metrodome lot, which you can enter at the intersection of South Fifth Street and 11th Avenue. Enter the Dome at Gate D. No cameras, recording devices, or outside cans, bottles, coolers, or containers are allowed at the Metrodome or Rollerdome, but concessions are available inside in case you get peckish.

Mall of America
60 East Broadway, Bloomington
(952) 883–8800
www.mallofamerica.com

This gigantic mall says only one thing about the state of American shopping: Fantasy moves product. And at this cement-and-plastic Bloomington behemoth, there's a lot of product to move. The largest shopping and entertainment complex in the United States, the megamall—at 4.2 million square feet—is the size of seven Yankee Stadiums and home to more than 400 stores, 71 restaurants, a 14-screen movie theater, an indoor amusement park, a golf course, and an aquarium. To make your shopping experience more pleasurable, the mall provides strollers, wheelchairs, changing stations in rest rooms, a post office, and lockers with secure key locks. In case you change your mind about shopping and decide to get married instead, there's also a wedding chapel conveniently located inside the mall.

Some 40 million annual visitors flock to the Mall of America in suburban Bloomington near Minneapolis-St. Paul International Airport. PHOTO: GREATER MINNEAPOLIS CONVENTION & VISITORS ASSOCIATION

Museums

The Bakken: A Library and Museum of Electricity in Life $
3537 Zenith Avenue South, Minneapolis
(612) 926–3878
www.thebakken.org

Established in 1975 by Earl E. Bakken, inventor of the first transistorized cardiac pacemaker and founder of Medtronic, a Twin Cities company on the cutting edge of electrocardio technology, this Tudor-style mansion houses an incredible collection of rare books, manuscripts, and more than 2,000 scientific thingamajigs that are all related to the role electricity plays in life. Bakken's fascination with the life-saving capabilities of electricity led to the establishment of this museum, and his similar interest in homeopathic medicine led to creating the herbal gardens outside the museum, full of Old and New World medicinal plants.

A $6 million renovation, completed in 1999, doubled the original size of the museum. The expansion created more space for exhibits and classrooms, added a workshop geared toward student experiments, and expanded the library. The most recent permanent exhibit, added to the collection in 2000, is "Benjamin Franklin and the Lightning Rod," telling the story of Franklin's experiments with electricity. The exhibit celebrates the 250th anniversary of Franklin's famous kite experiment, and it includes demonstrations of artificial lightning, the chance to build a toy version of Franklin's bells, exhibits of original books and letters printed or written by Franklin, an early thunder house, and much more from the museum's collection.

The Bakken Museum is open Tuesday through Saturday; the museum's research library is open Monday through Friday.

Bell Museum of Natural History $
University of Minnesota, 10 Church Street SE, Minneapolis
(612) 624–7083
www.bellmuseum.org

The Bell preserves an impressive collection of stuffed creatures that would interest 19th-century taxidermists as well as current students of the natural sciences. The animals are displayed in simulated natural environments, with background murals painted by renowned landscape artist Francis L. Jaques. These scenes are curious testaments to the exotic hobbies of scientists of the past, especially in regard to the exhibits displaying passenger pigeons and other now-extinct creatures.

The exhibits of stuffed birds, mammals, and fish are extremely clean and tastefully exhibited, with beautiful painted backdrops of seascapes and woodlands for the animals on display. The exhibits are primarily Northland animals and confined to North America, with emphasis on Minnesota wildlife including porcupines, bears, moose, and ground squirrels. There is also a temporary exhibit hall that features artwork, animal remains, and fossils from around the world, changing approximately every two months.

The Touch and See Room, located on the second floor of the museum, is a veritable paradise for children interested in the natural sciences. Living snakes, turtles, and lizards are on display in tanks around the room, and with assistance from one of the friendly attendants, children can even hold some of these creatures. The room is full of horns, antlers, bones, fossils, and rocks, all for the handling—there's even a big, leathery elephant ear for kids to pick up and examine. The third floor has a large butterfly and moth exhibit that traces the lives of these insects from egg to maturity, and a side room contains a photography exhibit focusing on bats.

The Bell Museum is closed Monday and major holidays. Admission is free to all every Sunday.

Hennepin History Museum $
2303 Third Avenue South, Minneapolis
(612) 870–1329
www.hhmuseum.org

Founded by the Territorial Pioneers Association in 1858, the Hennepin History Museum has long been dedicated to preserving the history of Hennepin County. Today Hennepin History Museum serves as the gateway to a wide variety of historical resources. Housed in the George H. Christian mansion, designed by Hewitt and Born, the museum offers a series of rotating exhibits focusing on everything from toys to technology. Past exhibits have highlighted Ojibwe and Dakota cultures, period clothing design, toys, quilt making, technology, innovations, local artists, and decorative arts. City Kids' Gallery is one place where touching the artifacts is not only allowed but encouraged.

The museum also contains more than 1,200 volumes on the city of Minneapolis and Hennepin County, as well as 3,500 photographs, extensive business records, and personal scrapbooks. Of special interest are the *Diaries of Gideon Pond*, early 20th-century real estate photos, and a collection of first editions on local history.

The Hennepin History Museum is open varying hours Tuesday through Sunday.

Minnesota Air National Guard Museum $
34th Avenue South, Minneapolis,
Minneapolis-St. Paul International Airport
(612) 713–2523
www.mnangmuseum.org
This small but historically important museum displays vintage aircraft and memorabilia of the Minnesota Air National Guard. The memorabilia—airplane pictures, portraits, helmets, patches—is crowded into a couple of cramped rooms in a hangar. The museum's focus is on local flyboys, and the

only globally relevant information pertains to when these local boys left town. Eighteen cool old planes are on display on the tarmac outside, though, including fighter jets, transports, and the terrifying black A-12, the CIA's favorite superfast spy plane.

Located on an active military base, the museum was closed and upgrades to the security of the building and site made in 2002–2003. The museum was reopened to the public in spring 2003; call for the hours.

Minnesota Children's Museum $$
10 West Seventh Street (Seventh and Wabasha), St. Paul
(651) 225–6000
www.mcm.org
Einstein said that "play was the highest form of research," and if you have children, you will appreciate the diversion this museum can offer your kids. Traveling exhibits have included items on Peter Rabbit and Mister Rogers, while permanent exhibits are interactive and give children a chance to crawl through simulated ant colonies, operate a giant crane to transport foam blocks, or take the stage in a mini TV studio. Look into the membership rate here, as it will give you and your family unlimited access to the premises throughout the year and a 10 percent discount off items at the amazingly fun Creative Kidstuff store located in the museum. This is an especially popular place for graduate students to take their

Insiders' Tip

The Arts and Museums Pass allows access to dozens of museums and historical sites in the Twin Cities. The cost is $20 for adults and $15 for children, and it is valid for five consecutive days. You can buy the pass at most museums and historical sites in the Twin Cities, Minneapolis and St. Paul visitor information centers, or by contacting the Greater Minneapolis Convention and Visitors Association at (888) 676-MPLS.

kids, as it keeps the kids entertained while letting education-minded parents comfortably take a study break. Recommended for children six months to 10 years of age and for parents looking to entertain their brood during the winter.

The Minnesota Children's Museum is open year-round Tuesday through Sunday; during summer the museum is also open Monday.

The Minnesota History Center   Free
345 West Kellogg Boulevard, St. Paul
(651) 296–6126 or (800) 657–3773
www.mnhs.org/places/historycenter

The History Center is an architectural masterpiece constructed from Minnesota's own Rockville granite and Winona limestone. The view of the city from several vantage points inside the museum is breathtaking. There are exhibits and events all year focusing on Minnesota's past. Encounter early settlers in Tales of the Territory or explore Families, which tells the story of immigrants and Native Americans who made the Land of 10,000 Lakes their home. The History Center also has a gigantic library of books and photographs about Minnesota events, regions, family genealogy, and other artifacts; visitors are allowed to pore through the collection for free.

The center is a wonderful resource of artifacts (dating back 11,000 years), historical texts, and changing and permanent exhibits that chronicle much of the history of the upper Midwest. Three of the permanent exhibits are specifically geared toward children. Grainland includes an authentic 24-ton boxcar and a model grain elevator that children can climb through as they learn how grain gets to the marketplace. Help Wanted: Work in Minnesota lets children and adults try on the roles of different Minnesota workers in the 1930s and 1940s, from a railway inspector who has to judge whether rail cars are safe to send on their way down the track, to a meat packer—see how many rubber pig's feet you can pack in a minute—or a dairy farmer who has to work the crank on a cream separator. The real kid pleaser is the Minnesota A to Z galleries, which feature a different Minnesota exhibit to match each letter (Z is Below Zero; B stands for Burma Shave).

Aside from the visual exhibits, the museum also presents lecture series and book readings from local historians and authors. Justice Rosalie Wahl, the first woman on the Minnesota Supreme Court, has spoken here on her experiences with task forces on gender bias and racial fairness, as has "Super V-man" John Velek, a Vikings football fan, who brought rare Vikings memorabilia from his collection to display temporarily at the History Center. The museum has also hosted musical exhibits from members of the St. Paul Chamber Orchestra and the Minnesota Youth Symphonies Solo Competition, in which 10 to 12 youth finalists perform in a two-hour solo competition. An extensive research library rounds out this amazing historical resource, housing maps, books, photographs, newspapers, and census records. Anyone can use these resources, and classes are available for those who want help. There is no admission charge to visit the museum, and parking in the museum's lot is only a couple of dollars. The History Center museum is closed Monday; the research library is open Tuesday through Saturday.

Minnesota Transportation Museum $–$$
various locations
(800) 711–2591
www.mtmuseum.org

Discover the history of transportation at the museum's several exhibit sites. Visitors may ride vintage streetcars and antique buses at Lake Harriet and Excelsior; steam and diesel-powered trains in Osceola, Wisconsin; or the restored steamboat *Minnehaha* on Lake Minnetonka. Additional sites include the restored Jackson Street Roundhouse in St. Paul as well as the restored "Princess" depot in Minnehaha Park.

The Como-Harriet Streetcar Line operates on weekends September through October 29. Streetcars run until dusk, beginning at 12:30 P.M. on weekends and 6:30 P.M. on weekdays. The line consists of restored streetcars from different periods of streetcar history—streetcar No. 78 is from the first generation of streetcars that replaced horse and buggies in the 1890s; No. 1300 was built in 1908 as part of an order for faster cars to be used on the Interurban line between Minneapolis and St. Paul. These cars, the exhibits in the Linden Hills depot, and the knowledgeable volunteers who operate the line, offer a fascinating glimpse of life in Minneapolis during the streetcar era from 1867 to 1954. You can also ride the museum's vintage motor buses on specially designated days and tour the car barns, where the museum's skilled volunteers maintain and restore the vintage streetcars.

The *Minnehaha* is an authentic 1906 steamboat. You can pick up the boat at the MTM Steamboat Division at 328 Lake Street in Excelsior (952–474–2115) several times a day on summer weekends. More than 90 years ago, a fleet of six steam-powered boats were launched into Lake Minnetonka. Designed to resemble streetcars, the boats were an extension of the Twin City Rapid Transit Company. For 20 years, the boats served the resorts, summer cottages, and Big Island Park. Five of the boats were scuttled near Big Island, three in 1926 and two more in 1928. In 1948, the last boat was sent to join the others at the bottom of the lake. Today, thanks to the efforts of the Minnesota Transportation Museum, visitors can rediscover the pleasure of a smooth water passage between Excelsior and Wayzata aboard the fully restored *Minnehaha*.

At Minnehaha Park is the Minnehaha Depot (651–228–0263), another branch of the Transportation Museum. It isn't hard to understand why Milwaukee Road employees once referred to the delicate, gingerbread-trimmed Minnehaha Depot as "The Princess." Built in 1875 to replace a smaller station on the first railroad line into the city of Minneapolis, the depot served as a recreational gateway to Minnehaha Falls and as a departure point for Fort Snelling personnel during both World Wars. Today active trackage in front of the depot still connects with the Canadian Pacific rail system.

At the Jackson Street Roundhouse, located at 193 East Pennsylvania Avenue in St. Paul (651–228–0263), you can watch the excavation and eventual restoration of the first railroad locomotive maintenance facility in Minnesota, built by the Minnesota and Pacific Railroad (which later became the Great Northern Railroad company) in 1862. The roundhouse and its companion buildings in the adjacent Empire Builder Park are the oldest known railroad buildings in St. Paul. In a city whose history has been so dominated by railroading, the Jackson Street Roundhouse is an extremely important historic facility. Future plans for the site include excavating the turntable pit and installing the original Great Northern turntable from the Minneapolis junction, and linking the Jackson Street Roundhouse Museum by rail to the St. Paul riverfront and the Science Museum.

The Science Museum of Minnesota $$
120 West Kellogg Boulevard, St. Paul
(651) 221–9444
www.smm.org

With eight indoor acres of both permanent and temporary exhibits that include an extensive collection of dinosaur, mammal, insect, and fish fossils, a geology exhibit, a reproduction of a big game hunter's lodge with a huge variety of preserved game animals, as well as nearly a whole floor dedicated to hands-on technology and weather demonstrations, this museum is guaran-

Insiders' Tip

An admittance stamp at the Minnesota Children's Museum lets you come and go from the building all day, so you can sneak out and get a decent lunch and still come back and play for no extra charge.

teed to bring out the scientist in adults and children. Previous temporary exhibits have included a collection of life-size mechanical dinosaur sculptures that visitors can manipulate with pulleys and a series on bats from around the world, while the museum's permanent collection includes an amazing fossil display—including an exhaustive collection of fossilized coprolites—displays of Minnesota's past and present, and a Human Body Gallery that demonstrates through models how everything from lungs to red blood cells work in the human body.

The Museum of Questionable Medical Devices, formerly located in Minneapolis, is now housed in the Science Museum. The offbeat and sometimes frightening collection chronicles the history of medicine from the 1790s to the present and includes such things as a 1920 phrenology machine that reads the bumps on your head to determine your true character.

The museum's education center also offers classes to kids on subjects as diverse as animation and film making and archeology—there's also a Collections Gallery where kids can bring in interesting rocks, seashells, and bones for the staff to positively identify with the option of exchanging their pieces for something in the museum's trading collection. For a less hands-on experience, but just as thrilling, check out the nation's first convertible dome Omnitheater and the 3D Multimedia Laser Theater, both located inside the museum.

Twin City Model Railroad Museum $
Bandana Square, 1021 Bandana Boulevard
East, St. Paul
(651) 647–9628
www.tcmrm.org

Since 1939 this museum has been dedicated to the promotion and understanding of the role played by railroads in the history and development of Minnesota. An extensive collection of railroad artifacts and art is also available, including a changing photo exhibit in the museum focusing on a different historic train or train line each month.

More than 3,000 square feet of transportation-related artifacts and displays make up the museum, the centerpiece of which is the scale model railroad of the recreation of the Twin Cities during the '30s, '40s, and '50s. Up to five trains at once glide through the depots and tunnels of the incredibly detailed model, while miniature streetcars seen running back and forth over the Stone Arch Bridge model are sometimes brought out to run on the tracks as well. Re-creations of historic steam engines like the Milwaukee *Hiawatha* can be seen pulling passenger cars in and out of the 1914 Great Northern passenger depot, peopled with tiny engineers, parked automobiles, and waiting passengers. The museum is closed Monday.

Kidstuff

We Minnesotans have a great love for our children, and it's no more evident than in the way our major metropolitan areas are laid out. In both Minneapolis and St. Paul, neighborhoods are centered around parks with community centers, swimming pools, and, in winter, ice-skating rinks—in most areas, these parks occur every 2 or 3 blocks. Public schools have initiated many after-school programs to help parents who can't be at home when the school day officially ends, and during summer these same schools offer fun classes for kids that include swimming lessons and summer sports. Even the state government has a special branch dedicated to the welfare and mental health of our children: the Department of Children, Families and Learning.

There are more than enough activities for your children when you come to the Twin Cities, from science and nature-oriented attractions to water parks and bumper cars. Most of the kid-oriented activities in the metro area are of the "highbrow" sort. For some strange reason, we like to drag our kids to museums and art events here an awful lot. Luckily, most places are fully prepared to receive and entertain children, even those without specific arts programs geared toward kids.

As for dining options, just about every restaurant in the Twin Cities is fine to take your kids—bars that double as restaurants in the daytime welcome underage patrons (accompanied by adults) until just before happy hour. We've included the listings at the end of this chapter because they are restaurants that specifically try to make children feel comfortable, from the menu to the service and the decor. We've also tried to pick places that are easy on the wallet, because kids don't always eat everything they order and traveling with a doggy bag full of expensive food can be a real pain.

Price Code

The following price code is based on the cost for general admission for one adult. Most sites offer considerably discounted tickets for children and seniors, and some allow discounts or even free entry for members of their respective organizations.

Free
$ . . . . $5 and under
$$ . . . . $6–$15
$$$ . . . . $16–$30
$$$$ . . . . $31 and up

Amusement Centers

Amusement City $
1870 Rice Street, St. Paul
(651) 487–1025

This is a fun way to spend an afternoon with your kids. The seasonally open, modest-size neighborhood amusement park has bumper boats, a miniature golf course, go-karts, batting cages, and an arcade. There's also a Naskart track with really, really fast cars for those with a valid driver's license. Most of the rides cost

$3.50 each; Naskart racing is $5.00 per ride. It's a little unimpressive looking when you first get there, but all the vehicles are meticulously maintained by the owners and are much better quality than cars and boats you usually find at similar facilities.

Knott's Camp Snoopy $$
Mall of America, 60 East Broadway,
Bloomington
(952) 883–8600
www.campsnoopy.com

Located right in the center of the Mall of America, Knott's Camp Snoopy, the largest indoor amusement park in America, has more than 25 rides and attractions for kids and adults alike. For the little guys, there's the Americana Carousel, a handpainted contemporary version of the classic carousel, and Li'l Shaver, a smaller, slower version of the roller coaster that circles the park (the Ripsaw Roller Coaster). For everyone else, there's the Skyscraper Ferris Wheel that takes visitors 74 feet high in the air, the Log Chute—a watery ride that includes a drop over a 40-foot waterfall—and more than enough other rides and features to take your mind off of shopping. If you like, there's a full-service child care facility at Camp Snoopy, Kids Quest, which charges by the hour and entertains kids with toys, video games, and heavily supervised walks around the park—a perfect place to drop your kids off while you take care of all your shopping. Admission to the park itself is free; you purchase tickets at the park to pay for the rides.

Valleyfair! $$$$
1 Valleyfair Drive, Shakopee
(952) 445–7600 or (800) 386–7433
www.valleyfair.com

There's nothing quite like spending the day at a cool water park in the middle of summer. With more than 75 rides, the upper Midwest's largest theme park has something to offer the littlest kid and the bravest adult alike. You can take an inner tube down a gently sloping canal for a relaxing, meditative ride, or choose the bumper cars and electric car tracks or exciting water rides like the Flume, which sends passenger

The largest indoor theme park in the United States, Knott's Camp Snoopy in the Mall of America thrills kids of all ages. PHOTO: GREATER MINNEAPOLIS CONVENTION & VISITORS ASSOCIATION

boats off a 50-foot drop at the end of the ride, and the Excalibur, a high-speed wooden roller coaster with a 105-foot drop and lots of quick twists and turns. There

Insiders' Tip

Day care is offered at the Mall of America at Knott's Camp Snoopy. No appointment is necessary.

are many rides for the really little ones, too, from bumble bee–shaped electric cars to Berenstain Bear Spooky Tree Children's Slide to an antique carousel.

Animal Adventures

Como Zoo   Free
1250 Kaufman Drive, St. Paul
(651) 487–8229
www.comopark.com

One of only four free metropolitan-area (in excess of one million people) zoos in the country, Como Zoo has been an institution in St. Paul for more than a century. The first Siberian tigers successfully bred in captivity were born here in 1958, and the big cat display is still one of the best features of the zoo, including a single breeding pair of lions that has had several healthy pairs of cubs over the past decade and have provided valuable insight to professionals and the public alike on how well lions do in captivity when allowed to stay together as a family instead of being separated immediately after mating and birth, as is customary at many other zoos. There is also a great primate display here, with about a dozen ring-tailed and brown lemurs, spider monkeys, a couple of breeding pairs of tamarins that have successfully given birth every spring (again, the babies are left with the parents to raise), and orangutans and gorillas that have been with the zoo more than 10 years. There's a seal show with some very friendly seals—you can buy little Dixie cups of fish at the zoo to feed the seals, too—bears, giraffes, zebras, buffalo, and a bird show in the warmer months. There's also a pair of wolves in a large, specially designed exhibit area that is designed to make the wolves feel comfortable having people watch them, with thick tree cover in the back of the enclosure for them to hide in when they don't feel like company.

But it doesn't stop at the animals. There's also an antique wooden carousel, Cafesjian's Carousel, for kids and adults to ride in a building near the entrance of the zoo, and in summer the zoo sets up a minicarnival with at least a dozen amusement park rides. In late October the zoo

opens in the evening for its annual "Zoo Boo," where kids come in their Halloween costumes and are given candy and gifts by the zoo staff. In winter the lot next to the zoo is turned into a snow-sculpture garden, and a giant sledding hill and tunnels are built for kids to play on and in.

Minnesota Zoo $$–$$$
13000 Zoo Boulevard, Apple Valley
(952) 431–9500 or (800) 366–7811
www.mnzoo.com

Located in the southern suburb of Apple Valley and housing more than 3,000 species of animals from five different continents, the Minnesota Zoo and its IMAX theater see more than a million visitors per year; the zoo is considered by wildlife experts to be one of the 10 best zoos in the country. The expansive grounds include an indoor tropical rain forest populated by an amazing variety of birds and animals, ranging from colorful African hornbills to a family of gibbons and a large and smelly South American tapir. There are also dolphins that officially perform for audiences every afternoon and unofficially any time enough people gather around their huge, glass-walled tank; a walk-through aquarium with sharks, fish, and deep sea plants; an education center where kids can pet everything from snakes to chinchillas, depending on what the zoo personnel bring in that day; and a Minnesota animal exhibit with beavers, foxes, fruit bats, and porcupines. Outside the main exhibit building, you can find ducks and swans, a prairie dog town, wild horses, camels, tigers, and many, many other animals, some of which are on the endangered species lists and are almost an exclusive at the zoo.

The newest exhibit at the zoo is the extremely hands-on Wells Fargo farm exhibit. This reproduction of a working family farm is surrounded by fields of crops—you can either walk up the hill to the farm itself or wait at the stationhouse for a tractor or horse cart to give you a ride. The farm has a huge selection of domestic animals, from beautiful show chickens and roosters to plow horses to many varieties of cows, including three

Trip to the Zoo: St. Paul's Como Zoo

To people expecting to find the same sad displays of animals rejected by other zoos that earmark most other free zoos in the country, Como Zoo will be a pleasant surprise. This zoo, a St. Paul institution for more than a century, actually supplies major city zoos with healthy animals from their successful breeding programs, especially from that of their internationally famous big cat program. Every two years there's a new pair of lion cubs from the zoo's extremely peaceful African lion couple. In the primate house, every spring brings new baby monkeys and tamarins.

Despite having such a great track record, the zoo itself has a lot fewer cosmetic flourishes than the newer, "virtual reality" exhibits that grace larger zoos. The bears are still in the small, fake stone exhibits that were built for them prior to 1970, and in winter the zebras and giraffes spend all their time inside pens the size of most people's living rooms. Yet the animals don't appear to be uncomfortable. Instead, they seem just as curious about the people who come to observe them as the zoo visitors are. The animals are calm, playful, and obviously healthy, and you don't have to spend much time at the zoo to see the distinctive personalities of the animals coming out. Casey the gorilla, the zoo's most famous escape artist, loves baby people, and if you visit the zoo with an infant in the wintertime, don't be surprised to see him come right up to the glass window and make rocking gestures with his arms, a big sappy look on his face. And Sparky, the star attraction of the seal show, sometimes gets so upset when children leave the window by his pool that he barks incessantly until they come back. The spider monkeys are always intensely interested in whatever toys children bring into the exhibit hall with them, and it's always hilarious watching the monkeys following nervous children from one side of their cage to another, climbing over one another to get a better look at whatever it is the child's purchased from the zoo's gift shop.

The secret to the zoo's success has much to do with the incredible amount of research that has gone into studying what animals need to be actually comfortable, from keeping animal families together and giving females near-total privacy with their newborns after giving birth, to the special toys placed in each animal's cage and allowing zoo volunteers that have formed bonds with specific animals to spend more time at those exhibits. Zoo director Victor Camp is especially proud of Como. "We really believe that Como Zoo is a place for generations of people," he says. "Grandparents come out here with their grandchildren, and they talk about how they brought their grandchild's parent out when he or she was a child and how they walked around the zoo and saw the Sparky show—it's just a wonderful place. The zoo is a place for people, and it's a place for animals, and it's a place to be up close and personal with the animals. And that's the goal of Como Zoo—we are connecting people with the wonders of the living world."

His favorite part of the zoo? "You know, I'm just part of the whole thing," he says. "All I can say is that sometimes you start out with some personal favorites, but then after a while, everything becomes your favorite. I've always wanted to work with animals, ever since I was a little boy, and this zoo is a place where I can work with a whole bunch of different kinds of animals, whether fish or amphibians or reptiles or birds or mammals. It's just a wonderful place to do that."

that were cloned. The chicken coop has an incubator with hatching eggs in it, and an assistant is on hand most hours to show children how to pet and hold the new baby chicks properly. There's also a petting pen full of goats, and you can even enter the pen to feed and play with the friendly animals.

UnderWater Adventures $$
Mall of America, 60 East Broadway,
Bloomington
(952) 883–0202 or (888) DIVE–TIME
www.underwateradventures.net

UnderWater Adventures is a huge (1.2 million gallons) walk-through aquarium featuring more than 3,000 different sea creatures from around the world in seven different displays. For a one-time admission charge, visitors can walk through an acrylic-walled tunnel that leads them underneath and through the middle of the three freshwater exhibits: Northwoods (featuring fish from Minnesota), Fisherman's Hollow, and the Mighty Mississippi, and four ocean exhibits: Shark Cove, Rainbow Reef, Seven Seas Gallery, and Starfish Beach, where children can touch a variety of harmless sharks and stingrays.

Berry Pickin'

A Minnesota summertime tradition, driving out to the country to pick fresh strawberries, blueberries, and apples is an important part of being a kid in the upper Midwest. For a small per-bucket fee, the following farms let visitors pick as much fruit as they can carry home. For apples, we suggest you stop by **Aamodt's Apple Farm,** 6428 Manning Avenue North, Stillwater (651–439–3127); the **Afton Apple Orchards,** 14421 South 90th Street, Afton (651–436–8385); or **Pine Tree Apple Orchards,** 450 Apple Orchard Road, White Bear Lake (651–429–7202). For strawberries and blueberries, try either the **Bauer Berry Farm,** 10830 French Lake Road, Champlin (763–421–4384); or **Berryland Farms,** 10900 Point Douglas Road, Cottage Grove (651–459–1359). The berries and apples you pick yourself will taste so much better than anything you can

UnderWater Adventures in the Mall of America offers the chance to walk among a gathering of sharks and other sea creatures while remaining dry and uneaten. PHOTO: GREATER MINNEAPOLIS CONVENTION & VISITORS ASSOCIATION

get at the grocery store, and you'll be lucky if any of the fruit you picked will last the car trip home.

Highbrow Entertainment (Arts and Culture)

The Children's Theatre Company $$$
2400 Third Avenue South, Minneapolis
(612) 874-0400
www.childrenstheatre.org

Since 1965 the Children's Theatre Company and its cast of incredibly talented children have been putting on performances at the Minneapolis Institute of Arts campus at the 746-seat facility. Most of the performances are based on children's stories and fairy tales, but many contemporary sources are used, such as Dr. Seuss—their rendition of *How the Grinch Stole Christmas* is an annual tradition—as well as C. S. Lewis's *The Lion, the Witch, and the Wardrobe*.

Minneapolis Sculpture Garden   Free
725 Vineland Place, Minneapolis
(612) 375-4444

Located right next to the Walker Art Center, this beautiful collection of large sculptures made by local and internationally known artists is a great place to take kids because it's outside, it's interesting, and it's free. Kids can run around and enjoy the 11-acre grounds without worrying about keeping silent while the grown-ups enjoy art—and who knows? They might learn something about art appreciation themselves. Right across the street is Loring Park, with rest rooms, a food cart that serves ice cream, and lots of sunny spots for a relaxing summer picnic.

Minnesota Center for Book Arts $
1011 Washington Avenue South, Suite 100, Minneapolis
(612) 215-2520
www.mnbookarts.org

The Minnesota Center for Book Arts, the largest independent book arts facility in the nation, offers classes to children and adults alike on making paper, binding books, and working in a letterpress printing studio. Kids can take their literary creations to the next level by making a beautiful cover out of found objects and binding their books using a variety of traditional methods, or they can create their own newspapers in the letterpress studio using both modern and antiquated letterpress equipment.

Northern Clay Center
2424 Franklin Avenue East, Minneapolis
(612) 339-8007
www.northernclaycenter.org

Kids of all ages get to play in the mud and create permanent monuments to their creativity at the Northern Clay Center. Classes and workshops are offered in ceramics, pottery, and glazing for the novice and master ceramist alike.

Sever's Corn Maze $$
15900 Flying Cloud Drive, Eden Prairie
(952) 974-5000

Since 1997 Sever's farm has been making incredibly detailed walk-through mazes in their expansive fields of corn, growing more and more complex as they become more experienced in maze-making. The maze for 2000 was modeled on the White House and received enough public attention that former President Bill Clinton stopped by to try out the maze while in Minnesota. Since then, thousands of people have come to Sever's farm to try their luck at the maze, which takes anywhere from 15 minutes to an hour to complete,

Insiders' Tip

Most museums have one day of the week where no group tours are allowed. It's a good idea to call ahead and ask which day that is before planning your visit.

depending on personal speed and skill level—maps are provided to guests as they enter the maze, and there are plenty of landmarks throughout to help you find your way about. The trails through the maze are seven feet wide, so you never feel trapped or claustrophobic, and it's a great place to meet and talk to other people trying to find their way through the maze. Also at Sever's farm is a courtyard that features live music, a kitchen that serves roasted sweet corn from the farm, as well as Minnesota's largest sandbox and smallest petting zoo.

Museums and Historical Attractions

American Swedish Institute $
2600 Park Avenue, Minneapolis
(612) 871–4907
www.americanswedishinst.com

Set in a spectacular, 33-room turn-of-the-20th-century mansion that looks more like a castle than a former residence, the American Swedish Institute is the largest and oldest museum of Swedish culture, arts, and history in the country. The outside of the building is decorated with gargoyles and three high turrets, while inside are beautiful stained-glass windows and hand-carved wooden furniture. If your kids have any interest in history or a love of mythical castles, this is about the closest they'll get to walking through a real one in this country. Exhibited at the museum are Scandinavian artifacts from the Turnblad family, including their clothes, family photographs, books, and toys. There are also fiddling and dancing groups that come through to entertain visitors, special festivals with music and food, and Swedish-language classes for kids and adults.

The Bakken: A Library and Museum of Electricity in Life $
3537 Zenith Avenue South, Minneapolis
(612) 926–3878
www.thebakken.org

Founded in 1975 by Earl E. Bakken, inventor of the first transistorized cardiac pace-maker, this Tudor-style mansion houses an incredible collection of rare books, manuscripts, and more than 2,000 scientific thingamajigs that are all related to the role electricity plays in life. Not suitable for children under age six.

Bell Museum of Natural History $
University of Minnesota, 10 Church Street SE, Minneapolis
(612) 624–7083
www.bellmuseum.org

While this type of museum has fallen out of favor with the increasing quality of zoos with live animal exhibits, this is actually one of the more pleasant traditional natural history museums in the country. The exhibits of stuffed birds, mammals, and fish are extremely clean and tastefully exhibited, with beautiful painted backdrops of seascapes and woodlands for the animals on display. The exhibits are primarily Northland animals and confined to the North American continent, with emphasis on Minnesota wildlife, including porcupines, bears, moose, and ground squirrels. There is also a temporary exhibit hall that features artwork and animal remains from specific parts of the world, changing approximately every two months. On the second floor is the Touch and See Room, where kids can view and even hold live snakes, turtles, and lizards—children are allowed and even encouraged to handle everything in the room, which houses a large assortment of horns, antlers, bones, fossils, and rocks. The third floor has a large butterfly and moth exhibit; a side room contains a photography exhibit focusing on bats.

Fort Snelling $$
Junction of Minnesota Highways 5 and 55, St. Paul
(612) 726–1171
www.mnhs.org/places/sites/hfs

Built on a high bluff overlooking the Mississippi and Minnesota Rivers in 1827, Fort Snelling was once the last United States outpost in the mostly unexplored wilds of the north and was the center of frontier commerce and government on the upper Mississippi. A variety of themed tours provide insight into what life was like at the fort, with costumed guides reenacting scenes from military, civilian, and American Indian life of the 1800s. Kids can join in the fun by taking up a musket and pretending to be a soldier, scraping hides with fur traders, or "working" in the laundry or kitchen of the fort.

Gibbs Farm Museum $$
2097 Larpentur Avenue, Falcon Heights
(651) 646–8629
www.rchs.com/gbbsfmz.htm

A point of interest to note for both politically correct parents and otherwise is that the history most spoken about at this archeological site is that of Jane Gibbs, a young girl raised by missionaries and used as an interpreter between the Dakota Indians and settlers for many years, and not that of her husband, Heman Gibbs, who helped build the two houses on the property as well as the barn in back. The Gibbses, who first moved to the Minnesota property in the 1840s from Illinois, lived for five years in a tiny sod house—replicated in astounding detail and now a part of the tour—before building the main house. The tour covers everything that's left of the original Gibbs property, from gardens full of plants indigenous to the area more than a thousand years ago, reconstructed Dakota bark lodges and tepees furnished with firepits, animal skins, and hunting tools, a barn complete with pigs, chickens, ducks, and many other animals that visit the farm on loan from the University of Minnesota's Agriculture Program, to the schoolhouse and the two houses that Heman built for his family. The main house is furnished with the artwork, furniture, photographs, and essentials from the Gibbses themselves and period pieces donated by members of the Historical Society, including a full kitchen with a wood-burning stove and a crank-operated washing machine. A word of warning, however; the general tour is not really suitable for fidgety children under age nine, as it takes about an hour and most of the tour involves listening to lectures on the history of the farm. However, the farm does put on seasonal events geared specifically toward children, including ghost story readings and refreshments around Halloween, and metal forging, crop gathering, milking demonstrations, and craft-making days throughout the summer.

Henry Sibley House Historic Site $
1357 Sibley Memorial Highway, Mendota
(651) 452–1596
www.mnhs.org/places/sites/hts

One of the last remaining buildings of Minnesota's oldest European-American settlement, the Henry Sibley House, once home to American Fur Company mogul and legendary boatman Henry Sibley, has been restored to its original splendor and furnished with mid-19th-century period pieces and a variety of exhibits. The Sibley House also schedules special "Children's Days" on an irregular basis, where kids get to dress up in traditional clothes and play games that settler and Native American children did up to 350 years ago, make scale models of tepees, and create rope, fishing lines, mats, and bowstrings out of plant fibers.

Minnesota Children's Museum $$
10 West Seventh Street, St. Paul
(651) 225–6000
www.mcm.org

While kids up to age 9 or 10 might still appreciate this wonderful resource, this really is geared to younger children, from infants to eight-year-olds. The great thing about this place is that all the exhibits are hands-on, and they're extremely well researched exhibits, too. We had no idea how much our own son would enjoy pretending to be a bus driver or a shopkeeper or a restaurant owner until he politely refused to leave the One World Gallery exhibit hall until all the possibilities the exhibit had to offer had been exhausted. There's also a mock recording studio, newspaper press, and TV studio, while in the World Works Gallery, kids can operate a crane to pick up blocks, build a house foundation out of rubber masonry, or learn how to make art out of recycled newspaper. The Earth World Gallery has a giant anthill (populated by giant ant statues and nests) that kids can crawl through, pulley-operated clouds that can be moved across the ceiling from a remote control, and a beaver dam and a giant hollow log that kids can climb in and out of.

For toddlers age six months to four years old, there's a wonderful playroom, the Habitot, that's set up like a nature preserve, with a giant "pond" playpen filled with plush lily pads and frog, turtle, and fish puppets at one end and a padded crawl-through cave filled with more stuffed animals and puppets at the other end. Changing rooms are connected to the exhibit, too, so parents don't have to rush to the other end of the building to take care of emergencies. At scheduled intervals throughout the day, musicians and storytellers set up camp on the first floor and invite children to huddle around and listen or even participate.

Another nice feature about this place is that as long as you leave your museum admission sticker on, you can leave the building and come back all day, which is great because their dining facilities consist of vending machines and there are a lot of great restaurants in the immediate vicinity to take the family instead.

The Minnesota History Center   Free
345 West Kellogg Boulevard, St. Paul
(651) 296–6126 or (800) 657–3773
www.mnhs.org/places/historycenter

The Minnesota History Center is a wonderful resource of artifacts (dating back 11,000 years), historical texts, and changing and permanent exhibits that chronicle much of the history of the upper Midwest. Three of the permanent exhibits are specifically geared toward children. Grainland includes an authentic 24-ton boxcar and a model grain elevator that children can climb through as they learn how grain gets to the marketplace, and Help Wanted: Work in Minnesota lets children and adults try on the roles of different Minnesota workers in the 1930s and 1940s, from a railway inspector who has to judge whether rail cars are safe to send on their way down the track, to a meat packer—see how many rubber pig's feet you can pack in a minute—or a dairy farmer who has to work the crank on a cream separator. The

real kid pleaser is the Minnesota A to Z galleries, which feature a different Minnesota exhibit to match each letter (Z is Below Zero; B stands for Burma Shave).

Murphy's Landing $$
2187 East Minnesota Highway 101, Shakopee
(952) 445–6900
www.murphyslanding.org

The Minnesota River's Restoration Project (i.e., Murphy's Landing) is a living-history site that preserves and interprets 19th-century life in the Minnesota River Valley. More than 40 period buildings once in danger of being razed were moved here from 1969 to 1972, with the intent of re-creating a 19th-century village. The village includes a fur trading post, a homestead, and a storefront, all of which are arranged in chronological order according to when they were built. The site is peopled by "villagers" who are clothed in period costumes and perform such duties as weaving, metalsmithing, and farming—visitors are encouraged to approach the villagers and ask them questions about what they are doing. Educational seminars and lectures are ongoing, and special seasonal events are planned around the holidays for history buffs of all ages.

Science Museum of Minnesota $$
120 West Kellogg Boulevard, St. Paul
(651) 221–9444
www.smm.org

With eight indoor acres of both permanent and temporary exhibits that include an extensive collection of dinosaur, mammal, insect, and fish fossils, a geology exhibit, a reproduction of a big game hunter's lodge with a huge variety of preserved game animals, and nearly a whole floor dedicated to hands-on technology and weather demonstrations, this museum is guaranteed to bring out the scientist in parents and kids alike. Previous temporary exhibits have included a collection of life-size mechanical dinosaur sculptures that visitors can manipulate with pulleys and a series on bats from around the world. The museum's education center also offers classes to kids on subjects as diverse as animation and filmmaking and archaeology. There's also a

The Science Museum of Minnesota on Kellogg Boulevard in downtown St. Paul offers world-class exhibits and hours of fun experiments for curious kids. The museum also houses a gigantic IMAX theater. PHOTO: TODD R. BERGER

Collections Gallery where kids can bring in interesting rocks, seashells, and bones for the staff to positively identify with the option of exchanging their pieces for something in the museum's trading collection and an IMAX theater that shows 3D nature films.

Twin City Model Railroad Museum $$
Bandana Square, 1021 Bandana Boulevard East, St. Paul
(651) 647-9628
www.tcmrm.org

A great treat for children and adults alike, this exhibit will particularly impress anyone even slightly interested in history, railroads, or miniatures. In existence in one form or another since 1939, the Model Railroad Club has been educating and entertaining the public with their model locomotives, building their incredible panoramic sets to scale to complete the illusion. The museum itself is set inside a former "Como depot"—a repair shop for passenger trains—while the exhibit inside

the museum is a wonderful scale model of the Twin Cities and the surrounding communities, including parts of the Mississippi River and the old Mill District in Minneapolis prior to 1950, when trains were still the main means of transporting goods throughout the country. Up to six different trains run at once through the model, disappearing into tunnels and climbing through the tree-filled landscapes with their tiny headlights blazing. The exhibit changes monthly sometimes, miniature streetcars can be seen running back and forth over the Stone Arch Bridge model, or steam engines like the Milwaukee *Hiawatha* pulling passenger cars in and out of the 1914 Great Northern passenger depot. There's a changing photo exhibit in the museum, too, focusing on a different historic train or train line each month. In the winter, the museum stays open a little later to show off their special "Night Trains" exhibit, where all the lights are turned off in the museum and the lights on the trains and miniature buildings become the only source of illumination in the room.

Parks (Favorites of Little Insiders)

**Marjorie McNeely Conservatory
at Como Park
1325 Aida Place, St. Paul
(651) 487–8200**

Located right next door to the zoo in Como Park, this beautiful glass-domed botanical garden is a fun place to take kids interested in plants and flowers. The garden is divided into six sections featuring palms, ferns, tropical food plants, bonsai trees, and seasonal flowers, as well as a Gallery Garden dedicated to showcasing youth artwork set among a changing selection of flowers and plants. In summer a side door opens up into the Como Ordway Memorial Japanese Garden, a Sansui (mountain and water) design created by

St. Paul's sister city, Nagasaki, Japan, especially for the park. Nature-loving children will love the decorative pathways that lead them to the center pond stocked with giant, friendly goldfish and past some of the most relaxed cottontail rabbits you will ever see.

**Minnehaha Falls   Free
Hiawatha Avenue at Minnehaha Parkway, Minneapolis**

Immortalized in the Henry Wadsworth Longfellow epic poem about the Ojibwe warrior Hiawatha, Minnehaha Falls and the park are both worth the hype. The best time to see the falls is right after it rains, because after a good rainstorm, the falls are so strong that you can barely see through the curtain of water, and visitors more than 100 feet away are sprayed with drops of cool water. Kids can walk down to the base of the falls and follow the stream at the bottom all the way to the Mississippi River. Along the way, kids can have fun spotting fish in the waters, tiny

The Marjorie McNeely Conservatory at Como Park in St. Paul offers a warm, green respite from the long Minnesota winters. PHOTO: SAINT PAUL CONVENTION AND VISITORS BUREAU

garter snakes, 13-striped squirrels in the woods, and boats and barges on the Mississippi. There are also statues throughout the park of notable local historic figures (including Hiawatha), the John H. Stevens House Museum, which is yet another "birthplace of Minnesota" site, a picnic area, and a playground. In winter the walkway down to the bottom of the falls is closed, but visitors get the rare opportunity to see what a powerful waterfall looks like when it freezes solid.

Nicollet Island Park   Free
Off Historic Main Street at East Hennepin Avenue, Minneapolis

In summertime this little island is a haven for woodchucks, muskrats, raccoon families, and rabbits, as well as geese, ducks, and squirrels so tame they come right up to you to be fed. In winter the park is converted into a giant ice-skating rink, with hot chocolate and warm treats available at the brick Pavilion building at the far end of the park. The view from the park is something you can't miss—located right in the middle of the Mississippi River and Minneapolis itself. You get a breathtaking view of the Minneapolis downtown area looming on one side of the river and the beautiful old brick buildings of St. Anthony on the other side. This is also the best place in the Twin Cities to spend Fourth of July with your family; the fantastic Boom Island fireworks display can be seen from anywhere in the park.

Restaurants That Like Kids (and vice versa)

Annie's Parlour
313 14th Avenue SE, Minneapolis
(612) 379–0744

Located just a couple of blocks from the University of Minnesota and the Bell Museum, Annie's Parlour is a great place to stop and get a burger. While the prices for adult food are fair but not super cheap, the kid's menu is extensive and extremely reasonable, and the portions are nearly as big as those served to adults, at about half

Insiders' Tip
In both Minneapolis and St. Paul, there's a park in every neighborhood for you to stop and let the kids get out and stretch their legs.

the price. The menu includes lots of hamburgers, chicken sandwiches served on white or dark rolls, huge baskets of french fries, and malts, sundaes, and banana splits. Annie's makes its own hot fudge to go with the sundaes, and it's very good. One drawback to the place is that it serves alcohol, which means that from 3:00 to 6:00 P.M. there's a happy hour—however, most of the people who come here are underage college kids and can't drink anyway and are just showing up for the great deals on food during this time. If you want to avoid the bar crowd, your best bet is to sit outside (if it's the right time of year) on the large porch that overlooks Dinkytown and the beautiful Minneapolis skyline.

Darl-etto Drive Inn
1440 Minnehaha Avenue, St. Paul
(651) 776–3470

Located in St. Paul's east side working-class neighborhood and a little hard to find (take Minnesota Highway 36 to White Bear Avenue and go south to Minnehaha), this old-school neighborhood Italian drive in restaurant is excellent for kids. The extremely reasonably priced menu includes everything from wonderful, thick meatball, sausage, or pizza sandwiches (for a little extra, you can order peppers, onions, or mushrooms on the sandwich), to hamburgers, Coney dogs, and fried shrimp baskets. The sandwiches come with either french fries or spaghetti on the side—we recommend getting the spaghetti because it is good, although a little messy to eat in the car. For dessert, there are ice cream shakes, malts, sundaes, and banana splits that are better than your usual burger-joint fare.

Davanni's Pizza & Hot Hoagies
2500 Riverside Avenue, Minneapolis
(612) 332–5551
www.davannis.com
Sixteen additional Twin Cities locations

A treat for discriminating adults and kids alike, Davanni's is one of the best places to get a pizza in the Twin Cities. The pizza is wonderful and just loaded with whatever toppings you order—the crust, in particular, is spectacular. There are two levels to the restaurant—the downstairs, which is small, and the upstairs dining room, which has large, comfortable booths and a great view through the large windows set next to each table.

Little Oven
1786 Minnehaha Avenue East, St. Paul
(651) 735–4944

Small and comfortable, this restaurant is a favorite after-work stop for people in the neighborhood. The best and most popular thing here is the flat-style pizza (the type most commonly made in the '70s, especially in the Midwest)—it's good, uncomplicated, and very cheap. There's also a good selection of steak, chicken, and turkey dishes on the menu, as well as desserts. This is a great place to take kids, and lots of people do.

Queen of Sheba Café & Restaurant
2447 West Seventh Street, St. Paul
(651) 690–0068

Another unusual choice for a restaurant to take kids, this is sort of fun because not only is it good food, but it's all food you can eat with your hands—and unless you specifically request silverware, that's what the waitstaff expects you to use at the table. The restaurant primarily serves Ethiopian food—stewed meat and vegetables spiced and served with injera (delicious, spongy pieces of flat bread) but the menu also has hot dogs, french fries, and hamburgers. It's a strange mixture of ele-

gant and casual, as the restaurant is beautifully decorated with hand-embroidered tablecloths and framed needlepoints, but many families take their kids here and the waitstaff is very friendly. There's also a counter at one side of the restaurant that serves Ethiopian coffee for grown-ups.

Snuffy's Malt Shop
244 Cleveland Avenue South, St. Paul
(651) 690–1846
1125 West Larpenteur Avenue, St. Paul
(651) 488–0241

This burger joint caters especially to kids, and not just because of their 19 different flavors of ice cream malts, including fudge banana and neapolitan. The decor itself is designed to entertain, with large cartoon characters of penguins and bears and other animals painted in bright colors all over the walls, and the waitstaff automatically brings crayons and paper to your table if you are accompanied by a child. The food is excellent for this sort of fare, too—the bread on the burgers and sandwiches is lightly toasted and the pickles are set to the side so you can decide if you actually want them in your burger or not. While it may initially seem like a rip-off to have to order fries or onion rings separately, since they're not included with the

Insiders' Tip

In springtime, Canada geese can be found anywhere along the Mississippi, and they expect to be fed. Most places don't sell popcorn or bread crumbs for them, so it's a good idea to be prepared and pick some up at the store before venturing out.

meal, be warned—half an order of Snuffy's fries or rings is big enough to feed two adults well, while a whole order can easily feed a family of four. They also offer flavored phosphates and sodas along with take-out ice-cream cones, and while the menu may seem limited, everything on it is made very, very well. The one drawback of the restaurant is that there is only one rest room, and you have to go through the kitchen and down a steep flight of stairs to get to it; that can be a real hassle if you have small children with you.

We All Scream For...

Conny's Creamy Cone
1197 North Dale Street, St. Paul
(651) 488–4150

A stop by Conny's is a must for kids when you're in the Como Park area. With 24 flavors of soft-serve ice cream (plus a ton of specialty treats, including M&M ice cream made right on the spot), kids have the option of either ordering standard ice cream flavors—strawberry, chocolate, etc.—or, for the more adventurous child, the raspberry and piña colada cones are pretty wonderful, too. And you can't beat the price—a small cone falls well under a dollar and is as big as most places' "large" cones.

Livingston's Organic Ice Cream
2037 Riverside Avenue, Minneapolis
(612) 333–5692

Don't let the word "organic" scare you away from this place. Livingston's has absolutely incredible homemade ice cream, made from hormone-free milk provided by local dairy cows. There are only two flavors of ice cream—chocolate and vanilla—but it's some of the best chocolate and vanilla ice cream you'll ever have, and the cones are big enough to happily split with someone. Occasionally, the owners have short-term specials like ice-cream floats made with specialty-bottled root beer, but even coming in to get an ordinary ice cream cone is an extraordinary treat. The atmosphere is like walking into someone's living room, and you can choose either to sit at a regular table to eat or kick back and relax in a comfy chair.

Shopping Kid-Style

The Basic Brown Bear Factory
154 North Garden, Mall of America, 60 East Broadway, Bloomington
(952) 883–0822

It's hard to say who this will mean more to—loving parents watching their child put together their very own special bear or making a surprise bear for their child or the ambitious child who gets to design his or her very own teddy bear. At any rate, there's no denying that the Basic Brown Bear Factory is a special toy store. The Bear Factory experts let you select an unstuffed bear from their wide selection of styles and help you stuff it on their stuffing machine. They then take it to their sewing station, where they sew it together for you, groom it, then let you pick out the clothes, ribbons, and other accessories to fully make it your bear. There are a wide choice of price ranges, too, with the cheapest being around $12 and the most expensive bears around $150.

Creative Kidstuff
10 West Seventh Street, St. Paul
(651) 225–6060
Four additional Twin Cities locations

This neat little toyshop chain offers a wide variety of educational and creative toys for kids and parents alike to salivate over.

> ### Insiders' Tip
> Most local festivals have exhibits and events aimed specifically at kids. See the Annual Events and Festivals chapter for our Calendar of Events for Kids.

Aside from all the cool toys, Kidstuff also has in-store Play Days, where kids get to try out some of the new toys on the market for free, visits by characters from TV and books, science demonstrations, great sales on already reasonably priced toys, and lots of other kid-oriented events, including face painting and magic shows.

Half Price Books
2041 Ford Parkway, St. Paul
(651) 699–1391
www.halfpricebooks.com
Four additional Twin Cities locations
This wonderful discount new and used book store has a great selection of children's books and toys, with everything from large volumes of fairy tales, picture books for toddlers, a whole shelf of dinosaur books, and another dedicated to "creepy" creatures like reptiles, spiders, sharks, and insects. It's easy to get carried away shopping here, because the books have been marked down so low you can buy three or four for what one good children's book usually costs.

LEGO Imagination Center
Mall of America, 60 East Broadway,
Bloomington
(952) 858–8949
It's amazing what you can build with LEGOs if you put your mind to it. The people who put this exhibit together obviously put a lot of thought and time into their creations, which include several gigantic robotic dinosaurs, a moon lander complete with astronauts, and the world's largest working LEGO clock tower. You can buy LEGOs and LEGO kits here, too, but the real treat is taking your kids to see all the things other people have made with the colorful little blocks.

Maud Borup Candies
790 Grand Avenue, St. Paul
(651) 602–9919
293 Como Avenue, St. Paul
(651) 488–8023
Where most specialty candy stores charge outrageous prices, Maud Borup is surprisingly reasonable. This is a fun place to take kids for a treat, whether it be seasonal candies such as jack-o'-lantern– or Santa Claus–shaped chocolates, nearly two dozen flavors of suckers, or mesh bags of chocolate pirate coins.

Annual Events and Festivals

Festivals are an important part of Minnesotans' life. In the winter, elaborate festivities like the Holidazzle Parade and the St. Paul Winter Carnival are a good way to stave off cabin fever, while the coming of spring is a time to get reacquainted with friends and neighbors you haven't seen since the first snowfall. In fact, as soon as the weather warms up, just about anything can kick off a festival, from an abundance of wildflowers blooming to a variety of charitable functions and building restoration projects. Entire city blocks are roped off for block parties in the summer, and the streets are filled with cars decorated with seashells, ribbons, sculptures, and big painted flowers. Just about every tiny town in the state holds at least one spring and summer festival, complete with parades, concession and merchandise kiosks, and live music.

The following calendar lists only events that have been around for a while and will continue to be around for a while. Some summers, it seems like the Cities are in a perpetual state of celebration, with neighborhood bars staging street concerts and churches organizing small carnivals in local parks. Other summers, certain festivities can't fit into certain budgets, and what may seem like an annual event may not actually occur for a few years, or may be cancelled altogether.

January

St. Paul Winter Carnival
Various locations around St. Paul
Fourth week of January through first week of February
(651) 223–4700
www.winter-carnival.com

The St. Paul Winter Carnival is by far the coolest celebration in the Midwest and one of the oldest winter festivals in the country. More than 50 events, including giant snow slides, ice mazes, amazing snow and ice-sculpture exhibits, live music, and sporting events such as dogsled racing and snowshoe hikes, are a part of this annual festival, with the crowning events being the King Boreas Grande Day Parade and the more decadent evening Vulcan Victory Torchlight Parade.

Twin Cities Food & Wine Experience
Minneapolis Convention Center,
1301 Second Avenue South, Minneapolis
Last weekend in January
(612) 371–5857 or (866) 895–8911
www.foodwineshow.com

Although tickets for this annual event get into the pricey range, around $50, you are highly unlikely not to get your money's worth if you come hungry. More than 280 Twin Cities restaurants; local, national, and international wineries; and other exhibitors serve up their gourmet specialties to the masses. Additional events (at an additional charge) include a silent auction to benefit Minnesota Public Radio, wine seminars, and wine lunches at restaurants throughout the Metro.

February

Kidfest
RiverCentre/Touchstone Energy Place,
175 Kellogg Boulevard, St. Paul
(651) 265–4800

Kidfest is Minnesota's longest running children's event, with multiple stages of live entertainment, dozens of free activities and games for kids of all ages, a video arcade, and Minnesota's largest inflatable playground (featuring a superslide, Velcro wall, maze, and sports challenges), all guaranteed to keep your kids busy for at least a day, maybe two. The weekend-long festival, part of the St. Paul Winter Carnival, features celebrity visits, which have included Nickelodeon's touring Franklin and the Magic Fiddle show, featuring Franklin the Turtle, as well as Swampmaster Jeff Quattrocchi and his live alligator show. Additionally, there's the perennial favorite, the petting zoo, a rain forest stage filled with exotic creatures, a minigolf area, pony rides, and trout fishing.

March

St. Patrick's Day Parade
Downtown St. Paul
(651) 292–3225

St. Paul's annual St. Patrick's Day Parade picks up at Fourth and Wacouta Streets

Insiders' Tip

The Twin Cities Infoline (612-379-CALL) provides an automated list of events, arts and entertainment, restaurants, sports scores, and other happenings throughout the Twin Cities metro area.

and heads west all the way down Fourth Street, ending at Rice Park. The parade features Irish music and performers, and food, drink, and merchandise kiosks are set up along the parade route for the remainder of the day.

The parade is all part of St. Paul's annual Irish Celebration, paying homage to the many Irish immigrants who settled in the city. Entertainment, crafts, Irish foods, and beer (Irish and otherwise) are all part of the festivities, centered around the Landmark Center in downtown St. Paul.

April

Minneapolis/St. Paul International Film Festival
Various locations, sponsored by U Film Society
First three weeks of April
(612) 627–4430
www.ufilm.org

For over 20 years, the Film Society's International Film Festival has gone from a weekend-long event to the present high-water mark where about 120 flicks from more than 40 different nations are screened during three full weeks in April. Some of the festival's participating theaters include the Oak Street Cinema, Reading Cinema, St. Anthony Main, Suburban World, Highland, Knollwood 4, and the Lakeville 18 theaters; specific venues change each year.

Ironman Bicycle Ride
Lakeville High School, Plymouth
Last Sunday of April
(612) 378–3773
www.pro-events.com

An annual event for more than 30 years, the Ironman Bicycle Ride takes more than 5,000 participating bicyclists through 33-mile, 66-mile, or 100-mile scenic tours through the Minnesota countryside. The $25 entrance fee goes to benefit Youth Hosteling International.

May

Festival of Nations
Various locations, St. Paul
(651) 647-0191
www.festivalofnations.com

Founded in 1932 and held generally in late April or early May, the Festival of Nations has been an event of the people who helped create it for their pleasure and the ethnic values they treasured. Its underlying philosophy has been that as Americans of all backgrounds—native citizens and naturalized citizens alike—share experiences, their differences become less significant and barriers to understanding are removed. Today Minnesota's largest multicultural event showcases more than 100 ethnic groups through food, dance performances, cultural exhibits, folk art demonstrations, an international bazaar, and more.

Cinco de Mayo Mexican Fiesta
District del Sol, St. Paul
First week in May
(651) 222-6347
www.districtdelsol.com

The Cinco de Mayo Mexican Fiesta lights up the District del Sol on the west side of St. Paul, across the Robert Street Bridge from downtown (for visitors, the "west" side of St. Paul is actually south of down-

The Cinco de Mayo Mexican Fiesta in the District del Sol across the Mississippi from downtown St. Paul brings many smiles to little faces. PHOTO: SAINT PAUL CONVENTION AND VISITORS BUREAU

town). Up to 100,000 people teem the streets of the Hispanic neighborhood to take in Mexican entertainment and food and to watch the Cinco de Mayo Parade.

Scottish Country Fair
Macalester College, 1600 Grand Avenue, St. Paul
First weekend of May
(651) 696-6239
www.macalester.edu/~scottish

Macalester's Scottish Fair draws crowds of up to 20,000 spectators and performers who participate in athletic competitions, bagpipes, bands, Highland dancing, Celtic music, and Scottish food, art, and crafts. From single-malt tasting seminars to log-tossing, it's all here, with a fair amount of bagpipes on the side.

Smalandskalaset
American Swedish Institute, 2600 Park Avenue, Minneapolis
(612) 871-4907
www.americanswedishinst.org

Held annually at the American Swedish Institute throughout the month, Smalandskalaset celebrates the history and culture of Smaland, Sweden. Glassblowing demonstrations, Swedish craft demonstrations, live music, food, and traditional folk costumes are just some of the things you can see at this event. For kids, there's Pippi Longstocking's Playhouse to explore.

St. Anthony Main Summer Concert Series
213 Southeast Main Street (St. Anthony Main), Minneapolis
(763) 591-9979

Throughout the summer, you can catch live music for free on the stage outside Tuggs Tavern, located right across the street from the Mississippi River.

In the Heart of the Beast May Day Parade
Powderhorn Park, 3400 15th Avenue South, Minneapolis
First Sunday of May
(612) 721-2535
www.hobt.org/mayday

For nearly 30 years, In the Heart of the Beast Puppet and Mask Theatre's annual

May Day parade has been as true a sign of spring coming back to the Twin Cities as robins choosing their mates. The brilliantly colored ensemble of friendly and scary creatures on stilts, children dressed as flowers, and other magical images travels all along Minneapolis's downtown Bloomington Avenue and ends in a colorful pageant in Powderhorn Park, where puppets sail across the pond in boats. This is probably the largest, funkiest celebration of spring in the entire Midwest, paired with an entire day of dance, music, fun, and food all along the parade route.

Eagle Creek Rendezvous
Murphy's Landing, 2187 East County Road 101, Shakopee
Memorial Day weekend
(952) 445–6901
www.murphyslanding.com
Historic Murphy's Landing hosts the oldest annual Minnesota fur trappers celebration, Eagle Creek Rendezvous, each Memorial Day weekend. Traditionally, fur trappers gathered to trade goods and celebrate winter's end at this event, and at Murphy's Landing the celebration is re-created in minute detail. More than 100 encampments are set up, with demonstrations including black powder shoots and tomahawk throwing.

June

Improv in the Parks
Lake Harriet Rose Gardens, 42nd Street and Lake Harriet Parkway, Minneapolis
Sunday, June through August
(612) 825–1832
Stevie Ray's Improv Troupe performs in the great outdoors, creating comedy sketches on the spot based on audience suggestions. Sometimes the troupe even incorporates unsuspecting audience members in the act. Bring something to sit on (blanket, lawnchair, etc.). The troupe performs twice each summer Sunday, at 4:00 and 7:00 P.M., although shows are canceled if it rains or the grass is wet. The shows are free.

Alive After Five Concert Series
Peavy Plaza, 11th Street and Nicollet Mall, Minneapolis
(612) 338–3807
Unwind after the workday with good food and music on the mall throughout June. Local and touring bands can be seen at the plaza, either for free or for a minimal charge, and drink and food kiosks are set up close to the stage.

Grand Old Day
Grand Avenue, St. Paul
First Sunday of June
(651) 699–0029
www.grandave.com
More than 250,000 people show up for this granddaddy of Twin Cities celebrations—the largest one-day street festival in the Midwest—with everything from giant Velcro walls for kids and adults to hurl themselves against to local bands performing well into the night. Fourteen entertainment stages, lots of food vendors and merchant kiosks, and various family attractions are featured during the event, as well as the early afternoon Grand Old Day parade.

The festival engulfs 20 city blocks and features rides, the Grand Old Day parade, and live music. Within its 20 blocks, Grand Old Day also boasts more than 150 outdoor vendors offering every delicacy imaginable, from Cokes, pizza, and corn dogs to gyros, egg rolls, and Jamaican beef.

Edina Art Fair
50th and France, Edina
First weekend of June
(952) 922–1524
Nearly 300 local, regional, and national artists whose works include clothing, dolls, woodcarving, and more are featured at this annual festival.

Stevens Square Community Summer Movies and Music Series
Stevens Square Park, Second Avenue and 18th Street, Minneapolis
(612) 871–7307
Stevens Square Park presents free movies and live music every Wednesday for six weeks, beginning in early June.

St. Anthony Park Art Festival
St. Anthony Park neighborhood, St. Paul
First Saturday of June
(651) 642-0411
www.sap.org

More than 100 artists showcase their goods annually in one of St. Paul's prettiest neighborhoods, with food and music available all along Como Avenue from Carter to Luther Seminary. You can find spectacular deals on truly unusual items, most of them made by some of the brilliant people who live in the neighborhood.

Tater Daze
Downtown Brooklyn Park
(763) 493-8122

Tater Daze began in the 1960s and celebrates Brooklyn Park's potato growing heritage. The weekend festival kicks off with a parade on the first night and is followed by a host of community events, including live music and lots of family activities.

Art on the Lake
Downtown Excelsior
(952) 474-6461

For more than 20 years, Excelsior's Art on the Lake has showcased the work of local artists through art competitions, demonstrations, and other related activities aimed to get the public interested in art. Live music and entertainment, as well as food and merchandise kiosks, are almost as important a part of this festival as the art itself.

Father Hennepin Festival
Downtown Champlin
(763) 923-7100

This is a family-oriented festival, featuring fireworks, powerboats, personal watercraft races, and amusement park rides.

South St. Paul Kaposia Days
Various locations, South St. Paul
(651) 554-3200

This family festival includes musical entertainment each day of the festival, parades, children's activities, a flea market and craft sale, royalty pageants, auto shows, bingo, water sports, fireworks, and athletic tournaments.

St. Louis Parktacular
Various locations, St. Louis Park
(952) 924-2550
www.stlouispark.org

St. Louis Park's annual citywide celebration features a carnival, parade with royalty, street dances, food vendors, bingo competitions, and a petting zoo for the kids.

Stone Arch Festival of the Arts
Mississippi Riverfront, Old St. Anthony
Main, Minneapolis
(612) 673-5123

More than 200 vendors, artists, bands, and street performers congregate along the riverfront on Father's Day weekend each year, making this a fun festival to either take Dad for the afternoon or shop for a present for him. Performances include kayak demonstrations by the Mississippi Whitewater Park, the Green Chair Project, and an "Art of Classic Cars" car show, featuring 125 vintage vehicles.

Midsommar Celebration
American Swedish Institute, 2600 Park
Avenue South, Minneapolis
Mid-June—call for specific dates and times
(612) 871-4907
www.americanswedishinst.org

Celebrate Midsommar in the Swedish tradition with music, folk dance, and food. Join the museum's costumed guides and performers in this traditional festival that celebrates everything good about summer.

Midsommar Dag
20880 Olinda Trail, Scandia
(651) 433-5053

The third Saturday of June kicks off the festival season in the picturesque town of Scandia, located at the edge of the metro area near Marine on St. Croix. Sponsored by the Gammelgarden Museum, the festival is a bright affair of parades, traditional Scandinavian dancing and costumes, and lots of food.

Buckhorn Days
Long Lake
Third weekend of June
(952) 497–5407

This weekend-long festival in the western suburb of Long Lake features live music, dancing, carnival games, fishing contests, "mad scientist" exhibits, a petting zoo, concession stands, and pony rides.

Earle Brown Days Festival
Downtown Brooklyn Center
Last week of June
(763) 569–3400

This annual festival, honoring civic leader activist Earle Brown, features a parade, fireworks, arts and craft fair, 10K run, ice-cream social, live music and entertainment, and special events aimed specifically at kids and teens, including a kids' fishing contest and lots of games.

Minnetonka Summer Festival
Various locations, Minnetonka
Last week of June
(952) 939–8316

This citywide festival includes family-oriented activities for all ages, including live entertainment, rides, games, food and craft vendors, and fireworks.

MSRA's Back to the '50s
Minnesota State Fairgrounds, St. Paul
Last weekend of June
(651) 641–1992
www.msra.com

Every year, the Minnesota Street Rod Association (MSRA) heads to the state fairgrounds to show off its members' street rods, classic, and custom cars dating from 1964 and older. More than 9,000 show cars can be seen at the event, which also features food and merchandise kiosks, family activities, commercial exhibits, and live music.

Twin Cities GLBT Pride Festival
Loring Park, 1382 Willow Street,
Minneapolis
Last weekend of June
(952) 852–6100
www.tcpride.com

The largest and probably the oldest annual gay/lesbian/bi/transsexual pride festival in the upper Midwest includes a parade, music, food, and more. An estimated 170,000 people show up for the festival over the course of the weekend.

July

Basilica Block Party
88th North Seventh Street, Basilica of St.
Mary, Minneapolis
First weekend of July
(612) 317–3511
www.basilicablockparty.org

All proceeds from this annual outdoor festival go to restore the historic Basilica of St. Mary, which in turn offers a huge variety of outreach and charitable programs to poor and impoverished people throughout the state. More than 30,000 people of all ages and denominations come to this event, which features big-name entertainment, food, drinking, and other community events.

Eden Prairie's 4th of July "Home Town"
Celebration
Downtown Eden Prairie
Fourth of July
(952) 949–8453
www.edenprairie.org

This celebration finishes with spectacular fireworks at the Eden Prairie Center at 10:00 P.M. Daytime activities at Round Lake Park include a mini-triathlon, kiddie parade, softball tournament, live music, games, and concession stands.

Mississippi Mile Fireworks Extravaganza
Old St. Anthony Main, Minneapolis Riverfront
Fourth of July
(612) 673–5123
www.mississippimile.org

One of the best Fourth of July fireworks displays in the Twin Cities, sponsored by the Mississippi Mile Promotions Committee. The best seat in the house is anywhere on Nicollet Island, where the fireworks seem to explode directly overhead.

Panorama of Progress
Downtown Lakeville
First week of July
(952) 985–9558
www.lakevillechambercvb.org

For more than 30 years, Lakeville has celebrated its Panorama of Progress festival, which features family entertainment including races, picnics, pet shows, dances, scholarship pageants, Fourth of July fireworks, and a parade.

Anoka Riverfest & Art Fair
Historic Downtown Anoka
Second Saturday of July
(763) 421–7130
www.anokaareachamber.com

This all-day riverfront festival includes a craft/artisan fair, historical society events, live music, youth activities, and, of course, lots of food.

Summer Movies and Music
Loring Park, 1382 Willow Street,
Minneapolis
(612) 375–7622

Every Monday night from mid-July through August, free live music followed by a movie selected to coincide with a current Walker Art Center exhibit can be seen at Loring Park on their outdoor movie screen.

Hennepin Avenue Block Party
Hennepin Avenue from 4th Street to 10th
Street, Minneapolis
Third weekend in July
(612) 331–8371

Part of the Minneapolis Aquatennial Celebration, this free outdoor concert always features big-name bands and even bigger crowds.

Minneapolis Aquatennial
Various locations around Minneapolis
Third and fourth weeks of July
(612) 331–8371
www.aquatennial.org

Royalty pageants, parades, boat races, and other events are featured in this citywide celebration of the 10 Best Days of Summer. The Aquatennial has one of Minnesota's largest parades, the nation's fourth-largest

The milk carton boat races are one of the many popular events of the Minneapolis Aquatennial.
PHOTO: GREATER MINNEAPOLIS CONVENTION & VISITORS ASSOCIATION

fireworks show, milk carton boat races, sand castle competitions, a triathlon, programs for juniors and seniors, and tons of family-oriented activities. One of the highlights of the celebration, the milk carton boat races, invites participants of all ages to create full-sized boats out of hundreds of sealed milk cartons and race the largest creation was Tetra Pak's 1993 25,000-milk-carton boat that held 150 passengers.

Rockin' Ribfest
Fourth Street and Nicollet Mall, Minneapolis
Last week of July
(612) 288–2002
www.rockinribfest.com

More than a dozen barbecue experts compete for titles while local and national music acts rock the parking lot. This is a great way to sample many of the best rib joints in the United States without busting a gut the first time out.

Insiders' Tip
Then-Vice President Richard Nixon served as the Aquatennial's Grand Marshal in 1958.

Lumberjack Days
Various locations, Stillwater
Last weekend of July
(651) 430–2306
www.lumberjackdays.com

This huge, weekend-long event features live concerts from major-label recording stars, tons of concession stands, Minnesota's fastest 10-mile and 5K runs, kids' events, a huge parade, and Minnesota's biggest fireworks display—all located in historic downtown Stillwater. Wine tasting, ice-cream socials, lumberjack exhibits, logrolling, pie eating, baking contests, and an authentic 19th-century baseball game are just a few of the events that you can expect to be torn between, not to mention the annual Treasure Hunt.

Blooming Days on Grand
Grand Avenue, St. Paul
Last Saturday of July
(651) 699–0029
www.grandave.com

Celebrate summer on St. Paul's Grand Avenue. This one-day event is made for strolling, shopping, and having fun. From 10:00 A.M. to 5:00 P.M., the businesses of Grand Avenue give out free flowers and desserts. Strolling along Grand Avenue will become even sweeter than normal, a visual spectacle of gardens and floral displays and exhibits of local artisans' work.

Taste of Minnesota
Minnesota State Capitol,
75 Constitution Avenue, St. Paul
First week of July
(651) 772–9980
www.tasteofmn.org

This huge event offers food prepared by more than 40 of the Twin Cities' best restaurants, dozens of national and regional performers, and an art bazaar. Each night concludes with fireworks.

August

Uptown Art Fair
Uptown Minneapolis, Lake Street and
Hennepin Avenue
First weekend of August
(612) 823–4581
www.uptownminneapolis.com

The Uptown Art Fair is the largest art fair in Minneapolis, featuring work from hun-

Fireworks over the State Capitol during the Taste of Minnesota. PHOTO: GREATER MINNEAPOLIS CONVENTION & VISITORS ASSOCIATION

Insiders' Tip

The Taste of Minnesota Festival is a good way to sample many local restaurants in one place.

dreds of local and national artists as well as food and live music. Painting, photography, sculpture, jewelry, ceramics, fiber, and Kids Activity Art, made from household items that typically end up in the trash, are just a few of the items on display and for sale at the event.

Powderhorn Festival of the Arts
Powderhorn Park, 3400 15th Avenue South, Minneapolis
First weekend of August
(612) 823-1141

The popular Powderhorn Festival of the Arts, which usually runs concurrent with the Uptown Art Fair, is a winning attraction for crafts-fair fans. The weekend-long festival—originally billed as an alternative to the "big one down the street"—has developed a flavor of its own, exposing an extremely eclectic variety of both artwork and artists to the public.

Minnesota Fringe Festival
Various venues in Minneapolis
First two weeks of August
(612) 872-1212
www.fringefestival.org

This annual celebration of theater has hundreds of performances in multiple venues throughout Minneapolis. Independent film, live theater, mime performances, and performance art are just some of the events during the festival.

Old Time Harvest Festival
Various locations, Jordan
First weekend of August
(952) 492-2062

This family-oriented festival has antique farm equipment displays, a fiddling contest, and an antique car show, as well as

demonstrations of threshing, sawing, spinning, and quilting. There's even an antique farm equipment parade in the afternoon.

Minnesota Irish Fair
Harriet Island, St. Paul
Second weekend of August
(952) 474-7411
www.irishfair.com

From bagpipes to bodhrans, corned beef to ceilis, this two-day celebration of Irish culture features Irish music, dance, theater, exhibits, sports, a marketplace, genealogy information, and a special children's area.

Minnesota State Fair
State Fairgrounds, 1265 Snelling Avenue North, St. Paul
Last two weeks of August
(651) 642-2200
www.mnstatefair.org

One of the largest fairs in North America—drawing crowds of several hundred thousand people a day—this fair has big name entertainment, exhibits, competitions, food, demonstrations, horse shows, auto races, a huge midway carnival, and food on a stick. There's also a bust of the festival's queen sculpted in butter, farm animal shows and competitions, a huge garden show, and juried arts and crafts from state elementary, high school, and college students.

Woodbury Days
Ojibway Park, Woodbury
Last weekend of August
(651) 714-3733, ext. 2
www.woodburydays.com

Woodbury Days is a community event with lots of activities for the whole family, including Midway Carnival Rides, games and food, the Woodbury Days Annual Bike Ride, inflatable slides, water fights, a petting zoo, the Rod & Custom Car Club Car Show, fireworks displays, daily parades, and live music.

Stiftungsfest
Downtown Norwood Young America
Last full weekend of August
(952) 467-3365
www.stiftungsfest.org

There's something for everyone at this celebration of German heritage and culture:

German choirs, dancers, polka bands, arts, crafts, ethnic foods, and beverages. Stiftungsfest, founded in 1861, is the oldest festival in Minnesota.

Minnesota Renaissance Festival
3 miles South of Shakopee on
Minnesota Highway 169
Mid-August through the end of September
(952) 445–7361 or (800) 966–8215
www.renaissancefest.com/minnesota-main.htm

Jump back in time to experience life in the 16th century, or at least the fun parts of it. For more than 30 years, Minnesota has been host to the largest Renaissance Festival in the United States. Food, fun, sword fights, games, comedy, dancers, singers, music, full-contact armored jousting tournaments, 12 stages of continuous entertainment, and royalty are regular staples of this annual event, which is open weekends in mid-August, Labor Day, and through the end of September. The site of the Minnesota Renaissance Festival is a bustling 16th-century village filled with hundreds of costumed villagers, period buildings, and a huge marketplace.

September

Excelsior Apple Day
Downtown Excelsior
First Saturday after Labor Day,
(952) 474–6461

Excelsior Apple Day is a main street festival with antiques, crafts, apples, produce, entertainment, food, and a children's red wagon and doll buggy parade.

Sunbonnet Day
J. R. Cummins Homestead, 13600 Pioneer
Trail, Eden Prairie
Mid-September
(952) 949–8453

Each September, Eden Prairie steps back in time with Sunbonnet Day—a time of ice cream socials, sack races, and games of Pennies in the Hay and Rolling Hoop.

Celebrazione Italiana
Washington County Fairgrounds,
Lake Elmo
Mid-September, call for specific dates
(651) 777–3556

An Italian celebration featuring entertainment, boccie ball, historical and cultural exhibits, and fabulous food.

Johnny Appleseed Bash
Utley Park, 50th Street & Woodale Avenue,
Edina
Third weekend of September
(952) 920–0595

Since the mid-1980s this family-oriented event has taken place in Utley Park. Food, live entertainment, a silent auction, a petting zoo, and pony rides are just a few of the things you can expect at this community-oriented festival.

Lone Oak Days
Historic Holz Farm, 4665 Manor Drive, Eagan
Third weekend in September
(651) 681–4660
www.eaganmn.com

Hayrides, farming demos, games, and self-guided tours of 1940s Holz Farm highlight Eagan's heritage festival. The center of the festival is the Lone Oak tree, which was once the community center/public bulletin board and is designated a Minnesota Heritage Tree.

Harvest Festival
Gibbs Farm Museum, 2097 West
Larpenteur at Cleveland, Falcon Heights
Third or last Sunday of September
(651) 646–8629

An annual event with food, music, and square dancing, usually taking place on the third or last Sunday of September. Guests can participate in crop gathering, kitchen duty, and other activities.

October

Twin Cities Marathon
Minneapolis and St. Paul
First weekend of October
(612) 925–3500
www.twincitiesmarathon.org

The Twin Cities Marathon's unique scenery and aesthetics have earned it the distinction as "the most beautiful urban marathon in America." It's also ranked as one of the nation's top marathons and one of the country's 13 Great Races. The 26.2-mile course begins near the Metrodome in Minneapolis and finishes at the State Capitol on John Ireland Boulevard in St. Paul. The course is easy to navigate, mostly asphalt, and very scenic with mile after mile of parkways, lakes, rivers, and tree-lined boulevards. Prospective runners should register early for the race, as this race attracts contestants from around the country. Good viewing spots include the Lake Harriet Rose Garden, the Lake Street Bridge, and the Capitol grounds.

Anoka Halloween
Downtown Anoka
www.anokaareachamber.com/
Anoka celebrates more than 80 years as the Halloween Capital of the World with two parades and many other activities for young and old alike. The town's huge Halloween celebrations have been held every year since 1920, with the exception of 1942 and 1943, when they were canceled because of World War II. The celebration boasts a wide variety of activities, beginning with a football game dubbed "the Pumpkin Bowl." Other events include card parties, bingo, horseshoe tournaments, costume contests, a haunted house, parades, and a 5K Gray Ghost Run.

November

Samhain Celtic New Year
Newell Park, Fairview Avenue and Pierce Butler Route, St. Paul
November First
(651) 641-0485
This celebration consists of traditional Irish music, food, storytelling, dancing, and games.

GLBT Film Festival
Bell Auditorium, University Avenue and 17th Avenue SE, Minneapolis
Mid-November
(612) 627-4430
www.ufilm.org

This successful festival is the largest annual gay and lesbian film event in the upper Midwest, showing a variety of documentaries and features.

Autumn Festival/Arts and Crafts Fair
Canterbury Park, 1100 Canterbury Road, Shakopee
Second week of November
(952) 445-1660 or (800) 574-2150
The largest crafts show in the upper Midwest, the Autumn Festival draws more than 500 vendors from all over the country.

Christmas at the Courthouse
Courthouse Building, Stillwater
Weekend before Thanksgiving
(651) 430-6233
Fine handmade crafts by local artists are displayed at the elegantly decorated Stillwater courthouse during "Christmas at the Courthouse." The building, beautifully decorated in Victorian style, resounds with laughter and music, while vendors in costume offer their wares to the public. Volunteers in period clothing offer jail tours, an exhibit, an old-fashioned tearoom, and music of the season. This event is considered the gateway to the holiday season in Stillwater.

Holidazzle Parade
Nicollet Mall, Minneapolis
Fourth week of November through December
(612) 616-7669
Costumed children, adults, and festooned floats covered with over one million colored lights make up the Minneapolis Holidazzle Parade. These free, 30-minute night parades head down Nicollet Mall from 12th to Third Streets, beginning at 6:30 P.M. Wednesday through Sunday from late November to just before Christmas. Fairy tale–themed floats, marching bands, celebrity grand marshals, and, of course, Santa in his sleigh can be seen in the parade.

Old-Fashioned Holiday Bazaar
Landmark Center, 75 West Fifth Street, St. Paul
Last week of November, call for specific dates
(651) 292-3225

Stroll through a marketplace of more than 60 exhibits featuring beautiful and unique gift items, all handcrafted by the area's finest artisans. Participating in this annual event is considered an important tradition by many, who like to get their Christmas shopping done the month before the holiday, instead of at the very last minute.

December

Capital Holiday
Various locations in downtown St. Paul
New Year's Eve
(651) 291–5608
www.capitalholiday.org

Every New Year's Eve, the 5-block radius around Rice Park is transformed into an arts and entertainment extravaganza. Featuring more than 125 acts on 25 indoor stages, the event showcases the finest arts and entertainment acts found in the Twin Cities. Music, food, and midnight fireworks in Rice Park are part of the celebration—lots of businesses on the New Year's Eve route keep their doors open well past midnight. Capital Holiday is a family celebration intended as an alternative to alcohol-oriented festivities else-where: No alcohol is served at the official event. Admission buttons are available in advance for $8.00 at all metro area Firstar Bank branches and the Science Museum of Minnesota, Minnesota Children's Museum, and Ordway Center for the Performing Arts box offices. Buttons are available at all major venues the night of the event for $10. Children age five and under are free.

Mississippi Mile Fireworks Extravaganza,
Minneapolis Riverfront, Old St. Anthony
Main, Minneapolis
New Year's Eve
(612) 673–5123

The New Year's Eve fireworks extravaganza on the Minneapolis riverfront, sponsored by the Mississippi Mile Promotions Committee, is just about the best free event in the Twin Cities. There's a family fireworks show at 8:30 P.M., and a second show at midnight. The real party is just over the bridge at Nicollet Island, where ice skating, cross-country skiing, snowshoeing, trolley rides, hayrides, displays of Holidazzle floats, and live music make for an incredibly festive evening. A dance follows the first fireworks display from 9:00 P.M. until midnight.

The Arts

The Greater Twin Cities have been dubbed a "cultural Eden on the prairie," where almost three million people support more than a hundred theater companies and classical music ensembles. Sir Tyrone Guthrie began the theatrical boom back in 1963, enrolling large-scale local assistance to establish the classical repertory company named after him. The cities now have more theaters per capita than anywhere in the United States apart from New York City.

Large Broadway productions, such as Disney's *The Lion King* and *Victor/Victoria*, got their start at the historic State and Orpheum Theatres in downtown Minneapolis. The city's regional theater jewel, the Guthrie Theater, consistently presents critically acclaimed contemporary shows. As a testimony to the strength of the theater scene, more than 30 smaller theater venues sprinkled throughout the city produce farcical ballets, cabarets, comedies, and other unique performances. Minneapolis and St. Paul are also serious museum towns, with a number of important collections housed in several world-famous buildings. Minneapolis is home to the Walker Art Center, the internationally renowned contemporary art museum on the southern edge of downtown Minneapolis, as well as the University of Minnesota's acclaimed Frederick R. Weisman Art Museum, housed in a distinctive metal building designed by Frank Gehry on a site overlooking the Mississippi River. Many, many more little galleries spread throughout the metro area take up any slack these museums might have missed, displaying everything from concrete anatomy molds to metal mechanical sculptures.

More than 90 performing arts groups and organizations flourish in the Twin Cities area, ranging from tiny neighborhood-based production companies to full-fledged touring troupes. The **Metropolitan Regional Arts Council** (2324 University Avenue West, Suite 114, St. Paul; 651–645–0402; www.mrac.org) keeps pretty good track of who's who and where in town.

Art Galleries

AZ Gallery
Northern Warehouse Building, 308 Prince Street, St. Paul
(651) 255–6624

This prominent Lowertown St. Paul gallery holds opening receptions on the first Friday of each month, hosting artwork premieres of two featured artists plus a group exhibit. The 2,000-square-foot gallery also puts on performing arts events throughout the year.

CIRCA Gallery
1637 Hennepin Avenue South, Minneapolis
(612) 332–2386
www.circagallery.org

CIRCA Gallery displays much new art, as well as old, in exhibits that show how a gallery with coherent vision can unite widely different artists. Everything from encaustic prairie landscapes with mottled-wax finishes to intensely colored abstractions fit into this vision, as do bronze sculptures inspired by primitive altars and acrylic paintings that look like aerial shots of bombed-out civilizations.

CIRCA Gallery's mission is to provide awareness and appreciation of a vast array of contemporary styles, media, and expressions. The gallery represents 40 regional and national artists, with an exhibition rotation every six weeks.

Dolly Fiterman Fine Arts Gallery
100 University Avenue Southeast, Minneapolis
(612) 623–3300

Dolly Fiterman Fine Arts represents American and European contemporary artists in a turn-of-the-20th-century landmark marble building. The gallery's collection emphasizes sculptures, painting, drawings, and graphics, and the gallery is known globally for its advanced and avant-garde international scope.

Works from artists like Lichtenstein and Moore encircle the main room and special exhibits are in the affordable range ($950 to $50,000). The clean white walls and the well-lit spaces make the vibrant modern art works, even the sketches, seem to pop off the walls. The layout allows for casual contemplation, and if you're lucky, the energetic Dolly Fiterman herself might come and show you around the gallery personally.

Flatland Gallery
208 Hennepin Avenue East, Minneapolis
(612) 378–3890

Hip, cool, and contemporary, Flatland Gallery provides an intimate home in vibrant northeast Minneapolis for the Twin Cities' most exciting young artists. Local anchorwoman Robyne Robinson from KMSP-TV opened the gallery to give local artists exposure, invigorate community awareness, and make art collecting a more affordable pursuit. Featured artists change monthly, and everything from blown glass works to mechanical sculptures have been shown here.

Groveland Gallery
25 Groveland Terrace, Minneapolis
(612) 377–7800
www.grovelandgallery.com

Groveland Gallery represents the work of 30 regional artists and specializes in contemporary representational painting and drawing. Established in 1973, this elegant gallery is located in a restored 1890s mansion and carriage house on the edge of downtown Minneapolis. Also on the premises is a second gallery, the Annex, which features work by emerging local artists. Exhibitions change every six weeks at both spaces.

Inside Out Gallery
Interact Center for the Visual and Performing Arts, 212 Third Avenue North, Suite 140, Minneapolis
(612) 339–5145
www.interactcenter.com

Inside Out is a cooperative studio for actors and artists with disabilites. Professional artists work as advocates and mentors on an ongoing basis, holding four exhibitions each year that are open to the public. The Inside Out theater company, which has been featured on local and national television spotlights, produces two major shows per year.

Intermedia Arts
2822 Lyndale Avenue South, Minneapolis
(612) 871–4444
www.intermediaarts.org

The graffiti on Intermedia's facade isn't just a nice concession to local taggers— giving them the space is part of the gallery's mission. More than perhaps any other gallery in town, Intermedia is dedicated to being a neighborhood space, with shows often focusing on the work of artists from the semibohemian streets of Lyn-Lake. As a result, Intermedia's exhibits lack the gloss and commercial appeal of other galleries' shows, but they do offer a compelling artistic window into the soul of a community.

Intermedia Arts presents more than 80 visual, media, and performing arts events each year. Past events include the Young Artists' Cabaret—an open-mic event extended to young performance artists of all persuasions, and the Wheels As Art exhibit, in which community members work with artists to decorate their bikes, wheelchairs, and in-line skates to lead a parade of similarly decorated motorized vehicles.

Katherine E. Nash Gallery
Willey Hall, 216 21st Avenue South, Minneapolis
(612) 624-7530

The mission of the Katherine E. Nash Gallery is to create an accessible environment for U of M faculty and students to exhibit their work and to show art in various media by diverse artists from regional, national, and international sources. Located in Willey Hall on the University of Minnesota's Minneapolis campus, the gallery is well lit and comfy, with a layout that prevents there from being a truly defined beginning or end to featured exhibitions. The gallery's programming has consistently balanced the needs of representing campus artists with bringing in outside genius.

Kellie Rae Theiss Gallery
Wyman Building, 400 First Avenue North, Suite 318, Minneapolis
(612) 339-1094
www.theissgallery.com

The Kelly Rae Theiss Gallery features original classical, surrealistic, and impressionistic paintings and sculpture. This intimate gallery exclusively represents local artists, both in solo and group exhibitions, on an eight-week rotation.

Minnesota Center for Photography
711 West Lake Street, Minneapolis
(612) 824-5500
www.partsphoto.org

The Minnesota Center for Photography offers a broad range of works from local and national artists. Ranging through the cute, creepy, conventional, commercial, and creative, there's something here for everyone with an interest in the photographic arts. The gallery encourages strong community involvement and is a good place for budding photographers to begin exploring the professional side of their craft.

Northern Clay Center
2424 East Franklin Avenue, Minneapolis
(612) 339-8007
www.northernclaycenter.org

Northern Clay Center's mission is the advancement of the ceramic arts. Ongoing programs include classes and workshops for children and adults at all levels of proficiency, seven exhibitions a year of functional and sculptural work by regional and national clay artists, studio facilities and grants for artists, and a sales gallery representing many of the top ceramic artists across the region and country.

No Name Exhibitions @ the Soap Factory
110 Fifth Avenue SE, Minneapolis
(612) 623-9176
www.soapfactory.org

No Name Exhibitions is an exciting, and expanding, nonprofit arts organization dedicated to supporting emerging artists, enhancing the public's understanding and appreciation of their artistic expressions, and fostering strength and vitality within the arts, cultural, and education communities of the Twin Cities. With its hardwood floors and old prefab office walls, the Soap Factory building could easily double as a phenomenal nightclub or revolutionary headquarters. No Name has put the space to good use, however, filling it with shows that are always well balanced between avant-garde sensibilities and good old-fashioned representationalism. No Name maintains an open-door submission policy, and artists and potential curators are invited to submit their work and proposals at the beginning of each year.

Each year, No Name presents several large-scale visual exhibitions featuring a wide range of media from local, national, and international emerging artists. New exhibitions open with special events and artists' talks that provide artists and their audiences with the opportunity to interact with one another. In addition to their visual arts exhibitions, No Name puts on an annual Fourth of July independent film festival, the Great Soapbox Derby, which pairs artists and families to build and race soapbox cars, and numerous musical and performance events.

Vern Carver & Beard Art Galleries
LaSalle Plaza, 800 Lasalle Avenue, Minneapolis
(612) 339–3449

Vern Carver & Beard is the oldest gallery in the Twin Cities. Founded in 1886 the gallery features fine original art by regional artists of past and present, antique prints, and art glass (stained glass, blown glass, etc). The gallery also provides custom framing for prints and paintings.

Art Museums

Frederick R. Weisman Art Museum
333 East River Road, Minneapolis
(612) 625–9494
www.weisman.umn.edu

The Weisman is impossible to miss—it's the huge metal structure on the east side of the Washington Avenue bridge that either looks stunningly beautiful or stunningly pretentious, depending on your mood and the time of year. On the outside, the museum faces the Mississippi River with an undulating, dramatic facade covered in polished aluminum, especially beautiful at sunset. In comparison, the interior is surprisingly conservative, and the modestly scaled and wonderfully lit galleries inside are so attractive that the *New York Times*

called them "possibly the five best rooms for viewing art in the world."

The mostly 20th-century permanent collection contains the world's largest assemblage of works by Marsden Hartley and Alfred Maurer as well as paintings and prints by Georgia O'Keeffe, Arthur Dove, and Robert Motherwell, among others. The entrance is dominated by Roy Lichtenstein's *World's Fair Mural*. Be sure to take in the river view from the tiny balcony, located one floor above the galleries.

A teaching museum for the university and the community, this sculptural stainless steel and brick landmark building designed by architect Frank Gehry provides a multidisciplinary approach to the arts through an array of programs and a changing schedule of exhibitions. Admission is always free.

The Minneapolis Institute of Arts
2400 Third Avenue South, Minneapolis
(612) 870–3000
www.artsmia.org

The Minneapolis Institute of Arts, one of the outstanding art museums in the country, features art and artifacts from around the world, from ancient sculptures to photography and film. Housed in a 1915 Beaux marble building designed by McKim, Mead, and White near downtown Minneapolis, the free museum contains a world-class collection of nearly 100,000 objects on three separate floors, representing artistic traditions and treasures spanning 5,000 years. Unlike many big-city art museums, which have the tendency to overwhelm casual visitors, the MIA can be easily explored in a few hours—and, unlike many big-city museums, no admission fee is charged.

Highlights of the museum include a small but exceptional collection of French Impressionist paintings, including works by Monet and van Gogh; an extensive collection of carved Oriental jades; *Lucretia*, considered by art historians to be the best Rembrandt in the country; and works by old masters such as Titian, El Greco, and Poussin as well as an exhaustive list of 19th- and 20th-century American and European artists. There's also an amazing collection of tapestries, photography, and prints to pore over as well.

The Minnesota Museum of American Art
Landmark Center, 75 West Fifth Street, St. Paul
(651) 292–4355
www.mmaa.org

Founded in 1927, the Minnesota Museum of American Art is an intimate, accessible museum located in the historic Landmark Center in downtown St. Paul. Home to one of the most extensive collections of American art in the country with more than 10,000 American paintings, drawings, and prints, the museum's permanent collection represents more than 130 years of art in the making. From paintings by Jacob Lawrence and George Morrison to sculpture by Evelyn Raymond, the galleries provide a glimpse at artwork that spans various media and styles. Traveling exhibitions along with an impressive museum shop make this a great place to find inspiration and marvel at the quiet of St. Paul. The museum also offers art exhibitions and classes for adults and children focusing on American art

Schubert Club Museum of Musical Instruments
Landmark Center, 75 West Fifth Street St. Paul
(651) 292–3267
www.schubert.org

Considering how small this museum actually is, its collection of keyboards, phonographs, and musical instruments is amazingly complete. Owned and operated by the Schubert Club, this museum is a popular stomping ground for music aficionados of all types, local and otherwise.

Walker Art Center/Minneapolis Sculpture Garden/Cowles Conservatory
725 Vineland Place, Minneapolis
(612) 375–7622
www.walkerart.org

For years, the Walker's been the foremost modern art museum in the state. The museum is the only place in town to consistently bring in artists who tweak, poke,

or outright stab at comfortable Midwestern sensibilities, organizing concept-centered shows with a sociopolitical awareness. The displays include a permanent collection of 20th-century American and international art, including works from Willem de Kooning, Andy Warhol, Sol LeWitt, and Dan Flavin; the Walker also sponsors vanguard music, dance, theatre, film, and video events throughout the year, as well as innovative education programs and visionary new media initiatives. Artists and filmmakers from around the globe have lectured and performed at the Walker, including filmmaker John Waters and composer Philip Glass. The popular monthly After Hours parties offer previews of new shows, live music, and cocktails.

Located right next to the Walker Art Center is the Minneapolis Sculpture Garden's beautiful collection of large sculptures made by local and internationally known artists. The 11-acre garden holds more than 40 sculptures by many different artists, including George Segal, Jenny Holzer, and Franz Lipschitz, set among tree-lined courtyards. The Garden is one of the most-visited sites in Minneapolis, for good reason—the works of art combined with the ever-changing landscape make it a year-round delight.

The garden's entrance is framed by a pair of monumental granite columns titled *Ampersand* by the sculpture's creator, Martin Puryear. The garden's most famous statue, however, is the whimsical *Spoonbridge and Cherry* fountain, a 55-foot spoon topped by a 15-foot red Bing cherry, designed by Claes Oldenburg and Coosje van Bruggen. The glass-walled Cowles Conservatory, located in the garden, is a

...fect place to hide from gloomy weather, with a changing display of blooming plants as well as a palm court dominated by Frank Gehry's *Standing Glass Fish*.

Cinema—Art House and Specialty Theaters

The Heights Theatre
3951 Central Avenue NE, Columbia Heights
(763) 788–9079

The Heights really is one of the last of the great one-screen theaters. Renowned for showing first-run films that are actually interesting, the Heights is a classic place to catch a film without being assaulted by the "Surround Sound/THX" onslaught coming through the paper-thin walls of the movie cell next to you. In fact, the Heights has been known to introduce movies with organ music from time to time. As an added extra bonus, refills on soda and popcorn are always free.

Landmark's Lagoon Cinema
1320 Lagoon Avenue, Minneapolis
(612) 825–6006

If you're into art house, indie, or critically acclaimed film fare, chances are you'll end up here a lot. Lagoon Cinema is part of the Landmark franchise, which consistently snatches up the best new films and markets them aggressively to a niche of self-described art housers. The facilities are relatively distinctive for a cineplex, with swirled carpet and abstract light trees. Even more impressive, the theater is designed for optimum view-friendliness—cushy yet supportive seats, no center aisles, and sharp floor inclines.

Oak Street Cinema
309 Southeast Oak Street, Minneapolis
(612) 331–3134
www.oakstreetcinema.org

What more could you want from a repertory house? Never mind that Oak Street offers a great variety of films, ranging from mainstream classics to obscure art house fare, with room to include work from all over the globe, too. And forget for a second that their occasional highlighting of rave-ups lets you be cheap and almost up-to-date about your moviegoing. Oak Street makes film obsession as entertaining as it could ever be. Oak Street's not too stuffy to include edgy crowd-pleasers, but still serious enough to give a fair share of time to Antonioni and Hitchcock films. With this kind of film resource in the city, it's a wonder people still rent videos.

Riverview Theatre
3800 42nd Avenue South, Minneapolis
(612) 729–7369
www.riverviewtheatre.com

The first impressive thing about this king of all budget movie theaters is the cool '50s lobby straight out of *The Jetsons*. And then there's the popcorn—it's one of the few places where you buy the popcorn because it tastes good. Ask for the Special—a budget price for a lot of popcorn and a huge soda. The theater itself is enormous, and the elevated-back seats allow you to sit back and put your feet up. In addition to their regular second-run fare, they play Asian films on Saturday at midnight for six bucks.

U Film Society
U of M Campus, Bell Auditorium, 17th Avenue SE at University Avenue SE, Minneapolis
(612) 627–4430
www.ufilm.org

Year after year, this very independent art house manages to keep world cinema projected on campus in spite of poverty. With the corporation of art cinema and "independent" distribution, U Film has had trouble booking the higher-profile titles, but its contributions to the community—most notably with the international and GLBT film festivals—are undeniable. Often, U Film is the only place to take a chance on an otherwise completely unknown film.

Uptown Theatre
2906 Hennepin Avenue South, Minneapolis
(612) 825–6006

Uptown is the granddaddy of all local single-screen theaters, boasting the biggest screen around and some of the roomiest seats. This place not only stands out as a great space to see films but also ranks as one of Minneapolis's landmarks.

Dance

James Sewell Ballet
528 Hennepin Avenue, Suite 205,
Minneapolis
(612) 672–0480
www.jsballet.org

Founded in New York City in 1990 by James Sewell, the James Sewell Ballet relocated to Minnesota in 1993. The ballet specializes in original contemporary ballet, and the beautiful performances run the gamut from classical choreography to improvisation of entire movements. During the Minnesota Twins playoff run in 2002, the troupe even improvised a movement to the live play-by-play broadcast of the American League Divisional Series. The James Sewell Ballet performs primarily at O'Shaunessy Auditorium on the College of St. Catherine's campus in St. Paul, but the troupe ventures to other venues across the Twin Cities at times and has performed across the country and internationally.

Ragamala Music and Dance Theater
711 West Lake Street, Suite 102,
Minneapolis
(612) 824–1968
www.ragamala.net

Ragamala presents original works of dance, music, and poetry based on the ancient classical dance of southern India, Bharatanatyam. The cross-cultural performances of the company have developed a strong reputation for innovation, and the company's school in Minneapolis has some 50 students studying the ancient form of dance. Ragamala performs across the country as well as at O'Shaunessy Auditorium on the College of St. Catherine's Campus in St. Paul and at the Southern Theater in Minneapolis.

Zenon Dance Company
528 Hennepin Avenue, Minneapolis
(612) 338–1101
www.zenondance.org

Zenon commissions original works of modern and jazz dance from emerging choreographers in Minnesota and New York as well as established masters. The high-energy performances of the company allow it to appeal to communities not regularly reached by dance troupes, from youth in poorer areas of Minneapolis to nursing home residents in outstate Minnesota. Zenon performs regularly in the Twin Cities as well as around the Midwest and operates a school teaching not only modern and jazz dance but also classical ballet, hip-hop, tap, and improvisational dance. Call Zenon or check out their Web site for upcoming performances.

Music Ensembles and Companies

Greater Twin Cities' Youth Symphonies
(GTCYS)
430 Oak Grove Street, Suite 205,
Minneapolis
(612) 870–7611
www.gtcys.org

Heralded as one of the world's largest youth music organizations, GTCYS boasts eight orchestras and a student body with 600-plus members. It presents fall, winter, and spring concerts, as well as the Celebrity Series and the Young Concerto Soloists Showcase. GTCYS sponsors a summer orchestra program and the Orchestral Institute of America. Auditions are held in late spring.

Minnesota Chorale
528 Hennepin Avenue, Suite 211,
Minneapolis
(612) 333–4866
www.mnchorale.org

Under the direction of Kathy Saltzman Romey, the Minnesota Chorale has become the state's preeminent symphonic chorus and ranks among the best in the nation. The 150-voice chorale is the principal chorus for the Minnesota Orchestra and the St. Paul Chamber Orchestra. Its nationally recognized Bridges series seeks to build musical and social bridges through artistic collaboration.

The Minnesota Opera
620 North First Street, Minneapolis
(612) 333–2700
www.mnopera.org

For more than 35 years, the internationally renowned Minnesota Opera has produced more American and world premieres than any other company in the United States. From January through May, more than 40,000 operagoers enjoy performances at the Ordway Music Theater in St. Paul. An anchor tenant at the acoustically perfect Ordway Center for the Performing Arts, the Minnesota Opera also offers classes at its Minnesota Opera Center in the Minneapolis Warehouse District ($15 to $20). Walk-ins are welcome.

The Minnesota Orchestra
1111 Nicollet Mall, Minneapolis
(612) 371–5656 or (800) 292–4141
www.minnesotaorchestra.org

The Minnesota Orchestra performs more than 200 concerts each year ranging from classical to pops. Performances are scheduled in Orchestra Hall, the Ordway Music Theater in St. Paul, and other Minnesota communities. A summer highlight is the Viennese Sommerfest.

The Minnesota Youth Symphonies
790 Cleveland Avenue South, St. Paul
(651) 699–5811
www.mnyouthsymphonies.org

The Minnesota Youth Symphonies are open to students of all abilities from elementary school through high school. Co-music directors Claudette and Manny Laureano oversee three full orchestras and a string ensemble. The MYS presents major concerts at Orchestra Hall in Minneapolis. Auditions are held at the end of August of each year.

The St. Paul Chamber Orchestra
408 St. Peter Street, Suite 500,
St. Paul
(651) 292–3248
www.stpaulchamberorchestra.org

With 33 members, the St. Paul Chamber Orchestra is about one-third the size of the

The Minnesota Orchestra in Minneapolis's spectacular Orchestra Hall. PHOTO: GREATER MINNEAPOLIS CONVENTION & VISITORS ASSOCIATION

average symphony orchestra. But that definitely doesn't mean they don't sound as "big" as any other orchestral ensemble. In fact, before 1800, when almost all European orchestras were chamber orchestras, they played in smaller chambers instead of concert halls. As the only full-time professional chamber orchestra in the United States, the SPCO has an extensive discography, approaching 60 recordings on about 15 labels. This ensemble presents more than 150 concerts annually and reaches millions more through radio broadcasts, and regional, national, and international touring.

The Schubert Club
Landmark Center, 75 West Fifth Street,
St. Paul
(651) 292–3267

The Schubert Club is Minnesota's oldest musical arts organization, presenting world-renowned artists and local and regional musicians to Twin Cities audiences through various grants and private funding. The Schubert Club Instrument Museum is located in the club's basement.

VocalEssence
1900 Nicollet Avenue, Minneapolis
(612) 547–1451

VocalEssence presents music for chorus and orchestra. The chorus offers innovative programming under the direction of founder Philip Brunelle.

Theaters and Performance Spaces

Acadia Cabaret Theater
1931 Nicollet Avenue South, Minneapolis
(612) 874–8702

The first thing audiences notice after entering the Acadia Cabaret is that the space wasn't designed to hold theater performances. The stage sits slightly higher than the ground in front of rows of very uncomfortable chairs designed to hold cafe patrons. In fact, the space acts as a second room for the Acadia Cafe during the day and is only converted to a theater in the evening. But all these eccentricities fade away when the shows start. Acadia hosts a wide variety of performance—music, improv, comedy, poetry, and performance art—and while it may not be the best theater space in town, they hold some of the most intense productions to be found.

Brave New Workshop Theatre
2605 Hennepin Avenue South,
Minneapolis
(612) 332–6620
www.bravenewworkshop.com

The country's longest-running satirical comedy theater, founded by Dudley Riggs in 1958, features original shows and improvisation six nights a week (every night except Tuesday). The Brave New Workshop is known for its satirical takes on pop-culture icons of the moment, from Prozac to *Who Wants to be a Millionaire* to the Christian Right, bringing cutting-edge shows like *Beanie Baby Barbecue* and *I Think, Therefore IBM* to the stage. The theater also offers classes dealing with the many different aspects of theater and hosts many student and alumni plays in its space.

Bryant Lake Bowl Theater
810 West Lake Street, Minneapolis
(612) 825–8949
www.bryantlakebowl.com

The Bryant Lake Bowl Theater space has become a mainstay of local performance acts, bringing live music (including opera), dance, comedy, and theater to an intimate stage tucked behind the bowling alley. On any given night, you may wander in and find the tiny performance area packed in support of a wide array of local talent. No matter where you decide to sit, make sure to take advantage of the extensive beer and wine lists.

Cedar Cultural Centre
416 Cedar Avenue South, Minneapolis
(612) 338–2674
www.thecedar.org

The Cedar offers an eclectic selection of world music throughout the summer months and into the fall. It perfectly fills the niche that the majority of Twin Cities venues have missed, booking acts that include the very best—and very often under-appreciated—of global and ethnic musicians, including folk, Irish, African, blues, and bluegrass. Some past performers include French guitar virtuoso Pierre Bensusan and American performer Ani DiFranco. The Cedar is also host to the annual Nordic Roots Festival, which brings Nordic and Nordic-style performers from around the world to play the week-long event.

Chanhassen Dinner Theatres
501 West 78th Street, Chanhassen
(952) 934–1525
www.chanhassentheatres.com

The Chanhassen Dinner Theatres complex is the nation's largest professional dinner theater, featuring four stages under one roof including its 600-seat main stage, and producing one lavishly costumed Broadway musical comedy after another, year-round. This facility is also the Midwest's largest employer of actors, giving many young hopefuls a paying gig right out of the gate.

Children's Theatre Company
2400 Third Avenue South, Minneapolis
(612) 874–0400
www.childrenstheatre.org

Since 1965, the Children's Theatre Company (CTC) and its cast of incredibly talented young actors and actresses have been performing at the Minneapolis Insti-tute of Arts campus's 746-seat facility. Most of the performances are based on children's stories and fairy tales, but many contemporary sources are used, such as Dr. Seuss—their rendition of *How the Grinch Stole Christmas* is an annual tradition—as well as C. S. Lewis's *The Lion, the Witch and the Wardrobe*. One of the country's leading theater groups for youths, the CTC produces an annual season featuring more than 350 mainstage performances and a touring production that performs in nearly 50 Midwest cities. Its public performances, school matinees, and Theatre Arts Training Program serve more than 300,000 people each year.

The Fitzgerald Theatre
10 East Exchange Street, St. Paul
(651) 290–1221

Opened in 1910 as the Schubert Theater and long known as the World Theater, this comfortable classic structure was renamed

The Fitzgerald Theatre, named after St. Paul's famous literary son F. Scott Fitzgerald, is the home of Prairie Home Companion, *the wildly popular radio show of another famous literary son of St. Paul, Garrison Keillor.* PHOTO: SAINT PAUL CONVENTION AND VISITORS BUREAU

in 1994 after St. Paul's famous literary figure and social gadfly, F. Scott Fitzgerald. The man behind the restoration and renaming of the theater is its well-known tenant, Garrison Keillor, host of the Public Radio International program *A Prairie Home Companion*. As St. Paul's oldest surviving theater space, now restored to its former elegance, The Fitzgerald Theatre presents its shows in a two-balcony, 1,000-seat hall with excellent acoustics and sightlines. The theater's many pleasant features make it popular with touring acts that could probably sell out much larger venues. The theater schedules classical, jazz, folk, country, and pop music events as well as film screening and theater productions.

Guthrie Theater
725 Vineland Place, Minneapolis
(612) 377–2224
www.guthrietheater.org

Anyone who knows American theater knows the Guthrie, the Minneapolis theater founded in the early '60s by legendary director Sir Tyrone Guthrie. The company's métier has always been intriguing interpretations of classic drama. The largest nonprofit theater between New York and San Francisco, the Guthrie is renowned for its productions of classic, comedic, and contemporary plays. The mainstay of Twin Cities professional theater, the Guthrie has a shared entry with the Walker Art Center. The Guthrie's season (six shows a year, and an annual *Christmas Carol* production) is more traditional than the smaller venues in town, choosing to stick to mostly classic and Broadway productions and not veering much into experimental territory.

The theater's larger budget productions and prominent location translate into ticket prices ranging from $15 to $45 on average, but the theater offers discount rush tickets 10 minutes before showtime and student discounts. Special access services include American Sign Language interpretation, wheelchair accessibility, and audio description.

Guthrie Lab
700 First Street North, Minneapolis
(612) 377–2224
www.guthrietheater.org

Essentially, the Guthrie Lab is the experimental wing of the Guthrie Theater. While the Guthrie Theater is known for its big-name, high-budget performances, productions at the Guthrie Lab are known for taking chances with much bolder productions. Their performances revolve around ingenious staging, costuming, and even lighting, and although the Lab is hidden deep within Minneapolis's Warehouse District, when you find it, you'll be blown away with what they can do with theater.

Hennepin Center for the Arts
528 Hennepin Avenue, Minneapolis
(612) 332–4478
www.artspaceprojects.org

This renovated turn-of-the-20th-century building in downtown Minneapolis has three main performance venues. On the top floor is the Bower-Hawthorne, a comfortable, medium-size theater that is home to the Illusion Theater, a company devoted mainly to local and world premieres of new productions. By putting on educational touring productions on abuse, healing, and other hot topics, the company has managed to avoid the fate that meets most young production companies—many of which have rented this same space—and has no trouble keeping grant money flowing in. On the second floor is the Little Theater, an intimate black box theater that's a great place to catch a variety of productions. The third venue is Studio 6A, a dance studio adapted to accommodate audiences, where you'll find modern dance by local companies. Performances and workshops are scheduled throughout the year—check back often for updated production schedules and events.

In the Heart of the Beast Puppet and Mask Theatre
1500 East Lake Street, Minneapolis
(612) 721–2535
www.hobt.org

In the Heart of the Beast's unique theater production is marked by elaborate costuming; stories are told through puppets or actors hidden behind gigantic masks, giving performances a mystical and magical quality. For more than 20 years, this unique theater company has used the ancient tradition of puppet and mask theater to explore issues, events, and values of contemporary society. Though some performances are adaptations of children's stories, all shows are a wonder for eyes of any age.

Puppets are hand-hewn by those involved with the show, and the traveling company stages shows both regionally and nationally. Residencies, educational programs, and special events are offered in the permanent facilities.

Jungle Theater
2951 Lyndale Avenue South, Minneapolis
(612) 822–7063
www.jungletheater.com

The Jungle Theater has a reputation for straightforward performances scripted by lesser-known or more poetic playwrights, offering a year-round season of plays from classic and contemporary sources in an intimate, off-Broadway setting. The red-velvet-seated theater has put on plays by Dylan Thomas and Tennessee Williams and was the site of the world premiere of playwright Karl Gaidusek's *Silver Lake*.

Mixed Blood Theatre
1501 South Fourth Street, Minneapolis
(612) 338–6131
www.mixedblood.com

Walking around Minneapolis's West Bank, it's hard not to notice Mixed Blood's sign and wonder what lurks beneath. Far from anything runaway imaginations may concoct, Mixed Blood is a professional theater company whose mission is to expose and promote the Twin Cities cultural melting pot. Founded in 1976 by Jack Reuler to provide voice and venue for actors of color, Mixed Blood has branched out into the working world to tackle hot topics like race, culture, gender, sexual orientation, and disability. The main stage is housed in a turn-of-the-20th-century brick firehouse, while the touring company itself performs in schools and office buildings throughout the region.

Northrop Auditorium
84 Southeast Church Street, Minneapolis
(612) 624–2345

Located on the University of Minnesota campus in Minneapolis, this is the primary venue for big-name dance company tours, and classical, jazz, and alternative music acts. The old, ornate theater has the grandiose feel of a palace, with high ceilings, velvet curtains, ornate gold and marble trimming, and beautiful acoustics. The annual Northrop Dance Season is an exceptional mix of traditional and cutting-edge dance performances from around the world, while the annual Jazz Series brings acts as varied as the Buena Vista Social Club and the Mingus Big Band.

Old Log Theater
5175 Meadeville Street, Excelsior
(952) 474–5951
www.oldlog.com

You could call the Old Log one of the Twin Cities' legendary theaters. When it was founded (in 1940), however, the forested shoreline around meandering Lake Minnetonka was not considered part of the Twin Cities but a distant retreat from the urban core, a summer playground for the wealthy. Now, of course, it's the leviathan of the western suburbs, but this large log cabin of a dinner theater—and America's oldest professional theater—still stands among the trees near the banks of Lake Minnetonka.

At the Old Log, you'll find American and British comedies with all of the slamming doors, mistaken identities, and double-entendres inherent in the genre. Typically running for about six months, the productions are crowd-pleasers for conservative audiences but are usually not adventurous enough for those who enjoy theater with an edge.

The Jungle Theater on Lyndale Avenue in south Minneapolis. PHOTO: TODD R. BERGER

Orchestra Hall
1111 Nicollet Mall, Minneapolis
(952) 371-5656

The Minneapolis counterpart to St. Paul's Ordway, Orchestra Hall is the place to go to hear the Minnesota Orchestra. The modern exterior can put you off a little, but once inside, visual distractions are kept to a minimum. The minimalist auditorium, which seats 2,400, has a large main floor with three balconies symmetrically girding it. Behind the natural wooden stage and on the ceiling loom what look like enormous sugar cubes hurled by some mythical giant. These blocks provide hundreds of surfaces that deflect sound, making Orchestra Hall among the most acoustically perfect theaters in the nation. The Minnesota Orchestra, Plymouth Music Series and visiting big-name soloists make this place a regular stop in their performance repertoire.

Ordway Center for the Performing Arts/The Ordway Music Theater
345 Washington Street, St. Paul
(651) 224-4222
www.ordway.org

While Minneapolis's Orchestra Hall is modern and glassy like the downtown around it, St. Paul's Ordway is elegant and Old World, conforming admirably to the high and somewhat stuffy standards set forth by its older neighbors, Landmark Center, the St. Paul Hotel, and the St. Paul Public Library. Both the hall and the lobby are tastefully designed, with the wooden walls of the auditorium making for outstanding acoustics, especially for a relatively small ensemble like the St. Paul Chamber Orchestra as well as touring Broadway productions like *Peter Pan*. Rich in contemporary details, the handsome 1,800-seat theater is laid out in the manner of a European opera house, with spacious lobbies overlooking Rice Park from a continuous, three-story bank of windows.

Orpheum Theatre
910 Hennepin Avenue South, Minneapolis
(612) 339-7007

When it opened in 1921, the Orpheum was the second-largest vaudeville house in the nation, with a seating capacity of 2,900. For a time in the mid-1980s, it was

Disney's *The Lion King*, while the expanded Orpheum stage also features epic Broadway shows, concerts, and plays.

Park Square Theatre
20 West Seventh Place, St. Paul
(651) 291–7005

Located in the heart of downtown St. Paul in the center of Park Square—a block-long brick street that's pedestrian-only—Park Square Theatre offers great professional theater in a reasonably large setting. The sets and costumes are beautiful, and there are no bad seats in the theater. The shows they stage range from contemporary plays to classical works.

Penumbra Theatre
270 North Kent Street, St. Paul
(651) 224–3180
www.penumbratheatre.org

As the only professional African-American theater company in the Twin Cities, the Penumbra has a large following and a great reputation. Founded by director Lou Bellamy with the mission of creating artistically exceptional productions that address the African-American experience, the troupe has a rich history of excellence that has included Pulitzer Prize–winning playwright August Wilson as a member. Recently the Penumbra worked in conjunction with the Guthrie to present *The Darker Face of the Earth* by Rita Dove, and their annual Christmas production of Langston Hughes's Black Nativity is an extremely popular event.

The Playwrights' Center
2301 East Franklin Avenue, Minneapolis
(612) 332–7481
www.pwcenter.org

This former church converted into theater space stands in the middle of the Seward neighborhood on Franklin Avenue (near the Second Moon Café). If people know about it, it's because they read the name in another theater's playbill—usually because the Playwrights' Center gave a donation to the performing company. However, behind the scenes, the center helps actors and writers workshop their new ideas. They also house the occasional performance—last

The near-acoustically perfect Ordway Center for the Performing Arts in downtown St. Paul is home to the St. Paul Chamber Orchestra and the stage of choice for many traveling Broadway shows. PHOTO: SAINT PAUL CONVENTION AND VISITORS BUREAU

owned by singer Bob Dylan and had seen better days. After the roaring success of the State Theatre renovation, the city stepped up to the plate in 1988, bought the Orpheum, and spent nearly $9 million on its restoration, which was completed in 1994. Today the Orpheum's most stunning element is the auditorium's glittering dome, lined with 30,000 silvery 4-inch aluminum squares and lit by a 2,000-pound brass chandelier.

Like the State Theatre, the Orpheum hosts both musical concerts and many of the Broadway musicals that come to town. The old-style marquee blinking over downtown can't be missed. The renovated theater has showcased the world premieres of *Victor/Victoria*, starring Julie Andrews, and

year they hosted Ten Thousand Thing's rave-reviewed, edgy version of *The Tempest*.

Plymouth Playhouse
2705 Annapolis Lane, Plymouth
(763) 553-1600
www.plymouthplayhouse.com

The Plymouth is the flagship space of Troupe America, which specializes in dinner-theater productions long on laughs and music. *Nunsense, Pump Boys and Dinettes,* and revues featuring the Twin Cities' own Lovely Liebowirz Sisters have had extended runs here. Their most recent long-running production, *How to Talk Minnesotan,* was adapted for the stage by the book's author, Howard Mohr.

Rarig Center
U of M Campus, 330 21st Avenue South, Minneapolis
(612) 625-4001

The Rarig Center, located on the West Bank, hosts University Theatre and Xperimental Theater productions throughout the year on three stages: the Rarig Mainstage, the arena theater, and the small black box theater. The Mainstage shows are usually the more popular ones, such as *As You Like It,* and the smaller theater spaces offer more experimental shows. The X Theater productions are written, directed, and performed exclusively by undergraduate U of M students. At University Theatre, student and professional actors, designers, and directors write and direct musicals, comedies, and dramas. *The Centennial Showboat* offers performances each summer aboard a sternwheeler riverboat anchored at Raspberry Island.

Red Eye Theater
15 West 14th Street, Minneapolis
(612) 870-0309

One of the smaller theater venues in the Twin Cities, the Red Eye Theater is by far the most experimental. Just off Nicollet Avenue, the Red Eye's theater space hosts a wide variety of film and video productions, theater, and dance events, both local and imported. The venue itself has become a sponsor of fringe performances over the last few years, and not just at the Red Eye itself. They've supported summer movies and music events at Stevens Square Park as well as the Open Reel program—an open mic opportunity for independent filmmakers to show their work. The Red Eye's performing space is a long, rectangular black box that's also used by other companies who enjoy its versatility and intimacy.

Roy Wilkins Auditorium
RiverCentre, 175 West Kellogg Boulevard, St. Paul
(651) 265-4800

Roy Wilkins Auditorium (named for the longtime NAACP head, a St. Paul native) is all that's left of the old St. Paul Auditorium. Half the auditorium and its adjoining theater were razed to build the Ordway Music Theatre. This cavernous hall, part of the sprawling RiverCentre complex, has seen a revival in recent years thanks to big-ticket touring dance DJs (Chemical Brothers, Moby) and cutting-edge rock acts (Marilyn Manson, Deftones). What Roy Wilkins loses in acoustics, it makes up for in breathing room. If a show has festival seating, you can quench your fanaticism and get quite close to the stage, or take a break and find respite near the exit doors.

Southern Theater
1420 Washington Avenue South, Minneapolis
(612) 340-1725
www.southerntheater.org

The Southern has increasingly become a venue for dance due to its recently rebuilt stage floor. Many local dance companies perform here, and everything from flamenco to classical Indian dance to modern dance can be seen in this venue. Exposed-brick walls enclose the auditorium, lending a comfortable warehouse-like feel to the performance experience. Every January the Southern hosts Out There, a notably high-quality series of theatrical performances.

ages Theatre Company
1111 Main Street, Hopkins
(952) 979–1111
www.stagestheatre.org

Stages, known until spring 1999 as Child's Play Theatre Company, produces plays for young audiences. Once housed in the Eisenhower Community Center, the company moved in 1997 to the Hopkins Center for the Arts. It offers acting, singing, and directing classes year-round for youth ages 5 through 18 at education centers throughout the Twin Cities.

State Theatre
805 Hennepin Avenue South, Minneapolis
(612) 339–7007

Downtown Minneapolis has become a theatrical center due in large part to the renovation of this gem of a theater in the early '90s. Painstakingly restored in 1991 to its former 1920s glory, which includes a golden proscenium arch, glittering chandeliers, and intricate murals, the 2,200-seat State Theatre now showcases a steady stream of touring plays and musicals, concerts, and lectures. Smaller than its neighbor the Orpheum Theatre (which is owned and managed by the same group), the historic State Theatre is similar in its beautifully restored interior, complete with a grand sloping balcony that hangs over the rear half of the main floor. Broadway touring productions sometimes set up shop here for months at a stretch. Rock concerts, comedians, and dance performances fill in the rest of the schedule.

Theatre de la Jeune Lune
105 North First Street, Minneapolis
(612) 333–6200
www.jeunelune.org

The Jeune Lune is located in the Warehouse District of downtown Minneapolis and is known for its elaborate and poignant commedia-style productions. The space itself is justification for buying the first ticket after that, most theater goers are hooked. The facade of the building was designed by renowned architect Cass Gilbert, and the theater is listed on the National Register of Historic Places.

The interior is a large bricked space, which lends itself to very authentic-looking street and/or exterior house scenes in a variety of plays.

This theater ensemble is known for its highly physical, visually spectacular productions. Jeune Lune's acclaimed *The 3 Musketeers* was the hit of the 1997 Spoleto USA Festival and toured in 1999 to Philadelphia's Wilma Theatre.

Theatre in the Round Players, Inc.
245 Cedar Avenue South, Minneapolis
(612) 333–3010
www.theatreintheround.org

Theatre in the Round, the oldest amateur theater in Minneapolis, performs a variety of drama and comedy on a unique arena stage. Because the audience surrounds the stage entirely, sets are minimal, making the action between the actors more intense. Props are also very important because of the lack of stage settings. Most of the plays presented are classics, but the players perform a few well-done area premieres each year. Company members call George Bernard Shaw their playwright in residence, and at least one Shaw comedy is offered yearly.

All About Books

Open Book—Book and Literary Arts Center
1011 Washington Avenue, Suite 100,
Minneapolis
(612) 215–2520
www.mnbookarts.org

The first literary arts complex of its kind in the nation, this renovated historic building opened in 2000. Visitors can watch the book printing and binding process from beginning to end, explore the exhibitions gallery, or simply stretch out on the sofa in the Literary Commons with a good book from the center's free library. Other amenities include occasional live performances, literary readings, writing workshops, family reading space, and a cafe. Located in the building is the Minnesota Center for Book Arts, the largest independent book arts facility in the nation; the Loft, which offers

The Minneapolis Institute of Arts houses a massive collection from many eras, styles, and media, as well as traveling exhibits ranging from the works of Vincent Van Gogh to Richard Avedon. PHOTO: GREATER MIN-

a variety of classes on writing and publishing; and an excellent performance space for visiting authors and lecturers. This place is fun to just walk around in, as so much of the original structure and facades were saved in the restoration process, including pieces of the original wallpaper, staircases that go nowhere, and ancient bakery and factory signs painted on the brickwork itself.

Parks

Minneapolis
St. Paul
Greater Metro Area

The Suburban Hennepin Regional Park District, commonly called Hennepin Parks, is an independent park district established by the state legislature in 1957 and is responsible for maintaining most of the parks around the Twin Cities metro area. As a special park district, Hennepin Parks is charged with the responsibilities of acquisition, development, and maintenance of large park reserves, regional parks, and regional trails for the benefit and use of the citizens of suburban Hennepin County, Scott County, the metropolitan area, and the state of Minnesota. Hennepin Parks' policy for planning and management of natural resources has distinguished it from other park and recreation agencies in Minnesota. The policy specifies that no more than 20 percent of a park reserve may be developed for active use and that at least 80 percent of a park reserve shall be restored to and retained in a natural state. As a result, once-rare osprey, bald eagles, sandhill cranes, and trumpeter swans are now nesting in the park reserves. Woodland and prairie restorations have been accomplished using native wildflowers, shrubs, and trees produced from seeds collected in the park reserves.

Twin Citians have the luxury of being able to walk past wetlands full of migratory waterfowl and turtles on their way to downtown Minneapolis, or through thickly forested areas housing species of rare native animals and birds just minutes outside St. Paul. Kids who grow up in the Twin Cities get to share in pleasures usually reserved for children who grow up in the country, whether it be fishing in one of the many regularly stocked urban lakes, berry picking, or just enjoying being surrounded by trees, songbirds, and wildflowers in parks practically in their own backyards. Even in the dead of winter, you'll find people outside enjoying cross-country skiing, snowshoeing, or ice fishing in the many city and suburban parks around the Twin Cities. Take a trip to any of the following, and you'll soon see why we Minnesotans are rabidly protective of our wilderness areas.

Minneapolis

Boom Island
Plymouth Avenue and Northeast Eighth
Street, Minneapolis
(612) 661–4800

Boom Island Park is a jewel in the crown of the nationally acclaimed Minneapolis parks system. Situated above historic Main Street, Nicollet Island, and the St. Anthony Lock and Dam, Boom Island is a veritable playground for families and tourists wishing to experience the majesty and beauty of the Mississippi River. The park is well used and threadbare in spots, but not enough to lose its luster as a popular destination point for picnicking, tossing a frisbee, sight-seeing on a riverboat, launching one's own boat, or simply relaxing by the river on the plaza overlooks.

Attention to details, with few notable exceptions, makes this park highly accessible to persons with disabilities. Low-grade rampways have been well integrated into the overlooks and boarding docks. Water fountains and the public telephone all incorporate current accessible features, and level asphalt pathways connect all the critical areas of the park. The park can serve as a nice starting or ending point on a journey on foot or by bike to the nearby Heritage Trail around historic Main Street and St. Anthony Falls or going north up the river to connect with the Mississippi

236

River Regional Corridor Trail that takes you to Anoka Riverfront Regional Park, Islands of Peace Park, and, eventually, East and West Coon Rapids Regional Parks.

The boat launch is located on the north side of the main parking area situated in a small, protected channel about 300 feet away from the water's edge and the dock area to the boat slips. Several sets of stairs and a wheelchair-access ramp go to the boat slip dock area, and a lovely promenade/plaza area is just downriver of the riverboat landing. This area provides a nice overlook to the river, as well as a stunning view of downtown Minneapolis. There is another small plaza area with wood decking adjacent to the boat landing, which affords visitors an opportunity to view the comings and goings of both the riverboats and the private boats being launched nearby.

Boom Island is also home to St. Anthony Falls' miniature "lighthouse," which sits on a prominent point overlooking the riverboat dock and river. The lighthouse is not functional, but makes a nice destination point for visitors, especially kids. The view is great from this area—almost like being out on the water.

Cleary Lake Regional Park
18106 Texas Avenue, Minneapolis
(952) 447–2171

The 1,045-acre Cleary Lake Regional Park, southwest of Burnsville, is one of the most popular year-round recreation spots in the southern metro area. A distinctive three-season pavilion, available by reservation, is a favorite Cities site for large group gatherings, while golfers find challenge in the par 3, nine-hole golf course and driving range. Water sports available include swimming, boating, and fishing in Cleary Lake. Winter activities include cross-country skiing on groomed trails and snowshoeing anywhere in the park except the ski trails. Boats, bicycles, in-line skates, and cross-country skis are available for rent at the visitor center; reservation picnic areas and group campsites are also available.

Loring Park
1382 Willow Street, Minneapolis
(612) 661–4800

Modeled after New York's Central Park, although about 800 acres smaller than the real thing, Loring Park is a hip city park with just about everything. For families and single adults alike, there's a large, beautiful lake (Loring Lake) full of mallards, wood ducks, and Canada geese that come up on the shore regularly, demanding handouts; friendly squirrels; lush, green rolling hills; and, in summer, free live music and movies in the outdoor amphitheater several nights of the week. There's also a concession cart parked conveniently near the amphitheater most nights, which sells snack foods and ice cream. The park is well maintained, with lots of paved trails that take you around Loring Lake and the stunning fountain and the bronze sculpture of Norway's esteemed violinist Ole Bull.

A short walk across the street takes you to either the Basilica of St. Mary or the internationally acclaimed Walker Art Center and its Sculpture Garden, depending on which way you point your feet.

Mill Ruins Park
On the Mississippi River at St. Anthony Falls, Minneapolis
(612) 661–4800

Mill Ruins Park is next to the Mill City Museum, the historic Crosby A Mill now preserved to celebrate the history of the flour mills that built the city of Minneapolis. The park overlooks the locks and St. Anthony Falls, and visitors can watch the barge traffic making its way through the locks and on down the Mississippi. The park connects to the Stone Arch Bridge, a pedestrian and bicycle pathway across the river, and to the bike trail system winding up and down the Mississippi and throughout the Twin Cities. A guided historical walking tour is available at the park (see the Attractions chapter for more information).

The parks that surround the Minneapolis Chain of Lakes are bucolic and wildly popular with sailboaters, in-line skaters, sun-worshiping twenty-somethings, and your average Minnesotan with cabin fever after a long winter. PHOTO: GREATER MINNEAPOLIS CONVENTION & VISITORS ASSOCIATION

Minneapolis Chain of Lakes/Rice Creek Regional Parks
Cedar Lake, 25th Street West and Cedar Lake Parkway
Lake Calhoun, Calhoun Parkway and Lake Street
Lake Harriet, 4135 Lake Harriet Parkway East
Lake Nokomis, Minnehaha Parkway East and Cedar Avenue
Lake of the Isles, 25th Street West and Lake of the Isles Parkway East
(612) 661–4800

About 2,500 acres of parkland surrounds Minneapolis's Chain of Lakes, which includes Lake Harriet, Lake Calhoun, Lake of the Isles, Cedar Lake, and Lake Nokomis. The lakes are all connected by Rice and Minnehaha Creeks, which makes canoeing through much of the parkland a fun trip that involves little or no docking to get from lake to lake. Both boat and shore fishing are extremely popular in the Chain of Lakes, and many fishing piers and easily accessed shore fishing sites can be found throughout the parks.

The lakes are surrounded by paved bike and walking trails, and the bike trails connect to the larger system surrounding and cutting across the city of Minneapolis, including the Cedar Lake Trail, the Minnehaha Creek Trail to the Mississippi (which will also get you to the St. Paul bike trail system), and the Midtown Greenway, which follows the railroad tracks along 29th Avenue through south Minneapolis and Uptown.

Thomas Sadler Roberts Bird Sanctuary, located on the north shore of Lake Harriet, consists of 13 acres of unapologetically wild land that attracts more than 200 bird species each year. The sanctuary is named for Thomas Roberts, the late Minneapolis physician and University of Minnesota ornithology professor who in 1932 wrote what remains the definitive work on local avian culture, *Birds of Minnesota*. Created by the Minneapolis Park Board in 1936 as Lyndale Park Bird Sanctuary, its name was changed after Roberts's death to honor the man who led so many field trips here.

Minnehaha Falls and Park
Hiawatha Avenue and Minnehaha
Parkway, Minneapolis
(612) 661–4800

This historic, well-used, and recently refurbished 193-acre regional park gives visitors little wonder where Henry Wadsworth Longfellow got the inspiration to write his epic poem *Song of Hiawatha*, which was inspired by accounts the poet had read about Minnehaha Falls, though he never actually visited them. The impressive falls are the primary destination point for most park visitors, with several wonderful overlook points and steps that take you all the way down to the bottom of the falls. From the bottom, you can pick up the Minnehaha Trail and follow it and the river to the Lower Glen area of Minnehaha Regional Park. There, you'll find a wide, open field, old stone bridges that cross the water at regular intervals, limestone cliffs, and areas of restored prairie and undeveloped wetlands. Throughout the park are statues, plaques dedicated to historic events, and historic buildings, including the historic Minnehaha Depot, built in 1875 to serve as a recreational gateway for visitors to the falls and as a departure point for soldiers from nearby Fort Snelling, and the Colonel John H. Stevens Home, which is open to visitors most weekends mid-May through mid-September.

The main area of the park, around the picnic areas and the falls, can be very busy during summer months. There are lots of walkers, bikers, and skaters, so keep one eye out as you go from overlook to overlook. One can easily walk south of the falls, however, and find quieter, more reflective surroundings in which to relax and enjoy the natural beauty of the park. Benches are strategically placed in and among statuary, gardens, and a unique pergola (covered walk). About 1 mile south of the main park entrance, there is a paved hike/bike trail that goes from Minnehaha Falls to Fort Snelling State Park. The trail is mostly paved, with a few sections in disrepair, but it's quiet, little used, and takes bicyclists and hikers all along the upper river bluffs and past a magnificent river overlook at a pedestrian bridge that crosses to the Old Soldier's Home.

The park is also connected to the Minnehaha Creek Bike Trail, which follows

Minnehaha Falls in southeast Minneapolis have inspired many, including the poet Henry Wadsworth Longfellow. PHOTO: GREATER MINNEAPOLIS CONVENTION & VISITORS ASSOCIATION

the creekbed all the way to Lake Harriet; the Mississippi River Trail leading north to the University of Minnesota; and downtown Minneapolis, and the St. Paul bike trail system via the Ford Parkway bridge.

Nicollet Island Park
off Historic Main Street at East Hennepin Avenue, Minneapolis
(612) 661-4800

In summertime this little island located in the middle of the Mississippi River is a haven for native wildlife of all sorts, including the occasional deer. In winter the park is converted into a giant ice-skating rink. Year-round, the park is a beautiful place for an afternoon or evening stroll—at night, the lights of downtown Minneapolis reflect off the Mississippi River, giving one the feeling of being downtown yet still walking through a quaint, small town, all at once. Horse and carriage rides are available from the nearby Nicollet Inn, and fireworks displays can be seen from the park's rolling green hills on New Year's Eve, Fourth of July, and during the Aquatennial celebration.

St. Anthony Falls Heritage Trail
Main Street, Minneapolis
(612) 627-5433

This amazing stretch of land is often overlooked because the entrance is tucked behind the giant Pillsbury flour mill, next to Minneapolis's historic Main Street retail area directly across the Mississippi River from downtown. This park and trail celebrate the founding of Minneapolis.

The Heritage Trail is a highly accessible asphalt multiuse trail (bike, hike, jog, and skate) that takes visitors on a 1.8-mile loop, connecting them to most of the historic and natural features of early Minneapolis, including natural vistas of the tree-lined banks of the Mississippi River as well as many ruined brick arches that served a variety of uses in the days of the area's bustling milling industry. The trail is widely interpreted along the way, making this an excellent "self-guided" trail, although visitors can also learn about the area in a comprehensive tour offered by the Minnesota Historical Society.

The centerpiece of the park, the Stone Arch Bridge, was built by railway baron James J. Hill in 1883 to speed his trains across the Mississippi. Now beautifully restored, the bridge provides a serene transit for walkers, joggers, and anybody who wants the best possible view of St. Anthony Falls, whose churning power first made Minneapolis a milling capital. Trail users can cross the river over the historic bridge, which offers a spectacular vista of the river, the downtown Minneapolis skyline, and the highly accessible St. Anthony Falls Lock and Dam at the other end. A beautiful promenade parallels the river on its west bank and is a favorite destination of noontime walkers and others who wish to sit, read, or watch the river flow by. There are plenty of overlooks and bench areas on the trail, and water and toilets are located at developed areas on both sides of the river.

The Minnesota Historical Society offers guided weekend walking tours of the St. Anthony Falls area, a nationally designated historic site containing architectural ruins, as well as significant buildings and bridges. Tours depart several times a day during summer weekends from the society's interpretive center at 125 Main Street SE, Minneapolis.

Como Park
1360 North Lexington Parkway, St. Paul
(651) 632–5111

This 450-acre urban park, more than 100 years old, is one of the most visited sites in the Twin Cities, offering large group picnicking areas and a conservatory, zoo, Japanese garden, a small amusement park with pony rides, and summer concerts and plays. There's also an 18-hole golf course that turns into a cross-country ski area in the winter; seasonal equipment rentals and refreshments are available at Como Lakeside Pavilion. (See Attractions chapter for more information on Como's facilities.)

In the middle of a tough Minnesota winter, there's no palliative like a visit to the lush, green-filled Marjorie McNeely Conservatory at Como Park, which houses such exotic plants as 125-year-old palm trees (botanical souvenirs from world tours of the city's elite) and papaya trees (grown in Como greenhouses from the seeds of grocery store papayas). Outside, the tea house in the Como Ordway Memorial Japanese Garden offers a traditional Chanoyu tea ceremony several times throughout the summer, as well as a beautiful goldfish pond stocked with giant, colorful, friendly fish.

The historic Cafesjian's Carousel, which operated for three-quarters of a century at the Minnesota State Fair, found a new home in summer 2000 at the park, just south of the conservatory. The carousel and its beautiful antique horses are available to the public during the summer, and a ride on the carousel is a great way to end a day at the park.

Crosby Regional Park and Hidden Falls Park
East Mississippi River Boulevard, St. Paul
(651) 632–5111

Hidden Falls Park dates back to 1887, when the area was identified as one of four major park sites for the City of St. Paul. The park got its name from both the small, spring-fed waterfall hidden deep inside the park and the historic Crosby Farm, formerly owned by English immigrant Thomas Crosby, who once farmed 160 acres of this land. Today, hiking and biking trails run along shady, wooded bottomlands next to the river and along the marshes of the two lakes before connecting to Mississippi River Boulevard. (If it's rained recently, bike slowly through the lower, shadier spots or a slippery patch of mud may wreck your outing.) The primary park features include a well-developed picnic area with pavilion and modern toilet facilities, a boat launch ramp, picnic sites, and access to a 7-mile-long hiking/biking path that follows the Mississippi River. A wide variety of panfish can be caught from the banks of the Mississippi River or from over the side of a boat.

The hiking/biking trail, which converts to a cross-country ski trail in the winter, takes users along the Mississippi River, where the flora and fauna of river life can be observed up close. Songbirds migrate and nest nearby, and deer and rabbits can be seen in the thick wooded areas around the park. At points along the trail, historic Fort Snelling can be seen on the high bluffs across the river. The Crosby Regional Park section has an open floodplain meadow, two lakes, and wooded areas.

Fort Snelling State Park
Post Road off Minnesota Highway 5, St. Paul
(651) 725–2389

For hundreds of years before Europeans arrived, generations of Dakota people lived in villages along the Mississippi and Minnesota Rivers that meet in what's now Fort Snelling State Park. The river confluence was believed to be the place of origin and center of the earth by the bands of Mdewa-kan-ton-wan Dakota, the "Dwellers by Mystic Lake." By the late 1600s Europeans had visited the area. In the 1820s historic Fort Snelling was built on the bluff above the two rivers to control the exploration, trade, and settlement on these waterways.

Established as a state park in 1962, the 3,400-acre park is located in the Mississippi River Sandplains Landscape Region at the confluence of the two great rivers. During the last Ice Age, retreating glaciers left thick moraine deposits over the bedrock in the area. As the glaciers melted,

Fort Snelling State Park, along the Minnesota and Mississippi Rivers near Minneapolis–St. Paul International Airport, offers miles of hiking and skiing trails less than fifteen minutes from both downtowns.
PHOTO: TODD R. BERGER

torrential meltwaters carved through the deposits to form the valleys of what are now the Minnesota, Mississippi, and St. Croix Rivers. Most of the park is on the Minnesota River floodplain and is thickly wooded with large cottonwood, silver maple, ash, and willow trees along the braided channels of the Minnesota River. Numerous picnic sites, a beach, and river and lake fishing invite visitors to enjoy the recreational opportunities offered by this historic and beautiful park nestled in the shadow of city freeways and airport flyways. The swimming beach, added in 1970, remains a popular recreation attraction in the park. In 1997 a new visitor center opened to the public.

Conveniently located in the heart of the Twin Cities, this park offers extensive hiking, bike, and ski trails that link to Minnehaha Park and the Minnesota Valley National Wildlife Refuge. Canoe on Gun Club Lake, play golf, swim in Snelling Lake, or hike or ski to Pike Island, at the confluence of the Mississippi and Minnesota Rivers. Interpretive exhibits and films on display in the Thomas C. Savage Visitor Center give visitors a good background on the history and resources of the park and area. Trails also allow visitors to hike up to historic Fort Snelling for a view of military life in the 1820s. The Pike Island Interpretive Center hosts exhibits concerning historic Fort Snelling and the region in general. Throughout the park, the forest bottoms and marshes have an abundance of wildlife consisting of white-tailed deer, foxes, woodchucks, badgers, and skunks. Visitors might also come across the native, nonvenomous fox snake, which is almost identical in appearance to a rattlesnake. Snapping, soft-shell, and painted turtles can be seen basking in the sun along the river or in one of the lakes.

During winter, the park maintains 10 miles of groomed cross-country ski trails and 6 miles of groomed skate-ski trails—snowshoeing is permitted anywhere in the park except on groomed ski trails. The park also has 7 miles of hiking trails available for use in the winter, with even more available during summer. Golf equipment and canoes are available for rent in the park, and naturalist programs ranging from bird-watching tours to nature and snowshoe hikes are offered year-round.

Indian Mounds Park
Earl Street and Mounds Boulevard, St. Paul
(651) 632–5111

Built to enshrine six 2,000-year-old Hopewell Indian burial mounds, Mounds Park occupies what was the choicest residential land in St. Paul in the 1860s. Today the bluffs of the park give visitors one of the best "aerial" views of the Twin Cities, with the Minneapolis skyline on the left, the St. Paul skyline on the right, and the Mississippi River below. The mounds are surrounded by metal rail fences but are easily seen and approached—the remains of the chiefs have long since been removed, but the mounds are still standing as a sacred memorial. Visitors are not permitted to climb upon the mounds, and a brass plaque describing the site stands near the brick pavilion. The park is also the site of the first visit by Europeans to the Twin Cities area; Father Louis Hennepin and two other Frenchmen were brought here in 1680.

Two more historic features nearby are the reconstructed aerial beacon used for many years by aircraft approaching the Holman Field airport directly across the river and the Carver's Cave outlook. Information about this beacon is posted on signage adjacent to the beacon tower located a short distance from the mounds. It's best to park at the Mounds parking lot, approaching this site via the asphalt path. The Carver's Cave overlook commemorates Jonathan Carver, a forward scout for Major Robert Rogers's expedition to find a Northwest Passage, whose travels brought him up the Mississippi River. In 1766 he discovered an ancient cave with artifacts and hieroglyphics along the bluff at about this point. A plaque at the overlook describes the history.

The park is actively used by families, groups, skateboarders, cyclists, hikers, and others. It is a well-worn park with old restrooms and access routes developed before accessibility was a concern, but there are plenty of picnic and play space for people of all ages and accessible parking spaces at many points in the park.

Lilydale/Harriet Island Park/Cherokee Park
South side of Mississippi River at Wabasha, St. Paul
(651) 632–5111

The river-oriented Lilydale/Harriet Island Park includes the natural area of the Lilydale portion below the river bluffs and Harriet Island itself. Harriet Island, situated on the Mississippi River across from downtown St. Paul, was one of the first recreational sites in the city. Named for pioneer schoolteacher Harriet Bishop, the park was a true island separated from the mainland by a channel of water until 1950, when the channel was filled. At the top of the bluffs is Cherokee Park, which has picnic grounds and good spots for viewing the entire park.

Harriet Island has long been a playground for St. Paul citizens who have come alone or with friends and family to fish, launch their boats, take a cruise on a historic riverboat, picnic, take walks, and simply enjoy nature. The park has landscaped river edges, beautiful flower gardens that also attract a huge variety of

Insiders' Tip
A daily or annual parking sticker is required to park in the lot at any Hennepin Park. To park for a full day, the charge is $5.00—however, for $25.00, you can buy a patron parking pass, which is good for the whole year. Call Hennepin Parks at (763) 559-9000 for more information.

native and migratory songbirds, and a marina from which park visitors can board several large paddleboats to tour the waterways.

Lilydale, formerly a residential community, extends to the west of Harriet Island and is now an undeveloped floodplain. It also used to be the site of former Twin City Brick Co.'s mining operations, until the company exposed extensive fossil beds, making the area well known among professional and amateur paleontologists, who are sometimes allowed to accompany professionals on guided digs at the park. A connected pond and about 200 acres of marsh and woodlands provide habitat for varied flora and fauna.

Mears Park
366 Sibley Street, St. Paul

Located near Galtier Plaza in the distinctive, anachronistic Lowertown neighborhood of St. Paul, Mears Park serves as the neighborhood's village commons. The park is a popular lunchtime and evening gathering spot and is filled with trees, flowers, benches, sculpture, and even a rippling creek. Summertime brings outdoor concerts, performances, events, and festivals. In winter the park's many trees are covered with hundreds of thousands of twinkling lights. Restored bridges across Interstate 94 serve as beautiful new gateways to the neighborhood.

Phalen Regional Park
Off Wheelock Parkway and East Larpenteur Avenue, St. Paul
(651) 632–5111

Founded in 1899, Phalen Regional Park surrounds the quiet residential area around Phalen and Round Lakes in northeast St. Paul, with 3.2 miles of paved trails, an amphitheater, a beach, an 18-hole golf course, and a picnic shelter and pavilion. The park is named for Edward Phelan (whose name was spelled various ways), the earliest settler of the land around Phalen Creek. The park's trails connect to the Gateway State Trail, a paved biking and walking trail stretching from downtown St. Paul to Pioneer Park, north of Stillwater.

Rice Park
140 Washington Street, St. Paul

In the shadow of Landmark Center, the Ordway Center for the Performing Arts, the St. Paul Public Library, and the St. Paul Hotel, St. Paul's Rice Park is a restful yet active square of greenery and monuments. Young trees provide a little shade during the day, but the park is at its best for summer concerts and as the ice sculpture hub of the annual St. Paul Winter Carnival.

Greater Metro Area

Afton State Park
6959 Peller Avenue South, Hastings
(651) 436–5391

Five miles south of the town of Afton, Afton State Park is a 1,702-acre wilderness area set along the St. Croix National Scenic Riverway. Opened in 1969 specifically to both preserve the native landscape and to give visitors the opportunity to see Minnesota wilderness up close, the park is located in a landscape of rolling glacial moraines and rocky bluffs, surrounded by thick hardwood woodlands and pine trees, with protected remnants of original prairie being aggressively restored by park management. In spring the grassy fields are sprinkled with prairie pasque flowers and woodland ephemerals. In summer and early fall, the landscape gives way to thick bunches of butterfly weed, puccoons, sunflowers, and blazing star. Throughout the park, visitors get picture-perfect glimpses of the slow-moving St. Croix River.

Among the activities visitors enjoy at Afton, bird-watching is one of the most popular. Red-tailed hawks hunt for rabbits, and eagles soar high above the bluffs. Native and migratory waterfowl can be seen along the riverbanks, while bluebirds, meadowlarks, and a huge variety of migratory birds make their homes in the prairie grasses here each year. The park is also home to an amazing diversity of wild animals native to Minnesota, including deer, fox badgers, squirrels, and wild turkeys. This is also a great spot for fishing, in both summer and winter; walleye, sauger, and smallmouth bass can be caught either

St. Paul's elegant Rice Park is one of many small parks breaking up the building-after-building atmosphere of downtown. PHOTO: SAINT PAUL CONVENTION AND VISITORS BUREAU

along the riverbank or over the side of your canoe.

Afton State Park has more than 20 miles of paved and groomed trails for horseback riding and hiking in spring and summer. In winter many of these trails are left open for cross-country skiers and snowshoers to explore. The park office has maps of the park available for visitors, and, while the park does not have a naturalist on staff, many activities are offered throughout the year by volunteers who lead snowshoe hikes, demonstrate bird-banding practices, and teach visitors how to identify many of the birds that visit the park. There are also several primitive camping sites with nearby access to hiking trails—reservations are needed from April to November but not from November to April.

For kids, Afton is a great place to play year-round. In summer Afton has a large, clean swimming beach near a picnic area and public rest rooms. In winter Afton has a great sliding hill for sleds, toboggans, and tubes, as well as a warming house to huddle in before and after playing in the snow. The visitor center offers many one-day classes for kids on flower and bird identification, hiking, snowshoeing, and cross-country skiing.

Anoka County Riverfront Regional Park
550 Bunker Lake Boulevard NW, Andover
(763) 757-3920

This Anoka County park's biking, hiking, and ungroomed cross-country skiing trails are right in the Twin Cities metropolitan area, offering nice views of the Mississippi River all along the trails. Canoes can be rented from the park, and fishing is permitted from the shore and the river. If you're lucky enough to hook some lunch, grills and picnic shelters are also available.

The Islands of Peace segment of the park, located north of Interstate 694, has been developed by the Foundation for Islands of Peace. Chase's Island and the adjacent riverfront land is used as a recreational facility for the general public, as well as adults and children with disabilities, and a reception center has a fireplace, rest rooms, library, a lounge, and meeting rooms for use by the public. A walk bridge and paved trail link the center to Chase's Island facilities, which include paved trails, shelter, river viewing, and picnic facilities—all with wheelchair access. The 57-acre Durnam Island segment, located in the river west of Chase's Island, has only recently been developed into nature trails to accommodate the disabled and the general public, with a boat shuttle service back and forth from the island.

The Anoka County Riverfront Regional Park also acts as a trailhead for the trail segment to the south along East River Road, connecting the Minneapolis trail system and the trail segment to the north to Islands of Peace in Fridley. An additional trail link to Brooklyn Center exists as well, with a trail crossing over the I–694 bridge.

Baker Park Reserve
County Road 19, between Minnesota Highways 12 and 55
(763) 559–9000

Located on Lake Independence in central Hennepin County, just a 20-minute drive from much of the metro area, Baker Park Reserve's 2,700 acres offer diverse outdoor activities in natural surroundings. Baker Park offers a 213-site campground, golf at the Baker National Golf Course, swimming and boating in Lake Independence, and a playground for kids. The kids' playground area is truly spectacular, almost fortresslike, and is one of the reasons that this is such a popular family park and a great place to take kids of all ages. Kids scramble over ramps, platforms, and paths made of recycled rubber mats that protect against minor falls and bumps and bruises from roughhousing.

In winter a sliding hill, a cozy warming chalet, and groomed cross-country ski trails are opened. In summer, paved hiking and biking trails wind through one of the remnants of a Big Woods forest. Boats, bikes, and skis are available for rent through the park's visitor center.

Bald Eagle–Otter Lakes Regional Park
5287 Otter Lake Road, White Bear Lake
(651) 407–5350

Bald Eagle–Otter Lakes Regional Park, comprising 884 acres, is located in White Bear Lake in the northeast corner of Ramsey County. The park is a large natural area in a developing suburban neighborhood, with extensive woods, wetlands, and grasslands. The park is home to many species of wildlife, including red foxes, deer, woodcocks, herons, turtles, minks, beavers, and muskrats. Two relatively rare species of wildlife, osprey and otters, have also been sighted in this park. More than 3 miles of paved and woodchip-covered hiking trails offer visitors the opportunity to experience nature up close. The two lakes at the park, Fish Lake and Tamarack Lake, are open to shore and lake fishing, and Fish Lake is a popular spot for ice fishers in winter.

The Tamarack Nature Center offers a variety of programs, including bird-watching tours, syrup-making, guided summer hikes, and winter snowshoe walks. Inside the nature center itself are mounted displays of many animals native to the area, several of which were made by famous taxidermist Walter Breckenridge, former director of the Bell Museum of Natural History.

Battle Creek Regional Park
East of McKnight Boulevard between I–94 and Lower Afton Road, Maplewood
(651) 266–6400

Battle Creek Regional Park, consisting of 1,840 acres located in the southeast corner of St. Paul and southern Maplewood, provides a large natural area in a highly developed urban environment. The park's extensive areas of woods, wetlands, and grasslands provide habitat for many species of wildlife, including deer, foxes, herons, egrets, and hawks. Biking and hiking trails offer visitors the opportunity to view the birds and animals as well as the beauty of the vegetation. Winter visitors can tour the park on groomed cross-country trails. A large picnic pavilion accommodates groups of up to 500 people, and smaller picnic shelters are also available. In summer the park has a weekly concert series that showcases everything from local alternative acts to acoustic jazz combos.

Baylor Regional Park
County Road 33, Norwood
(952) 467-4200

Baylor Regional Park is located in the extreme southwest corner of the Twin Cities, so far removed from the bright lights of the downtowns that it's a favorite observation point for junior astronomy clubs and amateur stargazers of all ages. Perched on the shoulder of Eagle Lake and surrounded by farmers' fields, Baylor preserves a rich mix of native habitats, from the large grove of mature maple trees that are tapped in early spring each year for maple syrup, to the floating boardwalk that carries visitors over wetland marshes to get a glimpse of turtles, waterfowl, and wildflowers.

The park also offers a 50-site tent and RV campground with 30 utility sites, two shower facilities, a swimming beach and bathhouse on Eagle Lake, two large picnic shelters, tennis courts, and 5 miles of hiking trails. A community room in the park barn is available with advance reservations for group usage. In winter the 5 miles of hiking trails turn into a neatly groomed cross-country ski trail, and a warming house is available for outdoor enthusiasts from 8:00 A.M. to sunset daily.

Bryant Lake Regional Park
6800 Rowland Road, Eden Prairie
(952) 941-4518

Bryant Lake Regional Park is located south of Minnesota Highway 62 and west of Shady Oak Road on Rowland Road and has a three-season concession plaza, three-season pavilion, a paved boat launch, a fishing pier, a swimming beach, a boat rental building, and 3 miles of turf and paved hiking/biking trails. The 170-acre park also provides habitat for deer, waterfowl, and songbirds; fishing, boating, swimming, and ice fishing are just some of the ways visitors can get close to the natural beauty of this metro-area park. Located in the suburb of Eden Prairie, the park is set in a vista of rolling hills that block out the surrounding city lights and sounds, making it a perfect spot for an urban escape.

Carver Park Reserve
7025 Victoria Drive, Victoria
(952) 472-4911

While visiting a park as large as Carver Park Reserve in the suburbs may seem natural today, it was quite controversial when first proposed. Carver Park was authorized for purchase on December 3, 1964, and a lawsuit requesting the purchase be found illegal was soon filed by developers who wanted the land for housing. The claim was rejected in April 1966, and Hennepin Parks went on to purchase parkland in Anoka, Scott, and Wright Counties. Today folks throughout the metro area are the beneficiaries of Hennepin Parks' early imperialist urges, and the trailblazer, Carver Park Reserve, is one of the crown jewels of the system, with 3,500 acres with lakeshore frontage on six major lakes.

At the head of the reserve is Lowry Nature Center, designed for adults, schoolchildren, and families alike. Lowry Nature Center offers programs that focus on Carver's abundant natural resources, ranging from fall bird migration and waterfowl watches to the springtime activity of maple syrup–making and stargazing in the summer, as well as tracking mink, voles, and foxes, and building snowcaves. The park itself is home to deer, foxes, owls, hawks, and many other animals that can be seen from roads and trails. Wetland animals can be seen from more than 1,700 feet of boardwalk that takes you through marsh and tamarack swamps. For small children, HABITATS, a creative education play area, features larger-than-life flowers to climb on, dragonfly eyes to peer through, and a beaver lodge to sit in.

Park facilities include a boat launch, 54 campsites at Lake Auburn, and four different lakes for canoeing, fishing, and ice fishing as well as trails for hiking, horseback riding, cross-country skiing, snowmobiling, and snowshoeing. On winter weekends the park turns a wood-heated barn into a warming house for outdoor enthusiasts, with snack counters and rest room facilities conveniently located nearby. Cross-country skis, Norwegian kick sleds, and bicycles can be seasonally rented from the park.

Clifton E. French Regional Park
County Road 9 on the north shore of
Medicine Lake, Plymouth
(763) 559–8891

Clifton E. French Regional Park, usually shortened to just "French Park" by locals, was named for the first superintendent of the Hennepin County Park Reserve District. Under French's direction, the Hennepin County park system underwent an unprecedented period of development through the '60s up until his retirement in 1984. Under his guidance, Hennepin Parks became the largest landowner in the county and acquired parcels in four adjacent counties.

Located on 310 acres on Medicine Lake—which was originally called I (mouth), CA-PA GO! (beaver), CA-GA-STA-KA (free from ice, broken), MDE (lake) by the Dakota Indians—French Regional Park features a variety of water-based activities. A self-guided canoe trail through the backwaters of beautiful Medicine Lake provides intimate views of wetland wildlife. Monthly outdoor education programs for the public feature such activities as maple syruping, bird-watching, and guided hikes to beaver lodges. The open landscape of rolling glacial hills is broken along the lake and lagoons with second-growth forest. Windy days can be chilly, but the fine vista of the downtown Min-

neapolis skyline in the late afternoon sun is well worth it. This is not a place to come for solitude. The park's central location attracts more than 20,000 skiers—half at night—during a good season.

The visitor center has a concession area with rental equipment, from cross-country skis to volleyballs. A creative play area is available for people of all ages and abilities, and a shuttle tram runs throughout the summer season between the visitor center and the swimming beach. French Park's playground recently won recognition from the Playground Appreciation Association, sponsored by the Minneapolis Public School System and voted on by kids of the schools themselves, for having the best "training ground" for tag players for its "many opportunities for climbing, rolling, running, falling, and navigating through cargo nets."

Coon Rapids Dam Regional Park
9750 Egret Boulevard, Coon Rapids
(763) 424–8172

Situated on the banks of the Mississippi River, the 610-acre Coon Rapids Dam Regional Park offers visitors the chance to see our nation's greatest river up close. The centerpiece of this large regional park is the newly refurbished Coon Rapids Dam, which spans the Mississippi River. A wide dam walkway, usable by pedestrians, bicyclists, and in-line skaters, allows visitors a unique opportunity to walk across a working dam, as well as affords a scenic view of the riverway above and below the dam.

Interpretive signs describing the history of the dam and various natural features related to the river line the bridge on the river side of the railing; the visitor center provides outstanding exhibits about the history and construction of the dam, especially focusing on the economic, cultural, and environmental impact the Mississippi River has on the lives of people who live and depend on having a clean and well-managed riverway that extends all the way south to New Orleans. Boating is allowed north of the visitor center, with a boat launch for accessing the north Mississippi River waterway through a naturally sheltered backwater.

Insiders' Tip

Persons age 65 and older who meet income eligibility standards can receive a free Park Patron package, which gives them free parking at parks year-round and discounts at a variety of golf courses and on rental equipment and items at the parks' gift shops.

Trout fishing is also allowed in Cenaiko Trout Lake, a beautiful lake stocked with rainbow and brook trout (Minnesota fishing license with State Trout Stamp affixed required), located at the east side of the park. Fishing piers are also located on the southern shore of Cenaiko Trout Lake, and bank fishing is reasonably clear with some brush and weeds. Bait and tackle supplies can be purchased at the visitor center for reasonable prices.

A 12-foot-wide pedestrian walkway is part of the recent restoration of the dam, and bicycles and in-line skate rentals are available at the visitor center for use on many of the paths. The Coon Rapids Dam Walk gives park visitors the opportunity to experience being on top of a dam. The stunning Native Prairie Restoration Area is on the nearby banks of the river, just past the visitor center entrance and extending to the picnic plaza. The park also has two well-developed and conveniently linked and accessible asphalt bike/hike trails—all part of the extensive Mississippi River Trail Corridor that leads users south into Anoka Regional Park and eventually connects users with the Minneapolis Parkway Trail System at Boom Island and the Heritage Trail at historic Main Street in Minneapolis.

Cottage Grove Ravine Regional Park
Half a mile east of Washington County Road 19 and Minneapolis Highway 61, Cottage Grove (651) 430–8368

This handsome 506-acre park stays pretty quiet except when the high school teams are practicing. The park name refers to the nearby town (organized in May 1858) and the wooded ravine that was formed in glacial times and may once have been a channel of the St. Croix River. The park is home to a variety of native Minnesota wildlife, including the pileated woodpecker. These spectacular birds have a flaming red crest and can reach 16 inches in height. If a loud jackhammering sound breaks the silence, you'll know they are close by.

In winter this is a great park for the experienced skier, with almost 150 feet in elevation change and some great downhill runs through heavily wooded, dramatic ravines. It is also a popular spot for ski skaters.

Crow-Hassan Park Reserve
West of Rogers on Sylvan Lake Road, Rogers (763) 424–5511

A visit to the 2,600-acre Crow-Hassan Park Reserve invokes images of the early pioneers as they crossed the wilderness in covered wagons. On the prairies of Crow-Hassan Park Reserve, those days are replicated with wagon rides during the annual Prairie Fest, not to mention in the wide, open spaces of the restored prairies themselves. No matter what time of year one visits, the prairie is colorful: Spring brings delicate blue and violet wildflowers, summer produces stands of tall grasses that dance in the breeze, fall offers a spectacular, fluorescent-hued display of reds and oranges, and winter leaves white snow, drifting like ocean waves. It's hard to imagine an endless sea of grass flowing from Minnesota to the Rocky Mountains now that trees, crops, houses, and billboards muddy the view. But one of the best places in the Twin Cities to catch a glimpse of that sweeping landscape is this park, where 600 acres of old farm fields have been transformed back into prairie.

The reintroduction of native grasses and forbs began here in 1969, using seeds from a two-acre remnant of virgin prairie located in the park near Prairie Lake. Other sources were also tapped to complete the collection of nearly 100 species that have been planted since, and with the reintroduction of native grasses and plants, native animals have slowly made their way back to the land as well. Deer, foxes, coyotes, trumpeter swans, hawks, and bald eagles may be seen from the many miles of trails that wind through the park as well as on the nearby Crow River.

For pet owners, more than 30 acres of open space allows dogs to run off-leash; a special permit is required and is available from Hennepin Parks Headquarters for about $25 per year. This is also a popular park for horseback riders, with more than 15 miles of trail dedicated for just this purpose. In winter, cross-country skiing and snowmobiling bring crowds of enthusiasts. The beauty about Crow-Hassan, though, is that in between the rolling hills, the deep prairie grass, and the thick tree cover, you can come out here and be as completely alone as you want to be, even if the park is at peak season.

Elm Creek Park Reserve
County Road 81 and Territorial Road, Osseo
(763) 424-5511

The Elm Creek Park Reserve, located northwest of Osseo, is a beautiful and varied park and nature reserve that makes a concerted effort to provide access to people of all abilities and ages. A swimming beach, creative play area, and a concession stand with volleyball, horseshoe, and bike rentals are located on the premises, and horse trails, cross-country ski trails, hiking trails, and bicycle paths interlace the entire park.

At 4,900 acres, Elm Creek Park Reserve is the largest in the Hennepin Parks' system. Wildlife is abundant in Elm Creek because of the numerous streams and marshes: Herons, ducks, and beavers can be viewed from miles of trails. Coyotes are also known to roam the wilds of Elm Creek Park Reserve, and while your chances of seeing one are slim, their presence attests to the wide expanse of undeveloped land contained here. Five lakes, three streams and wetlands, hardwood forest, and reclaimed farmland provide plenty of elbow room for wildlife and parkgoers alike.

The Eastman Nature Center provides stimulation for curious minds of all ages, with displays giving a concise overview of the reserve's habitat. From here, hikers can go on self-guided tours ranging from wildflower walks to a trip through turtle country. If the displays don't move you into the woods, the enthusiastic naturalists and creative courses (on tagging monarch butterflies, for example) offered here will. On late afternoon weekend days in January and February, Eastman packs them in to view the white-tailed deer that come here to feed.

Elm Creek also has a good-size creative play area and is another recipient of the Playground Appreciation Association Award, voted on by kids of the Minneapolis Public School System.

Hyland Lake Park Reserve
10145 Bush Lake Road, Bloomington
(952) 941-4362

When visiting the 1,000-acre Hyland Lake Park Reserve, one can hardly believe it's located in the middle of the bustling metropolis of Bloomington. The parklands, which include prairie lands, deciduous woods, and Normandale, Hyland, and Bush Lakes, have more than 9 miles of trails for hiking, an additional 5 paved miles for bicycling, and, in winter, 8 miles of groomed trail set aside for cross-country skiing. The first cross-country ski trail in the Twin Cities was cut here, near the old Bush Lake ski jump in the winter of 1965–66. Hyland Lake Park Reserve is now one of the finest and most popular cross-country facilities in the area.

On the lakes, there's a boat landing with a newly built rental/storage facility for canoes, rowboats, and paddleboats, as well as a large fishing pier for shore fishing. Bush Lake has a clean swimming beach with picnic shelters nearby. Skis, bicycles, paddleboats, and seasonal recreation equipment can be rented at the visitor center for reasonable rates.

The Richardson Nature Center, located inside the park, is home to deer, pheasants, and wild songbirds. Richardson's spacious center focuses especially on raptors and raptor recovery, with programs on eagles, owls, hawks, and falcons. You can see ospreys banded and meet live owls, hawks, and kestrels. Other classes taught by naturalists include how to build bluebird houses, identify birds and waterfowl, use natural plant materials to dye things—Easter eggs, yarn, paper—or create nature-friendly lawns.

Interstate State Park/Glacial-Pothole Trail
On Minnesota Highway 8 in Taylors Falls
(651) 465-5711

Carved by glacial meltwater, Interstate State Park follows the cliffs and bluffs bordering the beautiful St. Croix River. Established in 1895 when Minnesota and Wisconsin created separate parks across from each other on the St. Croix River, this was the first example of an interstate collaboration in the country. During the late 1930s, Interstate State Park received the highest number of visitors of any park in the state—327,496 in 1937 alone.

The main attraction of the park, besides the St. Croix, are the unusual basalt formations and potholes and greenstone cliffs that were formed before there was any complex life on Earth. The Precambrian basalt boulders make up the Glacial-Pothole Trail, which is amazing to explore. The Glacial Pothole Trail is a rough-hewn pathway through the maze of "potholes"—deep, perfectly circular holes carved into the hard basalt by glaciers—some of which are hundreds of feet deep and the deepest known glacial potholes in the world. Interstate State Park also holds annual wildflower exhibits, and some of the flowers that bloom here no longer naturally grow anywhere else in the state.

There is much to do at Interstate State Park. Visitors can climb the cliffs of the St. Croix River Dalles, canoe the flatwater, watch kayakers rush through the rapids, or relax on an excursion boat. Spring brings a great diversity of wildflowers and in fall, the St. Croix River Valley forest is ablaze in the autumn colors of red, gold, and orange. The geology that formed this park intrigues visitors and brings geologists from all over the world. At least 10 different lava flows are exposed in the park, along with two distinct glacial deposits and traces of old streams' valleys and faults. The park's visitor center is carved out of the dense, black basalt that makes up most of the Glacial-Pothole Trail and the Glacial Gardens. During the summer, a park naturalist provides tours of the glacial potholes, a landmark of the park, and programs detailing the natural history of the area. The park also has a 22-acre summer campground with 22 electric sites located near the Glacial-Pothole Trail and Glacial Gardens that fills up very quickly in the summer months—reservations are highly encouraged. Canoes can also be rented at the nearby boat dock, and can be reserved by calling the park.

Lake Elmo Park Reserve
1515 Keats Avenue North, Lake Elmo
(One mile north of I–94 on Washington County Road 19)
(651) 430–8370

The Lake Elmo Park Reserve is 2,165 acres of forest, wetlands, and prairie restoration lands. Eighty percent of the parkland is set aside for preservation and protection, and because of this, Lake Elmo is home to a huge variety of native animals, birds, reptiles, and fish. People come to Lake Elmo year-round for both shore and boat fishing, canoeing, hiking, swimming, and cross-country skiing. There are also four campgrounds with a total of 108 campsites, rest room facilities, lighted picnic shelters with electricity, hand pumps for water, and a two-acre swim pond that's regularly maintained by the park.

Lake Maria State Park
11411 Clementa Avenue NW, Monticello
(763) 878–2325 or (800) 246–2267

Visitors who come to Lake Maria State Park will enjoy one of the few remaining stands of the "Big Woods," a maple, oak, and basswood forest that once covered part of southern Minnesota. The park is perfect for hikers, backpackers, horseback riders, and cross-country skiers who enjoy the challenge of the rolling terrain. Take a stroll on the boardwalk that winds through a marsh. Backpack sites, located on remote lakes and ponds throughout the park, are just 2 miles from the trailhead parking lot. New log camper cabins, located near lakes and ponds, provide bunk beds for six people and a table and benches for campers who want more of the creature comforts.

The Big Woods was a forest that once occupied 3,030 square miles in south-central Minnesota. The forest was composed of maple, basswood, white and red elm, red oak, tamarack, and red cedar on the banks of numerous lakes. The trees were so thick that sunlight couldn't penetrate to the forest floor in some places. French explorers who came to the area called the forest "Bois Grand," or "Bois Fort," which was later amended by English settlers to the "Big Woods." Today, farms, towns, suburbs, and industry have replaced much of the Big Woods. Fortunately, the 1,590 acres located at the northern edge of what was once the Big Woods retain a remnant of the grandness of these original forests as Lake Maria State Park.

Today the park maintains more than 20 miles of summer hiking trails, 16 miles of groomed cross-country ski trails, and 3 miles of winter hiking trails. Snowshoeing is permitted anywhere in the park except on groomed ski trails, and snowshoes can be rented at the visitor center for about $6.00 a day. Boat and canoe rentals are available through the visitor center in summer, and three camper cabins and numerous secluded primitive campsites are available for rent year-round.

Although there is no full-time naturalist on staff, interpretive programs are available year-round. The marshes, potholes, and lakes here provide excellent habitat for wildlife, and approximately 205 different species of birds have been reported living in, or passing through the park on seasonal migrations. Visitors have seen bald eagles, Cooper's hawks, Franklin's gulls, osprey, egrets, loons, trumpeter swans, great blue herons, marsh hawks, and goldfinches, as well as screech, great-horned, snowy, and short-eared owls. Shrews, bats, moles, rabbits, woodchucks, red and gray squirrels, pocket gophers, beaver, mice, fishers, muskrats, mink, striped skunks, red foxes, and white-tailed deer also make Lake Maria State Park their home. Lake Maria is also one of the last remaining natural habitats of the endangered Blanding's turtle, easily identified by bright yellow spots on its shell.

Lake Minnetonka Regional Park
4610 County Road 44, Minnestrista
(952) 474–4822

This new 292-acre park features picnic areas, a visitor center, a fishing pier, a boat launch with 48 car or trailer parking spaces, a unique 1.75-acre upland swimming pond with chlorinated water, and a wheelchair-accessible swimming ramp that

extends into the pond. The visitor center, which was formerly a private residence, contains meeting rooms, a reception area, exhibits concerning the area around Lake Minnetonka and the people and activities associated with it, and an exterior garden area containing a huge variety of native medicinal and herbal plants.

The park has a nice fishing pier, with two seated angler stations, that allows people of all abilities the opportunity to not only enjoy fishing but also to sit on the water and enjoy the beautiful view of the lake. There's also a concession stand next to the changing rooms/bathrooms by the picnic area with accessible tables where folks can purchase goodies while enjoying the water. The beach is very well maintained, with large umbrellas located around the water for families to use to keep themselves cool on the hottest summer days.

Lake Minnewashta Park
Off Minnesota Highway 41 between MN 5 and Minnesota Highway 7,
Chanhassen
(952) 467–4200

Lake Minnewashta Park is a large, suburban park that contains remnants of the Big Woods that once covered this area. Some of the oak trees here are so old that they're more than 12 feet in circumference. An ambitious reforestation project that included the planting of 25,000 new hardwoods was completed a few years ago but will realistically take many years to re-create the leafy canopy that once covered the park.

This park is really tucked away and is

Insiders' Tip
Beer is allowed in cans or bottles in most parks, as is wine. However, kegs and hard liquor are not allowed.

visited mostly by locals, and at times, you probably have a better chance of seeing deer than people while visiting. Lake Minnewashta is a popular fishing lake, allowing powerboats, canoes, and sailboats in summer, and ice fishing in winter.

Lake Rebecca Park Reserve
9831 County Road 50, Rockford
(763) 972-2620

From canoeing on the Crow River to boat and ice fishing on Lake Rebecca, this 2,200-acre park reserve offers outdoor activities in settings that suggest you are much farther away from the metropolitan area than you actually are. Lake Rebecca Park Reserve's gently rolling landscape, with numerous wetland areas, provides a haven for wildlife, including deer, beavers, and waterfowl. This park reserve is also one of the sites for the trumpeter swan restoration program, and several overlooks along hiking trails provide glimpses of these swans, which are the world's largest waterfowl. Boats are available for rent from the park's visitor center, and nonmotorized boat launching is permitted. Reservation picnic areas and group campsites are also available.

Lebanon Hills Regional Park
Pilot Knob Road South of Cliff Road, Eagan
(651) 438-4671

Less than 30 minutes from both downtown Minneapolis and St. Paul, this Dakota County park covers more than 2,000 acres of lakes, marshes, beaches, and trails. Open year-round, the park is divided into east and west sections connected by an immense network of trails. Nearly every outdoor activity is available—swimming in Schultz Lake (one of the few local beaches with lifeguards present), RV and tent camping, hiking, picnicking, horseback riding, mountain biking, and cross-country skiing. Fishing and all non-motorized boats are allowed on Jensen Lake, and in winter, ice fishing is allowed on the lake as well.

Lebanon Hills is a popular destination for winter sports enthusiasts. The park has two great ski areas: the 4K skate-ski lanes just off of Johnny Cake Road offer long, tough uphills and fast, winding downhills and is definitely not a place for beginners (this area doubles as a mountain bike area in summer, and the rock-and-dirt trails don't hold snow all that well), and the 19.8K classic-track area, just east of Pilot Knob Road. The trail system was originally laid out for hiking and horse paths, so some downhill corners can be awkward for skiers. Cross-country ski and snowmobile trails snake through the park's wooded, hilly terrain, and hot cocoa and snacks are available at the warming house at Schultz Lake.

Long Lake Regional Park
1500 Old MN 8, New Brighton
(651) 777-1707

Long Lake Regional Park is located in the city of New Brighton in the northwestern part of Ramsey County. The 218 acres of parkland include 1.5 miles of shoreline on Long Lake and a natural area around Rush Lake, a nonrecreational lake. Rush Lake is surrounded by cattail marshes, oak woods, and a nine-acre restored prairie, seeded in 1987, which is now beginning to reach maturity and offers a beautiful display of prairie flowers that bloom throughout the summer.

The park features an extensive trail system, a beautiful swimming beach, and a large picnic area near the swimming beach. Visitors can watch mallards paddle through the cattail marshes, take a stroll through the oak woods, or bike around the nine-acre restored prairie. After a dip in Long Lake, make tracks to the beach house for snacks, rest rooms, changing rooms, and showers. A large picnic pavilion is complete with kitchen and public rest rooms, and the group picnic area features a game field, a volleyball court, hiking/biking trails, and a wheelchair-accessible play area. On the south end of Long Lake, you can launch your boat and park your trailer—or just fish off the pier. Although the grounds are spread out quite a bit (the fishing pier is a couple of miles away on the south end of Long Lake, while most of the park is on the north end of the lake), the layout of the park's facilities is actually very convenient. The pier has its own parking area with rest rooms and a clean water source, and access from there to the pier is a paved walkway that's level and free of obstacles. Seated angler stations are situated on the pier for additional comfort and convenience.

Minnesota Valley National Wildlife Refuge and Recreation Area
3815 East 80th Street, Bloomington
(952) 854-5900

Only minutes from the Twin Cities and the airport, Minnesota Valley National Wildlife Refuge and Recreation Area is dedicated to preserving the wildlife of Minnesota River habitats. This archipelago of river-valley land parcels functions as a federally managed nature preserve, particularly for waterfowl and migrating birds using the Minnesota River flyway. All told, 10,514 acres are at your disposal, including the Minnesota Valley Trail, which links Fort Snelling State Park and units of the Minnesota Valley National Wildlife Refuge to waysides and other public lands. The area is ideal for hiking, biking, cross-country skiing, mountain biking, and snowmobiling. The landscapes are just as diverse as the trail system and include wetlands, floodplain forest, remnants of farmlands settled in the late 1800s, and blufftop oak savanna. Wildlife observation and bird watching are popular activities year-round, while seasonally, canoeing, cross-country skiing, bicycling, snowshoeing, and camping give visitors additional views of the park.

In the Minnesota Valley Recreation Area you can see the only remaining building from the town of St. Lawrence, visit the Jabs Farm Homestead, or ride your bike across a 1900s railroad bridge.

Today, a brightly lit, modern interpretive center in the park contains engaging displays of Minnesota River Valley history, ranging from its pollution perils—and comebacks—to a primer on the glacial forces that created the valley. The refuge's real strength is in its programs led by talented naturalists, who offer field trips to the woodcock dancing grounds in spring and to the heron rookery in winter via cross-country skis. The wildlife refuge occupies only a fraction of the Minnesota Valley Recreation Area, which is classified as a Minnesota State Park and stretches about 75 miles from historic Fort Snelling to Le Sueur.

Murphy-Hanrehan Park Reserve
15501 Murphy Lake Road, Savage
(952) 447-6913

The glacial ridges and hilly terrain of northwest Scott County make Murphy-Hanrehan one of the most challenging cross-country ski areas found in the Twin Cities. With the exception of the trails, this 2,400-acre park remains undeveloped. The park's hilly terrain attracts mountain bikers, horseback riders, and endurance hikers in summer and cross-country skiers, snowmobilers, and especially brave downhill skiers in winter.

Noerenberg Memorial Gardens
2840 North Shore Drive, Wayzata
(763) 559-6700

In 1972 the last surviving child of Frederick and Johanna Noerenberg—heirs to the Grain Belt brewery fortune—bequeathed the family lakeside estate to Hennepin County. The bequest stipulated that the 73 acres of flower beds, shade trees, and ornamental grasses be opened to the public, and that the enormous Queen Anne house, built in 1890 and one of the first constructed on Lake Minnetonka's shores, be torn down to prevent a roving public from wandering through the intimate remains of the past. The bequest also called for a memorial to be constructed from the housing materials, which became the white-pillared colonnade that now stands on the grounds. The family grape arbor and gazebo/boathouse were also left standing; they are the sole man-made structures on the premises.

Today, the park features beautifully sculpted flower gardens that include a wide variety of unusual annuals and perennials, an assortment of grasses, and a large day lily collection. The park is a beautiful spot to stroll through and enjoy the flowers—however, part of the bequest of the Noerenberg family states that no picnics or boating activities are to be permitted on the premises, so mild hiking and sight-seeing covers the range of what park visitors can do here.

St. Croix Bluffs Regional Park
10191 St. Croix Trail South, Hastings
(651) 430–8240

Five miles south of Afton, this 579-acre regional park is made up of rolling hills, blufftop hardwood forests, and nearly a mile of scenic St. Croix River shoreline. Woodlands and ravines cut through tight bluffs to the riverbanks, making great bird-watching areas for everything from eagles to wild turkeys. The park is located on the west bank of the St. Croix River, and has 0.75 mile of river frontage. Swimming is not allowed in the St. Croix, but boating, fishing, and ice fishing are.

St. Croix National Scenic Riverway
401 Hamilton Street, St. Croix Falls, Wisconsin
(715) 483–3288

The St. Croix River stretches more than 150 miles and partially forms the boundary between Minnesota and Wisconsin. It is also the only river in the world that's protected along its entire length. Beginning near Gordon, Wisconsin, it flows southerly to St. Croix Falls. The Lower St. Croix flows from St. Croix Falls dam to Prescott, Wisconsin, where it joins the Mississippi River. The Lower St. Croix is deeper, wider, and slower moving than the Upper St. Croix, making it a great place to fish, canoe, water-ski, and swim. Hot air balloon rides are available year-round and provide an excellent view of the river and its lush banks from on high. Winter activities include ice fishing, downhill and cross-country skiing, tubing, snowmobiling, and sledding. Nearby Lake St. Croix is formed by a dam on the Mississippi River and is also very popular for water recreation.

Spring Lake Park Reserve
Off County Road 42, Hastings
(651) 438–4660

Enjoy the feel of northern Minnesota while hiking or skiing the scenic trails that wind through the woods and along the bluffs high above the Mississippi River. Spring Lake Park Reserve provides a scenic and peaceful setting for nature lovers to appreciate, as well as a model airplane flying field that will delight adults and children alike and a challenging, state-of-the-art archery trail. A youth campground with a heated lodge and an outdoor classroom is also available to youth groups interested in outdoor educational/recreational activities.

Square Lake County Park
Marine on St. Croix
(651) 731–3851

The 27-acre Square Lake County Park is known for having one of the clearest lakes in Minnesota, making it a popular spot for scuba divers, swimmers, and anglers alike. The lake is regularly stocked with trout and has a 950-foot clean sand beach, a concession stand where food and fishing supplies can be purchased, and rest rooms with showers.

Theodore Wirth Park
1339 Theodore Wirth Parkway, Minneapolis
(612) 661–4800

Theodore Wirth first toured the parkland he would oversee in January 1906 using two horses and a sleigh, crossing what was then open country as he traveled from park to park. Wirth spent the next four decades developing these natural resources into one of the finest municipal park systems in the country. After he retired, his favorite park of the bunch was named in his honor.

Theodore Wirth Park, or just Wirth Park, as it's usually called, is a huge chunk of land extending from Minneapolis at Glenwood Avenue to Lowry Avenue and from Vincent Avenue into Golden Valley. This beautiful 500-acre park surrounds Wirth Lake, which has a swimming beach as well as a boat launch. There's also an archery range, a playground, tennis courts, the Theodore Wirth Golf Course, and the Eloise Butler Wildflower Garden.

This is a popular park for locals in winter. Behind Theodore Wirth Park's great sledding hill (on the golf course's

10th fairway) is the lighted snow-tubing hill, which isn't too steep and has a tow rope. Cold, hungry snow-tubers will appreciate the nearby Swiss Chalet, which has a fireplace and serves fast-food fare such as burgers and fries. Completed in 1923, the Swiss Chalet is the perfect headquarters for a winter recreational retreat and is based on a miniature chalet that Theodore Wirth had brought back from his honeymoon in Switzerland years before. Both a skate-skiing course and an intermediate traditional trail start from the chalet. From the top of the skiing hill, the Minneapolis skyscrapers glittering in the afternoon sun may startle you with their closeness. This is known as one of the prettiest places in the Cities for nighttime skiing.

Named for schoolteacher Eloise Butler, who is buried in the bird sanctuary, the Eloise Butler Wildflower Garden and Bird Sanctuary is a favorite spot for urbanites to escape the realities of city life and walk among the brilliant wildflower plots that are tended as carefully as they were when Butler was still alive. Eloise Butler feared that the wild beauty of Minnesota would be destroyed the way the old-growth hardwood forests near her childhood home in Maine had been, and she set about to save it by turning the three acres of land she owned into an immense wild garden full of native plants and grasses. After her death, the Minneapolis Park Board created a preserve for native flora in her honor, which included her own original garden and has grown over the years to include an additional 12 acres. The park draws huge crowds of native and migratory songbirds, including meadowlarks, red-wing blackbirds, and finches.

Wild River State Park
10 miles north of Center City
(651) 583-2125

Wild River State Park was established to protect the area's natural and cultural resources and to provide recreational opportunities along the St. Croix River. The park's name, "Wild River," is derived from the fact that the St. Croix River was one of the original eight rivers protected by the U.S. Congress through the Wild and Scenic Rivers Act of 1968. Nearly 5,000 of the park's total 6,803 acres were donated by Northern States Power Company (now Xcel Energy).

Wild River State Park attracts people who enjoy camping, hiking, horseback riding, canoeing, interpretive programs, self-guided trails, and cross-country skiing. Day visitors can enjoy a leisurely paddle down the St. Croix River from the Sunrise River access to the southern park river access. The park provides opportunities for semimodern camping, group camping, backpack camping, canoe camping, and walk-in camping. Visitors who want modern amenities can reserve the guest house, which provides a living room, dining room, kitchen, and fireplace. The park also has two camping cabins, which include bunk beds, a table, and benches. An all-season trail center is a great spot to relax after hiking or cross-country skiing on the 35-mile trail system. A visitor center with exhibits and environmental education programs is open year-round.

Naturalist programs at the park are available year-round, to individuals as well as schools and other groups upon request. The park maintains 35 miles of groomed cross-country ski trails, 1.5 miles of packed hiking trails, and 1.5 miles of snowshoe trails—snowshoeing is permitted anywhere in the park except on groomed ski trails. Guided snowshoe tours include a visit to a beaver pond, identifying and following animal tracks, or a challenging trip down a short, steep slope to a hidden prairie (basic instructions on how to snowshoe are covered before the hikes, and snowshoes are provided at no charge for participants). The park also offers one-day classes on tapping maple trees for sap and making maple syrup.

Wild River provides habitat for a variety of wildlife. Hawks, owls, eagles, and a diversity of songbirds are common. The tracks of beaver, raccoons, foxes, coyotes, otters, mink, and deer are often seen in the soft earth or snow. Northern pike, walleye, and smallmouth bass are found in the St. Croix River. Squirrels and other small mammals thrive in oak forests and savannas; the prairie restoration sites are home to flocks of meadowlarks and sparrows.

William O'Brien State Park
**16821 O'Brien Trail North, Marine on St. Croix
(651) 433–0500**

A great "getaway" park only 45 minutes from the Twin Cities, the 1,520 acres of William O'Brien State Park provide a beautiful setting for quality recreation along the banks of the St. Croix River. The park is named for William O'Brien, a pioneer lumberman in the St. Croix River Valley, its man-made lake is named for O'Brien's daughter, Alice, who donated an additional 180 acres to the park in 1945.

O'Brien is an extremely popular camping spot, and in the summer, the first-come, first-served campsites fill up quickly, especially on weekends; campsite reservations are strongly encouraged. The lower campground offers great river views, while the upper has both sunny, open spots and deeply wooded ones. The park has 125 drive-in campsites, 61 electric with a 60-foot RV limit, two walk-in sites, seven wheelchair-accessible sites with wheelchair-accessible flush toilets and showers, four group camps, and a select number of camping cabins available to the public. Conveniently, the park's open picnic shelter sells firewood and ice to campers, and public phones are also available for campers' use.

Hiking trails offer quiet exploration of the park's rolling, wooded hills. For anglers, the channels of the St. Croix have northerns, walleye, bass, and trout. Ideal for canoeing, the river is also a migratory pathway that offers visitors an exciting diversity of sights and sounds. Canoes can be rented from the park for an outing on the St. Croix or on Lake Alice. Swimming in the river isn't allowed, but Lake Alice has a sandy beach and shallow water close to shore. On clear days you can see Taylors Falls from one overlook, and, although the park is heavily used, the 12 miles of hiking trails are rarely crowded. Many of these hiking trails (11.5 miles worth) become cross-country trails for intermediate and expert skiers during winter. The park maintains 12 miles of groomed cross-country ski trails and 11 miles of skate-ski trails—snowshoeing is permitted anywhere in the park except on groomed ski trails. The park also has a warming house for huddling in after playing in the snow.

> ## Insiders' Tip
> Dogs are permitted on Regional Trail corridors and on designated turf trails in all parks. Pets must be on a leash no more than 6 feet long, and owners must clean up after pets and dispose of pet feces in a sanitary manner.

Spectator Sports

Auto Racing
Baseball
Basketball
Football
Horse Racing
Hockey
Soccer

People in the Twin Cities love sports. It is, however, a love tempered by regional priorities and perspectives on life. There are sports fanatics in this town, men and women whose hearts bleed the purple of the Minnesota Vikings football team or have not missed a Twins game in decades, but most Twin Citians practice a little more restraint. They love the local teams but also value a summer trip "up north" to the cabin at the lake or a night at the numerous other entertainment options the Twin Cities offer.

Not surprisingly, given that downtown St. Paul is only 20 miles from the Wisconsin border and downtown Minneapolis another 10 miles away, the Twin Cities also have a large number of fans of Wisconsin sports teams. Although for those filled with Purple Pride for the Vikings, the Green Bay Packers are a hated NFC North rival, a sizable proportion of Twin Citians don the green and gold when the Packers come to town. The Vikings-Packers game at the Metrodome is almost always an extremely raucous affair, with tickets nearly impossible to come by. To the delight of Vikings fans, the Packers seem to come apart at the seams in the noisy Metrodome, even in playoff years. The Cities also draw heavily from western Wisconsin visitors, who come to town to see the Packers, Badgers, Bucks, and Brewers play the hometown teams because the Cities are a lot closer to home than Madison, Milwaukee, or Green Bay. The Golden Gophers–Badgers football game at the Metrodome (played every other year) routinely draws the largest crowd of the season to the stadium, and the University of Minnesota charges considerably higher ticket prices for this game than the Gophers other matchups—diehard attendees are willing to pay any amount necessary to view this heated rivalry.

The Twin Cities have an enormous wealth of spectator sports options. All of the major professional sports call the Twin Cities home, including Minnesota Twins baseball, Minnesota Timberwolves basketball, Minnesota Vikings football, and the most recent addition, Minnesota Wild hockey. The area also is home to the WNBA's Minnesota Lynx women's professional basketball team. Another spectator sports choice is University of Minnesota Big Ten collegiate basketball, football, hockey, as well as numerous additional men's and women's sports teams. And for those who enjoy watching independent minor league baseball outside in the summer, the area hosts the St. Paul Saints of the Northern League. The Twin Cities metro area also has auto racing.

In competition with spectator sports are an astounding array of summertime outdoor activities. In the Twin Cities, summertime is cherished because of Minnesota's often long and harsh winters. Hence, here in the "Land of 10,000 Lakes," unparalleled numbers of locals venture on weekend getaways to boats, cabins, and fishing, where they frequently bring a radio along for the Twins game or other sporting events. Twin Citians' love affair with spectator sports and summer sunshine is reflected in the tremendous success of the St. Paul Saints.

Twin Cities sports fans love winners. Win or lose, the teams receive support, but when they win, the area erupts. The Twins' two world championships in '87 and '91, as well as their improbable trip to the American League Championship Series in 2002 in a year Major League Baseball tried to contract the team, created a colossal public outpouring of local pride. St. Paul and Minneapolis streets were flooded with happy citizens waving their "homer hankies" and celebrating their team.

The collective bargaining agreement between the owners and players settled in August 2002 took contraction off the table—for a few years at least. The Twins, like the Vikings and the Golden Gophers football team, are trying to secure funding for a new stadium. Although the Twins' stadium desires seem to be the top priority (among the three teams vying for new stadiums) for state lawmakers, a time of soaring budget deficits and limited funds available from the city of Minneapolis mean that the fight for new stadiums is likely to go on for a while.

When Twin Cities sports teams lose, radio talk shows are flooded with calls criticizing and wondering where the teams went wrong. Despite the many activities available to Twin Citians, many locals live vicariously through their sports teams. After a Vikings loss the mood is somber when returning to work on Monday, especially if it's a loss to the Green Bay Packers.

Now is an exciting time for Twin Cities sports, with most teams competitive and the 2000 season's arrival of a new franchise, the Minnesota Wild of the National Hockey League. The Wild are the first professional sports team to call St. Paul home, in a state-of-the-art new facility, the Xcel Energy Center. "The X" has immediately improved the nightlife in St. Paul and has attracted a diehard fan base. The Vikings also have a bright future behind one of the NFL's best young passing teams, quarterback Daunte Culpepper and wide receiver Randy Moss.

When in the Twin Cities, be sure to watch our sports teams. There is definitely something for everyone. Unlike in many other cities, parking is relatively easy to attend games at Twin Cities sports facilities, which are surrounded by parking ramps and pay lots. Ticket prices are also more reasonable than many larger markets; always check ahead, since ticket prices do frequently change. The only exception is Minnesota Vikings games, which in recent years have routinely sold out before the start of the season; ticket prices start at around $50 per seat. If you want to see the Vikings, it is best to plan early to secure tickets.

Auto Racing

One Twin Cities spectator sports option is auto racing. There are two locations in the Twin Cities for fans of auto racing. NASCAR racing fans can catch their fill at these tracks during spring, summer, and fall.

Racing Series. Late-model NASCARs race at Elko Speedway. The track is ⅜ of a mile with an asphalt and granite aggregate surface and high banking.

Elko Speedway usually has races from April through September, with races beginning in the early evening on Friday and Saturday.

Elko Speedway
26350 France Avenue, Elko
(952) 461–7223 or (800) 479–3630

For more than 15 years, Elko Speedway has been affiliated with NASCAR. Over the past decade Elko Speedway has witnessed spectator counts double and competitor counts more than double, which comes as no surprise to fans of the track.

Elko Speedway is one of only 100 short racetracks in the nation sanctioned by NASCAR, and a member of the Winston

Raceway Park
1 Checkered Flag Boulevard, Shakopee
(952) 445–2257

Raceway Park also offers NASCAR racing. This track has had racing for more than 40 years and emphasizes racing in a safe family-oriented atmosphere. Raceway Park is in Shakopee, a beautiful town in the Twin Cities area, which is also home to Valleyfair Amusement Park.

The most talented local drivers race at Raceway Park. There are many racing events at the track geared toward children, such as novelty events.

Baseball

The Twin Cities offer several choices for baseball fans. The Minnesota Twins and the St. Paul Saints offer two distinctly different baseball options. The Minnesota Twins are in the American League Central Division of Major League Baseball, and they provide major league caliber baseball in the climate-controlled environment of the Hubert H. Humphrey Metrodome. In contrast, the St. Paul Saints play a whole other brand of baseball at Midway Stadium, where the Saints are an unaffiliated minor league team in the Northern League. Since the team's return in 1993, they have had consistent near sellouts because of the Twin Cities' love of outdoor baseball and the team's colorful marketing and promotions. Both the Saints and the Twins have devoted followers of their distinct brands of baseball.

Minnesota Twins
Metrodome, 34 Kirby Puckett Place,
Minneapolis
(612) 375-7454 or (800) 33-TWINS
www.twins.mlb.com

After the 1960 season, the Washington Senators relocated to Minnesota. Oddly, throughout the Twins' history in Minnesota, there has been talk of the Twins relocating. In the last decade, "the stadium issue" has been a nagging question for owner Carl Pohlad and Minnesota politicians. The Twins want a modern ballpark like Baltimore, Cleveland, Milwaukee, and many other cities have built in the past decade. However, Twins ownership has no legitimate plans to move.

In 2002 the Minnesota Twins shocked most of Major League Baseball by advancing to the American League Championship Series, where they finally fell to the eventual World Champion Anaheim Angels. For years under longtime manager Tom Kelly and the tight wallet of owner Carl Pohlad, the Twins organization cut salaries by signing young, unproven play-

ers. However, under new manager Rod Gardenhire in 2002, the Twins proved they were quite talented at spotting raw talent and developing young players into champions. Much of the championship team remains in Twins uniforms, and their future seems bright for the next few years.

When the Washington Senators arrived in Minnesota, they were renamed the Twins after the Twin Cities of Minneapolis and St. Paul. The Twins were the baseball team of the upper Midwest. Twins ball games were broadcast not only on WCCO radio in Minneapolis but also on affiliates in greater Minnesota and throughout the Dakotas. The Twins reliance on fans from throughout the upper Midwest would convince the Twins, Vikings, and local politicians that a domed stadium was necessary to guarantee that games were played and were comfortable for fans. But the Metrodome did not enter the picture until 1982.

The Twins played at Metropolitan Stadium in Bloomington, a large suburb south of Minneapolis and next to the Minneapolis International Airport, from 1960 through 1981. Metropolitan Stadium, or the Met, was an expanded minor league ballpark for the defunct Minneapolis Millers. Currently, the Met is the site of the Mall of America. The Met stadium's home plate remains on display at Knott's Camp Snoopy.

The Met was host to both the 1965 All-Star Game and World Series, where the Twins lost the best of seven series to Sandy Koufax and the Los Angeles Dodgers. Har-

Insiders' Tip

If you plan on attending a Twins game with your family, try the family pack, which includes four general admission tickets, hot dogs, soft drinks, and a parking pass.

mon Killebrew, Tony Oliva, and Bobby Allison led the powerful Twins sluggers in the late 1960s. In 1969 and 1970 the Twins would lose twice to the Baltimore Orioles in the American League Championship Series; the Twins would not return to postseason play until the '87 season.

The organization did not perform as well in the '70s, when the Twins had a .500 record during most of the decade. Fans became frustrated with owner Cal Griffith, who often traded stars such as Rod Carew, Bert Blyleven, and even Hall of Famer Harmon Killebrew to trim the payroll.

In 1982 the new Hubert H. Humphrey Metrodome opened in downtown Minneapolis. Attendance did not improve, and the Twins increasingly dismal performance on the field made sales at the gates plummet. The Griffith family decided they could no longer financially compete with the increasingly corporate-owned baseball clubs. In 1984 local banker Carl Pohlad purchased the Twins.

Ironically, Pohlad bought a team loaded with young talent that would win two World Series. The young Twins included sluggers Kent Hrbek, Gary Gaetti, and Kirby Puckett. The Twins became renowned for their power at the "Homerdome." Besides the Twins powerful hitting, they also had outstanding pitchers Frank Viola and Jeff Reardon. This core of players propelled the Twins to its first World Championship in '87.

The attendance for Twins games was tremendous even after they began to sputter with losing seasons in '89 and '90. The Twins began to rebuild and, retaining the core of Hrbek and Puckett, made some key acquisitions. The Twins beat Atlanta in seven games in the '91 World Series.

After the euphoria of the '91 World Series Championship, the Twins entered a decade-long stretch of losing seasons as they rebuilt with raw talent with the hope of eventually competing with such deep-pocket, deep-talent teams as the Yankees and Braves. Dedicated Twins fans were rewarded when their team won the Central Division crown in 2002 and beat the Oakland A's in the Divisional Series—only to lose to the Angels in the first American League Championship Series in the Metrodome since 1991.

The Twins continue to play at the Hubert H. Humphrey Metrodome, or "the Dome" in local parlance. The Dome, a large concrete structure capped with an expansive teflon bubble, is located in downtown Minneapolis and is surrounded by parking lots. Fans of the Dome enjoy its steady temperature, in the low '70s. Detractors find the Dome's environment sterile and dull and at times incredibly loud. The stadium has been renovated and revamped several times since opening in 1982 and is clean and comfortable, especially during a spring blizzard. However, there are some significant disadvantages for baseball fans. Seating down both the third base and first base lines requires patrons to crane their necks because of the sight lines, which were developed for football.

Visiting outfielders and infielders fielding pop-ups complain bitterly about the roof, which is almost exactly the color of a baseball. The Astroturf field, a bit of a dinosaur in Major League stadiums nowadays, makes for fast action, but the hard surface is also known to cause injuries to running and sliding players.

Despite its shortcomings, the Dome is an adequate professional baseball facility. Hopefully, in the near future the Twins and local politicians can amicably resolve further "stadium issues."

Twins tickets can be purchased several ways and are readily available. For the 2003 season, ticket prices ranged from $6.00 for upper deck general admission to $31.00 for the "lower club" area behind home plate. Of course, these prices are subject to change.

The Twins also have special offers and promotional events. An exceptional value is the family pack: for $29, four general admission tickets, four hot dogs, four soft drinks, and one parking pass are provided. The price is subject to change, but the family pack has been an ongoing promotion for more than a decade. Another special promotion is Twins Knothole Days games. Knothole Days allow a paying adult to bring children to games for free. The free seats are always upper level general admission, and the sponsor and number of children who get in for free frequently changes. However, this has been a popular promotion since the '70s.

Twins tickets are available on the team's Web site, by phone, and in person. The Twins ticket office is located on the west side of the Dome facing the Minneapolis downtown skyline. Twins tickets can also be purchased at Twins Pro Shops in Apple Valley and Roseville and by mail by writing to: Minnesota Twins Ticket Office SDS 12-1466, P.O. Box 86, Minneapolis, Minnesota 55486-1466; be sure to include $4.00 for shipping and handling, and provide the game dates, seating preferences, and a legible return address.

St. Paul Saints
Midway Stadium, 1771 Energy Park Drive, St. Paul
(651) 644–6659
www.spsaints.com

On September 6, 1995, the independent minor league St. Paul Saints had 4,637 fans attend their playoff game, while only 2,700 showed up for the Twins game. The Twins and Saints offer two distinct options for baseball fans. The Saints have the advantage of summer outdoor baseball, something Twin Citians have sorely missed since the Twins moved to the Dome in 1982.

The St. Paul Saints have a long history in the Twin Cities. Saints history dates back to the 1890s, when they were alternately called the Apostles. Even before the original incarnation of the St. Paul Saints, a rivalry had developed between various Minneapolis franchises. The Saints served as the minor league affiliate of several teams before forming their most famous partnership. In the '40s the Saints became the top franchise in the Brooklyn Dodgers farm system, and the Minneapolis Millers became the top New York Giants affiliate. Future Dodgers Duke Snider and Roy Campanella played with the Saints before becoming major league stars. The Saints continued to play in St. Paul until the Twins arrived after the 1960 season. However, this was not the end for the Saints.

The Saints returned to St. Paul on June 18, 1993. Led by team president Mike Veeck, son of Hall of Fame owner Bill Veeck, the Saints played a colorful brand of baseball in the Northern League. Special promotions such as movies after ball games, haircuts at Midway Stadium, and numerous tailgating events made for a unique baseball experience. While detractors pointed to the low caliber of play, the Saints consistently provided competitive and interesting ball. The first Saints season had 25 sellouts, and they won their first Northern League title. Midway Stadium expanded to 6,329 capacity for the 1994 season. The Saints continued their magic, winning three Northern League titles in their first four years.

In 1997 the Saints received national exposure when they signed Ila Borders, the first woman to pitch in an all-men's professional baseball league. Borders's career with the Saints was brief. She appeared in seven games without a win or loss decision, and she was traded to Northern League rival Duluth-Superior in June of the same year.

Since then the Saints have continued to shine, regularly winning titles and returning to the playoffs. The Saints success on the field and in attendance has drawn national attention. Stories on the Saints have appeared on ABC's *Nightline*, *60 Minutes*, MTV's *Buzzkill*, and *Wide World of Sports*. The Saints continue to provide an interesting alternative to Major League Baseball with their traditional version of the game.

The Saints create an ambience reminiscent of the glory days of the national pastime at Midway Stadium. All seats at the stadium have a great view of the game. There are also good concessions and the omnipresent tailgating. Because of long and harsh winters, Twin Citians love outdoor baseball—a beer, a hot dog, summer sun, and baseball.

The St. Paul Saints are a hot ticket in the Twin Cities. However, the methods of purchasing Saints tickets are limited. The Saints can be reached by phone at (651) 644-6659 for phone orders. In addition, tickets may be purchased at the stadium ticket office. Keep in mind that games can and frequently do sell out. As of this writing, it is not possible to purchase Saints tickets on their Web site or by e-mail.

Ticket prices are reasonable, considering there is not a bad seat at Midway Stadium, and in the past have ranged from $4.00 to $8.00, with special discounts for seniors and children age 14 and younger. The Saints accept Visa, MasterCard, and Discover cards.

Parking is readily available for a small fee in the large parking lot abutting Midway Stadium. Feel free to bring some food for tailgating.

Basketball

The Twin Cities have three options for basketball fans: the Minnesota Timberwolves of the NBA, the Minnesota Lynx of the WNBA, and the University of Minnesota Golden Gophers. The Wolves are coming off seven seasons in which they've made the playoffs. In 1999 the WNBA awarded an expansion team to the Twin Cities; the Lynx were not a great success on the court, but they were off the court and in the community. The Lynx have established a loyal fan base, and the organization is prepared for success. In contrast, the Gophers are rebounding after scandal rocked the University of Minnesota during the 1998–1999 season. Despite their recent travails, the Gophers are poised to be competitive in the Big Ten. The Minnesota Golden Gophers women's basketball team finally found success in the

2001–2002 season, making the NCAA tournament for only the second time in school history.

Minnesota Golden Gophers Men's Basketball
Williams Arena, 1925 University Avenue SE, Minneapolis
(612) 624–8080 or (800) U–GOPHER
www.gophersports.com/tickets

The Twin Cities are great places if you're a basketball fan. The area boasts both men's and women's professional teams as well as the collegiate Big Ten men's team, the University of Minnesota Golden Gophers. Unfortunately, in recent years our beloved Gophers have made major mistakes that resulted in severe NCAA sanctions. However, the program seems headed in the right direction under the guidance of coach Dan Monson.

Since the 1895–1896 season the Minnesota Golden Gophers basketball team has played in one of the most august and competitive conferences in collegiate sports, the Big Ten. Former NBA stars Mychal Thompson and Kevin McHale wore the Gophers' maroon and gold, as have a number of other NBA players currently playing and retired.

Gopher boosters abound in the Twin Cities. The University of Minnesota's enrollment consistently ranks in the top among U.S. colleges and universities, but because of the state's population, roughly four and a quarter million people, the Gophers have been at a disadvantage in the Big Ten against the more populous states that are the homes of Michigan and Ohio State.

In March 1998 the *St. Paul Pioneer Press* broke a story about widespread academic fraud in the Gophers basketball program. The University of Minnesota discovered the allegations were true, and the team put itself on academic probation. On October 24, 2000, the NCAA put the Gophers basketball team on probation until October 2004, eliminated five scholarships during the next three seasons, and rescinded the team's postseason wins in the 1994–1998 NCAA and NIT tournaments, including the Gopher's 1998 Final Four appearance.

Wisely moving on after the scandal that resulted in the firing of coach Clem Haskins, the Gophers made a solid decision in hiring Dan Monson, formerly of Gonzaga. Rebuilding the Gophers will be a tough project, but Monson is used to success, after taking little Gonzaga to the "Elite Eight" during the 1998–1999 season. Could he bring the same success to Minnesota's basketball program? Gophers fans hope so!

The Gophers play at Williams Arena, a great place to watch basketball. It is a beautifully renovated brick building that feels comfortable yet electric because of the University of Minnesota students and alumni who attend games at "the old brickyard."

You may purchase Gophers tickets by phone, on-line, or in person at Williams Arena. The University of Minnesota accepts Visa, MasterCard, Novus, and American Express. There is plenty of parking for Gophers basketball in several lots on Oak Street.

Minnesota Golden Gophers Women's Basketball
Williams Arena, 1925 University Avenue SE, Minneapolis
(612) 624–8080 or (800) U–GOPHER
www.gophersports.com/tickets

In 2002 the Minnesota Golden Gophers women's basketball team finished with their best record in more than 20 years, finishing 22–8 just one year after finishing a more typical 8–20. The Gophers finished second in the Big Ten (the best finish in the Big Ten standings in school history), advanced to the NCAA tournament, and finished the season ranked 19th in the country. The team also set attendance records, with 12,142 fans (a single-game record) watching the game against Michigan State on February 24, 2002. Attendance overall was up an astounding 301 percent from 2000–2001, and the women's team averaged 4,360 fans per game.

Under coach Pam Borton, who took over the team in 2002, the future of Golden Gophers women's basketball looks

Historic Williams Arena is the home of the University of Minnesota Golden Gophers men's and women's basketball teams. PHOTO: TODD R. BERGER

bright. Borton went 102–51 during her five years as an assistant coach at Boston College, and her success there as well as in a previous stint as coach at the University of Vermont gives the team proven leadership.

Golden Gophers women's basketball has been in action since 1973 and competed as part of the Big Ten for the first time during the 1982–1983 season. Tickets are available by phone, on-line, or in person at Williams Arena.

Minnesota Lynx
Target Center, 601 First Avenue North, Minneapolis
(612) 673–8400
www.wnba.com/lynx

After beginning play in 1999, the Minnesota Lynx are building a growing fan base because of their activities both on and off the court. As an expansion team, they face all the growing pains of other new WNBA clubs, plus, they are the first women's professional sports team in the Twin Cities to receive significant fan and media attention. However, they have met this challenge and are receiving the respect they deserve.

Over the years there have been several efforts to create women's professional sports leagues. Interest in professional women's sports dates back to women's professional baseball during World War II but has often lacked the financial strength to weather the early years, when it's difficult to turn a profit. After the United States women's basketball team won the gold medal at the '96 Summer Olympics in Atlanta, women's basketball became a popular spectator sport. When it looked like a league would be commercially viable, two women's professional basketball leagues formed—the ABL and the WNBA. The ABL declared bankruptcy after three seasons, freeing up more talent for the Lynx's inaugural season in the WNBA. Through their partnership with the NBA, the WNBA has the financial backing to grow.

The Lynx began their first year in the WNBA as a team dominated by rookies and players with one year of experience. Despite this, they had a strong start:

beginning the year with 10 victories and only five losses. However, the Lynx did not perform as well the rest of the season, and ended the year with a respectable 15–17 record, a spectacular inaugural season. In the Lynx's second year (2000), the team repeated its inaugural 15–17 record.

The Lynx have quickly built a steady fan base with the WNBA's brand of basketball. The WNBA may not be as flashy as the NBA, but it shines on many other levels. Women's basketball is more team oriented, with plenty of well-executed passes, plays, and teamwork. Both on and off the court, the WNBA puts a premium on community involvement.

The Lynx have several initiatives within the community that profoundly benefit the Twin Cities area. Events occur frequently, such as the "Great Basketball Dribble." Annually fans, coaches, and players dribble basketballs for early detection of breast cancer and breast cancer research. A number of other events are aimed at young children, including tickets for underprivileged kids and youth-beat reporter tryouts.

The Lynx share the Target Center with the Timberwolves; the season begins in late May and ends in early August. There are many seating options. Tickets are available in person at the Target Center and by phone. There is ample parking in the several municipal ramps behind the arena. Prices ranged from $8.00 to $84.00 in 2003.

Minnesota Timberwolves
Target Center, 601 First Avenue North, Minneapolis
(612) 337–3865
www.nba.com/timberwolves

Professional basketball has a long history in Minnesota, going back long before the Timberwolves' recent successes. The Wolves debuted during the 1989–1990 season, but did not reach the playoffs until the 1996–1997 season, a year after Kevin Garnett was picked in the '95 Draft. The Wolves 1999–2000 season was the most successful in the team's history, but the off-season was marred by tragedy.

The history of professional basketball is long and glorious in Minnesota. The first professional basketball franchise in the area was the Minneapolis Lakers. The Lakers were the dominant team of the era. Between 1949 and 1954, they won five NBA championships and were led by the game's first great big man, 6'10" center George Mikan. Then the Lakers struggled and would return to the NBA Championship only one more time in Minnesota, when they lost to Boston in '59.

Even the talents of one of the NBA's first superstars, Elgin Baylor, could not save the Lakers. After the 1960 season the Lakers left for Los Angeles, where they would become one of the greatest franchises in NBA history. Professional basketball would not return to Minnesota until 1989, except for the brief visits by the American Basketball Association's Minnesota Muskies and Minnesota Pipers for 1967–1968 and 1968–1969.

The Timberwolves arrived in Minnesota as part of a four-team NBA expansion. The Wolves and the Orlando Magic entered the NBA for the 1989–1990 season. Their first season was uneventful on the court but impressive at the gate in the Metrodome, where they set an all-time attendance record in their first season with 1,072,572 fans, or an average of 26,160 a game.

As an expansion team, the Wolves continued to have difficulty winning, even in the new Target Center. Seemingly every step forward was met with two steps backward. The Wolves set an NBA record in 1994–1995 by losing 60 games in four

consecutive seasons. However, after reaching their nadir, incremental improvement loomed on the horizon.

The Wolves' turnaround began when coach Bill Blair was fired and Phil "Flip" Saunders was hired in December 1995. Then the team selected 19-year-old Kevin Garnett in the '95 NBA Draft. The Wolves slowly began to win, winning 40 games, and made their first playoff appearance in 1996–1997 but were swept by the Houston Rockets.

The Wolves' success has continued with yearly playoff appearances and franchise records for games won. Kevin Garnett has emerged as one of the NBA's stars and the team has improved its record. For the 1999–2000 season the T-Wolves won 50 games for the first time, a franchise record. Unfortunately, the Wolves faced the Portland Trailblazers in the playoffs, losing in four games. The Wolves' bad luck continued in the off-season when a drunk driver killed guard Malik Sealy.

Despite these tragedies, the Wolves seem poised to compete with the NBA's elite. Kevin Garnett is one of the league's best and most mobile big men and is surrounded by a talented team, which includes Terrell Brandon and Joe Smith. The future looks bright for the Wolves at the Target Center.

The Target Center was specifically constructed for the Wolves in 1990. Despite the existence of the Met Center and the St. Paul Civic Center, both of which have since been razed, the Wolves constructed a single-sport arena. This has allowed the Wolves always to have the home field advantage. The Target Center was the first Twin Cities facility for one major league franchise. Since then, Minnesota's NHL expansion team, the Wild, has opened the Xcel Energy Center exclusively for the Wild, and the Wolves now share the Target Center with the WNBA's Minnesota Lynx. Nevertheless, the Target Center feels like, and is, the home of the Wolves.

The Target Center is ideally located at the intersection downtown of the Warehouse District and the theater district. The structure fits tightly on its lot and almost spills out onto the street. However, it is comfortable on the inside, despite its size. Target Center has a capacity of 19,006.

Wolves tickets for the 2002–2003 season ranged from $10 to $350 for a single game. There are also several ticket plans, including full-season, half-season, 14-, and 7-game plans. Tickets are available in person at the Target Center and by phone. There is ample parking in the several municipal ramps behind the arena.

Football

The Twin Cities have two great options for football fans. The Minnesota Vikings of the NFL have been consistently one of the league's best teams, while the Gophers, under coach Glen Mason, are rising to prominence in the Big Ten. These are exciting times for Twin Cities football fans, so come join us in our "Purple Pride" and Gopher spirit.

Minnesota Golden Gophers Football
Metrodome, 34 Kirby Puckett Place,
Minneapolis
(612) 624–8080 or (800) U–GOPHER
www.gophersports.com/tickets

Long before the Minnesota Vikings arrived as an NFL expansion team, the Gophers were the Twin Cities' principal football team. They play in one of the premier NCAA conferences, the Big Ten, which has presented a significant hurdle for the team. The football team, like their basketball counterparts, lacks the recruiting base of many other Big Ten schools. Nevertheless, the Gophers football team has sporadically risen to glory.

Despite the long history of Minnesota Gophers football, the team has made a paltry eight bowl game appearances as of 2003. Their first bowl game was not until they met Washington in the 1961 Rose Bowl and lost, 17–7. However, in 1962 they again returned to the Rose Bowl and defeated the UCLA Bruins. After winning consecutive Big Ten titles and bids to the Rose Bowl, they did not return to a bowl game until 1977.

When they did return, the Gophers again lost, this time to Maryland in the Hall of Fame Bowl. The Gophers were once again in the doldrums; they would have a winning season in 1981, but then went into a major tailspin.

In 1984 Lou Holtz was hired as head coach. The team posted a 4–7 mark in 1984, and the program seemed to be turning around. The next season the Gophers improved their record again, and they defeated Clemson in the Independence Bowl. Then, much to the dismay of Gopher fans, Holtz left town to take the Notre Dame job. Assistant coach John Gutekunst was hired as head coach and took the Gophers to the Independence Bowl, where they lost to Tennessee. The Gophers faltered under Gutekunst and his successor, Jim Wacker.

Then the Gophers made one of their best decisions: They hired Glen Mason as coach for the '97 season. Mason came from the Kansas football program and was known for rebuilding troubled programs. They responded by incrementally improving their record; for the '99 season they went 8–4, and received a bid to the Sun Bowl, where they lost to Oregon. The Gophers went 6–6 in 2000. But that was enough for a trip to the Micronpc.com Bowl but not enough to overcome North Carolina State, which won 38–30. Unwilling to dwell on that defeat, the Gophers rebounded in 2001, winning the Music City Bowl 29–14 over Arkansas, to finish 8–5 for the season. In recent years the Gophers football squad has risen to the upper tier of the Big Ten.

The Gophers have played at the Hubert H. Humphrey Metrodome since moving off campus, and the results have been mixed. At times the Gophers have had attendance problems. However, when the Gophers are winning, fans attend their games. Students are often not as rabid or as plentiful at the Dome, but it is a more comfortable venue during cold fall days.

Tickets for Gophers football games are available by phone, on-line, or in person at the Mariucci Arena ticket office on campus at 4 Oak Street SE, Minneapolis. You cannot buy Gopher football tickets at Metrodome ticket outlets. Single game tickets for the 2002 season ranged from

$15.00 to $29.50. Gopher football tickets are often a matter of supply and demand.

Minnesota Vikings
Metrodome, 34 Kirby Puckett Place,
Minneapolis
(612) 338–4537
www.vikings.com

Are the Vikings among the NFL's elite or aren't they? Will the Vikings find a solution to their "stadium issues?" Currently there are some big questions facing the Vikes both on and off the field. In the near future we will definitely find out.

The year 2000 celebrated the Vikings 40th season in the NFL. The Vikings became an expansion team during the 1961 NFL season, debuting in the Twin Cities during the autumn following the Twins' move from Washington, D.C.

In the Vikings' first regular season game, they surprisingly defeated the Chicago Bears 37 to 13. This was a great start for an expansion team, but they would not have a winning season until 1964, when they posted a 6–5–1 record. Still, the Vikings were building a solid team that increasingly improved its record.

The Vikings made a monumental decision when they hired Bud Grant as coach. On March 10, 1967, Grant took over and the Vikings responded by winning their first division title. The Vikings lost in the playoffs but were on their way to greatness under the stoic, strict tutelage of Grant, a future Hall of Famer.

In 1970 the Vikings lost in Super Bowl IV, the first of four Super Bowl appearances. The era of the famed "Purple People Eaters" began. The name came from the Vike's fierce defensive line led by Carl Eller, Alan Page, and Jim Marshall. The defense was so dominant in 1971 that Page was the first defensive player named as the NFL's Most Valuable Player. The Purple People Eaters developed a tradition of playing relentless, hard-nosed football regardless of the elements.

Vikings fans' dedication mirrored their heroes on the field; the Viking faithful went rabid even when the mercury often plummeted below zero. The home-field advantage at the old Metropolitan Sta-

dium spearheaded the Vikings' dominance in the NFC Central Division during much of the '70s. Unfortunately, the Vikings were defeated in all four Super Bowl appearances, and the franchise did not receive a championship ring. Many Vikings stars of the epoch have been underrecognized and have not received the place they deserve at the NFL Hall of Fame.

During the '80s the Vikings became less dominant, as many of the Purple People Eaters retired. In addition, the team left Metropolitan Stadium behind for the new Hubert H. Humphrey Metrodome. At the Dome the Vikings lost part of their home-field advantage when the frequently harsh climes of Minnesota's late fall and winter became a nonfactor in the climate-controlled stadium.

The Vikings did not reemerge as a dominant NFL team until the 1998 season. Posting a 15–1 record, the Vikings were a missed field goal away from defeating Atlanta and returning to the Super Bowl. The Vikings were picked by many pundits to go to the Super Bowl in '99 but, after a disappointing start, finished 10-6 and were defeated in the playoffs by the St. Louis Rams. The Vikings again found success in the 2000 season with quarterback Daunte Culpepper.

A couple of down seasons followed the success of 2000, with the Vikes going 5–11 under Dennis Green in 2001 and 6–10 under new coach Mike Tice in 2002. Despite sometimes less than stellar performances, the Vikings remain wildly popular among Minnesota sports fans.

In 1998 the Vikings were sold to Red McCombs, a multimillionaire from Texas. Concurrently, the Vikings had a great season, while McCombs, despite the Vikings long-term contract at the Dome, asked the Twin Cities for a separate, football-only stadium. As with the Twins' "stadium issues," political leaders have made numerous proposals, but so far none have been successful. Until a decision is reached, the Vikings will continue to play at the Dome.

The Dome is a multipurpose stadium that the Twins and the Vikings call home; however, the seats have better sight lines for football than baseball. When modified for football, the Dome seats 64,121 fans. As at Metropolitan Stadium before it, the Vikings have a tremendous home-field advantage at the Dome. Just as the Vikings had the elements and rabid fans in their corner, at the Dome Vikings fans cheer loud enough to create a near-deafening din. The Vikings' "Dome field advantage" acts as the twelfth man on the field at Vikings home games.

The Vikings have several community-based programs. The Vikings Children's Fund is the team's major fund-raising project. The team is given only one day off during the regular season, known as "community Tuesday." On Tuesday the Vikings perform a host of charitable activities in the area, including visiting area hospitals, the Ronald McDonald House, and area schools or helping with Special Olympics activities. The Vikings provide exciting football action on the field, and also make many contributions to the community off the field.

Minnesota Vikings tickets are available through Ticketmaster (651-989-5151; www.ticketmaster.com), or in person at the Metrodome ticket office. A limited number of single-game tickets go on sale in mid-July, but they sell out very quickly.

There is plenty of parking, with tremendous variation in prices. The lots next to the Dome are expensive, but north of Washington Avenue there is ample reasonably priced parking.

Horse Racing

With the demise of St. Croix Meadows Greyhound Track in nearby Hudson, Wisconsin, there is only one place in the Twin Cities metropolitan area where you can go to see live racing of our four-legged friends. Canterbury Park's horse racing is also the only sport in the Metro where gambling is legal. The price of admission is inexpensive—if you don't feel like gambling.

Canterbury Park Racetrack and Card Club
1100 Canterbury Road, Shakopee
(952) 445–7223 or (800) 340–6361
www.canterburypark.com

Canterbury Park has been the state's only horse track since 1985. Live racing begins in mid-May and runs through the beginning of September. The track is open year-round for simulcast racing.

Admission is reasonable, only $4.00 for grandstand or clubhouse tickets during the 2002 season. Anyone under age 18 must be accompanied by an adult and is admitted free of charge. Besides horse racing, the track also has a card club (see the Attractions chapter for more information). Parking at the track is free.

Canterbury Park is approximately 25 minutes from downtown Minneapolis and 15 minutes from the Mall of America.

Hockey

Minnesota is arguably the hockey capital of the United States. In fact, our love of hockey mirrors our neighbor to the north, Canada. Rarely, if ever, would you hear someone in the area refer to the sport as ice hockey; it is simply hockey. The Minnesota high school hockey tournament regularly draws near sell-out crowds each spring and is broadcast on local television with saturated media coverage and intense interest. Minnesotans get excited about high school hockey, just as Texas loves its high school football, and Indiana has high school basketball mania.

So it came as a shock to Twin Citians when the Minnesota North Stars relocated to, of all places, Texas, after the 1992–1993 season. In the interim, the Twin Cities still had Minnesota Golden Gophers men's hockey, but, unfortunately, they were no longer a hockey powerhouse. Finally, after a seven-year wait, professional hockey returned to the Twin Cities, this time in St. Paul—at the beautiful Xcel Energy Center.

The Golden Gophers men's hockey team has a rich tradition at the University of Minnesota. They are the only Western Collegiate Hockey Association (WCHA) team in the Twin Cities and the largest university team in the area. In a state with so many sports entertainment options, Gophers fans are diehards. They have been rewarded with a team that has consistently played high-caliber hockey in one of college hockey's toughest conferences, the WCHA.

The Gophers have a storied history in Minnesota. The first Gophers men's hockey team took the ice in 1921, but modern collegiate hockey in the Midwest began in 1951 when the Midwest Collegiate Hockey League was organized. The Gophers were charter members along with the teams of Michigan Tech and North Dakota. The conference changed its name to the WCHA two years later, and from the start the Gophers were at the top of the WCHA almost annually. They won the first two WCHA regular-season championships, although during the '60s they frequently lost the title to teams from Michigan, North Dakota, and Denver, who relied heavily on Canadian players.

In the '70s and '80s the Gophers returned to dominance and frequently won the WCHA tournament and regular-season titles. In 1974, 1976, and 1979, the Minnesota Golden Gophers won the NCAA national championship. However, under coach Doug Woog, the Gophers recruited only players from Minnesota, and the Gophers failed to win either the WCHA regular-season or the tournament title. After Woog's 14 years, the Gophers were not performing at the high standard Minnesota required, and he resigned after the 1999–2000 season.

The University of Minnesota then hired Don Lucia, who had guided WCHA rival Colorado College out of the doldrums and into the NCAA tournament multiple times and once all the way to the championship game. A former winner of the Spencer Penrose Award for National Coach of the Year, Lucia seemed a solid choice, and he didn't take long to prove the athletic decision-makers at the U profoundly correct in their confidence in him.

The year 2002 brought glory back to Golden Gopher hockey. The team battled mightily in the talent-rich WCHA, finishing the regular season in third place behind Denver and state rival St. Cloud State, with a conference record of 18–7–3 and 26–7–4 overall. They would drop one more game, the WCHA Final Five Championship game to regular-season champion Denver, but their record was more than good enough for a trip to the NCAA tournament—and a foot in the door is all the Gophers needed. In the quarterfinals the Gophers dropped Lucia's former team, Colorado College, 4–2 and then beat powerhouse Michigan in the semifinals 3–2. That set up a matchup with eastern power Maine, and the game will go down as a classic in NCAA collegiate history. With Maine up 3–2 in the closing minutes of the third period, the Gophers pulled their goalie to gain an extra attacker, leaving an open net. But the strategy succeeded; the Gophers tied the game with only 54.2 seconds remaining. The National Championship would be decided in overtime. Both teams put everything they had into the overtime period, but it was the Gophers, with 3:02 left in the first overtime, who finally got the game-winner. For the first time since 1979, the Golden Gophers reigned as National Champions.

The Gophers play at beautiful Mariucci Arena, a facility built specifically for the team. Here they have a significant home advantage behind the enormous enthusiasm of students and alumni.

Ticket prices ranged from $23 to $26 in 2003. Tickets can be purchased by phone, on-line, or in person at Mariucci Arena.

Plenty of parking for Gophers hockey is available in the lots across from Mariucci Arena on Oak Street.

Minnesota Golden Gophers Women's Hockey
Ridder Arena, 1815 Fourth Street SE,
Minneapolis
(612) 624–8080 or (800) U–GOPHER
www.gophersports.com/tickets

The Golden Gopher men's hockey team is not the only hockey team on the U of M campus, nor are they the only one with a recent national championship. Women's hockey is blossoming in Minnesota, from young kids all the way to Division I athletics. With the 1997–1998 season, the University of Minnesota finally had a women's hockey team, and the state's deep talent pool has made the Gophers' women's team a power from the start.

In their inaugural season, the Gophers posted a record of 21–7–3 under coach Laura Halldorson. They didn't let up in 1998–1999, finishing the season 29–4–3 and advancing to the national semifinals before bowing to New Hampshire 3–2 in overtime. But the Gophers were just getting started. In 1999–2000 the Gophers went 32–6–1 and won the AWCHA National Championship. Not bad for your third season of existence.

Since taking the title, the Gophers have continued their winning ways, with records of 23–9–2 in 2000–2001 and 28–4–6 in 2001–2002, winning the WCHA-Women's League regular season title both years. Haldorson continues to lead the Gophers, and the women's hockey team shows no signs of letting up. The success of women's college hockey in Minnesota is spawning interest in the game for young women across the northern states, and the historic expansion of women's hockey in Minnesota will go down in history as the impetus of great change in women's hockey at all levels.

The Golden Gophers women's hockey team is the only women's hockey team in the country with an arena built specifically for them. Ridder Arena, a gorgeous 3,400-seat arena next door to Mariucci Arena, opened for the 2002–2003 season and is considered by many to be the finest women's collegiate hockey arena in the country.

Tickets are available by phone, on-line, or in person at the Mariucci Arena ticket office. Tickets are a relative bargain, ranging from $4.00 to $9.00 for the 2002–2003 season. Parking is widely available at lots and ramps near Ridder Arena.

Minnesota Wild
Xcel Energy Center, 175 West Kellogg Boulevard, St. Paul
(651) 222–WILD
www.wild.com

The Minnesota Wild were an expansion team for the 2000–2001 NHL season. However, a lot of work went into luring professional hockey back to Minnesota after losing the North Stars. Many Twin Citians doubted professional hockey would come to St. Paul, but painstaking efforts by city officials and fans made it a reality.

The North Stars were the first professional hockey team in the Twin Cities. The Stars began as the Wild did, as an expansion team for the 1967–1968 season. The Stars were a beloved part of the local community, but as the team entered the '90s, owner Norm Green claimed they were losing money because of poor attendance at the Met Center. Green told local leaders the Stars needed a new home or they would exercise their expiring lease and leave the state. During the '93 season, Twin Cities officials called Green's bluff. Much to Twin Citians' surprise, the team moved to the greener pastures of a new arena and larger revenue streams in Dallas. As a community the Twin Cities was shocked. How could the NHL leave a state where hockey was so loved?

The Twin Cities wanted hockey back, but it would not return for seven years. During this time, efforts were made to persuade other NHL teams to relocate to the

St. Paul's Xcel Energy Center, a state-of-the-art hockey facility, is the home of the NHL's Minnesota Wild.
PHOTO: TODD R. BERGER

Twin Cities. Early efforts failed due to the Twin Cities' lack of interest in publicly subsidizing professional sports.

Finally, a local group of investors and businessmen led by Bob Naegele Jr. was able to convince the NHL to award an expansion team to Minnesota for the 2000–2001 season. The NHL decision to come to St. Paul, however, was incumbent on a new hockey-only facility. And build a new state-of-the-art facility they did—the Xcel Energy Center.

The Xcel Energy Center is located in downtown St. Paul. It is equipped with all the modern amenities that the previous facility, the Met Center, lacked. The Xcel Energy Arena features four 9- by 16-foot, high-definition scoreboards as well as two 16- by 24-foot, high-definition marquees outside the arena. A truly spectacular ribbon board circles the entire arena at the suite level, showing statistics and ads in 16.7 million shades of color. When the Wild score a goal, the lighthouse in the northeast corner of the arena sounds its foghorn, and the Wild fans go nuts.

Seating in the facility is comfortable and all seats have an excellent view of the action. There are 18,600 seats in the arena, with ticket prices ranging from $10 to $70. Tickets can be purchased for individual games through Ticketmaster at (651) 989-5151 or www.ticketmaster.com. They may also be bought at the box office at the Xcel Energy Center. Wild tickets are a very hot commodity in the Twin Cities, and you may have difficulty finding tickets at any price level after the season begins. When tickets become available for an upcoming game, the Wild typically run ads in the sports sections of the *StarTribune* and *St. Paul Pioneer Press.* However, the availability of tickets, especially for some seating, is not guaranteed. There are many readily available parking options in downtown St. Paul.

Before the first puck was dropped in the Wild's NHL inaugural season, the team established an important charitable initiative: the 10,000 Rinks Program. The program takes its name from the state's motto, the Land of 10,000 Lakes. The program is ambitious and sets out to accomplish several initiatives: youth hockey clinics, funding inner-city youth hockey, and a program for creating diversity in hockey. The Wild will also offer "life skills messages" for youth on their radio network.

The Minnesota Wild value children and seem to realize that the kids they are helping will in the future be the team's fan base and players. The first few years are difficult for expansion teams, but the Wild will prosper with the support of number one, its fans. Principal owner, Bob Naegele Jr., retired the number one symbolically in the Wild's first game to commemorate the importance of the fans to the team.

Soccer

Over the years, soccer has existed in various forms in the Twin Cities. Franchises have come and gone, but they have not lasted. The Thunder, the most recent soccer franchise, has called the Twin Cities home since 1994. Finally, the area seems prepared to support professional soccer. Hopefully the Thunder's continued success on the field will improve the team's attendance numbers.

Minnesota Thunder
National Sports Center, 1700 105th Avenue NE, Blaine
(763) 785-3668
www.mnthunder.com
Professional soccer has appeared in the Twin Cities in various franchises. All the franchises have had modest success, but not enough to remain in business. However, after several seasons the Thunder continue to increase their Twin Cities fan base.

The Minnesota Kicks were the first professional soccer team in Minnesota. They began as the Denver Dynamos of the NASL, when they relocated for the 1976 season. The Kicks had success, even drawing an average attendance of 32,775 for the 1977 season. Unfortunately, the Kicks went bankrupt after the 1981 season. Following that season, the Fort Lauderdale Strikers relocated to the Twin Cities. The Strikers played in the NASL and later made the jump to the MISL, an indoor soccer league. After the 1988 season the Strikers also folded, and soccer did not return to the Twin Cities for six years.

The Thunder arrived for the 1994 season in the USISL. They have been successful both on the field and in attracting fans. The Thunder have appeared in the A-League Championship three times in the past few years, losing the 2000 A-League Championship game to Rochester. The Thunder appear poised to continue their success.

The Thunder's slogan is "the world's game…Minnesota's team." As the area becomes increasingly more diverse, soccer has developed a larger fan base. Soccer is the world's most beloved team sport, and in the Twin Cities soccer is especially popular among children and teens. The Thunder's season ticket sales have steadily increased. These factors, and the team's success, bode well for the future of the Thunder.

The Thunder are the only Twin Cities professional team currently not playing in either Minneapolis or St. Paul. Their home field is the National Sports Center in Blaine, a suburb of the Twin Cities easily accessible by many highways and Interstate 35.

Tickets for individual Thunder games may be purchased for VIP or general admission seating; they ran only $15 and $10 for the 2003 season. Both are reasonable for professional sports tickets. The Thunder also offers discount tickets for youth ages 19 and younger. Tickets are available by phone or in person at the National Sports Center.

Dome Souvenir Plus & The Original Baseball Hall of Fame Museum of Minnesota

When you walk down Third Street en route to the Hubert Humphrey Metrodome, it's just about impossible to miss the building. A loudspeaker mounted on the outside of Ray Crump's deceptively small establishment invites passersby in, warning them that they'll be paying twice as much for the same souvenirs inside the Metrodome.

Few people passing by the brick storefront would confuse the building for the National Baseball Hall of Fame in Cooperstown, New York, but upon entering the store, they'll be amazed by the wealth of local and national baseball history. The museum also houses an impressive "Wall of Celebrities," featuring a rotating display of the store's 10,260 signed photos, baseballs, and bats. Besides the free museum, the adjoining Dome Souvenir Plus stocks extensive sports souvenirs and team-related merchandise for all the Twin Cities sports teams at reasonable prices.

Ray Crump arrived in Minnesota after the Twins relocated from Washington, D.C., for the 1961 season. Crump's career in Major League Baseball began as a batboy for the Washington Senators, where he would later assume the position of equipment manager. His career spanned 36 years with the Senators and then the Twins, where he was able to acquire the unique sports memorabilia found at the museum. An affable and insightful man, Ray Crump has written and published a book detailing his professional baseball experiences, *Beneath the Grandstands*.

Vintage Minnesota Twins collectibles are prominently displayed at the Original Baseball Museum, including the complete uniforms of retired Twins stars Harmon Killebrew, Tony Oliva, and Rod Carew. In addition, there is a special section dedicated to retired Twins great Kirby Puckett, as well as plenty of Twins '65, '87, and '91 World Series memorabilia. Also included is a prominent display focusing on the Washington Senators relocation to Minnesota. Unique displays include baseballs autographed not only by baseball stars but also by a wide array of non–sports stars; e.g., Jerry Lewis, Hubert Humphrey, and Louis Armstrong. The Elvis Corner displays numerous personal items from "the King of Rock 'n' Roll."

Crump's "Wall of Celebrities" includes autographed photos of such stars as Muhammad Ali, Hulk Hogan, Liberace, and Bill Cosby shown posing with a younger Ray Crump. Many of the photos were autographed long before the personalities became stars. "When I got the photo taken with Bill Cosby, no one knew who he was," says Crump. "He was some guy who had done a Jell-O commercial. I also have a baseball signed by Frank Sinatra, except he signed it 'Francis Sinatra.' Years later, this woman who worked for him told me he never signed anything except business papers 'Francis,' and that he never signed autographs with anything but 'Frank.'" Besides the memories and stories inside the museum, the Crump family has an impressive selection of Minnesota professional and collegiate sports merchandise.

When Ray Crump opened the museum and store, there was no Wall of Celebrities. These autographed photos of the stars were considered personal and cherished by the Crump family. Crump decided to display the autographs after making an observation: Many women seemed bored, while their husbands refused to leave the museum. He quickly realized after displaying the celebrity photos that this made the museum much more fun for the entire family.

And the focus of the museum is on family fun. "This is a family business," explains Crump. "My wife's right back there behind the counter most days, and my two sons frequently help me up front or in the snack bar. I like working at the snack counter better than the front of the store because it gives me a chance to talk to people more. I really enjoy talking to customers about the museum and all the souvenirs we've got here." At least one Crump family member will be available when the museum/store is open to serve the needs of Minnesota sports fans.

The amiable Crump gushes with interesting stories and minutiae about memorabilia and Major League Baseball. How many people can give you a detailed explanation of the differences between the National and American Leagues' method for taking attendance, or know that the Vikings lease at the Dome does not expire until 2011? If you have any questions about sports at all, Crump probably knows the answer or can tell you who does. As far as souvenir shopping goes, Dome Souvenir Plus has a huge selection of items at reasonable prices. Whether you are looking for a Twins hat, Vikings barbecue sauce, or a collectible Bobblehead doll, Dome Souvenir Plus has it.

Dome Souvenir Plus & The Original Baseball Hall of Fame Museum of Minnesota is conveniently located 1 block directly north of the Dome, across from gate A (910 South Third Street, Minneapolis). For further information call (612) 376–9707 or, to order merchandise, (888) 375–9707. They also can be visited at www.domeplus.com.

Summer Recreation

Basketball
Baseball and Softball
Biking
Camping
Canoeing and Rowing
Car Shows
Croquet
Disc Golf
Fishing
Football
Golf
Hiking
Horseback Riding
Horseshoe Pitching
Hot Air Ballooning
In-Line Skating
Miniature Golf
Nature Interpretation and Bird Watching
Paintball
Sailing and Sailboarding
Scuba Diving
Skydiving
Soccer
Sprints, 10Ks, and Marathons
Swimming
Volleyball

The advent of spring is a time of continuous celebration in Minnesota that carries well into late summer and fall. The trees explode with new, tiny green buds; spring wildflowers bloom purple and blue and white throughout the countryside and alongside city streets; and every lake and pond is busy with mallards, wood ducks, and Canada geese. Minnesotans know how to appreciate the warm weather, too, and it seems like every day free of winter's cold is spent in the great outdoors.

It's the very idea that "winter is just around the corner" that governs so much of the average Minnesotan's life. Casual visitors to the Twin Cities are often amazed by how much space inside the metro area is left unpaved and untouched, that near downtown Minneapolis, the banks of the Mississippi are covered with greenery and lined with thick forests. The only human concessions are the paved hiking trails and handrails that weave in and out of the cliffs along the river, and even these often degrade into muddy turf trails. In St. Paul the bird sanctuary of Harriet Island can be found just across the Mississippi from the bustling downtown area, set in a beautiful flower garden that just doesn't feel like it's actually in the middle of a city.

In short, the best way to describe what to do in the Twin Cities during the summer is Go Outside. In this chapter we've attempted to list not only where to go to play but also the local associations responsible for organizing many of the outdoor recreational events here. We've also listed some of the more reasonable places to rent gear in the Cities, from bicycles to canoes to scuba equipment. Whether you're looking for something for the whole family to do or just looking for a quiet, beautiful spot to escape from the busy world of city traffic and shopping malls, you're sure to find it in the Twin Cities. Here are just a few suggestions of places to go and things to do during your stay.

Basketball

Cities Sports Connection organizes men's and coed basketball leagues for players age 18 and over of all skill levels. Rec teams consist of players with lower to average skill proficiency and game knowledge, with a focus on sportsmanship, having fun, getting a good workout, and improving skills. Intermediate teams consist of players with average to good skill proficiency and game knowledge, with a focus on evenly matched, quality competition. CSC basketball leagues are offered in the fall (September–December), winter (January–March), and spring (March–May) seasons. No membership or non-member fees are charged to participate in CSC leagues, and teams play events all over the metro area and are not tied to one specific area. CSC provides paid officials for all league action and free T-shirts for all participants. Call (612) 929-9009, ext. 3, or write P.O. Box 24004, Minneapolis, Minnesota 55424-0004 for more information.

Twin Cities Sport & Recreation Club (612-871-5000), located at 2101 Hennepin Avenue South, Suite #107, can match you up with already-existing men's basketball teams or help you find people to fill out your own team.

Baseball and Softball

Cities Sports Connection organizes coed and men's softball and baseball leagues at all skill levels. CSC softball leagues are offered in the spring (April–June), summer (June August), and fall (August/September–October). Teams consist of 10 players (coed means 6 men/4 women) on the field at all times, with rosters of 15-plus people per team. CSC is open to all adults 18 or older—no membership or nonmember fees are charged to participate in CSC leagues. Call (612) 929-9009, ext. 3, or write P.O. Box 24004, Minneapolis, Minnesota 55424-0004 for more information.

If you're looking to form a softball team in the Twin Cities proper, the **Amateur Softball Association** can help. In Minneapolis contact the ASA at (612) 661-4895, or write ASA, Grain Exchange Building #200, Minneapolis, Minnesota 55415-1400. In St. Paul you can reach the ASA by calling (651) 266-6406 or by writing ASA, 25 Fourth Street West, St. Paul, Minnesota 55102.

United States Slowpitch Softball Association (write: USSSA, 3954 Bryant Avenue South, Minneapolis, Minnesota 55409; 612-825-2200) can help you put together a slow-pitch softball team. The association will send you the information you need or at least get you in touch with your local park and recreation department. The USSSA oversees suburban leagues, sets up tournaments, and helps teams find places to play. **Twin Cities Sport & Recreation Club** (612-871-5000), located at 2101 Hennepin Avenue South, Suite #107, can match you up with already-existing softball and baseball teams or help you find people to fill out your own team.

Biking

Minnesota has more miles of paved-to-trail bikeways than anywhere else in the country. Mountain biking trails wind their way through forests and along cross-country ski trails in the off-season, and easy-to-navigate paved trails follow the shores of nearly every metro area state park lake. Lakes, creeks, waterfalls, bluffs, rivers—you can bike near them all without ever having to leave the Twin Cities metro area.

Inside the Cities proper, there are four especially nice paved bike trails to choose from. In Minneapolis the **Grand Rounds Parkway** follows the perimeter of the Chain of Lakes and encircles the city. Considered the crown jewel of metropolitan biking, this 38-mile scenic trail traces the shorelines of Lake Nokomis, Lake Hiawatha, Shingle Creek, Bassett Creek, Minnehaha Creek, and part of the Mississippi River.

The other three trails are located in St. Paul. **Como Park**'s 1.7-mile bike trail circles Como Lake and heads toward the Como Park Zoo and Conservatory area.

The bike lanes along St. Paul's historic Summit Avenue offer a crosstown pedaling commuter and recreational biker paradise. PHOTO: SAINT PAUL CONVENTION AND VISITORS BUREAU

Hidden Falls/Crosby Farm's 6.7-mile bike path follows the shady, wooded bottomlands along the banks of the Mississippi and is an especially pleasant ride to take during the dog days of summer. **Phalen Park**'s 3.2-mile bike trail circles Lake Phalen and its beautiful swimming beach, a layout that makes it oh-so-convenient to stop riding and go in for a dip if you start to wear out.

Other parks in the metro area with paved biking trails include Anoka County Riverfront, Baker Park Preserve, Battle Creek, Bryant Lake, Bunker Hills, Burlington-Northern Regional Trail, Carver Park Preserve, Central Mississippi Riverfront, Cleary Lake, Clifton E. French, Coon Rapids Dam, Elm Creek Park Reserve, Fish Lake, Hyland-Bush-Anderson Lakes, Lake Elmo Park Reserve, Lake George, Lake Minnetonka Regional Park, Lake Rebecca Park Reserve, Lebanon Hills, Lilydale-Harriet Island, Long Lake Regional Park, Minnehaha Parkway, Mississippi Gorge, Murphy-Hanrehan Park Reserve, North Hennepin Trail Corridor, Rice Creek-West Regional Trail, Rum River Central, Snail Lake, Southwest Regional LRT Trail, Theodore Wirth, and the Wirth-Memorial Parkway (see Parks chapter for complete listings). For more information about biking in the Twin Cities, call the **Minnesota Community Bicycle Safety Project** at (612) 624-9719, the **Minnesota Department of Public Safety** at (612) 296-6652, or the **Minnesota Office of Tourism** at (800) 657-3700, or visit the latter's Web page at www.exploreminnesota.com.

To rent bicycles, there are several good places in the metro area to get geared up. In Minneapolis you can rent bicycles at reasonable prices from either **Calhoun Rental** (612-827-8231), at 1622 West Lake Street; **Campus Bikes** (612-331-3442), at 213 Southeast Oak Street; or from **Kenwood Cyclery** (612-374-4042), located at 2123 West 21st Street.

Several in-town organizations hold annual bike-riding marathons worth checking out. **The Minnesota Chapter of the Multiple Sclerosis Society** (612-335-7900; www.mssociety.com) holds three separate MS Bike Tours in the Cities each summer to raise funds for multiple sclerosis research and treatment. The **Twin Cities–Chicago AIDS Ride** (612-871-0002; www.aidsride.org) is a huge six-day biking event (more than 1,750 participants in 2000) that starts in Minneapolis and ends in Chicago, a mere 500 miles away.

The **Minnesota Cycling Federation** comprises bicycle racing clubs in the upper Midwest, whose purpose is the education and promotion of bicycle racing skills and safety and the promotion of races for bicycle racers. The Federation provides cycling enthusiasts with the most current information about area race calendars, race results, MCF member clubs, the NCS Velodrome, and the Youth Cycling League. You can reach the MCF by calling their hotline at (612) 729-0702.

Camping

Although plenty of people, mostly ice fishers and hunters, go camping in wintertime, camping is really something to enjoy with your family in the warmer months. Camping sites in the metro area are scarce and quickly snatched up, so it's a good idea to reserve a site at least two weeks in advance. To make camping reservations, call the campground directly and let them know specifically where you want to camp (by the water, near hiking trails, etc., or the name of the specific campsite) and when you want to do it. Campers under age 18 must be accompanied by a parent or guardian, and leashed pets are permitted in campgrounds but must not disturb neighboring campsites. A $5.00 nonrefundable service fee is charged for all campground reservations, as well as an additional charge of $5.00 per vehicle per night. Check-in time is 4:00 P.M., and checkout time is 3:00 P.M. The maximum length of stay per site is 14 days. No reservations are necessary for tent camping—however, these sites are given out on a first-come, first-served basis. For a free copy of the *Minnesota Alliance of Campground Operators' Minnesota Campgrounds and RV Parks*, call the **Minnesota Department of Tourism** at (800) 657-3700.

Baker Park Preserve (763-559-9000), located approximately 20 miles west of downtown Minneapolis on County Road 19, has several very small sites for RV camping, as well as one large, 210-site family campground. Marshview has access to a scenic hiking trail, a barn shelter for horses, and electrical hookups, and costs $80 per night to camp. Lake Katrina has three spaces available for camping and has immediate access to a bike trail and an overhead shelter for RVs to park under—cost is $40 per site. Oak Knoll, located near the main gate, has close access to biking trails, and showers and electrical hookups are available. The Half Moon campsite does not allow RVs or campers on the site but has a garage-type shelter for winter camping and fishing, with immediate access to fishing docks and boat launches. For primitive camping, Baker also has an area set aside for tent camping. Located next to the main bike trail, two to three tents can rent space for $6.00 per night. The large family campground has 27 sites with electricity, an RV dump station, showers, and wheelchair-accessible flush toilets. The daily fee for the group campground is $12 per site, $17 per site with electricity, plus parking fees of $5.00 per vehicle.

Take Minnesota Highway 7 west from Minneapolis and turn left onto County Road 11 to get to **Carver Park Reserve** (952-472-4911). Campsite **Parley Lake** has 200 sites for RV camping, at $60 per vehicle, while nearby **Lake Zumbra** has 105 camping spots available at $40 per space, with easy access to a public boat launch and a great fishing/ice fishing spot.

Cleary Lake Regional Park (952-447-2171), located near Prior Lake on Scott County Road 27, is very popular with campers, having six different campsites to choose from: Cleary Point, Oak Grove, Island, Red Pine, Norway Ridge, and Birchwood. All are located a short walk from Cleary Lake and its swimming beach, and Cleary Point has a small boat dock for canoes or sailboats. Campers and RVs are not allowed at Norway Ridge and Birchwood, and the Island camping site is only accessible by boat and has no fresh water available for campers—one canoe per group is provided to campers at Island, so transportation to the campsite isn't a big deal. Cleary Point, Oak Grove, and Island all charge $60 per night to camp; Red Pine, Norway Ridge, and Birchwood charge $40 per night.

Crow-Hassan Park Preserve (763-424-5511) can be found west of Rogers on Sylvan Lake Road and has 90 camping sites for RV camping; 70 of them cost $75 per night. The Blue Stem site allows horse camping for an additional $5.00 a night. Blue Stem is also a great winter camping spot, with skiing and hiking trails leading right into the campsite. The other 20 sites are at Crow River ($20 per night), which is right on the banks of the river and near a small boat launch perfect for canoes. The downside of the Crow River campsite is, of course, mosquitoes, so make sure you pack some bug spray and have adequate netting or screens on all windows. Crow-Hassan also has a small primitive campsite available for $6.00 per night, with room for two to three tents. Horses are allowed to camp at the tent site as well for an additional $5.00 a night.

Elm Creek Park Reserve (763-424-5511) is located northwest of Osseo between the communities of Dayton and Maple Grove. To get there, take County Road 81 northwest to Territorial Road and turn right to get to the park entrance. The park has two midsize camping sites for RV camping: Rush Creek and Hayden Lake. Both bank-side campsites charge $40 per night, and Hayden Lake has a boat launch and fishing spots nearby. Elm Creek also has a primitive campsite ($6.00 per tent per night) located near the visitor center and the main bike trail, with room for two to three tents.

Hyland Lake Park Reserve (952-941-4362) is located on East Bush Road in Bloomington and has one campground, Sumac Knoll. For $60 a night, RV campers can park right next to a scenic biking and hiking trail. A small overhead shelter is on-site in case of rain or hail.

Lake Rebecca Park Reserve (763-972-2620) is approximately 23 miles west of Minneapolis on County Road 50 off of Minnesota Highway 55. The park has 80 RV camping sites available at Sarah Creek and South Camp, all at $60 per night. This is an especially pretty camping ground, surrounded by dense woods full of deer and hiking/horse trails. Horse camping is allowed at both sites for an additional $5.00 per horse, and South Camp has a small garage shelter on the site for public use in case of poor weather.

Canoeing and Rowing

The benefits of canoeing are immeasurable. Not only is it a great way to stay in shape, but it's also a pleasant way to get close to nature without disturbing it with noisy motors or having to worry about getting hung up on waters too shallow for outboard motors. In the Cities there are several parks that are perfect for canoes and kayaks. **Lake Calhoun** in Minneapolis is a popular canoeing lake surrounded by swimming beaches and fishing piers. The lake also has a great view of the downtown Minneapolis skyline and is absolutely spectacular at sunset. Connected to Lake Calhoun is **Lake of the Isles.** Lake of the Isles is an especially beautiful place to take a

With numerous lakes within the Twin Cities Metro, canoeists can paddle in peace through some of the most beautiful areas in the Twin Cities. PHOTO: GREATER MINNEAPOLIS CONVENTION & VISITORS ASSOCIATION

canoe, with narrow waterways overhung with old stone bridges, wide areas full of friendly ducks and geese, and a small forested island in the middle of the lake. A city-run building on the Lake Calhoun grounds rents canoes and sailboats to park visitors.

Also in Minneapolis, and adjacent to Lake Calhoun, is **Lake Harriet,** another wide-open lake heavily used by canoes, sailboats, and motor boats alike. The lake has several public swimming beaches and a refreshment stand on its northwestern shores—the perfect place to stop after a heavy workout on the water.

Other metro area parks that have waterways suitable for canoeing include Anoka County Riverfront, Baker Park Preserve, Bald Eagle-Otter Lakes, Bryant Lake, Carver Park Preserve, Cleary Lake, Clifton E. French, Como, Coon Rapids Dam, Crow-Hassan, Fish Lake, Hidden Falls-Crosby Farm, Hyland-Bush-Anderson Lakes, Lake Byllesby, Lake Elmo Park Reserve, Lake George, Lake Minnewashta, Lake Rebecca Park Reserve, Lebanon Hills, Lilydale-Harriet Island, Long Lake Re-

gional Park, Martin-Island-Linwood Lakes, Minneapolis Chain of Lakes, Nokomis Hiawatha, Phalen-Keller, Rice Creek/Chain of Lakes, Rice Creek-West Regional Trail, Rum River Central, Snail Lake, and Theodore Wirth (see Parks chapter for complete listings).

The **Minneapolis Rowing Club** has participated in regattas around the country almost every year since its founding in 1877. The club sponsors classes on rowing for youths of all ages as well as beginning adult rowers. Annual dues are $300, with discounts offered to student members. Contact the club at (612) 729-1541, or write Minneapolis Rowing Club, P.O. Box 583102, Minneapolis, Minnesota 55458-3102 for more information.

To rent canoes in the Cities, **Wilderness Canoe Base** (612-522-6501), at 2301 Oliver Avenue North in Minneapolis, rents a variety of canoes, kayaks, and rafts for reasonable prices, as do **Midwest Mountaineering** (612-339-3433), at 309 Cedar Avenue South in Minneapolis and **Northwest Canoe Company** (651-229-0192), at 308 Prince Street in St. Paul.

Car Shows

For more than 30 years, the **Minnesota Street Rod Association** has been sponsoring car shows in and around the Twin Cities area with the purpose of promoting interest in the hobby and sport of street rodding. More than 13,000 enthusiasts belong to the MSRA, a fact that's never more apparent than when the association's annual Back to the '50s show comes to town and the streets of St. Paul are filled with beautifully restored vintage hot rods. For more information about MSRA and MSRA events, call (651) 641-1992 or write MSRA, 2510 94th Way, Brooklyn Park, Minnesota 55444-1185.

Croquet

Over the last couple of decades, interest in croquet has made a resurgence with young and old people alike in the Twin Cities. While no specific park areas in the Cities have been set aside for croquet, people often bring their garden sets along to city parks to play friendly competitions. Two organizations, the **Twin Cities Croquet Society** (612–321-0707) and **University Club of St. Paul** (651-222-1751), set up regular full-size matches around town during the summer months and invite outsiders to join in the fun.

Disc Golf

Sort of a combination of Frisbee and golf, disc golf now has an official home in the Twin Cities. Located in the relaxing Bryant Lake Regional Park in Eden Prairie, **Hennepin Parks'** first disc golf course is 12 holes in length and features a short course and a long course. The course is open for play from sunrise until sunset, and there is no fee to play aside from the Hennepin Parks daily parking fee of $1.00. Reservations are required for groups, leagues, or tournaments; call (952) 941-4518. Discs are available for rental from 11:00 A.M. to 8:00 P.M. weekdays and from 9:00 A.M. to 8:00 P.M. weekends at the con-cession area for $2.00 per hour, with discounts available for park patrons.

Fishing

Many of the 1,000-plus lakes in the Twin Cities metro area have either been stocked with fish by the DNR or are naturally just great fishing holes. For more information about licensing requirements and where to drop your line, see the Fishing and Hunting chapter.

Football

Cities Sports Connection offers coed and men's outdoor and indoor touch football leagues for all levels of player. Rec teams consist of players of low to moderate skill level. Intermediate teams consist of a mix of players with average to good skill proficiency and game knowledge. Competitive teams consist of players with good skill proficiency and game knowledge. CSC touch football leagues are offered outdoors in spring (April–June) and fall (September–November), and CSC leagues move indoors for their annual turf leagues in winter (Session I, December–February; Session II, February–April). CSC is open to all adults 18 or older—no membership or nonmember fees are charged to participate in CSC leagues. Call (612) 929-9009, ext. 3, or write P.O. Box 24004, Minneapolis, Minnesota 55424-0004 for more information.

Twin Cities Sport & Recreation Club (612-871-5000), located at 2101 Hennepin Avenue South, Suite #107, can match you up with already-existing coed touch football teams or help you find people to fill out your own team.

Golf

With hundreds of acres of flat open plains and gently rolling hills already present, it's only natural that Minnesota would be home to some of the most incredible golf courses in the country.

Year-round Twin Citians take to the Metro's lakes seeking finny creatures. PHOTO: GREATER MINNEAPOLIS CONVENTION & VISITORS ASSOCIATION

Three of these courses belong to the Hennepin Parks system and are located in the parks themselves (see Parks chapter for more information about individual parks). **Baker National Golf Course,** located in the Baker Park Preserve at 2935 Parkview Drive, Medina (763-473-0800), has both an 18-hole course and a 9-hole course with a driving range/practice area, clubhouse, pro shop, and snack bar on the premises. Rates for the Championship Course and the Evergreen Course are $30 and $12, respectively, with discounts available to seniors, juniors (17 and under), and park patrons. Golf carts are available for rental. The park enforces a strict 15-minute limit per hole per party; telephone

reservations for the courses are highly recommended.

Glen Lake Golf & Practice Center (952-834-8644), located in Glen Lake Park at 14350 County Road 62 in Minnetonka, is a nine-hole golf course with a driving range/practice area, clubhouse, snack bar, and golf store on the premises. Carts and clubs can be rented at the store, and groups from two to four are permitted on the course. General rates are $11 per person, with discounts available for seniors and juniors. Tee times may be reserved up to five days in advance. The course enforces a limit of 13 minutes per hole per party.

Cleary Lake Golf Course (952-447-2171), located at 18106 Texas Avenue in Prior Lake, is a nine-hole course with a visitor center, snack bar, and golf store on the premises. Clubs, pull carts, and power carts can be rented at the course, and balls can be purchased at the store. General rates are $9.00 per person with discounts available for juniors (under 15) and senior citizens on weekdays only. No alcoholic beverages are permitted on the course.

St. Paul has four golf courses located within the city's park system: Phalen, Como, and two in Highland Park. **Phalen Golf Course** (651-778-0424) at 1615 Phalen Drive in Phalen Park, opened as a 9-hole course in 1917 and has since expanded into an 18-hole course with a clubhouse and a banquet room that seats 225. The course plays to a par of 70, measures approximately 6,100 yards, and has a rating of 68.7 and a slope of 121. The course includes a driving range, a full-service pro shop, and a snack bar.

Como Golf Course (651-488-9673), located at 1432 North Lexington Parkway in Como Park, opened as a 9-hole course in 1929 and is now an 18-hole golf course with a clubhouse, a full-service pro shop, and a snack bar on the premises. Como is a short, hilly course that plays to a par 70, measures approximately 5,800 yards, and has a rating of 68.5 and a slope of 115.

Highland 18-Hole Golf Course (651-695-3774), 1403 Montreal Avenue, opened to the public as an 18-hole facility in 1927 and is the longest of the parks courses, measuring about 6,200 yards. It plays to a par 72 with a rating of 69.0 and a slope of 111 and has a full-service pro shop, a driving range, and food service operation similar to Phalen and Como. **Highland 9-Hole Golf Course** (651–695-3708), 1797 Edgcumbe Road, opened in 1972 and is a favorite of beginning golfers. The course plays to a par of 35, measures 2,900 yards, and has a rating of 33.3 and slope of 105 for the nine holes. The course includes a snack bar that also sells a limited line of golf supplies (balls, gloves, tees, etc.).

All the St. Paul parks courses charge the same rate scale of $24 per game, with discounts available to students (grades 6 to 12), seniors, and season ticket holders; reservations for courses may be made for an additional $2.00 charge.

River Oaks Golf Course (651–438-2121), located in Cottage Grove at 11099 South Minnesota Highway 61, has both a 9-hole course and an 18-hole golf course with a grass driving range. The course plays to a par 71 and measures approximately 6,483 yards total. General rates for the 9-hole course are $16 on weekdays and $17 on weekends; general rates for the 18-hole course are $23.50 for weekdays and $26.50 on weekends. Discounts are available to residents, juniors under 17, and

---

> ## Insiders' Tip
> The Minnesota Department of Natural Resources has many publications dealing with camping, fishing, hunting, and boating in Minnesota. Call them at (800) 285-2000 to have information mailed to you about any of these activities.

---

senior citizens. There is also a restaurant on the premises and a pro shop where golfers can rent carts and clubs.

The Falcon Ridge Golf Course (651–462-5797) is a favorite spot for corporate outings and charity tournaments. Located at 33942 Falcon Avenue in Stacy, the grounds include an 18-hole regulation course and a 9-hole short course, as well as a resident PGA golf professional available for individual or group lessons. General rates for the 18-hole course are $18 on weekdays and $24 on weekends; rates for the 9-hole course are $12 on weekdays and $14 on weekends. A pro shop where carts and clubs can be rented is located on the premises.

Hiking

Just about every park in the Twin Cities metro area has a hiking trail that wanders in and out of forests, follows rivers and streams, passes close by natural waterfalls, or follows along the shores of the Mississippi River. Area parks with easy to moderate paved and turf hiking trails include Anoka County Riverfront, Baker Park Preserve, Bald Eagle-Otter Lakes, Battle Creek, Baylor, Bryant Lake, Bunker Hills, Burlington-Northern Regional Trail, Carver Park Preserve, Central Mississippi Riverfront, Cleary Lake, Clifton E. French, Como, Coon Rapids Dam, Cottage Grove Ravine, Crow-Hassan, Elm Creek Park Reserve, Fish Lake, Hidden Falls-Crosby Farm, Hyland-Bush-Anderson Lakes, Lake Byllesby, Lake Elmo Park Reserve, Lake George, Lake Minnewashta, Lake Rebecca Park Reserve, Lebanon Hills, Lilydale-Harriet Island, Long Lake Regional Park, Martin-Island-Linwood Lakes, Minneapolis Chain of Lakes, Minnehaha, Minnehaha Parkway, Mississippi Gorge, Murphy-Hanrehan Park Reserve, Nokomis Hiawatha, North Hennepin Trail Corridor, Rice Creek/Chain of Lakes, Rice Creek-West Regional Trail, Rum River Central, St. Croix Bluffs, Snail Lake, Southwest Regional LRT Trail, Spring Lake, Springbrook Nature Center,

Theodore Wirth, Wirth-Memorial Parkway, and Wood Lake Nature Center (see Parks chapter for complete listing).

For more experienced hikers, **Fort Snelling State Park** in St. Paul (651-725-2389), at 1 Post Road, has 18 miles of turf hiking trails that wind through the park's nature preserve, and **Minnesota Valley State Recreational Area** in Jordan (952-492-6400), at 19825 Park Boulevard, has 47 miles of turf and paved hiking trails to explore. The **William Munger State Trail** runs all the way from St. Paul to Duluth—you can pick up the Gateway Segment of the trail in Phalen Park (see Phalen-Keller listing in Parks chapter for more information).

If you're interested in meeting other people interested in hiking, **Friends of the Mississippi River** (651-222-2193), located at 240 Summit Avenue in St. Paul, organizes bird-watching tours and wildflower hikes at different spots along the Mississippi River. For women who don't like hiking in the backwoods of Minnesota alone, St. Paul's **Becoming an Outdoors Woman in Minnesota** (651-296-6157), 500 Lafayette Road, organizes group hikes for women as well as other solo and group gender-specific outdoors experiences ranging from canoeing to big game hunting.

Horseback Riding

Many of the parks in the metro area allow horses to share paved and dirt paths with cyclists and pedestrians. The trick is finding a place to rent horses from, unless you brought your own horse along on vacation. Tourists and residents alike can rent horses at many locations throughout the metro area suburbs for an average of $15 an hour.

North of the Twin Cities, horses can be rented at **Brass Ring Stables,** 9105 NW Norris Lake Road, Elk River (763-441-7987); **Valley View Horse Ranch,** 5168 County Road 33, Buffalo (651-682-2928); **Bunker Park Stables,** 550 Bunker Lake Boulevard, Coon Rapids (763-757-9445); **Rockin' R Ranch,** 8540 Kimbro Avenue

North, Grant City (651-439-6878); and **Roselawn Stables,** 24069 Rum River Boulevard NW, St. Francis (763-753-5517).

In the eastern suburbs, horses can be rented at the **Diamond T Riding Stable,** 4889 Pilot Knob Road, Eagan (651-454-1464); the **Windy Ridge Ranch,** 2700 Manning Avenue South, Woodbury (651-436-6557); and **Woodloch Stable & Tack,** 5676 North 170th Street, Hugo (651-429-1303).

South of the Twin Cities and just outside Carver, horses can be rented at **River Valley Ranch,** 16480 County Road 45 (952-361-3361).

Parks in the metro area with specified horse paths are Baker Park Preserve, Bunker Hills, Carver Park Preserve, Crow-Hassan, Elm Creek Park Reserve, Lake Elmo Park Reserve, Lake Rebecca Park Reserve, Lebanon Hills, Murphy-Hanrehan Park Reserve, North Hennepin Trail Corridor, and Rum River Central (see Parks chapter for individual addresses and more information)

Horseshoe Pitching

If you don't particularly like riding horses but do like throwing their shoes around, there are two local organizations that sponsor horseshoe-throwing competitions around the Twin Cities metro area. In Minneapolis the **Minneapolis Horseshoe Club** (612-926-2285), at 5241 Zenith Avenue, organizes competitions and events throughout the summer. In Coon Rapids, Minnesota's oldest nudist resort, the **Oakwood Club Inc.** (763-408-9004; www.oakwoodclub.com) holds extremely informal competitions at their beautiful, secluded facilities adjacent to a state nature preserve.

Hot Air Ballooning

There's nothing quite as beautiful as riding a hot air balloon over the St. Croix River Valley in the middle of summer, when the rolling fields below are bright green and the water is at its bluest. **Balloon Adventures** (952-474-1662) and **Scenic Adventures Hot Air Balloon Flights** (612-432-7009) offer a variety of balloon adventures, from champagne rides to daylong trips. Call companies for specific takeoff times and sites. To learn how to pilot one of these big colorful beasts by yourself, **Wiederkehr Balloon Academy** in Lakeland (651-436-8172), located at 130 North St. Croix Trail, offers classes in balloon navigation.

In-Line Skating

In-line skating is a great way to keep up your ice-skating chops during the summer months and vice versa. And, while St. Paul has the bulk of the ice-skating rinks of the Cities, Minneapolis has more paved paths open to in-line skates.

Some of the parks that allow in-line skates to share paved walking paths are Lilydale-Harriet Island, Minneapolis Chain of Lakes, Nokomis Hiawatha, and Theodore Wirth (see Parks chapter for complete listing). Two other particularly nice places to skate are along Lake Calhoun and Lake of the Isles; both the trails follow the lakeshore all the way and are wide enough that you don't have to worry about knocking pedestrians over or being hung up behind them for too long.

Minneapolis also has two indoor skate parks. **Third Lair Skatepark** (612-724-4546; www.3rdlair.com), at 1201 East Lake Street, has a street course, miniramp, and bowl to take your skates on. The **Hubert H. Humphrey Metrodome** has 105,600 square feet of pavement to skate on and has on-site equipment rentals, including protective gear. For more information, call (612) 825-DOME or see www.roller-dome.com.

For more information about in-line skating events around town, **Friday Night In-Line Skating/MN In-line Skate Club** (612-540-2582; www.skate tour.com/Friday.htm) meets at the northwest corner of Second Avenue SE and University Avenue in Minneapolis every first, third, and fifth Friday of the month to skate through downtown Minneapolis.

Miniature Golf

Definitely a kid's sport or even a fun place to take a date, a round of miniature golf makes for a relaxing, mildly competitive evening out for the whole family. Although there aren't any miniature golf parks in the Twin Cities proper, there are several in the suburbs. **Adventures Garden Miniature Golf** (612-861-9169), located at 64th Street and Portland Avenue South in Richfield, is the largest of the bunch, with more than enough windmills and castles for any minigolf enthusiasts. In Eagan, **Grand Slam Sports and Entertainment Center** (651-452-6569), at 3984 Sibley Memorial Highway, has a midsize golf park that makes for a good quick night out. Last but not least, inside the Mall of America on the third floor is **Golf Mountain** (952-883-8899), a spectacular 18-hole minigolf park that overlooks Camp Snoopy and LEGO World.

Nature Interpretation and Bird Watching

Many of the metro area parks have ongoing wildlife conservation projects on the grounds open to the public, which are a great way to get an up-close look at Minnesota's wildlife. Bald eagles, hawks, egrets, deer, porcupines, and the occasional skunk are just a few of the many animals you might bump into while walking about in the Minnesota woods. In the Cities, raccoons and Canada geese are extremely plentiful along the banks of the Mississippi River. Some of the metro area parks that have specific areas set aside for nature interpretation include Bald Eagle-Otter Lakes, Baylor, Bunker Hills, Carver Park Preserve, Clifton E. French, Como, Coon Rapids Dam, Elm Creek Park Reserve, Harriet Island, Hidden Falls-Crosby Farm, Lake Minnetonka Regional Park, Lebanon Hills, Minneapolis Chain of Lakes, Noerenberg, Memorial Park, Rice Creek/Chain of Lakes, Springbrook Nature Center, Theodore Wirth, and Wood Lake Nature Center (see Parks chapter for complete listing)

Clifton E. French Regional Park (952-559-8891) organizes bird-watching tours and nature hikes from their visitor center—before the hike, park rangers demonstrate bird-banding techniques from capture to release. There is a $3.00 charge for the hike, and reservations are required a minimum of two days prior to the program.

Carver Park Reserve (952-472-4911) teaches beginning birders how to tell specific bird species apart by sight and sound. The classes are usually taught at the Lowry Nature Center at the park on the first Saturday of every month (call park in case of cancellation); there is no charge to participate.

Paintball

This could be considered either a winter sport or a summer sport, but, really, isn't it more fun running around outside in cut-offs and T-shirts, chasing down your opponents with mock artillery in the hot summer sun than dealing with the limited cover and even more limited area of an indoor range? You have your choice of outdoor or indoor paintball arenas at **Adventure Zone** in Burnsville (952-890-7961) at 13700 Nicollet Avenue, and at **Splatball Inc.** (612-378-0385), at 2412 University Avenue SE in Minneapolis. The biggest outdoor paintball center is St. Paul's **Paintball Park** (651-488-7700), at 1870 Rice Street. The park is open to groups of six or more (up to 24 participants per group), and reservations are required in order to play.

Sailing and Sailboarding

There's really nothing quite as pretty as the white triangles of sailboats bobbing in the placid waters of Minnesota's wide blue lakes. There's also nothing quite as pleasant as actually being on one of the boats, enjoying the hot summer sun as you dangle your fingers and toes over the edge of the boat into the cool, clear water. Many lakes in the metro area are perfect for sailing and sailboarding alike, including Lake Harriet in Minneapolis, White Bear Lake in White Bear Lake, Keller Lake in St. Paul, Lake Minnetonka in Minnetonka, Medicine Lake in Plymouth, and Lake Nokomis in Minneapolis.

State parks in the metro area that allow sailboats and sailboards in the park lakes (and provide convenient boat launches for the same) include Baker Park Preserve, Bald Eagle-Otter Lakes, Bryant Lake, Carver Park Preserve, Cleary Lake, Clifton E. French, Fish Lake, Hyland-Bush-Anderson Lakes, Lake Byllesby, Lake Elmo Park Reserve, Lake George, Lake Minnewashta, Long Lake, Martin-Island-Linwood Lakes, Minneapolis Chain of Lakes, Nokomis Hiawatha, Phalen-Keller, Rice Creek/Chain of Lakes, and Snail Lake (see Parks chapter for complete listings).

The **American Red Cross** in St. Paul (651-291-6704) offers sailing classes and events throughout the summer, as does **Blue Water Sailing School** at 2337 West

Sailboarders on Lake Calhoun in Minneapolis. PHOTO: GREATER MINNEAPOLIS CONVENTION & VISITORS ASSOCIATION

Medicine Lake Drive in Plymouth (763–559-5649); **Lake Calhoun Yacht Club and Sailing School** in Minneapolis (612–822-8328), at 3010 East Calhoun Parkway; and **Scuba Center** (612–925-4818), at 5015 Penn Avenue South in Minneapolis, and 1571 Century Point in Eagan (651–681-8434).

Scuba Diving

Yes, there is scuba diving in Minnesota. Divers from around the world come to Minnesota to dry-suit dive in the frigid waters of Lake Superior, where hundreds of shipwrecks, including the famous *Edmund Fitzgerald*, can be found miles off the coast and a variety of underwater life found only in this region can be studied up close. If you just feel like exploring the bottom of a less cold and much less deep lake, pretty much any spot that has a swimming beach is fine for diving and snorkeling. Classes on scuba diving, scuba certification, and gear rental are provided by **Scuba Center** (612–925-4818), at 5015

Penn Avenue South, Minneapolis and at 1571 Century Point, Eagan (651–681-8434); and **Scuba Dive and Travel** (612–823-7210), at 4741 Chicago Avenue South in Minneapolis. **FantaSea Scuba & Travel** (952–890-3483), at 3429 East Highway 13 in Burnsville, offers both classes and certification and arranges Minnesota scuba adventure packages for amateur and novice divers alike.

Skydiving

The **Minnesota Skydivers Club** offers both static line and tandem airplane jumps as well as freefall jumps to those that have satisfactorily completed five static line jumps and are at least 18 years old. Ground training is provided for beginning jumpers, with instruction given by jumpmasters and instructors who have been certified by the United States Parachute Association. For jump times and site information, contact the Minnesota Skydivers Club at (952) 431–1960; www.mnskydive.com, or write them at Minnesota Skydivers Club, Inc., 3536 West Frontage Road, Owatonna, Minnesota 55060.

Soccer

Cities Sports Connection offers coed outdoor and indoor soccer leagues at the following skill levels: Rec teams consisting of players of low to moderate skill level, intermediate teams consisting of players with average to good skill proficiency and game knowledge, and competitive teams consisting of competitive, higher-skilled players with good skill proficiency and game knowledge. CSC soccer leagues are offered outdoors in spring (April–June), summer (June–August), and fall (August/September–November). CSC also runs two indoor leagues, winter1 (November–January) and winter2 (February–April). CSC is open to all adults 18 or older—no membership or nonmember fees are charged to participate in CSC leagues. Call (612) 929–9009, ext. 3, or write P.O. Box 24004, Minneapolis, Minnesota 55424-0004 for more information.

Twin Cities Sport & Recreation Club (612–871–5000), located at 2101 Hennepin Avenue South, Suite #107, can match you up with already-existing soccer teams or help you find people to fill out your own team.

Sprints, 10Ks, and Marathons

The **Twin Cities Marathon, Inc.,** is a nonprofit corporation that organizes and directs the annual Twin Cities Marathon, TC 10 Mile, and Saturday events as a community service for the Minneapolis-St. Paul area. The Twin Cities Marathon is often referred to as the most beautiful urban marathon in America and runs alongside the Mississippi River and through many metro area parks. For more information, call (612) 925–3500 or write Twin Cities Marathon, Inc., 4050 Olson Memorial Highway, Suite 26.2, Minneapolis, Minnesota 55422.

The **Minnesota Distance Running Association** (MDRA) organizes running events throughout the metro area and beyond year-round, including the annual St. Patrick's Day Human Race, a USATF/MN 8K Championship race, a 5K noncompetitive walk/jog, competitive relay races, and youth runs of all lengths. For a $15 membership fee, members of MDRA receive a subscription to the organization's magazine, *Minnesota Running and Track*, the *Running Minnesota* annual with details about track events throughout Minnesota, and the chance to participate (for free) in the many training runs the association sponsors year-round to help runners get in shape for distance runs. To contact the MDRA, write to 5701 Normandale Boulevard, Edina, Minnesota 55424. For information about MDRA-sponsored races in the metro area, call the MDRA raceline at (952) 925–4749.

Swimming

Summertime is beach weather, and all together there are more miles of combined swimming beaches in Minnesota than even California or Florida. There are more than 1,000 lakes throughout the seven counties in the Twin Cities metro area, and almost all of them are used for one form of recreation or another. In Minneapolis, swimmers are welcome at Lake Calhoun and Cedar Lake—the former does not have lifeguards, but Cedar Lake does. At the northern edge of St. Paul, swimmers share Keller Lake with the occasional boater, while at the northwestern corner of St. Paul is beautiful Lake Josephine, a family outing tradition for residents and visitors of the area for generations. White Bear Lake in White Bear has five public areas set aside for swimming, and in Minnetonka the 1,500-acre Lake Minnetonka is surrounded by swimming beaches and boat launches. Outside Minneapolis, Plymouth's Medicine Lake has two public beaches with lifeguards and has an on-site outfitter that rents small boats and canoes. State parks in the metro area with swimming beaches are Baker Park Preserve, Bald Eagle-Otter Lakes, Baylor, Bryant Lake, Bunker Hills, Cleary Lake, Clifton E. French, Como, Elm Creek Park Reserve, Hyland-Bush-Anderson Lakes, Lake Byllesby, Lake Elmo Park Reserve, Lake George, Lake Minnetonka Regional Park, Lake Minnewashta, Lake Rebecca Park Reserve, Lebanon Hills, Long Lake Regional Park, Martin-Island-Linwood Lakes, Minneapolis Chain of Lakes, Nokomis Hiawatha, Phalen-Keller, Rice Creek/Chain of Lakes, Snail Lake, Square Lake Park, and Theodore Wirth (see Parks chapter for individual addresses and more information).

If you just want to take a quick dip in a pool, nearly every neighborhood park in the Twin Cities has a free wading pool for kids and adults alike to splash around in, while several parks have full-size pools for public use. In Minneapolis, full-sized public swimming pools can be found at **North Commons Water Park** (612–370–4945), at 1701 Golden Valley Road; **Rosacker Pool** (612–370–4937), at 1520 Johnson Street NE; and **Webber Pool** (612–370–4915), at 4300 Webber Parkway. In St. Paul, full-sized public swimming pools can be found at **Como Pool** (651–489–2811), in Como Park at Como Avenue and Lexington Parkway; **Highland Swimming Pool** (651–695–3773), at 1840 Edgcumbe Road; and **Oxford Pool** (651–647–9925), at North Lexington Parkway and Iglehart Avenue.

Volleyball

Cities Sports Connection offers indoor and outdoor (sand and grass) coed volleyball leagues at all skill levels, from the very

beginning volleyball player to the advanced, highly competitive player. CSC volleyball leagues are offered indoors in the fall (September–December), winter (January–March), and spring (March–May). CSC leagues move outdoors for early summer (May–July, sand), summer (June–August, grass and sand), and late summer (July–September, sand). CSC is open to all adults 18 or older—no membership or nonmember fees are charged to participate in CSC leagues. Call (612) 929–9009, ext. 3, or write P.O. Box 24004, Minneapolis, Minnesota 55424-0004 for more information.

Twin Cities Sport & Recreation Club (612–871–5000), located at 2101 Hennepin Avenue South, Suite #107, can match you up with already-existing sand or indoor volleyball teams or help you find people to fill out your own team.

Winter Recreation

Minnesota transforms itself during the winter. Familiar landmarks are completely obliterated by giant piles of soft, white snow, and the horizon stretches out seemingly forever, no longer blocked by the lush green foliage of the spring and summer landscape.

With the change in scenery comes a change in the mood and activities of the people. Summer streets are always packed with pedestrians, and the parks are full of picnicking families and nature lovers. However, when the temperature drops below 20 degrees F—and in January and February, below 0 degrees F—many of these same people couldn't be pried out of their houses for anything but the absolutely necessary drive to work or trip to the grocery store. Those that do venture outside engage in crazy, hyperactive sports like snowmobiling, sledding, ice hockey, and skiing to stay warm, while people trying to stave off cabin fever without having to actually deal with winter congregate at bars and bowling alleys for hours on end, just to avoid having to go back outside.

But you can't spend the whole winter inside, and, despite the frequently unreasonable cold, few people here go through a whole winter without going ice skating or sledding at least once. Following are examples of some traditional Minnesota winter activities to choose from (and the places to do them at), as well as a few nontraditional indoor activities that take you outside the home without leaving you out in the cold.

Bowling
Boxing
Broomball
Cat Shows
Cross-Country Skiing
Curling
Dogsledding and Skijoring Trails
Downhill Skiing and Snowboarding
Fencing
Formal Dancing
Health Clubs
Hockey
Ice Fishing
Ice Skating
Rock Climbing
Sledding/Tobogganing
Snow-Tubing
Snowmobiling
Snowshoeing
Yoga

Bowling

A great winter sport, bowling gets you out of the house and in someplace warm and friendly. **ABC Bowling Office** (612–522–7100), located at 3701 Fremont Avenue North in Minneapolis, organizes leagues and tournaments throughout the metro area. For gender-specific league and tournament information, contact the **Minneapolis Woman's Bowling Association** at (612) 529–1666, or write 3701 Fremont Avenue North, Minneapolis, Minnesota 55412-2013.

If you just want to bowl a couple of games with a friend, there are dozens of bowling alleys to choose from. The smoke-free **Brunswick Eden Prairie Lanes** (952–941–0445), located at 12200 Singletree Lane in Eden Prairie, is open until 6:00 P.M. daily. This is the original Twin Cities home of Cosmic Bowling, during which the lights fade to black, pins glow, fog machines blow, and laser lights keep time to '50s through '90s dance music. There's also a free playroom for kids to explore while their parents knock down pins. For family fun, head on over to the 36-lane **Earle Brown Bowl** (763-585-4912), located in Brooklyn Center at 6440 James Circle North. Earle Brown also features the very popular Extreme Bowling nights, where gutter lights glow and blink to the beat of disco music and the pins glow in the dark. People wait as long as 90 minutes to get a lane during Extreme Bowling, so show up early to reserve a lane. For retro-galactic bowling, **Stardust Bowling Lanes** (612-721-6211), located at 2520 26th Avenue South in Minneapolis, is where cosmic hipsters come to toss glow-in-the-dark bowling balls and drink reasonably priced fancy mixed drinks. One of Stardust's stellar promotions is their own version of lights-out Cosmic Bowling, which runs the first and third Saturdays of the month from 2:00 P.M. to 4:00 P.M. Be sure to select a blue- or orange-swirled ball—when the lights go out, these balls glow in the dark, along with the pins and the spacey murals of bowling pin–shaped rockets. **Park Tavern** in St. Louis Park (952-929-6810), located at 401 Louisiana Avenue, is another hot bowling spot. Every Saturday night, the Park Tavern holds Cosmic Moon Lite Bowl with a spacey light show and music added to the bowling experience, while Friday night is Electric Rock & Bowl, which draws in huge crowds of the young and hip. Be sure to show up early to reserve a lane on these nights, because the 20 in-house lanes are booked fast. **Bryant-Lake Bowl** (612-825-3737), 810 West Lake Street in Minneapolis, is a throwback to bowling alleys of the past. The 1950s-era lanes in this small bowling alley provide loads of atmosphere, and the BLB does not have electronic scoring, so you get to practice scoring by hand, something many of us haven't done since childhood. Bowling is cheap here, but the lanes are first-come, first-served, and no reservations are accepted. Expect to wait on busy weekend nights, although the numerous micro-brews on tap will make the wait enjoyable.

Boxing

No longer a sport confined to men alone, boxing rings have sprung up at health clubs all over the metro area, while those that have been long established have found new participants and audiences of both genders. In St. Paul, **Brunette Boxing Gymnasium** (651-779-6248), 1135 Arcade Street, holds both coed competitions and gender-specific competitions aimed at women boxers and those interested in learning self-defense. **Uppercut Boxing Gym** (612-339-9530), 1300 Nicollet Mall, is mostly open to training sessions with occasional competitions. To find out more about boxing competitions throughout the metro area, **BT Bomber Boxing Club** in St. Paul (651-228-0503), 440 Thomas Avenue, keeps track of those matters as well as schedules competitions in regional gyms for all levels of adults and youths.

Broomball

Similar to hockey, except using brooms instead of sticks and an actual ball instead of a puck, broomball is becoming an extremely popular sport throughout the world and here in the Midwest. The United States Broomball Association recently sponsored the first USBA broomball championships in Minneapolis, and there's already talk of holding the championships here on a regular basis. The **Minneapolis Parks and Recreation Department** (612-661-4800), 400 South Fourth Street, Suite 200, organizes broomball teams for competitions and informal meets. The **Twin Cities Sport Connection** (612-929-9009) organizes coed and men's broomball leagues for informal and intermediate competitions.

Cities Sports Connection (612-929-9009, ext. 3), also offers coed and men's broomball leagues of all skill levels. CSC broomball leagues are offered in winter (December–February) as well as indoors in the summer (June–August). CSC broomball teams consist of men's 5's, coed 6's (3M/2W and goalie), coed 7's (3M/3W and goalie), or coed 8's (4M/3W and goalie) players on the ice at all times. League fees include paid officials for all league games, official broomball game balls, a six-game league schedule and play-off tournament, stylish CSC T-shirts, and prizes for winners. Teams and individuals need to supply their own brooms and additional equipment as desired.

Cat Shows

Throughout winter, the **Saintly City Cat Club** organizes and sponsors cat shows in and around the Twin Cities. For more information or to receive a calendar of events, call the Saintly City Cat Club at (651) 455-8043.

Cross-Country Skiing

There's nothing quite as exhilarating as exploring the Minnesota backwoods on a pair of cross-country skis. As luck would have it, nearly every park in the metro area has well-groomed ski trails for enthusiasts and beginners alike, taking skiers through everything from heavily wooded marked forest paths to gently sloping open spaces with incredible views of frozen waterfalls, lakes, and streams. On top of that, nearly every golf course in the metro area doubles as a cross-country ski park as soon as there's sufficient snow to do so. In the Cities, St. Paul's **Como Park,** at 1432 North Lexington Parkway, has a 5K trail that loops around the park. Cross-country ski lessons are also offered at the park's pavilion on an irregular basis—call (651) 632-5111 for details. Also in St. Paul are **Fort Snelling State Park** (651-725-2389), which is located at 1 Post Road and offers 29K (18 miles) of groomed trails for cross-

When the snow falls, cross-country skiers shush around Minneapolis's Chain of Lakes. PHOTO: GREATER MINNEAPOLIS CONVENTION & VISITORS ASSOCIATION

country and skate-ski use; **Hidden Falls/ Crosby Regional Park** (651–632–5111), at Crosby Farm Road and Shepard Road, which has 4K of groomed trails for ski use; **Highland Nine Hole Ski Area** (651–266–6400), at 1797 Edgcumbe Road, which has a 5K groomed trackset for experienced skiers and a 3K loop across the street for beginners; and **Phalen Golf Course** (651–778–0424), at 1615 Phalen Drive, which has 10K of groomed trackset for cross-country skiers.

Metro area parks with groomed trails for cross-country skiers include Baker Park Preserve, Bald Eagle-Otter Lakes, Battle Creek, Baylor, Bunker Hills, Carver Park Preserve, Cleary Lake, Clifton E. French, Coon Rapids Dam, Cottage Grove Ravine, Elm Creek Park Reserve, Hyland-Bush-Anderson Lakes, Lake Elmo Park Reserve, Lake Minnewashta, Lebanon Hills, Long Lake Regional Park, Minneapolis Chain of Lakes, Minnehaha, Minnehaha Parkway, Mississippi Gorge, Murphy-Hanrehan Park Reserve, Nokomis Hiawatha, Rice Creek/Chain of Lakes, Rice Creek-West Regional Trail, Snail Lake, Spring Lake, Theodore Wirth, Wirth-Memorial Parkway, and Wood Lake Nature Center. (See the Parks chapter for complete listings.)

Cross-country ski gear can be rented or purchased in Minneapolis at **AARCEE**

Insiders' Tip

Minnesota winters are usually coldest (with many days consistently below 0 degrees F, depending on the year) between mid-January and mid-February, so if you are going to go out and play in the snow, your best bet is to do it before or after those weeks.

---

at 2910 Lyndale Avenue South (612–827–5746), and at **Midwest Mountaineering** at 309 Cedar Avenue South (612–339–3443). In St. Paul, ski gear can be rented or purchased at either **Finn-Sisu Racing Equipment** at 1841 University Avenue West (651–645–2443), or **Joe's Sporting Goods** at 935 North Dale Street (651–488–5511).

Curling

Resembling a combination of ice hockey and shuffleboard, curling has gone from being a popular sport confined mostly to Canada and the UK to being an Olympic event and a well-loved, albeit still relatively obscure, winter sport in the Midwest USA. The St. Paul Curling Club, the largest member-owned curling club in the country, organizes curling matches throughout the Twin Cities during the winter, with practice meets at indoor rinks arranged infrequently during the summer. For more information contact the **St. Paul Curling Club** at (651) 224–7408, or write 470 Selby Avenue, St. Paul, Minnesota 55102.

Dogsledding and Skijoring Trails

Dogsledding and skijoring—in which a skier is pulled along by a horse or a vehicle—are permitted on designated trails in some metro area parks. With the exception of the multiuse trail at **Baker Park Reserve,** a special-use permit is required for both activities; call the **Hennepin Parks Reservations** office at (763) 559–6700 for further information, permits, and maps.

Sections of snowmobile trails at **Crow-Hassan Park Reserve, Elm Creek Park Reserve,** and the **North Hennepin Trail Corridor** are also open for skijoring and dogsledding on weekdays during the day and weekends and holidays from 5:00 A.M. to 10:00 A.M. **Crow-Hassan Park Reserve,** located west of Rogers on Sylvan Lake

Road, has 5.5 miles of trail designated for dogsledding/skijoring use; **Elm Creek Park Reserve,** located northwest of Osseo on County Road 81, has 11 miles of trail designated for dogsledding/skijoring use; the **North Hennepin Trail Corridor,** connecting the Coon Rapids Dam Regional Park in Brooklyn Park to Elm Creek Park Reserve in Maple Grove, has 6 miles of trail designated for dogsledding/skijoring use. These trails are usually packed, so be prepared for lots of company. A special-use permit and annual Park Patron permit are required to use the trails.

Murphy-Hanrehan Park Reserve, located near Prior Lake on Scott County Road 75, has 4 miles of trail designated for dogsledding and horseriding—no snowmobiles are allowed. The trail is open all week during daylight hours and is not usually packed. A special-use permit and annual Park Patron permit are required in order to use the trails.

Baker Park Reserve, located 20 miles west of downtown Minneapolis on County Road 19, has 4 miles of trails set aside for dogsledding, skijoring, mountain biking, and snowshoeing. No special-use permit is required, but parking fees apply for all vehicles.

Downhill Skiing and Snowboarding

In the immediate Twin Cities metro area, there aren't a lot of options for downhill skiing or extreme snowboarding. But let's face it—this is farm and lumber country, and mountains don't really figure into our natural geography. For real downhill skiing, you have to make the three- to four-hour trek up to Duluth and the North Shore, where you'll find the **Giants Ridge Golf & Ski Resort** (218-865-4143; www.giantsridge.com), in the town of Biwabik off County Road 138; **Golden Eagle Lodge & Nordic Ski Center** (218-388-2203), at 468 Clearwater Road in Grand Marais; **Spirit Mountain** (218-628-2891), at 9500 Spirit Mountain Place in Duluth; and **Lutsen Mountains** (218-628-2891; www.lutsen.com) found halfway

between Duluth and the Canadian border at 467 Ski Road in Lutsen. All four ski areas are also resorts, and discounts are offered seasonally on rooms and lift tickets for those who purchase a combination of both—advance reservations are highly recommended.

Closer to home—but again, not as tall or as steep as the North Shore slopes—is **Buck Hill** in Burnsville (952-435-7174; www.buckhill.com) located at 15400 Buck Hill Road; **Hyland Ski Area & Snowboard Area** in Bloomington (952-835-4250; www.hylandski.com), at 8800 Chalet Road; **Afton Alps** (651-436-5245; www.aftonalps.com), located in Afton on County Road 20; **Welch Village Ski Area** (651-222-7079; www.welchvillage.com), located in Welch on Minnesota Highway 61 and County Road 7; and **Wild Mountain Ski** (651-257-3550 or 800-447-4958; www.wildmountain.com), located off Minnesota Highway 8 in Taylors Falls at 37350 Wild Mountain Road.

Fencing

The **Twin Cities Fencing Club** is one of the top fencing clubs in the country. Fencers from TCFC have represented the United States at international competitions, won national championships (both senior and junior), and earned medals at local, regional, and national competitions. Head Coach Roberto Sobalvarro has coached U.S. National Teams at the World Championships, World Cup competitions, and the U.S. Olympic Festival. The club serves fencers of all ages and all levels of experience, from beginner to National Champion. For more information about club events and to get current membership rates, call (651) 225-1990, or stop by the facility at 741 Holly Avenue in St. Paul.

Formal Dancing

What better way to chase away the winter blues and meet new people than dancing? Several clubs in the Twin Cities area have sprung up to bring like-minded dance partners together, including the **Twin Cities Rebels Swing Dance Club** in Bloomington (952–941–0906), which has regular swingin' get-togethers all over the metro area, and the **Twin Town Twirlers Square Dancing Club** (651–484–7696, www.tripletdance.com), which generally meets at the Fairview Community Center at 1910 West County Road B in Roseville. For more traditional dancers, the **Minnesota Chapter of the U.S. Amateur Ballroom Dancers Association** organizes events and competitions throughout the year; call (952) 483–5467 for more information.

Health Clubs

What better way to stay in shape and keep your beautiful summer tan than a health club membership? The Twin Cities proper have several full-size gyms and health clubs to choose from, many of which offer free child care and youth programs such as swimming lessons and martial arts. **Lifetime Fitness** has two locations in St. Paul—at 2145 Ford Parkway in the Highland Park neighborhood (651–698–5000), and at 340 Cedar Street (651–227–7777), in the downtown area. There is also a downtown Minneapolis branch at 615 Second Avenue (612–752–7000) in the Grand Hotel Minneapolis (branch is for executive members only), and several locations in the suburbs, including the women-only location at 2480 Fairview Avenue in Roseville (651–633–4444). The facilities include Cybex, Nautilus, Gravitron, and ski machines as well as stairclimbers. Aerobics, dance, and karate classes are offered, as are massage, tanning beds, personal training, nutrition seminars, and free child care. Reciprocity is included in regular membership fees, and this is the only health club chain in town that is open 24 hours a day.

Body Quest Fitness Center (612–377–7222), located at 245 Aldrich Avenue North in Minneapolis, is a sparer gym, catering especially to the art of body building. The club features a mix of equipment such as Cybex, free weights, and stairclimbers and has personal trainers and a massage therapist on site. Another weight-training gym, **Los Campeones Fitness & Body,** 2721 Franklin Avenue East in Minneapolis (612–333–8181), features free weights as well as Gravitron, Spinnaker 3000, and Hammer Strength machines, while the on-site pro shop offers vitamin supplements and tanning beds. **The Sweatshop Health Club** in St. Paul (651–646–8418), located at 171 Snelling Avenue North, offers a variety of personal weight-training programs, as well as kick boxing, t'ai chi, and Pilates mat classes, and has a free childcare facility on the premises. Voted "Best Workout" by *Glamour* and *Seventeen* magazines, **The Firm** (612–377–

Insiders' Tip

Every year, the American Red Cross, local television station WCCO, and various businesses donate supplies to the Winter Car Safety Kit project. These emergency car kits are sold at local stores for only $5, for which you get a flashlight and batteries, a snack food item, flagging tape, a candle, matches, a pencil and notepad for messages, a guide for safe winter travel, and other roadside necessities in one handy package.

3003), located at 245 Aldrich Avenue North in Minneapolis, offers weight training, spinning, and Pilates and has a masseuse on the premises.

A national standard in women's gyms, the **YWCA** has three branches in Minneapolis—in Downtown at 1130 Nicollet Mall (612-332-0501), in Midtown at 2121 East Lake Street (612-215-4333), and in Uptown at 2808 Hennepin Avenue South (612-874-7131). The YWCA also has one location in St. Paul at 375 Selby Avenue (651-225-9922). All facilities have indoor swimming pools, weight machines, fitness programs, and day care for children of all ages.

The **YMCA** has multiple locations throughout the Twin Cities metro area, including one in downtown Minneapolis in City Center at 30 South Ninth Street, (612-371-8750), and one in downtown St. Paul at 194 East Sixth Street (651-292-4143). All locations offer weight rooms, aerobic workout equipment, lap pools, gyms, and day care.

Hockey

Kids in Minnesota start playing hockey about as soon as they can walk, and both boys and girls participate in the sport with equal fervor. Every winter, parks in the Twin Cities metro area are flooded to make ice-skating rinks for skaters and hockey players, and formal and informal hockey teams are formed among children and adults alike. During hockey season, large amounts of television time are blocked off on more than one station to bring live coverage of local high school and college hockey playoffs.

Traditionally St. Paul has been a much more dedicated hockey town than Minneapolis, and it shows. St. Paul has the Minnesota Wild's Xcel Energy Center arena and is home to more than a dozen groomed ice hockey rinks, including the **Arlington Ice Skating Rink** at 665 East Rose Avenue (651-298-5701), **Battle Creek Ice Skating Rink** at 2076 Upper Afton (651-298-5737), **Conway Ice Skating Park** at 2090 Conway Avenue (651-298-5742), **Desnoyer Ice Skating Rink** at 525 Pelham Boulevard (651-298-5753), **Eastview Ice Skating Rink** at 1675 East 6th Street, (651-298-5710), **Edgcumbe Ice Skating Rink** at 320 South Griggs, (651) 298-5772, **El Rio Vista Ice Skating Rink** at 179 East Robie Street (651-298-5659), **Frost Lake Ice Skating Rink** at 1518 East Idaho Avenue (651-298-5712), **Griggs Ice Skating Rink** at 1188 Hubbard Avenue (651-298-4393), **Hazel Park Ice Skating Rink** at 919 North Hazel Avenue (651-298-5739), **Langford Ice Skating Park** at 30 Langford Park (651 298-5756), **Linwood Ice Skating Rink** at 860 St. Clair Avenue (651-298-5660), **Margaret Ice Skating Rink** at 1109 Margaret Street (651-298-5719), **Merriam Park Ice Skating Rink** at 2000 St. Anthony Avenue (651-298-5766), and **West Minnehaha Ice Skating Rink** at 685 West Minnehaha Avenue (651-298-5823).

If you're interested in forming a casually competitive hockey team or joining an already-existing one, **Twin Cities Sport & Recreation Club** (612-871-5000), located at 2101 Hennepin Avenue South, Suite #107, in Minneapolis, can match you up with already-existing hockey teams or help you find people to fill out your own team.

Ice Fishing

Most people who didn't grow up here don't believe this sport actually exists until they've been to Minnesota. Basically, you set up camp on top of a frozen lake, cut a hole in the ice, and wait for some sluggish fish to come along and snap up your bait. There are lots of fancy variations to this you can try, including bringing portable houses, space heaters, camping refrigerators, and televisions out onto the ice with you, but this is basically the blueprint to every ice fishing trip. For more information, see the chapter on Fishing and Hunting.

Ice Skating

Just about every park in the Twin Cities metro area, if not every park in Minnesota, has an area of the green that gets flooded every winter and turned into a free neighborhood ice skating rink. The two best examples of this are at **Nicollet Island** in Minneapolis and the **Como Park Lakeside Pavilion** in St. Paul, (651) 266-6400, 1360 North Lexington Parkway. Each winter at Nicollet Island, most of the park is converted into a Norman Rockwell scene of kids with earmuffs and white and black skates filling the three giant interlocking rinks, while adults look on sipping hot chocolate and coffee sold by vendors inside the cozy pavilion. The same goes for Como Park, except a good part of an entire lake is cleared of snow and turned into a gigantic ice skating rink—and yes, coffee and hot chocolate are served at the Como Park Pavilion, and during Winter Carnival, both are given to park visitors for free.

If you're looking for something more groomed than a neighborhood ice skating rink filled early in the morning by a bleary-eyed, pink-nosed park attendant with a hose, there are many "real" rinks to be found in St. Paul, something that Minneapolis strangely lacks.

In St. Paul, you can find well-groomed skate rinks at the **Arlington Recreation Center Rink** at 665 East Rose Avenue, (651) 298-5701; **Conway Recreation Center Rink** at 2090 Conway Avenue, (651) 501-6343; **Desnoyer Ice Skating Rink** at 525 Pelham Boulevard, (651) 298-5753; **Eastview Recreation Center Rink** at 1675 East 5th Street, (651) 772-7845; **Edgcumbe Ice Skating Rink** at 320 South Griggs, (651) 695-3711; **El Rio Vista Recreation Center Rink** at 179 East Robie Street, (651) 298-5659; **Griggs Recreation Center Rink** at 1188 Hubbard Avenue, (651) 298-5755; **Hancock Recreation Center Rink** at 1610 Hubbard Avenue, (651) 298-4393; **Hazel Park Recreation Center Rink** at 919 North Hazel Avenue, (651) 501-6350; **Langford Recreation Center Rink** at 30 Langford Park, (651) 298-5765; **Linwood Recre-**

When the lakes freeze in the Twin Cities Metro, everyone from ice anglers to skaters gets out on the lakes. PHOTO: GREATER MINNEAPOLIS CONVENTION & VISITORS ASSOCIATION

ation Center Rink at 860 St. Clair Avenue, (651) 298-5660; **Merriam Park Recreation Center Rink** at 2000 St. Anthony Avenue, (651) 298-5766; **North Dale Recreation Center Rink** at 1410 North St. Albans, (651) 298-5812; **Northwest Como Recreation Center Rink** at 1550 North Hamline, (651) 298-5813; and **West Minnehaha Recreation Center Rink** at 685 West Minnehaha Avenue, (651) 298-5823.

Again, in Minneapolis, your selection is much more limited when it comes to groomed skating rinks. **Edison Civic Arena** at 1306 Central Avenue NE, (612) 782-2123, opens up to the public for skating whenever there isn't a hockey game or practice in session, while just outside of Minneapolis in Brooklyn Park is the

Breck School Ice Arena (763-545-1614), 5600 85th Avenue, which opens to the public when there aren't classes being taught or competitions being held. Downtown Minneapolis recently converted the old Milwaukee Road Train Depot at Fifth Street and Washington Avenue into a year-round indoor skating rink. **The Depot Skating Rink** (612-339-2253), is a gorgeous ice sheet inside the historic, glass-walled depot. Skate rentals are available.

For information about ice skating, call the **Twin Cities Figure Skating Association** at (612) 934-4963. The association sponsors most of the ice skating events, lessons, and competitions in the Twin Cities through 14 metro area clubs that boast more than 1,200 members.

Rock Climbing

While there aren't any mountains or even too many steep hills in the Twin Cities metro area, there are several organizations that can help put together mountaineering excursions for solo or group climbers, as well as a few gyms with indoor climbing walls for varying skill levels.

REI (952-884-4315; www.rei.com), located at 750 West 79th Street in Bloomington, organizes annual trips to such destinations as the Summit Challenge in Nepal and the Kilimanjaro Climb. They can also direct you to local climbing spots favored by the staff and fellow customers alike. REI is a complete gear shop and can hook you up with anything you might need to prep yourself for any level of climb. The Bloomington store also has an indoor climbing wall available free to members and at a nominal fee to non-members.

Midwest Mountaineering (612-339-3433, www.midwestmountaineering.com), located at 309 Cedar Avenue in Minneapolis, is another great gear shop with information about local climbing spots for all levels of climber. Recently the store erected an on-site 31-foot-high vertical climbing tower made of both artificial and real (weather permitting) ice, available for public use with a full complement of guides to assist in your climb.

For indoor climbing, **Footprints Adventure Company and Climbing Gym** (952-884-7996), located at South James Avenue, Suite 3, in Bloomington, has several climbing walls for varying skill levels. **Vertical Endeavors Indoor Park and Climbing Camp** (651-776-1430), located in Seeger Square in St. Paul, has a wide variety of practice climbing options for all skill levels as well as on-site climbing instructors.

Sledding/Tobogganing

There aren't really rules regarding or areas set aside for sledding or tobogganing—most Twin Cities metro parks have great sledding hills either built or already existing for kids and adults to use. Just use your common sense and don't pick a hill that terminates in a busy street, and don't try to take your sled on a ski or snowboard slope. **Como Park** in particular has some

---

Insiders' Tip

Como Park offers a variety of family-related activities each winter, including kite-flying outings where they provide free kites to everyone, group snowshoe walks, and dog races. Call the Como Park Lakeside Pavilion at (651) 488-4920 or the Como Zoo and Conservatory Society at (651) 645-1014 for more information on winter events.

great areas built up especially for sledding/tobogganing—call (651) 488–9673 for more information.

Snow-Tubing

Unlike sledding or tobogganing, you actually have to have a decent hill in order to get real speed on an inner tube. Some of the places that have designed and built special hills for snow-tubing are **Eko Backen** (651–433–2422), at 22570 Manning Trail in Scandia; **Green Acres** (651–770–6060), at 8989 55th Street North in Lake Elmo; **Oak Hill Park** (952–924–2540), at 3400 Rhode Island Avenue South in St. Louis Park; **Staring Lake Park** (952–949–8442), at 14800 Pioneer Trail in Eden Prairie; **Trapp Farm Park** (651–681–4660), at 841 Wilderness Run Road in Eagan; **Valleywood Golf Course and Park** (952–953–2323), at County Road 38 and 125th Street in Apple Valley; and **Wirth Park** (763–522–4584), at 1301 Theodore Wirth Parkway in Golden Valley. Inner tubes can be rented at all of the aforementioned facilities for a nominal fee.

Snowmobiling

There's an incredible sense of freedom that comes with riding a snowmobile, and Minnesota has over 18,000 miles of public and private snowmobile trails that cross both wide open frozen lakes and follow paths cut through thick Minnesota forests. With just a few commonsense rules to "limit" the snowmobiler, this is a great way to see the outdoors in Minnesota. You can download a copy of the Snowmobiler's Safety Laws, Rules & Regulations from the **Department of Natural Resources** Web page at www.dnr.state.mn.us, or call the DNR at (800) 285–2000 to have them mail you a copy. You are required to have a Snowmobile State Trail Sticker ($16 per sticker) on your vehicle before you can take to the trails, so you'll probably want to give the DNR a call anyway. Alcoholic beverages are not allowed on snowmobiles at all, even if they're locked in a separate compartment—firearms may be transported on snowmobiles if they are unloaded and completely enclosed in a case. Maximum speed in Minnesota for snowmobiles is 50 MPH, and youth/young adult riders age 13 and under are not allowed to operate snowmobiles by themselves. All snowmobiles must be registered with the DNR, whether you're a resident or just a visitor.

You are allowed to ride snowmobiles anywhere within the seven-county metro area on your own land (although you'd better be on good terms with your neighbors if you try it in the Cities), on land that has signs posted saying SNOWMOBILES ALLOWED, and on land where you have express written or spoken consent from the owner or lessee. Parks within the metro area that have trails specifically groomed for snowmobiles include Baker Park Preserve, Carver Park Preserve, Cleary Lake, Crow-Hassan, Elm Creek Park Reserve, Hyland-Bush-Anderson Lakes, Lake George, Lake Rebecca Park Reserve, Lebanon Hills, Murphy-Hanrehan Park Reserve, and North Hennepin Trail Corridor (see Parks chapter for complete listings). Additional information on trails, trail maps, and snowmobiling events can be obtained by calling the **Minnesota United Snowmobilers Association** at (763) 577–

0185 or by writing them at 5131 Fern-
brook Lane North, Plymouth, Minnesota
55447-5321.

Snowshoeing

Snowshoeing may seem too clunky and
slow to be practical. However, the wide, flat
paddles make it possible to safely walk over
the top of snowdrifts that would otherwise
cause hikers to fall all the way through to
solid ground, making this an ideal means of
transportation after a fresh snowfall. Once
you've mastered walking in snowshoes,
you've no need to worry about getting the
cuffs of your pants wet with melting snow,
or getting trapped in unexpected deep
snowdrifts. Instead, you and your snowshoes will practically glide over the soft
snow, proving that for all their awkward
appearance, putting on a pair of these will
actually make your walk easier and faster.

The following parks have areas set
aside for snowshoers: Baker Park Preserve,
Bald Eagle-Otter Lakes, Baylor, Carver
Park Preserve, Clifton E. French, Como,
Coon Rapids Dam, Crow-Hassan, Elm
Creek Park Reserve, Hidden Falls-Crosby
Farm, Hyland-Bush-Anderson Lakes, Lake
Minnewashta, Lebanon Hills, Minneapolis Chain of Lakes, Minnehaha, Nokomis
Hiawatha, Rice Creek/Chain of Lakes, and
Theodore Wirth (see Parks chapter for
complete listings). Como Park holds guided
snowshoe hikes most full-moon nights
across the golf course/cross-country ski
area. Carver Park Reserve, Elm Creek Park
Reserve, Hyland Park Reserve, and Coon
Rapids Dam hold guided snowshoe hikes
led by a naturalist several times a month
during winter—reservations to participate
are required at least two days prior to the
hike, and there is a $6.00 fee per person
that includes snowshoe rental.

Yoga

Developed in India, yoga is a psycho-
physical discipline with roots going back
about 5,000 years. Depending on how you
approach it and what you want to get out

*A young snowshoer high-steps through the powder
in Minneapolis.* PHOTO: GREATER MINNEAPOLIS CONVENTION
& VISITORS ASSOCIATION

of it, yoga is a religion, an exercise routine,
or a great way to forget about being
trapped in a subzero climate. Hatha Yoga,
which includes postures and breathing, is
the form most popular in the West and is
actually part of Raja Yoga, the path of self-
control, while the path most followed in
India is thought to be Bhakti Yoga, the
path of devotion. Hatha Yoga classes are
taught throughout the Twin Cities,
including at the **Crocus Hill Health Center** in St. Paul (651-222-8517), 653 Grand
Avenue; and in Minneapolis at the **BKS
Iyengar Yoga Center** (612-872-8708),
2736 Lyndale Avenue South, the **Meditation Center** (612-379-2386), 631 University Avenue NE, and the **Yoga Workshop
of Minneapolis** (612-825-2554), 810
West 31st Street.

Hunting and Fishing

Hunting and fishing have been an important part of Minnesotans' lives and the state's economy since explorers first encountered the plentiful bounty of the area. Even before Europeans discovered the dense, rich hardwood forests that harbored deer, bear, moose, and elk, or the many lakes and streams that teemed with fish and furbearing animals like otter and beaver, nomadic indigenous peoples made this land of plenty their home in spring and summer. Much, much later, wealthy socialites from Chicago made annual treks to Minnesota to swim and fish in the beautiful, clear waters, giving rise to vacation and health resort towns all along the banks of Lake Superior, Lake Minnetonka, and many other Minnesota lakes.

These are traditions that stand today. There are literally hundreds of hunting and especially fishing resorts all over the state, many of which can sell you your fishing licenses right there on the premises, as well as bait, ammunition, and rod and boat rentals. **Hospitality Minnesota** (651-778-2400; www.hospitalitymn.com), and the **Minnesota Office of Tourism** (800-657-3700; www.exploreminnesota.com), issue an annual booklet that lists resorts in detail and will mail you a free copy if you call either number or contact them through either Web site.

While Minnesota has an incredible abundance of wildlife, hunters and anglers are always encouraged to be ethical, safe, and as responsible as they can possibly be. Minnesota wildlife conservation officers and the Department of Natural Resources (DNR) have been working hand in hand for more than 115 years to make sure that there will always be game and fish for future generations, and strict fines and imprisonment are some of the penalties imposed on poachers and careless hunters who disregard the laws. The DNR offers many valuable resources to hunters and anglers, including information booklets on the best places to go hunting and fishing, a regularly updated Web site (www.dnr.state.mn.us) with specific information about breeding and stocking programs for game animals and fish, and the convenience of applying for hunting and fishing licenses over the telephone for a nominal extra charge.

Many of Minnesota's pristine wildlife areas reflect the grandeur that amazed the first Europeans who came to this beautiful area. Minnesota's great outdoors offers a variety of unforgettable experiences for anglers and hunters of all levels.

Hunting

Although hunting and trapping have been established outdoor traditions in Minnesota since before the first European settlers came to the area, this is not to say that hunting itself is a casual recreation in the eyes of the law. Hunting is a heavily regulated sport in Minnesota, requiring specific licensing dependent on game targeted, whether you're hunting with firearms or bow and arrow, the area you plan to hunt in, and the age of the hunter. If you purchase a small game license but do not specify that you plan to hunt migratory birds (waterfowl, woodcock, snipe, rails, etc.), you are not allowed to hunt those birds; you must reapply for the same license and specify that you do plan to hunt migratory birds. Deer and big game licenses are awarded on a lottery basis depending on how many animals the Minnesota DNR considers an expendable excess.

Trespassing laws are very rigidly enforced, and if you're caught hunting on private property or on land that is not zoned for hunting, you'll be charged a minimum $50 fine for the first violation, a $200 fine for the second violation, and a $500 fine and loss of hunting license for the third violation. Exceptions to the trespassing laws include entering private land, on foot and without a weapon to retrieve a wounded animal that was lawfully shot or to retrieve a hunting dog. If a landowner does not allow you onto his land to retrieve a wounded animal, you must leave the private property immediately without the game animal.

Hunting dogs are not allowed to chase down, wound, or kill big game animals. A dog that is observed doing so may be legally killed by a person other than a DNR conservation officer between January 1 and July 14. Hunting dogs may not be killed by anyone other than a DNR conservation officer any other time, as many hunters legally use dogs to track upland game, waterfowl, rabbits, raccoons, foxes, and coyotes.

For current licensing rates for game hunting, call the **Minnesota DNR** at (651) 296-6157 or (800) 657-3929, or check out their Web site at www.dnr.state.mn.us. Most licenses, both hunting and fishing, can be picked up at almost any bait shop or convenience store near the popular hunting areas (more than 1,700 licensing facilities are spread throughout Minnesota), but for extra expedience, the DNR can immediately issue small game licenses electronically by calling (651) 296-4506 or (888) MINN-DNR, or through the DNR's Web site. Hunters are encouraged to apply for all licenses early, as the number of licenses issued is dependent on actual game availability.

Animal poaching is a serious crime in Minnesota. **Turn In Poachers (TIP), Inc.,** is a nonprofit organization founded by hunters and concerned citizens to stop poaching in Minnesota. TIP offers cash awards for information leading to a poacher's arrest; all tipsters remain anonymous. For more information call the toll-free TIP hotline at (800) 652-9093.

The following listings are only general rules that apply to hunting and trapping game in Minnesota. Most parks and wildlife preserves have specific rules and restrictions regarding hunting and trapping, and it's important to check with both the DNR and with the specific park/preserve in question before going out.

Big Game

When hunting big game (deer, moose, bear, etc., as dictated by law) in Minnesota, the minimum caliber of rifle, shotgun, muzzleloader, or handgun that can be used is .23 (.30 caliber M-1 carbine cartridges are not allowed), and only single-projectile ammunition can be used. Also, it's illegal to take down big game with a bow and arrow while in possession of a firearm, with the exception of hunting bear, where possession of a firearm while in possession of archery equipment is allowed. Bows must have a minimum pull of 40 pounds at or before full draw in order to effectively kill big game. Arrow heads used must have a minimum of two sharp metal cutting edges and be barbless. Crossbows are not allowed for either big or small game hunting, except by special permit given only to disabled hunters. Big game may only be hunted from one-half hour before sunrise to one-half hour after sunset.

Bear

Bear hunting is legal in northern Minnesota in specified areas around Duluth and along the border waters during Bear Season (approximately late August through mid-October), with the exception of white bears, which may not be hunted at any time. Residents and nonresidents can obtain bear hunting licenses from the DNR, which are usually made available by mid-March. More than 20,000 bear hunting permits were issued during the 2000 hunting season but the number of permits issued is dependent on actual animal population.

Deer

Open season for deer hunting generally begins in early November and lasts through early December. Archery season for deer traditionally begins in mid-September. Call the DNR for specific dates, as they vary from year to year depending on weather. It's recommended that hunters apply much earlier than the early-September application deadline for licenses, as a limited number are awarded, depending on game availability. Any deer brought down by a hunter must be tagged according to DNR specifications, and no one hunter may tag more than one deer per calendar year, with the exception of the Northwest Two-Deer areas in Kittson, Lake of the Woods, Marshall, Pennington, and Roseau Counties in northwestern Minnesota, where a hunter may tag one deer with a regular archery license and another with a regular firearms license. Both deer must be taken and registered in the county they were taken in. Chronic Wasting Disease (CWD), a fatal disease sometimes present in the wild deer and elk population in Minnesota, is a concern for many hunters. The federal government says it is "unlikely" that CWD can be transmitted from an infected animal to a human, and there are no known cases of this happening. The DNR takes samples voluntarily at several deer registration stations throughout the state, although the testing process may take several weeks or months. Brochures on proper tagging procedures and CWD are available at any of the 1,700 licensing stations across Minnesota, or from the DNR Information and License Center at 500 Lafayette Road, St. Paul, Minnesota 55155-4040, www.dnr. state.mn.us, (651) 296-6157.

A limited number of Special Area Permits are issued each year to hunters in places where the number of hunters must be limited to control the harvest or for public safety. Permits are awarded by a lottery system dependent on a head count and estimation of expendable deer available. Hunters who receive Special Area Permits may also hunt deer outside that Special Area if they apply to do so and have it specifically punched on their hunting license. Special Area Permits are issued for hunters in Rice Lake National Wildlife Refuge in Aitkin County; St. Croix State Park in Pine County; Gooseberry Falls State Park, Split Rock Lighthouse State Park, and Tettegouche State Park in Lake County; Afton State Park, Lake Elmo Park Reserve, and William O'Brien State Park in Washington County; Lake Bronson State Park in Kittson County; Zippel Bay State Park in Lake of the Woods; Wild River State Park in Chisago County; Frontenac State Park in Goodhue County; Elm Creek Park Reserve and Murphy Hanrehan in Hennepin County; Beaver Creek Valley State Park in Houston County; Miesville Ravine Park Reserve in Dakota County; Zumbro Falls Woods in Wabasha County; Lake Louise State Park in Mower County; Rice Lake State Park in Steele County; and Maplewood State Park in Otter Tail County.

Bow and arrow hunting is also permitted (with Special Area Permit) at Crow-Hassan Park Reserve in Hennepin County, Murphy-Hanrehan Park Reserve and Cleary Lake Regional Park in Scott County, and outside the city limits of New Ulm and Red Wing. Contact the DNR at (651) 296-6157 for information regarding specific dates open to bow and arrow hunting, as dates change depending on weather conditions and deer availability. (For specific details and contact information on metro-area parks listed, see Parks chapter.)

Elk

During years when elk hunting is permitted, the season is open only to residents of Minnesota, and hunters must apply in parties of two. Elk hunting permits are not issued every year; contact the DNR to find out more about whether there will be a hunt and for more information about applying for permits. Permits are issued by random drawing, and, like hunting for moose, the hunt is a once-in-a-lifetime event.

Moose

Minnesota's annual moose hunt is open only to Minnesota residents and is a "once-in-a-lifetime" event—each hunter is allowed to take down only one moose in his or her lifetime. Moose licenses are awarded annually on a lottery basis determined by actual animal populations. Some years, no moose permits are issued. Generally the moose hunting season runs from late September to mid-October. Contact the DNR for more specifics.

Small Game, Waterfowl, and Migratory Birds

Most small game and migratory bird hunting is sanctioned by the state in order to keep animal population levels down, as the natural enemies of most of the following—bears, wolves, coyotes, etc.—are in short supply in the modern world. However, while there are no real bag limits for many of the following, the DNR does require that hunters purchase proper licenses before taking any small game animals or migratory birds in order to get a rough estimation of how many animals and birds will be culled during a given hunting season. It's no accident that Minnesota has an abundance of wildlife in its parklands, wildlife preserves, and even in the cities. Careful monitoring of habitats and hunter/game interaction by Minnesota conservation officers has been an important facet of state government for more than a century, with the goal of creating safe hunting opportunities for residents and visitors to the state while preserving as much of the native Minnesota wildlife as possible.

Beaver, Mink, Muskrat, and Otter

It is unlawful to trap any furbearing animals within any state-owned game refuge without first obtaining a permit from the appropriate wildlife manager. Most of the state parks and state wildlife refuges allow trapping of furbearing small game as long as you get prior permission and have a small game hunting license.

Foxes, Raccoons, Squirrels, Rabbits

It is legal to hunt all of the above year-round throughout most of Minnesota. A small game hunting license is required, unless you are hunting on your own land.

Migratory Waterfowl

A State Migratory Waterfowl Stamp (State Duck Stamp), purchased from the DNR for a nominal fee, is required for hunting geese, ducks, and mergansers. All hunters—resident and nonresident—between the ages of 18 and 65 are required to have a valid State Duck Stamp in their possession while hunting migratory waterfowl, with the exception of those taking down waterfowl on their own property or who are in the U.S. Armed Forces and are stationed outside Minnesota with official military leave papers on their person.

Waterfowl hunting seasons and bag limits are set in late summer, and season dates are announced in early September. Contact the DNR for more information.

A special permit is also required for hunting Canada geese in season. During early September and late December, the entire state is open to hunting geese. Daily bag limits range from two to five geese per hunter, depending on the DNR-specified hunting zone, and shooting hours last from one-half hour before sunrise to sunset every day. Possession limits are double the daily bag limits. Migratory waterfowl must be transported in an undressed condition (with head and wings attached) at all times until delivery to either the hunter's home or to a commercial processing facility.

It is unlawful to take geese, ducks, mergansers, coots, or moorhens with lead shot or while having any lead shot in possession. Only nontoxic shot approved by the U.S. Fish and Wildlife Service may be used. These nontoxic shot restrictions are responsible for preventing lead poisoning of more than 400,000 wild ducks nationwide each year.

Wild Turkey

Spring and fall (check with the DNR for specific dates) are open for hunting wild turkey in Minnesota. Generally application deadlines for Wild Turkey Stamps are five or six months before the actual season begins. Smaller, quicker, and smarter than domestic turkeys, these native Minnesota birds can also fly up into trees to hide, making them a competitive target for traditional firearm and bow hunters alike. Although a small game license is not necessary for taking wild turkey, you must purchase a Wild Turkey Stamp from the DNR in order to legally hunt the birds. Bag limit is one bird of either sex in the fall season per hunter and one male bird per hunter in spring.

Only fine shot size Number 4 and smaller may be used to hunt turkey, and nothing smaller that a 20 gauge shotgun can be carried on turkey hunts. Bows must have a pull of no less than 40 pounds, and arrows must be sharp, have at least two metal cutting edges, and be at least $\frac{7}{8}$ inch in diameter. Poison- or explosive-tipped arrows may not be used to hunt any game animal or bird in Minnesota. Hunting dogs are not allowed on turkey hunts, and neither are electronic tracking devices. Every hunter who takes a wild turkey must personally present the bird for registration at one of the 1,700 registration stations throughout Minnesota; the feathers, head, and feet must remain on the bird until it is officially registered.

Some of the areas set aside for hunting wild turkey are Linn Lake Refuge in Chisago County, Claremont Refuge in Dodge County, Lost Lake Refuge in Fillmore County, Moscow Refuge and Albert Lea Refuge in Freeborn County, Rochester Refuge in Olmsted County, Nerstrand Refuge in Rice County, Stearns County Refuge in Stearns County, St. Croix River Refuge and Stillwater Refuge in Washington County, and Whitewater Refuge in Winona County.

Protected Animals

There is no open season for hunting bob-white quail, prairie chickens, cranes, swans, mourning doves, hawks, owls, eagles, herons, bitterns, cormorants, loons, grebes, or any other species of birds except specified game or unprotected birds. Crows may be taken without a license in season (September 1 through February 28) or at any time when they are doing or are about to do damage. There is also no open season for hunting caribou, antelope, gray wolf, wolverine, cougar, or spotted skunk ("civet cat").

Unprotected Species

Minnesota residents are not required to have a license to hunt unprotected species. Weasels, coyotes, gophers, porcupines, striped skunks, and all other mammals for which there are no closed seasons or are not under protected status may be hunted year-round. They may be taken in any manner, except with the aid of artificial lights or by using a motor vehicle to chase, run over, or kill the animal. Poisons may not be used except in accordance with restrictions stated by the Minnesota Department of Agriculture.

House sparrows, starlings, common pigeons, chukar partridge, quail other than bobwhite quail, mute swans, and monk parakeets are all unprotected and may be hunted year-round.

No person may take a wild animal with a firearm or by archery from a motorized vehicle except a disabled person with an appropriate permit on a stationary vehicle. Also, it's against the law to transport an uncased firearm or shoot from any motorized vehicle in Minnesota.

Fishing

In the "Land of 10,000 Lakes," it's no surprise that fishing is one of the most popular summer recreational activities. To meet the demand of thousands of dedicated anglers, the Minnesota DNR runs fisheries all over the state that are in charge of keeping the most popular lakes and fishing holes well stocked with walleye, pike, muskellunge, trout, bass, catfish, crappie, bluegill, and, in certain areas, Minnesota's newest popular catch of the day—salmon. Fishing licenses are available at any of the 1,700 licensing agents located at convenience stores, bait shops, and sports outfitters across the state. Since March 2000 the DNR has also been issuing fishing licenses electronically over the telephone (call 888–MNLicense for more information) and through their Web site at www.dnr. state.mn.us.

Regulations for fishing areas change per year according to species populations, so it's a good idea to call the DNR to request a current fishing guide or to ask about a specific fishing spot before heading out. The DNR's Web site regularly posts updated fishing information and regulation changes, if any.

Northern Pike

Although walleye is the most popular fish in Minnesota, the most widely spread game fish in the state is the northern pike. With its abundance of marshes and shallow streams, Minnesota has as much or more northern pike habitat than any other state. Given relatively clean water, an adequate food supply, and enough shoreline marshes and wetlands to spawn in, northern pike will propagate in abundance all on its own.

Northern pike does so well on its own, in fact, that stocking lakes with the fish is usually unnecessary. The feisty carnivorous fish, which can grow to weigh 20 pounds, will eat just about any other fish, and lakes with an abundance of northern pike tend to have low populations of all other fish. Eventually the food supply runs out, and pike populations start dropping off as well.

However, this practice of allowing pike populations to grow on their own has problems. It's every sport angler's dream to catch a giant trophy northern pike, but it usually takes at least 15 years for a northern pike to grow to weigh 20 pounds and another 10 to reach 30 pounds. You can usually count on a few 20-plus-pounders to be caught each year, but most northern pike caught are only two or three pounds on average. The DNR encourages anglers to view the northern pike as a trophy fish only, and that all small fish carefully caught and released can be caught again year after year for sport until they are big enough to be mounted.

Pike are a fun sport fish for all levels of angler, as they are fearless, toothy creatures and will snap at just about any bait you use. This makes catch-and-release tactics especially practical, as northern pike can be lured with harmless artificials as easily as live bait and tend to release their grip on artificials a lot easier than they do tasty organic bait.

Northern pike season generally runs mid-May through mid-February of the following year. Contact the DNR for specific season dates. A possession limit of three is in effect, and only one pike longer than 30 inches can be taken each day.

Northern pike are best caught in cool waters, so winter, early spring, and late fall are the best times to pursue these fish. Some of the state-managed lakes and streams known for their strong northern pike populations are Baudette River, Rainy River, and Winter Road River in Lake of the Woods County; Warroad River in Roseau County; Andrew Lake, Burgen Lake, and Rachel Lake in Douglas County; Big Birch Lake, Big Swan Lake, and Little Sauk Lake in Todd County; Coon-Sandwick Lake in Itasca County; Dudley Lake and Kelly Lake in Rice County; East Battle Lake, Twenty One Lake, and Norway Lake in Otter Tail County; Medicine Lake and North Twin Lake in Beltrami County; Sallie Lake and Melissa Lake in Becker County; Platte Lake in Crow Wing County; Reeds Lake and St. Olaf Lake in Waseca County; Sissabagamah Lake and Wilkins Lake in Aitkin County; and Stieger Lake in Carver County, Sturgeon Lake in Paine County, Ten Mile Lake in Cass County, and Sullivan Lake in Morrison County.

Bass

Bass are some of the scrappiest, most wildly gymnastic fish in Minnesota's waters and can fight an angler after being hooked for several hours before either wearing out or breaking completely free. Because of their aggressive reaction to being hooked, catch-and-release fishing is often not a viable option; these fish literally throw themselves into the air and against boats and rocks trying to escape, sometimes ripping hooks completely out of their bodies while doing so. Both smallmouth and largemouth bass are very strong for their size, and anglers should expect a good fight no matter what size the catch.

Largemouth bass are especially adaptable and prolific fish. They live and successfully spawn in a variety of conditions, and only very few stocked bass are required to populate a large body of water. Male largemouth bass viciously guard largemouth fingerlings until they're old enough to leave the nest, which almost guarantees that many of the tens of thousands of largemouth eggs laid each year will someday become full-grown fish. Consequently, stocking plays a very small role in largemouth bass management and is usually only done in newly filled basins, winterkill lakes, or chemically rehabilitated waters.

What largemouth bass do need to flourish is spawning areas with a firm bottom of sand, mud, or gravel; heavy cover such as beds of rooted aquatic weeds or logs large enough for fingerlings to hide in or under; and adequate dissolved oxygen levels in the water, especially in the winter, when the fish hibernate under ice. Largemouth bass are a warmwater fish and do best in waters that are as warm as 80 and 90 degrees. In winter, largemouth bass go into a state of near-hibernation, settling lethargically near the bottom of lakes until temperatures rise to a comfortable 60-degrees-plus again.

Smallmouth bass don't usually get much larger than two or three pounds, although those who catch them swear they're at least twice that big in the water because of their incredible strength. A native Mississippi watershed fish, smallmouth are abundant throughout the Mississippi River and its tributaries. The smallmouth is also naturally found in many Minnesotan lakes, though it is far less common in this environment than are largemouth bass. Unlike largemouth bass, smallmouth bass prefer to live in cool water and need to be in 60-degree water in order to spawn. Like the largemouth bass, though, smallmouth males guard their nests until the fingerlings are at least two weeks old, guaranteeing a successful population in any area they find comfortable enough to settle.

Stream-based smallmouth bass are migratory fish, and in late fall these migrations take them 50 miles or more from their spawning grounds to their "hibernacula"—places where large groups of smallmouth bass crowd together under the ice, eating and moving little while they wait out the winter.

Largemouth and smallmouth bass season generally runs mid-May through mid-February of the following year; the dates change year to year and depend on what part of the state you intend to fish. In 2003 it is illegal to catch and keep any smallmouth bass after September 8 (catch and release is okay). Contact the DNR for specific season dates. A six-fish possession limit of combined smallmouth and largemouth bass is in effect.

Some of the state-managed lakes and streams that are excellent for catching largemouth and smallmouth bass are Otter Tail River, Clitherall Lake, Fladmark Lake, and Annie Battle Lake in Otter Tail County; Bavaria Lake, Minnewashta Lake, Stieger Lake, and Waconia Lake in Carver County; Chisago Lake and South Lindstrom Lake in Chisago County; DeMontreville Lake, Jane Lake, and Olson Lake in Washington County; Flour Lake, Hungry Jack Lake, Pike Lake, and Two Island Lake in Cook County; Green Lake and Long Lake in Kandiyohi County; Little Sauk Lake and Moose Lake in Todd County; Mink Lake and Somers Lake in Wright County; Moccasin Lake and Portage Lake in Cass County; and Pelican Lake in St. Louis County, Pierz (Fish) Lake in Morrison County, Turtle Lake in Ramsey County, Bear Creek Reservoir in Olmsted County, Clear Lake in Waseca County,

Crooked Lake in Anoka County, and Little Mantrap Lake in Hubbard County.

All along the Mississippi River Valley and the Mississippi River itself are also very good places for catching smallmouth bass. Largemouth bass can be found in the warmer runoff pools and tributaries of the Mississippi River.

Catfish and Bullheads

Catfish and their close cousin, the bullhead, are incredibly hardy fish that can live on just about anything. Both fish, especially bullheads, are often stocked in urban ponds and lakes that have low oxygen levels due to high concentrations of algae or detritus, where they can be fished for fun by kids and those with limited mobility. Minnesota has two native catfish species, channel and flathead, and three species of bullheads—black, brown, and yellow. Found throughout the state, the fish prefer fertile waters but respond well to stocking programs that put them in waters other than where their populations would naturally occur. During winter, catfish and bullheads seek deep waters where boulders or logs provide refuge from currents, and sink into a torpor so deep that silt often collects on their bodies.

An old myth concerning catching catfish claims that they're armed with poisonous spikes and that they should be handled as little as possible. Truth is, while they do have sharp spines along the leading edges of the dorsal (top) fin and the two pectoral (side) fins that stand erect when the fish is alarmed, the spines are not poisonous, and any pain experienced comes from being poked by them and not from any toxin. As long as you avoid grasping the dorsal and pectoral fins, catfish and bullheads can be handled as safely as any other fish.

Flathead catfish, also called "mud cat" or "yellow cat," are most commonly found in Minnesota's large, slow-moving rivers, such as the Minnesota River, the St. Croix at Taylors Falls, and the Mississippi River below the Coon Rapids Dam. Distinguished by the broad, flat head from which it got its name, it is the largest catfish in Minnesota and has been reported to grow up to 100 pounds. Flatheads occupy deep pools with dense cover, such as logjams, and feed primarily on other fish—because they eat such great numbers of other fish, fish managers sometimes introduce them to lakes with large numbers of undesirable fish, such as carp, to try to control those populations. They have an acute sense of smell and therefore don't generally go for artificial lures, dead bait, or "stink bait," preferring live bait instead.

Channel catfish are steel gray and peppered with dark spots that disappear with age. Similar in appearance to the flathead, their distinguishing characteristic is their deeply forked tail. Much smaller than flatheads, rarely growing to exceed 20 pounds and usually averaging one to four pounds, channel cats can navigate much better in the faster waters of the Mississippi, St. Croix, Red, and St. Louis Rivers than flatheads do. While channel cats prefer deep, still, clean waters, they often move to murky waters to spawn, as the limited visibility protects their fry from predators.

Bullheads are the toughest of the catfish, requiring nothing but a puddle of warm water and some wet grass to survive. Ideally, though, these omnivorous fish prefer weedy, deep lakes and ponds with bottom cover (logs, thick weeds, etc.) for them to lay their eggs. All bullheads are relatively small members of the catfish family—yellow bullheads, found in southern Minnesota, weigh about a pound on average, while black bullheads and brown bullheads, naturally found in the Mississippi, Minnesota, St. Croix, and Red Rivers, usually don't grow to be longer than 10 inches.

Catfish are plentiful throughout the state and are not usually stocked in lakes or streams unless they're there to control other fish populations, or are stocked in inner-city ponds to give kids and those with limited mobility a chance to enjoy the sport of fishing.

As of 2003, the season for both bullhead and catfish is year-round. A possession limit of 100 fish is set for bullhead and 5 fish for catfish. Contact the DNR for more information.

Crayfish

Licensed anglers and children under age 16 may take home up to 25 pounds of crayfish for personal use during crayfish season, as determined by the DNR. Crayfish cannot be sold as bait or for aquarium use.

Frogs

Licensed anglers and children under age 16 may take or buy an unlimited number of frogs to use as bait only. Frogs that measure more than 6 inches (legs outstretched) may not be used as bait.

Minnows and Leeches

DNR commercial licenses are required in order to possess more than 24 dozen minnows or leeches. Minnows and leeches may not be taken from designated trout water except with a DNR permit.

Muskie and Tiger Muskie

The muskellunge is one of the largest and most elusive fish in Minnesota and is also one of the most prized trophy fish sought by sports anglers. Closely related to the northern pike, muskies can grow to surpass 40 inches long and weigh 30 pounds and up. Light-colored with dark bars running up and down their bodies, muskies can be silver, green, or brown, with large, strong, tooth-lined jaws for dragging down prey.

As with northern pike, stocking lakes and waterways with muskies is unnecessary. For one thing, they prefer larger fish as prey, so introducing them to a fishing lake only guarantees the eventual annihilation of the already-existing bass and trout populations. Muskie are also very particular about their environment, requiring well-oxygenated, cool water (60 degrees and cooler) that's clear enough for these sight-feeding fish.

Because muskies are perceived as trophy fish only, and because large muskies are scarce and usually very old, Minnesota imposes a possession limit of one muskie per licensed angler, with a minimum length of 40 inches (30 inches in Shoepac Lake within Voyageurs National Park).

The muskie season generally runs early June through mid-February of the following year. Contact the DNR for specific season dates.

Tiger muskie, a sterile hybrid of the northern pike and the muskellunge, has characteristics of both parents. Tiger muskies have distinct bars that run along their light-colored bodies similar to the bars on a full muskie, fins and tail lobes rounded like a northern pike's, and cheekscale patterns that fall somewhere between those of both fish. The hybrid grows slightly faster than either pure-strain parent and can exceed 30 pounds in less than 10 years. Because of their quick maturation rate and because they are sterile, tiger muskie are often stocked in lakes and streams in heavily fished lakes and streams throughout Minnesota, including some Twin Cities metro area lakes.

Some of the state-managed lakes open to fishing these amazing trophy fish are Bald Eagle Lake in Anoka County, Eagle Lake and Rebecca Lake in Hennepin County, Elk Lake in Clearwater County, Little Wolf Lake in Cass County, Owasso Lake in Ramsey County, and Plantanganette Lake in Hubbard County.

Mussels

With possession of a fishing license, a person may take a limited number (determined by the DNR) of dead mussels home if the harvesting is done by hand. It is illegal to harvest live mussels or clams.

Panfish

Panfish are not actually any particular species of fish but a blanket term referring to any number of small food fishes, especially those caught with hook and line, generally not available on the market. Minnesota has quite a few good-tasting "panfish," and it's common practice to take home a few of them to eat to make up for all the undersized trophy fish you caught and had to let go.

Crappies and bluegills are probably caught for eating more often than any other fish in Minnesota. Crappies are easy to catch and produce sweet-tasting fillets,

and they travel in schools, which make them even easier to find and catch. Bluegills are Minnesota's biggest and most popular panfish, found in about 65 percent of Minnesota's lakes and slow streams, including the backwaters of the Mississippi. Though they occasionally exceed a pound, an 8-inch bluegill is considered a big fish.

Closely related to the bluegill are the pumpkinseed, the green sunfish, and the orange-spotted sunfish. Like the bluegill, the pumpkinseed lives in many of Minnesota's lakes and streams. Almost as large as the bluegill, the pumpkinseed can be distinguished from its dark olive cousin by the bright orange spot at the tip of its ear flap. Green sunfish are a drab, gray color and are much smaller than pumpkinseed and bluegill—usually about 5 inches long. The brightest, smallest, and most colorful member of the sunfish family is by far the orange-spotted sunfish, which rarely reaches 4 inches long. Although their bodies are the same olive tones of the other sunfish species, orange-spotted sunfish are often streaked with orange-red lines on their cheeks and gill covers, while their stomachs and lower fins are tinged red. Because they're so small, orange-spotted sunfish aren't usually taken home by anglers, but they're very pretty to see in the water while you're fishing,

Black and white crappies are among Minnesota's most popular panfish. Black crappies are much more widely distributed than white crappies and can be found in most of the state's lakes. The two fish are very similar in appearance—in fact, the only real difference in appearance is that the black crappies are a slightly darker gray color than white crappies. Both fish rarely grow to weigh more than two pounds, and both species travel in large schools that are easy to spot.

Rock bass are stout and heavy compared with sunfish and crappies, measuring 10 inches on average and weighing around a pound. With its red eyes and brassy-colored, black-spotted flanks, it's an easy fish to identify when caught. Rock bass live in many streams and lakes in Minnesota, generally preferring well-oxygenated, hard-water walleye lakes with boulder and sand bottoms. White panfish and yellow bass, despite their names, are not related to largemouth and small-mouth bass. They're actually a cousin of the much larger Atlantic striped bass. Yellow bass populations are limited to the backwaters of the Mississippi below Lake Pepin, while the white bass can be found in the Minnesota River, the St. Croix, and the Mississippi and many of its tributaries and reservoirs. Both fish are thick bodied, occasionally exceeding two pounds.

The season for most of Minnesota's panfish runs year-round, with varying bag limits. Contact the DNR for more details.

Walleye, Sauger, and Perch

Walleye is the most sought-after fish in Minnesota, and Minnesota anglers and restaurant patrons alike go crazy over the thick-filleted perch. Each year, anglers in Minnesota catch and keep almost four million pounds of walleye, keeping the DNR's hands full stocking Minnesota lakes and rivers with the elusive fish.

The average walleye weighs one to two pounds, although some specimens caught have weighed in at as much as 10 pounds. The fish is torpedo shaped, with opaque, pearly eyes (for which the fish is named), and its color ranges from dark olive-brown to yellowish gold. Unlike its near cousin, the sauger, the walleye lacks spots on its dorsal fin, except for a dark patch on the rear base of the fin, which the sauger does not have. Also, the lower tip of the walleye's tail is white, while the lower lobe of the sauger's tail is all dark.

Both the walleye and the sauger are native fish, although walleye is much more commonly found in Minnesota's waterways than the sauger. The walleye prefers large, shallow lakes with gravel shoals, such as Mille Lacs, Leech Lake, Winnibigoshish, Upper and Lower Red Lakes, Lake of the Woods, and Lake Vermilion. However, because of its popularity as a game and food fish, the walleye has been introduced to waterways all over the state and now occupies more than 1,600 lakes and 100 warmwater streams throughout the Midwest. The walleye's low-level vision and sensitivity to light keep it hidden in the deep parts of lakes until dawn and dusk, at which point they come to the shallows to feed. Their diet consists almost solely of fish, and their biggest prey is yellow perch, which can't see well in the dark and are easily caught by the night-feeding walleye. Because of their sensitivity to light, the best time to catch walleye is at dawn or dusk, or when the skies are overcast.

Sauger are similar to walleye in appearance and habits, although their distribution throughout Minnesota is much more limited. They can usually be found in Lake St. Croix, the Minnesota River, the Mississippi River, Lake of the Woods, Rainy Lake, and Lake Kabetogama. Saugers seldom exceed three pounds and are generally much slimmer than walleye.

Yellow perch, cousin to both walleye and sauger as well as a shared common prey, are also found throughout Minnesota's lakes and streams. They're often infected with parasites, and even the healthy ones are usually too small to reasonably consider eating. Walleye and yellow perch populations often coincide with each other, and lakes where the yellow population is strong are also home to big, healthy walleye—who may not be hungry enough to be interested in bait.

Some of the state-managed lakes and streams that are especially good for walleye are Ann Lake and Knife Lake in Kanabec County; Big Sand Lake in Hubbard County; Big Stone Lake in Big Stone County; Borden Lake in Crow Wing County; Crane Lake, Kabetogama

Insiders' Tip

Kids under 16 and adults over 65 do not need a license to fish in Minnesota when accompanied by an adult with a fishing license.

Lake, Sand Point Lake, Little Vermilion Lake, Loon River, Namakan Lake, and Rainy Lake in St. Louis County; Crawford Lake, Wright Lake, and Somers Lake in Wright County; Farm Island Lake, North Big Pine, and South Big Pine in Aitkin County; Goose Lake and Green Lake in Chisago County; Lake of the Woods in Roseau County; Little Elk in Sherburne County; Little McDonald Lake and Norway Lake in Otter Tail County; Little Sauk Lake and Osakis Lake in Todd County; Red Lake in Beltrami County; and Stieger Lake and Waconia Lake in Carver County.

The season for walleye and sauger generally runs mid-May through mid-February of the following year, with a limit of six fish. The opening of walleye season is an annual event in Minnesota, opened with much fanfare by the governor casting a line in a chosen outstate lake with cameras clicking and TV cameras rolling. Perch season is year-round, with a limit of 10 fish per day. Contact the DNR for more details.

Salmon

Three species of Pacific salmon have been introduced to Lake Superior in the past few decades: the chinook (or king) salmon, the pink (or humpy) salmon, and the coho (or silver) salmon. All three species feed in Lake Superior until they reach sexual maturity and then swim up rivers to spawn and die. The chinook salmon has been the most successful of the three species, growing to weigh more than 30 pounds and being the most resistant to disease.

There is no closed season for salmon fishing—however, you must get a Trout and Salmon Stamp on your fishing license in order to legally catch them. Bag limits for catching all species of salmon change with each year as newly hatched young come back to Lake Superior to mature. Contact the DNR for more information.

Trout

Minnesota has four species of trout inhabiting its streams and lakes, two of which are native species (brook trout and lake trout) and two of which were introduced

to Minnesota waters in the late 1800s—the rainbow trout, originally from western North America, and the brown trout, which was brought over from Germany. Brown trout have done exceptionally well here and are the hardiest of the trout species, able to tolerate warmer and murkier waters than any other species in the state. In addition to a regular fishing license, anglers must buy a Trout and Salmon Stamp to fish in Minnesota's trout streams and lakes, including Lake Superior. Funds from stamp sales pay for habitat improvement and raising and stocking trout and salmon.

Most trout streams are located in southeastern Minnesota and along the North Shore. The southern streams are populated with mostly brown trout, some rainbow trout, and, where the water runs cold and clear, a few brook trout. Northern streams have mostly "brookies," while the deep, cold lakes up north and Lake Superior itself make a comfortable home for lake trout as well as a lake and brook trout hybrid called a splake. Also up north is a specific type of rainbow trout, called a steelhead, that lives only in Lake Superior and grows exceptionally large.

Out of all the trout species represented in the state, the pink-striped rainbow trout and the silvery steelhead are the most prized as gamefish among anglers; they put up a good, dramatic fight when hooked, sometimes leaping several feet into the air to free themselves from a line, as opposed to the brown trout, which is too suspicious to be easily lured by bait, and the brook trout, which is extremely gullible and will bite at just about anything floating in the water.

Hundreds of streams course through Minnesota's woods and farmlands. Some are naturally fertile and have always been excellent fishing holes; others are poor in nutrients and soil quality and have to be regularly stocked by the DNR. A good trout stream has rich siltbeds, a profuse insect population, and adequate groundwater, creating a suitable streambed ecology for healthy trout to flourish in. Though brown, rainbow, and brook trout have evolved over time to live and breed in cool, fast-moving streams, they actually grow much bigger when they're removed from streams and put in lakes. Because of this, the Minnesota DNR regularly removes young trout from streambeds and stocks about 160 deep, clean, coldwater lakes throughout the state to give anglers a chance to catch some real trophy trout. The DNR also stocks these same lakes with plenty of splake—a cross between a male brookie and a female lake trout. As with most other hybrids, splakes grow much faster and bigger than either of their parent species and are popular fish because they're big, they taste good, and they're very easy to catch.

Some of the state-managed stocked lakes open to trout fishing are Beaver Creek, Cold Spring Brook, West Indian Creek, and Zumbro River in Wabasha County; Bunker Hill Creek and Little Rock Creek in Benton County; Camp Creek, Canfield Creek, Duschee Creek, North Branch Creek, Root River, and Trout Run Creek in Fillmore County; Whitewater River and Trout Valley Creek in Winona County; Boys Lake, Thrush Lake, and Turnip Lake in Cook County; and Foster Arend Lake in Olmsted County, Square Lake in Washington County, Eagle Creek in Scott County, East Beaver Creek in Houston County, Hay Creek in Goodhue County, and Ann Lake in Carver County. Trout seasons and bag limits range widely, depending on the

species and where you are fishing. Stream trout (rainbow, brook, and brown) can be fished only in summer, although lake trout have both summer and winter seasons. Contact the DNR for more details.

Turtles

Licensed anglers and children under age 16 may take and transport turtles for personal use. Snapping turtles under 10 inches wide (from side to side at mipoint) may not be taken; Blanding's turtles and wood turtles are threatened species and may not be removed from water without a DNR permit.

Harmful Aquatic Species

Several plant and animal species introduced to Minnesota waters over the past 100 years, have caused severe damage to native species populations. Among these are zebra mussels, Eurasian watermilfoil, ruffe, and round goby.

Eurasian watermilfoil is a water plant similar in appearance to duckweed that reproduces quickly in shallow water and can interfere with water recreation as well as harm oxygen levels in lakes and ponds. Even the tiniest of fragments clinging to boats and trailers can spread the prolific plant from one body of water to another. Zebra mussels, originally from Asia, can quickly displace native mussels, disrupt lake ecosystems, and clog industrial equipment. Their microscopic larvae can accidentally be transported in bait buckets or by moving a boat from one confined body of water to another. The best way to prevent the spread of Eurasian watermilfoil and Zebra mussels is to make sure you wipe dry any excess water from your boat before moving it from one body of water to another, and dump bait buckets on land and dry them thoroughly before putting them back in water.

Ruffe is a small, perchlike fish from Europe that has taken over many parts of Duluth harbor, displacing many native fish. Also from Europe is the bottom-dwelling round goby, which has displaced many fish in Minnesota lakes and is a serious threat to the fisheries in the Great

Lakes, which it has already entered. The spread of both fish can be attributed to being transported from one body of water to another in bait buckets and livewells.

Ice Fishing

This sport is a longtime tradition of both Minnesotan and Alaskan anglers, inspired by Alaskan indigenous anglers who had no choice but to catch fish this way. The basic principle of ice fishing is to walk out on a deep lake with enough ice cover to safely support your weight (ice should be a minimum of 6 inches thick for walking, a foot or more for vehicles), cut a hole in the ice, and sink a hook through it with hopes of luring the few fish that aren't in a state of torpor to take your bait. Over the years, this simple idea has expanded to include portable ice fishing houses for anglers to sit in comfort while waiting for fish to bite, equipped with televisions, suspended heating elements, radios, furniture, and the requisite cooler stuffed with beer. Newer adaptations include a variety of ice boats (or "rigs")—a cross between a sled and a sailboat—and mechanical bobbers that are guaranteed to catch sleepy fish.

Your best bet in ice fishing is to stake out lakes and rivers known for having good trout or muskie populations, as these fish actually get more energetic as the weather grows cooler. Anything else you catch is most likely by accident, as most fish "sleep" in the winter and aren't normally interested in brightly colored bobbers or frozen chunks of bait.

Some metro area parks with lakes deep enough (and enough lively coldwater fish) for ice fishing include Baker Park Preserve, Bald Eagle-Otter Lakes, Bryant Lake, Carver Park Preserve, Clifton E. French, Como, Coon Rapids Dam, Fish Lake, Hidden Falls-Crosby Farm, Lake Byllesby, Lake George, Lake Minnewashta, Lake Rebecca Park Reserve, Lebanon Hills, Long Lake Regional Park, Martin-Island-Linwood Lakes, Minneapolis Chain of Lakes, Nokomis Hiawatha, Phalen-Keller, Rice Creek/Chain of Lakes, Snail Lake, and Theodore Wirth (see Parks chapter for complete parks listings).

Metro Fishing

Both Minneapolis and St. Paul have a surprising number of good fishing lakes within city limits, as do their nearby suburbs. At least 23 city lakes and rivers in the metro area are regularly stocked and monitored by the Minnesota DNR, with the purpose of providing safe, fun fishing lakes for urbanites, children, and those with limited mobility.

Some of the best fishing lakes in Minneapolis are Lake Calhoun, Lake of the Isles, Cedar Lake, Lake Harriet, and Lake Nokomis. Lake Calhoun, located about 3 blocks west of Lake Street and Hennepin Avenue, is a deep (82 feet deep in spots) fishing and boating lake with largemouth bass, northern pike, crappie, sunfish, tiger muskie, walleye, perch, catfish, and carp swimming in its waters. Rental canoes are available at the concession stand, which also sells fast food but no bait. Calhoun has a couple of great fishing piers and three swimming beaches.

Connected to Lake Calhoun by a canoe-navigable channel is Lake of the Isles, located by land just south of Franklin Avenue and 1 mile west of Hennepin Avenue. Many of the same types of fish as in Lake Calhoun are in these waters, with a huge population of sunfish and crappies, much to the delight of the many species of waterfowl that also frequent these waters.

Cedar Lake, located just south of Interstate 394 and east of Minnesota Highway 100, is stocked with healthy populations of largemouth bass, northern pike, crappie, sunfish, tiger muskies, perch, carp, and catfish and is a great shore fishing spot due to the deep water right next to shore. Anyone willing to bushwhack along the brushy banks can usually find some good-size largemouth bass hanging out along the lake's north shore.

Lake Harriet, another great Minneapolis fishing and boating lake with waters as deep as 87 feet in places, is located 1 mile west of Lyndale Avenue just north of 50th Street. Shore fishing at Lake Harriet is surprisingly good, considering that most of the really deep water is near the middle of the lake, and muskies, bass, sunfish, perch, catfish, and walleye can be caught here. The lake has a fishing pier and a boat rental facility nearby as well as a swimming beach and playground.

Lake Nokomis, located south of Minnehaha Parkway between Cedar and Hiawatha Avenues, is one of the best crappie lakes in the Twin Cities. Because it gets more sun and warms up quickly, the north shore fishing pier is the best spot to stake out in the spring. Also found in Lake Nokomis are northern pike, sunfish, tiger muskie, carp, bullhead, perch, and walleye.

St. Paul has a couple of excellent fishing spots for more serious anglers—meaning no picnic area, no playground, and little or no paved paths leading down to the water. Hidden Falls Regional Park, located just south of Ford Parkway, is an excellent summer fishing spot for walleye, catfish, crappie, sunfish, white bass, smallmouth and largemouth bass, northern pike, and carp. If the water level is high, anglers can fish from the grassy picnic area, but if it's low, you must descend a steep bank to reach the water.

Pike Island and Snelling Lake, both located in St. Paul's Fort Snelling State Park, are two rustic yet excellent fishing holes. Pike Island is good for early-season walleye fishing, as the fish pass here while moving upstream to spawn below Ford Dam. The best fishing is where the channel north of Pike Island meets the Mississippi River, where you can catch carp, catfish, smallmouth bass, walleye, white bass, and crappie. Snelling Lake actually has some good paved paths leading to the shoreline, although to get to the really good fishing areas, you have to stand in the marsh. There's also a good fishing pier here, from which you can catch largemouth bass, crappie, sunfish, northern pike, carp, and bullhead.

Other metro area parks that have areas set aside for fishing include Anoka County Riverfront, Baker Park Preserve, Bald Eagle-Otter Lakes, Baylor, Bryant Lake, Carver Park Preserve, Central Mississippi Riverfront, Cleary Lake, Clifton E. French, Como, Coon Rapids Dam, Fish Lake, Lake Byllesby, Lake Elmo Park Reserve, Lake George, Lake Minnetonka Regional Park, Lake Minnewashta, Lake Rebecca Park Reserve, Lebanon Hills, Lilydale-Harriet Island, Long Lake Regional Park, Rice Creek/Chain of Lakes, Rice Creek-West Regional Trail, Rum River Central, Snail Lake, and Theodore Wirth.

Becoming an Outdoors Woman in Minnesota (651–296–6157), at 500 Lafayette Road in St. Paul, and **Women Anglers of Minnesota** (612–339–1322) offer angling, ice fishing, and shore fishing classes for women interested in either taking up the sport or finding other women to fish with.

Day Trips and Weekend Getaways

Any way you point your vehicle, you're sure to end up somewhere extraordinary. Minnesota is dotted with hundreds of little towns settled in the early days of the state, and just about all of them are worth exploring. Although there are more than enough attractions and sights in the Twin Cities themselves to fill up your time here, there's nothing like a good long road trip through the countryside to clear one's mind of the hustle and bustle of the Metro life.

The best time (we think) to hit the road is early spring, the last two weeks of April and the first two weeks of May, or when autumn is in full swing, the last two weeks of September and the first two weeks of October. There is nowhere better to see the changing of the seasons than out in the country, amid the old hardwood forests that line the state highways and the charming old farmhouses—many of which are still in use—that dot the gently rolling fields and coulees outside the Cities. Having said that, here is a sampling of the road trips well worth taking from the Twin Cities.

Duluth

Located right on the shore of Lake Superior and a major shipping port, Duluth was once the fastest-growing city in the country and was expected to surpass Chicago in size by 1870. When Jay Cooke, the wealthy Philadelphia land speculator, picked Duluth as the terminus of the Northern Pacific Railroad, Lake Superior Railroad, and Mississippi Railroad, Duluth's future appeared very prosperous. Unfortunately, Jay Cooke's empire crumbled when the stock market crashed in 1873, and Duluth almost disappeared from the map. However, by the late 1800s, with the continued boom in lumber and iron mining and with the railroads completed, Duluth again bloomed. By the turn of the 20th century, there were almost 100,000 inhabitants, and it was again a thriving community. At its economic height, more millionaires lived in Duluth than anywhere else in the world.

Much of this history is reflected in present-day Duluth, both in the fantastic architecture and in the huge boats that serve as floating museums at the Maritime Visitor Center museum. The signs that Duluth is once again experiencing an economic revival have never been more obvious. Most of the old warehouses by the Maritime Center and along the harbor have been converted into picturesque shopping centers and family-owned restaurants, many with the original facades left intact to give a historical perspective of what the region once looked like. Uphill from busy Canal Park Drive, the streets are lined with row houses and redbrick churches, many of which have been closed up but left intact. While driving up the steep roads in Duluth is a little nerve-wracking (especially in winter), the harbor looks absolutely stunning from the heights. An incredible stretch of blue water dotted with white sailboats and gigantic ore boats greets you, while the far, far shore of Lake Superior is barely visible even on the clearest days.

For more information on the sights and attractions of Duluth, call the **Duluth Convention & Visitor Bureau** at (218) 722-4011 or (800) 4-DULUTH, or check out their extensive Web page at www.visit duluth.com.

Getting There

Getting to Duluth from the Twin Cities is easy. Just take Interstate 35 E north or I-35 W north (depending on where you are in the Twin Cities). The highways merge into I-35 north of the Metro, and the interstate shoots straight north to Duluth.

Attractions

Most of Duluth's attractions are located around the Duluth Harbor, so it's easy to walk from one to the next to make a full day of sight-seeing. The newest of Duluth's offerings to visitors and locals alike is the **Great Lakes Aquarium** at 353 Harbor Drive (218-740-FISH; www.gl aquarium.com), which houses the largest freshwater aquarium in America. While the main focus of the GLA is the gigantic aquarium that houses every known species of fish from Lake Superior (including several giant sturgeons), there are also many hands-on exhibits geared toward children. One of the favorites is a joystick-operated microscope hooked up to a video monitor that's focused on a tank full of carnivorous water bugs. For more squeamish children, a very friendly otter on the first floor loves to show off for visitors. Ticket prices are $5.95 for children up to age 14 and $10.95 for everyone else.

Right next door to the aquarium at 350 Harbor Drive is the **S.S. *William A. Irvin*** (218-722-7876; www.williamairvin. com), a giant ore ship-turned-museum. The ship is open for tours for most of the year, with a special "Ship of Ghouls" exhibit around Halloween. For serious maritime buffs, there's also the **Lake Superior Maritime Visitor Center**, 600

Duluth's historic lift bridge allows freighters from all over the world to reach the city's inner harbor. PHOTO: TODD R. BERGER

Lake Avenue South (218–727–2497), owned and operated by the U.S. Army Corps of Engineers. Movies, model ships, and rotating exhibits are housed here both inside and outside the museum year-round. For an extensive listing of maritime films, events, and dinner cruises all around the harbor, you can also call the Lake Superior Marine Museum Association at (218) 727–2497.

At 506 West Michigan Street inside the depot is the **Lake Superior Railroad Museum** (218–733–7590), which houses a rotating exhibit of historic railway cars, locomotives, and engines, most of which can be boarded for a close-up view of turn-of-the-20th-century machinery. On permanent display is a dining car china exhibit, the William Crooks (Minnesota's oldest engine), and the oldest known rotary snowplow in existence. The depot is also home to the **Duluth Children's Museum.** The depot is full of hands-on exhibits for kids as well as education programs and tours, the Duluth Art Institute, the St. Louis Historical Society, and a performing arts wing where community and touring ballet companies, plays, and concerts take place throughout the year.

One block away from the depot, at 72nd Avenue West and Grand Avenue, is the **Lake Superior Zoological Gardens** (218–733–3777), which is home to more than two dozen endangered and threatened species from around the world. Admittedly on the small side, the zoo is considered more a preservation project and educational tool than a major tourist attraction.

For a little highbrow entertainment, check out the **Karpeles Manuscript Library Museum** at 902 East First Street (218–728–0630). This museum displays a rotating selection of original manuscripts from all over the world, including a Civil War photography exhibit and a collection of original folk tales written in the 17th century. The **Tweed Museum of Art,** located on the University of Minnesota Duluth Campus at 10 University Drive (218–726–8222), features nine separate galleries and exhibits dating all the way back to the 15th century. For a glimpse of what life was like for the well-to-do during the Iron Range boom, the historic **Glensheen Estate** at 3300 London Road (888–454–GLEN), holds tours of its seven-acre grounds throughout most of the year (call for times and reservations).

For wintertime fun, head to **Spirit Mountain,** just outside Duluth, for cross-country and downhill skiing, tubing, and, of course, snowboarding. Spirit Mountain has five chairlifts (including a covered one for skiers wanting to take a little break from the cold), and the 175-acre site has 23 separate downhill runs geared for all levels of skiers and a huge freestyle park for snowboarders. If you haven't tried tubing before, we highly recommend it—it takes the least amount of concentration of all the downhill sports and is just a blast. Spirit Mountain has all sorts of package plans for extended stays in the area, including discounts on lodging, meals, and lift tickets, so give them a call before you head up.

Accommodations and Camping

Right on the waterfront and steps away from Canal Park Drive, the following hotels are relatively new buildings designed with easy access to the hot spots of Duluth in mind. The **Canal Park Inn** at 250 Canal Park Drive (218–727–8821 or 800–777–8560), features an indoor heated pool and hot tub, and all adult guests receive a complimentary full hot breakfast each morning. The **Hampton Inn** at 310 Canal Park Drive (218 720–3000 or 800–HAMPTON) offers the same amenities with the added bonus of allowing children age 18 and under to stay free, while the **Inn on Lake Superior** at 350 Canal Park Drive (218–726–1111 or 888–ON–THE–LAKE) offers a lakefront view with its balcony suites. Downtown lodging is, to be expected, more affordable than the lakefront hotels. At 131 West Second Street is the **Best Western Downtown** (218–727–6851 or 800–528–1234), located close to the skyway system that connects downtown Duluth. Two blocks away at 200 West First Street is the **Holiday Inn** (218-722-1202 or 800-477-7089), which has two pools and a sauna on the premises. Also downtown is the **Radisson Hotel** at 505 West Superior Street (218-727-8981 or 800-333-3333), **Fitger's Inn** at 600 East Superior Street (218-722-8826 or 888-FITGERS), and the **Voyageur Lakewalk Inn** at 333 East Superior Street (218-722-3911 or 800-258-3911).

Duluth also has many beautiful bed-and-breakfasts designed to make guests feel right at home. In town is the **Mathew S. Burrows Inn** at 1632 East First Street (218-724-4991 or 800-789-1890), the **Ellery House** at 28 South 21st Avenue East (218-724-7639 or 800-355-3794), and the **Firelight Inn** on Oregon Creek at 2211 East Third Street (218-724-0272 or 888-724-0273). All of these establishments are historic landmarks furnished with period antiques, built around the turn of the 20th century with only a few modern conveniences added to the original designs.

While there aren't any campsites in Duluth proper, there are several notable ones right outside the city limits. Five miles south of Duluth is **Buffalo Valley Camping,** located at 2590 Guss Road, Proctor (218-624-9901), which has a full bar and restaurant at the campsite as well as showers and electrical, sewer, and water hookups for RVs. Take exit 239 off I-35 and you'll find the **Knife Island campsite**

at 234 Minnesota Highway 61, Esko (218-879-6063), located right in the middle of the ghost town of Slateville and the adjacent abandoned logging camp. Water and electrical hookups are available at more than half the 20 available sites, and firewood is provided by the camp for an extra $5.00 a night.

Shopping

Unless you're just out for groceries, most of your Duluth shopping is going to take place around the museums and walkways in the Canal Park Drive and Lake Avenue area. Here, original warehouse structures from Duluth's manufacturing past have been converted into shopping malls and restaurants, while new structures have been built to integrate perfectly with the brickwork of the older buildings.

If you're into antiquing, the **Canal Park Antique Mall** at 310 Lake Avenue South (218-720-3940), is your best bet. The largest antiques and collectibles mall in Duluth is where you're sure to find that perfect knickknack for yourself or souvenir to take home to family and friends. If you prefer collecting old literature, **Old Town Antiques & Books** at 102 East Superior Street (218-722-5426) is also a good place to stop.

And while you're on Superior Street, try out **Torke Weihnachten Christmas & Chocolates** at 600 East Superior Street (218-723-1225 or 800-729-1223) for both specialty candies and imported hand-blown Christmas ornaments. Check out the wonderful **Electric Fetus,** 12 East Superior Street (218-722-9970) for the best selection of records, CDs, and tapes in this part of the state (visit its sister store in Minneapolis when you come back).

Along the Canal Park area is the **DeWitt-Seitz Marketplace** at 394 Lake Avenue South, home to both **Hepzibah's Sweet Shoppe** (218-722-5049), with their wonderful homemade and imported candies, and educational toy store **J. Skylark Company** (218-722-3794). Outside the mall and along Lake Avenue are even more gift shops—this is a great place to catch up on your window-shopping in the summer.

Insiders' Tip

The University of Minnesota-Duluth offers reasonably priced accommodations for senior citizens during the summer months. Call the campus at (218) 726-8222 for more information and rates.

Restaurants

Traditional American fare dominates the restaurant scene in Duluth, with steakhouses on the high end of the scale and hamburger and french-fry joints at the low end. In the Fitger's Brewhouse complex at 600 East Superior Street is **Bennett's on the Lake** (218-722-2829) and **Fitger's Brewhouse Brewery and Grill** (218-726-1392). The first is very fancy and almost requires you call ahead for reservations on weekends. The second is much more fun, offering live music entertainment most weekends, homebrewed beer, and gourmet sandwiches. There are also five separate Grandma's restaurants along the Lakeway, as well as Perkins Family Restaurants just about everywhere. For Asian food, we recommend **Taste of Saigon** in the Dewitt-Seitz Marketplace at 394 Lake Avenue South (218-727-1598)—their food and selection are as good as the portions are large and generous. For late-night dining and carousing, **Schooners Nightclub** at 250 Canal Park Drive (218-727-8821) offers food, alcohol, billiards, and live entertainment on weekends, while the **Top of the Harbor** and **Skyview Lounge** at the Radisson Hotel on 505 West Superior Street (218-727-8981), is a rotating restaurant and bar that revolves to give you a full view of the city every 72 minutes.

An invaluable resource to pick up when in Duluth is the local free paper, *Ripsaw*—each issue has a restaurant review section and calendar of events that is informative to even the most experienced of Duluth visitors. Very well written and fun to read even if you don't need help picking out something to do for the day, *Ripsaw* is available at most retail centers and newsstands around town.

Hinckley

Established in 1885, the little town of Hinckley—population 1,291—is rich with fishing holes, hiking trails, natural beauty, and history. The site of the Great Hinckley Fire in 1894 that killed more than 400 people, Hinckley is a monument to a community's triumph over tragedy. For more information, contact the **Hinckley Convention and Visitors Bureau** at (320) 384-0126 or (800) 996-4566; www.hinckley mn.com.

Getting There

From the Twin Cities, take either I-35 E or I-35 W north until they merge into I-35 north in Lino Lakes, then follow I-35 all the way to the Hinckley exit. From there you can go west into downtown Hinckley, or east on Minnesota Highway 48 to the Hinckley Grand Casino.

Attractions

Hinckley's history stretches back to the early 1800s, to the days when it was mostly fur trading posts and Ojibwe lands. The Great Hinckley Fire destroyed most of the original settlements, but what could be saved is on display or documented at the **Hinckley Fire Museum** at 106 Old Highway 61 South (320-384-7338), open May through October. A large obelisk memorial has also been set up in the town cemetery to commemorate the disaster. The route of the railroad used by settlers fleeing the Great Hinckley Fire is now the **Willard Munger State Trail,** the longest paved hiking trail in the country, stretching from Hinckley all the way up to Duluth. In winter the trail is open to snowmobilers and cross-country skiers and in summer to hikers, bicyclists, and horseback riders.

The other major attraction in the area is the Mille Lacs Band's **Grand Casino Hinckley,** 777 Lady Luck Drive (800-472-6321; www.grandcasinosmn.com/Grand CasinoHinckley), located 1 mile east of I-35 on Minnesota Highway 48 just outside Hinckley. The casino features more than 2,000 slot machines, blackjack tables, poker tables, pull tabs, and live bingo competitions. There are also two restaurants and five cocktail lounges on site, as well as live music at the Silver Sevens Lounge, the Grand Casino Hinckley Convention Center, the Grand Casino Amphitheater, and Tobies Lounge, all located at or right next to the main building of the casino.

For nature lovers, there's **St. Croix State Park** (320–384–6591), located 15 miles east of Hinckley on Minnesota Highway 48, then 5 miles south on County Road 22. St. Croix State Park is Minnesota's largest state park, with 33,000 acres of campsites as well as hiking, horse, snowmobile, and ski trails. There's also a swimming beach and six canoe landings along the St. Croix River. Twelve miles north of Hinckley on I–35 is **Banning State Park** (320–245–2668), which is the home of the beautiful Kettle River. Canoe and kayak rentals are available on site—this is a great place to catch a glimpse of the native wildlife (porcupines, raccoons, etc.) while traveling down the river. There is limited camping available, so it's a good idea to call and check with the park before making long-term plans.

Annual events in Hinckley include the Great Trail Sled Dog Race in January; the VFW Bunny Fair in April; Little Britches Rodeo, Corn and Clover Festival, and Grand Celebration & Pow Wow in July; the Arts & Crafts Festivals in August and November; and Santa Days in December.

Accommodations

There are quite a few places to spend the night at Hinckley, both at the Grand Casino or in town. The **Holiday Inn Express,** I–35 at exit 183 (320–384–7171 or 800–558–0612), offers a complimentary breakfast, an indoor swimming pool, and 24-hour casino shuttle service, while the **Days Inn** at 104 Grindstone Court (800–559–8951), has an indoor pool and sauna and allows kids under age 17 to stay for free (when accompanied by an adult, of course). **The Hinckley Gold Pine Inn** (320–384–6112), at the Minnesota Highway 48 exit off I–35, has snowmobile trails that lead right off the parking lot, a free 24-hour shuttle service to take you to the casino, and a coin laundry on the premises. The **Grand Hinckley Inn** (800–737–8675) is located right next to Grand Casino Hinckley, and has rooms with private hot tubs, and an indoor pool. The two bed-and-breakfasts in the area are the **Dakota Lodge,** located 12 miles east of Hinckley on Minnesota Highway 48 (320–384–6052), which has rooms with individual whirlpools and fireplaces, and the small and cozy **Down Home Bed & Breakfast** in town (320–384–0396 or 800–965–8919), which offers sled dog rides during the winter months and opens an outdoor Jacuzzi in summer.

Shopping

Many shops in Hinckley are located in the downtown area on Main Street. **Just Like New!,** 114 East Main Street, (320–384–7741), lets you roll a die to decide what your discount will be on Amish furniture and clothes, handcrafted knickknacks, collectibles, and toys. **Antiques America Mall** at Tobies Mill, located at the junction of I–35 and Minnesota Highway 48 (320–384–7272), houses 50 dealers of antiques and collectibles, and **The Mill House** (320–384–6046) carries homemade fudge, afghans, and quilts as well as sculpture and pottery made by local artists.

Your options at the neighboring Grand Casino Hinckley are much more limited. It's only fair to note here that cigarettes sold on Indian reservations are much, much cheaper than those sold off the reservations, and that you can buy cartons of them at extremely reduced prices at the Grand Casino, which is run by the Mille Lacs Band of Ojibwe. Other than that, though, the casino isn't the greatest place to purchase gifts for friends and family, unless they like cigarettes, previously used casino playing cards, or Vikings paraphernalia.

Restaurants

Most of the dining establishments in Hinckley are fast-food restaurants, with just a few exceptions. **Tobies Mill** (320–384–6174) has a pizza parlor (Tobies Pizza Express), a family restaurant (Tobies Restaurant), and a bar (Tobies Lounge) all in the same building.

Dining options at the **Grand Casino Hinckley** are a little better—however, we must warn you that the casino is a serious smoking establishment and even the non-smoking sections of the restaurants get a little congested. **Cherry's Snack Bar** located at the junction of I-35 and Minnesota Highway 48 is a good place to stop for lunch, while **Grand Buffet** is a good place to stop for dinner, if you can get in. There's usually a long line to get into the buffet, so you may want to try **Grand Grill Americana** or **The Winds Steakhouse** instead, which aren't as good a deal as the buffet but are less crowded and farther away from the noise of the casino.

Nightlife

Like most other small towns, the doors close pretty early here, so all the nightlife (after 6:00 P.M.) is at or near the **Grand Casino Hinckley.** The **Silver Sevens Lounge** is mostly cover bands; **Tobies Lounge** has nightly karaoke during the week and live bands Saturday and Sunday. The **Grand Casino Convention Center** brings in well-known lounge and Golden Oldies singers as well as the occasional comedian, and the **Grand Casino Amphitheater** is a 5,000-seat outdoor affair that books top country stars and the occasional pop star.

New Ulm

Founded in 1856 by two German immigration societies, today nearly everything about New Ulm reflects the town's German heritage. The shadow of the Hermann Monument, set high on a hill just outside the business district, rises in the distance and is visible from just about anywhere in town. Often referred to as the "City of Charm and Tradition," New Ulm's colorful history is reflected in its attractions and many seasonal festivals.

Getting There

New Ulm is easily accessible by taking U.S. Highway 169 South from the Twin Cities to Minnesota Highway 99 West. From there, go west on U.S. Highway 14 (the Laura Ingalls Wilder Highway), which will take you into downtown New Ulm.

For further information, brochures, or directions, be sure to visit the **New Ulm Area Chamber of Commerce/Visitors Information Center** at One North Minnesota Street (507-233-4300 or 800-4-NEW-ULM), located a short walking distance from most of the area attractions, shopping, and restaurants.

Attractions

At the forefront of New Ulm's attractions is the **Hermann Monument.** Representing the Teutonic hero, Hermann Arminius of Cherusci, the monument overlooks the city from the bluff on Center and Monument Streets. Dedicated in 1897, the monument stands 102 feet tall in Hermann Heights Park—a beautiful park with a panoramic view of the city below. The Hermann Monument is open Memorial Day through Labor Day and costs a nominal fee of $1.00, but you may visit the adjoining Hermann Heights Park year-round for free.

Another attraction is the **Glockenspiel/Schonlau Park** at Fourth and Minnesota Streets. The glockenspiel is one of the few free-standing carillon clock towers in the world. The glockenspiel chimes at noon, 1:00, 3:00, and 5:00 P.M. daily and features a revolving stage of 3-foot-high characters, including a bricklayer, a brewer, and an American Indian dressed in 19th-century period clothing. There is no charge to visit the glockenspiel.

Brown County Historical Society and Museum at Center and Broadway Streets (507-233-2616) provides an excellent overview of the history of the New Ulm area. The building was once the New Ulm Post Office, and was placed on the National Register of Historic Places in 1970. The Brown County Historical Society houses three floors of regional history: a Dakota Indian exhibit, a Brown County settlers area called "Made in Brown County," seasonal displays, and much more. All of the information is insightfully presented with great detail, and the admission charge is a meager $2.00.

New Ulm is filled with many beautiful, historical homes, but the **John Lind Home,** at the intersection of Center and State Streets (507-354-8802), is especially aesthetically pleasing and historically significant. This lovely structure is an excellent example of Queen Anne–style architecture and was the home of the 14th governor of Minnesota and the first Swedish member of the United States Congress, Minnesota Representative John Lind. Admission is a $1.00-per-person donation. Tours are available on a limited basis; however, especially in winter, please call for more information.

Beer brewing was New Ulm's first industry. The **August Schell Brewing Company,** 1860 Schell Road (507-354-5528 or 800-770-5020), was founded in 1860, and since its inception Schell's has produced premium-quality crafted and specialty beers at reasonable prices. Before the emergence of the popularity of "microbeers," Schell's was the area leader in providing libations. Tours of the brewery, gardens, and park are available on a limited basis. The brewery tour and tasting cost $2.00. Schell's recently purchased the Grain Belt brand of beer, a well-known Minnesota brew of American lager formerly made in the Twin Cities. If you can't make it to Schell's Brewery, be sure to visit one of New Ulm's restaurants and bars for a bottle or draught of Schell's Bock, Dark, Original, or 1919 Root Beer.

New Ulm has a wealth of additional attractions. For lovers of the classic children's book *Millions of Cats,* author Wanda Gag's childhood home and the place she wrote many of her classic books is here. **The Wanda Gag Home,** 226 North Washington Street (507-359-2632), is open on weekends in June, July, and August and during the rest of the year by appointment.

Yet another attraction of historical significance is the **Turner Hall,** at the intersection of First Street South and State Street (507-354-4916). The New Turnverein opened in 1856 and was dedicated to improving the health of New Ulmers through gymnastics and exercise. Parts of the Turner Hall building date back to 1865, including 70 feet of murals in the Ratskeller. The Turner Hall is free and open daily to the public 10:00 A.M. to 10:00 P.M.

In addition, New Ulm has a full slate of annual festivals and events. New Ulm celebrates Christmas with traditional German hoopla. Included are **Santa's Parade of Lights,** which celebrates the arrival of Santa Claus on the Friday evening after Thanksgiving; traditional German **St. Nicholas Day,** December 6; and **German Christmas in German Park,** with food, caroling, and holiday activities. There are several more festivals in New Ulm. **Fasching,** a German version of Mardi Gras, occurs annually in late February or early March concurrent with **Schell's Bockfest.** Another important event in New Ulm is **Heritagefest,** held annually during two weeks in July. And last, but certainly not least, is **Oktoberfest,** which features traditional German food and music.

Accommodations

New Ulm has ample accommodations, including bed-and-breakfasts as well as hotels. As with all other aspects of New Ulm, most of the accommodations have a German flavor.

The Holiday Inn, at 2101 South Broadway Street (507-359-2941 or 877-359-2941), is the largest hotel in New Ulm. It hosts Oktoberfest for two weekends each fall and has a swimming pool, restaurant, and cocktail lounge for your convenience. The **Budget Holiday,** 1316 North Broadway Street (507-354-4145), is a newly renovated hotel. Another New Ulm hotel is the **Colonial Inn** at 1315 North Broadway Street (507-354-3128 or 888-215-2143), a relatively small, 24-unit hotel that offers free HBO during your stay.

The New Ulm area also has many bed-and-breakfasts. Two of the bed-and-breakfasts are located outside New Ulm. The **Innis House Bed & Breakfast** is 5 miles north and 5 miles west of New Ulm on County Road 5 (507-359-9442 or 800-597-3964). In contrast to the German omnipresence in the city of New Ulm, an Irish theme pervades the Innis House, which takes its name from a Gaelic word for "island." For golfers, there are five golf courses within a 20-mile radius of Innis House. Another bed-and-breakfast option is the **W. W. Smith Inn** at 101 Linden Street SW in Sleepy Eye (507-794-5661 or 800-799-5661). Located 14 miles from New Ulm, the W. W. Smith Inn has much to offer lovers of bed-and-breakfasts. Listed on the National Register of Historic Places, this elegant Queen Anne structure was constructed in 1901 for a wealthy area banker. Finally, we come to a New Ulm bed-and-breakfast, **Deutsche Strasse B&B** at 404 South German Street (507-354-2005 or 866-226-9856). Five rooms are available, two with queen-size beds, and three with full-size beds. Also included is a choice of full or continental breakfast.

Shopping

If you're looking for specialty shops with a German flair, you'll find it in New Ulm. New Ulm boasts businesses devoted to antiques, crafts, sweets, dolls, and sausages. The vast majority of shops are conveniently located on Minnesota and Broadway Streets, in the heart of beautiful old downtown New Ulm. **Edelweiss Flower Haus,** 209 North Minnesota Street (507-354-2222), specializes in flowers, and shoppers can watch floral artists create arrangements before their eyes. Another fine shop is **Muggs Fabric** at 101 North German Marktplatz (507-359-1515), which features a variety of quilting and fabric supplies, books, patterns, and gifts. In addition, there is **Maria's Creative Touch,** 202 North Minnesota Street (507-354-1888). Maria's offers handcrafted gifts such as pottery, dried floral arrangements, bears, and candles. Another New Ulm craft shop is **NadelKunst, Ltd.,** 212 North Minnesota Street (507-354-8708), specializing in basketry, knitting, crocheting, and many lesser-known crafts.

Of course, New Ulm has stores that specialize in German merchandise: the **Guten Tag Haus,** 127 North Minnesota Street (507-233-HAUS), and **Domeier's New Ulm German Store,** 1020 South Minnesota Street (507-354-4231). Unlike the aforementioned businesses, Domeier's is located 10 blocks south of the downtown business district. **Lambrecht's,** 119 North Minnesota Street (507-233-4350), sells two entire floors of gift items, from greetings cards and framed prints to lace, lamps, and shirts.

For those who prefer eating the items they purchase, New Ulm has several options. **Fudge and Stuff's,** 210 North Minnesota (507-359-5272), specialty, of course, is fudge, but they also carry cappuccino, espresso, coffee, and tea, as well as art and gift items. At the **Schell's Brewing Co. Gift Shop,** Schell's Park (507-354-5528), there is something for every shopper. Naturally, there are many Schell collectibles, plus gourmet food and novelty items.

Restaurants

Surprisingly, German food does not dominate New Ulm's restaurant options. German food is often included with traditional American fare. Certainly the place to start when discussing New Ulm's restaurants is the **Veigel's Kaiserhoff,** 221 North Minnesota Street (507-359-2071). The Kaiserhoff's most popular dish is their barbecue ribs, and for more than 62 years, diners have enjoyed the restaurant's unique version of this all-American

Insiders' Tip

New Ulm shops have limited hours, with many closing as early as 5:00 P.M., so call ahead or arrive early to maximize your New Ulm shopping experience.

favorite. Of course the menu also includes many German favorites such as bratwursts, schnitzels, landjaeger, and German chocolate cake. Finally, don't forget to wash down the Kaiserhoff's cuisine with a delicious Schell's beer, brewed in New Ulm. Another restaurant with heavy German influences is the **Heidelberg** at 2101 South Broadway Avenue (507–359–2941). The Heidelberg is conveniently located for travelers in the New Ulm Holiday Inn and serves American food and German specialties.

Traditional American food is also popular in New Ulm. **V's Kitchen** (Hy-Vee), 2015 South Broadway Avenue (507–354–8255), is a local cafe-style restaurant. The **Ulmer Café,** 115 North Minnesota Street (507–354–8122), is right in the middle of New Ulm's shopping area, and features breakfast and lunch in a hometown cafe.

For families, **Happy Joe's,** 1700 North Broadway Street (507–359–9811), specializes in food kids and adults love, such as pizza and chicken. There is also a smorgasbord at Happy Joe's, which outside Minnesota is called an all-you-can-eat buffet. **DJ's,** 1200 North Broadway Avenue (507–354–3843), is another family diner featuring lunch and dinner specials daily.

Besides German-influenced restaurants, there are a few Chinese restaurants in New Ulm. The **Ming Garden,** 106 North Minnesota Street (507–354–1628),

offers Chinese and American food in the center of New Ulm's business area. A more authentic Chinese restaurant is **Main Jiang House,** 206 North Minnesota Street (507–354–1218). Finally, New Ulm has several sandwich, burger, pizza, and taco chain restaurants.

North Shore Drive

The North Shore Drive, officially U.S. Highway 61, is lined with rental cottages, bed-and-breakfasts, RV parks, and motels, while the shore is dotted with rent-by-the-day boat docks and marinas. The first real town outside Duluth is Two Harbors, a virtual mecca of fast-food chain restaurants and gift shops, while any actual residences themselves are relatively new and tucked away some distance from the downtown area. Two Harbors is a good place to sit down and get a bite to eat or rest for the night before heading on to the beautiful parks that make up the attractions in this area, or pick up a bag of regionally grown wild rice, fresh honey, fruit preserves, or a lighthouse-shaped refrigerator magnet.

Attractions

Thirteen miles northeast of Two Harbors on US 61 is **Gooseberry Falls State Park** (218–834–3855), an amazing series of relatively untouched waterfalls that are open to the public to walk out on—literally. This is not recommended for those struggling with a fear of heights, as it's possible to climb to the very top of the waterfalls via hiking trails and walkways and walk right to the edge of the rocky face to peer over the edge, without having to deal with the presence of pesky handrails or safety mesh. A recently built visitor center features exhibits on Lake Superior and the history of the park itself.

Split Rock Lighthouse State Park (218–226–6372), also on US 61 about 20 miles northeast of Two Harbors, has been a landmark on the Lake Superior shore since 1910. Now a state-run historic site, it and

Insiders' Tip

If you're making any road trips during winter, make sure you're prepared—put something heavy (like a sandbag) over each drive wheel for weight. Tire chains are illegal in many parts of the state, so don't bother packing them.

the neighboring three lighthouse keeper's houses and fog signal building have been restored to their original turn-of-the-20th-century appearance and opened to visitors and tour groups. The attached History Center shows films and exhibits on the lighthouse, commercial fishing, and shipwrecks through most of the summer.

For more energetic travelers, the **Superior Hiking Trail** winds through the forested ridgeline of the coast for nearly 200 miles. There're also many small and midsize fishing lakes and tiny craft shops to be found all along the drive—call the Superior Hiking Trail Association in Two Harbors (218) 834-2700; www.shta.org.

Accommodations and Camping

The Lighthouse Bed & Breakfast, at the harbor in Two Harbors (218-834-4814 or 888-832-5606; www.lighthousebb.org), is one of the few B&Bs on the Great Lakes housed inside a working lighthouse, built in 1892. The B&B has three rooms decorated with period antiques, and all have a view of Lake Superior. For more pedestrian comforts, **AmericInn Lodge and Suites,** 1088 US 61 West, Two Harbors (800-634-3444), offers guests an indoor pool and sauna, while just outside Two Harbors on the shoreline is the **Grand Superior Lodge,** 2826 US 61 (218-834-3796 or 800-834-3796), a beautiful resort with individual log homes, an on-site restaurant and cocktail lounge, and an indoor pool and spa. A more rustic resort is the **Heinz Beachway Motel & Cabins,** 5119 North Shore Drive, Duluth (218-525-5191, www.lake-superior-explorer.com/beach), with full kitchenettes, evening campfires, and playgrounds for the kids. The motel and cabins are open May through October. If camping out is more your style, the **Wagon Wheel Campground,** 552 Old North Shore Road, Two Harbors (218-834-4901), is a pleasant lakeside campground with water and shower facilities, electrical hookups, and an on-site dump station.

Shopping

It's a tradition of ours to make the trek up to the North Shore every summer for one reason—wild rice. The tiny one-quarter pound bags of wild rice you get at the supermarket in the Cities usually cost you a couple of dollars, while just about every store in Two Harbors on up sells four-pound bags for around $8.00. Wild rice is much richer than domestic rice and adds a wonderful, hearty dimension to soups, poultry stuffing, and anything else that calls for rice.

All along the North Shore Drive can be found tiny houses converted into shops where you can buy anything from jars of wild clover honey to homemade preserves to lighthouse-shaped refrigerator magnets and, of course, fish bait. **Beaver Bay Agate Shop and Museum,** 1003 Main Street in Beaver Bay, is exactly what it sounds like, with jewelry and keychains made from agates found along the Lake Superior shoreline as well as man-made artifacts and geological marvels found in the area on permanent display, **Buddy's Wild Rice,** 724 Seventh Avenue, Two Harbors (218-834-5823), sells a wide selection of preserves, honey, wild rice, and sculptures commemorating the Split Rock Lighthouse, while **Country Crafts** in Two Harbors at 721 Seventh Avenue carries a wide variety of country-themed knickknacks.

Actually listing the shops along the North Shore Drive is a tricky business, because the area is so tourist-related. Not many people are willing to brave the winding roads that follow Lake Superior during winter, or the little stores that line the roadside, and winter sometimes lasts three-quarters of the year here.

But the remote shops in the sticks and in the small towns dotting the North Shore Highway all the way to the Canadian border often sell unique and/or memorable items and are worth a browsing stop. In particular, the beautiful town of Grand Marais, about 110 miles northeast of Duluth on US 61, is a haven for many artists, and the downtown region is alive with galleries and studios.

Restaurants

If you're more comfortable dining at familiar restaurant chains, then Two Harbors is the place to stop before heading on up the Lake Superior coast. Pretty much every fast-food chain in America is represented here, including Burger King, Dairy Queen, Pizza Hut, and Hardee's. If you're more interested in sticking to family owned-and-run establishments, there are plenty of those to choose from, too, either in Two Harbors or along the North Shore Drive. For lunch fare and sandwiches, try **Judy's Café,** at 623 Seventh Avenue, Two Harbors (218- 834-4802), or for a variety of fresh fish dishes, **Lou's Fish House,** 1319 US 61, Two Harbors (218-834-5254). For an elegant dining experience, try the **Northern Lights Restaurant** on US 61 in Beaver Bay (218-226-3012), and for informal, family-style meals, there's **Our Place** on Minnesota Highway 1, Finland (218-353-7343). And if you're just looking for a muffin and a cup of coffee, **Vanilla Bean Bakery and Café,** 812 Seventh Avenue, Two Harbors (218-834-3714), provides a cozy atmosphere to enjoy both.

Red Wing

Perhaps best known as the home of the Red Wing Shoe Company, Red Wing is a charming little town with a beautiful, regal downtown composed of refurbished old warehouse buildings and absolutely amazing churches that date back to 1855. Set deep in a valley surrounded by beauti-ful fishing lakes, scenic hilltop views, rivers, picturesque farms, and apple orchards, Red Wing has the added advantage of being populated by some of the most genuinely friendly and helpful people you'll ever meet.

Getting There

You have two choices here: You can either take the scenic drive to Red Wing via US 61 from St. Paul, or you can get on a train at the Amtrak station in St. Paul (730 Transfer Road; 800-872-7245) and take it all the way to the historic **Old Milwaukee Depot** at 420 Levee Street (800-231-2222) in Red Wing. You may want to stop by the depot while in Red Wing anyway, since it doubles as the visitor center and there are lots of maps, brochures, and free local newspapers with restaurant coupons and information on events and happenings around town. The depot, established in 1904, is located next to downtown Red Wing and all its sights, too, so there's no need to worry about transportation unless you have plans outside of town. This is especially a good option if you're coming to Red Wing to do some antiquing, since all the antiques shops in town are located right in the downtown area.

If you opt to drive, a good alternative to US 61 is taking Interstate 94 East out of the Twin Cities into Wisconsin to Wisconsin Highway 35 South just east of Hudson. Follow WI 35 to Bay City, and then turn on to U.S. Highway 63 West to cross the Mississippi to Red Wing. WI 35 is a two-lane highway that passes through beautiful old hardwood forests and gently sloping farmlands dotted with old farmhouses, stone silos, and shallow creeks. From Prescott to Bay City, WI 35 roughly follows the Mississippi River, providing spectacular views of the waterway and the bluffs across the river on the Minnesota side.

However, if you want to get to Red Wing quickly, US 61 out of St. Paul can save you about 15 minutes off your total driving time. There's not much to look at until you get to Hastings, Minnesota.

Insiders' Tip

No tickets are sold at the Red Wing Amtrak station, so make sure you buy a round-trip ticket at the Twin Cities station.

Once you pass through Hastings, though, it's all trees and farmland again.

For more information about the area, contact the **Red Wing Visitors and Convention Bureau,** 418 Levee Street; (651) 385-5934 or (800) 498-3444; www.red wing.org.

Attractions

A good place to start exploring Red Wing is **Bay Point Park** on Levee Street. Located right on the Mississippi River, this is also the home of **Boathouse Village,** one of the only remaining "gin pole" boathouse installations in the country. The village looks just like a bunch of little houses floating in the water, with floating walkways connecting the "neighborhood" together. Close by is **Levee Park,** located just behind the historic 1904 Milwaukee Depot. Both parks have picnic tables and play areas for kids.

Located at the corner of Third Street and East Avenue at 773 Third Street is the historic **Sheldon Theatre** (651-385-3667 or 800-899-5759; www.sheldontheatre.org) the country's first municipal theater. First opened in 1904, the theatre was such an unabashed collection of sculpture, arches, marble columns, and gilded plaster detail, it was once described as a "jewel box." Nowadays, the 466-seat theatre is used for everything from classical performances and rock concerts to lecture series and plays. If you just want to walk in and look at the inside of this beautiful building, the extremely helpful men and women at the ticket counter will gladly let you in to take a peek.

As well as being rich with historical architecture, Red Wing also has its share of museums, including the somewhat unconventional **Red Wing Shoe Museum,** 314 Main Street (651-388-8211 or 800-733-9464), www.RedWingshoe.com. Owned and operated by Red Wing Shoes, the museum treats visitors to exhibits imparting the history of the company as well as an interactive display where kids and adults can go through the process of making a pair of shoes. There are also film clips from 1925 about the early days of the factory and a series of first-hand "shoe tales" visitors can read. About 9 blocks away at 1166 Oak Street is the **Goodhue County Historical Museum** (651-388-6024; www.goodhuehistory.mus.mn.us), which contains more than 150,000 paintings, photographs, geological and natural history displays, and artifacts concerning Goodhue County from prehistory to the present.

At the end of Fifth Street is majestic **Barn Bluff,** immortalized by Henry David Thoreau in 1861 after he hiked to the top. The bluff is listed on the National Register of Historic Places, and several marked paths and stairways are available to hikers of varying skill levels. A much easier climb (or drive) to the top of the bluffs is in **Memorial Park,** located at the end of Seventh Street. On your way to the top of **Sorin's Bluff,** you'll find hiking trails, bike paths, and caves that may or may not be wise to explore. From either bluff, you get a great view of Red Wing and the Mississippi River, as well as the beautiful valley and tree-covered bluffs that stretch around the town. For another view of the valley, **Red Wing River Boat Rides,** located at the Levy Wall (651-455-7983), offers relaxing, one-hour boat rides along the rugged bluffs of the Mississippi River. Be sure to bring your binoculars, as everything from deer, beavers, bald eagles, and wild turkeys have been seen on these rides. Cold soda is available for sale on the boat, but otherwise no food is served on the boats. Passengers are encouraged to pack a picnic lunch to take with them for the trip.

In wintertime, Red Wing and its neighbor, Welch, became ski country. Twelve miles northwest of town, just off US 61, is the **Welch Village Ski Area** (651-222-7079 or 800-270-1838; www.welchvillage. com), which features some of the best downhill skiing in the state. Right next door, **Welch Mill,** at 14818 264th Street Path (800-657-6760), offers canoe and inner tube rentals and to-and-from shuttle service to the Cannon River in spring and summer. For cross-country skiers, there's the **Cannon Valley Trail** in Cannon Falls, nearly 20 miles of countryside that follows the original Chicago Great Western Railroad line that once connected Cannon Falls and Red Wing. Call (800) 766-6000 for information and to purchase required ski passes. Nine miles to the south of Red Wing on US Highway 61 is the **Mt. Frontenac Ski Area** (800-488-5826), which features the highest vertical drop in southeast Minnesota.

Ten miles north of Red Wing and just off US 61 is the glamorous **Treasure Island Resort and Casino** (651-388-6300 or 800-222-7077; www.treasureisland casino.com), a tropical-themed casino and hotel that features 44 blackjack tables, 2,500 slot machines, a 40-foot man-made waterfall, and smoking and nonsmoking gambling areas. The casino is decorated with fake shipwrecks and palm trees, and the slot machines and gambling tables are spread far enough apart that the casino never feels too crowded. The attached hotel has an indoor pool with another waterfall, a fitness room, and a child care facility, while outside is a campground with 95 pull-through sites and a 137-slip marina.

Accommodations and Camping

If you plan to spend the night in Red Wing, you have many options. The most elegant of the hotels in the area is downtown Red Wing's historic **St. James Hotel** at 406 Main Street (651-388-2846 or 800-252-1875; www.st-james-hotel.com), established more than 125 years ago and a member of the National Trust's Historic Hotels of America. The elegant hotel has only 60 guest rooms, so you'll definitely want to call way ahead of time to make reservations.

Many beautiful old houses in Red Wing have been converted to bed-and-breakfasts and inns over the past decade. Most of them are on the National Register of Historic Places, and many were former residences of Red Wing Shoe Company tycoons. In fact, the **Golden Lantern Inn** at 721 East Avenue (615-388-3315 or 888-288-3315; www.goldlantern.com), wasn't just home to one Red Wing Shoe president—three former presidents of the company once lived here. The Golden Lantern has since added whirlpools and fireplaces to the rooms and offers a full breakfast each morning to visitors. A few streets over is the **Red Wing Blackbird Bed and Breakfast** at 722 West 5th Street (651-388-2292), which has two large guest rooms with whirlpools and private bathrooms, while nearby at 1105 West Fourth Street is the **Moondance Inn** (651-388-8145; www.moondanceinn.com), which offers a five-course gourmet brunch to weekend guests and rooms with private bathrooms and double whirlpools.

For more conventional lodging, there's an **AmericInn Motel** at 1819 Old West Main (651-385-9060 or 800-634-3444), which offers guests a free continental breakfast and has a pool and sauna on the premises; a **Best Western Quiet House & Suites** next to the Pottery Place Shopping Mall off US 61 (651-388-1577 or 800-528-1234; www.quiethouse.com), offers both indoor and outdoor pools as well as complimentary coffee in every room; a **Super 8 Motel** at US 61 and Withers Harbor (651-388-0491 or 800-800-8000), has an indoor pool and allows pets to stay with guests for a small additional fee; and the **Parkway Motel** at 3425 US 61 West (651-388-8231 or 800-762-0934), has snowmobile trails, hiking trails, fishing lakes, and a golf course within walking distance.

If you're more happy "roughing it" while on vacation, there's the **Hay Creek Valley Campground** (651-388-3998 or 888-388-3998), located 6 miles south of Red Wing on Minnesota Highway 58. The campground has a heated swimming pool and a restaurant, the Old Western Saloon, on the premises and borders a stocked trout stream. Right next to the campground is the Hardwood Forest State Park with trails laid out for horseback riding, hiking, snowmobiling, and areas set aside for in-season hunting.

Shopping

Antiques addicts beware—Red Wing has some amazingly good deals on antique furniture, toys, jewelry, and collectibles in general. The two main shopping areas in town are situated right by each other, too. There's the Downtown District, which is composed of beautiful old warehouse buildings and storefronts that have been refurbished and turned into antiques stores, thrift stores, and restaurants, while about 9 blocks away, down Old West Main Street, is the Historic Pottery District, where you can buy antiques from **Al's Antique Mall** at 1314 Old West Main Street (651-388-0572), or watch local potters make original, salt-glazed pottery at the **Historic Pottery Place Mall** at 2000 Old West Main Street (651-388-1428).

The Downtown District has the widest variety of shops to choose from. At **Memory Maker Antiques** in the Boxrud Building at 415-419 Main Street (651-388-3033), you can find beautiful antique rhinestone jewelry, porcelain vases, music boxes, and a huge selection of old photographs and vinyl LPs for sale at ridiculously low prices, while down-

stairs, at **Twigges of Galena Ltd.**, 415 Main Street (651-388-7881), you can buy brand-new glass, brass, and ceramic candleholders as well as a wide assortment of handmade candles at extremely reasonable prices. Down the street at 329 Main Street is **Amish Heirlooms** (651-385-0500), where you can find handmade linens, folk art, exquisitely stitched quilts, and warming blankets. In the **Riverfront Shopping Centre** at 320 Main Street are many more shops, including **Main Street Toys** (651-385-8775), where you can pick up everything from handmade wooden puzzles to art supplies and books for your kids.

Restaurants

While the majority of Red Wing's restaurants can be categorized as traditional American fare, quite a few add a unique twist to those traditional dishes. The **Staghead Restaurant** at 219 Bush Street (651-388-6581), featuring the culinary skills of former Hüsker Dü bassist Greg Norton, offers a changing and eclectic menu of steak and venison dinners, Italian dishes, and specialty sandwiches; the restaurant also has a huge wine list and more than 30 imported and domestic beers on tap. This restaurant has received enough attention statewide for its food menu and wine list that it gets lauded in Minneapolis/St. Paul newspapers pretty much every time there's a significant menu change, or rumor of one. **Old Fashioned Foods** at 1920 West Main Street (651-388-8916), serves 15 different homemade soups for lunch, including vegetable beef barley and corn chowder and ham, while the nearby **Fiesta Mexicana,** 2555 Old West Main Street (651-385-8939), serves authentic Mexican food for the lunch and dinner crowd and is quite possibly the only nonchain Mexican restaurant you'll find within a 50 mile radius. **Bev's Café** at 221 Bush Street (651-388-5227) offers classic home-style meals from hash to roast beef dinners and a fish fry on Friday. For a very elegant evening, the historic St. James Hotel's restaurant, **The Port of Red Wing** (651-388-2846; call ahead for reservations), serves a limited but tantalizing dinner menu, with live piano music Friday and Saturday evenings.

If you just want a cup of coffee and something to munch on while you read the paper, you're in luck. Red Wing has several cozy little nooks to grab a cup of java, including **Lily's Coffee House & Flowers** at 419 West Third Street (651–388–8797), which serves soups, sandwiches, pastries, coffee, and espresso drinks; **Braschler's Bakery and Coffeeshop** at 410 West Third Street, (651–388–1589), makes its own pastries and muffins to accompany its large menu of caffeinated beverages; **Tale of Two Sisters Tea Room and Gift Shoppe** at 204 West Seventh Street (651–388–2250), offers a full English garden tea or just a cup of coffee to patrons, depending on your tastes.

For the sports bar fan, **Andy's Bar** at 529 Plum Street (651–388–3351), has several TVs with satellite hookups to accompany its menu of beer, burgers, and chicken dinners, while in downtown proper, the **Barrel House,** at 223 Main Street (651–388–9967), serves light food, pizza, and beer, with daily happy hour specials.

In the Area

Twenty-three miles south of Red Wing across the Mississippi River on WI 35 is the historic town of **Pepin, Wisconsin.** Named after the Pepin brothers, who were two of the first French trappers in the area, the village was settled in 1846 and was known for years as a steamboat boomtown and a vacation spot for wealthy Chicago socialites who summered on Lake Pepin. This is the place to visit if you're interested in fishing, boating, or bird-watching—the 13,000-acre Tiffany Wildlife Area, right next to Lake Pepin, is a regular roosting spot for bald eagles and hawks, while Lake Pepin itself has several beautiful marinas with public docking ramps.

Perhaps the most famous of Pepin's residents was Laura Ingalls Wilder, immortalized in *Little House on the Prairie*. Every third full weekend of September,

Pepin celebrates Laura Ingalls Wilder Days with events including a Laura Look-Alike Contest, a parade, demonstrations of traditional crafts and industries, live theatrical productions, and other activities inspired by Wilder's writings. For more information about Laura Ingalls Wilder Days, contact The Laura Ingalls Wilder Days Committee, Pepin Visitor Information Center, P.O. Box 274, Pepin, Wisconsin 54759, or call (715) 442–3011.

Stillwater

While Stillwater is technically considered a Twin Cities outer-ring suburb, it's still a good half hour's drive from the Cities themselves, especially in wintertime. Long in competition with the Twin Cities for everything from being the state's logging and industry capital to making a bid for the state capital itself, Stillwater is a beautiful riverside city with much to offer antiques shoppers, architecture connoisseurs, book collectors, and nature lovers alike. There's more than enough to do in the Stillwater area to make it at least a day trip, if not a relaxing weekend getaway.

That the economy is on an uphill climb in Stillwater has never been more apparent—everywhere you go, brick-and-wood storefronts have been restored and repainted, and specialty stores, wineries, and espresso bars have set up shop where there were once just thrift shops and diners. Along with all of its parks and bicycle trails, there's sure to be something here that appeals to you and your family.

For more information about Stillwater, check out www.ilovestillwater.com, or call the **Stillwater Chamber of Commerce** at (651) 439–4001.

Getting There

Take Minnesota Highway 36 East until you reach Stillwater.

Attractions

Whether your interest lies in shopping for antiques or taking long, beautiful nature hikes or just taking some time to yourself to catch up on some fishing, Stillwater and the St. Croix River have much to offer in all of the above, and more. In spring-time (approximately late March), you can catch sight of **bald eagles** sunning them-selves on breaking ice floes in the river. In summer the town comes to life with the **Rivertown Art Fair** (third weekend in May, Lowell Park; 651-430-2306) and the Saturday morning farmers' markets.

Stillwater is known for being a festival town, and its appearance changes drasti-cally depending on whatever holiday is coming up. In mid-June you can catch the **Stillwater Art Crawl & Festival** (651-439-1465), during which all the local gal-leries open their doors to the public; dur-ing the third weekend in June is the **Taste of Stillwater Festival** (651-439-4001), where all the local restaurants and chefs set up shop outside and invite passersby to taste their wares. The last weekend in July is **Stillwater's Lumberjack Days,** a city-wide street festival complete with parades, live music, and logrolling competitions. December 1 through 24 is the **Victorian Holidays** in Stillwater, when the town gears up for Christmas with daily winter events and special weekend celebrations.

From Stillwater you can ride the beau-tiful "floating wedding cake" **steamboats** that travel up and down the St. Croix River on a daily basis through spring and sum-mer. The *Andiamo* takes passengers for a long and relaxing ride along the limestone cliffs overhung with oaks and firs that make up most of the river valley (contact Andiamo Enterprises, 651-430-1234, www.andiamo-ent.com. If solo boating is more your style, you can rent fishing boats and equipment from either **Beanies** at Maui's Landing (651-436-8874) or kayaks from **P.J. Asch Otterfitters** at 413 East Nelson Street (651-430-2286; www.pjasch otterfitters.com).

Another great way to see Stillwater and the St. Croix is from the air—in a hot air bal-loon. **Aamodt's Hot Air Balloons** (call 651-351-0101 or 866 5-HOT-AIR) for launch sites and to make reservations, or check their Web site at www.aamodts balloons.com for more info) have been tak-ing satisfied passengers up into the air for years. There's also the **Minnesota Zephyr** at 601 North Main Street (651-430-3000 or 800-992-6100; www.minnesotazephyr. com), an elegant, refurbished dining train that takes passengers on a three-hour trip through Stillwater and along the bluffs of the St. Croix River Valley. The trip includes a five-course white linen dinner and the musical stylings of the Zephyr Cabaret, which performs hits of the '40s and '50s for your pleasure. Another option is the **Still-water Trolley** at 400 East Nelson Street (651-430-0352; www.stillwatertrolley.com), for a narrated trip through the older neigh-borhoods and downtown of Stillwater—the trolley is enclosed and climate controlled, so don't be afraid to take this trip in win-ter. Speaking of winter, many of the sports stores in town rent cross-country skis and snow gear. **St. Croix Outfitters** at 223

Insiders' Tip

In 1994 Stillwater was declared America's first "Book Town," an international designation sponsored by Welshman Richard Booth to honor notable book-friendly towns worldwide. Stillwater's multiple antiquarian and new booksellers line Main Street downtown. For more information about Stillwater's bookstores, visit www.booktown.com.

South Main Street (651–439–4891) is a good place to start.

Accommodations and Camping

Stillwater boasts a variety of bed-and-breakfasts housed in quaint old hotels and Victorian mansions listed on the National Register of Historic Places as well as modern hotels with the expected amenities. The **Lumber Baron Hotel** at 101 South Water Street (651–439–6000) is a beautiful red-brick building that's located right by the St. Croix and is furnished with turn-of-the-20th-century period pieces. The 150-year-old **Harvest Restaurant & Inn** at 114 Chestnut (651–430–8111) features wood-burning fireplaces and double Jacuzzis in the rooms, as well as an outdoor dining area set in a hidden garden. Eight miles south in Hudson, Wisconsin, is the **Baker Brewster** at 904 Vine Street (715–381–2895), a classic Victorian inn that features English tea parties, rooms with fireplaces and whirlpools, wine and cheese tasting, and the always-fun murder mystery evenings.

If you're just looking for a comfortable hotel room to spend the night, **Holiday Inn Stillwater** at 2000 Washington Avenue (651–275–1401), fits the bill nicely. The **Best Western Stillwater Inn,** 1750 West Frontage Road (651–430–1300), is located along Minnesota Highway 36 southwest of downtown. The comfortable hotel offers everything from basic rooms to suites with cozy Jacuzzis. The nearby **Super 8 Motel** (651–430–3990 or 800–800–8000), lets kids younger than age 12 stay for free and includes free HBO with the regular hotel cable TV.

For RV campers, there's the **Golden Acres RV Park & Picnic Area** at 15150 North Square Lake Trail (651–430–1374), which has 54 campsites with water, electrical, and sewer hookups available (no tent camping allowed). The campsite, located right on the banks of Square Lake, has a nice swimming beach and a reputation for being a good place to go fishing.

Shopping

Stillwater is antiques central, with shops that sell everything from collector's dolls and teddy bears to handmade Amish quilts and furniture. At the Main Street Square shopping mall at 124 South Main Street, you can buy pottery, jewelry, and vintage clothing at **Country Charm Antiques** (651–439–8202) or consignment clothing at **Nearly New!** (651–430–1188). **Seasons Tique** at 229 South Main Street (651–430–1240) carries beautiful Christmas tree ornaments and decorations from around the world all year long. For the larger budget, **Enigma** at 213 South Main Street (651–439–2206) carries new and antique furnishings from Europe and Asia, and the **J. P. Laskin Company** at 306 East Chestnut Street (651–439–5712) carries handmade American goods made by Amish people and Native Americans, as well as handblown glass artifacts.

Stillwater has a huge selection of independent bookstores to choose from. **St. Croix Antiquarian Booksellers** at 232 South Main Street (651–430–0732), carries more than 110,000 books on history, art, philosophy, Americana, and everything in between, while **Loome Theological Booksellers** in the Old Swedish Covenant Church at 320 North Fourth Street (651–430–1092) specializes in secondhand and out-of-print books on theology, religion, and philosophy. **The Valley Bookseller,** 217 North Main Street (651–430–3385; www.valleybookseller.com), is an independent bookstore selling new titles. The beautiful store is bright and sunny and features a strong children's section, a large selection of fiction and local history titles, and an exotic bird aviary in the middle of the store.

Restaurants

As we mentioned before, Stillwater has no shortage of coffeehouses and espresso bars. At the **Dreamcoat Café,** 215 South Main Street (651–430–0615), you can order sandwiches or ice cream to go with your coffee—on weekend nights, local acoustic acts perform at this neighborhood cafe. At the other end of Main, **Supreme Bean Espresso Café** at 402 North Main Street (651-439-4314) serves delicious croissant sandwiches and pastries that you can take outside to eat on their patio.

There are just as many places to go for dinner in Stillwater, too. Featuring a beautiful view of the St. Croix as well as traditional American fare is the **Dock Café** at 425 East Nelson Street (651-430-3770; www.dockcafe.com). **Brine's** at 219 South Main Street (651-439-7556) serves hot deli sandwiches, soups and salads, and the famous "Brine Burger," which is a heck of a lot better than it sounds. For German food, try the **Gasthaus Bavarian Hunter Restaurant** at 8390 Lofton Avenue North (651-439-7128), which features live accordion music Friday evenings.

For more refined dining, **La Belle Vie** at 312 South Main Street (651-430-3545) has an award-winning menu of Mediterranean seafood, chicken, and pasta dishes. The historic **Lowell Inn** at 102 North Second Street (651-439-1100) serves elegant multicourse dinners in a variety of themed rooms.

Stillwater is also the home to several wineries with on-site tasting rooms, including **Aamodt's Apple Farm/Saint Croix Vineyards** at 6428 Manning Avenue (651-430-3310) and **Northern Vineyards Winery** at 223 North Main Street (651-430-1032). Call ahead for an appointment at either place, just in case they're already booked.

In the Area

Just south of Stillwater and across the St. Croix River is the city of **Hudson, Wisconsin,** which is basically like a little Stillwater. There are plenty of antiques stores, jewelry stores, and coffee shops, as well as beautiful storefronts and turn-of-the-20th-century architecture throughout the downtown area. On the south end of

Coulee Road is the turnoff to Birkmose Park, which, if you take the drive to the top, gives you a great view of the harbor as well as several imposing-looking Native American burial mounds. Hudson is also the home of the **San Pedro Café** at 426 Second Street (715-386-4003), which features a variety of excellent pasta dishes with a Caribbean flair, such as linguine with jerk chicken and tomato-flavored Alfredo sauce.

North of Stillwater on Minnesota Highway 95 is the **Boomsite,** a large body of water where fresh cut trees once poured in through the river mouth and were then collected by the hardworking men of Stillwater's logging past. Now the Boomsite is a wonderful park surrounded by forest with an easily accessible path down to the beach. This is a beautiful, well-maintained park that makes a fun place to stop and relax and let the kids run around before getting back on the road.

Taylors Falls

In order to properly appreciate autumn in Minnesota, a drive to Taylors Falls in the last two weeks of September or the first two weeks of October is absolutely necessary. During this time, the leaves of the trees growing in the mineral-rich soil turn fluorescent shades of scarlet, gold, and yellow, looking more like bright springtime flower petals than dying tree leaves.

But don't just visit in the fall. Taylors Falls is just as beautiful in springtime, with millions of tiny purple, white, and blue wildflowers springing up even between the smallest of sidewalk cracks. In fact, each spring Taylors Falls holds several wildflower symposiums in Interstate State Park to celebrate the season. In the warm months, bird-watching is a popular pastime all along the St. Croix River, and canoes and other small boats can be rented at Interstate State Park for those who want to get a closer look at the natural beauty of the cliffs that line the river. For more information, you can either call the Taylors Falls Chamber of Commerce at (651) 465-5133 or visit their Web page at www.taylorsfalls.com.

Getting There

We, of course, recommend taking the scenic route up to Taylors Falls from the Twin Cities. If you take U.S. Highway 94 East to MN 95 North all the way to Taylors Falls, you'll be treated to scenes of beautiful old hardwood forests and the St. Croix River all the way. If you just want to get to Taylors Falls, the quickest route is to take either I-35 E north or I-35 W north (depending on where in the Twin Cities you are) to I-35, then take I-35 North to U.S. Highway 8 East and follow US 8 all the way to Taylors Falls. It's a little less scenic, being a major highway and all, but you'll travel through the cute towns of Chisago City, Stockholm, and Center City, and you can still get a glimpse of the beautiful St. Croix Valley along the last few miles.

Attractions

Taylors Falls attractions run the gamut of breathtaking, cliffside views of a landscape carved out by Ice Age glaciers to wild water park rides to self-guided tours through a historic neighborhood with houses dating back to the 1850s. You can take a trip down the St. Croix on your own in a rented canoe, or get on a steamboat for a relaxing bird-watching tour.

The centerpiece of the Taylors Falls, Minnesota, and the St. Croix Falls, Wisconsin, border is **Interstate State Park,** just off Highway 8 in Taylors Falls, (651) 465-5711, known for its rare flora and fauna. Perhaps the most distinguishing feature of the park, however, are the jet-black granite formations scattered throughout the region. Believed to once be full-sized mountains, the dense stone was slowly eroded by glaciers into solitary pillars, winding towers, and the deepest glacial potholes in the world. The potholes are really something to see. It's nearly impossible to see the bottom of the deepest ones. So much groundwater seeps into

the holes that the park has to regularly pump the water out. However, it's amazing to see how thousands of years of erosion can shape even the densest rock into these near-perfect, soft-edged circles that curve their way nearly 100 feet down through solid granite.

Aside from the unique geological formations, Interstate State Park is crisscrossed with nature trails that lead visitors through thick forests (again, breathtaking in the height of autumn), up into the greenstone cliffs and Precambrian basalt flows that encircle the Minnesota side of the park, and then into open fields of tiny purple trilliums and other native wildflowers. Bird-watching is another popular pastime in the park. Eagles and their hatchlings can be seen almost every summer. For another view of the park and its wildlife, catch a ride on the riverboat *Taylors Falls Princess*. The boat dock is located right next to the entrance to Interstate State Park, and you can either buy tickets at the dock or make reservations by calling (800) 447-4958. You can also rent canoes at the dock to take on the river.

For man-made entertainment, head over to **Wild Mountain.** To get there, take a left off US 8 in Taylors Falls, follow MN 95 to County Road 16, and take CR 16 to Wild Mountain. Park visitors of all ages can play on one of the giant waterslides, float down an 800-foot stream in an inner tube, slide down one of the two 1,700-foot-high alpine slides, or race around on the park's go-kart track. In winter, Wild Mountain becomes a ski and snowboard park, with more than 100 acres of beginner, intermediate, and advanced skiing terrain.

Bench Street Antiques & Mercantile in downtown Taylors Falls at 364 Bench Street (651-465-6100) sells comprehensive maps and self-guided walking tour packets for about $2.50. The guides contain detailed information on when the houses in Taylors Falls were built and a little of each building's history. While most of the historic houses in Taylors Falls are private residences and not open to tourists, you can stop by the **Folsom House Museum** at 272 West Government

Street (651–465–3125). Listed on the National Register of Historic Places, along with the rest of the Angel Hill neighborhood, the Folsom House is a five-bedroom Greek Revival home furnished with the original furniture, books, family pictures, and memorabilia belonging to Minnesota State Senator W. H. C. Folsom and his family in the 1800s. The home is open to tour groups from Memorial Day weekend to mid-October each year.

Accommodations and Camping

Although most of the historic houses in Taylors Falls are closed to the general public, a few of them have been converted to bed-and-breakfasts. The **Cottage Bed & Breakfast,** 950 Fox Glen Drive (651–465–3595; www.The-Cottage.com), was originally designed as an 18th-century English country house and offers guests a spectacular view of the St. Croix River. The house is furnished with English and French Country period pieces and is minutes away from several state parks and Wild Mountain. Even more interesting—especially from a historical perspective—is the **Old Jail Bed & Breakfast** at 349 Government Street (651–465–3112; www.oldjail.com). Exactly what it sounds like, the Old Jail has three furnished suites available to rent either by the day or by the week, each with its own private bathroom, kitchen, sitting room, and entrance. The Old Jail is located a short walk from the St. Croix River, Interstate State Park, and downtown Taylors Falls. Having just as good a view as any other place in town but offering much more conventional accommodations is the **Pines Motel** at 543 River Street (651–465–3422).

For campers, **Wildwood RV Park & Campground,** located right next to Wild Mountain on County Road 16 (800–447–4958; www.wildmountain.com), offers a variety of sunny, shaded, or isolated campsites for both tents and RVs, with immediate access to hiking and bicycle trails, a swimming pool, and a miniature golf course. The campsite also has well-maintained showers and flush toilets, as well as water, electrical, and sewer hookups. **Camp Waub-O-Jeeg,** located 2 miles north of Taylors Falls on CR 16 (651–465–5721), offers both traditional, "primitive" campsites and those with electrical hookups and is set in a thick forest a short walk from the banks of the St. Croix River. The campsite is open from mid-April through mid-October, and it's highly recommended that you make reservations at least a week in advance.

Shopping

Bench Street Antiques at 364 Bench Street (651–465–6100), and its downtown neighbors, **Johan's Antiques** at 424 Bench Street (651–465–7604), and **Newbery House** at 418 Bench Street (651–465–6802), all sell reasonably priced antiques, mostly relevant to the Taylors Falls area. Bench Street Antiques especially carries interesting merchandise, from old books and antique dual-blade ice skates to yellowing black-and-white photographs of Taylors Falls and its past residents.

Restaurants

The **Drive In Restaurant** at 572 Bench Street (651–465–7831) is a quaint, '70s-style drive-in with wonderful burgers, shakes, and homemade root beer served by waitresses in hoop skirts wearing roller skates. Patrons of the Drive In also get to enjoy a great view of the St. Croix and the steamboats passing by while they eat either in their cars or at one of the picnic tables set up outside the restaurant.

For family-style indoor dining, stop by **Romayne's Restaurant** at 391 Bench Street (651–465–4405). For grown-ups, **Border Bar & Grill** at 367 Bench Street, (651–465–6275) is a good place to stop by for burgers and beers.

If you're just looking for a cup of coffee, you're in luck—Taylors Falls has one of the nicest coffeehouses in Minnesota. Located next door to the oldest independent public library in the state, **Coffee Talk,** 479 Bench Street (651–465–6700), is a beautifully renovated Victorian house with a small front porch and a gigantic, beautiful flower garden with lots of comfortable, quaint wicker furniture and chairs spread around in the back. Inside, the establishment is decorated with brightly colored flowers and seasonal gourds, hand-painted furniture for both adults and children, and plenty of seating for customers both upstairs and down. The menu includes various espresso and coffee drinks and tasty bakery items, but the main sell of this place is the beautiful, morning glory–covered trellis that leads the way to the closest thing to a 19th-century English garden you may ever walk into.

In the Area

While driving up to Taylors Falls on MN 95, a stop at the little village of **Marine on St. Croix** is a must. The community, composed of stately old houses surrounded by fantastic flower gardens and ancient hardwood and conifer forests, is so still and quiet and beautiful it feels completely apart from the rest of the world. Established in 1838 as a lumber town, Marine has kept the look of a 19th-century settlement while becoming less an industrial town and more an out-of-the-way retreat for artists and writers. Inspired by the forests, ancient stone silos, and farmhouses that pepper the landscape and, of course, the St. Croix River, they create their art. Writer Garrison Keillor once compared Marine to his mythical hometown of Lake Wobegon, while the directors of such films as *Grumpier Old Men, Beautiful Girls* (which was also shot in nearby Stillwater), and *The Cure* all chose to film on location here.

Marine on St. Croix is mostly made up of residences, but there are several places worth stopping by. The 2-block downtown district on Judd Street, now on the National Register of Historic Places, has a gas station and general store, perfect for making pit stops, and the Village Scoop ice cream parlor. The **Brookside Bar and Grill,** 140 Judd (651–433–5132), has a real spring-fed stream running through its basement to keep the beer cool. There are also plenty of cross-country skiing and hiking trails that start in town and head out into the forests.

If you take US 8 to Wisconsin Highway 87 out of Taylors Falls, you'll come to **St. Croix Falls, Wisconsin.** Located on the other side of the St. Croix River, the historic downtown area has many antiques shops and farm stores to pick up knickknacks and produce. The countryside around the town is dotted with llama and ginseng farms, ancient farmhouses, and about a dozen abandoned one-room schoolhouses that date back to the time when wealthy landowners built schools on their land for their own as well as their employees' children.

If you take US 8 all the way to Wisconsin Highway 63, you'll reach the town of **Turtle Lake, Wisconsin,** home to the St. Croix Casino & Hotel, 777 US 8 and WI 63 (800–U-GO-U-WIN). An easy-paced, almost neighborly feeling casino decorated like a big game hunter's lodge, the St. Croix holds special events for visitors almost monthly, including a Polkathon and a Native American Talent Showcase.

Relocation

Minneapolis-St. Paul has always been an attractive place for relocation, given the region's consistently strong economy versus the rest of the nation, the high quality of life, access to world-class educational resources, the numerous corporations based in the Metro, lower crime rates than comparable metropolitan areas, and a vibrant cultural scene. Not surprisingly, many persons relocating to Minneapolis-St. Paul come from neighboring states, new Twin Citians accustomed to the cold. In recent years, however, thousands of Hispanic, Hmong, Somali, and Russian immigrants have chosen to come to Minnesota, adding new faces and languages to the Twin Cities community.

Although some of the quirks inherent to the Twin Cities may be hard for newcomers to understand (ice fishing, annual New Year's Day swims in area lakes—after a hole has been cut in the ice, Twin Citians' inability to merge smoothly into freeway traffic, onramp meters on freeways, "snow emergencies," and the rivalry between Minneapolis and St. Paul), the friendly nature of Minnesotans and the conveniences of the 14th largest metropolitan area in the country will quickly make just about anyone feel at home.

This chapter provides information to aid newcomers to the Twin Cities, including details about looking for work, buying real estate, renting, and neighborhoods, as well as listings for useful resources such as libraries, motor vehicle departments, and tourism bureaus (which have relocation packets to send out in addition to comprehensive area info). If you don't find what you are looking for here, ask a native; nine times out of ten, the famous quality of "Minnesota Nice" will come through and they will steer you in the right direction.

Finding a Job

The Twin Cities is a mecca for jobs in many industries, including manufacturing, banking, retail, airlines, information technology, medicine, law, publishing, state government, insurance, and many other fields. The following are a few sources to consult as you look for your perfect job.

Temp Agencies

Temp agencies, particularly in an ailing economy, can often find short- or long-term employment in a variety of fields.

They can also be very useful for newcomers to an area who have not yet secured a full-time job, as a way to pay the bills until the dream job comes along. All the national temp agency chains have offices in the Twin Cities, as do many local agen-

Insiders' Tip

Some of the largest employers in Minnesota are in Maplewood, with several thousand employed by 3M alone.

339

cies and specialized businesses that hire temp workers only in certain industries. The following are a few places to get you started.

Adecco Employment Services
900 Second Avenue South,
Minneapolis
(612) 339–1153
101 East Fifth Street, St. Paul
(651) 224–4040
www.adecco.com
Multiple additional locations in the Twin Cities

Adecco specializes in clerical, data entry, word processing, administrative, and light industrial jobs.

Allied Professionals
3209 West 76th Street, Edina
(952) 832–5101
www.alliedprofessionals.com

Allied focuses on medical and dental temporary positions, including jobs for nurses, X-ray technicians, dentists, medical secretaries, and senior assistance.

Freelance Creative Services
7835 Telegraph Road, Bloomington
(952) 941–0022
www.freelancecreative.com

Freelance Creative Services matches workers with jobs in creative fields, including graphic design, marketing, technical writing, editing and proofreading, and Web design.

Pro Staff
City Center, Third Floor, 920 Second Avenue South, Minneapolis
(612) 339–2220
Norwest Center, Skyway Level, 55 East Fifth Street, St. Paul
(651) 291–7811
www.prostaff.com
Multiple additional locations in the Twin Cities

Pro Staff is a national company specializing in hiring temps for companies looking for workers in the fields of accounting, creative services, office support, information technology, and engineering.

Strom Engineering
10505 Wayzata Boulevard, Minnetonka
(952) 544–8644
www.stromengineering.com

Strom Engineering finds temporary positions for engineers, information technology specialists, drafters and designers, and engineering technicians.

Teachers on Call
8120 Penn Avenue South, Bloomington
(952) 703–3719

Educational professionals can get their foot in the door with the help of Teachers on Call.

Employment Agencies

There are many employment agencies in the Twin Cities. Some specialize in certain fields, while others place candidates in jobs in a broad variety of fields. Keep in mind that some employment agencies charge a substantial fee to help you find a job; others charge their fee to the employer that hires you. Ask plenty of questions before you sign anything.

The Affiliates
800 Nicollet Mall, Minneapolis
(612) 349–2810
www.affiliates.com

The Affiliates specialize in helping workers in the legal field find jobs, including lawyers, legal secretaries, and support staff.

Career Professionals
4930 West 77th Street, Suite 260, Edina
(952) 835–9922
www.gocpi.com

Career Professionals focuses on recent college graduates, finding entry-level positions in customer service, marketing, financial industries, sales, retail, and administrative settings.

Creative Group
800 Nicollet Mall, Minneapolis
(612) 333–7990
www.creativegroup.com

Creative Group serves clients looking for work in marketing or advertising, including art directors, copywriters, graphic designers, Web site developers, marketing managers, and similar positions.

Thomas Moore, Inc.
608 Second Avenue South, Minneapolis
(612) 338–4884
www.thomasmooreinc.com

Thomas Moore matches accountants, financial professionals, and information technology specialists with jobs at Twin Cities companies.

State Agencies

Minnesota WorkForce Center
777 East Lake Street, Minneapolis
(612) 821–4000
2455 University Avenue West, St. Paul
(651) 642–0363
www.MNWorkForceCenter.org
Multiple additional locations In the Twin Cities

The Minnesota WorkForce Center is operated by the state. They offer free or inexpensive services, including access to their huge database of available jobs, help with résumés and interviewing skills, free local faxing, and free computer usage. After registering with the agency, you can have descriptions of available jobs of interest e-mailed directly to you on a regular basis. Positions available run the full spectrum of the Twin Cities economy, including education, human services, state government, executive management, and much, much more.

Classified Ads

The two major dailies in the Twin Cities, the *St. Paul Pioneer Press* and the *StarTribune,* have exhaustive classified job listings, particularly in their Sunday editions. The listings in the *StarTribune* are generally more extensive, although the *St. Paul Pioneer Press* is stronger in listings for jobs in the East Metro. If you're not in the Twin Cities and can't just pick up a copy of the Sunday paper, both newspapers allow you to search the classifieds on their Web sites for free (visit www.startribune.com or www.

twincities.com/mld/pioneerpress).

There are also several national Web sites that allow you to search for jobs in the Twin Cities based on specific criteria. Some allow you to post your résumé to the site for free, and some will e-mail job openings that match your criteria to you.

Finding a Place to Live

The Twin Cities have recently gone through an explosion in the value of homes and skyrocketing rents. The average price of a home has risen to $190,000 in the metropolitan area, nearly double what it was in the mid-nineties, and rental units are going for an average $840 per month, also up considerably from just a few years ago. With continuing low mortgage rates, home values are likely to continue to rise for the foreseeable future, but happily the vacancy rate of rental units throughout the Metro has steadily risen in the past couple of years (due largely to former renters buying houses), which should have somewhat of a stabilizing effect on rents. The following are a few places to get you started on your search for a new home in the Cities.

Buying

Real Estate Agencies

Following is a list of some of the major, national agencies that work through franchised operations in the Twin Cities metro area, as well as the larger independent agencies that are based here. Many allow you to search for houses through their Web sites.

Century 21–Luger Realty
4536 France Avenue South, Edina
(952) 925–3901 or (800) 328–0092
www.century21luger.com

Century 21 is one of the largest residential real estate franchisers in the world, with more than 6,300 independently owned and operated franchised broker offices in more than 28 countries and territories worldwide. Its local, independently owned branch, Century 21–Luger Realty, was founded by Jim and Judy Luger in 1976. It has achieved the highest honor conferred by Century 21, the Centurion Award, ranking it among the top 3 percent of all Century 21 offices worldwide. The company has also earned the coveted Quality Service Award, resulting from a client satisfaction rating of over 95 percent. Luger Century 21 represents the entire Twin Cities metro area, including the outlying suburbs, and there are both English- and Spanish-speaking representatives on-site for customer convenience.

Coldwell Banker Real Estate
Burnet-Minneapolis Lakes, 3033 Excelsior Boulevard, #100, Minneapolis
(952) 920–5605
Burnet-Highland Park, 1991 Ford Parkway, St. Paul
(651) 698–2481
www.coldwellbankmn.com

The Minnesota division of Coldwell Banker national, Coldwell Banker Burnet makes a genuine effort to make buying and selling homes as convenient as possible for clients, connecting potential buyers with local, accredited mortgage companies and payment plans specifically suited to each individual. As with all of their offices nationally, Coldwell Banker guarantees a return decision on all loan applications the same day they're filed—if not, clients are awarded $250 for their patience, and if they don't meet the agreed closing date on a property, they'll reduce your interest rate by ⅛ percent (call for details as certain restrictions apply). More than 120 Coldwell Banker Burnet offices serve the Twin Cities metro area, both the Cities and the surrounding suburbs.

The Minneapolis Lakes office is Coldwell Bankers #1 office nationally and is equipped to handle all your relocation needs, as well as setting up mortgages and refinancing for existing properties in the entire Twin Cities metro area, with an emphasis on properties in Minneapolis and St. Paul proper. More than 175 sales associates report to the Chain of Lakes office, and their strong intraoffice net-

working and communication with other offices and brokers ensures that your needs are broadcast to the largest possible audience of buyers and sellers. The Minneapolis Lakes office serves the Minneapolis and St. Paul residential communities as well as the immediate suburbs of Richfield, Edina, Bloomington, and St. Louis Park.

In St. Paul, the Highland Park office deals with properties in St. Paul, Mendota Heights, Highland Park, Lilydale, Inver Grove Heights, and Eagan. Sixty-nine sales associates report to the office, including associates specially trained to help hearing-impaired and Japanese-speaking clients. All Coldwell Banker Burnet offices are equipped with up-to-date real estate software and technology, and reciprocity is practiced with other real estate agencies at all offices.

Counselor Realty Corporate Office
7766 MN 65 NE, Minneapolis
(763) 786–0600
www.counselorrealty.com

Established in 1964, Counselor Realty is a local Minnesota company with strong ties to the community and 11 branches throughout the metro area in Brooklyn Park, Coon Rapids, Edina, Maple Grove, Spring Lake Park, Wayzata, White Bear Lake, Savage, Alexandria, and Brainerd. Counselor Realty prides itself on providing superior service tailored to each client's individual needs, as well as total integrity and honesty with clients. The agency has built its reputation through word-of-mouth referrals from satisfied customers over the years and has firmly established itself with the local community by involvement through local charities and causes.

Edina Realty
5309 South Lyndale Avenue, Minneapolis
(612) 827–3551
1050 Grand Avenue, St. Paul
(651) 224–4321
www.edinarealty.com

Founded in 1955 by Emma Rovick, a Minnesotan housewife with three kids and a $2,000 loan, Edina Realty Home Services was built on a strict standard of quality and service that lives on today. Now part of a company that comprises the second-largest independent real estate broker in the nation with a mortgage (Edina Realty Mortgage) and a title division (Edina Realty Title), Edina has more than 70 independently run offices throughout the Midwest. As the first Minnesotan real estate company to own a mortgage and title company, to have computer services for sales associates, and to have a 24-hour interactive real estate hotline number, Edina Realty has experienced unprecedented growth in the past decade. Edina realtors pride themselves in being able to match customers with their first-choice, affordable dream house as quickly and efficiently as possible without pressuring customers to settle for anything. Their Web site has many tools available for home buyers to use, including a mortgage calculator and full listings of all of the homes Edina represents. There are two Edina offices in the Twin Cities proper, and 40-plus throughout the metro area suburbs.

Prudential Plus
4901 West 77th Street, Suite 125, Edina
(952) 835-4400
www.prudential.com

With six offices in the Twin Cities metro area, Prudential Realty is part of the Metrowide Group of Prudential Realty, which provides its independently run offices with a regional support group and national relocation information and services, making it a favorite relocation service among businesses nationwide. As an added bonus, if you buy a home through Prudential, Prudential will buy your former residence from you at a mutually agreeable price if they can't sell it within six months. All offices have in-house closers and information on mortgages and home insurance on-site, making it an especially complete real estate agency to deal with.

RE/MAX Results
11200 West 78th Street, Eden Prairie
(952) 829-2900
1071 Grand Avenue, St. Paul
(651) 251-4800
www.remax.com

RE/MAX Results is not only the Twin Cities' oldest and largest RE/MAX broker-age, but it is also one of the nation's top five ranked firms in sales per associate. RE/MAX Results specializes in corporate relocations, and, as such, has one of the largest number of Corporate Relocation Specialists (CRPs) on staff in the United States. The CRP designation represents the highest level of achievement earned through the Employee Relocation Council (ERC). All RE/MAX Results associates either hold the designation or have been thoroughly trained in the relocation process. RE/MAX Results has six strategically located offices to service the metro area's strongest and fastest-growing markets, including Eden Prairie, Plymouth, and Wayzata.

Roger Fazendin Realtors
1421 East Wayzata Boulevard, Wayzata
(952) 473-7000
www.rogerfazendin.com

Founded in 1965 by Roger Fazendin, Roger Fazendin Realtors is the largest family-owned and operated residential real estate company in Minnesota. The company has expanded from its humble beginnings of Fazendin and a couple of realtors to include his son, Dan Fazendin, who now owns the company, and Dan's wife, Lynn, and their son, Dan Fazendin Jr., as well as 31 other professional real estate agents and a dozen other employees. Dan Sr. has served as president of the Minneapolis Association of Realtors, chairman of the Regional MLS committee, and president of All Points Relocation Service, and the agents that work under him are supremely qualified, practicing broker reciprocity and having good connections within the local financial community. All of their listings are available for viewing through their Web site, including color photos and basic floor plans.

Other Sources for Finding Homes

Both Twin Cities newspapers carry extensive listings of homes for sale in the Metro, particularly in their Sunday editions. Pick up a paper, or check out their Web sites: *Star Tribune* at www.startribune.com or *St. Paul Pioneer Press* at www.twincities.com/mld/pioneerpress.

There are also numerous more general sites on the Internet for searching for homes in the Cities. The following sites allow you to search by city and other specifics, with additional information about finding movers, financing, contacts, and more.

www.realestate.com
www.realtor.com
www.e-zhomesearch.com

Renting

The Twin Cities offer a remarkable variety of rental properties, from historic apartments with hardwood floors, beautiful woodwork, and lots of character to modern apartments in complexes with many amenities.

There are several ways to find an apartment in the Cities. One easy option is to consult with an agency. Two agencies in the Twin Cities with excellent reputations are **Spectrum Apartment Search** (2756 Hennepin Avenue South, Minneapolis, 612-870-0525; 2133 Hudson Road, Suite B, St. Paul, 651-730-0979; www.apartmentsearch.com) and **Apartment Mart** (telephone referrals only; call 612-927-4591 for Minneapolis and western suburbs; 651-224-9199 for St. Paul and eastern suburbs; 952-890-3222 for the southern

Metro; or 763-560-6865 for the northern Metro). Neither business charges a fee to the renter to locate an apartment.

Both Twin Cities newspapers carry extensive listings of apartments and houses for rent in the Metro, particularly in their Sunday editions. Pick up a paper, or check out their Web sites: *StarTribune* at www.startribune.com or *St. Paul Pioneer Press* at www.twincities.com/mld/pioneerpress.

There are also several national Web sites that allow you to search for apartments in the Twin Cities. The following sites should provide some good leads.

www.rent.com
www.apartmentlivingguide.com
www.apartments.com
www.springstreet.com

If you are looking for a roommate, one option is to contact **Roommate Referrals,** 1600 West Lake Street, Suite 105, Minneapolis; (612) 827-5565. For a fee they can match you up with persons looking to share their apartments or, if you've already found a place, with persons looking to move in with someone else. They provide a list of matches, giving you multiple options and allowing you to screen potential roommates by telephone.

Neighborhoods

Few places have such defined neighborhoods as the Twin Cities. Each neighborhood in the Cities themselves has distinct

Insiders' Tip
If you ever have any trouble with a rental company or landlord, contact the Tenants' Union (612-871-7485), located at 610 West 28th Street in Minneapolis. A nominal membership charge (under $20) entitles you to repeat visits in case you have more questions—the people at the Union can provide you with information about legal recourse and your rights as a renter.

personalities, churches, and often religious, ethnic, or social groups, as well as city parks and schools specific to the neighborhood, independently owned markets and delis, and active planning committees that do everything from petition city government for roadwork and cleanup crews after natural disasters to organize big neighborhood events like live music in the parks and evening and weekend educational seminars. Moving from one neighborhood to another is almost like moving to another town at times, with benefits and drawbacks to each new location. With more than 80 specific neighborhoods in Minneapolis and another 20-plus in St. Paul, new residents have the opportunity to choose exactly what kind of place they'd like to live in, whether it's in swanky, funky Uptown Minneapolis or the vibrant, artistic, mixed-ethnic community of Frogtown in St. Paul.

Minneapolis

Como

The Como community of Minneapolis is named after Como Avenue. The thoroughfare continues on to Como Park in St. Paul, where another residential community is located. The Minneapolis Como neighborhood is filled with middle-income homes. Van Cleve Park is a matter of pride for the community and includes baseball fields, a pool, and a community center.

Downtown

Downtown is one of the Twin Cities' quickest growing neighborhoods. After several decades of residents moving out of the downtown area, the area is expanding rapidly as high-rises and renovations replace once vacant or dilapidated properties. There are numerous living options in downtown Minneapolis, including apartments, condominiums, and lofts. In the past few years all three types of properties have been developed next to the old milling district and beside the Warehouse District. So you're in luck if you're looking to live downtown; however, remember most properties garner a premium price for the myr-

iad amenities the neighborhood affords.

The possibilities of living downtown are almost endless. There are numerous employment opportunities, and without the daily headache of commuting. In addition, the cultural and shopping opportunities abound—where else are so many four-star restaurants, performing arts, and a wide variety of stores accessible by walking? And when the weather becomes inclement, most buildings downtown are connected by skyways, so a downtown resident doesn't have to bear the unpleasant elements.

Linden Hills

One of the Twin Cities' most expansive neighborhoods, Linden Hills has several compelling reasons to purchase a residence in this charming neighborhood. Linden Hills is nestled between Lake Calhoun and Lake Harriet, two of "The City of Lakes" most breathtaking bodies of water. Its location isolates the area from the bustle of Uptown and Downtown but allows easy access to the lakes, which offer almost infinite possibilities in recreation, from bicycling and walking to riding a sailboat on a sunny summer day.

Linden Hills's appearance is reminiscent of a small town. Various specialty shops and restaurants are located on Linden Avenue. The restaurants are remarkably diverse, offering choices ranging from barbecue to Hmong cuisine. The idyllic shopping district is one of the many selling points of one of Minneapolis's hippest neighborhoods.

Marcy Holmes

Marcy Holmes is named after the two neighborhood parks located within the community. The neighborhood is a healthy mix of students, senior citizens, college professors, and young families. Beautiful Victorian houses sit side by side with apartments in this community next to the University of Minnesota.

Another great part about living in Marcy Holmes is its proximity to various Minneapolis attractions. The historic St. Anthony neighborhood borders Marcy Holmes, and the James J. Hill Stone Arch

Bridge, now a pedestrian bridge, offers one of the best views and shortcuts to downtown. Home prices are low compared with the rest of the city.

Prospect Park

The Prospect Park neighborhood is recognizable because of its water tower, which overlooks the Minneapolis community. The water tower, no longer in use, sits atop the highest point in Minneapolis and is one of the most scenic vistas in the area. The neighborhood is composed mainly of classic, expensive homes that sit on the many winding roads surrounding the water tower. The homes in Prospect Park are some of the most attractive in the Twin Cities. Prospect Park has easy access to all of the Twin Cities major thoroughfares.

Seward

Seward is the Twin Cities' idealistic, former hippie neighborhood. The area is lined with beautiful old homes, and many have lovely gardens. The neighborhood also has many schools, and diverse shopping options. Ethiopian restaurants and diners coexist in this neighborhood, where community is emphasized. Numerous churches of various faiths as well as New Age and wellness businesses exist in this charming community.

Uptown

The Twin Cities' hippest neighborhood, Uptown is the community that locals visit for fun. Others choose to live in this wonderful cosmopolitan hub because of the numerous cultural amenities. An example of comfortable high-density living, the area is packed with a variety of restaurants and retail shops. Calhoun Square, an urban shopping center, is at the center of the area's shopping scene.

A favorite spot for summer recreation and relaxation, Uptown is walking distance from Lake of the Isles and Lake Calhoun. The community effervesces with excitement each summer when it hosts the Uptown Art Fair. As a result of the excellent living in the Uptown neighborhood, rents and home prices are generally expensive.

St. Paul

Como Park

Not to be confused with the Como neighborhood in Minneapolis, St. Paul's Como neighborhood is centered around Como Park, Como Zoo, and Como Lake. Residents here have the pleasure of being located near many pleasant neighborhood coffeeshops and restaurants, and many of the bungalows and smaller two-story homes are reasonably priced.

Frogtown

Arguably St. Paul's most ethnically diverse community, the Frogtown District has been a magnet for poets, artists, and immigrants for many years. And, with some of the lowest property values in the city, who could blame them? In the 1990s, urban revitalization programs sold houses here for under $40,000, allowing homebuyers to take possession with no money down and delayed mortgage payments. Property values for these same houses are on the rise (with the rest of St. Paul), as are the small storefronts and restaurants owned by the Thai, African-American, Vietnamese, Cambodian, and Hmong residents that populate this area.

Highland Park

Highland Park, in the southwestern corner of the city and bordered by the Mississippi River, is a delightful area of the city, with many bungalows, larger two-story homes, and a smattering of upper-tier properties. The area surrounds the shops and restaurants centered at the intersection of Ford Parkway and Cleveland Avenue South, with numerous specialty retailers, bookstores, ethnic restaurants (as well as fast-food fare), and a major grocery store within a short drive from home. Almost surprisingly, given the pleasant nature of the neighborhood, Highland Park is also home to the Twin Cities Ford Plant, producing Ford Ranger pickups and other vehicles in the expansive factory on the banks of the Mississippi. However, the tree-lined streets, quiet boulevards, and bike paths of the neighborhood show no hint of industrial sprawl.

Macalester-Groveland

Macalester-Groveland is one of the Twin Cities' premier urban neighborhoods. The neighborhood has several excellent schools and is filled with numerous excellent businesses. The name of the neighborhood is in part derived from Macalester College, a highly respected liberal arts institution of higher learning, which has a significant presence in the area. An important part of the local community is the nationally recognized independent bookseller, Ruminator Books. The area also includes many diverse restaurants and shops.

Merriam Park

This attractive St. Paul neighborhood was named after the Merriams, a prominent Twin Cities family. The community is ideally located almost halfway between downtown St. Paul and Minneapolis. An important part of the neighborhood is the University of St. Thomas.

East Suburbs

Afton

Nestled between wooded river bluffs and the St. Croix River, the historic town of Afton is a rural community of approximately 3,000. Located on the eastern edge of Washington County, the quiet residential community has a small business district comprised of restaurants, marinas, unique shops, and services. The village is surrounded by parks, farms, and nature preserves, and the residential area is made up of mostly upper-bracket houses.

One of Afton's best-known landmarks is the Afton Alps Recreation Area. Open year-round, Afton Alps offers skiing, snowboarding, snow-tubing, golfing, and mountain biking in a beautiful scenic setting.

Bayport

Settled more than 150 years ago, Bayport, known as South Stillwater until 1922, was known as a "bootlegger's paradise" during Prohibition. Today, the small community boasts a charming downtown area, including a park, several marinas, and quaint little shops and restaurants in a downtown made up of turn-of-the-20th-century brick-and-wood buildings. Formerly built on the lumber industry, Bayport's main employer is Andersen Windows, the country's largest producer of windows and patio doors.

Insiders' Tip

Residents of the Como Park neighborhood often remark about how beautiful it is to hear the wolves at Como Zoo howling at night, especially in winter.

Lake Elmo

With the growth of the Twin Cities metro area, city dwellers seeking the quiet life have found Lake Elmo. Located on the old mail trail between Stillwater and St. Paul, the city boasts a big blue lake of the same name and eight other smaller lakes as well.

Settled in 1880 and incorporated in 1920, Lake Elmo is another historic town that has kept its quaint, turn-of-the-20th-century feel. Because it has resisted growth as its neighbors have expanded, it has retained its small town feel as well. Downtown Lake Elmo is made up of old brick-and-wood buildings and an old grain elevator, all of which have been turned into first-class restaurants, antiques shops, and other businesses. Lake Elmo is also home to the Washington County Fairgrounds and an annual August county fair. The town's population is around 7,000 residents.

Mahtomedi/Grant

Founded in the mid-1800s as a Methodist summer colony, Mahtomedi soon became a desirable location for summer homes and resorts due to its proximity to beautiful White Bear Lake. Both Mahtomedi and the nearby former township of Grant, one of Minnesota's newest cities, are dotted with hobby farms and working farms as well as natural areas set aside for parkland. White Bear Lake is deep enough for water-skiing and boating in the summertime, and is a popular ice fishing spot in the winter.

Many of the homes in Grant are located on the rolling acres of hobby, horse, or agricultural farms, while Mahtomedi offers more variety, including townhouses, condominiums, and newer residential developments centered around small parks.

Maplewood

The city of Maplewood was originally not much but farmland lying on the outskirts of St. Paul near the town of North St. Paul. In the past 30 years, however, Maplewood has earned an identity separate from St. Paul as an attractive community in which to work, live, and raise a family.

Maplewood's three most distinct features are the Maplewood Community Center—containing a fully appointed fitness center with a pool, a senior lounge, and a craft center—the Maplewood Mall, and the worldwide corporate headquarters of the 3M company, a major employer in the area.

Like many other Twin Cities suburbs, Maplewood is rich in parks and recreation areas. The city-funded Maplewood Nature Center offers environmental programs for children and adults, with interactive displays and marked trails for seasonal use.

Marine on St. Croix

Established in 1839 as a lumber town, Marine on St. Croix is now one of the prettiest, greenest little towns you'll ever come across. Located next to the St. Croix River and about 45 minutes from St. Paul and Minneapolis, the town is made up of old, New England–style houses with elaborate flower gardens lining the roads and sidewalks, old-growth hardwood trees, and little creeks running through the town that terminate in waterfalls in the city's parks. Marine on St. Croix was also used as the location site for several big-budget Hollywood films, including *Grumpier Old Men, The Cure,* and *Beautiful Girls.*

North St. Paul

Founded in 1870 by developer Henry Castle as Castle Site, this lakeside community was primarily farmland until 1880, when it became a major manufacturing hub in the area. Today the area manages to combine the benefits of a bustling commercial and industrial district with the feel of a quiet residential area, with tree-lined neighborhoods, a historic downtown area, and many community events along the shores of Silver Lake.

Stillwater

Founded in 1839 by trader Joseph Renshaw Brown, Stillwater is a town that's worn many nicknames in its past and present. The best-known one, of course, is the "Birthplace of Minnesota." Stillwater's also been called "The Queen of the St. Croix" because of its booming lumber industry, "North America's First Book-town" because of its many specialty and antiquarian bookstores, and "Prison City" because of the huge territorial prison built here in the mid-1800s. Modern Stillwater is home to a wide selection of restaurants and antiques shops, as well as beautiful parks and picturesque marinas.

Stillwater is home to some of the finest examples of 19th-century residential architecture in the state. A short drive from the downtown area are homes built in the Queen Anne, Second Empire, and Stick styles of the 1800s as well as the Prairie style of the 1900s. Many of the older homes have been restored and reopened as bed-and-breakfasts.

Not surprisingly, given the beautiful setting and vibrant community, Stillwater properties are some of the most expensive in the region, particularly if you have your heart set on a Victorian masterpiece with a turret and big front porch.

White Bear Lake

Created as a health resort town in the 1880s, White Bear Lake is a bustling business and residential community set on the clear waters of White Bear Lake. Located just 20 minutes from St. Paul, White Bear Lake has a beautiful, turn-of-the-20th-century downtown area with modern residential areas situated around parks and wetlands. Golf courses, beaches, lakes, and nature trails can be found within the city limits, and White Bear Lake itself is the largest lake within the metropolitan area, making it a great place for boating and fishing in the summer, and cross-country skiing and ice fishing during the winter.

Woodbury

With both beautiful residential neighborhoods and a thriving business community, Woodbury has enjoyed a population explosion over the past 10 years. Originally named "Red Rock Township" by the first settlers who came to the area in the 1840s, the area was later named after Judge Levi Woodbury of New Hampshire, who never actually set foot in the city. Many of the original settlers came here from the eastern United States and from Germany, Sweden, Denmark, Ireland, and Switzerland.

Today commercial development has helped create a strong community with a high quality of life, making Woodbury a great place to live and do business. Although most of Woodbury is strictly residential, the city is also home to a diverse group of businesses, from large corporations to small businesses and retail outlets. Some of Woodbury's industries and employers are 3M, State Farm Insurance, and the Woodbury Health Care Center.

Citizens of Woodbury enjoy four community parks: the Bielenberg Sports Center, Carver Lake, Ojibway, and Tamarack Nature Preserve, the last three of which are more than 120 acres of parkland connected by paved and turf trails. Woodbury has many neighborhood parks, too, with amenities such as basketball courts and ballfields.

South Suburbs

Apple Valley

Originally a small farming community named "Lebanon," Apple Valley and its low-cost farmland first started drawing city developers as early as 1960. When the city was incorporated in 1968, the area was renamed "Apple Valley" for developer Orrin Thompson Homes' habit of putting an apple tree on every single family lot. Located 12 miles south of Minneapolis off Minnesota Highway 38, Apple Valley today is a small business and residential community that is approximately 75 percent developed and 25 percent parks, marshes, woodlands, and wilderness conservatories. Apple Valley is also home to the Minnesota Zoo, one of the state's best-known attractions.

Bloomington

With its proximity to the Minneapolis-St. Paul International Airport and more than 25 hotels with 6,200 sleeping rooms, Bloomington is often the first and last stop of visitors to the Twin Cities. Home of the Mall of America and several prestigious golf courses and country clubs, as well as more than 90,000 residents, Bloomington is a city in the middle of an economic boom. Because of Bloomington's proximity to Minneapolis and St. Paul, this is a choice community for those who don't want to live in the Cities but have to commute there for work. Surrounded by open country and maintained parklands, Bloomington is also the home of the world's first virtual high school: Mindquest, which has students enrolled from as far away as India through the Internet.

Eagan

In Eagan's early days, a tree now known as the Lone Oak Tree served as a communication center for the city. Public notices and announcements were posted here as the town of Eagan grew into a modern city around it. The Lone Oak Tree was recently designated as a Minnesota Heritage Tree, and commemorative oaks have been planted throughout Eagan to honor the tree. Eagan was also once known as the Onion Capital of the United States, due to the thousands of onions Eagan once shipped out all over the country in the late 1800s.

Aside from its rich agricultural history, Eagan has a thriving business community as well. Major employers in the area include Cray Research, Blue Cross–Blue Shield, Northwest Airlines, West Publishing, and Coca-Cola. Eagan also borders several beautiful, large parks, including Lebanon Hills Regional Park and the Caponi Art Park, which features an outdoor sculpture garden.

Eden Prairie

Eden Prairie's history can be traced back to the mid-1800s, when an 1851 treaty opened the land west of the Mississippi River to settlement. According to legend, the town Eden Prairie was named by American author Elizabeth Fry Ellet, who visited the area at the request of the *New York Times*. She described the area in her resulting article as the garden spot of the territory, and the name "Eden Prairie" was coined.

Today, Eden Prairie is a refuge for commuters who want a quiet, beautiful home to escape to after a busy day at work. Surrounded by parklands, including Bryant Lake Regional Park and its boating and fishing lake, Eden Prairie is now one of the fastest-growing suburbs in the Twin Cities metro area.

Prior Lake

Located in the southwestern Twin Cities suburbs, Prior Lake is centered around the 16-square-mile lake that shares its name. Named for landowner and railroad employee Charles H. Prior, who brought the Chicago, Milwaukee, and St. Paul Railroad lines through the town, Prior Lake has been a summer spot for tourists and a busy port of business since 1872.

Of Prior Lake's attractions, perhaps the best known is Mystic Lake Casino, Minnesota's largest gaming and entertainment establishment. Prior Lake is also home to the world-class Wilds golf course, designed by Tom Weiskopf and Jay Morrish. The Wilds was recently rated fourth-best new public golf course in the United States by *Golf Digest* magazine.

However, it's the proximity of residents to the eponymous lake that makes water recreation the number one activity in the area. With its many swimming beaches and boating marinas, Prior Lake is a favorite resort spot for watersport enthusiasts. Lakeside living, however, is linked with expensive homes; the farther you get away from the waterfront, the more reasonably priced the houses get.

Savage

A steamboat landing, located at the point where the Credit River meets the Minnesota, marks the birthplace of the town of Hamilton. The early history of this community, renamed Savage in 1902 for Minneapolis businessman Marion Willis Savage, was largely shaped by its transportation connection to these two major waterways. In 1941 Cargill, Inc. moved to Savage and set up massive shipbuilding yards to construct oceangoing oil tankers for the U.S. Navy.

The present-day city of Savage is a dynamic community offering many housing options, all with easy access to the surrounding urban areas. An interesting mix of older homes and new construction, Savage is the fastest-growing and most populated community in Scott County.

West Suburbs

Deephaven

A small city surrounded by protected bays and woodlands, Deephaven is located on the south shore of Lake Minnetonka. The city is close to the water, in fact, that few of its residents live more than 1 mile from the beaches of this beautiful lake. Deephaven has more than 76 acres of parkland, with Thorpe Park being the largest, offering picnic areas, a lighted hockey rink, basketball courts, and many flower gardens.

Excelsior

The historic town of Excelsior is a perfect blend of the old and the new, combining a villagelike atmosphere of antiques shops and inns with modern hotels and restaurants. First settled in 1853, downtown Excelsior is full of old buildings and houses that date back to the turn of the 20th century, which have been made into part of the Lake Minnetonka Historical Society's guided tour route. Excelsior also borders Carver Park Reserve and its 3,500 acres of parkland, campgrounds, and horseback and snowmobile trails, as well as Minnewashta Regional Park and its public swimming beach.

Minnetonka

Residents of this Twin Cities metro suburb may just have the best of both worlds—a thriving, competitive business community set in a beautiful residential area. Minnetonka has more than 40 city parks and is set close to the shores of Lake Minnetonka. Careful city planning over the years has allowed its beautiful woodlands, wetlands, and creeks to survive intact inside the city itself.

Orono

Once known as Starvation Point, the village was renamed and organized as Orono in 1899. The population of Orono grew over the years at a purposefully slow pace in order to preserve much of the wildlife, wetlands, and farmlands in the area. This picturesque residential community is surrounded by many neighborhood and city parks, including Noerenberg Memorial Park, and five public marinas. City ordinances require minimum sizes for residential lots, so each homeowner has at least two acres of land, and many homeowners own five acres of land.

Wayzata

Pronounced "why-Zeh-tah," Wayzata is a small city located on the north shore of Lake Minnetonka. The name comes from the Dakota's god of the north, a giant who blew cold winds from his mouth. Today this area is a beautiful spot for a weekend retreat as well as a luxurious residential area with access to many downtown specialty shops, restaurants, and boutiques. The town also has the only free trolley service in the Twin Cities, which takes visitors and residents to and from work and play all during the summer months.

North Suburbs

Forest Lake

Founded in 1855 by Louis Scheil, a German immigrant, this area has long been a summer haven for tourists from Chicago and beyond and is now known as one of the most popular resort towns in the area. The city has managed to keep its small-town charm even with the introduction of many big city conveniences, especially the outstanding medical care and the many businesses that have moved into the area. Activities in Forest Lake are centered around Lakeside Memorial Park, where outdoor concerts and other cultural events take place at the gazebo in summer. Ice skating and ice fishing are popular in winter.

New Brighton

The land around New Brighton was originally inhabited by the Dakota and Ojibwe tribes. They were drawn to the area for its rich farmland and abundant wetlands, which were perfect for growing wild rice. French and English settlers first came to the area in the mid-1800s, looking for land to homestead and farm. By 1858 the settlement was named Mounds View Township, which was later broken up into the communities of New Brighton and Mounds View. Today New Brighton has a population just over 22,000, and many of the residents work within the city limits at the various industries that have been established here.

Roseville

Rose Township was originally named for Isaac Rose, one of the first white settlers in the area. Rose and his family settled on a claim near what is now St. Anthony Road and Fairview Avenue—look for the historical marker if you happen to pass by. When the federal government ordered a survey of the area, Rose went to work on the surveying team, and, as a result, the township was named for him. In 1948 the area was organized and incorporated as the towns of Roseville, Falcon Heights, Lauderdale, and part of St. Paul.

Today Roseville is a mostly residential community of pleasant houses with expansive gardens, specialty shops, and restaurants. The city of Roseville also owns 23 park sites, ranging in size from 2 to 220 acres, including a large concert amphitheater in Central Park. The John Rose MN Oval & Roseville Ice Arena has huge indoor and outdoor rinks available for hockey, figure skating, open skating, and speedskating. High school hockey games are held here on a regular basis, and the public is allowed to attend for a nominal charge.

Roseville's biggest housing boom took place in the early '70s; as a result, most of the residential areas are filled with split-level ramblers and bungalows.

Shoreview

Socrates A. Thompson, the first white settler on the land that makes up present-day Shoreview, came to the area from St. Paul looking for a good place to farm. He decided on the east shores of Turtle Lake and was soon joined by other settlers from as far away as Germany and Switzerland.

In 1941 the U.S. government opened the Army Arsenal plant on the west side of Shoreview, bringing many new workers into the area. This expanse of residential property turned Shoreview from a small, lakeside, rural community into a Twin Cities suburb, and the township was officially made a city on January 1, 1974.

Today Shoreview is approximately 95 percent developed, surrounded by expanses of farmland, lakes, and woods. The land and houses formerly belonging to struggling immigrant farmers are now sold at a premium. Residents enjoy proximity to the Twin Cities, as well as a strong sense of community exemplified by the opening of Shoreview Commons in 1990, which is now home to the town's city hall, library, and community center.

Vadnais Heights

Since its humble roots as a small rural farming community, Vadnais Heights has grown into the successful, thriving residential suburb and business community it is today. Within the city limits can be found many open, protected wetlands, lakes, and ponds, around which have sprung idyllic neighborhoods with relatively expensive houses. A solid industrial core and many service manufacturing jobs employ more than 5,000 residents, while many others make the easy commute into the Twin Cities.

Libraries

Hennepin County Library
17524 Excelsior Boulevard, Minnetonka
(952) 847–5725
www.hclib.org
Twenty-five additional locations in Hennepin County suburbs

The suburban Hennepin County Library system has locations throughout the Minneapolis suburbs. Borrowing privileges are available to suburban Hennepin County residents. In addition to the general library collections, the Hennepin County Library offers an eLibrary through its Web site and at branch libraries, with many databases available in languages commonly spoken in the seven-county metro area, including Hmong, Somali, Russian, and Spanish. The library also has KidLinks and TeenLinks collections of electronic resources for children, including children's search engines and word processing, as well as easy electronic information about the library's holdings of materials for children and teens.

The Hennepin County Library's hours vary widely by location; call for more information.

Minneapolis Public Library
250 South Marquette Avenue, Minneapolis
(612) 630–6000
www.mplib.org
Fourteen additional locations in Minneapolis
The central Minneapolis Public Library moved to a temporary location on the skyway level in the former Federal Reserve Bank building at 250 South Marquette Avenue in 2002. The library will remain in the bank building during the construction of the new central library on the site of the old library building, which is scheduled for completion in 2006.

The former site of the library dated from 1961, and although the library has some 2.5 million items in its collection, the largest of any public library in the state and the fourth largest of any public library in the country, the previous building (razed in 2003) allowed direct access in browsable stacks to only about 15 percent of the library's holdings. Items from the remainder of the collection, generally books and other items more than 10 years old, had to be requested from a librarian and pulled from subterranean stacks by a library employee and sent to the library floor for a patron's review—not the most efficient system for researchers, students, and the general public looking for a variety of books on a given subject. Research

could be very time consuming. And the sixties-era building suffered from some of the same architectural maladies of other public buildings built in that era.

The temporary library allows access to about half the library's holdings on open shelves and the rest by request through a librarian. Similarly, the new library now taking shape in downtown Minneapolis will allow direct access to 50 percent of the library's holdings, a huge improvement over the 15 percent access of the old library. Architect Cesar Pelli designed the new library, which will also offer a much larger children's book area, a public commons, a cafe, a retail bookstore, a center for teens, a computer training room, meeting rooms, and a 235-seat auditorium. The new library will be connected to the downtown skyway system, a feature the old library building lacked. At the time of this writing, it is uncertain whether the Minneapolis Planetarium, which was housed in the old library building, will be part of the new library, pending a decision on funding for the project by the state of Minnesota.

The design for the new library will make the building a landmark in downtown Minneapolis. The five-story building will have an exterior of clear, patterned, and opaque glass, allowing patrons to browse and read using largely natural lighting throughout the building. The specially designed glass will also protect the library's collections from ultraviolet damage. Bands of Minnesota stone will form layers between the glass panels. The see-through building will provide a more integrated feel for the library with the surrounding downtown community, not to mention spectacular views of the Minneapolis skyline and Warehouse District.

The temporary library is open 9:00 A.M. to 6:00 P.M. Monday through Friday, and 10:00 A.M. to 6:00 P.M. Saturday. Patrons can enter the library from the plaza on the Nicollet Mall side of the building, from Marquette Avenue, and from the skyway across Marquette Avenue (the skyway is closed on weekends). Minneapolis residents can obtain a library card at the central library and all branch locations; residents of other Twin Cities communities can use library cards from their local library to check out materials from the Minneapolis system after registering at the library.

Ramsey County Library
Administrative Offices, 4570 North Victoria Street, Shoreview
(651) 486–2200
www.ramsey.lib.mn.us
Six additional locations in Ramsey County suburbs

The Ramsey County Library allows residents of the St. Paul suburbs of Arden Hills, Maplewood, Mounds View, North St. Paul, Roseville, Shoreview, and White Bear Lake convenient access to general books and other materials. Although suburban libraries in Ramsey County date from the 1920s, the Ramsey County Library system was established in 1951. Today the seven libraries house more than one million items, and patrons can also access the Internet from library terminals, use Microsoft Word at all branch libraries except North St. Paul, and enjoy such amenities as a Dunn Bros. cafe in the Roseville branch library. Any resident of the seven-country metropolitan area can get a library card. Hours vary widely, depending on the individual library's policies; call for more information.

St. Paul Public Library
90 West Fourth Street, St. Paul
(651) 266–7000
www.stpaul.lib.mn.us
Twelve additional locations in St. Paul

The elegant St. Paul Public Library building in downtown St. Paul dates from 1917. Having reopened in 2002 after a $15.9 million renovation, the beautiful Italian Renaissance Revival building brashly shows off its historical and artistic interior. The renovation included restoration of the building's detailed hand-painted ceilings, Mankato stone and plaster details, and compressed cork floors, as well as updating the library's telecommunications connections to allow high-speed Internet access. As a result of the renovation, the library building is finally connected to downtown St. Paul's skyway

The recently remodeled St. Paul Public Library on Rice Park downtown. PHOTO: TODD R. BERGER

system via a tunnel between the St. Paul Hotel and RiverCentre. Other features include an enlarged Children's Room, larger public browsing areas, a cafe on the first floor, and a new entrance from Kellogg Boulevard.

The central library's collection includes some 350,000 items. Patrons can browse the collection on Monday 11:30 A.M. to 8:00 P.M.; Tuesday, Wednesday, and Friday 9:00 A.M. to 5:30 P.M.; Thursday from 9:00 A.M. to 8:00 P.M., and Saturday from 11:00 A.M. to 4:00 P.M. Although the central library is closed on Sundays, several of the St. Paul Public Library's branch locations are open that day. Borrowing privileges are available to any resident of the seven-county metropolitan area.

University of Minnesota Libraries
110 Wilson Library, West Bank Campus,
Minneapolis
(612) 626–2227
www.lib.umn.edu

The University of Minnesota–Twin Cities Libraries contain the largest collection of materials in the state, including some 6 million books, 45,000 periodical subscriptions, 5.7 million microforms, 2.6 million government documents, and 400,000 maps. The library system's extensive holdings are housed in five major libraries and 11 branch locations on the U's campuses in Minneapolis and St. Paul. In addition to the main Wilson Library general collection, the system includes such specialized collections as the Veterinary Medical Library on the St. Paul campus, the Science and Engineering Library within Walter Library on the East Bank of the Minneapolis campus, and the Eric Sevareid Journalism Library in Murphy Hall on the East Bank. The U of M Library is also the regional depository for Minnesota and South Dakota of all publications produced by the U.S. Government Printing Office, and the library boasts more than one million full-text journal articles stored in electronic databases.

University students, faculty, staff, and research assistants enjoy free borrowing privileges to the library's collections. The general public can borrow books and other materials from the library by joining the Friends of the Library, with a mini-mum donation of $60 annually, or by requesting an interlibrary loan at a public library. The hours of Wilson Library and the other libraries and collections on campus vary widely, depending on the individual library's policies and the academic schedule of the university. Call Wilson Library for more information.

Motor Vehicle Registration and Driver's Licenses

As a new resident of Minnesota, you have 60 days after moving to the Twin Cities to register your vehicle and obtain a driver's license if your vehicle is registered in another state and/or you have a driver's license from another state. Commercial vehicle drivers have 30 days to obtain a commercial driver's license.

To obtain Minnesota plates and register your vehicle, you will need the current vehicle registration card or certificate of title, your insurance information, the odometer reading from your vehicle, a driver's license (or other valid form of identification) from another state, and, if you are leasing your vehicle, a copy of the leasing agreement. The cost to register your vehicle is based on set fees for plates, filing, public safety tax, and title, as well as on the value of your vehicle for the registration tax. For passenger cars the title fee is $2.00, the filing fee is $7.00, the public safety vehicle fee is $3.50, and the plate fee

Insiders' Tip

You don't need to be a resident of the town or county where the Motor Vehicle Registrar Office is located to obtain a driver's license or vehicle plates there, and it is often a much shorter waiting time at suburban offices than at the main offices in Minneapolis and St. Paul. For a full list of Twin Cities registrar offices, contact the Minnesota Department of Public Safety at (651) 296-6911 or www.dps.state.mn.us.

is $3.00 for standard plates. Personalized and specialized plates (such as Critical Resources plates) are an additional charge. The registration tax for first-time registration of a vehicle in Minnesota is based on the value of the vehicle but will be no more than $189. Subsequent renewal fees will be no more than $99. The tax for cars older than 10 years is set at $35 for new registration and renewals.

If you have a valid driver's license from another state, you will need to pass a knowledge test and vision check to obtain a Minnesota driver's license. If your license from another state has been expired for more than a year or you move to Minnesota from another country, you will also need to pass a skill (road) test. You will need to present your current driver's license when applying for a Minnesota license. A regular driver's license for adults over 21 costs $37.50; for those under 21, it's $17.50.

Motor Vehicle Registrar Offices are located throughout the seven-county metropolitan region. The following offices serve Minneapolis and St. Paul.

Driver and Vehicle Services
Government Center, 300 South Sixth Street,
Minneapolis
(612) 348–8240

Driver and Vehicle Services
Sears, 425 Rice Street, St. Paul
(651) 291–4267

Tourism Bureaus

Both Minneapolis and St. Paul have convention and visitor bureaus with a wealth of information about the Cities, including relocation information, lists of resources, current arts and sporting events listings,

Insiders' Tip

The Saint Paul Convention and Visitors Bureau offers a Saint Paul Fun Pass, which entitles the bearer to discounts at hotels, restaurants, stores, and attractions throughout the Twin Cities.

restaurants, real estate agents, neighborhoods, and much, much more.

The **Greater Minneapolis Convention and Visitors Association,** 33 South Sixth Street, Minneapolis (612-661-4700 or 888-676-6757; www.minneapolis.org), offers a visitor guide, a very complete listing of visitor and resident resources, travel/hotel reservations, events calendars, and discounted tickets to certain events. You can also obtain an Arts and Museum Pass through the association, allowing access for a set fee to numerous Twin Cities museums.

The **Saint Paul Convention and Visitors Bureau,** 175 West Kellogg Boulevard, Suite 502, St. Paul (651-265-4900 or 800-627-6101; www.stpaulcvb.org), offers detailed information about the city's attractions, restaurants, hotels, neighborhoods, and more. A free visitor kit, with much information useful to new Twin Citians, is available through the bureau. You can also get an Arts and Museum Pass here, as well as buy discounted event tickets and other specials from area businesses.

Senior Scene

Retirement
Communities

Services and
Programs In the
Metro Area

Support Programs

The Twin Cities and its suburbs are home to more than 100 retirement communities and nursing homes, many of which are located on scenic lakefronts or surrounded by parklike grounds. This chapter covers just a few of the residences senior citizens have to choose from in the greater Twin Cities metro area and is in no way meant to be all-inclusive. For more information about nursing homes, call the Minnesota Department of Health at (651) 215–5800, Care Providers of Minnesota at (952) 854–2844, the Minnesota Health and Housing Alliance at (651) 645–4545, or the AARP at (952) 858–9040.

Today, more and more emphasis is placed on senior citizens receiving assisted care in their own homes instead of relocating to a group nursing home. With more than 60,000 senior citizens in Minnesota in need of day-to-day care, many nursing homes are filled to capacity, and most opt to stay relatively small and intimate in order to provide quality care to residents. To accommodate the growing senior population in the state, many hospitals and managed care facilities offer assisted living options to seniors that are covered by either Medicare or their own insurance plans. These services range from having a nurse stop by on a regular basis to having a home care worker live full-time with seniors, helping out with everything, including grooming, medication, shopping, and housekeeping.

Senior citizens are a vital force in the Twin Cities, as evidenced in many successful political campaigns that have run primarily on senior concerns and issues. This is in no small part because of the Twin Cities' being home to some of the most dynamic senior rights advocacy groups, including the Gray Panthers, the AARP, the Minnesota Senior Federation, and many of the other lesser-known organizations that are listed in this chapter. These groups have effected positive change in the way the government, employers, and businesses view senior citizens by continuing to be important and aggressive in the community. They have also changed for the better the way senior citizens are treated in nursing homes and medical facilities across the country.

Retirement Communities

Alterra Sterling House
1005 Paul Parkway, Blaine
(763) 755–2800
11372 Northwest Robinson Drive, Coon Rapids
(763) 754–3500
5891 Carmen Avenue East, Inver Grove Heights
(651) 306–0919
305 East Thompson Avenue, West St. Paul
(651) 453–1803

Alterra Sterling House, known nationally as a pioneer in senior care, offers assisted living to older adults who want to retain their independence while receiving the personal services they need. Residents live in their own private apartments, complete with kitchens and private bathrooms, receiving the individual care and personal assistance they need in a comfortable, cheerful, homelike atmosphere. This allows residents to enjoy privacy, yet still have access to a full-time professional staff that caters to their personal needs.

Bethany Covenant Home
2309 Hayes Street NE, Minneapolis
(612) 781–2691

Located in northeastern Minneapolis, Bethany Covenant Home is a 16-room Christian facility that provides care to senior citizens that require assistance in their day-to-day living. Their supportive and sensitive staff provides assistance with such activities as dressing, bathing, medication management, and anything else that may be needed to help residents retain their independence. A licensed nurse supervises medical management; rehabilitation services include physical, occupational, speech, and intravenous therapy.

Studios and one-bedroom apartments are furnished and decorated by the residents, creating a cozy, familiar homelike atmosphere. Each unit has a private bathroom, carpeting, drapes, individual climate control, master TV antenna, telephone outlets, and an emergency call system.

Colonial Acres Health Care Center
5825 St. Croix Avenue North, Golden Valley
(763) 544–1555

Located in the metro suburb of Golden Valley, Colonial Acres' professional health care team excels in meeting individualized needs, from subacute care to rehabilitation to continuing care. The on-site Special Care Unit offers individuals with Alzheimer's or progressive memory loss the highest quality nursing care in a Christian environment. The facility provides personalized dining areas, comfortable lounges, specially designed activity programs, and an enclosed outdoor yard—a safe, secure environment for residents. A specially trained staff is on-site to offer support to families and residents to cope with Alzheimer's progression through monthly support groups and individual counseling.

The Commons on Marice
1380 Marice Drive, Eagan
(651) 688–9999
www.commonsonmarice.com

The Commons on Marice is an elegant senior living community offering independent and assisted living, a progressive memory center and intergenerational learning opportunities. Their luxurious apartments include a full kitchen and a private bathroom with a walk-in shower equipped with grab bars. The residents' common grounds include a two-story atrium where residents can tend a garden, enjoy entertainment, or simply gather for conversation with neighbors. The library, fireplace, lounge, and billiards room also provide residents with additional opportunities to gather.

The Commons' main claim to fame is their fine dining—all meals are prepared from scratch by an executive chef, using only the finest ingredients. All meals are chosen by residents from a changing and extensive menu, and meals are taken when the resident chooses to do so and not on any predetermined schedule. There's also an ice cream parlor, an Intergenerational Learning Center, a chapel, and a Wellness Center offering everything from massage to aromatherapy. The Commons offers around-the-clock staffing, a 24-hour emergency call system and daily "I'm OK" checks, and has programs aimed at three levels of living, from independent residences to assisted living to a special Memory Center for residents with Alzheimer's.

Covenant Manor Retirement Community
5800 St. Croix Avenue North, Golden Valley
(763) 546–6125 or (800) 296–4114
www.covenantretirement.com

Covenant Manor is the first accredited continuing-care retirement community in Minnesota—one of only 260 in the nation to achieve this honor. Loving care is the essence of Covenant Retirement Communities, from assistance with daily activities to rehabilitative care following injury or illness to long-term skilled nursing care. Established in 1886, Covenant Manor provides homes to more than 5,000 senior adults in 15 retirement communities found throughout the country.

Apartments of various sizes include a full kitchen and balcony, and some are equipped with dens and fireplaces as well. Housekeeping, maintenance, dining services, and amenities such as recreational facilities all contribute to residents' comfort, and regular group activities are scheduled. Beyond services and amenities, residents enjoy the comforts of a community that cares for them physically, socially, emotionally, and spiritually. Wellness programs, exercise facilities and programs, dietary services, and residential and nursing services are all a part of the Covenant facilities, and everything from assisted living to rehabilitative care is available from a licensed skilled nursing facility located right on the grounds.

Lake Ridge Manor at Ebenezer Covenant Home
130 Lake Boulevard, Buffalo
(763) 682–1434

Located just 30 minutes west of Minneapolis in a quiet rural community, Ebenezer Covenant Home combines exceptional professional health care with personal attention to help residents achieve their highest level of ability and independence. Providing a family-like, Christian community, the home's gracious common grounds overlook beautiful Lake Buffalo, where many of the home's group activities take place. A licensed nurse supervises medical management; rehabilitation services include physical, occupational, speech, and intravenous therapy.

Residents are in charge of personally furnishing their single or double (private or semiprivate) residences. Each apartment has a private bathroom, carpeting, draperies, individual climate control, a master TV antenna, telephone outlets, and an emergency call system. Both short- and long-term care is available.

Phalen Shores
958 East Ivy, St. Paul
(651) 771–6201

Phalen Shores is a senior community for active seniors, offering one- and two bedroom apartments a short paved walk from beautiful Lake Phalen. Each apartment is individually climate controlled by residents and is equipped with a 24-hour Urgency Call System. Heated underground parking spaces are available to residents with vehicles, and regularly scheduled van transportation is available to seniors without transportation to run errands and participate in recreational activities.

RidgePointe
12600 and 12800 Marion Lane West, Minnetonka
(952) 540–6200
www.ridgepointeseniorliving.com

RidgePointe apartments offers one- and two-bedroom residences surrounded by gardens to active, independent seniors and adults. The complex is located conveniently near a variety of shopping centers, restaurants, medical facilities, theaters, and cultural centers. The complex itself has a group and private dining room, a fitness center with a whirlpool spa, a hair salon, a convenience store, and a hobby room on site. There's also daily scheduled transportation to shopping, medical appointments, and church services for residents; and amenities figured into the apartment rent include weekly housekeeping, a complimentary continental breakfast, all utilities except telephone and electric, basic cable television, individual climate control, and centrally located elevators in each four-home apartment building. For recreational purposes, there's a card room, a complete library, a billiards room, and a tropical atrium and art gallery connecting the resident buildings.

> ## Insiders' Tip
> For up-to-date information about retirement communities in the Twin Cities, *New Lifestyle* magazine has a great Web site at www.NewLifeStyles.com with regularly updated community overviews listed.

Twin Lake North
4539 38th Avenue North, Brooklyn Center
(763) 533–1168

Twin Lake North's manor-style homes are surrounded by beautiful grounds that allow residents countrylike comfort with city convenience. One- and two-bedroom apartments are available, and rent includes an attached garage with remote, heat, water, and trash removal. Many apartments include private balconies, and all apartments have walk-through kitchens with dishwashers and garbage disposals and controlled entrances to each four-apartment building.

Services and Programs in the Metro Area

A plethora of organizations in the Twin Cities are concerned with protecting the welfare of our growing senior community. These organizations deal with everything from helping senior citizens and their families choose a suitable retirement community to matching grandparentless children with volunteer senior citizens. For more information about senior advocacy groups in the Twin Cities, contact the AARP at (952) 858–9040.

Alzheimer's Association,
Minneapolis-St. Paul Chapter
4550 West 77th Street, Edina
(952) 830–0512

The Alzheimer's Association is available to answer any questions you may have about Alzheimer's disease and to direct you to services, educational workshops, support groups, and information.

CARELINK
(952) 854–2884
www.carelinkusa.com

CARELINK is an interactive resource to link families with long-term care facilities throughout Minnesota. Up-to-the-minute information gives caregivers current resources to better define individual plans of care for senior citizens.

DARTS
1645 Marthaler Lane, West St. Paul
(651) 455–1560
www.darts1.org

DARTS provides professionally coordinated transportation and in-home services for Dakota County seniors and their families. As a volunteer-based, nonprofit organization, DARTS pioneers services that support the full participation of seniors in community life, seeking out group activities and volunteer opportunities for seniors in the metro area and providing transportation to those functions.

Elder Learning Institute
(612) 624–7847

ELI is a voluntary, noncredit education and service program for older adults. It is a program of University College at the University of Minnesota and an affiliate of the Elderhostel Institute Network. The organization offers courses, luncheon programs, informal summer programs, educational tours, service opportunities, and special events. Courses are offered for an eight-week session each fall and spring and a six-week session each winter that meet weekly for one-and-a-half- to two-hour sessions. Courses focus on a wide range of interests—literature, psychology, world cultures, history, politics, economics, science, wellness, and the arts.

Estates in Transition, Inc.
(952) 938–5253

Estates in Transition, Inc., has been helping individuals with household organization, financial management, and personal and care management since 1982. They are particularly concerned with senior advocacy in all the aforementioned cases.

EverCare Minnesota
(612) 603–8515

EverCare provides enhanced, personalized care to frail senior citizens at their place of residence, utilizing nurse practitioner/physician teams who provide geriatric-focused care and case management services. EverCare currently makes housecalls to patients in more than 100 nursing homes and seven senior apartment complexes in Minnesota.

Friendly Visitors
(612) 331–4063
Friendly Visitors arranges weekly visits between adults of all ages and a homebound senior for a friendly chat and some personal assistance.

Gay & Lesbian Community Action Council
Sabathani Center, Suite 204, 310 East 38th Street, Minneapolis
(612) 822–0127
Call the Gay and Lesbian Community Action Council to receive a confidential copy of *Resources for Older Gays and Lesbians* for yourself, family, or friends. This resource includes several social groups, family and individual support, medical and mental health, housing, employment (volunteer, stipended, and paid), job search help, and many other services to make lives more comfortable.

Gentle Transitions
7001 Cahill Road, Edina
(952) 944-1028
Gentle Transitions is a fully insured moving company that provides moving services for relocating senior citizens, offering pre-move planning, sorting, and packing, through to unpacking, settling into a new home, coordinating all arrangements with utility and phone companies, and house closure.

Grandfriends
(612) 331–4063
Senior volunteers play the role of grandparents at community child care centers and homes, allowing both children and seniors to benefit from intergenerational companionship.

Gray Panthers of the Twin Cities
3255 Hennepin Avenue, Minneapolis
(612) 822–1011
The long-established Gray Panthers have worked on local, state, and national levels to fight ageism and press for legislation

that promotes age equality. Call for membership information as well as a listing of meeting times.

HandyWorks of Hennepin and Anoka Counties
Greater Minneapolis Council of Churches
(612) 870–3660
HandyWorks' chore and home maintenance services provide assistance to older adults and people with disabilities with household chores and minor home repairs to help them continue to live independently in their own homes. For some people, HandyWorks is a solution to a temporary situation—an illness or recovery from an injury. For others, HandyWorks becomes an essential service to help them remain living in their homes by providing routine cleaning, yard work, and snow removal.

Hearing Through Older Ears
DOORWAYS, 444 Cedar Street, St. Paul
(651) 223–5130
Hearing Through Older Ears (HTOE) is a program of DOORWAYS, a nonprofit agency in St. Paul that has been around since 1936. Hearing Through Older Ears teaches seniors and members of the general population how to live with a hearing loss.

Home Instead Senior Care Caregivers
3947 Excelsior Boulevard, St. Louis Park
(952) 929–5695
Home Instead provides 75 different non-medical companionship and helper services. Home-based care services can be scheduled for just a few hours or 24 hours a day.

Jewish Family and Children's Services of Minneapolis
13100 Wayzata Boulevard, Suite 400, Minnetonka
(952) 546–0616
Jewish Family and Children's Services of Minneapolis is dedicated to helping older adults maintain their autonomy, independence, and safety. Their Older Adult Services staff includes social service and nurse case managers who are specialists in the field of aging and are knowledgeable

about community resources—the staff also includes professionals who speak both Yiddish and Russian. One phone call to JFS puts you in touch with a case manager who will answer your questions and schedule a time for an in-home visit. Some of the services offered include housecleaning, personal grooming, Kosher Meals on Wheels, in-home health services, transportation to medical and dental appointments, grocery shopping, consultation with family and caregivers, household financial management, volunteer visitors, and individual and family counseling. Fees are based on income and ability to pay.

Lutheran Social Service
2414 Park Avenue South, Minneapolis
(612) 872–1719

Volunteer opportunities are available through Lutheran Social Service for individuals age 60 or older who would enjoy helping children through the Foster Grandparent Program or assisting homebound, isolated elderly through the Senior Companion Program. Enrolled volunteers receive a tax-free hourly stipend plus reimbursement for transportation expenses.

Metropolitan Area Agency on Aging, Inc.
1600 University Avenue West, Suite 300, St. Paul
(651) 641–8612

The Metropolitan Area Agency on Aging is one of 670 Area Agencies in the United States and the largest of the 14 Area Agencies on Aging in Minnesota. This state-designated agency is responsible for admin-

istering funds from the Older Americans Act for the Twin Cities area. They receive approximately $6.1 million annually from federal and state government funds to support a range of services through grants to community organizations. Their purpose is to support resources that help older people live independently and make our communities better places in which to grow old.

Metropolitan Elderly Health Promotion Project
165 Western Avenue North, St. Paul
(651) 221–0331

The Metropolitan Elderly Health Promotion Project provides outreach, education, literature distribution, and referral information to promote health and wellness among senior citizens of color in the Twin Cities metropolitan area.

Minneapolis YWCA
Encore Plus, 1130 Nicollet Mall, Minneapolis
(612) 332–0501, ext. 3183

The YWCA helps older women stay healthy and live longer through free information, free breast and cervical exams, free transportation, free child care, and free groceries.

The Minnesota Board on Aging
444 Lafayette Road North, St. Paul
(651) 296–2770

The Minnesota Board on Aging is committed to providing leadership in an effort to ensure that the needs of the state's 700,000 older citizens are met. The board provides many opportunities and programs to enhance the quality of life in this rapidly growing segment of our population. Programs include Senior Linkage Care (800–333–2433), Eldercare projects, legal advocacy, coordinated health insurance, counseling, congregate housing services, nutrition programs, and services as an ombudsman for older Minnesotans.

Minnesota Department of Veteran Affairs
20 West 12th Street, St. Paul
(651) 297–4932

The Minnesota Department of Veteran Affairs provides information to seniors on

---

Insiders' Tip

For informed referrals to medical programs, specially trained personnel, or special housing arrangements, call the Minnesota Home Care Association at (651) 635-0607.

---

benefits for former armed forces personnel in Minnesota.

The Minnesota Relay Service
(800) 627–3529 (TDD or Voice)

The Minnesota Relay Service connects deaf, hard of hearing, and speech-impaired to hearing people via the telephone, 24 hours a day, 365 days a year. There are no restrictions on the length or the number of calls placed by users. Specially trained operators relay conversations between people who use TDDs and people who use telephones, reading TDD users' typed messages and typing the telephone users' verbal responses, relaying conversations exactly as received. All calls are confidential.

Minnesota Senior Federation
1885 University Avenue, Suite 171,
St. Paul
(651) 645–0261 or (800) 365–8765
www.mnseniors.org

The Minnesota Senior Federation is dedicated to maintaining a democratic, grass-roots organization that trusts in the common sense of its members. Uniting seniors and their own organizations, the MSF acts as a body of peers, leaders, and decision makers, influencing state policies regarding seniors and providing community information and services to benefit people of all ages with an emphasis on health, housing, retirement planning, and spiritual issues. The MSF publishes several monthly newsletters and magazines that are available to their members—call for current membership information and dues.

Neighbor to Neighbor
1021 Marion Street, St. Paul
(651) 488–0507

Neighbor to Neighbor provides resources to senior citizens such as ongoing health and wellness monitoring through their "miniclinics" and foot care clinics, health and wellness education in numerous community locations, a weekly Parkinson's Support Group, and their Senior Aide Program that offers retraining to workers age 55 and over so that they can reenter the workforce after updating skills.

Recovery, Inc.
(612) 824–5773

Recovery, Inc., organizes and sponsors free self-help groups for depression, anger, frustration, fear, and anxiety throughout the Twin Cities.

RSVP
2021 East Hennepin, Suite 130,
Minneapolis
(612) 331–4063

The Retired and Senior Volunteer Program invites retired and semiretired persons to make volunteering a part of their lives. RSVP provides free assistance in locating volunteer opportunities, along with supplemental insurance and limited reimbursement of travel and meal expenses. Volunteer opportunities are available throughout the seven-county metro area.

St. Paul Parks and Recreation
300 City Hall Annex, 25 West Fourth Street,
St. Paul
(651) 266–6370

The Saint Paul Parks and Recreation "Special Programs" section invites senior citizens at least 55 years of age to spring into new activities. On a bimonthly basis, the Special Programs staff publishes a newsletter called *The Pioneer Spirit*, listing upcoming activities and registration materials—call the above phone number to get a copy mailed to you. More than 13 weekly groups meet throughout the year, with activities such as gym bowling, darts, cards, dice, senior choir, and table games.

Satin Dolls & Company
(612) 545–0501

Satin Dolls is a volunteer group of senior dancers and entertainers associated with the Lenox Community Center of St. Louis Park. The sometimes risqué troupe travels throughout the Minneapolis area presenting 45-minute shows of dance routines interspersed with specialty acts at senior centers, organization meetings, nursing homes, fairs, churches, and synagogues. Donations presented to the volunteers are given to the Lenox Senior Center in support of their programs, which have been featured on local television numerous times and have received favorable write-ups in several publications. If you are a senior citizen who tap-danced during your youth, or have had recent dancing experience, the Satin Dolls urge you to apply for an audition. Singers, instrumentalists, and masters of ceremonies are also invited to apply.

Senior Community Services
10709 Wayzata Boulevard, Suite 111, Minnetonka
(952) 541-1019

Senior Outreach provides in-home counseling and case management to frail elderly and their families throughout suburban Hennepin County to help older adults remain independent as long as possible. The broad range of services offered includes transportation, personal care, homemaking, medical care, finances, respite help, volunteer visitors, and assistance with health insurance. Their staff meets with seniors in their own homes to identify and connect with the combination of services that will fit their specific needs. Any Medicare-eligible beneficiary in Hennepin County may utilize this service.

Senior Dining (Volunteers of America)
5905 Golden Valley Road, Golden Valley
(763) 546-3242

Volunteers of America's Senior Dining offers seniors a delicious and nutritious noon lunch combined with the bonus of dining with other people. Meals are served in more than 40 pleasant dining locations in Hennepin and Anoka Counties, and anyone age 60 or older may be a guest. Make reservations ahead of time—most sites require a two-day advance reservation. The cost is a very reasonable suggested donation, although no one with a reservation will be denied a meal due to an inability to contribute. Call for times, locations, and reservations—additional volunteers are always needed to help with organizing events and coordinating transportation.

Senior Services Program
RHS Resource Center, 3730 Toledo Avenue North, Robbinsdale
(763) 522-0850

RHS's Senior Services Program offers several programs for seniors, from a variety of writing and art classes to one-day seminars on how to improve your memory. You can also learn how to improve your bridge game and how to use a computer, as well as attend informative seminars on sexuality, prostate health, sleep, colds and flu, skin cancer, hearing tips, and the benefits of humor.

Seniors Agenda for Independent Living
1114 Hennepin Avenue, Glencoe
(800) 223-7292

SAIL is an opportunity through coordinated efforts to be a catalyst for change in the way the world views senior citizens, developing and offering services to a growing population in a cost-effective and dignified manner. Assistance is available to seniors to match their wants and needs with local services that will allow them to remain safe and independent in their own home or community.

TeleFriends
(612) 331-4063

Senior volunteers monitor, via telephone, children who are at home alone after school.

University of Minnesota Elderhostel
136 Nolte Center, University of
Minnesota, Minneapolis
(612) 626–1231
www.elderhostel.org

Elderhostel, a residential educational program for people age 55 and older, is offered on 53 campuses in Minnesota and an additional 1,900 sites around the world. This "learning vacation" provides opportunities for older adults to take noncredit courses in a wide variety of subjects while enjoying extracurricular activities with others who share similar interests. During each Elderhostel week, students enjoy about 22 hours of instruction. No homework, tests, or grades—just learning for the pleasure of learning. Visit the Elderhostel Web site or call the above phone number to be put on all Elderhostel mailing lists.

Support Programs

Adult Day Programs
(612) 331–4063

Adult Day Programs offers long-term, daily support for seniors, including transportation and day care for adults with social activities, lunch, field trips, and more.

Elder Ride
(612) 339–0655

Elder Ride provides van rides for seniors to medical appointments, social services, grocery shopping, VOA Senior Dining, and recreation.

Insiders' Tip

Many travel agencies offer substantial discounts to senior citizens, as well as tour packages tailored specifically for senior citizens.

Grandparents As Parents
(612) 529–7721

Grandparents as Parents offers intensive, one-to-one support for grandparents raising their grandchildren.

Special Access
(612) 529–7721

This organization offers comprehensive, hands-on assistance for people of color to gain access to needed social services.

West Metro Coordinated Transportation
(612) 331–4063

WMCT plans, develops, promotes, and coordinates transportation resources for older adults in Hennepin County.

Child Care

There are more than 290 child care providers and preschools in the Twin Cities metro area, ranging from small, home-based day care centers that cater to infants and toddlers to public schools that have specialized programs for children as young as two years old. Minnesota law has set specific guidelines for child care providers, including mandatory licensing for all providers, with the exception of having a friend or relative watch your child. Minnesota's licensing procedure for potential child care providers is a strict one, too, requiring thorough background checks, drug testing, proof of completion of a child development course and a family day care training program, and unannounced site inspections that continue long after the license is actually granted. On top of this, providers must have at least $100,000 in liability insurance for each child enrolled, as well as a $25,000 policy on the facility itself. Minnesota law also dictates that each day care must adhere to specific adult-to-child/infant ratios, usually of no more than six preschool-aged children per adult or two infants per adult.

The upside of this is that parents are able to rest much easier knowing their children are placed in such rigidly monitored day care facilities. Most day care centers in the Twin Cities have large, fenced-in play areas attached; serve one or two hot, homemade meals that meet USDA guidelines; and are run by people willing to go through rigorous screening procedures to become day care providers. The downside is, of course, that child care costs in the Twin Cities are easily above the national standard, costing parents between $4,000 and $11,000 per year per child, with an average monthly bill of about $600. The following listings are by no means exhaustive but should give you a good foundation for your search for child care.

After-School Care

As part of their continuing effort to both get parents involved in school and to keep public schools an important focus of their community, almost every school in Minneapolis and St. Paul offers some sort of after-school program for children, continuing education classes for adults, or weekend activities open to both children and adults. The newest innovation in this trend to turn public schools into true community hubs is the **Beacons Project** (612-625-6025) in Minneapolis. Offering everything from baby-sitting classes and career exploration to wall climbing and digital camera workshops, the Beacons Project is a bold approach to keeping inner-city kids interested in school long after they're let out of class. For information regarding after-school activities in your neighborhood, contact Minneapolis Public Schools at (612) 668-0000 or www.mpls.k12.mn.us, or the St. Paul Public Schools at (651) 767-8100 or www.stpaul.k12.mn.us.

Montessori Schools

Founded by Dr. Maria Montessori more than 85 years ago, Montessori education has gained growing favor with the public over the past decade. In Minnesota, many

Montessori schools have been incorporated into the public school system, bringing their tradition of encouraging independent thinking and cultural literacy to inner-city children who might otherwise not have the financial option of attending the formerly private schools. As all Montessori schools generally allow children as young as three to attend classes, a Montessori education is a viable alternative to traditional day care.

When choosing a Montessori school for your child to attend, it's important to remember that no two Montessori schools are exactly alike. One might put an emphasis on arts and crafts, while another might concentrate primarily on math and science. Curriculums are subject to change, too, so the only way to know for sure what type of Montessori school is in your neighborhood is to personally check it out—which the schools strongly encourage anyway, as parent involvement is just as vital a part of the system as the students and teachers themselves. One word of warning: Montessori preschool classes fill up very quickly, and parents are encouraged to apply to their school(s) of choice at least six months in advance.

In Minneapolis, Montessori schools that have specifically pre-K (from one year old on up) and kindergarten classes are **Bernie's Montessori School** (612–333–5460) at 115 Second Avenue South and **Children's Village Montessori** (612–378–7730) at 2812 University Avenue SE. In St. Paul there is **Children's House Montes-**

sori (651–690–3403) at 1194 Randolph Avenue and **Oak Hill Montessori School** (651–484–8242), at 4665 Hodgson Road.

Group Day Care Centers

New Horizon Child Care
2733 Park Avenue, Minneapolis
(612) 871–0233
111 Marquette Avenue, Minneapolis
(612) 332–7866
2204 Lower Afton Road, St. Paul
(651) 735–7311
1385 Conway Street, St. Paul
(651) 778–9441
www.newhorizonchildcare.com

One of the largest child care providers in the Twin Cities with more than 60 branches in the metro area alone, New Horizon Child Care aims to give children under their care a safe place to play as well as a head start on their future academic careers. New Horizon has an actual curriculum for children, based on their age and developmental levels, which includes art, drama, computer, music, reading classes, field trips, lots of storytelling, and indoor and outdoor exercise (depending on weather). Infants as young as six weeks old are accepted into their program, as well as children as old as 12.

Children's World Learning Center
3708 West 44th Street, Minneapolis
(612) 922–6727
807 Second Street SE, Minneapolis
(612) 379–0857
525 Huron Street SE, Minneapolis
(612) 623–4642
2070 Burns Avenue, St. Paul
(651) 731–1815

With some 40 locations in the Twin Cities metro, this all-purpose day care is extended to children as young as 6 weeks old to kids as old as 12, with the exception of the Minneapolis facility on Second Street SE, which only takes infants age six weeks to five months. The facilities offer transportation to and from home, and meals are provided three times a day.

Insiders' Tip

The Greater Minneapolis Day Care Association (612-341-1177) connects parents to day care centers and child care providers in the Twin Cities metro area.

Nannies

Although there aren't a lot of nanny resources in the Twin Cities, the resources available have exemplary reputations. The state required screening process of the nannies and the potential hiring parents, as well as the extra screening completed by the individual agencies themselves, ensures you will let a quality child care professional into your home who understands your needs as a parent for your child. Nanny care is not just for infants, either—all the agencies listed below have nannies qualified to take care of infants 1 month old to children 14 years old.

Above & Beyond Nannies, Inc., 10936 Territorial Drive, Burnsville; (952) 894-0200; www.the-nanny.net

Nannies From the Heartland, 5490 Balsam Lane North, Minneapolis; (763) 550-0219; www.nanniesheartland.com

Nanny Professionals, 245 Sixth Street, Suite 703, St. Paul; (651) 221-0587; www.nannyprofessionals.com

Church-Based Care

Many of the hundreds of churches in the Twin Cities metro area offer weekday and/or weekend day care for young children—a condition that depends primarily on congregation support and interest as well as finding volunteers or permanent staffers to run these programs. Therefore, it would be difficult to mention specifically all the churches that do offer day care, just because these programs are sometimes offered only in the summertime or are even canceled altogether due to lack of community support. Your best bet is to call the churches directly to find out if they are offering day care—church-based care generally costs about $100 per week for full-time care.

Saint Mathews Christian Childcare (651-646-6484), located at 701 North Lexington Parkway in St. Paul, is a Christian-oriented day care that offers children ages one to five years old such activities as drama, dance, and music classes. **Calvary Lutheran Pre-Kindergarten** (763-545-5659), located at 7520 Golden Valley Road in Golden Valley, is another Christian-oriented day care for children ages three to five, with an academic curriculum that encourages children to start reading and writing prior to entering the public school system. **Holy Trinity Child Care Center** (612-724-7652), located at 2730 East 31st Street in Minneapolis, is Lutheran-based but offers nondenominational programs, concentrating more on developing the social and interactive skills of their wards, ages three to seven. Their one stipulation for acceptance into their program is that children must be toilet-trained.

Special Needs

Ronald McDonald House
608 Southeast Ontario Street,
Minneapolis
(612) 331–5752

The Minnesota Chapter of the Ronald McDonald House has provided comfort and care to families throughout the Twin Cities through establishing emergency care funds, free lunch programs, and domestic violence shelters across Minnesota. The cornerstone of Ronald McDonald House Charities, Ronald McDonald Houses worldwide have been a beacon of hope to children and families in need since 1974.

Crisis Nursery of Anoka County–Childrens Home
500 Northeast Osborne Road, Fridley
(763) 785–9222

Minnesota Crisis Nurseries offer a variety of emergency care family services, including help for battered women, teen parents, and abused or neglected children. One of their many great services is their open-door policy to parents facing desperate situations—Crisis Nurseries will take in children and infants from troubled homes for up to 48 hours. Another policy is to take in any infants brought in, no questions asked, and place them with adoption agencies.

Support Groups

Chrysalis–A Center for Women
4432 Chicago Avenue South, Minneapolis
(612) 871–0118

Chrysalis holds a wide selection of parenting classes for new and experienced mothers alike, with a special emphasis on helping couples with children deal with divorce or separation—some of these classes are required by Minnesota law for divorcing couples to attend. Child care is provided during counseling and classes, and counseling is extended to children ages 6 to 17 whose parents are facing separation.

Fathers' Program
Episcopal Community Services
123 North Third Street, Minneapolis
(612) 338–6558

Fathers' Program is a resource specifically aimed at unmarried, noncustodial fathers, ages 18 to 30, who are having difficulty with employment, making child support, or visitation issues. The program also offers personal and vocational counseling, job placement services, parenting classes, mediation and educational planning, as well as regularly scheduled father-child activities.

Fathers' Resource Centers
430 Oak Grove Street, Minneapolis
(612) 521–3409

With locations in Minneapolis, St. Paul, Burnsville, Blaine, and Hopkins, Fathers' Resource Center has a variety of programs aimed at single, married, or divorced fathers who want to improve their relationship with their children, including anger management groups, parent education classes, and support groups. The center also has information for fathers on legal issues, including referrals and up-to-date information on public policy and child support issues.

Parents Anonymous of Minnesota
(800) 487–2111

Parents Anonymous is a national non-profit organization that provides an outlet for parents to vent their joys and frustrations about being parents. Support groups, led by a Parent Group Leader, assist parents who want to improve their parenting by providing models, information, and ongoing support while parents learn new child rearing techniques or improve upon old ones. The groups provide a place for parents to experience adult contact and share new ideas and experiences with parenting. Groups are community-based, and there are no waiting lists or dues.

Southside Family Nurturing Center
2448 18th Avenue South, Minneapolis
(612) 721–2762

Southside Family Nurturing Center offers parenting classes to men, women, and couples alike. Among the classes offered are the prevention of abuse and neglect, parent and child activity nights, anger management, and therapeutic group discussions and individual counseling.

Insiders' Tip

Parent support groups are a great place to meet other parents who can provide tips and insight on the Twin Cities' day care programs.

Education

Public Schools
Private Schools
Higher Education

Education is a matter of considerable civic pride in the Twin Cities and is viewed as essential to the area's continued success in the future. Efforts are made throughout the area's school districts to incorporate the entire community in improving the quality of education, and the influence of K–12 education is felt beyond the confines of the students in the classroom in important areas such as parent involvement, athletics, and local school boards. The state of Minnesota places a premium on education, and therefore an astounding number of local residents are directly or indirectly involved in the school system. Education has always been highly valued in the Twin Cities, and Minnesota as a whole, thus parents, politicians, and educators usually work together. The end result is one of the best states for education in the nation.

This section's focus is on metro area public education, particularly Minneapolis and St. Paul. In addition, there are profiles of a few of the area's excellent private preparatory schools, both nonsectarian and parochial, and profiles of institutions of higher education.

Public Schools

Organization

The organization of Minnesota public education (K–12) is based on a stable and efficient school board government. A significant issue with state school districts is consolidation, especially in rural areas.

As Minnesota's population has swelled, the number of school districts has shrunk. Moreover, many suburban school districts have rapidly expanded to immense megadistricts, but they have shrewdly avoided the political difficulty of dividing districts. Today the state of Minnesota has 426 school districts. Included in this figure are numerous types of school districts from traditional K–12 districts to significantly less numerous but growing charter districts. Also counted are one experimental district, Pine Point, within the Park Rapids District, as well as cooperative, intermediate, education, and enhanced paired districts; all the different types of school districts have missions and objectives specified by the state of Minnesota. The state encourages innovation in education, which along with school consolidation means the number of school districts is remarkably ephemeral.

All districts are subject to review, and are granted powers by the state legislature and government. When the school districts are negligent, their powers may be rescinded and inspected by the Minnesota School Board Association (MSBA). The MSBA frequently serves as a surrogate for direct state intervention in the school districts. Founded in 1920, the MSBA was the eighth organization of its kind in the nation. The administrative body comprises 14 directors, appointed from local school boards, and meets once a month to decide general issues for the district's local school boards.

The governance and structure of Minnesota school boards includes minimal variation. School boards' size and lengths of elected terms differ, and they are frequently authorized to make personnel, curriculum, and budget decisions. The Minneapolis school district is the largest in the state, with 47,661 students enrolled for the 2002–2003 school year, and is governed by seven "at large" elected school board members, who serve four-year terms.

371

School District 623, the Roseville Area School District, in minor contrast, elects six members every odd year.

Both state and local government make enormous financial appropriations to Minnesota public education. The state of Minnesota serves approximately 850,000 K–12 students annually. The state is fervently committed to providing a quality education for all students. In addition, the Twin Cities have made efforts to improve education. During the November 2000 election the state's two largest school districts, St. Paul and Minneapolis, approved referendums for further education financing. Moreover, the Twin Cities have an important organization dedicated to improving Twin Cities K–12 public education, the Association of Metropolitan School Districts, which represents 260,000 students from numerous school districts including Minneapolis, St. Paul, Edina, North St. Paul-Maplewood-Oakdale, and Bloomington, to name only a few of the 26 member districts. Organization is an essential component of Minnesota, and Twin Cities, K–12 public education, and efforts are continually made to better serve the area's most important resource—children.

Grade Level

The nomenclature used in Twin Cities public education follows the national standard for dividing grades. Most area school districts are divided into elementary (K–6 or K–5), junior high (7–8 or 7–9) or middle school (6–8), and high school (9–12). The state's two largest school districts, Minneapolis and St. Paul, significantly contrast each other in matters of grade level. Minneapolis has a standardized district-wide system of elementary (K–5 or K–8), middle school (6–8), and high school (9–12). St. Paul's grade level nomenclature is significantly more varied and innovative. Demarcation of grades in St. Paul includes elementary (K–8 or 1–8), middle school (6–8), junior high (7–8), high school (9–12), as well as innovative 4–6, K–12, and 4-year-old programs. Twin Cities suburban public schools frequently use a system similar to Minneapolis for grade levels, and although junior highs continue to persist, middle schools over the past couple of decades have become much more prevalent.

Standards

Minnesota, unlike many other states, did not develop statewide standards until 1993. Because Minnesota consistently has had a 90 percent graduation rate (18- to 24-year-olds), many argued against the trend toward state graduation standards. At the beginning of the '90s, the Minnesota Department of Education (shortly thereafter reorganized as the Department of Children, Families, and Learning) and the Minnesota Board of Education jointly initiated efforts in developing a statewide graduation standards program. The Minnesota State Graduation Standards were approved by the legislature in 1993. However, implementation has been fairly slow, as the state did not want to undermine the excellent public education provided in Minnesota. All Minnesota public middle school/junior high and high school students began participating in the system, but the 9th grade class of 1996–1997 was the first to have the entire "basic standards" apply toward graduation, which gets to the specifics of the "standards."

The Minnesota State Graduation Standards are divided into two parts, the basic standards and the high standards (profile of learning). The basic standards are a "safety net" to ensure that students graduating from Minnesota high schools are competent in seven core areas: mathematics, government, science, safety, physical health, geography, and reading. Students are required to pass written exams in reading and math, which are first given in 8th grade. The writing component of the basic standards is first offered in 10th grade. Students may retake the exam in another academic grade if they fail on their first attempt. The basic standards are straightforward in comparison to the high standards.

The high standards are a performance-based measurement of students' achieve-

Groveland Park Elementary School in the Mac-Groveland neighborhood of St. Paul. PHOTO: TODD R. BERGER

ment. Teachers must fold the standards into their daily classroom curriculum and provide opportunities for students to meet the graduation standards. They present many difficulties for school districts throughout the state, which must revise curricula to incorporate the standards into their lesson plans. The profile of learning develops students' academic abilities in nine mandatory areas and one optional area, in an effort to develop specific skills for the workplace or post-secondary education. There are 48 content standards in the 10 learning areas, and students must complete 24 of 48 content standards, which include both required and elective areas, in learning areas one through nine. Enumerated in the Minnesota Graduation Standards are 10 areas: read, view, and listen; write and speak; arts and literature; math applications; inquiry; scientific applications; decision-making; people and cultures; resource management; and world languages (optional). The high standards are assessed by teachers using rubrics, which assign points based on quality of performance. As the example

shows, the high standards are bureaucratic in language and function and have been routinely criticized since their implementation. In fact, the 1999 legislature launched an unsuccessful attempt to abolish the profile of learning, and the 2003 legislature may attempt the same.

Despite the discontent with some aspects of the Minnesota State Graduation Standards, they are probably here to stay. Standards are an important part of education nationally, and that alone is an important impetus promoting their survival. The basic standards are viewed by many as an essential safeguard, which requires all graduates of Minnesota high schools to be at least literate. Nationally there are many critics who feel not enough of the standards are tested and that the system relies too much on performance standards. In contrast, some feel that the flexibility of the standards is their strength and allows Minnesota's and, in particular, the Twin Cities' excellent teachers to incorporate standards into their curricula. The standards are, and likely will continue to be, a hotly discussed issue for years to come in Minnesota education.

Curriculum

The curriculum in Minnesota schools varies widely across school district boundaries. However, the state, especially the Twin Cities, has in many ways standardized its curriculum. Whereas many regions are contentious about issues such as evolution, Twin Cities public schools accept and teach this scientific theory in the classroom. Technology has played a role in statewide curricula by both enriching and streamlining activities. The importance of computers as a technological tool cannot be underestimated, especially when the state's computer-to-teacher ratio is 1:9. In addition, the Minnesota Graduation Standards have had a profound impact on curricula statewide, as districts must comply with the requirements of the standards and incorporate them into the classroom. However, districts do, without a doubt, vary in the types of curricula they teach, and the way they are taught in the classroom. In addition, the state has numerous charter schools, which specialize in innovative approaches to curriculum. As laboratories for schools, curricula at charter schools are enormously diverse. Many Twin Cities school districts, like Minneapolis and St. Paul, offer this wide spectrum of curriculum possibilities.

Textbooks

Textbooks differ from school to school based on the decisions of school boards and/or classroom teachers. As a result, teachers use numerous textbooks in the myriad subject areas taught in Minnesota public education. The state has enacted laws regarding textbooks; however, they do not delve into content but rather compulsory availability. Minnesota statute 123B.42 addresses the accessibility of textbooks for all public education students. The commissioner of the Minnesota Department of Children, Families, and Learning is given regulatory power in verifying the law is followed, and public students are not denied access to textbooks. The textbooks used in public school classrooms differ significantly; however, parents have largely permitted school districts to use the textbooks and materials deemed appropriate, of course with some positive parent and taxpayer input. Textbooks have not been as much of a political football in the Twin Cities as other regions of the United States. Hence, the best available textbooks, with occasional controversial subject matter, are permitted in the classroom, which is an important part of the high-quality education provided in the Twin Cities.

Teachers

Minnesota has one of the nation's premier public education systems because of numerous factors. Central to the state and the Twin Cities success are the 55,862 teachers statewide. Funding and class size are important, but nothing can overshadow passionate, well-educated, committed, student-centered teachers. The state of Minnesota contributes to the superior quality of education by having relatively strict requirements for teaching. Education Minnesota, the state's teachers' union, also makes a considerable contribution by espousing and promoting only the highest caliber of members in its ranks. The strength of teaching in Minnesota can be attributed to a number of factors, from the Department of Children, Families, and Learning to individual school districts, but quality education begins with each individual teacher's commitment to the children of Minnesota.

Requirements for teaching in Minnesota are more rigorous than in many other states. First, in order to receive a license, prospective teachers must attend an institution accredited by the state. Then they must successfully complete classes in a specific area of study; e.g., English, social studies, mathematics, or science. In addition, the state has designated requirements for teachers, which vary depending on the grade levels in which the license can be used. All licensed teachers in the state must pass a course in human relations. Since 1973 each teacher's education institution has been required to provide a course addressing race, culture, socioeconomic status, and general interpersonal communication. Specific licenses have additional requirements. For example, in social studies, and most prospective grade 6–12 disciplines, teachers must take a number of state specified courses in teaching technology, assessment, kinesiology, special education, and drug and alcohol abuse. Beyond academic requirements, passing a relatively simple test of general knowledge, the Praxis I, is required. Finding employment as a teacher in the Twin Cities is highly competitive, especially in liberal arts subject areas such as social studies and English. However, math, science, and special education teachers, in contrast, are in high demand. Minnesota sets high standards in teacher education, which are manifest in the excellent classroom instruction in the area.

An important institution for Twin Cities educators is Education Minnesota, which represents the teachers of the state. Education Minnesota developed after the first merger at the state level of the nation's two largest unions of the Minnesota Federation of Teachers (affiliate of the American Federation of Teachers) and the Minnesota Education Association (affiliate of the National Education Association). The 1998 merger was completed in an attempt to improve the bargaining position of Minnesota's teachers.

Minnesota's teachers are highly esteemed throughout the nation. Almost 37 percent of Minnesota teachers have received advanced degrees. The average salary among Minnesota teachers is $43,330 annually, and statewide the student/teacher ratio is 16:1. Students are the Twin Cities future, and the area is fortunate to have such excellent teachers.

Special and Gifted/ Talented

Special and gifted/talented instruction are important components of Twin Cities education. Over the past couple decades local educators have moved toward integrating special education students in the classroom to reflect society at large. The largest school district in the state, Minneapolis, has developed an approach to special education that is followed by most school districts statewide. Of the 128 schools in the Minneapolis school district, only 6 are special education–only facilities. In contrast, gifted/talented students have increasingly had opportunities available segregated in school districts, or off campus, to engage their academic strengths.

Both St. Paul and Minneapolis emphasize diagnosing and beginning special education students as early as possible. Thus, both schools have early-childhood special education programs, which follow the proscriptions of state law: Students who are assessed to require additional educational enrichment prior to K–12 education receive it. St. Paul addresses these students with the Early Childhood Special Education program (ECSE). Minneapolis has a similar pre–K–12 program and promotes "job seeking and job retention skills" for high school special education students. Twin Cities special education integrates these students in the classroom so that they can fully participate in the community as adults.

Minnesota special education is among the best in the nation because of the stringent requirements of its teachers. Statewide, master's degrees or greater are required for all special education teachers. The Twin Cities has many nationally recognized special education programs; in particular, the University of Minnesota was ranked fifth by *U. S. News & World Report*. The University of Minnesota sponsors many important special education outreach programs, such as the Institute on Community Education, which provides social support to individuals with developmental problems. Minnesota bolsters special education with specific programs, and so does gifted and talented education.

Gifted and talented students are targeted with specific programs to meet their educational needs. St. Paul addresses gifted education at the elementary level with "DISCOVER," where students are assessed and identified for enriched education. Also, most elementary districts have Schoolwide Enrichment Models (SEMs), with programs for gifted students and teachers to meet their needs. At the senior high level, the International Baccalaureate program provides a challenging liberal arts curriculum. For Minneapolis talented students, there is the "Gifted Catalyst Program," which develops the strengths and talents of this important student group. Another essential part of gifted education statewide is a post-secondary option, where Minnesota high school students enroll in college and university classes and earn coursework toward graduation.

Gifted and special education students are both important to Twin Cities education. Twin Cities school districts recognize the value of all their young citizens and the pivotal role they play in the area's future success.

Alternative Education

The seven-county metropolitan area of the Twin Cities features several programs to meet the individual needs of students. Alternative education programs lead to degrees for nontraditional students who have dropped out of school or require a more flexible learning experience. The state features 145 area learning centers (ALCs), with many other options available within the Twin Cities. From night school GED programs to charter schools, the state has always been an innovator in education for every student.

School Choice

School choice is central to Twin Cities public education, where intense efforts have been made to serve all the area's students. A highly debated subject nationally, the Twin Cities have without great commotion implemented school choice programs. Integration in the Twin Cities has been relatively civil over the past few decades; compliance has occurred largely through district-wide magnet programs in both St. Paul and Minneapolis, which provide all area students with extensive choices in public education.

Minnesota state statute allows students to attend the public school of their choice, regardless of the community they live in and where their parents pay taxes. If the student is of low socioeconomic status, in some cases transportation may be provided free of charge. As long as there is space in the school, and the student completes registration before individual district's deadlines, then he or she is ensured admittance. Because of the success of open enrollment, the idea of vouchers has only been bandied about but not considered a serious public education option. The success of Minnesota school choice can in part be attributed to the relative parity in funding between Twin Cities school districts. If this condition did not exist, local public education expert Joe Nathan of the nationally recognized Center for School Change argues that school choice would surely fail. Minnesota is proud of the equitable school choice system developed by the state, which offers educational opportunity to every child.

Magnet schools are a major component of Twin Cities school choice. Both Minneapolis and St. Paul districts have school choice programs. Minneapolis has a combination of magnet and community schools, where specific magnet programs and comprehensive options are available.

Comprehensive takes a general, wide-breadth approach to curriculum, whereas the magnets feature a wide array of options. Some of the programs included at the high school level are the Academy of Travel and Tourism, Aviation and Aerospace, Communication and Technology, Education, International Baccalaureate, Automotive and Liberal Arts, and several more specific areas of study. There are also magnets available beginning in kindergarten, as well as community schools, which make it easier for families to participate in their particular elementary school's education policies. Minneapolis school choice provides almost infinite options for Minneapolis's children.

The St. Paul district's magnet system is similar to Minneapolis's, with some minor differences. In the jargon of St. Paul public education, there are magnet/city-wide and neighborhood schools. Again, the system is developed as a voluntary form of desegregation, and offers numerous educational opportunities in specific and broad areas of study.

In both districts, magnet programs admission is competitive; however, the majority of students get into the program they desire during their first application. Magnet programs are an important part of the Twin Cities' school choice program, which offers specialized education for every area student.

Charter Schools

Minnesota has, throughout its history, been an innovator in education. The state passed the nation's first charter school law in 1991, and since then, both locally and nationally, there has been an exponential growth of charter schools.

Minnesota sparked the movement, and has numerous charter schools to meet students' needs. As a laboratory for innovation in education, Twin Cities charter schools have distinguished themselves. Charter schools are independent educational entities, where experiments are permitted in the classroom. Minneapolis alone sponsors seven charter schools. The charter schools vary widely in curriculum

and environment. "The Cyber Village Academy" is a school dedicated to serving students with "a serious challenge to learning." Annually, approximately 150 homebound students participate in this program for students who may otherwise fall behind or drop out of school. "The Heart of the Earth" serves Twin Cities American Indians in a K–12 school, while Minneapolis's five other charter schools provide educational opportunity for students who may have otherwise given up on education. St. Paul also has several charter schools to meet the needs of specific student groups, including the Acorn Dual Language School, which is a school for students whose first language is Hmong or Spanish, and City Academy, where "hard to teach learners" receive an education. The state has allowed charter schools to emerge and to satisfy the needs of underserved student populations.

The Twin Cities were an early laboratory for charter schools. Detractors have argued against the charter school movement because of the low performance of some of these students on standardized tests. But advocates of charter schools point out that these students come from disproportionately low socioeconomic backgrounds and include many more special education students. Minnesota has always provided education for as many students as possible, and through charter schools, educational opportunities are open to more area students with special needs and abilities. Given Minnesota's educational history, it's not surprising the state would develop unique schools to save students from falling through the cracks.

Homeschooling

Homeschooling is another sector of Minnesota education to experience significant growth in the past couple decades. Throughout the nation, Christian families have most frequently "unschooled" their children, and Minnesota is no exception to this trend. However, there are a number of homeschoolers who are not primarily motivated by faith. Numerous organizations have appeared recently to meet the requirements of homeschoolers and the complex labyrinth of local, state, and federal laws with which they must comply.

Minnesota state laws are mandated to guarantee a high-quality homeschooling education. Minnesota has several laws that protect students from being denied a compulsory education (M. S. 120 A. 22. Subdivision 9), which also set minimum curriculum requirements for schools across the state, including homeschools. Numerous other statutes ensure that homeschool teachers are competent, as well as address numerous other issues relevant to quality of education. Plus, homeschool students are required annually to successfully complete a state exam to prove that they are being provided with a sufficient education. For the most part, homeschool students have scored well academically compared with their peers. Homeschooling is yet another option for Twin Cities students, requiring substantial planning and hard work by parents and teachers.

Athletics

Athletics play a significant role in Twin Cities education by developing a bridge between students and the local community. In addition, enthusiasm for school is generated by extracurricular activities. The number of sports available for both boys and girls to participate in varies greatly across school district boundaries. Most schools have boys' baseball, soccer, football, basketball, and hockey. For young women sports include soccer, softball, basketball, gymnastics, and hockey. Girls' hockey is by far the fastest growing sport in the state, the result of the sport becoming available at most large Minnesota high schools in the past few years. Over the years, the Twin Cities have produced a number of outstanding athletes of both genders.

Local residents support their area athletic teams with an outpouring of enthusiasm. March in Minnesota is tournament time, when high school sports fans become captivated with state champi-

onships over three successive weeks. Minnesotans love high school hockey. The Minnesota High School Hockey Tournament draws sellout crowds regularly, and enormous television ratings, as the Twin Cities and greater Minnesota schools engage in annual rivalries. The men's and women's basketball tournaments are also well received throughout the state, as is the annual state football championship the day after Thanksgiving, the Prep Bowl.

The Minnesota State High School League (MSHSL) is the organization that oversees the state's interscholastic athletics and fine arts programs. As a nonprofit, the MSHSL promotes fairness and good sportsmanship by standardizing rules and also acts as a bureaucratic force protecting the integrity of statewide athletics. Since 1916 the MSHSL has overseen athletic and fine arts programs, where students have "gone to state." Each year more than 200,000 students participate in MSHSL-sanctioned events.

Parent Involvement

Parents are encouraged to actively participate in their child's education, whether it's in the classroom or in local school board elections. In fact, Minneapolis has one of the nation's most proactive programs for parent involvement.

The first place parents can involve themselves is at the local polling place. There they can support school board members who espouse an agenda most

> ### Insiders' Tip
> Extensive homeschooling information is available from the Minnesota Homeschoolers Alliance, P. O. Box 23072, Richfield, Minnesota 55423; (612) 288-9662 or (888) 346-7622.

closely resembling their own. In addition, school districts periodically have levies or referenda regarding funding. In the 2000 election, St. Paul and Minneapolis each passed a referendum to increase K–12 public education spending. Twin Citians are usually willing to support more taxes if they believe it will markedly improve K–12 public education.

The Twin Cities school districts also have specific initiatives for parent involvement. In 1996 the Minneapolis school district adopted family involvement standards, the only program of its kind in an urban school district. The program bridges the gap between students, parents, and the community to promote learning. Training and access to resources help families enrich their student's educational experience. Parent involvement creates an important link between Twin Cities children and the community.

English Language Learners (ELL)

In the past decade the Twin Cities have undergone a significant transformation in student composition, particularly in the two largest urban districts, Minneapolis and St. Paul. Both districts have bent over backward to ensure a worthwhile education for these students, who hold in their minds the future of the area. English Language Learners have always been a significant part of student demographics; however, currently there has been a serious expansion of the ELL, which is not a historical first. In the late 19th and early 20th centuries, large groups of Czech, German, Swedish, Norwegian, Polish, Jewish, and numerous other immigrant children entered Twin Cities public schools. ELL programs have been established to make the transition of Hmong, Somali, Tibetan, Bosnian, Hispanic, Amharic (Ethiopian), Russian, and many other students whose first language is not English, easier. Every child is needed to participate in the Twin Cities dynamic economy and community. The Minneapolis K–12 school guide is an excellent example of the school's commitment to ELL education; on the very first page, seven languages ask, "Do you speak a language other than English?"

ELL instruction is paramount to the Minneapolis public schools. Minneapolis is the most diverse school district in the state, with school attendance figures for 2001–2002 at 45 percent African American, 14 percent Asian American, 11 percent Hispanic American, 4 percent Native American, and 26 percent Caucasian students. Minneapolis schools have 24 percent ELL students or approximately 12,000 in the district. An ELL student must meet two requirements: The student's first language is not English, and he/she scores poorly on an English reading or language proficiency test. Throughout the district specific ELL programs are available at most schools. For example, the Ericcson Community School has Hmong and Spanish ELL programs. ELL programs are also significant parts of many area school districts, especially St. Paul. With 51,275 ELL students statewide, serving this population will continue to be a major objective of public education.

Private Schools

The Twin Cities are home to a wide variety of nationally respected private schools. Many of the schools are denominational parochial institutions, but in most cases they include children of diverse faiths in their student body.

Unlike in many other areas of the nation, especially urban areas, private schools in the Twin Cities have been de-emphasized because of the exceptional quality of education in the area. In contrast with many other large metropolitan areas, the Roman Catholic Church does not dominate parochial education but instead plays a significant role in many Catholic private education institutions sprinkled throughout the Twin Cities, with the greatest concentration in St. Paul.

Miscellaneous Christian denominations have their own private schools in the Twin Cities. Curricula in these schools vary widely, from faith-centered instruction to substantially academically rigorous programs. The area also features schools with innovative academic programs, which mirror charter schools with one exception—tuition. Of course, a considerable concern regarding private schools is the cost of tuition. Many of these schools are quite expensive; however, many do offer scholarships for children with low socioeconomic status. Admission is another difficult matter, since some of the schools have fairly rigid admission requirements for K–12 education.

Minneapolis

Minnehaha Academy
3100 West River Parkway, Minneapolis
(612) 729–8321
www.minnehahaacademy.net

Minnehaha Academy offers a pre-K through 12 education with a distinctly Christian orientation. The school's approach to teaching and curriculum does not endorse a particular Christian denominational outlook but does emphasize "challenging minds and nurturing souls."

Minnehaha Academy has three campuses: one in suburban Bloomington and two Minneapolis campuses, idyllically located on West River Parkway overlooking the Mississippi River. Founded in 1913, Minnehaha Academy was established to educate children in Christian faith. Since then the school has expanded but continues its mission of providing an excellent education rooted in faith.

St. Paul

Cretin-Derham Hall
550 South Albert Street, St. Paul
(651) 690–2443
www.cretin-derhamhall.org

Cretin-Derham Hall (CDH) is one of the premier private high schools in the Twin Cities area. The school is recognized throughout the area for providing a disciplined Catholic education. Besides their outstanding academic reputation, CDH is respected statewide as an athletic powerhouse, especially in football and baseball,

where they almost annually compete in state championships.

Cretin-Derham Hall's roots date back to 1871. The Christian Brothers founded Cretin High School exclusively for young men, and in 1905 the Sisters of St. Joseph Carondelet founded Derham Hall. The schools did not merge until 1987, creating a much larger coeducational Catholic high school. After all these years Catholic values remain central to the school's academic experience. CDH inculcates in its students such values as leadership, service, diversity, and equity. These values are promoted throughout a CDH education, from the classroom to the football field.

Cretin-Derham Hall has been a name synonymous with athletic success in the Twin Cities. The level of skill and talent that CDH athletes display on the field always astounds area sports fans. Many CDH athletes have gone on to national success after graduating. In baseball the school boasts major league great Paul Molitor. The school is also renowned for developing football players who went on to successful college, and even NFL careers. Former Florida State quarterback and Heisman Trophy winner Chris Weinke is one of the most recent CDH stars to achieve enormous success after graduation.

Friends School of Minnesota
1365 Englewood Avenue, St. Paul
(651) 917–0636
www.fsm.pvt.k12.mn.us

A school developed by parents, educators, and members of the Quaker community, the Friends School of Minnesota is in the fine tradition of Quaker education nationally. The Friends School prepares children with a specific Quaker curriculum in grades K–12.

The curriculum at the Friends School is characterized by several teaching techniques. One important aspect of the school's academic experience is a weekly silent meeting, where students and staff are allowed to reflect on the events of the day. In addition, as a part of the Quaker tradition, students also have daily moments of reflection. The curriculum emphasizes "hands-on" education, especially with the young children. The school has a community focus in the classroom, and "group gatherings" are a regular component of the curriculum, where students discuss group dynamic problems. Essential to the educational experience at the Friends School is the inquiry process, which encourages students to be thirsty for answers when learning.

St. Paul Academy and Summit School
1150 Goodrich Avenue, Goodrich Campus,
St. Paul
1712 Randolph Avenue, Randolph Campus,
St. Paul
(651) 698-2451
www.spa.edu

St. Paul Academy and Summit School provides a private education on two beautiful campuses in St. Paul. The school's mission is to prepare students for life by providing academically challenging programs.

Another area private school that developed as the result of a merge, St. Paul Academy and Summit School are the result of consolidation to create a coeducational school. St. Paul Academy was founded in 1900 to educate young men, and Summit School first opened its doors in 1917. The two schools have been one since 1969 and have provided an excellent college preparatory education in beautiful, historic facilities.

North

Totino-Grace
1350 Gardena Avenue NE, Fridley
(763) 571-9116
www.totinograce.org

Totino-Grace, a private Catholic high school, serves the northern Twin Cities suburbs. The school's mission centers on learning, faith, service, and community. As the second largest of the 13 Catholic high schools in the Archdiocese of St. Paul and Minneapolis, the school has an annual enrollment of more than 1,000. Totino-Grace is a relative latecomer among Catholic parochial schools and was founded in 1965 to meet the needs of the rapidly expanding Twin Cities north suburban area. Since then, the Twin Cities

---

Insiders' Tip

Totino-Grace High School is named in part for Jim and Rose Totino, owners of Totino's frozen pizzas, who made a large donation to the private Catholic school.

---

have expanded much farther with suburbanization, but Totino-Grace remains an important area Catholic high school.

South

Academy of Holy Angels
6600 Nicollet Avenue South, Richfield
(612) 798-2600
www.ahastars.org

The Academy of Holy Angels, one of the Twin Cities' most picturesque campuses, is equipped with excellent education facilities. The campus is on 26 acres in suburban Richfield, where the school actively pursues a diverse student population.

Beyond the beautiful campus, the facilities have several important selling points. The 700 students in grades 9 through 12 have ample academic resources available. Besides amenities such as a theater, four computer labs, and a library with more than 12,000 books, there is a television studio. The school also has excellent athletic facilities, which include a domed football stadium, two gyms, and a weight room with modern exercise equipment. The Academy of Holy Angels specializes in a Catholic education with state-of-the-art education facilities.

The International School of Minnesota
6385 Beach Road, Eden Prairie
(952) 918-1800
www.sabis.org

The International School of Minnesota (ISM) is a private preparatory school for pre-K through 12th grade. The school is a member of the SABIS School Network that includes 20 schools worldwide and traces its history back to 1886 in Lebanon.

Located in Eden Prairie, a southern suburb of Minneapolis, ISM has an impressive 55-acre campus beside Bryant Lake. The school was founded in 1986 with an enrollment of only 24 students; since then the school has rapidly expanded to over 700 students. There are numerous academic opportunities available at ISM. High school students at ISM have advanced placement programs in many academic fields, such as art, biology, history, French, English, and several more college-level courses.

East

Hill-Murray School
2625 Larpenteur Avenue East, Maplewood
(651) 777–1376
www.hill-murray.org

Hill-Murray is a respected Catholic private high school for the east metropolitan Twin Cities. The school enrollment is 940 students for grades 7 through 12, and it has an impressive 14:1 student/teacher ratio. Academics with a moral perspective are emphasized at Hill-Murray, and the results show in student standardized test performance. In addition, during the 1999–2000 school year, 96 percent of the school's graduates attended college.

Athletics are another important aspect of a Hill-Murray education. There are 22 varsity sports teams, and the Pioneers excel in many, especially hockey, where they have regularly competed in state high school tournaments. Hill-Murray has provided an excellent Catholic education for more than 40 years.

West

Blake School
Blake Campus, 110 Blake Road, Hopkins
Highcroft Campus, 310 Peavey Lane, Wayzata
Northrop Campus, 511 Kenwood Parkway,
Minneapolis
(952) 988–3420
www.blakeschool.org

Blake School is one of the area's elite private preparatory schools and provides a nonsectarian, coeducational experience. The school features three campuses in the western Twin Cities metropolitan area and one next to the Walker Art Center in Minneapolis. The three campuses are the result of the school's interesting history, and each facility offers a wide array of educational options for Blake students.

The Blake School grew out of three separate private schools. The Northrup Collegiate School was founded in 1900, the Blake School (a boys' school) in 1907, and the Highcroft Country Day School in 1958. In 1972 these three highly respected independent schools merged. The result was the pre-K through 12th grade program, which continues today as the Blake School. The school's academic programs are challenging and intensive. Though the school is nonsectarian, it does promote a specific set of values, which include respect, love of learning, integrity, and courage. In addition, all students participate in artistic, academic, and athletic activities designed to prepare Blake students for higher education.

Breck School
123 Ottawa Avenue North, Golden Valley
(763) 381–8100
www.breckschool.org

The Breck School is recognized as one of the Twin Cities' finest private schools. The school offers Episcopalian values in the curriculum and is coeducational. Breck has a beautiful campus just outside Minneapolis and features 37 acres for school activities.

Higher Education

It's hard to imagine a metropolitan area with more diverse quality higher education options than the Twin Cities. The possibilities are seemingly endless; not only does the area boast numerous nationally recognized colleges and universities but also highly esteemed community colleges and technical institutes, transcending the traditional notion of trade schools, preparing students to participate in the area's dynamic economy. Education is structured to serve every member of the Twin Cities community, from recent immigrants to single parents.

The area's higher education institutions have long, storied histories, and many are nationally recognized for excellence. The University of Minnesota celebrated its sesquicentennial in 2001. Throughout its history, the school has shaped the quality of public education available in the state and has provided a relatively inexpensive undergraduate education through significant state subsidies. The area's community colleges are evenly distributed throughout the Twin Cities in order to serve as a "feeder system" for the University of Minnesota system and the Minnesota state colleges and universities. Another feature of Twin Cities' higher education is the many nationally recognized private colleges located in the area. The present epoch is fraught with abundant and dramatic change, but local innovations in education have arisen to meet these demands.

Higher education includes all learners in the community, as demonstrated by the prominence of continuing education, which has become an increasingly essential component of most school's missions. As a result, area colleges and universities have extensive, flexible continuing education programs to satisfy the needs of nontraditional students and adult learners. "Distance learning" is an innovative means for busy adults to complete undergraduate and professional degrees.

Numerous Twin Cities graduate programs and schools are nationally recognized for educational excellence and professional training. For more information on specific educational programs, most area higher education institutions have Web sites. *Peterson's 4-Year Colleges* is also a good source of information on Minnesotan institutions. Also, several area institutions are mentioned in *The 331 Best Colleges* by Princeton Review. Throughout Minnesota's history, higher education

excellence has been a paramount political and civic objective. The state's success is reflected in the tremendous accomplishments of area higher education alumni in the Twin Cities, greater Minnesota, and throughout the world.

Minneapolis

Augsburg College
2211 Riverside Avenue, Minneapolis
(612) 330–1001 or (800) 788–5678
www.augsburg.edu

Located approximately 1 mile from downtown Minneapolis, Augsburg College is the Twin Cities' Evangelical Lutheran institution of higher learning. Despite the school's origins, the college provides a distinctly secular education, though it retains its affiliation. The college, founded in Marshall, Wisconsin, in 1869, relocated to Minneapolis in 1872. Since then, Augsburg has grown substantially in scope and enrollment, with annual enrollments of slightly more than 3,000 students.

Teaching students is at the core of an Augsburg education, and it is reflected in many programs and activities. Professors concentrate on teaching rather than research and publication. Average class size is only 19, which is a tremendous advantage for students and affords ample opportunity for interactions with professors. Another asset is the plentiful multicultural support programs, ranging from Pan-African and Pan-Asian to Hispanic/Latino students. Students recovering from alcoholism can receive the support they require through "Step Up," a sobriety outreach program.

Featured at Augsburg are programs in most disciplines. For many majors, the college has an area of emphasis, such as "Sociology-Crime and Community" or "Social Psychology." Augsburg also offers majors not found at some other institutions of higher learning, e.g., Nordic Area Studies and Interdisciplinary Studies. Nordic Area Studies reflects the heritage of the region and the continuing influence of Scandinavian Lutheran culture.

Activities abound at Augsburg and enrich students' educational experience. Participating in nine male and eight female intercollegiate sports, the "Auggies" are members of Division III of the NCAA in the MIAC (Minnesota Intercollegiate Athletic Association). In addition, more than 50 clubs and organizations are on campus, including forensics, cheerleading, and the student newspaper.

Capella University
222 South Ninth Street, 20th Floor,
Minneapolis
(888)–CAPELLA
www.capellauniversity.edu

Capella University is the Twin Cities' first, and only, "distance learning" undergraduate and graduate school, primarily offering their courses on-line. In addition to Capella's on-line campus, the school offers directed studies programs. About 1,500 students are enrolled at the school in more than twenty nations worldwide.

Since receiving accreditation in 1997, the school has received significant media attention for its high-tech version of higher education for the 21st century. The school offers 400 accredited on-line classes, which are accessible anywhere and anytime a computer is available. In addition to coursework, Capella offers the on-line "cybrary," the school's Internet version of a library. The university has five primary schools: Business, Technology, Psychology, Human Services, and Education. Conferred degrees at Capella University include B.S., M.S., and Ph.D. Adult students are the most common group in the student body. Distance learning provides the opportunity for people to earn a degree, take a class for personal enrichment, or receive an advanced degree and ascend up the occupational ladder, despite the encumbrances of their busy lives.

Dunwoody Institute
818 Dunwoody Boulevard, Minneapolis
(612) 374–5800
www.dunwoody.tec.mn.us

Dunwoody Institute is an excellent Twin

> ## Insiders' Tip
> E-learning is a rapidly expanding service area of the economy; Minneapolis based Capella University reflects this trend, and was named one of the 500 fastest growing companies by *Inc. Magazine.*

Cities unified trade school. The institute is a nonprofit that offers 16 technical programs. Founded in 1914, Dunwoody has trained more than 250,000 students for technical careers during its history. Located next to the breathtaking Walker Art Center Sculpture Garden, the school sits on the edge of downtown Minneapolis and has one of the most panoramic views of the city, where many of its students move on to successful careers in various trades.

Dunwoody Institute is recognized as one of the premier trade schools in the nation. Just a few programs offered at Dunwoody are Applied Electronics, Automation Technology, Auto Collision Repair, Heating and Cooling Systems, and Architecture Drafting/Estimating. A unique opportunity for trade education at Dunwoody is the national Baking Center, "the only national nonprofit educational institution in the United States devoted exclusively to traditional baking." In addition, there are continuing education and Web-based tech classes, such as night classes offered for construction industry trades. Dunwoody Institute recognizes the importance that trades continue to play in the Twin Cities' dynamic economy by providing a high quality education, and their placement results demonstrate the institution's success—95 percent of graduates are placed in their field of study after graduation.

Minneapolis College of Art and Design
2501 Stevens Avenue South, Minneapolis
(612) 874-3700 or (800) 874-MCAD
www.mcad.edu

Minneapolis College of Art and Design (MCAD) is the leading art educator in the Twin Cities. Since 1886 MCAD has served area art students. Today, the art college shares a large portion of the state-of-the-art Minneapolis Institute of Arts (MIA) building. MIA is one of three excellent art museums in Minneapolis, all within a few miles of MCAD, plus there is a plethora of art-related businesses in the area.

For art students, there is an area of study for everyone at MCAD. Programs are available in almost 20 fields, which include Film/Video, Graphic Design, and Photography, plus business friendly areas of art, such as Furniture Design and Advertising Design. In order to create well-rounded art students, besides the rigorous studio art portion of most majors, important foundation and liberal arts courses are also required.

MCAD confers many specialized graduate degrees. Offered are Masters of Fine Arts programs as well as graduate one-year post-baccalaureate and certificate programs in Design, Fine Arts, and Media Arts. MCAD also has continuing education courses, open to the general public, which include distance learning and exhibition programs.

Minneapolis Community and Technical College
1501 Hennepin Avenue, Minneapolis
(612) 341-7000 or (800) 247-0911
www.mctc.mnscu.edu

Minneapolis Community and Technical College (MCTC) is dedicated to serving the increasingly diverse Twin Cities student population with liberal arts and career/technical programs. The focus at MCTC is on creating an environment where recent high school graduates, working adults, and continuing education students are comfortable and excel together in various educational fields.

Diversity is a major commitment at MCTC for several reasons. As the Twin Cities most ethnically diverse school of higher education, MCTC has an important mission: providing a quality education to students who speak more than 80 languages and dialects. In part, this is accomplished by the English as a Second Language program, which serves these frequently skilled students, who may need to improve their English language proficiency to receive better jobs and further contribute to the burgeoning Twin Cities economy. Besides the ethnic diversity at MCTC, the average age of the student body, 29.6 years, is decidedly nontraditional. MCTC offers numerous programs, which students can transform into successful careers. A few of the most popular programs are liberal arts disciplines, Law Enforcement, Nursing, and Computer Support. Associate in Arts (AA) and Associate in Science (AS) degrees are popular at MCTC, as are numerous technical certificate programs.

Another important aspect of MCTC is technology. The school has dedicated and continues to allocate substantial funds and resources for technology. The school provides courses on-line, an important initiative that will grow in the tech-intensive future. The New Technology Center/Library is another significant part of the MCTC's future; it will certainly further technological opportunities for students.

MCTC's location is another tremendous asset. The community college abuts Loring Park, one of the Twin Cities' most beautiful parks, and is within walking distance from all downtown Minneapolis's attractions and employers.

The University of Minnesota–Twin Cities
231 Pillsbury Drive SE, 240 Williamson Hall, Minneapolis
(612) 625-2008
www1.umn.edu/twincities

The University of Minnesota–Twin Cities pervades all aspects of the area's culture from sports, education, research and development to medicine, law, politics, and business. Known in the Twin Cities as the U of M, or simply the U, the institution is the flagship of Minnesota public higher education and a matter of tremendous civic pride. With an annual undergraduate and graduate student enrollment of near 50,000, the U of M dominates southeast Minneapolis and is omnipresent throughout the Twin Cities.

The University of Minnesota public education system includes five campuses. Outstate campuses are located in Crookston, Duluth, Morris, and Rochester. The University of Minnesota–Twin Cities has two campuses. The vast majority of programs are on the Minneapolis campus, where the administration is housed. The St. Paul campus is much less urban, with 155 acres of beautiful property devoted to numerous agriculture and natural resources programs.

The academic options at the U of M are seemingly endless. The two largest colleges are the College of Liberal Arts (CLA) and the Institute of Technology (IT). Eleven U of M programs are ranked in the top 10 in the nation, including Chemical Engineering, Psychology, Geography, Economics, and Forestry. Besides the 20 distinct colleges of the U of M, there is University College, the continuing education program, which is important in serving Twin Cities nontraditional students. The University of Minnesota is nationally renowned for quality education and research.

Since 1851 the U has served the Twin Cities in various guises. The school was founded seven years before Minnesota statehood as a preparatory school. During the Civil War the fledgling institution struggled with great difficulty to continue. It was not until the appointment of the first University of Minnesota president, William Watts Folwell (1869 to 1884), that the school emerged as the state's foremost institution of higher learning, a role it would not relinquish in its history. The U of M experienced significant ebb and flow until the post–World War II era, when the august Big Ten school's enrollment, mirroring national trends, swelled far beyond previous proportions. In summer 1997 the University of Minnesota's 14th president, Mark Yudof, took office. One of his major goals was preserving and renovating the school's numerous historic buildings.

In 1999 the University of Minnesota opened the new McNamara Alumni Center and Gateway Center. The building is the culmination of decades of work and fund-raising. The new complex is an example of the ongoing reciprocal relationship between U of M students and alumni; the U of M gives to its students, who in turn give back to the school and the Twin Cities. The University of Minnesota has produced alumni in almost every imaginable field. Two vice presidents and Democratic Party nominees for president of the United States, Hubert H. Humphrey and Walter Mondale, attended the U of M. The school also counts five alumni members in the Pro Football Hall of Fame: Bud Grant, Leo Nomellini, Alan Page, Bobby Bell, and Bronko Nagurski. The list of alumni also includes Seymour Cray, the founder of Cray Research and an important figure in the development of the supercomputer. In addition, Earl Bakken, who created the first battery-operated pacemaker and founded Medtronic, is an important medical technology alumnus, as is 1998 Nobel Prize winner Dr. Louis Ignarro, who was instrumental in the development of Viagra. Another U of M Nobel Prize winner is Norman Borlaug, who received the award in 1970 for engineering the "green revolution," which resulted in unprecedented food yields for feeding the Third World. University of Minnesota alumni have had enormous impact on the Twin Cities by creating 1,500 technological companies, which contribute $30 billion annually to the state economy.

Many University of Minnesota activities serve as an important link to the Twin Cities community at large.

The U of M newspaper, the *Minnesota Daily*, has operated for more than a century and is regarded nationally as one of the nation's best college newspapers. The University's radio station, KUOM, better known as Radio K, provides student radio programming from dawn to dusk daily. Many *Minnesota Daily* and KUOM alumni have moved on to success in the Twin Cities and national media. As a link to the University of Minnesota, the alumni association publishes a bimonthly magazine,

Minnesota, a glossy publication filled with facts about the school and its history.

The University of Minnesota is one of the most important Twin Cities institutions. The numerous successes of the school are a matter of tremendous civic pride and link the school and community.

Walden University
155 Fifth Avenue South, Minneapolis
(612) 338–7224 or (800) WALDEN U
www.waldenu.edu

Walden University is a graduate school with programs in Education, Psychology, Management, and Health and Human Services. The university takes its name and mission from Henry David Thoreau, who stated: "It is time that we had uncommon schools, that we did not leave off our education when we begin to be men and women." This is the school's mission through its numerous graduate programs, which specialize in advanced degrees for professional fields. For example, teachers might choose the Ph.D. or M.S. in education for a promotion or to earn a larger salary in their profession. Ph.D.s and M.S.s are also conferred in Health and Human Services, Management, and Psychology. Walden student dissertations are posted in the school's newspaper, *The Walden Ponder*, at the Web site. Accredited by the Central Association of Colleges and Schools, Walden University regularly places its graduates in faculty positions at small colleges, community colleges, and professional colleges throughout the nation.

St. Paul

The College of St. Catherine
2004 Randolph Avenue, St. Paul
(651) 690–6000 or (800) 945–4599,
ext. 6000
www.stkate.edu

The College of St. Catherine's motto is "redefining women." Located on an idyllic 110-acre wooded campus, 5 miles from downtown St. Paul, the college champions the cause of women's higher education.

As the largest Roman Catholic liberal arts school for women in the state, the College of St. Catherine, or St. Kate's, has a notable history in the Twin Cities, state, and nation. Founded in 1905 by the Sisters of St. Joseph Carondelet, their mission is improving women's educational opportunities. Despite this, St. Kate's does offer limited programs for men at their much smaller campus in Minneapolis, as well as the graduate school. The College of St. Catherine has been, and continues to be, a groundbreaker in the area of women's education.

St. Kate's emphasizes a distinctly Roman Catholic spiritual and ethical approach to education. Offered at the college are more than 30 different fields of study and more than 70 areas of concentration, from Art and Biology to Theater and Theology. Liberal arts is the most popular area of study, while Health Care is an important option. The College of St. Catherine is the Twin Cities' oldest and largest health care educator and includes highly regarded programs in Nursing, Occupational Therapy, and Pre-med. The college has consistently been an innovator in offering education to women normally underserved by higher education.

One of St. Kate's greatest educational innovations was the creation of "Weekend College" in 1979. Weekend College is an innovative initiative to meet the needs of working women's thirst for a college edu-

The College of St. Catherine on Cleveland Avenue in St. Paul. PHOTO: TODD R. BERGER

cation. Classes meet every other weekend on Friday evening, Saturday, and Sunday. Twelve practical, career-oriented majors are offered in the Weekend College program, including Elementary Education, Accounting, Communication, and Nursing. Programs like Weekend College extend educational opportunities to students who would not otherwise, or as quickly, receive a college education, and this is one of the many ways St. Kate's shines as an institution of higher education.

The College of St. Catherine has created a rich, modern educational experience. St. Kate's curriculum emphasizes depth and breadth and is reflected in critical inquiry, multicultural studies, and interdisciplinary teaching in the classroom. These are only a few of the reasons the College of St. Catherine is one of the nation's premier Catholic women's colleges.

Concordia University–St. Paul
275 Syndicate Street North, St. Paul
(651) 641–8278 or (800) 333–4705
www.csp.edu

Concordia University provides higher education in a Christian environment. The origins of Concordia date back to 1893, when the Lutheran Church–Missouri Synod created a high school to prepare students for its ministry. However, the school did not become coeducational until 1950 and began granting bachelor's degrees in elementary education in 1962 for the first time as a college.

Today, educational opportunities are available in numerous fields. Liberal arts, business and health care are popular areas of study. In addition, the college continues to offer many specialized career majors in the ministry, such as Directors of Church, Parish Music, Christian Outreach and Christian Education, as well as Pre-seminary Studies.

Hamline University
1536 Hewitt Avenue, St. Paul
(651) 523–2207
www.hamline.edu

Hamline University is Minnesota's oldest university. The United Methodist Church organized the school in 1854 in Red Wing.

Shortly thereafter, it relocated 50 miles north to its present site in St. Paul. Hamline was a progressive area leader in higher education, and was the third coeducational college in the United States. The cornerstone of Hamline's curriculum is liberal arts, which it emphasizes as a transformational tool in creating responsible citizens.

Hamline offers degrees and majors in numerous areas of study. Undergraduate bachelor's degrees in liberal arts disciplines are the most popular certificates granted. Also conferred are master's, doctorate, and law degrees. The campus is composed of approximately 3,000 students in areas of study ranging from the familiar disciplines, such as History, Art, and Anthropology, to Urban Studies, Latin American Studies and Musical Studies. Besides the Hamline Law School, there are several additional graduate programs: the School of Public Administration and Management, the Graduate School of Education and the Graduate Liberal Studies Programs.

The Hamline Plan is a specific curriculum program instituted university-wide, which outlines and targets the institution's specific educational goals. Throughout a student's education they are exposed to an interdisciplinary focus—students are educated in particular majors, but taught to think beyond the confines of their specific fields. Hence, students in all areas of study are expected to improve their abilities in several key areas (writing, speaking, computing, and reasoning) regardless of their major. Another essential component of the curriculum is "culture and issues." Students are encouraged to consider how culture interacts with such issues as gender, race, and age. Finally, the curriculum promotes "work and leadership" through seminars, internships, and career development courses. The overall goal of Hamline's curriculum is creating good citizens through a liberal arts education, which the school has consistently accomplished over its history.

Luther Seminary
2481 Como Avenue, St. Paul
(651) 641-3456
www.luthersem.edu

Luther Seminary educates ministers for the Evangelical Lutheran Church in America (ELCA). It is the largest of eight ELCA seminaries in the United States. The seminary expanded over 50 years to its present size after the consolidation of six area institutions serving a similar function. The campus is located on a pastoral bluff in St. Paul, where they provide degree programs in Old Testament, New Testament, History of Christianity, Christian Lay Ministry, and Family Ministry; also offered are Graduate Studies and Doctor of Ministry programs.

Macalester College
1600 Grand Avenue, St. Paul
(651) 696-6000
www.macalester.edu

Macalester College is a preeminent private liberal arts college. The college is respected locally and nationally for maintaining high academic standards and championing internationalism and multiculturalism. Macalester is also the recipient of enormous endowment monies, particularly from the DeWitt-Wallace fund, which helps underwrite the costs of tuition, through scholarships and other awards, for students of low socioeconomic status.

Macalester was founded in 1874 by the Reverend Dr. Edward Duffield Neill. A superintendent for Minnesota Territory Schools, Neill did not move the college to its present site until 1885. In its early years the college received significant financial support from philanthropist Charles Macalester, for whom the college was named.

Macalester College's diversity is reflected in the exceptional students it attracts from the nation and abroad. Nestled in the exquisite Macalester-Groveland neighborhood, the college creates an excellent learning environment. Macalester's demographics consistently have represented one of the most diverse schools of higher education in the nation. The college's enrollment was 1,795 full-time students in 2002, with 61 percent of the student body coming from outside the state of Minnesota and 15 percent international students.

More than 30 majors and minors are offered at Macalester, including Geography, Russian, and Classics, as well as African-American Studies, Women's and Gender Studies, Urban Studies, and several interdepartmental fields. A major area of focus at Macalester is the arts, particularly music and theater. Macalester hosts four or five theater productions a year. In addition, the college features extensive organized music groups, which include: Symphony Orchestra, Mac Jazz, New Music Ensemble, Festival Chorale, Flying Fingers (a traditional bluegrass group), the Electric Guitar, and several other diverse music organizations.

Metropolitan State University
700 East Seventh Street, St. Paul
(651) 772–7777
Minneapolis Campus
730 Hennepin Avenue, Minneapolis
(612) 341–7250
www.metrostate.edu

Metropolitan State University provides flexible and affordable education to non-traditional students in the Twin Cities. Convenience is emphasized in order to provide educational opportunities toward earning bachelor's and graduate degrees.

Metro State has served the Twin Cities since 1971. The university's original objective was to offer a program for working adults. This has remained Metro State's focus, though the university has broadened its objectives. In 1983 the first graduate program, Master of Management and Administration, was launched. Today Metro State's enrollment is approximately 8,500 annually and continues to support education of diverse and underserved student populations.

Metro State offers more than 30 majors. Most majors are training toward occupations, such as Accounting, Social Work, Law Enforcement, and Nursing. Metro State Accounting students frequently distinguish themselves by annually placing in the top 10 percent on the CPA exam.

Metro State campuses are conveniently located to facilitate greater academic success. The Dayton's Bluff neighborhood,

Metropolitan State University in St. Paul serves working adults from across the Metro. PHOTO: TODD R. BERGER

just outside downtown St. Paul, is the largest campus. Another campus is in the heart of downtown Minneapolis. In addition, Metro State has three smaller campuses strategically placed throughout the Twin Cities, which minimize the time students must spend getting to school and brings classes closer to their homes.

Musictech College
19 East Exchange Street, St. Paul
(651) 291-0177 or (800) 594-9500
www.musictech.com

Musictech began in 1985 as "the Guitar Center of the Twin Cities" but since its inception has rapidly expanded into other music-related fields. The school is now known as a "college of contemporary music and recording arts." Professional musicians, music technicians, and educators formed the school to serve the needs of the burgeoning local music scene. Classical and traditional music schools of higher learning were already established in the Twin Cities, but a formal school for studying popular and rock forms was strikingly absent—Musictech filled this gap. Students have many options for study at Musictech, such as guitar, bass, percussion, vocals, recording engineer, music theory, brass and woodwind, and music business. The programs confer Associate of Applied Science in Music degrees and diplomas. Musictech is a relatively recent addition to Twin Cities higher education, and it offers educational opportunity to one of the Twin Cities' greatest cultural resources—musicians.

Northwestern College
3003 Snelling Avenue North, St. Paul
(800) 827-6827
www.nwc.edu

Northwestern College is a nondenominational, conservative, private Christian college. In recent years Northwestern has undergone significant growth; for the 2002-2003 academic year enrollment was 2,480 students. Part of the growing enrollment is linked to the expansion of the adult degree completion program, Focus, and the Center for Distance Learning. Both are recently added programs at Northwestern, which is an important part of the college's history. Expanding and adding programs to meet students' needs is essential.

Northwestern College began as the Northwestern Bible and Missionary Training School in Minneapolis in 1902. Over time, educational and vocational opportunities have been greatly expanded, with the creation of the Northwest Theological Seminary in 1935 and the College of Liberal Arts founded in 1944. Then the college acquired a former Roman Catholic seminary in 1970; the large, wooded, gated campus was renovated and reopened as Northwestern College in 1972.

Christian doctrine is central to the educational mission at Northwestern College. Despite firm established Christian doctrines, students follow remarkably diverse faiths. For the 2000-2001 academic year, Northwestern had students representing 44 religious denominations. Unlike with many of the Twin Cities commuter campuses, 63 percent of students live on campus, and, reflecting current higher education trends, the college student body is composed of 61 percent women. Northwestern College offers a distinctly conservative Christian education option for Twin Citians.

St. Paul Technical College
235 Marshall Avenue, St. Paul
(651) 846-1500
www.saintpaul.edu

St. Paul Technical College (SPTC) is a remarkable educational institution. Foremost among its accomplishments is its astounding job placement statistics; consistently 90 to 100 percent of its students find positions in their field of study. Technically-trained employees are highly sought by Twin Cities employers. SPTC provides more than 50 occupational fields, which include formal trades such as Cabinet Making, Carpentry, and Auto Body Repair, as well as numerous medical and computer service occupations, e.g., Medical Laboratory Technician and Computer Programmer. Deaf Education is another prominent field of study at SPTC. SPTC offers an affordable education in numerous fields, and most importantly, they place students in frequently high-paying and rewarding trades on completion of their programs.

University of St. Thomas
2115 Summit Avenue, St. Paul
(651) 962–5000
www.stthomas.edu

In 1885 Archbishop John Ireland founded St. Thomas Aquinas Seminary. This higher education institution quickly grew beyond the bounds of its original purpose, as a high school, college, and seminary, with only two departments, Theology and Classics. However, the Twin Cities largest Catholic university was prepared to gradually expand into numerous other areas of study.

The first four-year baccalaureate degrees were conferred by then St. Thomas College in 1910, and the school received accreditation for the first time in 1916. The college increased its liberal arts emphasis and broadened its demographic in 1977, when it became coeducational and accepted women for the first time. After this enormous change, St. Thomas expanded at an accelerated pace. Today the school is composed of 54 percent undergraduate women, with more than 75 major fields available.

St. Thomas has evolved into a private Catholic university with a liberal arts emphasis. Traditional majors such as Theology, Latin, and Classical Languages have been retained, as well as more popular majors such as History, English, or Geography, plus recent majors like Justice and Peace Studies. The annual enrollment at St. Thomas is approximately 10,000 students. During the 2000–2001 school year, 4,915 students were undergraduates. Graduate programs and continuing education are two significant places for student enrollment. St. Thomas began offering graduate education and social work programs in 1996, plus its Business and Psychology graduate programs, as well as a proposed Law School.

Continuing education is another paramount focus at St. Thomas. Since New College opened in 1975, the needs of part-time, adult, and nontraditional students have been readily met with innovative methods, such as off-campus classes to make convening easier. The program changed its name to the School of Continuing Studies in

The historic campus of the University of St. Thomas in St. Paul. PHOTO: TODD R. BERGER

1998, to reflect its commitment to students following a nontraditional educational path.

St. Thomas boasts several campuses. The main campus is 78 acres approximately halfway between downtown Minneapolis and St. Paul, on the western edge of historic Summit Avenue, where St. Paul's old money resides. In addition, since 1992 the Graduate Department of Psychology, the School of Education, and the Graduate School of Business have called downtown Minneapolis home, in a beautiful state-of-the-art facility that is the envy of many larger educational institutions. St. Thomas also owns smaller campuses in out-state Owatonna and the Mall of America.

Student activities abound at St. Thomas. Both men and women have a large slate of intercollegiate sports, such as basketball, swimming, cross-country running, and men's and women's hockey. Besides sports, St. Thomas publishes a newspaper to serve the university community, the *Aquin*. The seminary also publishes *Catholic Digest*, a world-renowned Catholic magazine. The University of St. Thomas is a coeducational Catholic higher education institution that specializes in liberal arts education.

William Mitchell College of Law is one of three law schools in the Twin Cities. PHOTO: TODD R. BERGER

William Mitchell College of Law
875 Summit Avenue, St. Paul
(651) 227–9171 or (888) WMCL-LAW
www.wmitchell.edu

In 2000 William Mitchell College of Law celebrated its centennial as a legal educator. During this time the institution has had many different names, but the goal has remained the same: providing a quality legal education for recent college graduates or, more frequently, students returning to school after a long absence. Over the past century William Mitchell has offered a legal education for students strapped for time; in fact the institution began as a night school for people who could not give up the wages of their day jobs. William Mitchell College was prescient in creating a flexible schedule where nontraditional students could succeed, which is one of the

many reasons the school has shiningly persisted for a century.

William Mitchell is the only Twin Cities higher education institution solely dedicated to legal education. It began as the St. Paul College of Law in 1900, then in 1956 merged with the Minneapolis-Minnesota College of Law to form the William Mitchell College of Law (named after a 19th-century Minnesota Supreme Court Justice).

Alumni of William Mitchell are an important group in Twin Cities government and law. The school's most famous graduate is Supreme Court Chief Justice Warren E. Burger of St. Paul, who attended one of the four predecessor law schools of William Mitchell. The Warren

E. Burger Library was built in 1990 in his honor and is one of the finest law-school libraries in the nation.

North

Anoka-Ramsey Community College
11200 Mississippi Boulevard NW, Coon Rapids
(763) 427-2600
Cambridge Campus
300 Polk Street South, Cambridge
(763) 689-7000
www.an.cc.mn.us

Anoka-Ramsey Community College (ARCC) has served the north metropolitan Twin Cities since 1965. As the suburbs of Minneapolis and St. Paul have expanded, Anoka-Ramsey has grown to meet the area's needs. The college is part of the Minnesota State Colleges and Universities (MnSCU), which was established to guarantee a quality education.

After opening the first campus in Coon Rapids, presently one of the Twin Cities' fastest growing suburbs, they added the Cambridge Campus in 1978 and shrewdly anticipated an area that would undergo significant urbanization. The community college provides a post-secondary education for students of all ages.

Anoka-Ramsey's student demographics mirror many other area community colleges. Developed by the state colleges as a "feeder system" for four-year degrees, 54 percent of the student body intends on transferring to a four-year program, the average student is approximately 22 years old, and more than 90 percent work while attending ARCC. In addition, the student body is predominantly female, composed of 65 percent women and 35 percent men.

Numerous programs can be started, and in some cases completed, at Anoka–Ramsey. They range from Accounting, Art, Astronomy, Music, and Law Enforcement, to Spanish, Sociology, Mathematics, and Zoology. The community college offers Associate in Arts (AA) and Associate in Science (AS) degrees. Anoka–Ramsey is one of the many fine community colleges that serve the Twin Cities area.

Bethel College and Seminary
3900 Bethel Drive, Arden Hills
(651) 638-6400
www.bethel.edu

Bethel College offers a four-year liberal arts education with an evangelical Christian perspective. Approximately 2,700 students attend the college, nestled on 214 wooded acres on the shore of Lake Valentine.

The Baptist General Conference created Bethel Seminary in 1871. Preceding Bethel College was a secondary academy and a junior college, before the liberal arts college was formed in 1948. In recent years, Bethel has undergone significant expansion and even added master's programs in Nursing, Education, Communication, Counseling Psychology, and Organizational Leadership.

NEI College of Technology
825 41st Avenue NE, Columbia Heights
(763) 781-4881
www.neicollege.org

Since 1930 NEI College of Technology has provided education in electronics and related fields. During this time, the field of electronics has undergone revolutionary changes, as careers have disappeared and new ones have been created. NEI has kept up with these changes and its programs reflect it. Computer-related fields are important at NEI, a private nonprofit institution. Two general programs are offered: Electronics, the more hands-on field, and Information Management Systems, which is a more applied area of study. For those studying Electronics, there are several specialized areas offered at NEI: Computer Repair, Biomedical Electronics, Aviation Electronics, and Network Systems.

North Hennepin Community College
7411 85th Avenue North, Brooklyn Park
(763) 424-0702 or (800) 818-0395
www.nh.cc.mn.us

North Hennepin Community College (NHCC) serves the northern Twin Cities. The 80-acre campus has an annual enrollment of 8,000 students, with 3,000 full-time students. NHCC has many liberal arts programs, which earn credit toward bachelor degrees. Associate in Arts (AA) and Associate in Science (AS) are transferable to all Minnesota State Colleges and Universities (MnSCU) schools as well as the University of Minnesota. Also offered at NHCC are career-oriented programs, such as Nursing and Accounting, and professional development and enhancement classes. Continuing education is another important part of NHCC's mission; it is reflected in the 5,000 part-time students enrolled at the community college. Numerous classes are offered to enrich people's lives in the community.

NHCC has a vast array of clubs for student participation. Among the options available for student involvement is the student newspaper, as well as career-oriented clubs such as the Student Nurse Association and Business Leaders of America. NHCC provides educational opportunities tailored for all members of its community.

United Theological Seminary
3000 Fifth Street NW, New Brighton
(651) 633-4311
www.unitedseminary-mn.org

United Theological Seminary (UTS) is the Twin Cities' ecumenical theological school. More than 20 denominations are represented at UTS, where their mission is "To prepare women and men for effective ordained and lay leadership in church and society." Building bridges and creating worldwide Christian unity is the focus at UTS, where tolerance, empathy, and diversity are central to the seminary's educational program.

UTS's history is fairly brief in the Twin Cities, but its origins date back to two separate organizations outside the area in the 1860s. The seminary's antecedents are rooted in the Evangelical and Reformed Church Seminary of Plymouth, Wisconsin (founded in 1862), and the Yankton School of Theology, which began serving the German Congregational churches in South Dakota in 1869. Not until 1960 did the seminaries merge and form UTS.

A progressive theological education is provided at UTS. Instruction reflects recent developments in curriculum, and the educational experience at UTS emphasizes field learning as well as classroom study. Interdisciplinary perspectives are included within the curriculum of all fields at the seminary. Also of paramount importance to UTS is supporting students of diverse racial, ethnic, sexual orientation, and denominational traditions.

The programs offered at UTS include a variety of options for theology students. Programs for becoming ordained ministry, lay ministry, academic vocations, professional, and individual enrichment are offered. Degrees include conferred master's degrees in Divinity, Arts in Religion and Theology, Religious Leadership, and Women's Studies. Doctor in Ministry is also offered. There are also specialized programs, which are available at few other seminaries, including Indian Ministries, Rural Ministries, and Religion and Arts. United Theological Seminary is prepared to meet the challenges the church faces in the 21st century because it addresses diversity and issues important in contemporary society.

East

Century College
3300 Century Avenue North,
White Bear Lake
(651) 779-3300 or (800) 228-1978
www.century.mnscu.edu

Century College is dedicated to creating educational opportunity for its community in the east metropolitan Twin Cities. Students of all ages may attend the college based on their needs, whether to build a foundation for a four-year degree or solely for the joy of learning as a continuing-education student. There are classes to satisfy almost everyone's interest.

Century College was created when Lakewood Community College and Northeast Technical College merged in 1996. However, both institutions already had long histories serving the area. Since

1967 Lakewood has provided an inexpensive education for many students, who otherwise wouldn't have been able to afford it. Northeast Technical College has performed a similar function for students since its inception in 1968.

More than 60 technical and occupational programs are offered at Century College, as well as more than 100 degrees, certificates, and diplomas. Students with limited financial means may begin a four-year degree program in numerous subject areas, such as English, Geography, and Biology by earning Associate of Arts (AA) and Associate of Science (AS) degrees. When students complete their AA or AS and transfer to the University of Minnesota system or the Minnesota State Colleges and Universities (MnSCU), all credits are accepted toward a BA or BS.

Another important function of Century College is continuing education. Century College serves more continuing-education students than any other college in Minnesota, making up 55 percent of the student body. Century College is an important component of Twin Cities higher education.

Minnesota School of Business and Globe College
7166 10th Street North, Oakdale
(651) 730-5100
5910 Shingle Creek Parkway, Brooklyn Center
(763) 866-7777
1401 West 76th Street, Richfield
(612) 861-2200
1455 County Road 101 North, Plymouth
(612) 861-2000
www.globecollege.com

Minnesota School of Business has four Twin Cities campuses. There are also campuses in the northern suburb of Brooklyn Center, Richfield in the southern suburbs, and Plymouth, west of Minneapolis. At all locations Globe College offers a quick-track to many careers in business as well as technical fields. Also included are Accounting, Dental Assistant, Paralegal, Medical Assistant, Software Developer, and E-Commerce Design. There are many other career paths available at Globe College. Besides regular classroom instruction, Globe College offers distance education, which allows students to take classes on-line. Minnesota School of Business and Globe College provide excellent opportunities for students who quickly begin a career.

South

Argosy University
5503 Green Valley Drive, Bloomington
(952) 921-9500
www.argosyu.edu

Medicine is an important part of the Twin Cities economy, and Argosy University has the most comprehensive allied Health Care Associate programs in the area. Students can pick from numerous health care programs at MIM. Here are a few of the Associate degree programs available: Histotechnology, Radiologic Technology, Dental Hygiene, Medical Laboratory Technician, Veterinary Technology, and Radiation Therapy.

Brown College
1440 Northland Drive, Mendota Heights
(651) 905-3400
www.bi.careered.com

Brown College is an important local technical and trade school. The school boasts many graduates from its programs in local television and radio positions. Brown provides an education that employs its students in their fields of study. Since it opened in 1954, the range of programs at Brown has rapidly expanded.

Today Brown College has eight programs in fields as varied as Culinary Arts and Visual Communications. The Culinary Arts program was added in 1998 and is a member of Le Cordon Bleu French cooking school. Le Cordon Bleu began in Paris in 1895; since then, exclusive, limited culinary arts programs have been licensed by the institution. Brown College offers this august school, which prepares chefs for the Twin Cities restaurant scene. Another important program is the Department of Visual Communications, where students first develop traditional computer skills, which build from basics to advanced skills, such as computer animation and multimedia production. Also of note at Brown is the Radio and Television Broadcasting Program, where many local media technicians and producers have received their education. In addition, Brown has Digital Electronics and Computer Technology, Telecommunications, PC/LAN, and e-Commerce programs. Brown College has specialized programs important to the Twin Cities from modern computer high tech to culinary arts.

Inver Hills Community College
2500 East 80th Street, Inver Grove Heights
(651) 450-8500
www.ih.cc.mn.us

Inver Hills Community College fulfills the needs of students working toward a four-year degree, to improve job skills, or simply to explore subjects of personal interest. The community college is one of the many excellent two-year and continuing-education institutions in the Twin Cities and serves the south and east suburbs of St. Paul.

The community college offers numerous programs for degrees and certification. The Associate in Arts, or AA degree, is a popular stepping-stone toward receiving four-year degrees in more than 50 academic areas, which include Sociology, Economics and Nursing, as well as more uncommon major fields, such as Fish, Game, and Wildlife, and Public Health Education. Another important two-year degree is the Associate in Science, or AS, which is more career oriented (e.g., Accounting, Criminal Justice, Aviation, and Construction Management). The Associate in Applied Science is a two-year degree aimed at immediate employment upon completion, and includes Medical Secretary, Building Inspection, and Management/Marketing. Finally, Inver Hills offers several vocational certificates. The certificates qualify students for various vocations, or can be used to improve jobs already held. Many high demand technical degrees are available, especially computer-oriented programs, including Desktop Publishing, Medical-Office Systems, Computer Applications and many more. Inver Hills Community College

serves its community by providing programs that fit the needs of the area.

KRS Computer & Business School
5100 West 82nd Street, Bloomington
(952) 835-1410 or (877) 835-1410
www.gokrs.com

Computers and their relationship with business is an important nexus in the Twin Cities high-tech economy. KRS Computer & Business School specializes in educating students in these fields. Central to KRS's educational mission is finding employment for its students, especially since a significant portion of the student body attend the higher education institution to find more financially rewarding jobs.

The programs available at KRS prepare students for the business world. There are several Associate in Applied Science programs, such as A+ Certification and Windows Network Administration. In addition, KRS offers diplomas in Computerized Accounting, Office Administration, C++ with MCSD, and numerous other programs.

The facilities at KRS are state of the art, with 10,000 square feet of space divided into 100 classrooms. In the classrooms, there are on average 15 students or less, allowing for easy interaction between students and faculty. The omnipresent computer technology and unlimited student computer labs are available six days a week for student academic support. Twin Citians looking for a career in technical and business fields will find opportunities abound at KRS, which is "a Microsoft authorized academic training provider."

Normandale Community College
9700 France Avenue South, Bloomington
(952) 487-8210
www.normandale.mnscu.edu

Normandale Community College serves the needs of the southern Twin Cities by offering associate degrees, certification programs, and classes for personal enrichment. The community college is easily accessible from Interstate 494 and is located on a 90-acre site, complete with the beautiful Normandale Japanese Garden. Founded in 1968, the school has an enrollment of 7,000 students and is the largest community college in Minnesota. Normandale offers programs in numerous occupational fields, including Law Enforcement, Radiologic Technology, Hospitality Management, Dental Hygiene, and Computers/Information Management. Other popular programs include two-year liberal arts degrees.

Northwestern Health Sciences University
2501 West 84th Street, Bloomington
(952) 888–4777 or (800) 888–4777
www.nwhealth.edu

Northwestern Health Sciences University offers classes in a frequently overlooked portion of medicine: "natural approaches to health and health care." There are programs in Acupuncture and Herbal Studies, Professional Massage, Integrative Health and Wellness, and the College of Chiropractic. The university's origins are as a chiropractic school, but it has grown to include the aforementioned programs as well as graduate programs.

The university recently received accreditation for master's programs in Oriental Medicine and Professional Acupuncture. The Oriental Medicine program requires more than 3,000 hours of instruction over four years, with 200 hours' observation and greater than 600 hours' clinical practice. Not nearly as rigorous are undergraduate programs, which are approximately two years in duration. Programs are also offered for nontraditional and/or adult learners. All students must complete foundation, core, and clinical courses before completing their program. Another important activity before graduation is a "summary paper" about their field of study, written with the help of a faculty member. The summary paper develops students' analytical skills and requires reflection in their chosen field of study. As medical technology increases, Northwestern Health Sciences University's programs have experienced growing importance as ancillary adjuncts for medicine.

West

Rasmussen College
12450 Wayzata Boulevard, Minnetonka
(952) 545–2000 or (800) 852–0929
3500 Federal Drive, Eagan
(651) 687–9000 or (800) 852–6367
www.rasmussen.edu

Rasmussen College has been a two-year college for business and professional careers since 1900. During the past century, the college has expanded the number of programs available. Presently, there are nine majors. Students may chose from Information Technology, Accounting, Child Care Specialist, Medical Records, Restaurant Management, and other fields of study. The programs are flexible and allow students to expeditiously embark on new careers.

Students can determine the pace at which they want to complete their program—in as little as nine months or over the standard period of two years. Institutions like Rasmussen are essential to the Twin Cities economy, by quickly creating qualified employees for high-demand careers. The college has two convenient Twin Cities locations, Minnetonka, in the western suburbs, and Eagan, in the southern suburbs. In addition, Rasmussen College has campuses both north and south of the Twin Cities metropolitan area. Many things have changed in the past century, but some have stayed the same. Two-year degrees continue to lead to specific careers. Unlike in the past, the rapidly changing high-tech economy demands that the workforce change professions frequently and with easy transitions. Workers facing this conundrum, or recent high school graduates looking for a fast track to a career, can look to Rasmussen College, which provides these opportunities in high-demand career fields.

Health Care and Wellness

Minnesota has enjoyed a reputation for being a medical industry hub and site of health care innovation for decades, even before the founding of the world-famous Mayo Clinic and Medtronic, the company started by Earl Bakken, inventor of the first battery-operated external and internal heart pacemakers. Ironically, a good deal of this reputation came from rumors started by PR agents in territorial times, who were horrified to find that the rest of the country likened Minnesota to an American Siberia. With the hordes of health-challenged immigrants who moved to the state in the 1850s to 1870s to follow these claims of rejuvenation came doctors and scientists who were just as willing to test the healing powers of Minnesota's climate, including Dr. William W. Mayo, whose sons founded the Mayo Clinic in Rochester, and Dr. Brewer Mattocks, who wrote the highly partisan book *Minnesota as a Home for Invalids*.

Even today, Minnesota, especially the Twin Cities region, is a major force in the medical community. Fairview-University Medical Center in Minneapolis is world renowned for its innovations in the treatment of cancer and leukemia with bone marrow transplant therapy, and the Hazelden Foundation is one of the foremost addiction recovery centers in the country. North Memorial Health Care in Robbinsdale designed the I Can Cope cancer program adopted nationally by the American Cancer Society and is also the site for the first hospital-integrated emergency transportation system in Minnesota.

The medical industry is strong in the Twin Cities as well. Medvision, Urilogics, St. Croix Medical, St. Jude, and 3M are all regional medical supply manufacturers and research centers, providing hospitals and home patients with everything from artificial organs and life support systems to surgical gloves, heart catheter leads, and hearing aids.

Minnesota's health care system has been at the top of the field for many, many years. The strong emphasis on research that the Mayo Clinic started at the turn of the 20th century has been carried out all over the state, ensuring that hospitals in the Twin Cities and throughout Minnesota will continue to keep far ahead of the times.

Hospitals and Hospital Cooperatives

Abbott Northwestern Hospital
800 East 28th Street, Minneapolis
(612) 863-4000
www.abbottnorthwestern.com

Abbott and Northwestern hospitals were merged into the Abbott Northwestern Hospital Corporation in 1970, and in 1982 Abbott Northwestern's board of directors approved the creation of a new parent corporation, LifeSpan Inc. It was designed so that other hospitals and companies could join it in the future. LifeSpan originally included Abbott Northwestern Hospital, the Sister Kenny Institute, and Eitel Hospital. LifeSpan merged with Health One on March 1, 1993, to form HealthSpan Health

Systems Corporation, the second-largest not-for-profit secular health care system in the United States. Twin Cities metropolitan area hospitals involved in the merger were Abbott Northwestern in Minneapolis, United in St. Paul, Unity in Fridley, and Mercy in Coon Rapids. On December 7, 1993, the boards of directors of HealthSpan and Medica approved a letter of intent to merge the two organizations and form Allina Health System, a not-for-profit integrated health care system committed to enhancing the health status of the communities it serves. Allina owns or manages 17 hospitals, including Abbott Northwestern, two nursing homes, and clinics in more than 40 locations throughout Minnesota, Wisconsin, and North Dakota.

Abbott Northwestern Hospital has grown to become the Twin Cities' largest health care provider, with a tradition of compassionate care, outstanding service, and leadership in education and clinical research. The huge facility treats a wide range of health-related issues, from family practice to cosmetic medicine and surgery, cancer treatment, neuroscience, and behavioral studies.

Children's Hospitals and Clinics
Children's-Minneapolis, 2525 Chicago Avenue South, Minneapolis
(612) 813–6100
Children's-St. Paul, 345 North Smith Avenue, St. Paul
(651) 220–6000
Children's-West, 6050 Clearwater Drive, Minnetonka
(952) 930–8600
Children's-Ridges, Fairview Ridges Hospital, 201 East Nicollet Boulevard, Burnsville
(952) 892–2202
Children's-Roseville, Twin Lakes Health, 1835 West County Road C, Roseville
(651) 638–1670
Children's Clinics-Woodwinds, 1875 Woodwinds Drive, Woodbury
(651) 232–6800
Children's-St. Francis, St. Francis Regional Medical Center, 1455 St. Francis Avenue, Shakopee
(952) 403–3360
www.childrenshc.org

Children's Hospitals and Clinics was created by the merger of the children's hospitals in St. Paul and Minneapolis. With 268 staffed hospital beds at their main Minneapolis and St. Paul campuses, they are the largest children's health care organization in the upper Midwest with services available in all major pediatric specialties.

Comfort is an important facet of each Children's Hospitals facility. Each child's room has a VCR, television, and radio. Videos are available for checkout, and a computer on a rolling cart, stocked with CD-ROM games, can also be brought into your child's room. Many rooms feature built-in beds for a parent to sleep in. A handicapped-accessible garden of sculptures, flowers, and wild plants soothes visitors and provides a place to eat, relax, and play. Several floors of the hospital have decks with lawn furniture and grills. Playrooms full of toys, colorful play structures, art supplies, and games are on each floor of the hospitals. Playrooms are the center of activities, including cooking, movie days, visits from zoo animals, and bingo. Special efforts are also made to accommodate children who need to stay in their rooms.

Children who are away from school 15 consecutive school days or longer can continue their studies with a teacher from the St. Paul public school system. Sessions are limited to one 50-minute session per day. You will be asked to sign an authorization form to permit your child to participate in the school program. The child life special-

> **Insiders' Tip**
> For health questions while in Minneapolis, call the Hennepin County Health Department at (612) 347-4747. In St. Paul call the St. Paul-Ramsey County Health Department at (651) 266-1200.

ist will communicate your child's needs to the hospital-based schoolteacher.

Fairview Health Services
Fairview-University Medical Center,
Riverside Campus, 2540 Riverside Avenue,
Minneapolis
(612) 273-6000
Fairview-University Medical Center,
University Campus, 420 Delaware Street SE,
Minneapolis
(612) 273-3000
Fairview Southdale Hospital,
6401 France Avenue South, Edina
(952) 924-5000
Fairview Ridges Hospital
201 Nicollet Boulevard, Burnsville
(952) 892-2000
www.fairview.org

Established in 1965, Fairview Southdale's 390-bed facility offers a wide range of health services and advanced medical technology.

The hospital specializes in maternal and newborn care, cardiac care, oncology, mental health treatment, eye care, vascular, spine, neurology, neurosurgery, urology, orthopedic surgery, and joint replacement. On an outpatient basis, they offer a comprehensive 24-hour emergency department, urgent care for evenings and weekends, diagnostic radiology and imaging, and a same-day surgery center. They also offer a wide selection of health education and wellness programs at the hospital and in community settings. They believe that offering the finest in health care includes addressing the physical, emotional, and spiritual needs of their patients and their families.

Fairview-University Medical Center partners with the internationally renowned University of Minnesota's Organ Transplant and Blood and Marrow Transplant research programs. Fairview-University Medical Center also provides clinical services to the world's oldest and second-largest blood and marrow transplant program. Transplants here, along with cutting-edge technology and research at the university's nationally recognized Cancer Center, have improved survival rates of patients with cancer and diseases of the immune system.

Fairview-University Medical Center's program is one of the largest pediatric blood and marrow transplant centers in the world, one of the first unrelated-donor transplant centers, and a world leader in the field of hematopoietic stem cell transplantation to treat metabolic disorders.

Hennepin County Medical Center
701 Park Avenue, Minneapolis
(612) 347-2121
www.hcmc.org

Hennepin County Medical Center (HCMC) is a public teaching hospital in downtown Minneapolis owned and operated by Hennepin County, governed by the seven-member Hennepin County Board of Commissioners, and affiliated with the University of Minnesota Medical School. HCMC is the centerpiece of Hennepin County's health services system, which includes the HMO Metropolitan Health Plan, the physician group practice Hennepin Faculty Associates, and a network of community clinics. HCMC is home to a variety of research departments and provides specialized and general medical care, often through hospital referrals.

The Minneapolis Medical Research Foundation is the third-largest nonprofit medical research organization in Minnesota. The MMRF was founded by a group of concerned physicians and citizens 45 years ago at Minneapolis General Hospital (now HCMC). The MMRF has a long history of innovative research resulting in clinical breakthroughs, such as the world's first dual lung transplant, the Midwest's first kidney transplant, and Minnesota's first blood dialysis. It continues to serve the citizens of Hennepin County through its 14 designated programs: Alternative Medicine, Brain and Immune Disorders, Cancer Center, Children's Hunger and Growth, Diabetes and Obesity, Heart Disease, HIV/AIDS, Kidney Research, Berman Center for Clinical Outcomes, Sleep Disorders, Smoking Prevention, Trauma/Shock/Sepsis, Traumatic Brain Injury, and Women's Health.

Because HCMC serves many patients from the Native American community, an Indian Health Advocate is available to ensure that the special needs or cultural preferences of Native American patients are treated with sensitivity and respect, and that both American Indian health practices and Western medicine can be brought to the care of the patient.

Mayo Clinic Rochester
200 First Street SW, Rochester
(507) 284-2511
www.mayoclinic.org/rochester

The world-famous Mayo Clinic has been a pioneer in medical research and disease treatment for more than a century, and, while it is located almost 90 miles south of the Twin Cities, the very existence of the hospital is one of the reasons there is such a strong medical community in Minnesota. Mayo Clinic Rochester, the original Mayo Clinic, began its research program in 1901, when Dr. Henry Plummer joined the Mayo Clinic as the fourth partner and urged the two Drs. Mayo to invest as much time in research as they did in treatment. This course of action led to some incredibly revolutionary discoveries that changed the face of medicine, including developing a method for staining fresh-frozen tissue from surgical specimens so that they could be studied under a microscope for diagnostic purposes; the isolation of thyroxin, a system for grading cancer (created in 1920) that is still used all over the world today; and the creation of the Sheard-Sanford Photelometer photoelectric eye, the BLB mask for high-altitude pilots, the

leprosy and tuberculosis suppressant Promin, the first human centrifuge, Cortisone, and the Gibbon Pump. The Mayo Clinic Rochester was also the site for some of the earliest successful heart transplants and open-heart surgeries.

Today more than 2,000 physicians and 35,000 allied health staff work in the Mayo system, treating nearly half a million patients annually. Their specialties include (but are far from being limited to) cancer treatment, dermatology, diagnostic radiology, Native American studies and medicine, internal medicine, cardiovascular disease treatment, allergy studies and treatment, plastic surgery, HIV study, and general practice/family medicine.

Mercy Hospital
4050 Coon Rapids Boulevard, Coon Rapids
(763) 236-6000
Unity Hospital
550 Osborne Road, Fridley
(763) 236-5000
www.mercy-unity.com

Mercy and Unity Hospitals are nonprofit hospitals that have been serving the northern Minneapolis-St. Paul metropolitan area for many decades. Together, Mercy and Unity are dedicated to providing cost-effective, quality healthcare to the more than 250,000 households in the neighboring 26 communities and nearby out-of-state towns. Mercy and Unity Hospitals are affiliated with Allina Health System, the largest integrated health care system in Minnesota.

Mercy Hospital is located in Coon Rapids, and Unity Hospital is located in Fridley. The hospitals function as virtually one entity, with shared resources to help ensure quality, cost-effective care. Mercy and Unity respond to a wide range of health care needs with specialty services including Behavioral Health, Cardiac, Emergency, Family Centered Care, Oncology, and Orthopedics/Neurosciences. The hospitals also offer medical transportation, health education, and support groups. In addition, Mercy Hospital provides specialized services for senior citizens, such as

Meals on Wheels, Hot Meals for Shut-ins, and the Senior Identification Program.

North Memorial Medical Center
3300 Oakdale Avenue North, Robbinsdale
(763) 520–5200
www.northmemorial.com

Located in the northwestern Twin Cities suburb of Robbinsdale, the independently owned North Memorial is a familiar face in an always-changing health care community. North Memorial's history of responding to the health care needs of its communities has lasted for more than four decades and continues to be the main ingredient to its success.

North Memorial's early leadership in emergency care was one of the factors that led to its being the successful emergency and trauma services center it is today. The first totally integrated hospital-based medical transportation system in the state of Minnesota began at North Memorial, which now includes two helicopters, 100 ambulances, and 575 employees. North Memorial also founded the I Can Cope cancer education program that is now used in hospitals throughout the country and by the American Cancer Society.

St. Francis Regional Medical Center
SouthValley Health Campus, 1455 St. Francis Avenue, Shakopee
(952) 403–3000

Founded in 1938 by five Franciscan Sisters, St. Francis Regional Medical Center is jointly sponsored by the Benedictine Health System and Allina Hospitals and Clinics. St. Francis has also developed a strong presence in Shakopee by working in close harmony with area primary care physicians, including Crossroads Medical Center, Valley Family Practice, Jonathan Clinic, Spinal Designs International, and Orthopedic Medicine & Surgery Ltd. The Medical Center has 63 private rooms and a Family Birth floor with 14 rooms, as well as the St. Francis Cancer Center, St. Francis Breast Care Center, Children's-St. Francis Pediatric Unit (affiliated with Children's Hospitals and Clinics), St. Francis Rehabilitation and Sports Medicine, St. Francis Health Services, and several primary and specialty clinics.

St. Joseph's Hospital
69 West Exchange Street, St. Paul
(651) 232–3000

The first hospital in Minnesota, St. Joseph's was founded by the Sisters of St. Joseph of Carondelet in 1853. Today the downtown St. Paul Catholic hospital serves patients in the eastern Metro, with specialties in heart care, cancer care, mental health and chemical dependency treatment, and maternity care. St. Joseph's operates a 24-hour emergency room and comprehensive services for inpatient care. The hospital has been a member of the HealthEast Care System since 1987, which operates several hospitals, clinics, and rehabilitation centers throughout the eastern Metro. The respect and compassion routinely shown by staff members at the hospital reflects the vision of the founders of this historic hospital.

United Hospital
333 North Smith Avenue, St. Paul
(651) 220–8000

United Hospital is a premier acute care medical facility in St. Paul. A part of the Allina Health System, United has 572 beds, offers staffing privileges to more than 1,000 physicians, and employs more than 3,000 professionals. The hospital facilities include a Birth Center, a Pain Center, the Nasseff Heart Hospital, and a Center for Breast Care; the hospital specializes in behavioral health studies and treatment, emergency care, heart/lung medicine, oncology, rehabilitation services, and surgery.

United Hospital is St. Paul's largest private not-for-profit hospital and a premier health care provider. In 1994 and 1995 United was selected one of the top 100 hospitals in the United States.

Saint Joseph's Hospital in downtown St. Paul is the oldest hospital in Minnesota. PHOTO: TODD R. BERGER

Rehabilitation Centers

Hazelden Foundation and Renewal Center
15245 Pleasant Valley Road, Center City
(651) 213–4000 or (800) 257–7800
www.hazelden.org

Hazelden has a history spanning more than 50 years of pioneering leadership in the care of chemically dependent people and their families. It is internationally recognized for its broad spectrum of interrelated services and continuum of care, which includes assessment and rehabilitation for adolescents and adults, aftercare and family services, renewal services, extended care and continuing care, professional development, counselor training, and clergy training and counseling. A nonprofit organization dedicated to helping people recover from alcoholism and other drug addiction by providing residential and outpatient treatment for adults and young people, Hazelden offers programs for families affected by chemical dependency as well as training for a variety of professionals. Hazelden is also known as the world's premier publisher of information on chemical addiction and related areas.

New Beginnings
190 North Shore Drive, Waverly
(763) 658–5800 or (800) 487–8758
www.newbeginningsatwaverly.com

New Beginnings is nationally recognized for its treatment of alcohol, cocaine, methamphetamine, and other drug dependencies, providing intensive and individualized treatment programs for adults and adolescents. New Beginnings offers a unique treatment environment. Located on several acres of private wooded lakeshore property in the converted summer home of former Vice President Hubert H. Humphrey, away from the noise and tension of urban life, the program components are designed to help men and women overcome the physical, emotional, spiritual, behavioral, and social aspects of addiction. New Beginnings programs were founded on the belief that people who are suffering from addiction deserve treatment that is specifically designed for them.

New Beginnings at Waverly offers intensive individualized treatment programs that include residential and outpatient levels of care. All dimensions of addiction are addressed under the principle that successful treatment demands the efforts of an interdisciplinary team that includes the patient, family, clinicians, and other professionals.

HMOs

HealthPartners
8600 Nicollet Avenue South, Bloomington
(952) 886–7000
www.healthpartners.com

HealthPartners Medical Group is one of Minnesota's largest medical groups, with more than 570 physicians practicing in primary care and in 35 medical and surgical specialties. HealthPartners and its related organizations provide health care services, insurance, and HMO coverage to nearly 650,000 members at its facilities throughout Minnesota, which include the Health-Partners Medical Group and Clinics, RiverWay Clinics, HealthPartners Central Minnesota Clinics, HealthPartners Dental Group and Clinics, Regions Hospital, Regions Hospital Foundation, HealthPartners Research Foundation, HealthPartners Institute for Medical Education, and Group Health, Inc. To provide even greater access to health care services and facilities across the state, HealthPartners has developed long-term contractual relationships with 70 medical groups at more than 700 sites. These other providers share Health-Partners' commitment to managing care effectively, beginning with prevention and primary care.

HealthPartners Dental Group is a group practice of more than 55 dentists, including specialists in oral surgery, periodontics, endodontics, prosthodontics, and pediatric dentistry. The HealthPartners Dental Group provides both prepaid and fee-for-service dental and oral-care services in 17 HealthPartners dental clinics. In addition to the HealthPartners Dental Group, HealthPartners has developed contractual relationships with Park Dental, the Premier Dental Group, and many independent dental offices. For many enrollees, this provides a choice of more than 900 general and specialty den-

tal providers across the state of Minnesota or in adjoining states.

Special Clinics

HealthEast Wound Care
Bethesda Rehabilitation Hospital,
559 Capitol Boulevard, St. Paul
(651) 232–2500

HealthEast Wound Care is a comprehensive outpatient program that treats patients with chronic, nonhealing wounds caused by diabetes, vascular disease, pressure, or trauma. Wounds or sores that are located on the legs or feet need quick attention to ensure fast and proper healing. HealthEast Wound Care provides treatment with specialized doctors and nurses, who use the latest technology in wound healing. Positive outcomes have exceeded 90 percent for patients visiting HealthEast Wound Care.

Phillips Eye Institute
2215 Park Avenue, Minneapolis
(612) 336–6000

Phillips Eye Institute is a premier specialty center devoted exclusively to the diagnosis, treatment, and care of eye disorders and diseases. Located in Minneapolis, the institute is a unique facility that has integrated the latest technologies available in eye care with unprecedented staff expertise. Phillips Eye was originally designed to function as a freestanding eye specialty

---

Insiders' Tip

The Minnesota Traveler Resource Line at (612) 676-5588 can direct travelers to health care facilities as well as information about out-of-state insurance coverage.

center associated with Mount Sinai Medical Center and was named for Mount Sinai's largest benefactor, Jay Phillips.

Nearly 8,000 patients a year visit the institute for refractive surgery (LASIK), vision rehabilitation, and other inpatient services. The institute also has an established Pediatric Ophthalmology department for its younger patients.

Health Associations

Alzheimer's Association
(952) 830–0512 or (800) 232–0851

American Cancer Society
Minneapolis (612) 925–2772
St. Paul (651) 644–1224

American Diabetes Association
(763) 593–5333

American Heart Association
(952) 835–3300 or (800) 242–8721

American Lung Association of Minnesota
Minneapolis (952) 835–3300
St. Paul (651) 227–8014

American Parkinson's Disease Association
(800) 908–2732

American Red Cross
(651) 291–6789

Arthritis Foundation of St. Paul
(651) 644–4108

United Way
Minneapolis (612) 340–7400
St. Paul (651) 291–8300

Counseling

Catholic Charities, Archdiocese of St. Paul and Minneapolis
(612) 664–8500

Jewish Family and Children's Service
(952) 546–0616

Lutheran Social Services of Minneapolis
(612) 871–0221

Media

A good way to familiarize yourself with a new city is to head down to the local newsstand and pick up a newspaper. Visitors to the Twin Cities will be surprised to find out exactly how much free literature is available to newcomers, offering information on everything from arts and entertainment to fringe politics, as well as two major local daily newspapers. The scope of print media in the Twin Cities is especially vibrant and, in a time when the majority of television and radio stations are run by nationally based corporations, is an invaluable source of local-specific information to both travelers and residents alike.

Daily Newspapers

St. Paul Pioneer Press
345 Cedar Street, St. Paul
(651) 222–5011 or (800) 950–9080
www.twincities.com/mld/pioneerpress

The *St. Paul Pioneer Press* is Minnesota's oldest newspaper, founded as the *Minnesota Pioneer* in 1849. The original *Pioneer* merged with the *St. Paul Press* in 1861, and in 1909 the *Pioneer Press* was acquired by the *St. Paul Dispatch*. They operated together for the next eight decades, with the *Dispatch* publishing in the afternoon and the *Pioneer Press* in the morning. The paper was acquired by the Ridder family in 1927 and, in 1974, Knight Ridder. The *Pioneer Press* and the *Dispatch* were combined into a single all-day newspaper in 1985 as the *Pioneer Press Dispatch* The "Dispatch"

The St. Paul Pioneer Press *is one of two major dailies in the Twin Cities.* PHOTO: TODD R. BERGER

was dropped when the afternoon publication ceased in 1990.

Today the paper is known as being on the cutting edge of news journalism. Winning three Pulitzer Prizes, including one for breaking the Gopher basketball scandal, the paper was named one of the nation's Top 20 Sunday sports sections in 1998. The newspaper retains bureaus in Washington, D.C., and at the State Capitol in St. Paul. It also has a North Metro bureau in Shoreview, a Metro West bureau in Minneapolis, and a Wisconsin bureau in Hudson, Wisconsin. While it has a smaller readership and distribution than Minneapolis's *StarTribune*, it has arguably just as good coverage of the area and is only 25 cents on weekdays and $1.00 on Sunday as opposed to the *StarTribune's* 50 cent daily price tag and $1.75 on Sunday.

StarTribune
425 Portland Avenue, Minneapolis
(612) 673-4000
www.startribune.com

Since 1867, the *StarTribune* has been a part of the Twin Cities community with an outstanding newspaper that's read by 1.5 million people each week and an on-line network of services that has become the region's preferred source for on-line information. Originally composed of four different Minneapolis papers: the *Minneapolis Tribune*, the *Minneapolis Times*, the *Minneapolis Daily Star*, and the *Minneapolis Journal*, the papers merged in 1941 when the Cowles family purchased the *Tribune*. In 1998 Cowles Media Company merged with McClatchy Newspapers, a family-owned company with roots in the newspaper business since 1858. The new organization is called the McClatchy Company, of which The Star Tribune Company is a subsidiary.

Bigger than the *Pioneer Press*, especially in the Employment/Job Search and Business sections, the *StarTribune* is considered the leading area paper in sports coverage as well. Their main sportswriter, Sid Hartman, is considered the ultimate "homer"—that is, a Twin Cities–biased booster sportswriter—and has been with the paper for so long that staffers joke he was there when the first issue hit the streets.

Magazines

Minnesota Monthly
600 U.S. Trust Building, 730 Second Avenue South, Minneapolis
(612) 371-5800 or (800) 933-4398
www.minnesotamonthly.com

Full of interviews with local political figures and celebrities, restaurant reviews, and a variety of features ranging from controversial reports on small town sexual harassment suits to staying healthy longer, *Minnesota Monthly* is a vibrant publication that showcases all the facets of Minnesota and its people. A monthly publication, it can be bought at most magazine racks and bookstores in the Twin Cities. *Midwest Home and Garden* and *Minnesota B&Bs* are also published by Minnesota Monthly Publications. The former is full of recipes, garden secrets, and interior designing tips; the latter features reviews of B&Bs from around the state as well as interviews with their owners.

Mpls/St. Paul Magazine
MSP Communications
220 South Sixth Street, Suite 500, Minneapolis
(612) 339-7571

For nearly 30 years, *Mpls/St. Paul Magazine* has been providing readers with up-to-date information on Twin Cities events and dining, as well as features on local celebrities and important members of the community. The magazine also runs travel articles, lodging information outside the metro area, and universally pertinent features concerning health, beauty, child-rearing tips, and everything in between.

Utne Magazine
1624 Harmon Place, Minneapolis
(612) 338-5040
www.utne.com

Utne is a nationally distributed monthly magazine that reprints articles from thousands of alternative media sources, providing interesting perspectives on current events, environmental issues, lifestyles, politics, books, and the arts. The magazine hosts a popular on-line discussion room, Cafe Utne (accessible through the magazine's Web site), with postings about many of the topics the magazine covers.

Other Publications

Business

Twin Cities Business Monthly
MSP Communications
220 South Sixth Street, Suite 500, Minneapolis
(612) 339–7571
www.mspcommunications.com/pubs/tcbm
Twin Cities Business Monthly, published by the same company that publishes *Mpls/St. Paul Magazine*, includes profiles of successful businesspeople and companies in the metropolitan area and information about business education, technology, and other topics of interest to business-oriented readers.

Ethnic Community

Asian American Press
417 University Avenue, St. Paul
(651) 224–6570
www.aapress.com
Not only does *Asian American Press* cover news of interest to Asian Americans in the Twin Cities region but it also provides excellent coverage of international news geared to the Asian population, from local business profiles to politics to festival information (local and other) to the struggles new immigrants have adjusting to life in a new country.

The Circle Newspaper
3355 36th Avenue South, Minneapolis
(612) 722–3686
www.thecirclenews.org
Approximately 25,000 Native Americans from various tribes live in the Twin Cities, and *The Circle* monthly newspaper is dedi-

cated to publishing news, arts information, community calendars, and resource information for Native Americans in the region.

Gente de Minnesota
Latino Communications Network
2019 East Lake Street, Suite 7, Minneapolis
(612) 729–5900
www.latinocom.net
Published in Spanish, *Gente de Minnesota* is a weekly newspaper that serves the Hispanic population of the Twin Cities with local, national, and international news, as well as sports, entertainment, and Spanish-language TV program listings.

Hmong Times
379 University Avenue West, St. Paul
(651) 224–9395 or (800) 229–9577
www.hmongtimes.com
With some 70,000 Hmong residents, the Twin Cities have the largest population of Hmong of any urban area in the world. The community is served by the English-language *Hmong Times*, with news, community information, religion, sports, and agriculture coverage. Published twice a month, the newspaper reaches a wide audience among the community, which began settling in Minnesota after the Vietnam War.

Family Papers

Family Times
P.O. Box 16422, St. Louis Park
(952) 922–6186
Voted best specialty publication in America for three years running, *Family Times* truly is geared to the entire family. News about children and senior events alike is listed here, as well as wellness information for everyone in the family. There's an extensive theater section in the back as well as a decent calendar of events for all members of the family.

Good Age
570 Ashbury Street, Suite 305, St. Paul
(651) 917–1212
www.wilder.org/goodage

This senior-oriented monthly publication contains more than 40 pages of information on health care issues and developments dealing with medical expenses, support groups, and nursing homes, as well as lots of advice and tips on how to stay at your peak physical and mental shape for as long as possible. There's also information on less age-specific things like filing taxes and shopping for a new house.

Minnesota Parent
1750 Yankee Doodle Road, Suite 108, Eagan
(651) 454–5145
www.parenthoodweb.com

Presenting itself both as a support group and a how-to guide to parenting, *Minnesota Parent* contains information on essentials like enrolling your children in school to helping them survive a divorce. The greatest part of this magazine, however, is the exhaustive calendar of events in the back, containing times, prices, and contact info for just about every museum and park in town.

The *Minnesota Women's Press*
771 Raymond Avenue, St. Paul
(651) 646–3968
www.womenspress.com

The biweekly print flagship of Minnesota's Feminist Voices, the *Minnesota Women's Press* provides a very fair and open-minded view of women in politics and feminist issues that affect women and

men alike, as well as profiles and interviews with political personalities and prominent women in the Twin Cities. The publication is extremely well written by members and volunteers of MFV as well as outside contributors, many of them prominent businesswomen and writers from the area.

Senior Times
P.O. Box 16422, St. Louis Park
(763) 541–9363

The sister publication of *Family Times*, the award-winning *Senior Times* is specifically geared toward the senior community. The paper is full of news about living on your own and adjusting to retirement, as well as tons of information about senior events and activities around the Twin Cities and surrounding communities.

Food and Entertainment

Buon Gusto
P.O. Box 65147, St. Paul

This is a fun little food-related publication that's released bimonthly and carried at most gourmet grocery stores and some restaurants. Covering everything from haute cuisine to Minnesota hot dishes and carrying many interviews with local chefs and restaurant owners as well as reviews of local cooking supply stores, this newsletter has information for the weekend cook and professional alike. It also has a lot of really great recipes, usually about six in every issue.

City Pages
401 North Third Street, Suite 550, Minneapolis
(612) 375–1015
www.citypages.com

Since the '70s, when it was called *Sweet Potato*, *City Pages* has been consistently providing great coverage of local politics, music events, and Twin Cities culture in general. The weekly calendar and A-List deliver the best information on what to do with your spare time, whether it be catching a lecture at the university or seeing a show at your neighborhood coffeehouse,

---

Insiders' Tip
Pick up a copy of *City Pages* or *Pulse*... of the *Twin Cities* to get an idea of what's happening in town— both weeklies have a good calendar of entertainment events in both cities.

while the interviews with notable Minnesotan artists and musicians are both entertaining and informative. The restaurant reviews are also worth noting, serving up the good and not-so-good news about area eateries.

Lavender
2344 Nicollet Avenue, Suite 300, Minneapolis
(612) 871–2237 or (877) 515–9969
www.lavendermagazine.com

The best known of the local gay and lesbian publications, *Lavender* is a 90-plus-page glossy publication containing interviews, features, events calendars, and book and music reviews of interest to the gay, lesbian, and transgendered population. Published biweekly, it's carried in record stores, coffee shops, and bars throughout the Twin Cities.

Pulse . . . of the Twin Cities
3200 Chicago Avenue South, Minneapolis
(612) 824–0000
www.pulsetc.com

Founded in 1996, the *Pulse...* provides decent coverage of music, art, and film community activity happening throughout the Twin Cities, as well as many controversial political feature stories. Available at most convenience stores and alternative media venues in the area, *Pulse...* officially hits the streets every Wednesday, although slow press dates sometimes keep it from actually being available until later in the week.

Rain Taxi Review of Books
P.O. Box 3840, Minneapolis
www.raintaxi.com

Distributed nationally, this quarterly publication contains tons of book reviews (all genres) as well as interviews with established and up-and-coming authors from around the world.

Skyway News
3225 Lyndale Avenue South, Minneapolis
(612) 825–9205
www.skywaynews.net

Another free weekly newspaper distributed throughout the Twin Cities, *Skyway News* provides information on local politics and events, interviews with local and national celebrities, a calendar of art and music events, and a decent map of the skyway system of downtown Minneapolis.

Twin Cities Blues News
P.O. Box 65671, St. Paul

Full of information about new blues recordings, blues acts coming to town, and reviews of regional blues festivals, this publication contains some of the more interesting music interviews in town with both old and new bluesmen (and women). Released monthly and carried in record stores and coffee shops throughout the area, this is full of essential blues info to even the most casual of enthusiasts.

Health, Religion, and Support Publications

Catholic Digest
2115 Summit Avenue, St. Paul
(651) 962–6725
www.catholicdigest.org

This 60-plus-year-old national magazine, published by the University of St. Thomas in St. Paul, aims to provide more than two million readers of all ages the tools and motivation to lead happier, more successful, and more fulfilling lives. Featuring articles ranging from health, psychology, humor, adventure, and family to ethics, spirituality, and Catholic heritage, the magazine also runs articles about and interviews with "successful" Catholics, from saints through the ages to modern-day heroes.

The Edge
Leap Productions
14590 Bowers Drive NW, Ramsey
(763) 427–7979
www.edgenews.com

Falling somewhere between being a New Age and Christian publication, *The Edge* contains articles about miracles and biblical prophesies and articles about how they've been fulfilled—reincarnation, faith healing, and archeological excavations that may or may not prove the existence of

God. The paper is distributed throughout most of the Midwest during the first week of every month and is carried at most bookstores in the Twin Cities.

Fate Magazine and New Worlds of Mind & Spirit
P.O. Box 64383, St. Paul
(651) 291–1970

Both publications are out of St. Paul's Llewellyn Press, which is the nation's biggest publisher of New Age and spiritual books, tarot cards, and Wicca-related material. *Fate Magazine* is a nationally distributed publication with news about retreats, interviews with high-profile members of the New Age community, and articles about breakthroughs in natural healing therapies. *New Worlds of Mind & Spirit* is a free and mostly locally distributed publication containing book and music reviews, horoscopes, and one or two features about Wiccan holidays and the Pagan lifestyle.

The Phoenix
7152 Unity Avenue North, Brooklyn Center
(763) 560–5199
www.phoenixrecovery.org

This monthly publication is full of features written by recovering alcoholics and drug addicts struggling to stay clean and sober. It's very well written and a valuable support source for those in recovery or trying to take that next step into recovery.

Wellness
P.O. Box 897, Stillwater
(715) 259–3385
www.tcwellness.com

This monthly paper is an excellent source of information about alternative healing techniques, breakthroughs in homeopathic and alternative medicines, and features written by practitioners of alternative medicine. There's also a lot of information on where to find alternative and homeopathic doctors and treatment centers in the Twin Cities area, from massage therapists to herbal venders.

Neighborhood Free Publications

Almost every neighborhood in the Twin Cities has a free paper that can either be found in neighborhood convenience stores or is sent directly to your residential mailbox. These papers cover local news, school district announcements, flea market schedules, city council efforts on the part of the district in question, and sometimes, like in the *Villager*, news that affects the entire city. Here are just a few listings of neighborhood papers and the areas they cover:

Northeaster—Northeast Minneapolis
Southwest Journal—Southwest Minneapolis
Southeast Angle—Southeast Minneapolis
The Villager—St. Paul, Highland Park area
The Riverview Times—Harriet Island St. Paul riverside community
Midway/Como Monitor—St. Paul Como Park area
Grand Gazette—St. Paul Summit Hill/ Grand Avenue area
Seward Profile—Minneapolis, Seward/ Cedar-Riverside/Cooper/North Longfellow neighborhoods

Sports

Minnesota Motorcycle Monthly
3604 Orchard Avenue North, Robbinsdale
(763) 521–8313
www.motorbyte.com/mmm

This publication contains everything from reviews of new motorcycle gear to motorcycle vacation tips to full-length travel logs contributed by readers and staff writers. Check out the anti–Harley Davidson "Geezer with a Grudge" column for some really scintillating insight into the mind of a longtime motorcycle owner.

Twin Cities Sports Magazine
3009 Holmes Avenue South, Minneapolis
(612) 825–1034
www.twincitiessports.com

This monthly free magazine covers all aspects of personal sports in the Metro, with features on such things as in-line skating at the Metrodome, profiles of athletes, and a very detailed calendar of events. The magazine can be found at many restaurants, bars, grocery stores, and bookstores in the Twin Cities.

Radio Stations

AM Stations

KFAN–1130 AM
7900 Xerxes Avenue South, #102, Minneapolis
(651) 989–1130
www.kfan.com

KFAN is the Twin Cities sports radio leader. The Fan features interesting sports talk and occasional discussions about current affairs. The talk personalities on KFAN are the station's strength. Morning drive host Dan Cole, "the Common Man," is a seasoned veteran of local talk, who offers an offbeat look at various topics. The Fan is also the radio home of the Minnesota Timberwolves basketball games.

KKMS–980 AM
2110 Cliff Road, Eagan
(651) 405–8800

KKMS is a Christian talk radio station owned by Salem Communications It features the Salem Radio Network and Family News in Focus. In addition, KKMS, oddly enough, broadcasts St. Paul Saints baseball coverage, which, despite their name, is a secular organization.

KLBB–1400/KLBP–1470 AM
331 South 11th Street, Minneapolis
(612) 321–7200

KLBB or Club 14 is the Twin Cities big band jazz, vocal jazz, and easy listening station. On a regular basis Club 14 spins Benny Goodman, the Mills Brothers, Frank Sinatra, Artie Shaw, and much more. KLBB has stayed true to its format. The recent swing craze spearheaded by bands such as Big Bad Voodoo Daddy caused the station's popularity to briefly skyrocket, but since then things have returned to normal, and the program schedule remains as it has for years—emphasizing big band jazz. The station simulcasts the same programming on KLBP, which is in Brooklyn Park and serves the Twin Cities north metro area.

KSGS–950 AM
7001 France Avenue South, Suite 200, Edina
(952) 836–1041

KSGS is known by its nickname "Solid Gold Soul." They specialize in soul, funk, and R&B classics that are absent from the other local commercial stations. Solid Gold Soul has carved out a niche in the Twin Cities with few rivals.

KSTP–1500 AM
3415 University Avenue, St. Paul
(651) 646–TALK
www.am1500.com

KSTP is one of many Hubbard Broadcasting Inc. media stations in the Twin Cities. Since its origin as WAMD in 1923 as a dance station and its subsequent consolidation and renaming in 1928, KSTP has served the Twin Cities.

In recent decades KSTP has specialized in conservative talk radio. The station airs a combination of nationally syndicated personalities, including Rush Limbaugh, Dr. Laura Schlesinger, and Paul Harvey, and local programs such as *Garage Logic* with Joe Soucheray, and a political talk show that features "Minnesota's Mr. Right" Jason Lewis. Another interesting on-air personality is Barbara Carlson, a former Minneapolis city council member and mayoral candidate, who offers her brash opinions for weekday morning drive time.

KTIS–900 AM/98.5 FM
3003 Snelling Avenue North, Roseville
(651) 631–5000

KTIS is a religious music and talk station, with frequencies on the AM (900) and FM (98.5) dials.

KUOM–770 AM
University of Minnesota, 610 Rarig
Center, 330 21st Avenue South,
Minneapolis
(612) 625–3500
www.radiok.org

The Twin Cities' largest and most popular college radio station is KUOM or, as it is known locally, Radio K. Radio K plays alternative, techno, ska, hip-hop, and much more. They feature music from independent labels and local music as well as major label music. Radio K has the most diverse playlist in the Twin Cities. Plus Radio K's schedule abounds with piquant specialty programs, such as *Radio K International*, *Rude Radio* (a ska, dub, and reggae show), and *Cosmic Slop*, which spotlights forgotten music and some hits of the '70s. Additionally, there is *Off the Record*, a program devoted to local and recently released music, which features weekly performances by local bands in Studio K.

KYCR–1570 AM
2110 Cliff Road, Eagan
(651) 405–8800

KYCR is a Twin Cities Christian radio station featuring Christian talk, music, and lectures and discussions about religious matters.

WCCO–830 AM
625 Second Avenue South, Minneapolis
(612) 370–0611
www.wccoradio.com

WCCO Radio was, until the '90s, the undisputed leader in news and talk. In the past decade, ratings have slid as demographics aged, yet WCCO remains a vital force on Twin Cities radio. The station continues as the broadcast home of Minnesota Twins baseball as well as University of Minnesota Golden Gopher football and basketball.

WMNN–1330 AM
331 South 11th Street, Minneapolis
(612) 321–7200
www.wmnn.com

Every 10 minutes WMNN features Twin Cities "weather and traffic together." So if you're curious whether or not it will rain on your trip to the Como Zoo or Lake Calhoun, check out WMNN. In addition, the station broadcasts local and national news and sports coverage.

FM Stations

KBEM–88.5 FM
1555 James Avenue North, Minneapolis
(612) 668–1735
www.jazz88fm.com

Jazz 88 focuses on light jazz, fusion, classic jazz, and cool jazz but also programs that include exotica, Latin, and bluegrass music. Besides jazz KBEM features traffic information every 10 minutes during morning and afternoon drive time. Jazz 88 also features programs that focus on Twin Cities jazz.

KDWB–101.3 FM
100 North Sixth Street, #3066, Minneapolis
(612) 340–9000
www.kdwb.com

KDWB plays contemporary hits, with an emphasis on dance, especially on the weekend evenings. The station has been popular with local teens for decades because of its programming. If you want to hear hits, KDWB is where Twin Citians go.

KFAI–90.3/106.7 FM
1808 Riverside Avenue, Minneapolis
(612) 341–3144
www.kfai.org

Since 1978, KFAI has served the Twin Cities with an extremely wide array of programming. This community radio gem began in a church loft and has over the years grown to two frequencies: the original 90.3 and, in 1994, the 106.7 signal for St. Paul and eastern Twin Cities suburbs.

KFAI programming is remarkably diverse. Prominent features of the program schedule are arts, public affairs, world music, community affairs, jazz, and rock. In addition, KFAI hosts several weekly bilingual programs to serve the local immigrant communities. KFAI features Khmer, Hmong, Somali, Eritrean, and Ethiopian programs.

KMOJ–89.9 FM
501 Bryant Avenue North, Minneapolis
(612) 377–0594

KMOJ is the Twin Cities home to soul, jazz, blues, and reggae. It is one of only two area community radio stations. KMOJ gives its community, North Minneapolis, a voice on the air with music and public discussions of issues important to the neighborhood. Beyond North Minneapolis, KMOJ is enjoyed by many throughout the Twin Cities.

KNOW–91.1 FM
45 East 7th Street, St. Paul
(651) 290–1212
www.mpr.org

KNOW is the Twin Cities Minnesota Public Radio news, information, and talk station. The programming consists of a mix of local, nationally syndicated, NPR, and BBC broadcasts. KNOW has an MPR sister station at KSJN, which emphasizes classical music.

KQQL–107.9 FM
60 South Sixth Street, Minneapolis
(612) 333–8118
www.kool108.com

If you are looking for golden oldies, KOOL 108 is the Twin Cities frequency on the FM dial. The station is known for "good times, great oldies" and plays a surprisingly diverse chunk of rock music. If you love classic rock check out the *Saturday Night Oldies Party*.

KQRS–92.5 FM
2000 Southeast Elm Street, Minneapolis
(612) 617–4000
www.kqrs.com

KQ 92 is the Twin Cities' most popular classic rock station. It began as an early FM maverick radio station in the late '60s, but in the '70s began to take on its classic rock position. Since then KQ has been enormously popular—so popular, in fact, it caused the local affiliate with the *Howard Stern Radio Show* to leave the area and change formats. Morning talk show host Tom Barnard, a derivative midwestern version of Stern, is so popular that KQ's rat-

ings now regularly eclipse local radio ratings leader WCCO. Beyond the "The KQ Morning Crew" led by Barnard, the station plays a consistent rotation of Pink Floyd, Led Zeppelin, Foreigner, and Tom Petty.

KSJN–99.5 FM
45 East Seventh Street, St. Paul
(612) 290–1212
www.mpr.org

KSJN is Minnesota Public Radio's Twin Cities classical station.

KSTP–94.5 FM
3415 University Avenue, St. Paul
(651) 642–4141
www.ks95.com

KS 95 has held the honor of being the Twin Cities' favorite Top 40 station for decades and continues to play "the best variety of the '80s, '90s, and today!"

KTCZ–97.1 FM
100 North Sixth Street, Suite 306C, Minneapolis
(612) 339–0000
www.cities97.com

Cities 97 is the Twin Cities adult contemporary station. KTCZ's motto is "music you thought was too good to hear on the radio." Cities 97 regularly showcases deeper, nonhit tracks by artists such as Sting, Los Lobos, and Steely Dan.

KXXR–93.7 FM
2000 Southeast Elm Street, Minneapolis
(612) 617–4000
www.93X.com

93X is the station for fans of acts like the Red Hot Chili Peppers, Korn, and Metallica. The station serves up nonstop new metal and industrial music.

WCAL–89.3 FM
St. Olaf College, 1520 St. Olaf Avenue, Northfield
(612) 798–9225 or (888) 798–9225
www.wcal.org

WCAL has a storied local and national history in radio. The radio channel began as a student's physics project more than 80 years ago at St. Olaf College. Then, in 1924,

WCAL became the first listener-supported radio station when a newspaper received funds to keep the fledgling frequency on the air. Since 1971 WCAL has been a member of National Public Radio; the station was one of only 90 charter members nationally. WCAL is loved in the Twin Cities because of its classical music programming. But also featured are jazz, talk, and syndicated NPR shows.

WLKX–95.9 FM/KBGY–107.5 FM
15226 West Freeway Drive, Forest Lake
(651) 464–6976
www.spirit.fm

WLKX/KBGY is a Twin Cities adult contemporary Christian channel. WLKX reaches the Metro, northern suburbs, and western Wisconsin; KBGY reaches the Metro, southern suburbs, and a wide area of southeastern Minnesota.

WLTE–102.9 FM
625 Second Avenue South, Suite 550,
Minneapolis
(612) 343–2329
www.wlte.com

WLTE plays a large selection of light rock; some perennial favorites are the Eagles, Air Supply, Anita Baker, and Phil Collins. The station also features some unusual specialty programs. One particularly interesting show is *On the Air With John Tesh*. It is a weekly program about music and musicians hosted by New Age guru and former *Entertainment Tonight* cohost John Tesh.

Television Stations

TPT2–Channel 2
172 East Fourth Street, St. Paul
(651) 222–1717
www.tpt.org

TPT2 is the Twin Cities public television station. It recently changed its call letters from KTCA to TPT2 to signify its commitment to the community. Of course, TPT is an acronym for Twin Cities Public Television. TPT2 has continually served the community with a healthy mix of national PBS and local public television programming.

TPT2 features more children's television programming than any other Twin Cities station. *Sesame Street* and *Teletubbies* are featured on the daily schedule, as well as *Newton's Apple*, a locally produced science program for the past 15 years.

For adults, TPT2 has national PBS hits such as *Frontline*, the *NewsHour with Jim Lehrer* and countless national public television specials. Additionally, TPT2 has created a wealth of locally produced programming. Local public affairs programs like *Almanac*, and *Newsnight Minnesota* distinguish the station and serve the community.

WCCO–Channel 4
90 South Eleventh Street, Minneapolis
(612) 339–4444
www.wcco.com

WCCO has a long history in television and radio in the Twin Cities. In fact, the acronym, WCCO, stands for Washburn and Crosby Company, the former name of the Twin Cities–based international corporation, General Mills. However, WCCO has lost some of its local focus as both the television and radio station have been owned by the CBS Corporation for well over a decade.

WCCO continues to link itself through "the Home Town Team," the WCCO news team, as well as several other programs and initiatives to the community. One is *Hometown Heroes*, where WCCO-TV encourages Twin Citians to nominate people who make significant contributions to the community; later some of the outstanding local citizens nominated are interviewed and honored on WCCO news. Another WCCO community-based program is *Community 4 Kids,* where adults in the community mentor troubled area youths.

If you are interested in further information about WCCO, check out their Web site, which has lots of detail about programming and local television personalities. In addition, surveys are available on the Web site regarding matters of public interest to the Twin Cities. Information from surveys is frequently used on the air by the WCCO news team. It is yet another effort to connect the station to the community.

KSTP–Channel 5
3415 University Avenue, St. Paul
(651) 646–5555
www.kstp.com

KSTP is recognized locally and nationally as an innovator in the television industry. Hubbard Broadcasting, Inc., owns KSTP, as well as additional stations in New Mexico and New York. KSTP was the first television station in the Twin Cities, signing on the air on April 27, 1948. It also was the first full color television station and the first to broadcast daily newscasts in the nation.

News is important to KSTP and its "Eye Witness News Team." KSTP was a local pioneer in investigative journalism and weather reporting. "Weather Center 5" is always a step ahead of the competitors in weather technology and forecasting; whether you are going up north for the weekend or are concerned about an ominous storm, KSTP and its meteorologists have the answers. It is also the only affiliated station that remains under local ownership, which is reflected in the station's news and programming. KSTP is the Twin Cities ABC affiliate but has its own unique identity because of the strong local ownership.

KMSP–Channel 9
11358 Viking Drive, Eden Prairie
(952) 944–9999
www.kmsp.com

In 2002 the Twin Cities UPN affiliate, KMSP Channel 9, and the Fox affiliate, WFTC Channel 29, switched call letters and places on the TV dial—an effort by the Fox network, which owns both stations, to reach a larger audience with a Fox channel bunched together with the other major stations in the Cities.

Fox has made a lot of progress in the Twin Cities market since debuting in the late '80s. Fox has definitely eroded some of the Big Three networks' market share in the Twin Cities, particularly among younger viewers.

Fox News Sunday is the network's competition against such Sunday news institutions as NBC's *Meet the Press* and CBS's *Face the Nation.* They carry plenty of Twin Cities sports. NFL football and Major League baseball are featured prominently on Fox. In addition, professional hockey is on Fox; the Twin Cities NHL team, the Wild, is broadcast locally on Fox and also UPN's WFTC.

KARE–Channel 11
8811 Olson Memorial Highway, Minneapolis
(763) 546–1111
www.kare11.com

KARE is the Twin Cities home of NBC. Besides NBC programming, it consistently has the highest-rated news broadcasts at 6:00 P.M. and 10:00 P.M. Paul Magers and Diana Pierce have co-anchored on the ever-popular six and ten o'clock broadcasts for well over a decade. Besides great ratings, KARE also has created local initiatives such as "11 Who KARE," which recognizes citizens who have made significant contributions for the betterment of the Twin Cities. In addition, KARE produces programs like *Whatever,* aimed at teens. *Whatever* features teen reporters examining subjects of interest to the group, which is frequently underserved by national and Twin Cities media.

KMWB–Channel 23
1640 Como Avenue, St. Paul
(651) 646–2300

KMWB is the Twin Cities WB network affiliate. KMWB airs WB programs, such as *Dawson's Creek,* plus syndicated programming, movies, and infomercials. *The Jerry Springer Show* calls KMWB its Twin

Cities home. There are also plenty of reruns of *Roseanne, Spin City,* and *The Nanny* to sate the viewing appetite of Twin Citians.

WFTC–Channel 29
1701 Broadway Street NE, Minneapolis
(612) 379–2929
www.wftc.com

WFTC is the Twin Cities Paramount, or UPN, affiliate. After many years as an independent, WFTC now airs UPN programming. However, the station retains its unique version of television news.

Previously, former U.S. Senator Rod Grams served as the station's news anchor; today, their news team is much younger and loquacious, especially on *Good Day Minnesota*, which airs weekdays from 6:00 A.M. until 9:00 A.M., and offers a local alternative to the other networks' national morning programs.

KPXM–Channel 41
10700 Old County Road 15, Suite 285,
Plymouth
(763) 417–0041
www.paxtv.com

PAX TV recently bought this longtime independent station. One of the many goals at PAX is to buy low-performing stations and make them competitive. PAX TV is very new to the Twin Cities. So far, they lack a local presence and are still developing much of their programming schedule.

PAX TV became the seventh national television network in November 1997, started by Lowell W. "Bud" Paxson, who developed the Home Shopping Network. The station airs popular reruns such as *Diagnosis Murder, Touched By An Angel,* and *Dr. Quinn, Medicine Woman.* In addition, the network develops made-for-television movies and original programs.

KSTC–Channel 45
3415 University Avenue, St. Paul
(651) 645–4500
www.kstc45.com

KSTC is an interesting newcomer to Twin Cities television. The channel specializes in expanded news coverage and creative programming. Hubbard Broadcasting, Inc., owns KSTC and is the parent company of KSTP. But KSTC, unlike KSTP, is not an ABC affiliate, which permits much greater leeway in programming. In organization, KSTC is a "duoply," the first allowed by the FCC (permitting more than one station in a designated market area).

KSTC aims at expanding its sister station, KSTP's, news programming. In addition to KSTP's 10:00 P.M. news, news coverage now begins at 9:00 P.M. on KSTC. This allows more in-depth stories and commentary. KSTC will also have a public affairs program, *At Issue,* on Saturday evening.

Besides in-depth news coverage, KSTC also broadcasts creative and quirky programs. The weekly program schedule includes *Horror Inc.*, a Saturday late-night program featuring, of course, horror movies. In addition, there are the *Saturday Three Stooges Marathon* and *The Big Bad Movie,* a nightly movie hosted by two local comedians, and much more unique programming to round out the interesting schedule. KSTP has a long history in the Twin Cities—its sister station, KSTC, is an independent newcomer without a network affiliate, which allows it to make atavistic, creative programming decisions.

Worship

An amazing variety of religious groups are represented in the Twin Cities, with hundreds of churches—many of which are on the National Register of Historic Places—spread throughout the Twin Cities. Besides established groups such as the Catholic Church, Judaism, Evangelism, Lutheran, Mennonite, Islam, and Methodist, newer groups of immigrants have brought new traditions, celebrations, and orders to the area. Among these new arrivals are the Hmong people from Asia. More Hmong live in Minnesota than any other state as of the 2000 census, and every December the Hubert H. Humphrey Metrodome is the site of the Hmong New Year celebration. The event is spectacular, with beautiful costumes, parades, traditional dancing, and singing. The event brings Hmong immigrants from all over the country to the Twin Cities, as well as curious non-Hmong residents of the area. To encourage more people to come to the celebration, the annual event was recently renamed the Hmong-American New Year in hopes that the entire Twin Cities community would feel welcome to participate and not just the immigrant population. As Minnesota's nonwhite, non-Christian population continues to grow, organizations like the Minnesota Cultural Diversity Center have been arranging more and more open festivals celebrating the metro area's cultural richness both in social customs and religious observances.

It is this openness and acceptance of new cultures and religions that makes the Twin Cities so special. While Catholicism has long been one of the primary faiths in the area, as evidenced by the many beautiful old Catholic churches throughout the region, this is also the home base of the Billy Graham Evangelistic Association. In late December, Muslims can be seen walking to mosque to celebrate Ramadan, dressed in beautiful traditional robes that stand out brightly against the piles of white snow. Earlier in the month, street celebrations of Hanukkah, complete with food and live music, are a regular tradition in both Twin Cities downtown areas. Many cultures and religious groups have found a home here in the Cities, and no sooner does a new group move in than organizations spring up to welcome and support them in their new home. And for those wishing to experience new cultures themselves, there's nothing that says "welcome to the neighborhood" quite like attending a Minnesota polka mass!

Churches and religious centers are an important aspect of Minnesota culture, and vice versa. Most neighborhoods in the Twin Cities are traditionally built around churches, and these churches, many of which have been there since the 1890s and earlier, are an integral component of their neighborhoods. Churches in the Twin Cities have made an effort to remain an active part of the community, setting up soup kitchens and sleeping quarters for homeless people, FoodShare and FoodShelf grocery bag giveaways, and shelters for battered women, orphans, and runaways. On the lighter side of things, many religious centers in the Twin Cities also double as reasonably priced day care centers during the workweek, and most have regular festivals and picnics open to the church community as well as nonmembers, sponsor neighborhood rummage sales for charity, and arrange summer camps for kids.

If you're looking for volunteer opportunities, any and all the religious centers in the Twin Cities would be more than happy to have your help. **Loaves and Fishes Too** (1917 Logan Avenue South, Minneapolis; 612-377-9810) is the primary local service for providing free dinners to disadvantaged families throughout the Twin Cities. Operating from six strategically located facilities, Loaves and Fishes Too serves hot, nutritious meals to 1,200 to 1,800 persons every night.

The **St. Paul Ecumenical Alliance of Congregations/Interfaith Action,** located at 2720 East 22nd Street in Minneapolis (612–333–1254), is a dedicated force behind much of the urban revitalization programs in the Twin Cities. Established specifically to organize urban neighborhoods and give community leaders the support they need to impact social and political conditions in the Cities, the Alliance offers scholarship programs and creates cleanup teams in lower-bracket neighborhoods.

Lutheran Social Service of Minnesota, located at 2485 Como Avenue in St. Paul (651–642–5990), started in 1865 when a Swedish pastor and his congregation began taking in children orphaned by poverty and tragedy. The congregation soon opened the Vasa Children's Home to serve orphans and from there grew into what it is today: the largest nonprofit social service agency in the Midwest, offering crisis shelters, group homes, counseling, and adoption services for people of all income levels and religious affiliation. The Lutheran Social Service helps more than 100,000 disabled citizens, senior citizens, and children each year.

The **Minnesota Center for Corporate Responsibility,** located at 1000 LaSalle Avenue, Suite 153 in Minneapolis (651–962–4120) is not a religious organization, but it has many similarities to religious charities and groups. The purpose of the center is to promote corporate responsibility by serving as a regular forum for exchanging ideas on how businesses can better improve their communities, whether by charitable actions or by establishing scholarships in public schools. Minnesota businesses traditionally give 5 percent of their annual profits to charity, so it's only natural that establishments such as the Center for Corporate Responsibility exist in the middle of downtown Minneapolis.

No matter what your religious persuasion, two important stops in the Twin Cities are **The Basilica of St. Mary** and **The Cathedral of St. Paul.** The Basilica of St. Mary, or just "the Basilica," as locals call it, is the second-largest basilica in the Midwest and the first basilica built in the United States, taking 18 years to build before holding its first Mass on May 31, 1914. Located at 88 North 17th Street off Hennepin Avenue in Minneapolis (612–333–1381; www.mary.org), the Basilica has ingrained itself firmly into the community around it, organizing events ranging from amazing bell choirs open to the public to full-scale annual summer rock concerts—the Basilica Block Party—of which proceeds go to help maintain the historic building. The Basilica also has an amazing Martin Luther King Day celebration that brings in national acts, and the wonderful Minnesota Sinfonia performs here regularly.

The Cathedral of St. Paul, located at 239 Selby Avenue in St. Paul (651–228–1766; www.cathedralsaintpaul.org) and impossible to miss once you're in St. Paul's Capitol district, took more than 50 years to complete and is absolutely stunning. The gigantic building, topped with a 175-foot-high dome, is filled with carved marble statues of saints, gold accents, painted murals, and large stained-glass windows. The cathedral dome is an important landmark of the city, lending St. Paul a European feel that the rest of the Midwest can only envy. A recently completed $35 million renovation of the historic cathedral resulted in replacing the copper domes, cleaning and sealing the granite walls, repairing interior damage, and updating the lighting, heating, and cooling systems. The replacement of the main copper dome involved 60 roofers and more than 100 craftspeople (carpenters, electricians, ironworkers, and plumbers) to put the new 70-ton dome in place. The spectacular results have returned St. Paul's great landmark to its historic state. The cathedral is the working headquarters of the archdiocese and has a regular attending congregation of more than 2,500. Many regularly scheduled choral and orchestral concerts are held here (the acoustics are spectacular).

Minnesota FoodShare

Minnesota FoodShare is just one example of how the many diverse religious and neighborhood communities in the Twin Cities come together to help people in need. FoodShare, one of the region's largest and most successful charities, is the result of what happens when neighborhood religious centers with soup kitchens and grocery bag giveaways put aside their surface differences and get together to form an actual organization. Members of the FoodShare project include Catholic Charities, the Minnesota Rabbinical Association, and the Minnesota Council of Churches, as well as many members of the business community, including several popular nightclubs. Organized officially in 1982, Minnesota FoodShare now delivers literally millions of pounds of food each month to people in need through neighborhood churches, grocery stores, and home delivery programs.

One church that has been an active member of Minnesota FoodShare is Pastor Paul's Mission. For more than 21 years, Pastor Paul Arnopoulos has been helping feed homeless and disadvantaged Minnesotans through Disciples Ministry Mission in north Minneapolis, an area that even now is still struggling with poverty. Every day, staff members hand out bags of groceries and cook hot meals for families in need, handing out approximately 14 million pounds of food each year. More than 12,000 families from Minnesota and Wisconsin depend on the mission for help, and Pastor Paul has dedicated his entire life to making sure they get it.

Supporters of the mission and the FoodShare project come from a variety of unlikely sources. The most well-known one is the Acoustic Garage Sale, a rock benefit put on each year by the First Avenue nightclub. Each January, First Avenue brings in several dozen local and national acts to play the Main Room stage, and all door proceeds go directly to Pastor Paul's Mission. Concertgoers also have the option of bringing in canned and boxed food in lieu of the door price, and that, too, is taken to the mission. After the show, well-known local and national music personalities donate musical instruments, autographed photographs, albums and CDs, and other items to be auctioned off for additional money for the mission.

Another aspect of Minnesota charities is that they all work together to feed those in need. The charities keep in touch with one another, and if one charity is having trouble meeting its neighborhood's needs, another pitches in to bring any surplus they have. This network of charities makes Minnesota's foodshelves among the most successful in the country.

Other Worship Resources and Organizations

Archdiocese-St. Paul and Minneapolis
266 Summit Avenue, St. Paul
(651) 291–4410

Bethesda Lutheran Homes & Services Inc.,
275 North Syndicate Street, St. Paul
(651) 603–6279

Billy Graham Evangelistic Association
1300 Harmon Place, Minneapolis
(612) 338–0500

Catholic Defense League
3499 Lexington Avenue North, Arden Hills
(651) 766–7896

Good News For Israel
6408 Minnetonka Boulevard, St. Louis Park
(952) 926–7369

Greater Minneapolis Council of Churches
1001 East Lake Street, Minneapolis
(612) 721–8687

Islamic Center of Minnesota
1401 Gardena Avenue, Fridley
(763) 571–5604

Joint Religious Legislative Coalition
122 Franklin Avenue West, Minneapolis
(612) 870–3670

Minnesota Zen Meditation Center
3343 East Lake Calhoun Parkway, Minneapolis
(612) 822–5313

St. Paul Area Council of Churches
1671 Summit Avenue, St. Paul
(651) 646–8805

Unitarian Universalist Association
122 Franklin Avenue West , Suite 303,
Minneapolis
(612) 870–4823

Wat Lao Minneapolis
1429 Northeast Second Street, Minneapolis
(612) 789–9382

The ornate entryway of St. Luke's Catholic Church in St. Paul. PHOTO: TODD R. BERGER

Index

About the Authors

Photo: Bonnie Platt

Todd R. Berger

Todd R. Berger, a freelance writer and editor based in St. Paul, is the author of *Lighthouses of the Great Lakes* and the editor of 11 anthologies on pets, wildlife, and the outdoors. He has also edited more than 100 books written by other authors, including travel titles on the Midwest, Pacific Northwest, Southwest, and Florida; wildlife; photography; alcoholism and other addictions; and dog training.

Holly Day

While not actually a Minnesota native, Holly Day has spent the past five years immersing herself in Twin Cities culture, working as a freelance editor and writer for a variety of local publishing houses and as a frequent contributor to *Pulse of the Twin Cities* and *City Pages*. Nationally, her writing has appeared in over 2,000 magazines and newspapers, including *Music Alive!*, *XLR8R*, and *The Long Islander*. She currently lives in Minneapolis with her writing partner and favorite photographer, Sherman Wick, and their son, Wolfegang Day Wick.

Sherman Wick

Sherman Wick was born and raised in suburban Stillwater, Minnesota, a city central to Minnesota's history and today an outer-ring suburb of the Twin Cities. His exploration of the Twin Cities started as a small child when his paternal grandmother began taking him to Minnesota Twins baseball games, and on innumerable trips to area attractions with his parents and siblings. He is a freelance writer and photographer.